HANDBOOK OF AMERICAN POPULAR LITERATURE

HANDBOOK OF AMERICAN POPULAR LITERATURE

Edited by M. THOMAS INGE

Greenwood Press
NEW YORK
WESTPORT, CONNECTICUT
LONDON

Library of Congress Cataloging-in-Publication Data

Handbook of American popular literature / edited by M. Thomas Inge.
   p. cm.
  Includes index.
  ISBN 0–313–25405–2 (lib. bdg. : alk. paper)
  1. American literature—History and criticism—Bibliography.
2. Popular literature—United States—History and criticism—
Bibliography. 3. United States—Popular culture—Bibliography.
4. Books and reading—United States—History—Bibliography.
I. Inge, M. Thomas.
Z1231.P74H36 1988
[PS169.P64]
016.81′09—dc19   87–32294

British Library Cataloguing in Publication Data is available.

Library of Congress Catalog Card Number: 87–32294
ISBN: 0–313–25405–2

First published in 1988

Greenwood Press, Inc.
88 Post Road West, Westport, Connecticut 06881

Printed in the United States of America

The paper used in this book complies with the
Permanent Paper Standard issued by the National
Information Standards Organization (Z39.48–1984).

10 9 8 7 6 5 4 3 2 1

For my sons,
Scott and Michael

Contents

Preface

Despite the diversions of other media for entertainment and information, America remains a nation of book readers. Thousands of copies of hardcover and paperback books are published daily and the largest share of them are in popular literature. Because of increasing demands on the part of its patrons, the public library has in the last decade made available more popular fiction than ever before.

Most of this material falls into distinct and recognizable genres, such as the romance, science fiction, fantasy, the detective novel, the Western, and popular history or biography. So popular are two of these genres—science fiction and the spy novel—that they have moved out into mainstream American literature. The *New York Times* best-seller list today is as likely to include a novel of science fiction or international intrigue as the latest work by John Updike or Saul Bellow. In fact, some writers like Kurt Vonnegut, Jr., have crossed over from science fiction to general fiction, while others like Norman Mailer have been attracted by the murder mystery. When Truman Capote published *In Cold Blood*, he combined elements of the detective story with the aesthetics of mainstream fiction. It may become increasingly difficult to distinguish between popular and so-called serious literature if this trend continues.

Critics of popular literature have observed that its best writers combine elements of the familiar with the innovative, or as John G. Cawelti describes them in his influential study of formula fiction *Adventure, Mystery, and Romance* (1976), convention and invention. Cawelti believes that these have quite different cultural functions: "Conventions represent shared images and meanings and they assert an ongoing continuity of values; inventions confront us with a new perception or meaning which we have not realized before." Both of these functions, he notes, are important to culture: "Conventions help maintain a culture's stability while inventions help it respond to changing circumstances and provide new information about the world." If these perceptions are accurate, then formula fiction would seem an ideal form of literary expression in these rapidly changing times. In the meantime, it would be helpful to begin to place these books into the larger perspectives of American literature and culture.

The intent of this collection of bibliographic essays is to provide access to the body of existing commentary and scholarship on several of the main forms of popular literature of the past and present. Thus there are essays on detective and mystery novels, fantasy fiction, gothic novels, historical fiction, popular history and biography, pulps and dime novels, romantic fiction, science fiction, verse and popular poetry, and Westerns. Also discussed are what some consider to be ephemeral forms of literature—comic books and Big Little Books—as well as two forms that are traditionally considered to occupy an area between popular and mainstream writing—children's literature and young adult fiction. There is also a general essay on the phenomenon of the best seller.

Each essay follows a standard format where applicable: a survey of the historic development of the form of literature, a critical guide to the available reference works, a discussion of research centers and collections of primary and secondary materials, an evaluative overview of the histories and criticism on the subject, and a checklist of works cited and journals in the field. Ten of these essays were first published in my *Handbook of American Popular Culture* (1978–81) and have been thoroughly revised and updated for their appearance here. Two of the original contributors could not participate in this revision, so their essays have been supplemented by others (Best Sellers and Verse and Popular Poetry). Additionally, five essays were written especially for this book: Big Little Books, Comic Books, Fantasy, Popular History and Biography, and Young Adult Fiction.

I am grateful to all the new and old contributors for their effort and support of this project and to John Baldwin for his cheerful assistance.

M. Thomas Inge

HANDBOOK OF AMERICAN POPULAR LITERATURE

1.

Best Sellers

SUZANNE ELLERY GREENE and
ROBERT G. SEWELL

Books that became best sellers have received widely varying amounts of attention from literary critics and analysts, historians, and students of societal values and behavior. Those best sellers that scholars determined to be of intrinsic literary merit have been written about many times over and generally are still widely read. A few books, judged to typify the thought of a particular period or considered to have played some major role in influencing the course of history, are read and written about as historical documents. The vast majority of best-selling novels and nonfiction works have simply been forgotten until quite recently. Those books considered to be lacking in literary merit were relegated to a category of popular entertainment unworthy of serious study. With the growing interest in popular culture, however, an increasing number of people have chosen, particularly in the last decade, to study these books either for their own content and style or as a tool for broader historical or social analysis.

Whenever an attempt is made to use a medium like popular books to study the attitudes and values or behavior of a given time period, or as these change over time, the question of cause and effect must be considered. Do best sellers receive wide acceptance because they reflect their times? Or do they influence their readers to espouse new values and undertake new modes of life? The best answer is both. If all the best sellers of a given period are surveyed it will be apparent that they differ widely, both in their subject matter and concerns and in their value systems. Some will closely resemble those of a preceding era. Others will appear to be the product of a rebel, writing about a hoped-for future. It may be that the best sellers are most useful for tracing changes in dominant attitudes, beliefs, and behavior patterns as they take place over the decades. If popular books are to be used as a reflection of society, it is very important to determine the precise identity of the readers.

Another important trend in best-seller research is to view the production of the best seller as a complex social and economic phenomenon of interest in and of itself. John Sutherland in *Bestsellers* has described this interest as follows:

One of the useful aspects of bestsellers is that we cannot see them as isolated texts with single minds behind them. We have to see them as books: things which are made and are successful in so far as they sell, not just things which are composed and are successful in so far as they are critically evaluated. Nor are bestsellers entirely made by their "authors"; a whole string of agents, editors and salesmen could—if copyright law and literary convention allowed—claim "credits" in an essentially corporate venture. (P. xii)

Other research has refined the notion of best seller and distinguishes several types of best sellers. There is the "fast seller," which has a relatively short but spectacular period of "bestsellerdom" before it fades from the scene. There is the "steady seller," characterized by continuous popularity but never a very high rate of sales at any particular time. A "true best seller" has characteristics of both the fast seller and steady seller. There is also the best-selling author whose individual works may not have truly exceptional sales but whose name alone continues to sell books at something better than the break-even level. Writers of the romance and other types of genre fiction often fall into this category. A related phenomenon is the "best seller formula," determined by marketing research and sales analysis. A variety of authors, sometimes in fiction factories, produce works following these formulas supposedly guaranteed to make best sellers. Finally, there is the "blockbuster," which is orchestrated by authors, publishers, and most importantly the writer's agents. The work becomes a product that can be produced in a whole variety of media, as a hardback, mass paperback, an advertisement, and television and film adaptations.

While mention will be made of specific types of genre fiction such as the mystery and romance, the primary focus of this essay is on the phenomenon and concept of the best seller. It will provide a brief account of the predominant groups of books that were popular in the United States from colonial times to the present and will be a guide to the reference works and resources most useful to those who wish to study best sellers more thoroughly.

HISTORIC OUTLINE

Before a historic overview of American best sellers can be undertaken, several points must be established. The first is the nature of the best sellers to be considered. Although the Bible, several cookbooks, and a few other reference works have outsold most other books in the United States, these are excluded from this study. All other fiction and nonfiction works are considered. Second, in such a brief account, only the major trends can be noted. The best sellers of a given period are never homogeneous. Within every period, books more typical of an earlier era continue to appear and gain popularity. During this century, the number of popular books has grown so rapidly that broad categorizations are exceedingly difficult to establish. The function of this overview is to provide a brief account of the major new developments and leading trends in best-selling literature from colonial times to the present.

The first press in America opened in 1638 in Cambridge, Massachusetts, in conjunction with Harvard College. Its early output consisted of almanacs, sermons, catechisms, and *The Whole Booke of Psalmes*, generally known as *The Bay Psalm Book* (1640). Most books were imported from England, and booksellers reported sales of romances, collections of poetry, school books, and religious books. By the 1660s, American presses had begun to publish books in large enough editions and of sufficiently general interest that their products began to gain a wide circulation. Religious books dominated the market, while books about peculiarities of the New World, especially tales of captivity among the Indians, also gained a large readership.

Traditionally, the first American best seller is said to be *The Day of Doom*, a versified account of the final judgment day written by Michael Wigglesworth in 1662 and printed by Samuel Green in Cambridge. Even a century later, some school children were required to memorize the seemingly endless stanzas about people doomed to an eternity in hell and about the lucky few who were chosen by God for heavenly bliss. In 1664 appeared the first of four editions printed over thirty years of Richard Baxter's collection of sermons, *A Call to the Unconverted*. This was translated by John Eliot for circulation among the local Indian tribes. Books such as *The Pilgrim's Progress* by John Bunyan, reprinted in Cambridge in 1681, *Husbandry Spiritualized* (1709) by John Flavel, an anonymous *The History of the Holy Jesus* (1745), and James Hervey's *Meditations and Contemplations*, published in Philadelphia in 1750, mark a continuation of the wide appeal of religious subjects.

The Captivity and Restoration of Mary Rowlandson (1682) and John Williams's *The Redeemed Captive* (1707) exemplify the popular captivity tales. Adventure stories complete with massacres, survival through various sorts of cleverness, an eventual return home, all punctuated by Christian devotion, made lively reading for colonists who felt threatened by God's order and by the wilderness outside their small towns. These narratives provide a valuable indication of the English settlers' attitudes toward the Indians as well as their heavy reliance on God.

As the colonial period progressed, literary concerns grew wider, and the philosophical points of view of the authors became more varied. During the 1740s, American editions of Samuel Richardson's sentimental and didactic tale *Pamela* (1744) and Alexander Pope's *Essay on Man* (1747) were best sellers. The decade before the Revolution was marked by the appearance of political best sellers representing all points of view: John Dickinson's conservative *Letters from a Farmer in Pennsylvania* (1768), a treatise entitled *Conciliation with America* (1775) written by Edmund Burke, and Thomas Paine's provocative *Common Sense* (1776).

The titles of the best sellers that were published from the 1770s until the end of the eighteenth century sound like a reading list for an English literature course. Many of these works came to be considered classics, and despite the Revolution, the majority were authored by Englishmen. This list includes such novels as *The Vicar of Wakefield* (1772) by Oliver Goldsmith, *Clarissa* (1786) by Samuel Richardson, *Tristram Shandy* (1774) by Laurence Sterne, and *Charlotte Temple* (1794) by Susanna Rowson. Poetry such as John Milton's *Paradise Lost* (1777), William Cowper's *The Task* (1787), and an edition of Robert Burns's *Poems* (1788) sold well. Thomas Paine's *Age of Reason* (1794) and Benjamin Franklin's *Autobiography* (1794) were both widely read. *The Federalist* (1788), arguing for the adoption of the new constitution, had a large audience. *Paradise Lost* and John Fox's *Book of Martyrs* (1793) indicate that religion had not been forgotten although it was relegated to a less central position than it had held a century earlier. It is quite evident that the readers of best sellers had a wide range of interests, were heavily influenced by British literary culture, but also read many American products.

History and heroism dominated the best sellers of the first three decades of the nineteenth century. Books written in America about American subjects predominated for the first time. Parson Mason Weems's *Life of Washington* (1800), in which the cherry tree story first appeared, was read avidly, even in rural areas where it was carried by itinerant book peddlers. Washington Irving's *History of New York* (1809) and his later *Sketch Book* (1819) enjoyed wide sales. Jane Porter's novels about patriotic heroes, *Thaddeus of Warsaw* (1804) and *Scottish Chiefs* (1810), helped prepare the way for the enormous success of the tales of adventure and nationalism by Sir Walter Scott, including *Guy Mannering* (1815), *Rob Roy* (1818), *Ivanhoe* (1820), and *Kenilworth* (1821). James Fenimore Cooper created a prototype American hero and his adventures in *The Spy* (1821) and the Leatherstocking stories of *The Pioneers* (1823). *The Last of the Mohicans* (1826) and *The Deerslayer* (1841) were almost as widely read as Scott's novels. The popularity of Scott and Cooper continued through the century.

The 1830s and 1840s are marked by long lists of books that sold extremely well, in part because of the new practice of issuing cheap reprints of recent popular books. First in newspaper format, then in paperbound books, best sellers became available in twenty-five-cent editions. From this time on, cheap editions of popular books were always on sale for readers who could not afford the more expensive originals. Charles Dickens was an enormously popular author whose novels of sentiment and social reform were snatched up on issue. His sickly children, impoverished innocents, and evil rich men reduced thousands of American readers to tears and helped prepare the way for the American-produced, tear-jerking, sentimental novels that followed.

Dickens's works were not the only ones whose sales benefited from the inexpensive reprints. Readers who had not bought the earlier dollar editions of Scott and Cooper could now afford book purchases. Imitators of Scott, Cooper, and Dickens abounded. The best known was Joseph Holt Ingraham, who wrote thrillers such as *The Pirates of the Gulf* (1836), religious novels such as *The Prince of the House of David* (1855), and novels about life in the city such as *Jemmy Daly, or the Little News Vendor* (1843). Historical novels such as *The Last Days of Pompeii* (1834) by Edward Bulwer-Lytton and *The Three Musketeers* (1844) by Alexandre Dumas were popular, as were histories such as Jared Sparks's *Life of Washington* (1839), William Prescott's *Conquest of Mexico* (1843), and Thomas Macaulay's *History of England* (1849). Maria Monk's *Awful Disclosures* (1836), an anti-Catholic tract purporting to reveal the scandals of life in a nunnery, added a bit of sensationalism to the best-seller lists.

Mid-nineteenth-century America supported the rise of the sentimental domestic novel, often written by and about women and problems such as poverty, prostitution, drunken and perfidious husbands and lovers—all presented from a woman's point of view. Nathaniel Hawthorne complained that "America is now wholly given over to a d---d mob of scribbling women." Some examples of the more famous products of this group include *The Wide, Wide World* (1850) by Susan Warner and *The Lamplighter* (1854) by Maria S. Cummins. T. S. Arthur's *Ten Nights in a Bar-Room* (1854), written in a similar vein, was used as a temperance tract by various prohibition societies. Mrs. E.D.E.N. Southworth, the most prolific of the best-selling women authors, wrote over sixty novels, including *Ishmael* (1864) and *Self-Raised* (1864), which sold over two million copies each.

While the sentimental novels dealt with many of the problems that concerned the nation's reformers, the most divisive issue of all was largely ignored in the best sellers of the day. *Uncle Tom's Cabin*, written in 1852 by Harriet Beecher Stowe, was one of the few that directly attacked the slavery system and wielded an enormous impact in converting many disinterested readers into active opponents of slavery. Stowe's tear-jerking episodes and moralistic base closely resembled those of the other sentimental writers. *Uncle Tom's Cabin* stands as one of the few examples of a novel that clearly had a major impact on popular thought. Swinging many Northern readers to an antislavery position, the book gained acceptability by emphasizing the physical brutality and destruction of families inherent in slavery while omitting the questions of political rights and racial equality which, at that point, seemed an issue only to the most radical abolitionists.

The period of the late nineteenth and early twentieth century is marked primarily by the diversity of the popular forms, with no one innovation predominating. Sentimental and domestic novels, religious books, local color stories, historical fiction and nonfiction, adventures, some rather sensationalist exposés, and a few detective stories all gained wide readership throughout the period. Despite the fact that very few of these are read today, even by students of literary history, the period is important in that it marked out the broad categories of fictional best sellers as they have continued to the present day. Limitations of space permit only brief examples of these types to be given.

While Laura Jean Libbey produced sentimental domestic novels of the prewar sort, a new group of "glad-books" began to appear. Many centered on a child character and became children's classics. These include *Rebecca of Sunnybrook Farm* (1904) by Kate Douglas Wiggin and *Pollyanna* (1913) by Eleanor Porter. Grace Livingston Hill and Gene Stratton-Porter produced other glad-books, called "molasses fiction" by their critics, that remained best-selling types through World War I.

Religious novels like *St. Elmo* (1867) by Augusta J. Evans and *Barriers Burned Away* (1872) by Edward Payson Roe paved the way for some enormously popular writers like Lew Wallace, whose *Ben-Hur* (1880) sold over a million copies through the Sears, Roebuck and Company mail-order catalog alone. Charles Sheldon's *In His Steps* (1897), in which he presented accounts of how contemporary people would change their lives if they really followed Christ's teachings, sold even more copies. Harold Bell Wright, in books like *The Shepherd of the Hills* (1907) and *The Eyes of the World* (1914), combined religious morality with the strenuous outdoor life and a love story, thus putting together a very successful formula that combined several of the most popular subjects of fiction. Lloyd Douglas, who later produced novels like *The Magnificent Obsession* (1929) and *The Robe* (1942), followed in this same tradition.

Not all historical novels were religious. Winston Churchill's historical stories such as *Richard Carvel* (1899) and *The Crisis* (1904) made him one of the most popular writers of the turn of the century. Owen Wister's *The Virginian* (1902) put before the American reading public a character who is sometimes described as the first cowboy hero. Westerns and other masculine adventure stories grew in popularity. Zane Grey, whose more than fifty novels were read by millions, remained on the best-seller lists from the appearance of *The Spirit of the Border* in 1906 through 1924 with *The Call of the Canyon*. Writers like H. Rider Haggard and Rudyard Kipling set their adventures in the more exotic settings of Africa and India. Jules Verne's fantasies about outer space and the world beneath the sea moved even farther away from the familiar. Mystery stories like those of Arthur Conan Doyle in the late nineteenth century and Mary Roberts Rinehart in the early twentieth century marked the beginning of the rise to predominance of yet another sort of escapist adventure.

Two new kinds of literature caused an enormous sensation in the early twentieth century. The muckrakers' exposés about business, industry, and politics were read avidly. Books like Upton Sinclair's *The Jungle* (1906) about the Chicago meatpacking business shook the public. More sensationally, Elinor Glyn's *Three Weeks* (1907) drew both enthusiastic readers and official banning with its vivid account of a seduction scene and the following affair between an Englishman and a princess.

The questioning and criticism of society's traditional values and behavior patterns grew more pronounced and more popular during the 1920s. Readers turned away from political questions and emphasized a search for meaning in the life of the individual. Even Sinclair Lewis's social criticisms like *Main Street* (1920) and *Babbitt* (1922) showed the effect that forced conformity had on the individuals involved. More typical of the best-selling novels of the decade were *The Sheik* (1921) by Edith M. Hull and *The Private Life of Helen of Troy* (1925) by John Erskine, in which the characters simply took off and did their own thing. Nonfiction lists were dominated by histories, biographies, and fad books such as *Diet and Health* by Lulu Hunt Peters (1924), crossword puzzle books, and sagas of the South Seas.

The 1930s saw a swing back to historical novels. The leading characters almost invariably stood as successful examples of the old American rugged individualism. In books like *Drums Along the Mohawk* (1936) by Walter D. Edmonds and *Northwest Passage* (1937) by Kenneth Roberts, the heroes prevailed against overwhelming odds by dint of their own hard work and intelligence. Two epics headed the best-seller lists for two consecutive years: *Anthony Adverse* by Hervey Allen in 1933 and 1934 and *Gone with the Wind* by Margaret Mitchell in 1936 and 1937. An obvious search for stable, moral values appeared in novels like Pearl Buck's *The Good Earth* (1931) and Lloyd Douglas's *The Magnificent Obsession* (1929) and *Green Light* (1935). Despite the severity of the Depression and the rising tide of nazism in Germany, neither fiction nor nonfiction best sellers dealt deeply with either problem until the very end of the decade.

Best sellers that appeared during the years from World War II to the present can be treated as one unit, despite some changes that have taken place. The major noticeable feature of all these books, both individual works of fiction and the aggregate yearly lists of both fiction and nonfiction, is the recognition of the complexity of the world. Politics, religion, sex, psychology, health, love, and many other topics are combined in one book and certainly over the lists of books. Especially during the years from 1955 to the mid–1970s and into the 1980s concerns with personal physical and mental health and financial well-being became prominent. Several major trends can be picked out of the enormous variety, which itself is the most outstanding feature of the period since 1945.

From the appearance of *Mein Kampf* on the best-seller list of 1939 through the middle 1950s, both fiction and nonfiction lists revealed a very wide interest in World War II and subjects related to it. Other than that, the best sellers reflected few political concerns until after 1955, when books like *On the Beach* (1955) by Nevil Shute, *Dr. Zhivago* (1958) by Boris Pasternak, *Exodus* (1959) by Leon Uris, and *The Ugly American* (1959) by William Lederer and Eugene Burdick heralded increasing political awareness. The Watergate affair during the Nixon presidency was the subject of several best sellers, two by the reporters Carl Bernstein and Bob Woodward, *All the President's Men* (1974) and *The Final Days* (1976), as well as by participants in the Watergate affair such as John Dean and Charles Colson.

The historical romantic adventure story, a leading type of best seller for so long, declined in favor of novels like those mentioned above that treat contemporary problems and, a new favorite, suspense stories like two that came out in 1969—*Airport* by Arthur Hailey and *The Salzburg Connection* by Helen MacInnes. Many books, like Peter Benchley's sensational *Jaws* (1974), were made into films, which led to still higher book sales.

In the category of best sellers in fiction during the 1970s and 1980s, several authors are consistently represented. Among them are Judith Krantz, Robert Ludlum, Danielle Steel, and Louis L'Amour. John Le Carré's caustic spy novels have been on the best-seller lists since his first novel, *The Spy Who Came in from the Cold*, was published in 1964. He has had five just in the period from 1974 to 1986. James A. Michener's massive historical novels, *Centennial* (1974), *Chesapeake* (1978), *The Covenant* (1980), *Space* (1982), and *Poland* (1983), have all been best sellers. The horror stories of Stephen King, *The Dead Zone* (1979), *Firestarter* (1980), *Different Seasons* (1982), *Pet Sematary* (1983), and *It* (1986), represent a remarkable string of overwhelming successes. Novelists more in the tradition of the "serious" novel, including Norman Mailer, E. L. Doctorow, Kurt Vonnegut, Jr., and Saul Bellow, have also made the best-seller lists in the 1970s and 1980s, but less frequently than the more prolific authors listed above.

Another strong trend since World War II is the increasingly explicit descriptions of sex, both in the fictional characters' actions and in nonfiction best sellers such as A. C. Kinsey's *Sexual Behavior in the Human Male* (1948) and the William H. Masters and Virginia E. Johnson study, *Human Sexual Response*, published in 1966. Continuing in this line are Alex Comfort's hugely successful *The Joy of Sex*, an illustrated sex manual published in 1973, and a more sociological study, *The Hite Report: A Nationwide Study of Female Sexuality* (1976) by Shere Hite.

Popular science, psychology, business, and health and fitness books received wide readership. Eric Berne's *Games People Play* (1965) and Jean Nidetch's *The Weight Watcher's Cook Book* (1968) are two such books of the 1960s. Among the upbeat popular psychology books which have graced the best-sellers lists are Thomas Harris's *I'm O.K., You're O.K.* (1969) and Dr. Wayne W. Dyer's contributions, *Pull Your Own String* (1978) and *The Sky's the Limit* (1980). Bill Cosby's *Fatherhood* (1986) was the fastest-selling hardback book in U.S. publishing history with a record 2.4 million sales in one year. The book's popularity was certainly furthered by its release around Father's Day and the fact that Cosby played a father on a top-rated television sit-com. A work of health and fitness, which benefited from the celebrity status of the author as well as a media tie-in, was *Jane Fonda's Workout Book* (1981). The video cassette linked to the book was part of the VCR revolution. An example of the intense interest in business and financial success is Thomas J. Peters and Robert H. Waterman's *In Search of Excellence: Lessons from America's Best-Run Companies* (1982). Based on the success of the book, a television series and seminars for business people were developed by the authors.

From even a brief, oversimplified historical survey of American best sellers, it is clear that they do change drastically both in topics and in style, reflecting changes in the attitudes and the values of the readers. These are useful tools for looking at popular concerns in any given period and tracing their changes over a period of time.

REFERENCE WORKS

Surprisingly few reference works on best sellers are available to the researcher. Information on best sellers can be found in broader-based works on literature, intellectual history, and the publishing trade, but the researcher must dig a bit to find the specific information sought. Several exceptions to this generality provide the clear starting point for any study of American best sellers.

The classic study is Frank Luther Mott's analysis of best-selling books, *Golden Multitudes*, published in 1947. Although it treats books published only through 1945, it is clearly the most useful reference for the beginning researcher. Particularly valuable are the listings in appendixes A and B of the "overall best sellers in the United States" and the "better sellers." In appendix A, Mott lists all books believed to have sold 1 percent or more of the total population at the beginning of the decade in which they appeared. Appendix B lists the runners-up. One possible drawback in working from Mott's list is that his use of cumulative sales figures leads to the inclusion of books that did not sell well when they first came out. In the main text of *Golden Multitudes*, Mott analyzes the major schools of popular literature and gives brief excerpts from many of the books he mentions.

James D. Hart's *The Popular Book* of 1950 is the other available survey that combines listings and historically organized analyses of best sellers. His list is selective and is not based on specific sales requirements. Hart's study provides an exhaustive bibliography for each chapter.

The other basic reference in the field is *80 Years of Best Sellers* by Alice Payne Hackett and James H. Burke. Hackett and Burke list the top ten best sellers for each year from 1895 to 1975, based on yearly sales figures. Separation of fiction and nonfiction lists begins in 1917. After each year's list, the authors present a very brief account of the connections between the books and annual events. Total sales figures for top best sellers and separate lists of novelty books, home reference books, cookbooks, juveniles, mysteries, religious novels, and Westerns provide a good starting place for the topical researcher. Most of the figures here come from the trade journal *Publishers Weekly*.

For more detailed information, one can go straight to the source, *Publishers Weekly* published by R. R. Bowker, which has reported on best sellers since 1912. A literary magazine, the *Bookman*, contains lists from 1895, when it began publication. In spite of inconsistent and confusing indexing and presentation of information on best sellers, *The Bowker Annual of Library and Book Trade Information* is the best single reference source on recent best sellers. The annual began publishing lists of best sellers in the 1963 edition. Since that time, the categories and number of titles on the top best-sellers lists have changed. The general categories of fiction and nonfiction are stable, but lists of paperback best sellers have been given only infrequently. The annual list of best sellers has grown from five, to ten, to fifteen, and recently a list of runners-up expands the list to thirty. Since the 1974 edition, a brief essay on best sellers identifying trends and characteristics of best-selling books in America has been attached to the list. A listing of sources for comparisons with other nations can be found in another trade reference, *The Book Trade of the World*, edited by Sigfred Taubert and Peter Weidhaas. In four volumes, it provides basic information on the book business throughout the world and a list of references for more detailed study.

A number of books exist that list books and/or authors and provide very brief information on each. These would provide a useful starting place for facts on a particular writer or best seller. Listing both books and authors are James D. Hart's *The Oxford Companion to American Literature*, which has been updated several times, and *American Authors and Books, 1640–1940* by William J. Burke and Will D. Howe. Material on recent writers can be found in *Contemporary Authors: A Bio-Bibliographical Guide to Current Authors and Their Works*. Volume 1 came out in 1962, and a cumulative index appears regularly. One other possibly useful book in this category is *America in Fiction* by Otis W. Coan and Richard G. Lillard, which, by its own description, provides an annotated list of novels that interpret aspects of life in the United States. The extensive, annotated bibliography in the Literature subdivision of Popular Culture in *American Studies: An Annotated Bibliog-*

raphy, edited by Jack Salzman, is another useful resource for popular literature study. Randy F. Nelson's *The Almanac of American Letters* is an entertaining and informative work, full of interesting anecdotes, odd facts, charts, dates, biographies, statistics, and essays, including one on best sellers, to supplement more formal histories of American literature.

Since there is not space in this chapter to list material on specific authors or books, it should be pointed out that the *Library of Congress Catalog* and the *National Union Catalog* would contain listings of most books under author, title, and subject headings. The two national bibliographic utilities, OCLC and RLIN, are data bases from which cataloging information and holdings for library materials in academic and public libraries throughout the country can be derived. These data bases may be searched on-line from the traditional access points of author, title, and subject headings as well as through key word searching. The *Readers' Guide to Periodical Literature* lists articles from selected periodicals by topic and author. Scholarly journal articles were indexed from 1907 to 1965 in the *International Index to Periodicals*. In 1966, it became the *Social Sciences and Humanities Index*, and in 1974, this index split into two separate publications, the *Social Sciences Index* and the *Humanities Index*. Another useful index is *Library Literature*. All of these are available on-line and in CD ROM.

RESEARCH COLLECTIONS

The most useful secondary material can be found in any large library. The best sellers themselves may be more difficult to locate. Recent best sellers are held in the collections of most large public libraries. Certainly, the nearest public library is the place to begin. When that source is exhausted, the easiest thing is to use the inter-library loan facilities to locate and borrow specific books not available locally. Should you want to work in one place with a large collection of best sellers, the places to go are the New York Public Library and the Library of Congress in Washington. Their holdings are extensive; most books can be obtained through inter-library loan facilities, however.

In his article "Trash or Treasure? Pop Fiction in Academic and Research Libraries," Robert G. Sewell presents a rationale for the collection of popular fiction as research materials for academic libraries and describes numerous popular culture collections in such libraries. In most cases, however, such collections are special collections of "genre fiction," or publishers series such as Big Little Books, not necessarily "best seller" as the term is being used here. But there are some library collections of interest to our concerns. The Popular Culture Library at Bowling Green State University, the mecca of academic popular culture studies, has a collection of over 50,000 books, comic books, dime novels, Big Little Books, and mass paperbacks. The Russel B. Nye Popular Culture Collection at Michigan State University, named after the popular culture scholar, has especially noteworthy and relevant materials for best-seller research. It is available in the Special Collection Department of the Library, which has produced many useful finding aids for the Nye Collection. The University of Minnesota Library owns the Hess Collection, consisting of 70,000 dime and nickel novels published between 1860 and 1890, including an almost complete set of the Beadle and Adams dime and nickel novel series, listed in Albert Johannsen's *The House of Beadle and Adams*. The New York Public Library owns a collection of over 13,000 volumes of nineteenth-century American literature, as well as vast holdings of popular twentieth-century literature, which special efforts are being made to preserve, especially through microfilming. The Center for Research Libraries in Chicago, whose catalogs and handbooks are available at member libraries throughout the nation, has several collections that might be useful in best-seller research. The center's American Culture series consists of microfilm copies of 5,200 works published by 1876. The titles are listed in the *Bibliography of American Culture, 1493–1875*, compiled by David R. Weimer. A collection of American fiction on microfilm of about 12,000 volumes also resides at the center, the titles of which are listed in a bibliography of that name compiled by Lyle Wright. The center also owns a collection of nineteenth-century books and 40,000 volumes of children's literature. The Mugar Memorial Library at Boston University has a valuable research collection in its Twentieth Century Archives, including manuscripts, journals, diaries, reviews, and correspondence as well as published works of a number of twentieth-century authors, some of whom are best-selling ones. Undoubtedly the richest resource for best sellers is the Library of Congress. The major reason for this is the fact that since 1870 two copies of every copyrighted American work have been deposited in the library. There are as well a number of special collections in the Rare Book and Special Collection Division which are of importance to best-seller research. These include the Armed Forces Edition Collection (an archival set of paperbacks published for the American Armed Forces, 1943–47), the Big Little Book Collection, the Dell Paperback Collection (a virtually complete set from 1943), and the Pulp Fiction Collection.

HISTORY AND CRITICISM

Presenting a survey of the history and criticism of best sellers necessitates dividing the material into manageable categories; the most basic category consists of writings about the best sellers themselves, both overall surveys and period studies. The readership of the best sellers merits considerable attention, especially by the student who is looking for reflections and indications of changes in popular attitudes and values. For whom or to whom do these books speak? Studies in the history of publishing often provide information on the marketing and buying of the books and some interesting sidelights on the stories of individual best sellers. These as well as separate studies often provide information about book clubs and the appearance of various cheap editions, both of which have resulted in major changes in the makeup of the reading public. Published reviews provide an indication of the critical acclaim of a book and of what the potential reader thought he was getting. Excluded from this survey are studies of specific types of books such as mysteries and Westerns, which are treated elsewhere in this volume. Also omitted are biographies of individual authors and works on individual best sellers; these can be easily located in any subject index. Almost no anthologies of excerpts from best sellers exist. The few books that do include reprinted material are treated in this section since they all contain criticism as well.

Except for the lack of anthologies, enough general work on overall patterns of best sellers exists to give the beginning student or researcher a sound start. Russel B. Nye's widely used book on the popular arts in America, *The Unembarrassed Muse*, includes several chapters on popular literature, which form an excellent condensed survey. *Golden Multitudes* by Frank Luther Mott and *The Popular Book* by James D. Hart are the two major books that survey and analyze popular literature from the colonial period to the time of their writing (1947 and 1950, respectively). Both include inquiries into the readership, methods of circulation, and publishing trends, as well as commentary on the best sellers themselves. Nye and Hart assembled extensive bibliographies that are very useful. Geoffrey Bocca's book on best sellers is both wide ranging and fun to read as the title suggests: *Best Sellers: A Nostalgic Celebration of the Less-Than-Great Books You Have Always Been Afraid to Admit You Loved.*

The few books that do contain excerpts from best sellers do not deal with them exclusively. While they might be useful for classroom assignments, they would be of little value to the serious researcher who would have to read much more extensively. Three such collections do, however, deserve mention. *America Through the Looking Glass: A Historical Reader in Popular Culture*, edited by David Bruner et al., has selections from best sellers and other popular writing, both fiction and nonfiction. These are arranged chronologically and have been chosen as mirrors of the contemporary culture. While they are extremely well-chosen selections, the majority of the material does not come from best sellers. *Understanding American History Through Fiction*, edited by Warren A. Beck and Myles L. Clowers, also includes portions of a number of best sellers and other fictional works as well. These selections are arranged around such topics as manifest destiny, slavery, the growth of American capitalism, and World War II. These volumes would be a valuable addition to an American history course, but they do not contain enough material on best sellers to be useful for specialized research. One anthology, Donald McQuade and Robert Atwan's *Popular Writing in America*, contains an extensive section of excerpts from best sellers, both fiction and nonfiction. Selections include not only the standard ones like *Uncle Tom's Cabin* and *Poor Richard's Almanac*, but also portions of *Tarzan of the Apes, I, The Jury* by Mickey Spillane, *The Godfather, Love Story*, Emily Post's *Etiquette*, and Dale Carnegies's *How to Win Friends and Influence People*. This book would be the most useful to use for a classroom unit on best-selling literature but, once again, is far too limited for advanced work. All three of these books contain interpretive material relating chosen selections to the events and culture of their times.

Although the field is not overcrowded, a few other general interpretive efforts are available. Leo Gurko's *Heroes, Highbrows and the Popular Mind* touches on a lot of material germane to a study of best sellers. Gurko describes the most typical heroes of American popular literature and connects changes in these types to changing world conditions. His analysis is perceptive. Another analytical book containing many insightful comments is *The Half-World of American Culture* by Carl Bode. The author of both historical and literary studies, Bode here includes a number of best sellers in the material he uses to make cross-century comparisons. Q. D. Leavis's book, *Fiction and the Reading Public*, contains a section of analysis and comparison of old and recent best sellers, as well as the patterns, styles, and contents of "literary" and "popular" books. The author deals with books that were best sellers in Great Britain and in the United States and with the reading public of both countries. John G. Cawelti's *Adventure, Mystery, and Romance* is a theoretical study of formulas seen in Westerns, detective and crime fiction, and social melodrama. He develops a methodology that can be applied to other popular literary formulas. The title of James O'Donnell Bennett's book, *Much Loved Books: Best Sellers of the Ages*, tempts the reader in the field, but this series of articles from the Chicago *Tribune* is not particularly useful. Robert Bingham Downs's collection of essays, *Famous American Books*, consists of five- to ten-page studies of fifty books designed to illustrate and illuminate the impact of books on the course of history. He includes a number of best sellers, from the early *Day of Doom* down through Ralph Nader's *Unsafe at Any Speed*. His selections and analyses are quite good. Bernard Rosenberg and David Manning White edited *Mass Culture: The Popular Arts in America*, which contains a section on mass literature and includes chapters on the question of formula, who reads what books and why, and the role of paperback books. All these are applicable to any study of best sellers. A work that studies a rather technical aspect of the field is James Calvin Craig's *The Vocabulary Load of the Nation's Best Sellers, 1662–1945*. One final slim volume, a classic primarily because of its title, cannot go unmentioned. *Lincoln's Doctor's Dog* by George Stevens considers how a book becomes a best seller and concludes that, at least in 1938, word-of-mouth publicity led to the greatest sales. Stevens recounts stories about a number of best sellers, treating *Anthony Adverse* in the greatest detail.

A number of good period studies exist, some written specifically about popular literature, others more generally about the cultural life of a particular era. A work on colonial culture, *Literary Culture in Early New England, 1620–1730* by Thomas Goddard Wright, contains a remarkable listing of books held in public and in private collections, good material on the Boston booksellers, and provides interesting information on the reading elite. Although the emphasis is on high culture, the book's value is enhanced by providing the information necessary to make comparisons between elite and popular literature. Russel B. Nye's work, *The Cultural Life of the New Nation, 1776–1830*, contains a chapter entitled "The Quest for a National Literature," which concentrates more heavily on best sellers. The entire book provides a fine survey of the culture of the period. A more specialized study, Herbert Ross Brown's *The Sentimental Novel in America, 1789–1860*, includes many best sellers in its analysis. Other studies of early American novels include *The Rise of the American Novel* by Alexander Cowie and *The Early American Novel* by Lily D. Loshe.

Several books exist that treat best sellers of the mid-nineteenth century. A good starting place is Carl Bode's *The Anatomy of American Popular Culture, 1840–1861*, a thorough study that includes a section on "popular print" containing an analysis of fiction and nonfiction and comparing trends of that time with those of earlier periods. Bode considers both the works and their reception. Helen Papashvily's *All the Happy Endings* treats popular novels, as does a dissertation by Dorothy C. Hockey, "The Good and the Beautiful: A Study of Best Selling Novels in America, 1865–1920." Quentin Reynolds's *The Fiction Factory*, a history of the publishing firm of Street and Smith, contains some interesting material on best sellers of the late nineteenth century. Grant C. Knight wrote a study on the final years of the nineteenth century, *The Critical Period in American Literature, 1890–1900*, which integrates the literary and social history of the time. No overall study exists connecting best sellers with the course of nineteenth-century history, and other than the books by Bode and Knight, most of the available material is literary criticism, not serious analysis of the popular culture.

More has been written about twentieth-century best sellers than about those of the preceding periods. Clearly the place to begin research is *80 Years of Best Sellers* by Hackett and Burke. In addition to the invaluable compilation of the yearly best sellers, the book contains a bibliography that includes most of the major articles written about best sellers during the century. Because that source is so complete, those articles will not be relisted here.

A number of volumes have been published on American literature of the twentieth century. The vast majority of those limit their concern to the critically acclaimed books rather than to the best sellers. A few best sellers, such as novels by Ernest Hemingway, William Faulkner, and Thomas Wolfe, are included in literary histories, but most are not. For points of comparison, it might be useful to look at standard works like Alfred Kazin's *On Native Grounds* and Malcolm Cowley's *The Literary Situation*; the latter treats a wider range of authors than does the former. Another useful volume, not specifically on best sellers, is John Hohenberg's work *The Pulitzer Prizes*. Hohenberg lists the prize winners, many of which were best sellers, and analyzes changing patterns in the selections, relating them to the course of world and national events.

A number of books study the best sellers of one decade or make comparisons over several decades. An excellent example is Erik Lofroth's *A World Made Safe: Values in American Best Sellers, 1895–1920*. Grant C. Knight's integration of literature and social history, *The Strenuous Age in American Literature*, discusses many best sellers that appeared between 1900 and 1910. A Radcliffe College dissertation by Anna Lee Hopson entitled "Best Sellers: Media of Mass Expression" thoroughly compares the popular novels written from 1907 to 1916 with those written from 1940 to 1949. She concentrates on courtship and kinship relations. Suzanne Ellery Greene's *Books for Pleasure: Popular Fiction 1914–1945* uses best sellers as a reflection of changes in popular attitudes and values and treats such categories as political and religious involvement and beliefs, race and ethnicity, class relationships, family, and sex. The detailed methodology presented might prove useful to others working in this field. *Novelists' America: Fiction as History, 1910–1940* by Nelson Manfred Blake shows how a group of novels can be used to study social conditions and popular concerns. Although he concentrates on elite writers, best-selling authors like Sinclair Lewis and John Steinbeck are included. The book's bibliography lists general works about American fiction and biographical and critical studies of the individual authors.

Although much of the material on best sellers since World War II exists in the form of reviews, journal articles, or studies of individual writers, there are an increasing number of books that make useful introduction to the period. Among these are *The Novel Now* by Anthony Burgess; *Recent American Fiction: Some Critical Views*, edited by Joseph J. Waldmeir; *Working for the Reader* by book reviewer Herbert Mitgang; *A Question of Quality*, edited by Louis Filler; *Bright Book of Life* by Alfred Kazin; John Sutherland's *Bestsellers: Popular Fiction of the 1970s*; and *The American Dream and the Popular Novel* by Elizabeth Long. Most of these are collections of essays although Burgess's book provides a unified thematic study, as do Sutherland's and Long's. Sutherland not only surveys the most spectacular blockbusters of the 1970s, he also analyzes the international character of recent American best sellers, particularly the link between the United States and England. Long traces the changing ideas of success in the American dream as represented in best sellers from 1945 to 1975.

Publishers Weekly, whose best-seller listings began in 1912, has printed reviews of most major books since it first appeared in 1872. The *Library*

Journal prints some long reviews and many one-paragraph overviews designed primarily for librarians who are considering purchase. They are organized in topical sections. Since 1967, R. R. Bowker has published an annual volume of selections of reviews under the title *Library Journal Book Review*. Another early journal, the *Bookman*, calculated national best sellers from its first year in print and reviewed most major books that appeared from 1895 until it ceased publication in 1933. The *New York Times Book Review* became a separate section in 1896. Arno Press published a bound index to reviews from 1896 to 1970. In 1951, the *Times* published *A Century of Books*, a selection of one hundred reviews. Although the *New York Times* does not include every book published, its reviews, like those of the *Bookman*, provide much detail and a critical analysis. The *Booklist*, a publication of the American Library Association, tends to give very brief reviews of a large number of books. The *Saturday Review of Literature*, which became the *Saturday Review* in 1951, contains long reviews of all books that its editors have judged to merit discussion. One of the newest nationally circulated publications in this field is the *New York Review of Books*, which publishes detailed reviews and represents a comparatively elitist point of view. It should be noted that all these journals contain advertisements which are useful in understanding what the publisher wishes to convey to potential purchasers about his books.

Three indexes can aid significantly in a search for reviews of a particular book. The *Book Review Digest* prints indexes by subject and author and publishes a cumulative index every five years. It provides very brief excerpts that indicate the range of reviews. These can then be found in their entirety. Another good source for listings of reviews is provided by the *National Library Service Cumulative Book Review Index, 1905–1974*. In 1965, the Gale Research Company began publishing the *Book Review Index*, which provides simple listings of reviews by author and by year.

Numerous histories of the publishing industry and of the individual publishing houses contain some information on best sellers, especially as these are seen from the publisher's point of view. Some also consider the impact of factors like the first International Copyright Law of 1891, which gave a boost to American authors by cutting into the sale of cheap editions of pirated European works. Many books try to analyze the influence of developments like the growth of the paperback industry and the appearance of book clubs. Two excellent and thorough histories of the general field provide more than enough information for most readers. John William Tebbel's multivolume *A History of Book Publishing in the United States* contains a short section devoted to best sellers and numerous valuable charts. A briefer study, *Book Publishing in America* by Charles Allen Madison, includes a chronology of major events, information on the book clubs and inexpensive reprint editions, and a thorough bibliography that provides titles of many histories of individual publishing houses, memoirs, literary histories, criticism, and topical studies. *Books: The Culture and Commerce of Publishing*, by Lewis A. Coser, Charles Kadushin, and Walter V. Powell, presents a comprehensive, sociological perspective on the contemporary publishing scene in the United States. The most cynical and disparaging view of modern publishing in America is Thomas Whiteside's *The Blockbuster Complex: Conglomerates, Show Business and Book Publishing*. Whiteside analyzes trends in publishing which no longer view the book as a text but as a multimedia property. An intelligent response to Whiteside's criticism is found in Elizabeth Long's *The American Dream and the Popular Novel*.

Several other sources deserve mention in this section. Charles Lee's history of the Book-of-the-Month Club, *The Hidden Public*, would be useful for someone interested in the relationship between best sellers and book clubs. It should be noted that most of the book clubs will provide the researcher or interested student with lists of their selections and perhaps other material on their operations. A number of studies of the paperback industry exist, including *Paperback Books: A Pocket History* by John Tebbel, *The Paperbound Book in America* by Frank L. Schick, and *Paper-Bound Books in America* by Freeman Lewis. Two anthologies that contain useful material on publishing history, book clubs, and cheap editions are the *Bowker Lectures on Book Publishing* published by the R. R. Bowker Company, and *Books and the Mass Market* by Harold K. Guinzburg, W. Frase, and Theodore Waller.

Whenever best sellers are used as a tool to study the people who read them, it is essential to ascertain as precisely as possible the makeup of that reading public at the time under consideration. Most scientifically prepared studies have appeared since 1930 and treat only contemporary statistics. However, one excellent study, entitled *Literacy in Colonial New England* by Kenneth A. Lockridge, shows a method for analyzing such information from an earlier period. Three thorough studies treat reading during the Depression: Orion Howard Cheney in *Economic Survey of the Book Industry 1930–1931*, Douglas Waples in *Research Memorandum on Social Aspects of Reading in the Depression*, and Louis R. Wilson in *The Geography of Reading* consider book sales and library distribution and correlate them with geographic, cultural, and economic factors. Irving Harlow Hart noted in an article, "The One Hundred Leading Authors of Best Sellers in Fiction from 1895 to 1944" in *Publishers Weekly*, that for the period 1919 to 1931 there was an 80 percent correlation between bookstore best sellers and books with the highest library circulation. Several articles reprinted in Rosenberg and White's *Mass Culture: The Popular Arts in America* deal with questions of reading habits and availability of books in the 1950s; the most useful are Bernard Berelson's article "Who Reads What Books and Why" and Alan Dutscher's account of "The Book Business in America." Roger H. Smith's *The American Reading Public: What It Reads* is a study from the 1960s. Janice A. Radway's *Reading the Romance: Women, Patriarchy, and Popular Literature*

Hart, Irving Harlow. "The One Hundred Leading Authors of Best Sellers in Fiction from 1895 to 1944." *Publishers Weekly*, 149 (January 19, 1946), 285–90.

Hart, James D. *The Popular Book: A History of America's Literary Taste*. New York: Oxford University Press, 1950.

———. *The Oxford Companion to American Literature*. New York: Oxford University Press, 1983.

Hockey, Dorothy C. "The Good and the Beautiful: A Study of Best Selling Novels in America, 1865–1920." Ph.D. dissertation, Case Western Reserve University, 1947.

Hohenberg, John. *The Pulitzer Prizes*. New York: Columbia University Press, 1974.

Hopson, Anna Lee. "Best Sellers: Media of Mass Expression." Ph.D. dissertation, Radcliffe College, 1951.

Johannsen, Albert. *The House of Beadle and Adams*. 3 vols. Norman: University of Oklahoma Press, 1950–62.

Kazin, Alfred. *Bright Book of Life*. Boston: Little, Brown, 1973.

———. *On Native Grounds*. New York: Reynal and Hitchcock, 1942.

Knight, Grant C. *The Critical Period in American Literature, 1890–1900*. Chapel Hill: University of North Carolina Press, 1951.

———. *The Strenuous Age in American Literature*. Chapel Hill: University of North Carolina Press, 1954.

Leavis, Q. D. *Fiction and the Reading Public*. London: Chatto and Windus, 1965.

Lee, Charles. *The Hidden Public: The Story of the Book-of-the-Month Club*. New York: Doubleday, 1958.

Lewis, Freeman. *Paper-Bound Books in America*. New York: New York Public Library, 1952.

Library Journal Book Review. New York: R. R. Bowker, 1967-.

Link, Henry C., and Harry Arthur Hopf. *People and Books*. New York: Book Industry Committee, 1946.

Lockridge, Kenneth A. *Literacy in Colonial New England*. New York: Norton, 1974.

Lofroth, Erik. *A World Made Safe: Values in American Best Sellers, 1895–1920*. Acta Univ. Ups., Studia Anglistica Upsaliensia 45. Uppsala, Sweden, 1983.

Long, Elizabeth. *The American Dream and the Popular Novel*. Boston: Routledge and Kegan Paul, 1985.

Loshe, Lily D. *The Early American Novel, 1789–1830*. New York: Columbia University Press, 1907; Ungar, 1966.

Lyles, William H. *Putting Dell on the Map: A History of the Dell Paperback*. Westport, Conn.: Greenwood Press, 1983.

McQuade, Donald, and Robert Atwan. *Popular Writing in America*. New York: Oxford University Press, 1974.

Madison, Charles Allen. *Book Publishing in America*. New York: McGraw-Hill, 1966.

Mitgang, Herbert. *Working for the Reader: A Chronicle of Culture, Literature, War and Politics in Books from the 1950s to the Present*. New York: Horizon Press, 1970.

Mott, Frank Luther. *Golden Multitudes: The Story of Best Sellers in the United States*. New York: Macmillan, 1947.

National Union Catalogue. Ann Arbor, Mich.: J. W. Edwards, 1958-.

National Union Catalog Pre–1956 Imprints. 754 vols. London: Mansell, 1968–81.

Nelson, Randy F. *The Almanac of American Letters*. Los Altos, Calif.: William Kaufman, 1981.

New York (City) Public Library. *Dictionary Catalog of the Research Libraries at the New York Public Library 1911–1971.* 800 vols. New York: New York Public Library, 1979.

Nye, Russel B. *The Cultural Life of the New Nation, 1776–1830.* New York: Harper and Row, 1960.

———. *The Unembarrassed Muse: The Popular Arts in America.* New York: Dial Press, 1970.

Papashvily, Helen Waite. *All the Happy Endings.* New York: Harper, 1956.

Radway, Janice A. *Reading the Romance: Women, Patriarchy, and Popular Literature.* Chapel Hill: University of North Carolina Press, 1984.

Reynolds, Quentin. *The Fiction Factory: From Pulp Row to Quality Street.* New York: Random House, 1955.

Rosenberg, Bernard, and David Manning White. *Mass Culture: The Popular Arts in America.* Glencoe, Ill.: Free Press, 1957.

Salzman, Jack, ed. *American Studies: An Annotated Bibliography.* 3 vols. Cambridge: Cambridge University Press, 1986.

Schick, Frank L. *The Paperbound Book in America.* New York: R. R. Bowker, 1958.

Sewell, Robert G. "Trash or Treasure? Pop Fiction in Academic and Research Libraries." *College and Research Libraries,* 46 (November 1984), 450–61.

Smith, Roger H. *The American Reading Public: What It Reads.* New York: R. R. Bowker, 1964.

Stevens, George. *Lincoln's Doctor's Dog.* Philadelphia: J. B. Lippincott, 1938.

Sutherland, John. *Bestsellers: Popular Fiction of the 1970s.* London: Routledge and Kegan Paul, 1981.

Taubert, Sigfred, and Peter Weidhaas, eds. *The Book Trade of the World.* 4 vols. New York: R. R. Bowker and K. G. Saur, 1972–84.

Tebbel, John William. *A History of Book Publishing in the United States.* New York: R. R. Bowker, 1972 (vol. 1) and 1975 (vol. 2).

———. *Paperback Books: A Pocket History.* New York: Pocket Books, 1964.

Waldmeir, Joseph J., ed. *Recent American Fiction: Some Critical Views.* Boston: Houghton Mifflin, 1963.

Waples, Douglas. *Research Memorandum on Social Aspects of Reading in the Depression.* New York: Social Science Research Council, 1937.

Weimer, David R., comp. *Bibliography of American Culture, 1493–1875.* Ann Arbor, Mich.: University Microfilms, 1957.

Whiteside, Thomas. *The Blockbuster Complex: Conglomerates, Show Business and Book Publishing.* Middletown, Conn.: Wesleyan University Press, 1981.

Wilson, Louis R. *The Geography of Reading.* Chicago: American Library Association and University of Chicago Press, 1938.

Wright, Lyle, comp. *American Fiction: A Contribution Towards Bibliography.* 3 vols. San Marino, Calif.: Huntington Library, 1957–69.

Wright, Thomas Goddard. *Literary Culture in Early New England, 1620–1730.* New Haven: Yale University Press, 1920.

Indexes

Book Review Index. Detroit: Gale Research, 1965–.

Humanities Index. New York: H. W. Wilson, 1974–.

International Index to Periodicals. New York: H. W. Wilson, 1905–74.

Library Literature. New York: H. W. Wilson, 1933–.

National Library Service Cumulative Book Review Index, 1905–1974. Princeton, N.J.:
  National Library Service Corporation, 1975.

New York Times Book Review Index. New York: Arno Press, 1973–.

Readers' Guide to Periodical Literature. New York: H. W. Wilson, 1904–.

Social Sciences and Humanities Index. New York: H. W. Wilson, 1966–74.

Social Sciences Index. New York: H. W. Wilson, 1974–.

Periodicals

Book Review Digest. New York, 1905–.

Booklist. Chicago, 1905–.

Bookman. New York, 1895–1933.

Journal of Popular Literature. Bowling Green, Ohio, 1985–.

Library Journal. New York, 1876–.

New York Review of Books. New York, 1963–.

New York Times Book Review. New York, 1896–.

Publishers Weekly. New York, 1872–.

Saturday Review. New York, 1952–.

Saturday Review of Literature. New York, 1924–51.

2.

Big Little Books

RAY BARFIELD

"Big Little Book," like "Levis," "Xerox," and "Coke," is a trademark that has become firmly lodged as a generic term—in this case, for parallel product lines of several publishers, primarily from the Great Depression and World War II decades. Emerging from a finely tuned sense of the five-and-dime or variety store market, the Big Little Books, Better Little Books, New Better Little Books, Big Big Books, Little Big Books, Jumbo Books, Fast Action Books, and related series became prized possessions of children in a wide socioeconomic range of American homes, especially from 1932 to about 1950. Relatively recent attempts at reviving the Big Little Book genre have been moderately successful, but the earlier series remain the best remembered.

Most nostalgists will think of Big Little Books as the inch-or-so thick (thus "big"), almost 4″ wide and 4½″ tall (thus compact or "little") volumes issued first by Whitman Publishing Company, then by Saalfield Publishing Company, the Five Star Library, and others. The majority were hardbound or "board-covered," cased-in books with bright four-color covers, selling for ten or fifteen cents. Generally the left-hand text pages, set in ten or twelve lines of rather large type, faced black-and-white illustrations, sometimes drawn by the publishers' staff artists but more often adapted by them from comic strip panels or movie stills. Speech balloons were usually eliminated, and illustrations were extended or trimmed to fit the available space. The initial Big Little Books were slightly larger than their successors, but even after the major publishers had settled on a standard shape to fit the hands of seven- to twelve-year-olds, they continued to experiment with format variations as a way of defining several subseries and of maximizing their shares of the children's book market. The peak period of Big Little Book production also saw the development of penny and nickel versions as well as book lines for advertising giveaways and premiums. Smaller or thinner than the ten- and fifteen-cent volumes (and sometimes directly condensed from them), these types shared the emphases of the full-length Big Little Books on licensed comic strip and film characters, with a sprinkling of publisher-created protagonists.

Usually printed in single editions numbering hundreds of thousands of copies per title, Big Little Books were often scorned by public school teachers and librarians, while children's book reviewers and the book-trade press seldom found cause to notice them. The absence of such "official" endorsement notwithstanding, and despite the vulnerabilities of their highly acidic paper and fragile spines as well as sacrificial offerings to World War II paper recycling drives, tens of thousands of 1930s and 1940s Big Little Books survive. Many carry birthday or Christmas gift inscriptions from mothers, aunts, or grandfathers who might never have dreamed of investing in "those ol' *comic* books." For buyers, the Big Little Books' bindings gave them a kind of legitimacy, and they functioned both as objects and as reading (or looking) matter.

Sometimes seen as having finally "lost out to" comic books, to television, or simply to changing times, the early Big Little Books have now assumed the status of memory-evoking, period-characterizing artifacts. Copies in merely presentable to mint condition bring many times their modest original prices as they circulate in the relatively small but avid collectors' market. Several collectors' guides have been published, but academic-scholarly interest has been limited chiefly to the illustrative purposes of the social historian.

HISTORIC OUTLINE

Obviously the long and colorful tradition of children's illustrated books forms the broad background to the development of Big Little Books. Also, early newspaper comics reprint volumes from such publishers as the Frederick A. Stokes Company and Cupples and Leon stand as general predecessors to the comic book experiments of George Delacorte (1929), the Ledger Syndicate, and M. C. Gaines (1933) and equally to the first Big Little Book, *The Adventures of Dick Tracy*, adapted by Whitman from Chester Gould's Chicago *Tribune* strip in 1932. More specifically, however, the Big Little Book emerged from the ironic outcome of one event—the near-collapse of the Western Printing and Lithographing Company after a major creditor's default in 1916—and from the shaping skills of Samuel Lowe, who guided Western's Whitman division through more than twenty highly successful years.

In promotional brochures and in several drafts of an in-house company history, the story of Western Printing and Lithographing Company (which changed its name to Western Publishing Company in the summer of 1960) reads like a romance of American capitalism. According to *Western Ways*, an unsigned brochure, the company began to take shape in 1907, when Edward H. Wadewitz (1878–1955), part-time bookkeeper for the West Side Printing Company in Racine, Wisconsin, fell heir to that modestly equipped firm "partly in lieu of wages." He and Roy A. Spencer (1880–1956), a veteran newspaper pressman, secured a $1,500 loan and, with three other employees, continued operating from the basement of a State Street hat store. A younger brother, William R. (Bill) Wadewitz, who would become company president in 1957, began his career by pushing a two-wheeled delivery cart through the streets of Racine. In 1910 the firm was incorporated as Western Printing and Lithographing Company, and by 1914 its job-printing orders had reached $100,000, a dramatic contrast to the first-year sales of $9,000 less than a decade earlier.

The year 1916 brought the crisis out of which the young firm found a new and major direction. Western found itself principal creditor of a Chicago book publisher, the Hamming-Whitman Company, which declared bankruptcy. As the anonymous promotional book *The Story of Western, 1907–1965* tells it, "Western had on its hands many thousands of completed books and work in process, for which it could never hope to collect from its customer." Making the best of its dilemma, "Western, on Feb. 9, 1916, acquired 'all the assets of said Hamming-Whitman Company of every nature and description, including office furniture, manufactured stock, work in process, unprinted stock, copyrights, plates, dies, drawings, contracts, orders for stock, material and all goodwill. . . .' " Two weeks later Whitman Publishing Company was organized as a wholly owned subsidiary, and Western was launched toward its eventual long-term status as the world's largest producer of children's books, games, and so on.

Soon after World War I, Samuel Lowe (1884–1952) became Whitman's president and began the innovations that assured its success. Setting up an "activity room" in which to try out children's books and games, he took careful note of the mock-up items that drew the greatest interest of the company's young guests. In the early 1930s he tested dummy copies of the first five or six Big Little Books there before taking them to a New York trade show, where they gained the approval of chain store buyers. In 1933, the year after the initial Big Little Book was published, Lowe led Whitman into an exclusive long-term contract for the production of books featuring characters from Walt Disney Studios, and *Mickey Mouse* became one of the earliest Big Little Book titles to reach the Woolworth, Kresge, Kress, and other chain store counters. Lowe's association with Whitman and his general direction of its line continued until 1940, when he set up the company that carried his name. At his death in 1952, *Publishers Weekly* credited Lowe with bringing Whitman to a production level of "more than 6,000,000 volumes a year," adding, "He had a genius for sensing the trends in the mass market for books and he had courage and ingenuity in trying out new ideas." The Big Little Book was one of the ideas on which he gambled and won hugely.

Whitman's format–establishing 700 series Big Little Books, published between 1932 and 1936, included titles suggesting a wide variety of appeals. *The Big Little Mother Goose Book* (at 576 pages, the longest Big Little Book ever published), *The Big Little Paint Book* (published in hardcover and soft-cover editions of slightly differing sizes and lengths), and *Once Upon a Time* were meant for very young children; adaptations of *Robinson Crusoe*, *Treasure Island*, and *The Spy* borrowed the high culture legitimacy of literary classics; *The World War in Photographs* served an educational function; *Buffalo Bill and the Pony Express*, *Cowboy Stories*, and *Billy the Kid*, among others, satisfied appetites for Wild West material. Mickey Mouse was featured in five 700-series titles, one of them offered in four length, size, and cover variations. *Tom Beatty, Ace of the Service*, the first of many G-man titles from the 1930s, was offered in a "New Size Detective Series," while the 4½" × 5" "Movie Size" included Clyde Beatty in *Lions and Tigers* (sometimes mistakenly thought to be the first Big Little Book because it bears an unusual number, 653), Lionel Barrymore in a much-altered film version (released to theaters as *The Sea Beast*) of *Moby Dick*, Katharine Hepburn in *Little Women*, Charlotte Henry in *Alice in Wonderland*, and Ken Maynard in *Gun Justice*. Curiously, Robert Ripley's newspaper panel *Believe It or Not!* was assigned the movie size. The first two Dick Tracy, the first two Little Orphan Annie, and the first Mickey Mouse titles as well as *Houdini's Big Little Book of Magic* were among the ten books sharing the initial size (3⅞" × 4⅜" × 1½"), while many other of the 700-series comic strip adaptations, including those retailing the adventures of Chester Gump, Buck Rogers, Smitty, Tarzan of the Apes, Moon Mullins and Kayo, Tailspin Tommy, Skippy, Alley Oop, and Tiny Tim, appeared in the slightly smaller dimensions that were to become standard. The 700 series, in addition to the experimental air suggested by its variety of subjects and book sizes, is characterized by a degree of disdain for bibliographic nicety: on some books, the copyright date given is that of the source material in its original form, and other books list only the Whitman publication date.

Succeeding and partially overlapping the 700 series were the two 1100 series published between 1934 and 1937. Of the 128 titles assigned 1100 numbers (with many numbers repeated from the first series to the second), 111 were offered in the standard size, 15 appeared in the movie size, and 2 film adaptations were given unusually large dimensions (5¼" × 6¼"). New titles carried established characters into the 1100 series, and Flash Gordon, Don Winslow of the Navy, Skeezix from *Gasoline Alley*, Terry and the Pirates, Mandrake the Magician, Felix the Cat, Jungle Jim, Smilin' Jack, the Phantom, Popeye, and Donald Duck were added. Both Herman Brix and Johnny Weismuller were featured in adaptations of Tarzan films, and Tom Mix, Buck Jones, and Tim McCoy appeared in B-Western novelizations. From animated cartoons came Betty Boop and Oswald the Lucky Rabbit, the second of these being little more than a badly drawn promotional effort for Carl Laemmle Studios. *The Laughing Dragon of Oz*, the sole early period Big Little Book version of an L. Frank Baum novel and today one of the rarest Whitman titles, appeared in the first 1100 series, and the second 1100 group saw emerging or increasing emphases on characteristic 1930s themes and preoccupations: crime and police methodology (*G-Man on the Crime Trail, In the Name of the Law, G-Man vs. the Red X, Secret Agent X–9, Radio Patrol, Dan Dunn, Secret Operative 48, On the Trail of the Counterfeiters*), aviation (*Flying the Sky Clipper with Winsie Atkins, Tailspin Tommy and the Island in the Sky, Jimmie Allen in the Air Mail Robbery, Skyroads with Hurricane Hawk*, Capt. Eddie Rickenbacker's *Hall of Fame of the Air, Smilin' Jack and the Stratosphere Ascent*), and the ominous international picture (*Dr. Doom, International Spy, Faces Death at Dawn*). *Little Annie Rooney and the Orphan House* and *Apple Mary and Dennie Foil the Swindlers* (from the Martha Orr strip later reshaped into *Mary Worth*) brought Depression-era poverty into close view, but *Perry Winkle and the Rinkeydinks, Kayo in the Land of Sunshine, Silly Symphony Featuring Donald Duck, Mutt and Jeff*, and *Popeye Sees the Sea* were pure, cloudless fun. Although the source material of most 1930s titles depicted blacks as subservient and perpetually astonished, the second 1100 series book *Joe Louis, the Brown Bomber*, illustrated with Wide World Press Service photographs, emphasized its subject's heroic dimensions. Within the second 1100 series, the Joe Louis biography and *The Texas Ranger on the Trail of the Dog Town Rustlers* share the same number (1135), another sign of casualness in the publisher's numbering system.

Between 1937 and 1949 Whitman produced six 1400 series, most with distinctive innovations or format adjustments. During the first 1400 series (1937–38) Whitman redubbed its line "Better Little Books" in seeking to minimize consumer confusion of its Big Little Books with Saalfield Publishing Company's Little Big Books, calculatedly similar in name and almost identical in evolved format. Through overprinting, Whitman blacked out the circular logos carrying the "Big Little Book" designations on about a dozen already-prepared titles. These have been termed "transition books" by Larry Lowery, author of an especially useful collector's guide, who also sees the first 1400 series as the demarcation line between the Golden Age and the Silver Age in Big Little Book publication. Other noteworthy features of the first 1400 series include movement toward standardizing length (at 432 pages); the introduction of Blondie and Dagwood from the comic page, Gene Autry from the movies, and Charlie McCarthy, the Gang Busters, and Jack Armstrong from radio as central characters; and a new emphasis on Whitman-commissioned or staff-produced titles, several of which were clearly meant for girl readers: *Mary Lee and the Mystery of the Indian Beads* (written and illustrated by Alice Andersen), *Kay Darcy and the Mystery Hideout* (written under the pen name Irene Ray by Judy Bolton novel series author Margaret Sutton), and *Peggy Brown and the Runaway Auto Trailer* (authored by Kathryn Heisenfelt and, like a number of other Whitman titles of the period, carrying the distinctive artwork of Henry E. Vallely, a veteran illustrator for Chicago newspapers).

While the second 1400 series (1937–38) continued the innovations begun in the first, the third (1939–41) pushed toward a slicker, more "commercial" appearance. The traditional back-cover illustrations (often panoramic extensions of front covers) were replaced by promotional lists of Big Little Book characters or, on some volumes, by explanations of the new "See 'em move" or "Flip it" feature, simulating movie animation through small serial drawings added to the upper right corners of the right-hand illustration pages. The third 1400 series also brought the first Big Little Book adaptations of Fred Harman's Red Ryder, done in a dashingly sketchy style, and when Whitman's negotiations for bringing Superman to Big Little Books failed, the publisher created its own *Maximo, the Amazing Superman*, with art by Henry E. Vallely and text by Big Little Book veteran Russell R. Winterbotham.

The fourth (1941–43) and the fifth (1943–46) 1400 series introduced All Pictures Comics, in which no typeset text was needed because the speech balloons of the adapted comic strips were retained. *Keep 'Em Flying, U.S.A, for America's Defense, Steve Hunter of the U.S. Coast Guard, Ray Land of the Tank Corps, U.S.A., Pilot Pete and His Dive Bomber*, and *Allen Pike of the Parachute Squad, U.S.A.*, all originated by the Whitman staff, shared a cover-art style which approximated that of comic books from the same period. Wartime paper shortages pushed the standard length from 432 pages in the fourth series to 352 in the fifth. In the fifth series the no-reissue policy was modified to permit abbreviated versions of earlier Blondie, Donald Duck, and Mickey Mouse titles. Popular characters introduced in the early to mid–1940s included Roy Rogers and Bugs Bunny.

In the late 1940s, signs of trouble were clear. The sixth 1400 series (1946–49) saw another length reduction (to 288 pages) and an increasing tendency to concentrate on the most popular comic strip characters. An altered format, projecting a new leanness at slightly more than 3″ wide and 5½″ high, was called a New Better Little Book. In contrast to the exuberant variety seen in the fifty titles of the 1943–46 fifth 1400 series, the new format, also designated the 700–10 series, yielded only fifteen books featuring Walt Disney, Walter Lantz, and Warner Brothers cartoon characters, the most popular Western characters, and one each of Blondie and Tarzan. Single primary colors were carried through each volume in a belated attempt to counter the comic book's four-color appeal.

Through most of the 1950s, Big Little Book production was suspended, and Whitman promotional material of that period almost entirely ignored the fact that the company had manufactured and hugely profited from millions of these books. A tentative revival came in 1958 with the release of six titles constituting the medium-sized Big Little Book TV Series: *Wyatt Earp*, Walt Disney's *Andy Burnett on Trial*, *The Buccaneers*, *Gunsmoke*, *The Adventures of Jim Bowie*, and *Sir Lancelot*. The 2000 series, closer to the traditional Big Little Book dimensions and featuring comic strip as well as television characters, was issued from 1967 to 1969. Illustrations were printed in four colors, and some titles were twice reissued with reprint-distinguishing endpapers.

By the 1970s, the Woolworth stores that had temptingly displayed the original titles had been largely supplanted by suburban K-mart outlets, and in 1973 the newer chain spurred Whitman to produce yet another series, the 5700 group. Called "a BLB Classic," some of these glued softcover or "limpbound" titles were revisions of much earlier titles. The black-and-white books in the series revived the "Flip it" feature, while the remaining titles had four-color illustrations. These books were several times reprinted, their cover prices escalating from twenty-nine to seventy-nine cents. After completing its K-mart contract, Whitman has continued to develop modest numbers of titles, finally releasing a Superman (in 1980) and mixing established and new favorites: Popeye, the Lone Ranger, Tom and Jerry, the Incredible Hulk, Spiderman, and the Pink Panther.

Always a flexible enterprise, Whitman Publishing Company issued a number of subsidiary series, especially in the mid- to late 1930s. Some were for direct sale in the same stores that stocked "regular" Big Little Books; others were wholesaled as "prizes" to be given away at shoe stores, movie theaters, and gasoline stations. For many of the mid–1930s softcover premiums, Whitman eliminated about one-third the length of the basic-line originals, and the back covers were reserved for Cocomalt, Amoco Gas, or other sponsors' ads. On Tarzan (brand) Ice Cream and Buddy Book premiums, the back covers served as coupons to be collected to earn further premium books. Contemporary with these were boxed sets called Wee Little Books (1934–35), published six titles to a set and featuring Mother Goose rhymes, biblical characters, Mickey Mouse, and Little Orphan Annie. Three-to-a-box Top Line Comics sets featured popular comic strip characters, and the fourteen Big Big Books of 1934 to 1938 were essentially enlarged (to 7¼" × 9½" × 1¼") Big Little Books about Little Orphan Annie, Dick Tracy (two titles), Skippy, Tarzan, Buck Rogers, Mickey Mouse, Popeye, Tom Mix, Buck Jones, and Terry and the Pirates. The Famous "Funnies" Cartoon Books and the nickel Famous Hardbound Cartoon Books of the same years were thinner (sixty-four to sixty-eight pages) variations on the same adapt-a-comic theme. In 1938 and 1939, Whitman introduced five series of thirty-two-page penny books measuring 2½" × 3½", ranging from the Famous Comic Strip Story series (Dick Tracy, Smokey Stover, the Texas Ranger, and others) to the Fun Book series (*Dreams, Hobbies, Learn to Be a Ventriloquist*) and a ten-item Walt Disney Picture Book series. Three Tall Comic Books, more than 8" high, were devoted to Andy Panda, Bugs Bunny, and Mickey Mouse. In short, Whitman Publishing Company, developer of the Big Little Book, stretched the genre to include many types of subjects, lengths, and dimensions.

If Whitman Publishing Company had a dramatic beginning, its chief competitor in the inexpensive juveniles field evolved quietly in the years after Arthur Saalfield purchased the publishing interests of Akron's Werner Manufacturing Company, a major book-binding firm, in 1899. Passing through three generations of the family whose name it bore, the Saalfield Publishing Company was especially well-known for its paper doll and coloring books. In 1934, two years after Whitman had defined the genre with its *The Adventures of Dick Tracy*, Saalfield challenged its Wisconsin competitor by introducing six oblong Little Big Books, available in hardcover or softcover versions. The Saalfield entries featured Popeye, Just Kids, Tim Tyler, Little Annie Rooney, the Katzenjammer Kids, and Krazy Kat, and these were followed in the same year by various-sized adaptations of other comic strips (*Brick Bradford, Polly and Her Pals*), literary classics (*Black Beauty, Tom Sawyer*), and motion pictures (Our Gang comedies, Jackie Cooper in *Peck's Bad Boy*, Laurel and Hardy, Shirley Temple). The second year of Saalfield's Little Big Book production brought such diverse film adaptations as *The Story of Will Rogers*, Bela Lugosi in *Chandu the Magician*, and Claudette Colbert and Clark Gable in *It Happened One Night*. Boy Scout and sports subseries appeared in 1936 and 1937, yielding such titles as *Tommy of Troop Six, The Hockey Spare, The Winning Point*, and *Stan Kent, Freshman Fullback*.

By 1938, Saalfield Little Big Books had settled into a shape closely imitative of Whitman's Big Little Books. Although Whitman continued to emphasize licensed comic strip characters, Saalfield's 1938 list was chiefly made up of staff-produced (and often amateurishly drawn) cowboy titles. The same year saw the series title changed to Jumbo Books, but Saalfield continued to use its now-established length (400 pages) and size. Western titles were dominant during the 1938–40 span of Jumbo Books production, supplemented by a sprinkling of G-man titles and comic strip characters, including Li'l Abner, Major Hoople of *Our Boarding House*, Abbie an' Slats, and Napoleon and Uncle Elby. After 1940, Saalfield withdrew from the Big Little Book field but continued to produce handsome children's books of other kinds. Its *Peanuts* coloring books were highly successful in the mid–1960s, but the firm folded in the early 1970s.

The Saalfield series is potentially confused with the Little Big Books and Little Big Classics published between 1934 and 1939 by McLoughlin Brothers of Springfield, Massachusetts, founded in 1828 and recognized by John Tebbel as the nation's first publisher of children's books. Most of these half dozen or so titles, however, are for very young children, and the format is more traditional than that of the Saalfield and Whitman books.

Dell Publishing Company and Fawcett Publishing Company are best known for comic books and other types of softbound publications—paperback novels, how-to-do-it books, and similar mass market lines—but both firms made brief forays into the Big Little Book market. Fawcett produced only four of its Dime Action Books, all issued in 1941 and all recycling stories of Bulletman and Bulletgirl, Captain Marvel, Minute-Man, and Spy Smasher from *Whiz Comics* and *Master Comics*. The Dime Action title echoes that of Dell's Fast Action series of the late 1930s and early 1940s. Identified by a diamond-shaped cover logo containing the series name, Dell's Fast Action Books were editorially prepared and printed by Whitman and featured that company's most popular Big Little Book characters. Fast Action Books, all softbound, were taller than the standard Whitman titles. Particularly sought by contemporary collectors is the Fast Action representation of Edgar Rice Burroughs's *John Carter of Mars*, with drawings by Alex Raymond, best remembered for his work on the *Flash Gordon* and *Secret Agent X–9* comic strips.

Recalling Whitman's early movie series format, four books spotlighting radio comedians were published in 1934 and 1935 by the Goldsmith Publishing Company, the juveniles imprint of M. A. Donohue and Company. Each sixty-four-page book had a cover photograph of its subject, and the interior drawings preserve early work of Henry Vallely, whose thin, agile line would take on a more mature firmness in later Whitman and Dell Fast Action titles. The Goldsmith stories of Eddie Cantor, of Jack Pearl in his Baron Munchausen persona, of Ed Wynn as the Fire Chief, and of Joe Penner as proprietor of a vaudeville-inspired duck farm incorporated a large amount of fantasy and were aimed at a younger readership than most Whitman and Saalfield books. In a foreword to each Goldsmith book the Juvenile Educators League "heartily approve[d]" the radio program being adapted, and one of the final pages showed a cartooned bronze plaque which read, "Our ideal—to publish good books for red blooded boys and girls, without any thing in the stories or illustrations which may cause fright, suggest fear, or glorify mischief."

In 1933 and 1934, using the book dimensions that became standard for Whitman Big Little Books (but with generally fewer pages), the World Syndicate Publishing Company issued five High Lights of History Series titles. All five—*Buffalo Bill, Daniel Boone, Kit Carson, Pioneers of the Wild West*, and *The Winning of the West*—were adapted from the 1920s newspaper educational feature of the same title, written and illustrated by J. Carroll Mansfield. Three books were offered in alternate bindings, apparently on the assumption that cartoony board covers would appeal to Big Little Book-conditioned young buyers, while the simulated leather covers suggested a more traditional appeal to gift-buying elders.

Another New York–based early Whitman competitor was Engle-Van Wiseman Book Corporation's Five Star Library, published in 1934 and 1935, just as the Big Little Book format was becoming well established. The taller-than-wide Five Star Library books were principally adaptations of feature and B-Western films from RKO, Columbia, Universal, Warner Brothers, Monogram, and other studios. Popular child star Jackie Cooper was featured in *Oliver Twist* and *Dinky*, and Mickey Rooney as Puck grinned from the cover of the volume based on Max Reinhardt's romanticized 1935 film of *A Midsummer Night's Dream*. Franklin Delano Roosevelt figured centrally in *The Fighting President*, from a Universal release, while Rex, King of the Wild Horses, dominated the book version of Columbia's *Stampede*. Cowboy stars Tim McCoy (in both Western and aviation stories), John Wayne, Buck Jones, and Ken Maynard appeared in Five Star Library books, while Katharine Hepburn in *The Little Minister* and Douglas Fairbanks, Sr., in *Robin Hood* lent special star quality to the series.

Using a circular logo similar to Whitman's, the Lynn Publishing Company released a series of film and comic strip adaptations in 1935 and 1936. Among the feature films novelized were 20th Century Fox's *Les Miserables*, with Fredric March and Charles Laughton, and *Call of the Wild*, starring Loretta Young and Clark Gable; *Ceiling Zero*, with James Cagney and Pat O'Brien, from Warner Brothers; Paramount's *Trail of the Lonesome Pine*, with Henry Fonda and Fred MacMurray; and, from MGM, Ronald Coleman in *A Tale of Two Cities* and Wallace Beery and Jackie Cooper in *O'Shaughnessy's Boy*. Chic Young's *Blondie and Dagwood* was a four-color offering, unusual for the date, but most of Lynn's comic art titles were adapted from less well-known strips. Young's brother Lyman was the artist for *Curley Harper at Lakespur*, and another Lynn book, *Donnie and the Pirates*, was Darrell McClure's imitative tribute to the success of Milton Caniff's China-based comic strip.

If Saalfield, Lynn, the Five Star Library, and others were Whitman Publishing Company's competitors in the early years of Big Little Book–format publication, still others have essayed the genre since Whitman returned to the field in the late 1950s. Despite its intermittent production, Whitman has retained its dominance, while Ottenheimer's book versions of television cartoons, Waldman and Son's Moby Illustrated Classics, and further recent series have continued to redefine the genre's scope.

Ottenheimer Publishers of Baltimore, incorporated in 1890, began issuing softcover Big Little Book–sized books in 1977. All are stories of the Flintstones, Yogi Bear, and Huckleberry Hound, licensed from Hanna-Barbera Productions. Ottenheimer's Flintstones title *The Mystery of Many Missing Things* is a reworking of *The Case of the Many Missing Things*, published by Whitman in 1968.

Waldman and Son, publisher of a mix of children's materials reminiscent of Saalfield's catalog in earlier years, came to the Big Little Book field in 1977 with its Moby Books, distinguished by a silhouette logo of an apparently cheerful whale. The initial set included condensations of *Heidi*, *A Connecticut Yankee in King Arthur's Court*, *Little Women*, and *Treasure Island*, while *The Merry Adventures of Robin Hood*, *The Count of Monte Cristo*, *Moby Dick*, and two titles each by Charles Dickens and Mark Twain were among the 1979 editions. In 1983 the series was further extended by twelve titles, including Kipling's *Captains Courageous*, Lew Wallace's *Ben-Hur*, Alexandre Dumas's *The Man in the Iron Mask*, H. G. Wells's *The Time Machine* and *The War of the Worlds*, and more from Dickens and Twain. In contrast to the single-dime price tag of Depression-era Whitman and softcover Saalfield titles, the latest Moby Books are marked for sale at $1.25.

Less sustained recent forays into the publishing of Big Little Books deserve mention. In 1977 the McDonald's fast food chain issued *The Wizard of Oz*, *Tom Sawyer*, *Black Beauty*, and *A Christmas Carol* as premiums over a two-month period in much the same way that it attracts customers through periodic offerings of cartoon character dolls and drinking glass sets. Four years later, a Punxsutawney, Pennsylvania, science fiction illustrator, Joe Wehrle, Jr., evoked the Big Little Book genre in his privately published *Cauliflower Catnip*, the adventures (with adult overtones) of a feline detective. Andrews and McMeel, a Universal Press Syndicate affiliate, gathered panels from Tom Wilson's newspaper cartoon into *Ziggy's BIG little Book* in 1983 and *Alphabet Soup Isn't Supposed to Make Sense!—Ziggy's BIG little Book 2* in 1984. In these efforts and in those of Whitman, Ottenheimer, and Waldman and Son, the Big Little Book continues to evolve, though on a considerably less ambitious scale than it once achieved.

REFERENCE WORKS

Mentioned only incidentally in film encyclopedias and in histories of comic art, Big Little Books have been given detailed consideration in seven guides of varying scopes and ambitions. Meant primarily for latter-day collectors, all provide at least general information on the genre's development. Two create numbering systems for keeping track of the hundreds of titles published, and most suggest market values for copies surviving in rough to mint condition. Even the sketchiest of these guides will act as a starting point for the resourceful researcher, while the best of them contains a considerable amount of detail equally useful to the collector and to the scholar.

In 1970, Dale Manesis published 300 copies of a pamphlet entitled *Whitman: A Listing of Big Little Books and Related Publications Printed by the Whitman Publishing Company*; the back-page statement of bibliographic data provides the alternate title *List of Whitman Material*. This twenty-four-page guide begins with the caveat that a full list of Whitman titles might be a "near-impossible" achievement, since "it is unlikely that even Whitman has a complete record of all items it published." On subsequent pages, lists of Big and Better Little Books are alphabetized by titles, followed by lists of premiums and their sponsors (if known), Dell Fast Action Books, Big Big Books, nickel and penny books, the Chubby Books for very young readers (omitted by most guides), Wee Little Book sets, Walt Disney Story Books, and partial listings of the Racine publisher's paint books, puzzles, playing cards, coloring sets, and games featuring Big Little Book characters. Having the tentative and apologetic qualities of a pioneering effort, the Manesis guide is most useful in its listings, incomplete though they are, of the secondary publications that most later accountings have passed over.

Michael Resnick's 1973 *Official Guide to Comic Books and Big Little Books*, which achieved its second edition in 1977, assigns its last thirty pages to an alphabetical listing of various publishers' Big Little Books titles, preceded by a page-and-a half overview. The listing comes within a respectable distance of being complete to the date of its publication, but it does not specify publishers, authors, artists, copyright dates, or publishers' numbers. Designation of penny books is inconsistent.

Also in 1973, James Ashton of Ashton Publications in Middletown, Indiana, issued the first of a projected annual series of price guides. The 131-page *Ashton's Big Little Book Catalog* was designed primarily to create "advertising savings" by suggesting a title-and-condition coding system as an alternative to the publishers' own sometimes confusing spine numbers. Identifying authors but not artists (where they are different), the Ashton guide gives a reasonably full accounting of Whitman and Dell Fast Action, Saalfield, Engle-Van Wiseman Five Star Library, World Syndicate, and Lynn series through the 1960s and adds a brief definition of grading standards, an editorial defense of Big Little Books as the first reading matter of a generation of American children, and short sketches of Whitman's and Saalfield's roles in the field. Illustrated pages from 1930s Whitman and Saalfield wholesale catalogs are usefully reproduced.

Issued in 1981 and still available (from Educational Research Corporation, P.O. Box 1242, Danville, CA 94526) is *Lowery's The Collector's Guide to Big Little Books and Similar Books*, in many ways the best of the guides yet published. Larry Lowery's 380-page book divides Big Little Book publication into Golden, Silver, and Modern ages and then, publisher by publisher, gives details on each book, cataloged within the publishers' numerical series. Lowery's own numbering system reflects the order of the books' publication, and each of the three major period divisions in his guide begins with a brief account of "The Setting," the historical and social milieu in which the books appeared. Lowery also summarizes each publisher's history and product range.

Each entry in the Lowery guide indicates the year of publication; author, artist, or movie studio providing the material; book size, specified to the fraction of an inch; length; type of binding used; and details of cover or length variations. For some comic strip adaptations, original newspaper dates are given, and for titles based on radio programs, the initial broadcast dates and networks are identified. Almost all entries include small photographs of the book covers, scaled to reflect the cover dimensions of the series to which they belong.

Although it does not claim to offer a full listing of Latin American, Dutch, British, and other foreign editions, the Lowery guide gives a well-detailed treatment of the Big Little Book, omitting only a few recently discovered titles or printing variations listed in the same author's more recent (and more compact) *Collector's Price Guide*, described below. In addition to the types of material already mentioned, *Lowery's The Collector's Guide* contains sections dealing with grading standards and preservation problems, and each one of the three major period divisions ends in a "Collector's Record" where holdings and prices paid may be noted.

A more recent Big Little Book guide, bearing a 1983 copyright, is James Stuart Thomas's *The Big Little Book Price Guide* from Wallace-Homestead Book Company's collectibles series. After a paragraph or two about each publisher, Thomas provides an alphabetical list of titles, specifying artists and writers, publishers' numbers, and copyright dates. No distinctions are made among the seven Whitman series, but the Thomas survey does account for some Big Little Book related series not detailed in other guides. These include the Samuel Lowe Company's 1949 Swap-It cowboy books and Whitman's mid–1940s Mystery and Adventure Series hardbacks, also known as the Authorized Editions (2300 series). Because the Thomas guide repeats minor omissions and errors made in the Lowery book, its publisher has withdrawn it in settlement of a copyright infringement suit. In an open letter published in *Comics Buyer's Guide*, Thomas has protested his innocence and has pledged to bring out a second edition.

Late 1987 saw two further Big Little Book guides being prepared for publication. Robert M. Overstreet, a collector of these volumes for more than a quarter century and well known for his periodically revised comic book price guides, has provided a brief introduction to the Big Little Book and an alphabetical titles list in a section of *The Official Overstreet Price Guide Companion*, a pocket-sized book of more than 500 pages, which also lists selected comic book titles and prices. Annual revision of the *Companion*, published by Ballantine, is planned. Meanwhile, the earlier-mentioned Larry Lowery has produced *The Big Little Book Collector's Price Guide*, updating his own price estimates but attempting to hold them within the range asked or paid by seasoned collectors. This book is not intended to be a replacement for or a direct revision of *Lowery's The Collector's Guide*; rather, it is a more handily portable volume listing series and publication number, date, size, page count, author, and artist, and, where useful, a "Collector's Note" about distinctive features or publication variations for particular titles. Pop-up books and peripheral Disney material receive more detailed consideration here than in the initial Lowery guide, full revision of which lies two or three years in the future, according to its author-publisher.

RESEARCH COLLECTIONS

Since Big Little Books have never been anthologized and, with the exception of a few rewritten and redrawn titles in a late revival series, were not reprinted, the researcher will necessarily seek the 1932–50 titles in large collections, the fullest of which are generally in the hands of private collectors. However, the Library of Congress and several academic libraries hold sizable numbers. Because of the relatively fragile nature of this material, most libraries forbid circulation and inter-library loan, but photocopying policies vary widely. Some libraries prefer—a few insist—that researchers traveling to their collections give prior notice of their needs.

As a copyright depository collection, the Library of Congress's Rare Book and Special Collections Division holds one of the largest publicly accessible concentrations of Big Little Books. In a recent inventory the division's staff counted 520 titles (328 Whitman, 104 Saalfield, 26 Dell, 12 McLoughlin Brothers, 11 Lynn, and 39 others). Big Little Books might also be found in other divisions of the library but have not yet been systematically identified. As is true of many large collections, recent publications are not included in the Rare Book and Special Collections Division's holdings, inventory lists of which may be consulted in its reading room.

Two university libraries place Big Little Books in the contexts of outstanding children's literature collections. The Kerlan Collection in the Children's Literature Research Collections at the University of Minnesota's Walter Library, well known for its dime novel holdings, contains 561 cataloged Big Little Books. The Department of Special Collections at the Kenneth Spencer Research Library, the University of Kansas, Lawrence, sees Big Little Books as components of its science fiction holdings and especially of its late eighteenth- to early twentieth-century children's books. The aim here is for "a representative sampling of the genre," not completeness. According to Spencer librarian Alexandra Mason, "Reasonable mail requests for information will be answered." Visitors may access Big Little Books by author and, for most Whitman Big Little Books and Better Little Books, by series. Whitman titles are dominant in the Spencer Library's selection of about 150 Big Little Books from the 1930s and 1940s.

The Popular Culture Library at Bowling Green State University, Bowling Green, Ohio, also holds about 150 Big Little Books, chiefly Whitman books from the 1932–50 period, although a few later titles appear in the mimeographed inventory list. In recent years the Popular Culture Library has moved increasingly toward a closed-stacks situation to protect its vulnerable materials, but visitors will find that the library's operating hours during the academic year are generous. The inter-library loan policy allows staff photocopying of chapters or articles only, but at present, patron photocopying is unrestricted.

Other university libraries contain large to medium-sized collections. The Department of Special Collections in the Shields Library at the University of California at Davis has 230 cataloged Big Little Books, and the Special Collections Department at the Northwestern University Library, Evanston, Illinois, counts 114 volumes, four Saalfield and the remainder Whitman. The latter collection will microfilm any of its volumes at the user's expense. An author-title listing is available in Northwestern's Special Collections Department; these books are not included in the Main Library's cataloging system.

About fifty leading-publisher Big Little Books have been placed, as a representative sampling of the genre, within the renowned Comic Art Collection at Michigan State University in East Lansing. Particularly noteworthy here is the availability of correspondence from Gaylord Du Bois about his career as a Big Little Book and comic book writer. The titles are fully cataloged, and *Comic Art Collection*, a quarterly limited-circulation newsletter from the Russel B. Nye Popular Culture collection, has begun a register of Big Little Book research libraries.

Smaller samplings of Big Little Books may be found in interesting juxtapositions with related material in other academic collections. The Archive of Popular Culture at the University of Pittsburgh Library's Special Collections Department has only a handful of titles, but it also owns more than eighty 1920s and 1930s Whitman novels, uncataloged at present. The Library of Communication and Graphic Art at the Ohio State University in Columbus houses titles based on Milton Caniff's *Terry and the Pirates*, and the general Special Collections division holds the Big Little Books related to another celebrated state son, Eddie Rickenbacker. Kent State University's libraries received much of the Saalfield Publishing Company archival material when that firm was dissolved, but few Little Big Books and Jumbo Books arrived there with the large inventories of Saalfield coloring and activity books, paper dolls, and fiction reprints. Apparently the Saalfield Little Big Book and Jumbo Book file copies found their way into the collectors' market.

Whitman Publishing Company's own file copies were sold to a collector-dealer some time ago, but researchers wanting information on the Racine-based company that pioneered the genre will find it useful to consult the library of the State Historical Society of Wisconsin, 816 State Street, Madison 53706. An assiduous gatherer of materials related to Wisconsin interests, this institution has brought together (and made available in hard copy or microfilm) numerous Whitman promotional brochures and catalogs and several typescript and printed in-house company histories. The *Big Little*

Times periodical has also been microfilmed by the State Historical Society of Wisconsin. All materials are carefully cataloged.

Still other contexts for Big Little Books are provided by three private or semiprivate collections, all of which require advance notice for research use. For comparing newspaper strip–based titles with the form in which they originally appeared, researchers might consult the San Francisco Academy of Comic Art, 2850 Ulloa Street, San Francisco 94116, and the research department of the Museum of Cartoon Art, Comly Avenue, Rye Brook, NY 10573. In Canada, Doug Kendig maintains the Comic Research Library at Tappen, B.C. VOE 2X0. Mainly a gathering of comic strips and related memorabilia, the Comic Research Library does hold 380 Big Little Books, which may be seen by appointment. Reference questions sent by mail are cheerfully handled.

HISTORY AND CRITICISM

Very little formal academic criticism on Big Little Books has been attempted. In two chapters of his *G-Men: Hoover's FBI in American Popular Culture*, Richard Gid Powers has shown how the crime titles illustrate a once-insignificant Washington agency's expanding influence: "The Comic Strip G-Man" documents J. Edgar Hoover's negative reaction to *Secret Agent X–9*, which was adapted to two Big Little Books, while the later chapter "The Junior G-Men" draws illustrative details from the Whitman books *Junior G-Men and the Counterfeiters* and *G-Man on the Crime Trail*. A more general approach may be found in Francis J. Molson's *Journal of Popular Culture* article "Films, Funnies and Fighting the War: Whitman's Children's Books in the 1940s," which sees Big Little Books as one part of the publisher's output. Beyond listing featured characters and titles, this study provides few details on Big Little Books per se.

The *Big Little Times*, a bi-monthly publication for members of the Big Little Book Collectors Club of America, was begun by John Stallknecht in 1982 as a continuing supplement to *Lowery's The Collector's Guide to Big Little Books and Similar Books*. Early issues were made up of quizzes, question and answer pages, collectors' letters, and lists of titles and characters. Larry Lowery, serving as editor since the beginning of volume 2, has brought an increasing variety of content and a degree of graphic polish to the periodical. Each issue spotlights one or more characters adapted to or created for Big Little Books. The films, radio series, cereal premiums, and other media featuring these characters are detailed, background on artists and writers is given, and each such article ends with a full bibliographic description of all the titles and related series in which the character under consideration appears. The *Big Little Times* also reprints newspaper clippings and magazine articles, chiefly from hobbyists' periodicals, about Big Little Books and their collectors, and it has treated such subjects as Big Little Book editorial bloopers, printing and binding errors, trademarks, copyrights, newly discovered length and cover variations, and the care and storage of these books. This bi-monthly's ads give a good sense of the availability or rarity of particular titles in the collectors' market. Subscriptions to and back issues of the *Big Little Times*, as well as a listing of most club members, are available through the Big Little Book Collectors Club of America, P.O. Box 1242, Danville, CA 94526.

If the study of Big Little Books has been more fully a collectors' than an academic interest, writers of popular period histories and memorabilia "catalogs" have found them richly evocative, especially of Depression-era childhood. In the *1930–1940* volume of the staff-written Time-Life series *This Fabulous Century*, the "Dream Factory" chapter recalls them as "squat, 400-page cubes of type and pictures," and one spread places five Flash Gordon Big Little Books beside an example of Alex Raymond's Sunday newspaper page and a Flash Gordon movie serial still. In *The Great American Depression Book of Fun*, John O'Dell places these books in the context of the "toys, games, and high adventures" of the period, and four books jointly written by Robert Heide and John Gilman make much of Big Little Books as period artifacts. In their *Dime-Store Dream Parade: Popular Culture 1925–1955*, now out of print, Heide and Gilman boldly assert, "Few things represent the 'feel' of the 1930s more than a Big Little Book," and this statement is repeated in their latest collaboration, *Starstruck: The Wonderful World of Movie Memorabilia*, which also contains a "Hollywood Big Little Books" subsection. In their *Cartoon Collectibles*, focused on every type of Disney collectible, Big Little Books are seen as "a child's first introduction to the novel form," while their *Cowboy Collectibles* shows Western titles among various kinds of items featuring B-Western stars and fictional characters.

The Big Little Book has had its critics—and not necessarily published ones. For young readers the story illusion was sometimes shattered when the illustrations lost synchronization with the text, one racing pages ahead of the other. Sometimes the preordained page count ran out before the plot line did, creating a huddled or a very abrupt ending, as in *Chester Gump at Silver Creek Ranch*, where Chester and a friend are left "trying to get out of the cavern to safety," with only a vague suggestion of their escape, which is "another story." Some unamused judges, perhaps forgetting that the publishers drew on a variety of sources, including their own writers and artists, have condemned Big Little Books for their Procrustean ways of adapting comic strip material, altering the source drawing's dimensions, and replacing its speech balloons with crosshatching or architectural doodling.

For others, the Big Little Book, its faults admitted and digested, served as an agent of imagination and even as a definer of experience. Authors of recent best sellers have seen the genre in that way. In *World's Fair*, his novel of late–1930s New York City boyhood, E. L. Doctorow uses the newsstand purchase of a Flash Gordon Big Little Book as a crystallizing detail in the young protagonist's perception of "New York and its excitements." In *Growing Up*, a Pulitzer Prize–winning evocation of small-town childhood in the Depression, Russell Baker remembers his sources of delight: "My idea of a perfect afternoon was lying in front of the radio rereading my favorite Big Little Book, *Dick Tracy Meets Stooge Viller*." Baker also recalls with characteristic irony that the unassigned profits of his *Saturday Evening Post* sales were "mine to squander on vices of my choice, which were movies, Big Little Books, and two-for-a-penny Mary Jane bars." Likewise, the illustrator Maurice Sendak, as quoted in Selma G. Lanes's book, has remembered the vivid impression that a Big Little Book made on him: "I must have been five or six years old, and in the next apartment lived a girl my age who had marvelous books, like the Big Little Book of *David Copperfield*, with photographs of Freddie Bartholomew in it. That's who I thought David Copperfield was for a very long time."

BIBLIOGRAPHY

Books and Articles

Ashton, James E. *Ashton's Big Little Book Catalog and Price Guide, 1973*. Middleton, Ind.: Ashton Publications, 1973.

Baker, Russell. *Growing Up*. New York: Congdon and Weed, 1982.

Doctorow, E. L. *World's Fair: A Novel*. New York: Random House, 1985.

"Fiftieth Anniversary Observed by Saalfield." *Publishers Weekly*, 157 (March 11, 1950), 1350–51.

Heide, Robert, and John Gilman. *Cartoon Collectibles: Fifty Years of Dime-Store Memorabilia*. Garden City, N.Y.: Doubleday, 1983.

———. *Cowboy Collectibles*. New York: Harper and Row, 1982.

———. *Dime-Store Dream Parade: Popular Culture 1925–1955*. New York: E. P. Dutton, 1979.

———. *Starstruck: The Wonderful World of Movie Memorabilia*. Garden City, N.Y.: Doubleday, 1986.

Kaiser, John W. "The History of Big Little Books." *Big Little Times*, 4 (September–October 1985), 9–10.

Knapp, Ed. "Big Little Books." *Rarities*, 4 (May–June 1983), 50–57.

Lanes, Selma G. *The Art of Maurice Sendak*. New York: Harry N. Abrams, 1980.

Longest, David. *Character Toys and Collectibles*. Paducah, Ky.: Collector Books, 1984.

Lowery, Larry. *The Big Little Book Collector's Price Guide*. Danville, Calif.: Educational Research and Applications, 1988.

———. *Lowery's The Collector's Guide to Big Little Books and Similar Books*. Danville, Calif.: Educational Research and Applications, 1981.

Madison, Charles Allen. *Book Publishing in America*. New York: McGraw-Hill, 1966.

Manesis, Dale. *Whitman: A Listing of Big Little Books and Related Publications Printed by Whitman Publishing Company*. Milwaukee: Dale Manesis, 1970.

Molson, Francis J. "Films, Funnies and Fighting the War: Whitman's Children's Books in the 1940s." *Journal of Popular Culture*, 17 (Spring 1984), 147–54.

Mussey, Virginia Howell. "Books—Five Cents, Ten Cents and Up." *Publishers Weekly*, 134 (October 1, 1938), 1280–83.

Nuhn, Roy. "Big Little Books: Giant Action in Tiny Packages." *Collectors' Showcase*, 2 (February 1983), 38–42.

"Obituary Notes: Samuel T. Lowe." *Publishers Weekly* 161 (February 23, 1952), 999.

O'Dell, John. *The Great American Depression Book of Fun*. New York: Harper and Row, 1981.

Overstreet, Robert M. *The Official Overstreet Price Guide Companion*. New York: Ballantine, 1987.

Powers, Richard Gid. *G-Men: Hoover's FBI in American Popular Culture*. Carbondale: Southern Illinois University Press, 1983.

Resnick, Michael. *Official Guide to Comic Books and Big Little Books*. 2d ed. Florence, Ala.: House of Collectibles, 1977.

"Samuel Lowe Organizes Firm to Issue Cheap Books." *Publishers Weekly*, 138 (November 16, 1940), 1905.

The Story of Western, 1907–1965: Fifty-Eight Years of Progress in the Graphic Arts. [Racine (?)], Wis.: Western Publishing, [1965].

Tebbel, John William. *A History of Book Publishing in the United States*. 4 vols. New York: R. R. Bowker, 1978.

Thomas, James Stuart. *The Big Little Book Price Guide*. Des Moines, Iowa: Wallace-Homestead, 1983.

———. "Open Letter: Price Guide Claims Are Disputed." *Comics Buyer's Guide*, issue 647 (April 11, 1986), 48.

Time-Life editors. *This Fabulous Century*. 6 vols. New York: Time-Life Books, 1969.

Western Ways: Products and Practices of the Western Publishing Company. [Kenosha, Wis. (?)]: Western Publishing, [1962 (?)].

Periodicals

Big Little Times. Danville, Calif., 1982-.

Comics Buyer's Guide. Iola, Wis., 1970-.

3.

Children's Literature

R. GORDON KELLY

The relationship between children's literature and the mainstream of the nation's literary and intellectual life was particularly close in the late nineteenth century, when, for example, three successive editors of the *Atlantic Monthly*, Thomas Bailey Aldrich, Horace Scudder, and William Dean Howells, all, at one time or another, wrote expressly for children. In this century, however, there has been significantly less overlap. Few major twentieth-century American authors have written for children, and in the development of higher education, the study of children's books was relegated to the intellectual periphery of schools of education and library science. Until recently, writing about children's books, as well as the books themselves, issued with a few notable exceptions from a cozy enclave cut off in large measure from modern literary and intellectual trends. As a consequence, "children's literature" all too often designates a narrowly belletristic tradition that excludes much that is of interest in the history of books for children, including works of great popularity. From the ubiquitous primers of the seventeenth and eighteenth century to the phenomenally popular stories of Horatio Alger in the nineteenth and the adventures of Nancy Drew and the Hardy boys in the twentieth, some children's books, however undistinguished in literary quality, have reached very large numbers of readers. Moreover, much of the literature directed to children is "popular" literature in the sense that it is highly conventional and intended to appeal to the largest possible audience. This is as true of the moral tale, the principal form of antebellum fiction for children, as it is of the works of Alger and the numerous series books produced early in this century under the direction of Edward Stratemeyer, to cite only three of the most conspicuous examples of popular children's literature. Thus there is ample justification for including a chapter on children's books in a handbook on popular literature.

Although there has been an increasing interest in the history and criticism of children's literature in the last twenty years, much of the work that has appeared reflects a conventional and unimaginative belletristic orientation, lacking scope and theoretical sophistication. Fortunately, the most interesting and promising work in the field deals with the cultural significance of popular books for children: the antebellum moral tale, the novels of Alger, and the Oz fantasies of L. Frank Baum. Children's books are especially deserving of a contextualist approach because they give form and specificity, in ways considered appropriate for impressionable minds, to matters of crucial importance: cultural definitions of what is; what is good, true, and beautiful; and what things go together. Children's books are an accessible, readily available feature in an elusive enterprise—the creation, maintenance, and modification of meaning in society. We have hardly begun to examine children's books in America from this perspective and to locate them in the cultural contexts in which they were written, read, and selectively preserved and made available to successive generations of American children.

HISTORIC OUTLINE

The following summary of the history of books for children in the United States departs in two important ways from the capsule histories to be found, for example, in most textbooks on children's literature. First, it emphasizes changes in the social and intellectual factors shaping the creation of children's books. One does not have to be a philosophical idealist to admit that concepts of the child and his or her needs constitute crucial aspects of an author's intention, nor need one be a Marxist to accept that changes in technology can significantly affect the production of books, including books for children. Second, I have not assumed that the development of literature for children can easily or unambiguously be interpreted as an increasingly faithful delineation of social reality appropriate to the child's needs and interests, for the very concept of these needs and interests has undergone significant change in the last two centuries and is changing even now.

Histories of children's literature have often been written as if fidelity to life and a due regard for the true nature of the child are asymptotic with the present—that as we approach the present, books for children, with numerous exceptions duly noted, are, on balance, both truer to life and truer to what we take to be the essence of childhood than books published decades or centuries ago. The view is understandable though scarcely pardonable. The children's books of colonial America especially lie on the far side of a cultural divide that few would-be historians of children's literature have endeavored to cross, being content to dismiss books written before the first quarter of the nineteenth century as narrowly sectarian, gloomy, and morbid, to note a few of the charges leveled at them by modern commentators. What is being condemned is not the literature so much as the view of human nature, including child nature, that pervades the primers and catechisms, those most popular of children's books produced in the seventeenth and eighteenth centuries. However, literature for children was more diverse than that, for in addition to the religious manuals and conduct books, there were biography, fiction, animal stories, riddles, fables, nursery rhymes, fairy tales, and picture books. A leading historian of early books for children only slightly overstates the situation when he observes: "Speaking broadly, I know of no kinds of children's books published today which were not also published in the seventeenth century."[1] Moreover, it is clear that writers for children sought in a variety of ways to appeal to and influence the mind of the child reader—as they understood it—since a major aim was to arouse in the child the desire for saving knowledge.

The emergence of modern children's literature is conventionally dated from the middle of the eighteenth century and credited, rather too narrowly, to the entrepreneurial genius of John Newbery, whose first venture in colorfully printed books written to amuse as well as edify children was *Pretty Little Pocket Book* (1742), by which time books for children had been highly vendible for several decades. From the 1750s, Newbery's little books were imported or pirated by American printers and booksellers, most notably Isaiah Thomas in Worcester, Massachusetts.

Americans remained heavily dependent on British books for children until well into the nineteenth century, but in the 1820s, the spirit of literary nationalism began to stir interest in the creation of a truly American literature for children. Much of the literature was religious, though not narrowly sectarian. Interdenominational tract societies, such as the American Sunday School Union, established in 1818, and the American Tract Society, founded the following year, produced vast quantities of books and pamphlets for the religious and moral edification of American youth, most of it presented in the attractive format that derived from Newbery and his American imitators.

The future of American children's literature, however, did not lie in the efforts of the tract societies but in the work of such popular and prolific antebellum moralists as Jacob Abbott and Samuel Griswold Goodrich, better remembered as the genial, avuncular Peter Parley. Goodrich eventually wrote over one hundred books designed to introduce his young readers to the facts of geography, history, and natural science in an informal and entertaining way—often by employing a travelogue format. Abbott, trained as a Unitarian minister, was even more prolific than Goodrich. In a series of books devoted to the educational and moral development of a good boy, Rollo, Abbott managed to hint at how an individualized child character might be created, and in a later series, the *Franconia* stories, he drew on his childhood memories of Maine in describing a group of children growing up in a rural village.

Until the 1850s, the moral tale, designed primarily to instruct the young in the civic virtues of obedience, piety, self-reliance, and self-discipline, was the principal form of secular fiction addressed to American children, but in the decade before the Civil War, there was a perceptible broadening of children's literature. William Taylor Adams, writing as Oliver Optic, introduced more adventure into boys' books while still adhering, in an early book like *The Boat Club* (1855), to the moral values of the day. Like the adventure tale, stories of family life, later a staple of girls' fiction, also have their origins in the 1850s in such popular works as *The Wide, Wide World* (1850) by Elizabeth Wetherell (Susan Bogart Warner) and Maria Cummins's *The Lamplighter* (1854), both of which illustrate the rewards accruing to faith, fortitude, and patience. Even fantasy, a form generally uncongenial to the New England temperament, can be traced to the 1850s in the work of the minor transcendentalist Christopher Pearse Cranch, *The Last of the Huggermuggers* (1855).

After the Civil War, American children's literature flowered in a manner that surprised even the most hopeful critics of children's books a decade before. Most of the differences that set off early nineteenth-century books for children from their counterparts in the 1870s and 1880s can be traced in large measure to the altered views about the nature and needs of children typically held by children's authors, publishers, and later librarians. By 1850, the concept of infant depravity ceased to be a major factor in shaping books for children and was replaced by a conception of the child as innocent and good.

Childhood came to be acknowledged as a separate stage of life valuable in itself, a time during which the child's capacity for wonder and imagination could be freely and safely indulged. This view of childhood affected virtually every aspect of child nurture from discipline to clothing and diet and had a profound effect on books for children. The extraordinary achievements in children's literature from 1865 to the turn of the century are owed directly and decisively to widespread acceptance of this altered view of the child.

Other factors of a more mundane sort also contributed to the expansion, diversification, and specialization of publishing for children that occurred after the Civil War. Population increases and comparatively high levels both of income and of literacy in the United States contributed to a rapid expansion of audiences for books of all kinds. Developments in printing technology speeded up the process of publication, making possible more attractive books at lower prices. Improvements in transportation, especially the creation of a continental rail system, meant that the market for children's books could be organized on a national basis. The growth of public education and the founding of public libraries also stimulated the demand for children's books.

To these demographic and technological factors, which in isolation merely describe a capacity for growth, must be added factors of belief and value. The development of literature for children after the Civil War was owed not only to the new views of childhood described earlier but also to the profound faith in the social and individual benefits of education—a faith deeply rooted in democratic thought—and to a conception of art, which, in its more exalted formulations, promised a kind of secular salvation through works of imaginative genius.

As a consequence of these views, writers for children, as well as editors and publishers, rejected the overt didacticism that had characterized the antebellum moral tale and sought to shift the emphasis in children's books from instruction to entertainment and pleasure. Nevertheless, this shift in emphasis can be overstated. The rejection of a particular form of moralizing after 1860 did not entail rejecting the moral values espoused by earlier writers, such as Goodrich and Abbott. Self-reliance, courage, and independence, if not religious faith, composed a core of values that underwent little change in the course of the century, although the literary forms in which they were expressed changed markedly. An astute student of the change correctly observes: "The assertion of freedom from moral didacticism, far from being a move toward aesthetic autonomy, was made within a definite and circumscribed moral framework."[2]

Much of the history of children's literature in the last third of the nineteenth century is foreshadowed in books and periodicals that appeared in the five years following the Civil War. The most notable single work is Louisa May Alcott's *Little Women* (1867), which provided a model for much subsequent fiction centered on family life. Earlier practitioners of the boys' adventure story, such as Oliver Optic, were joined by Harry Castlemon (Charles Austin Fosdick) and Horatio Alger, Jr., whose *Ragged Dick* (1868) was the first of more than one hundred novels depicting the rise (or, often, the restoration) to respectability of impoverished, often homeless, boys. A popular sentimental girls' series began in 1868 with the publication of *Elsie Dinsmore* by Martha Farquharson Finley.

The works of Castlemon, Alger, and Finley defined a gray area of literary and moral respectability—not as objectionable as the dime novels and story papers, a rank undergrowth of cheap, sensational fiction that flourished despite the contempt heaped upon it by custodians of the nation's cultural life—but certainly not as praiseworthy as the work of Harriet Beecher Stowe, John Townsend Trowbridge, Louisa May Alcott, and a host of other, mainly New England, writers who dominated the quality juvenile periodicals of the period: *Our Young Folks, Riverside Magazine, Wide Awake, Youth's Companion*, and pre-eminently *St. Nicholas*. In the thirty years following its establishment in 1873, *St. Nicholas*, under the able editorship of Mary Mapes Dodge, made available to American children the work of the best regarded juvenile authors in Britain and the United States.

With the turn of the century, new types of children's books appeared, but there was little change in the social and intellectual factors underlying the creation of children's literature. Interest in folk and fairy tales, formerly limited almost exclusively to British materials and the work of the Brothers Grimm and Hans Christian Andersen, broadened to include the traditional tales of other countries. Animal stories became popular after the turn of the century, with the publication of Alfred Ollivant's *Bob, Son of Battle* (1898), Jack London's *The Call of the Wild* (1903), and the work of Ernest Thompson Seton. An even more popular new form was the school sports story, which reflected the increasing prominence of athletics in the national life in the 1880s and 1890s. The Frank Merriwell stories of Burt L. Standish (Gilbert Patten), derived in large measure from the dime-novel tradition, but the work of more ambitious juvenile novelists, such as Ralph Henry Barbour, owed much to Thomas Hughes's widely read story of life at Rugby, *Tom Brown's School Days* (1857).

Such books as Kate Douglas Wiggin's *Rebecca of Sunnybrook Farm* (1903) and Dorothy Canfield Fisher's *Understood Betsy* (1917) were notable contributions in the early twentieth century to the well-established domestic story tradition inaugurated by *Little Women*, while L. Frank Baum enriched the rather thin tradition of American fantasy with *The Wonderful Wizard of Oz* (1900) and more than a dozen sequels. Another staple of juvenile publishing, the series adventure for boys, underwent development at the turn of the century at the hands of Edward Stratemeyer, who followed up his success with the Rover Boys by creating the Motor Boys, the Bobbsey Twins, and Tom Swift, among others. Retaining control of each series' concept, Stratemeyer hired writers willing to work to his formula and published their work under a series pseudonym. Following his death in 1930, Stratemeyer's production-line methods of quality control were successfully continued by his daughter, Harriet Stratemeyer Adams, who created Nancy Drew.

Stratemeyer's rationalization of series book production has an analogue in the world of quality publishing for children. The growth of children's libraries and the professionalization of children's librarianship in the late nineteenth and early twentieth century, together with the establishment of National Book Week in 1919, the appointment in the same year of Louise Seaman Bechtel as children's book editor at Macmillan, and the concentration of children's book reviewing in the hands of librarians and educationists—all influenced the creation of children's literature, especially after 1920, in ways that are not yet well understood. Part of the effect, however, has been to maintain critical standards that appear to have changed little since the 1870s.

The decade of the 1930s saw the publication of some notable examples of the family story and the juvenile historical novel as well as some excellent retellings of traditional folk tales. The picture book, however, is the principal form of children's book in which there has been dramatic improvement, owing largely to new color printing processes. The achievements of writers in the 1930s notwithstanding, the history of American children's literature in the century following the Civil War is marked by a proliferation of types but a singular continuity of underlying cultural values and assumptions.

The mid–1960s witnessed dramatic changes in the world of children's books, changes that had their proximate origins in the civil rights movement, the sexual revolution, and the emergence of the youth culture. Increased sensitivity to racial, ethnic, and gender discrimination combined with a less protective (or more honest) attitude toward children to permit franker and more explicit treatment of a range of social themes—divorce, drug abuse, mental illness—than had been earlier permitted in books for children. The roots of what came to be called the "new realism" go back to the 1950s. Writers like Judy Blume, Norma Klein, and Robert Cormier subsequently colonized the world made familiar by J. D. Salinger's *The Catcher in the Rye* (1951) and by Paul Goodman's nonfiction counterpart, *Growing Up Absurd* (1956).

Coincident with the introduction of new themes and conventions of realism, federal support for public and school libraries sustained a boom in children's book publishing in the late 1960s. The reduction of that support in the 1970s translated directly into less institutional buying, still the major support for the industry, and the subsequent recession of the early Reagan years was particularly hard on children's book publishing. Several companies stopped publishing children's books altogether (McGraw-Hill, Follett, Coward-McCann), while others cut back substantially (Doubleday and Scribner's, for example). Reduced institutional buying over the last decade has been offset to a point by increased space given over to children's books in bookstore chains, but the rising cost of publishing, together with reduced institutional buying and a markedly more conservative political and social climate in the early 1980s, has put pressure on publishers to come up with books designed for the largest possible audience. The most significant new trend in the early 1980s has been the commercial success of preteen and teenage romance series, following the introduction of Scholastic's Wildfire imprint. With print orders averaging 150,000 per title, other publishers were quick to follow Scholastic's lead. Condemned by their critics as trashy, sexist, and socially conservative, the romance series created the large audiences demanded by the new economics of publishing.

A second important trend in recent years is the proliferation of books for very young children that can be traced to both a rising birthrate and greater parental concern with early childhood development. The picture book remains a growth area in children's publishing and a staple in the growing number of children's bookstores established in the last decade.

The realism inaugurated in the 1960s continues to run side by side with the new romance, however. The turn toward social conservatism in the 1980s has not yet restored the family story to its former place of honor or relative innocence. The insufficiency of parents remains the norm, and home, no longer a safe or stable refuge, is typically a scene of misunderstanding and lack of communication between adults and their children. Teenage suicide and child abuse, both widely publicized in the early 1980s, have become prominent themes realistically treated in books for children. Whether the new realism is, on balance, a good or a bad thing, it remains the most durable and visible, if increasingly problematic, legacy of the changes that overtook American society in the 1960s.

REFERENCE WORKS

Until the late sixties, the study of children's literature was carried on principally in library science and elementary education programs that prepared school and children's librarians and teachers. In the last fifteen years, courses in children's literature have emerged as popular offerings in departments of English as well. Literary scholars have added substantially to the large and growing body of writing about books for children by those in the fields of librarianship and education. Reference works on children's literature reflect the institutional biases of those who, until recently, were the principal custodians of books for the young.

Several relatively comprehensive guides to the field of books for children are *Children's Literature: A Guide to Reference Sources*, by Virginia Haviland, former head of the children's division, Library of Congress, and *The World of Children's Literature*, by Anne Pellowski. Haviland's *Guide* is a selective annotated bibliography of books, articles, and pamphlets on the history, selection and evaluation, illustration, authorship, and principal genres of books for children. The scope of the volume is limited largely to the professional literature of librarianship and education, however; there are few references to the substantial body of writing about children's literature by historians, literary scholars, and the occasional psychologist or sociologist who has ventured into the field. Regular supplements to *Children's Literature* are planned, the first of which appeared in 1972 with citations to books and articles published from 1966 to 1969; the second in 1977.

Anne Pellowski's *The World of Children's Literature* is an international bibliography of monographs, series, and multivolume works, organized by country, relating to various aspects of writing for children, including the history and criticism of children's books, library work with children, criteria and techniques of writing for children, lists of recommended books, and children's reading interests. An elaborate index permits the reader to locate items about a given author, type of children's book, or theme. The brief historical introduction to children's literature in the United States is unusual for its account of social factors shaping the production of books for children in this country.

These two reference guides are supplemented by two more recent works: Mary Meacham's *Information Sources in Children's Literature* and *Books About Children's Books* by Virginia L. White and Emerita S. Schulter, an annotated bibliography of over one hundred books published between 1967 and 1977.

Doctoral dissertations, which are not covered in the foregoing reference guides, are indexed in W. Bernard Lukenbill's *A Working Bibliography of American Doctoral Dissertations in Children's and Adolescents' Literature, 1930–1971*, which is supplemented by Dianne L. Monson and Bette Peltola, *Research in Children's Literature*, which lists over 300 studies from the period 1960 through 1974. Since 1973, *Phaedrus: An International Annual of Children's Literature Research* has listed dissertations in the field. Edited by James Fraser, head of the library at Fairleigh Dickinson University, *Phaedrus* is the best source of information on current research and writing about children's literature, broadly defined by Fraser as "the media environment of the child and adolescent."

In addition to its invaluable bibliographies, *Phaedrus* publishes research articles and is the principal source in this country for information about children's literature research abroad. Current research and criticism also appear in *Children's Literature* (formerly subtitled "The Great Excluded"), the *Lion and the Unicorn*, and *Children's Literature in Education*.

Children's Literature, currently published by Yale University Press, is the journal of the Children's Literature Association. Issued annually, it emphasizes critical approaches to books for children, rarely offering articles on popular authors or social issues. The association's *Quarterly*, while sharing the rather narrow critical focus of *Children's Literature*, is a livelier forum for the membership, drawn principally from the ranks of English departments. The *Lion and the Unicorn*, published since 1977, is a theme- and genre-centered journal with aesthetic preoccupations similar to those which inform *Children's Literature*. *Children's Literature in Education*, now a joint venture of British and American professors, grew out of a 1969 British conference on the role of children's fiction in education. With its roots in the problems of schools, *Children's Literature in Education* has always had a broader mandate than the critical journals founded in the 1970s in this country. The *Horn Book Magazine*, long the only American periodical devoted exclusively to children's literature, publishes critical articles and reviews of children's books as well as occasional historical studies. These, unfortunately, are rarely the work of professional historians and all too frequently fail to add measurably to our understanding of the history of children's books in the United States. Articles on children's literature also appear regularly in *Top of the News*, the quarterly journal of the Children's Services Division and Young Adult Services Division of the American Library Association.

Biographical information on children's authors and illustrators is almost an industry of its own. The most comprehensive reference guide is Adele Sarkissian's *Children's Authors and Illustrators*, which lists over 20,000 writers and artists whose work is available in English. The work also serves as an individual guide to the principal sources of biographical information such as Stanley J. Kunitz and Howard Haycraft's *The Junior Book of Authors*; Muriel Fuller's supplemental *More Junior Authors*, and Doris DeMontreville and Donna Hill's *Third Book of Junior Authors*. With Elizabeth Crawford, DeMontreville edited the *Fourth Book of Junior Authors and Illustrators*. A *Fifth Book* appeared in 1983, edited by Sally Holmes Holtze. Other sources of biographical information include Anne Commire's series *Something About the Authors* and Miriam Hoffman and Eva Samuels's *Authors and Illustrators of Children's Books: Writings on Their Lives and Works*, containing articles on or by fifty notable contemporaries. *Twentieth-Century Children's Writers*, edited by Daniel Kirkpatrick, collects 600 entries consisting of a short biography, complete bibliography, and a brief critical essay on English language authors of fiction, poetry, and drama for children. A second edition appeared in 1983. Brian Doyle's *The Who's Who of Children's Literature* provides accounts of over 400 British and American authors, from 1800 to the present, some of whom, like L. Frank Baum, creator of the Wizard of Oz books, are rarely mentioned in histories of children's literature. Two articles by David L. Greene describe limited circulation, special interest periodicals devoted to children's authors, such as *Newsboy*, the journal of the Horatio Alger Society, and the *Baum Bugle*, published by the International Wizard of Oz Club: "Children's Literature Journals: Author Society Journals and Fanzines" and "Children's Literature Periodicals on Individual Authors, Dime Novels, Fantasy."

For biographical information on illustrators, the standard source is *Illustrators of Children's Books, 1744–1945*, by Bertha E. Mahoney Miller, Louise P. Latimer, and Beulah Folmsbee, which provides information on 500 illustrators whose work has appeared in picture books in this country. Supplements appeared in 1958 and 1968. Martha E. Ward and Dorothy A. Marquardt's *Illustrators of Books for Young People*, with 750 entries, is also valuable.

The most complete listing of contemporary books for children is *Children's Books in Print*, an annual trade bibliography published by R. R. Bowker since 1970. Its companion volume, *Subject Guide to Children's Books in Print*, lists books under 7,000 categories. Other indexes include: *Subject and Title Index to Short Stories for Children*; *Subject Index to Poetry for Children and Young People*; and Norma O. Ireland's *Index to Fairy Tales, 1949–1972*,

Including Folklore, Legends, and Myths, in Collections. Children's Catalogue, first published in 1909, is a selection aid for librarians. The fifteenth edition, listing over 3,400 titles, appeared in 1986. For years this annotated catalog was the basic tool for selecting books for children's libraries, but it is now generally supplemented by other selection aids, some of which are noted below. A basic guide to the many selection aids available is *Selecting Materials for Children and Young Adults,* a bibliography of bibliographies, describing nearly 300 titles published before 1979.

An invaluable historical bibliography of books for children is D'Alte A. Welch's "A Bibliography of American Children's Books Printed Prior to 1821," originally published serially in the *Proceedings of the American Antiquarian Society* and then reprinted as a single volume in which, unfortunately, the valuable notes on the British originals of American books were eliminated. Primarily interested in books intended for leisure reading, Welch excluded from his bibliography school books, catechisms, conduct manuals, and other popular materials that were intended solely or primarily for instruction. The usefulness of the bibliography is enhanced by Welch's survey of private and institutional collections of early American juveniles as well as by notes indicating libraries that own copies of the books listed.

Specialized bibliographies for children's literature are numerous. Many are listed in *Selecting Materials for Children and Young Adults,* noted above. For the vast literature of the dime novel, Charles Bragin's *Bibliography of Dime Novels, 1860–1964* provides valuable guidance. Deidre Johnson's *Stratemeyer Pseudonyms and Series Books* is an equally valuable guide to the Stratemeyer syndicate's numerous popular series. Dorothy Blythe Jones, *An "Oliver Optic" Checklist,* catalogs the series, nonseries stories, and magazine publications of the prolific William Taylor Adams, who also wrote under the pseudonyms Gayle Winterton, Warren T. Ashton, and Brooks McCormick.

Genre bibliographies include Barbara K. Harrah's *Sports Books for Children,* which lists 3,500 titles that were in print in January 1977. Historical fiction set in America and in print in 1964 are listed in Seymour Metzner, *American History in Juvenile Books.* Ruth Nadelman Lynn, *Fantasy for Children,* lists over 2,000 titles published in the United States between 1900 and 1982 for children in grades 3–8. A bibliographical appendix covers research sources, including a selection of dissertations.

Selecting Materials for Children and Young Adults lists a number of guides to books which counter racial, ethnic, and gender stereotypes. The following books supplement that listing or, like Augusta Baker's pioneering *The Black Experience in Children's Books,* deserve to be mentioned here. Arlene B. Hirschfelder's *American Indian Stereotypes in the World of Children* includes chapters on children's toys and textbooks as well as storybooks. Joan E. Newman, *Girls Are People Too!,* lists over 500 books, nearly all published after 1970, depicting nontraditional female roles.

Images of the future in books for children can be explored using Lillian Biermann Wehmeyer's *Images in a Crystal Ball*. Nearly 1,000 books with sales over 100,000 are cited in Jean S. Kujoth's *Best-Selling Children's Books*. Judith and Kenyon Rosenberg's *Young People's Literature in Series* extends the coverage offered by Frank M. Gardner's earlier compilation *Sequels*. In volume 1, the Rosenbergs list over 1,400 works of fiction published since 1955, omitting series for children under the age of seven as well as series lacking in literary merit such as the adventures of the Hardy boys and Nancy Drew. Like many lists in the field, the *Young People's Literature in Series* is not as inclusive as its title implies.

Over 400 children's periodicals are listed in R. Gordon Kelly's *Children's Periodicals of the United States*, the most extensive compilation to date. Lavinia G. Dobler's *The Dobler World Directory of Youth Periodicals* provides selective international coverage through 1970. The pre-eminent American children's magazine, *St. Nicholas* (1873–1944), is indexed by Anna Lorraine Guthrie (through 1920) and more selectively, by John McKay Shaw, *The Poems, Poets and Illustrators of St. Nicholas Magazine, 1873–1943*.

Some students of children's literature have argued that the serious reviewing of children's books did not really begin until just after World War I with the work of Anne Carroll Moore in the *New York Herald Tribune*. This view is rendered indefensible by Richard L. Darling's excellent monograph, *The Rise of Children's Book Reviewing in America, 1865–1881*. Darling demonstrates beyond cavil that children's books were widely reviewed in periodicals of all kinds and frequently judged by critical standards not significantly different from those in use during the last sixty years.

In recent years the reviewing of children's books has been increasingly restricted to a handful of specialized professional periodicals, of which the most important in terms of affecting a book's commercial success are *School Library Journal*, and *Booklist and Subscription Books Bulletin*, the latter published by the American Library Association as a selection guide for small and medium-sized public libraries, as well as schools and junior colleges. The *New York Times Book Review*, the *Horn Book Magazine*, *Language Arts*, *English Journal*, and the *Bulletin of the Center for Children's Books*, published at the University of Chicago, also do extensive reviewing of children's books. Much of this reviewing activity is superficial, however, with few reviews in excess of 300 words. Reviews since 1975 are listed in *Children's Book Review Index*. *Children's Literature Review*, edited by Ann Bloch and Carolyn Riley, excerpts reviews of children's books. Forthcoming children's books are announced, though not reviewed, semiannually (February and July) in *Publishers Weekly*.

Lists of selected children's books are legion. As already noted, *Selecting Materials for Children and Young Adults* briefly annotates nearly 300 titles. The following citations merely hint at the number and diversity of available selection aids. *Bibliographic Index*, under the heading "Children's Literature," provides the best current guide to children's book lists, since pamphlets and periodical articles are included in addition to books. *Aids to Media Selection for Students and Teachers* is available from the United States Office of Education. A comparable guide, Ingeborg Boudreau's *Aids to Choosing Books for Children*, is published by the Children's Book Council. Ellin Greene and Madalynne Schoenfeld's *A Multi-Media Approach to Children's Literature* lists films, records, and other nonprint materials generally neglected by list makers who restrict their definition of children's literature to books. *Notable Children's Books, 1940–1970* is an influential compilation of annual lists prepared by a committee of the Children's Services Division of the American Library Association. Similar compilations from the Center for Children's Books at the University of Chicago are Mary K. Eakin's *Good Books for Children* and Zena Sutherland's *The Best in Children's Books*. *Best Books for Children*, compiled by Eleanor B. Widdoes, lists some 4,000 titles that are reevaluated yearly against such standard guides to book selection as *Booklist*, *School Library Journal*, and *Children's Catalogue*.

Issues in Children's Book Selection, by Lillian Gerhardt, is a rewarding collection of twenty-nine essays culled from *School Library Journal* by Gerhardt, the journal's editor. The articles, principally by librarians and teachers of librarianship, discuss the assumptions, the professional and social context, and the dilemmas of evaluating books for children in a period characterized by increasingly realistic delineations of social problems in books for children. The historical development of approved lists of books has not received the systematic attention the subject deserves, but Esther Jane Carrier's *Fiction in Public Libraries, 1876–1900*, especially the chapter "Fiction for Young People," reveals the terms of the debate over appropriate principles of selection that concerned late nineteenth-century librarians.

Material on the Newbery and Caldecott awards, given annually to the best work of fiction for children and best illustrated book respectively, is available in Bertha E. Mahoney Miller and Elinor W. Field, *Newbery Medal Books, 1922–1955* and *Caldecott Medal Books, 1938–1957*; and Lee Kingman, *Newbery and Caldecott Medal Books, 1956–1965*. These volumes are especially valuable for the authors' acceptance papers reproduced in them. Irene Smith, *A History of the Newbery and Caldecott Medals*, describes the initiation of the awards and the criteria used and gives brief biographical accounts of the winners. Recent work supplements these older sources of information. Linda Kauffman Peterson and Marilyn Leathers Solt, *Newbery and Caldecott Medal and Honors Books*, provide annotations for runners-up in the medal competition as well as for the medal books. Jim Roginski's *Newbery and Caldecott Medalists and Honor Book Winners* duplicates information available in other sources but provides a complete bibliography of works by authors who have been medalists or honor book winners and indicates the location of research collections holding authors' papers. Nancy Larrick's popular *A Parent's Guide to Children's Reading*, now in its fifth edition, is a comprehensive manual for parents seeking to foster and sustain a love of reading and good books in their children.

The presence of sexism and racism in children's literature has been an issue for two decades. Representative studies dealing with the nature and incidence of stereotypes are discussed below, but several guides to literature purportedly free of stereotypes deserve to be noted here. *Human- and Anti-Human–Values in Children's Books*, published by the Council on Interracial Books for Children, provides both an evaluation of selected children's books and outlines a procedure for determining the presence of sexism, racism, and elitism in a given book. The procedure merits careful scrutiny, however, since it hinges on matching aspects of a book's content, mainly elements of characterization, to predetermined stereotypes and indicating the presence or absence of a match—a relatively inflexible and crude form of values analysis. Compilations of materials deemed nonsexist are *A Guide to Non-Sexist Children's Books*, edited by Judith Adell and Hilary D. Klein, and *Positive Images: A Guide to Non-Sexist Films for Young People*, edited by Linda Artel and Susan Wengraf.

Two textbooks have long been pre-eminent in the field of children's literature. May Hill Arbuthnot's *Children and Books* was first published in 1947. A seventh edition, edited by Zena Sutherland following Arbuthnot's death, appeared in 1986. *Children's Literature in the Elementary School*, by Charlotte Huck, first published in 1961 and most recently revised in 1979, aims to introduce prospective elementary teachers to the various types of literature for children and offers an outline for a classroom literary program. Other textbooks include William Davis Anderson and Patrick Groff's *A New Look at Children's Literature*, an interesting but flawed effort to found a literary approach to books for children on the principles of archetypal criticism; and James Steel Smith's *A Critical Approach to Children's Literature*, which also attempts to show how books for children could be judged primarily on literary rather than nonliterary criteria. Rebecca J. Lukens, *A Critical Handbook of Children's Literature*, approaches the teaching of children's literature by defining and illustrating fundamental literary concepts, such as plot, character, and setting, and then attempting to establish prescriptive norms for what constitutes a good plot, effective characters, etc., in an abstract and absolute sense.

Several recent textbooks are concerned more with contemporary social issues and the depiction of social reality in children's books than with considerations of literary merit. *Now Upon a Time*, by Myra P. Sadker and David M. Sadker, and *Children's Literature: An Issues Approach*, by Masha K. Rudman, are organized topically and treat such issues as racial and ethnic stereotyping in children's books or the handling of sexuality.

Several collections of essays on children's literature are valuable. Virginia Haviland's *Children and Literature: Views and Reviews* contains over seventy essays concerning the history, major genres, and the development in several foreign countries of children's literature. *Only Connect*, compiled by Sheila Egoff, collects articles published mainly in the 1960s that deal with children's literature as "an essential part of the whole realm of literary activity." Emphasized are the relationship between children and books, fantasy in children's literature, the relationship of children's authors to their work, and the characteristics of the contemporary literary situation. In a 1980 revision of *Only Connect*, eleven essays from the first edition were dropped to make room for nine essays on aspects and issues in children's books of the 1970s. Sara I. Fenwick, *A Critical Approach to Children's Literature*, reprints papers of the Thirty-first Annual Conference of the Graduate Library School at the University of Chicago. The conference, taking its theme from Lillian H. Smith's influential *The Unreluctant Years*, emphasized approaches to the study and evaluation of literature "that can provide for children satisfying and worthwhile experiences of joy, inspiration, self-imagination and increased wisdom." *The Hewins Lectures, 1947–1962*, edited by Siri Andrews, is a collection of addresses given annually in commemoration of the pioneer children's librarian Caroline M. Hewins. Most are devoted to historical topics, especially the work of New England authors of the last century such as A.D.T. Whitney, Eliza White, Laura Richards, and Lucretia Hale. Nicholas Tucker's *Suitable for Children? Controversies in Children's Literature* draws heavily on British writing but brings together a fine set of essays on fairy stories, comics, and children's classics. Articles on the value of children's literature round out the collection. Somewhat dated now, and drawn largely from journals in education and library science, Evelyn R. Robinson's *Readings About Children's Literature* treats such topics as book selection and evaluation, the history of children's books, illustration, fairy tales, and fiction. Some fifty articles on all phases of children's literature that appeared originally in the *Horn Book Magazine* between 1949 and 1966 are collected in *Horn Book Reflections on Children's Books and Reading*, edited by Elinor Whitney Field.

A particularly lively collection of personal essays is Selma G. Lanes's *Down the Rabbit Hole*. Concerned with the quality of children's books but not given to repeating pious inanities, Lanes is a sensitive, informed, and incisive commentator on topics ranging from the demise of *St. Nicholas Magazine* to the recent proliferation of picture books and the value of Dr. Seuss. Lanes also has some acute and useful things to say about the constraints imposed by the economics of the children's book trade. Louise Seaman Bechtel's *Books in Search of Children* consists of speeches and essays by Macmillan's pioneer children's editor. Another editor, Jean Karl, in *From Childhood to Childhood*, reflects upon the making of children's books from the vantage point of twenty years' experience. Two books by influential children's librarians are Frances Clarke Sayers's *Summoned by Books* and

Lillian H. Smith's *The Unreluctant Years*, arguably the most influential statement of the standards and goals for the criticism of children's books that has appeared since World War II.

RESEARCH COLLECTIONS

Brief overviews of the history and diversity of collections of children's literature are provided in two useful articles: James H. Fraser, "Children's Literature Collections and Research Libraries," and Frances Henne, "Toward a National Plan to Nourish Research in Children's Literature." Carolyn W. Field's *Subject Collections in Children's Literature* is indispensable. Supplementing it is *Children's Authors and Illustrators: A Guide to Manuscript Collections in United States Research Libraries*, by James H. Fraser with Renee I. Weber, which its compilers intend as a first step toward a national union catalog of manuscript collections. Articles on collections appear occasionally in *Phaedrus*, e.g., "Research Collections in New England," by Ruth Hayes, Priscilla Moulton, and Sarah Reuter, which describes nearly fifty collections of children's books held by New England colleges, universities, historical societies, public libraries, and religious associations.

The rich holdings of the Library of Congress are summarized by Virginia Haviland in "Serving Those Who Serve Children: A National Reference Library of Children's Books." The two-volume *Children's Books in the Rare Book Division of the Library of Congress* reproduces the card catalog of the collection. The origins and development of the outstanding collection of colonial and antebellum books for children housed at the American Antiquarian Society is described by Frederick E. Bauer, Jr., "Children's Literature and the American Antiquarian Society." A similar survey of the Pierpont Morgan Library collection is Gerald Gottlieb's "Keeping Company with the Gutenbergs." *Early Children's Books and Their Illustration*, with text by Gerald Gottlieb and a fine introductory essay by the noted British social historian J. H. Plumb, includes descriptions of a few American books, but this sumptuously produced catalog of an exhibit at the Pierpont Morgan Library is essential to any serious student of American children's literature. Another of the outstanding collections of children's books in the country is at the Free Library of Philadelphia. *Early American Children's Books*, by A.S.W. Rosenbach, catalogs some 680 items printed before 1836 that form the nucleus for a now greatly augmented collection. A *Checklist of Children's Books, 1837–1876*, recently completed by Barbara Maxwell, extends Rosenbach's coverage of this important collection.

Unlike Rosenbach and other notable collectors of children's books, Irvin Kerlan, who gave his collection to the University of Minnesota, concentrated his efforts primarily on twentieth-century materials (initially, award-winning books), but in addition to books, he also collected correspondence, original illustrations, manuscripts, book dummies, and press proofs, thus permitting the study of a work from its inception to its final form. *The May Massee Collection*, by George V. Hodowanec, describes a research collection at the William Allen White Library, Emporia State University. Massee, the nation's second children's book editor, worked first at Doubleday (1922–32) before going to Viking, where she remained until 1960. The collection consists of books for which she served as editor as well as manuscripts, correspondence, and original artwork.

HISTORY AND CRITICISM

Two collections of essays offer useful starting points for a consideration of recent critical trends. *Crosscurrents of Criticism*, edited by Paul Heins of the *Horn Book Magazine*, reprints essays from that journal from the period 1968–77. The forty-nine essays in Robert Bator's *Signposts to Criticism of Children's Literature* supplement *Crosscurrents* but typically offer more range and depth.

In an earlier article, "American Children's Literature: An Historiographical Review," R. Gordon Kelly described and evaluated the development of historical writing on children's literature in America. Owing to limitations of space, that discussion cannot be reproduced here, and interested readers are referred to it. The most comprehensive historical work in the field is still *A Critical History of Children's Literature*, by Cornelia Meigs, Anne T. Eaton, Ruth Hill Viguers, and Elizabeth Nesbitt, which dates from 1953. Although outdated, often in error, and primitive in conceptualization, the work is essential for anyone interested in the history of children's literature. The most authoritative brief account of the development of literature for children in this country is Fred Erisman's essay "Children's Literature in the United States, 1800–1940," but some older discussions of children's books in America are still useful: Algernon Tassin, "Books for Children"; Charles Welsh, "The Early History of Children's Books in New England"; and especially Elva S. Smith, *A History of Children's Literature: A Syllabus with Selected Bibliographies*; and Rosalie V. Halsey, *Forgotten Books of the American Nursery*. Smith's *History* was reissued in a revised and enlarged edition in 1980 under the joint editorship of Margaret Hodges and Susan Steinfirst.

Fortunately, there are several monographs and recent articles that partially offset the inadequacies of Meigs's *A Critical History*. William Sloane's *Children's Books in England and America in the Seventeenth Century* convincingly argues that, contrary to Meigs and others, seventeenth-century books for children were varied both in subject matter and the means chosen to appeal to youthful minds. Still valuable as an account of the popular primers of the eighteenth century, Paul Leicester Ford's *The New England Primer* includes a reprint of a 1727 edition, the oldest copy extant. Monica M. Kiefer's *American Children Through Their Books, 1700–1835*, based on research undertaken in the Rosenbach collection, relies uncritically on early, unreliable historians of children's books and is more concerned with changing conceptions of childhood, revealed in an array of historical documents and artifacts, than with books for children.

Anne Scott MacLeod's *A Moral Tale: Children's Fiction and American Culture, 1820–1860* is the best study to date of the didactic fiction of the antebellum period. Particularly valuable are her efforts to relate the moral tales to the social dislocation of the period. *A Moral Tale* largely overshadows John C. Crandall's "Patriotism and Humanitarian Reform in Children's Literature, 1825–1860"; but "Values Expressed in American Children's Readers, 1800–1850," by Richard DeCharms and Gerald H. Moeller, is still useful, in part for the method of content analysis employed in the study.

The thirty-five years between the end of the Civil War and the turn of the century saw an expansion and diversification of children's literature as well as a shift in emphasis from instruction to entertainment. Many of the changes can be traced in the children's periodicals of the period. John Morton Blum's *Yesterday's Children* is both an excellent anthology compiled from *Our Young Folks*, the prototypical New England literary magazine for children, and a cogent analysis of the social values expressed in its pages. Lovell Thompson's *Youth's Companion* is a rewarding anthology of articles and stories from the pages of the most popular and longest-lived of American juvenile periodicals. R. Gordon Kelly's *Mother Was a Lady* analyzes the structure of values exemplified in the major children's periodicals of the post–Civil War period, including *St. Nicholas*, *Youth's Companion*, and *Our Young Folks*. *Children's Periodicals of the United States*, edited by Kelly, profiles 100 American periodicals for children and, as noted earlier, lists over 400 periodicals with their dates and places of publication. Still helpful is Frank Luther Mott's standard work, *A History of American Magazines*. Also worth consulting is Betty Longeneker Lyon's dissertation, "A History of Children's Secular Magazines Published in the United States from 1789 to 1899."

The business of publishing books for children is a relatively neglected area of study, but three monographs on important nineteenth-century publishers by Raymond Kilgour deserve mention: *Estes and Lauriat*; *Messrs. Roberts Brothers, Publishers*; and *Lee and Shepard*. The latter, a year-by-year account of books published and monies paid to authors, includes material on the public reception of the firm's books as well as biographical information on house authors and brief descriptions of selected books brought out by the firm. John Tebbel's three-volume history of American publishing is the standard account. Recent trends can be explored through Robin Gottlieb's *Publishing Children's Books in America, 1919–1976*, an annotated bibliography of articles appearing in trade journals such as *Publishers Weekly* and in the principal journals used by librarians. George V. Hodowanec's guide to the May Massee collection, cited earlier, is also relevant. Children's book publishers are listed in *Children's Books in Print*. Supplementing that list is Wendy Osterweil's directory, *Alternative Press Publishers of Children's Books*. In *Getting Books to Children*, Joseph Turow takes a sharply focused, case-study approach to publisher-market relations.

Society and Children's Literature, edited by James H. Fraser, reprints papers that explore the relationships between children's literature and the social context in which it is produced, evaluated and read. A reliable overview of changes in children's literature at the end of the nineteenth century is Russel B. Nye's "The Juvenile Approach to American Culture, 1870–1930." Arthur Prager, in *Rascals at Large; or, the Clue in the Old Nostalgia*, writes affectionately but incisively about the popular heroes of his childhood reading: the Hardy boys, Tom Swift, Don Sturdy, Bomba the Jungle Boy, and a host of other series characters whose exploits go unsung in the standard histories. In *Golden Multitudes*, a history of best sellers, Frank Luther Mott gives incidental coverage to the popular reading taste of American youth from colonial times throughout the 1930s.

Substantial interpretive and critical studies of children's authors are not numerous, despite the recent increase of scholarly interest in the field. *A Sense of Story*, by the British critic and children's author John Rowe Townsend, is a thoughtful assessment of nineteen contemporary British, American, and Australian writers. Even so venerated an author as Louisa May Alcott has attracted relatively little first-rate commentary. Much of the best work on individual children's authors has been done not by literary scholars but by historians interested in popular authors who, like Horatio Alger and L. Frank Baum, may have considerable cultural significance but, in the view of the custodians of children's literature, little literary significance. Especially neglected are the popular and prolific antebellum writers like Jacob Abbott. Carl J. Weber's *A Bibliography of the Published Work of Jacob Abbott* includes a biographical sketch of Abbott, but the best account of his work can be found in MacLeod's *A Moral Tale*.

One of the most notable students of Louisa May Alcott's writing is Madeleine B. Stern. *Louisa's Wonder Book* reprints a heretofore unknown Alcott juvenile and provides a revised bibliography of Alcott's writings. Earlier work by Stern, and other significant commentary on Alcott's writings, are described and evaluated in Alma Payne's bibliographical essay "Louisa May Alcott."

On Horatio Alger, the recent work of Gary Scharnhorst and Jack Bales, *The Lost Life of Horatio Alger, Jr.*, is indispensable. Still valuable are John Seelye, "Who Was Horatio?"; Robert Falk, "Notes on the 'Higher Criticism' of Horatio Alger, Jr."; and Frank Gruber, *Horatio Alger, Jr.: A Biography and Bibliography*. Still the best single essay on Alger, R. Richard Wohl's "The Rags to Riches Story: An Episode in Secular Idealism," can be supplemented by John G. Cawelti's discussion of Alger in *Apostles of the Self-Made Man*, which places Alger in the context of earlier fiction about street children, and Michael Zuckerman's "The Nursery Tales of Horatio Alger, Jr." Dee Garrison, "Custodians of Culture in the Gilded Age: The Public Librarian and Horatio Alger," describes librarians' efforts to counter Alger's popularity in the late nineteenth century.

The popular Oz books by L. Frank Baum have also attracted the interest of cultural historians. Baum's life and work are ably described in *The Wizard of Oz and Who He Was*, by Martin Gardner and Russel B. Nye. Fred Erisman, "L. Frank Baum and the Progressive Dilemma," analyzes the differences between the Oz books and Baum's more realistic series, Aunt Jane's Nieces. Henry Littlefield, "The Wizard of Oz: Parable on Populism," argues for a coherent pattern of political reference in *The Wonderful Wizard of Oz*, Baum's first Oz book. S. J. Sackett, "The Utopia of Oz," reconstructs the Utopian vision allegedly informing the Oz series.

Commentary on other popular children's authors varies considerably in quality. Fred Erisman writes incisively on the school sports stories of Ralph Henry Barbour, "The Strenuous Life in Practice," and the books of Kate Douglas Wiggin, "Transcendentalism for American Youth"; but Jacob Blanck's *Harry Castlemon, Boys' Own Author* is disappointingly brief in its discussion of Castlemon's widely read adventure stories. The vastly popular Elsie Dinsmore books are given an indifferent and unsympathetic analysis by Janet Elder Brown, *The Saga of Elsie Dinsmore*. Nathaniel Hawthorne's contributions to children's literature are ably, if briefly, discussed by Alexander C. Kern in "A Note on Hawthorne's Juveniles," and more recently, and at greater length, by Mary S. Mattfield in "Hawthorne's Juvenile Classics."

Daniel Roselle's *Samuel Griswold Goodrich* is the best account of the life and work of the prolific and influential antebellum children's author who created the appealing persona of Peter Parley. John L. Cutler's *Gilbert Patten and His Frank Merriwell Saga* is a sympathetic biographical and literary analysis of a popular author generally ignored in the standard histories of children's literature. The work of Frank R. Stockton, a frequent contributor to *St. Nicholas* and one of the few American fantasy writers for children in the nineteenth century, is competently examined by Martin I. J. Griffin in *Frank R. Stockton: A Critical Biography*.

Several studies have dealt with various genres of children's literature. A particularly fine example is *The Uses of Enchantment*, a Freudian inquiry into the significance of fairy tales for the psychological development of young children, by the gifted psychotherapist Bruno Bettelheim. An earlier, neglected study on the same topic is Julius E. Heuscher, *A Psychiatric Study of Fairy Tales*. Renewed appreciation of the picture book in the last fifteen years has stimulated an interest in the historical development of this form of children's book. Barbara Bader, *American Picturebooks from Noah's Ark to the Beast Within*, is a comprehensive survey, while Joyce Irene Whalley's *Cobwebs to Catch Flies* is limited to illustrated books of the eighteenth and nineteenth century. Also valuable is Donnarae McCann and Olga Richard, *The Child's First Books: A Critical Study of Pictures and Texts*. *Thursday's Child*, by Sheila Egoff, provides a genre-by-genre overview of trends and patterns in books of the 1960s and 1970s by one of the most astute observers of children's book publishing. Bobbie Ann Mason gives a feminist reading of the Nancy Drew mystery books in *The Girl Sleuth*.

Carolyn T. Kingston's *The Tragic Mode in Children's Literature* is an interesting and ambitious effort to delineate a form of tragedy, based on an Aristotelian framework, that is appropriate to children's literature, one occupying a middle ground between ignoring suffering and offering the too complete exposure to "life's rawness" that characterizes great tragedy, according to Kingston.

The last twenty years have seen a number of studies which analyze the treatment of ethnic or racial groups in books for children. One of the earliest and most influential analyses, Nancy Larrick's "The All-White World of Children's Books," reported that fewer than 10 percent of the 5,000 trade books for children published in the period 1962–64 included black characters. Among the most comprehensive studies of the image of blacks in children's literature is Dorothy M. Broderick's *Image of the Black in Children's Fiction*, which treats books published from 1827 to 1967. Rudine Simms, *Shadow and Substance*, examines the Afro-American experience in books published between 1965 and 1979. Black stereotypes in series fiction are described by Paul C. Deane, "The Persistence of Uncle Tom." *The Black American in Books for Children*, edited by Donnarae McCann and Gloria Woodward, is a useful collection of readings on the topic. The two editors subsequently produced a second collection of readings on racism, *Cultural Conformity in Books for Children*. Jane Bingham's "The Pictorial Treatment of Afro-Americans in Books for Young Children, 1930–1968" summarizes her doctoral research.

Analyzing an ill-defined sample of books popular in the last one hundred years, J. P. Shepard, "The Treatment of Characters in Popular Children's Fiction," finds that villains in the selected books are typically unattractive, non-Caucasian, and either very rich or very poor. A more elaborate research effort, but limited to books published between 1945 and 1962, is reported by D. K. Gast in "Minority Americans in Children's Literature." His content analysis procedures yielded evidence of widespread stereotyping of ethnic minorities in children's literature, although Gast suggests that much of it is positive and complimentary. His conclusions were subsequently challenged by G. T. Blatt, however, in an essay "The Mexican-American in Children's Literature." Taken together, these representative articles suggest that the problem of typification in children's literature has hardly begun to be resolved at a conceptual level. Neither Gast nor Blatt, for example, provides a basis for discriminating necessary typification from unwarranted stereotyping.

On the delineation of sex roles in children's literature, the following are helpful: Lenore J. Weitzman et al., "Sex Role Socialization in Children's Picture Books"; Alleen P. Nilsen, "Women in Children's Literature," a survey of two decades of Caldecott Award books; and Susan K. Rachlin and Glenda Z. Vogt, "Sex Roles as Presented to Children by Coloring Books."

NOTES

1. William Sloane, *Children's Books in England and America in the Seventeenth Century* (New York: King's Crown Press, 1955), pp. 4–5.
2. E. Geller, "Somewhat Free: Post Civil War Writing for Children," *Wilson Library Bulletin*, 51 (1976), 175.

BIBLIOGRAPHY

Books and Articles

Adell, Judith, and Hilary D. Klein, eds. *A Guide to Non-Sexist Children's Books.* Chicago: Academy Press, 1976.

Aids to Media Selection for Students and Teachers. Compiled by Kathlyn J. Moses and Lois B. Watt. Washington, D.C.: U.S. Office of Education, 1976.

Anderson, William Davis, and Patrick Groff. *A New Look at Children's Literature.* Belmont, Calif.: Wadsworth, 1972.

Andrews, Siri, ed. *The Hewins Lectures, 1947–1962.* Boston: Horn Book, 1963.

Artel, Linda, and Susan Wengraf, eds. *Positive Images: A Guide to Non-Sexist Films for Young People.* San Francisco: Booklegger Press, 1976.

Bader, Barbara. *American Picturebooks from Noah's Ark to the Beast Within.* New York: Macmillan, 1976.

Baker, Augusta. *The Black Experience in Children's Books.* New York: New York Public Library, 1971.

Bator, Robert, ed. *Signposts to Criticism of Children's Literature.* Chicago: American Library Association, 1983.

Bauer, Frederick E., Jr. "Children's Literature and the American Antiquarian Society." *Phaedrus*, 3 (Spring 1976), 5–8.

Bechtel, Louise Seaman. *Books in Search of Children.* New York: Macmillan, 1969.

Bettelheim, Bruno. *The Uses of Enchantment: The Meaning and Importance of Fairy Tales.* New York: Alfred A. Knopf, 1976.

Bingham, Jane. "The Pictorial Treatment of Afro-Americans in Books for Young Children, 1930–1968." *Elementary English*, 48 (November 1971), 880–85.

Blanck, Jacob. *Harry Castlemon, Boys' Own Author.* New York: R. R. Bowker, 1941.

Blatt, G. T. "The Mexican-American in Children's Literature." *Elementary English*, 45 (April 1968), 446–51.

Bloch, Ann, and Carolyn Riley, eds. *Children's Literature Review.* Detroit: Gale Research, 1976.

Blum, John Morton, ed. *Yesterday's Children: An Anthology Compiled from the Pages of "Our Young Folks," 1865–1873.* Boston: Houghton Mifflin, 1959.

Boudreau, Ingeborg. *Aids to Choosing Books for Children.* New York: Children's Book Council, 1969.

Bragin, Charles. *Bibliography of Dime Novels, 1860–1964.* rev. ed. Brooklyn, N.Y.: Dime Novel Club, 1964.

Broderick, Dorothy M. *Images of the Black in Children's Fiction.* New York: R. R. Bowker, 1973.

Brown, Janet Elder. *The Saga of Elsie Dinsmore: A Study in Nineteenth Century Sensibility.* Buffalo, N.Y.: University of Buffalo, 1945.

Brown, Sterling. *The Negro in American Fiction.* Washington, D.C.: Associates in Negro Folk Education, 1937.

Carrier, Esther Jane. *Fiction in Public Libraries, 1876–1900.* New York: Scarecrow Press, 1965.

Cawelti, John G. *Apostles of the Self-Made Man.* Chicago: University of Chicago Press, 1965.

Children's Book Review Index. Detroit: Gale Research, 1975-.

Children's Books in Print. New York: R. R. Bowker, 1970-.

Children's Books in the Rare Book Division of the Library of Congress. 2 vols. Totowa, N.J.: Rowman & Littlefield, 1976.

Children's Catalogue. 15th ed. New York: H. W. Wilson, 1986.

Commire, Anne, ed. *Something about the Author.* Detroit: Gale Research, 1971.

Crandall, John C. "Patriotism and Humanitarian Reform in Children's Literature, 1825–1860." *American Quarterly,* 21 (Spring 1969), 3–22.

Cutler, John L. *Gilbert Patten and His Frank Merriwell Saga: A Study in Sub-Literary Fiction, 1896–1913.* Orono: University of Maine, 1934.

Darling, Richard L. *The Rise of Children's Book Reviewing in America, 1865–1881.* New York: R. R. Bowker, 1968.

Deane, Paul C. "The Persistence of Uncle Tom: An Examination of the Image of the Negro in Children's Fiction Series." *Journal of Negro Education,* 37 (Spring 1968), 140–45.

DeCharms, Richard, and Gerald H. Moeller. "Values Expressed in American Children's Readers, 1800–1850." *Journal of Abnormal and Social Psychology,* 64 (February 1962), 136–42.

DeMontreville, Doris, Donna Hill, and Elizabeth Crawford, eds. *The Fourth Book of Junior Authors and Illustrators.* New York: H. W. Wilson, 1978.

DeMontreville, Doris, and Donna Hill, eds. *The Third Book of Junior Authors.* New York: H. W. Wilson, 1972.

Dobler, Lavinia G. *The Dobler World Directory of Youth Periodicals.* 3d ed. New York: Citation Press, 1970.

Doyle, Brian. *The Who's Who of Children's Literature.* New York: Schocken, 1968.

Eakin, Mary K., comp. *Good Books for Children: A Selection of Outstanding Children's Books Published 1950–1965.* 3d ed. Chicago: University of Chicago Press, 1966.

Egoff, Sheila, ed. *Only Connect.* Toronto: Oxford University Press, 1969. 2d ed. 1980.

———. *Thursday's Child: Trends and Patterns in Contemporary Children's Literature.* Chicago: American Library Association, 1981.

Erisman, Fred. "Children's Literature in the United States, 1800–1940." In *Lexicon Zur Kinder-und Jugendliteratur*. Edited by Klaus Doderer. vol. 2. Weinheim and Basel/Pullachbei. Munich: Beltz Verlag and Verlag Dokumentation, in press.

————. "L. Frank Baum and the Progressive Dilemma." *American Quarterly*, 20 (Fall 1968), 616–23.

————. "The Strenuous Life in Practice: The School and Sports Stories of Ralph Henry Barbour." *Rocky Mountain Social Science Journal*, 7 (April 1970), 29–37.

————. "Transcendentalism for American Youth: The Children's Books of Kate Douglas Wiggin." *New England Quarterly*, 41 (June 1968), 238–47.

Falk, Robert. "Notes on the 'Higher Criticism' of Horatio Alger, Jr." *Arizona Quarterly*, 19 (Summer 1963), 151–67.

Fenwick, Sara I., ed. *A Critical Approach to Children's Literature*. Chicago: University of Chicago Press, 1967.

Field, Carolyn W. *Subject Collections in Children's Literature*. Chicago: American Library Association, 1982.

Field, Elinor Whitney, ed. *Horn Book Reflections on Children's Books and Reading*. Boston: Horn Book, 1969.

Ford, Paul Leicester, ed. *The New England Primer*. New York: Teachers College Press, 1962.

Fraser, James H. "Children's Literature Collections and Research Libraries." *Wilson Library Bulletin*, 50 (October 1975), 128–30.

————, ed. *Society and Children's Literature*. Boston: Godine, 1978.

Fraser, James H., with Renee I. Weber, comps. *Children's Authors and Illustrators: A Guide to Manuscript Collections in United States Research Libraries*. New York: K. G. Saur, 1980.

Fuller, Muriel, ed. *More Junior Authors*. New York: H. W. Wilson, 1963.

Gardner, Frank M., comp. *Sequels*. 4th ed. London: Association of Assistant Librarians, 1955.

Gardner, Martin, and Russel B. Nye. *The Wizard of Oz and Who He Was*. East Lansing: Michigan State University Press, 1957.

Garrison, Dee. "Custodians of Culture in the Gilded Age: The Public Librarian and Horatio Alger." *Journal of Library History*, 6 (October 1971), 327–36.

Gast, D. K. "Minority Americans in Children's Literature." *Elementary English*, 44 (January 1967), 12–23.

Gerhardt, Lillian, ed. *Issues in Children's Book Selection*. New York: R. R. Bowker, 1973.

Gottlieb, Gerald. *Early Children's Books and Their Illustration*. New York: Pierpont Morgan Library, 1975.

————. "Keeping Company with the Gutenbergs." *Wilson Library Bulletin*, 50 (October 1975), 154–56.

Gottlieb, Robin. *Publishing Children's Books in America, 1919–1976: An Annotated Bibliography*. New York: Children's Book Council, 1978.

Greene, David L. "Children's Literature Journals: Author Society Journals and Fanzines." *Phaedrus*, 2 (Spring 1975), 16–20.

————. "Children's Literature Periodicals on Individual Authors, Dime Novels, Fantasy." *Phaedrus*, 3 (Spring 1976), 22–24.

Greene, Ellin, and Madalynne Schoenfeld. *A Multi-Media Approach to Children's Literature: A Selective List of Films, Filmstrips, and Recordings Based on Children's Books*. Chicago: American Library Association, 1972.

Griffin, Martin I. J. *Frank R. Stockton: A Critical Biography*. Philadelphia: University of Pennsylvania Press, 1939.

Gruber, Frank. *Horatio Alger, Jr.: A Biography and a Bibliography*. West Los Angeles, Calif.: Grover Jones, 1961.

Guthrie, Anna Lorraine, comp. *Index to St. Nicholas, Volumes 1–45*. New York: H. W. Wilson, 1920.

Halsey, Rosalie V. *Forgotten Books of the American Nursery*. Boston: Goodspeed, 1911.

Harrah, Barbara K. *Sports Books for Children: An Annotated Bibliography*. Metuchen, N.J.: Scarecrow Press, 1978.

Haviland, Virginia. "Serving Those Who Serve Children: A National Reference Library of Children's Books." *Quarterly Journal of the Library of Congress*, 22 (1965), 300–316.

———, ed. *Children and Literature: Views and Reviews*. Glenview, Ill.: Scott, Foresman, 1973.

———, ed. *Children's Literature: A Guide to Reference Sources*. Washington, D.C.: Library of Congress, 1966.

Hayes, Ruth, Priscilla Moulton, and Sarah Rueter. "Research Collections in New England." *Phaedrus*, 3 (Spring 1976), 13–21.

Heins, Paul, ed. *Crosscurrents of Criticism: Horn Book Essays, 1968–1977*. Boston: Horn Book, 1977.

Henne, Frances. "Toward a National Plan to Nourish Research in Children's Literature." *Wilson Library Bulletin*, 50 (October 1975), 131–37.

Heuscher, Julius E. *A Psychiatric Study of Fairy Tales: Their Origin, Meaning, and Usefulness*. 2d rev. ed. Springfield, Ill.: Charles C. Thomas, 1974.

Hirschfelder, Arlene B. *American Indian Stereotypes in the World of Children: A Reader and Bibliography*. Metuchen, N.J.: Scarecrow Press, 1982.

Hodowanec, George V., ed. *The May Massee Collection: Creative Publishing for Children, 1923–1963, A Checklist*. Emporia, Kans.: William Allen White Library, Emporia State University, 1979.

Hoffman, Miriam, and Eva Samuels. *Authors and Illustrators of Children's Books: Writings on Their Lives and Works*. New York: R. R. Bowker, 1972.

Holtze, Sally Holmes. *Fifth Book of Junior Authors and Illustrators*. New York: H. W. Wilson, 1983.

Huck, Charlotte. *Children's Literature in the Elementary School*. 3d ed. New York: Holt, Rinehart and Winston, 1979.

Human- and Anti-Human–Values in Children's Books: A Content Rating Instrument for Educators and Concerned Parents. New York: Council on Interracial Books for Children, 1976.

Ireland, Norma O., ed. *Index to Fairy Tales, 1949–1972, Including Folklore, Legends, Myths, in Collections*. Westwood, Mass.: Faxon, 1973.

Johnson, Deidre. *Stratemeyer Pseudonyms and Series Books: An Annotated Checklist of Stratemeyer and Stratemeyer Literary Syndicate Publications*. Westport, Conn.: Greenwood Press, 1982.

Jones, Dorothy Blythe, comp. *An "Oliver Optic" Checklist: An Annotated Catalog-*

Index to the Series, Nonseries Stories, and Magazine Publications of William Taylor Adams. Westport, Conn.: Greenwood Press, 1985.

Jordan, Alice M. *From Rollo to Tom Sawyer*. Boston: Horn Book, 1948.

Karl, Jean. *From Childhood to Childhood*. New York: John Day, 1970.

Kelly, R. Gordon. "American Children's Literature: An Historiographical Review." *American Literary Realism*, 6 (Spring 1973), 89–108.

————. *Mother Was a Lady: Self and Society in Selected American Children's Periodicals, 1865–1890*. Westport, Conn.: Greenwood Press, 1974.

————, ed. *Children's Periodicals of the United States*. Westport, Conn.: Greenwood Press, 1984.

Kern, Alexander C. "A Note on Hawthorne's Juveniles." *Philological Quarterly*, 39 (April 1960), 242–46.

Kiefer, Monica M. *American Children Through Their Books, 1700–1835*. Philadelphia: University of Pennsylvania Press, 1948.

Kilgour, Raymond. *Estes and Lauriat: A History, 1872–1898*. Ann Arbor: University of Michigan Press, 1957.

————. *Lee and Shepard: Publishers for the People*. Hamden, Conn.: Shoe String Press, 1965.

————. *Messrs. Roberts Brothers, Publishers*. Ann Arbor: University of Michigan Press, 1952.

Kingman, Lee, ed. *Newbery and Caldecott Medal Books, 1956–1965*. Boston: Horn Book, 1965.

Kingston, Carolyn T. *The Tragic Mode in Children's Literature*. New York: Teachers College Press, 1974.

Kirkpatrick, Daniel, ed. *Twentieth-Century Children's Writers*. New York: St. Martin's Press, 1983.

Kujoth, Jean S. *Best-Selling Children's Books*. Metuchen, N.J.: Scarecrow Press, 1973.

Kunitz, Stanley J., and Howard Haycraft, eds. *The Junior Book of Authors*. 2d ed. New York: H. W. Wilson, 1951.

Lanes, Selma G. *Down the Rabbit Hole: Adventures and Misadventures in the Realm of Children's Literature*. New York: Atheneum, 1971.

Larrick, Nancy. "The All-White World of Children's Books." *Saturday Review of Literature*, 48 (September 11, 1965), 63–65.

————. *A Parent's Guide to Children's Reading*. 5th ed. Garden City, N.Y.: Doubleday, 1982.

Littlefield, Henry. "The Wizard of Oz: Parable on Populism." *American Quarterly*, 16 (Spring 1964), 47–58.

Lukenbill, W. Bernard. *A Working Bibliography of American Doctoral Dissertations in Children's and Adolescents' Literature, 1930–1971*. Champaign: University of Illinois Graduate School of Library Science, 1972.

Lukens, Rebecca J. *A Critical Handbook of Children's Literature*. Glenview, Ill.: Scott, Foresman, 1976.

Lynn, Ruth Nadelman. *Fantasy for Children: An Annotated Checklist and Reference Guide*. 2d ed. New York: R. R. Bowker, 1983.

Lyon, Betty Longeneker. "A History of Children's Secular Magazines Published in the United States from 1789 to 1899." Ed.D. dissertation, Johns Hopkins, 1942.

McCann, Donnarae, and Gloria Woodard. *The Black American in Books for Children: Readings in Racism*. Metuchen, N.J.: Scarecrow Press, 1972.

———, eds. *Cultural Conformity in Books for Children: Further Readings in Racism*. Metuchen, N.J.: Scarecrow Press, 1977.

McCann, Donnarae, and Olga Richard. *The Child's First Books: A Critical Study of Pictures and Texts*. New York: H. W. Wilson, 1973.

MacLeod, Anne Scott. *A Moral Tale: Children's Fiction and American Culture, 1820–1860*. Hamden, Conn.: Archon, 1975.

Mason, Bobbie Ann. *The Girl Sleuth: A Feminist Guide*. Old Westbury, N.Y.: Feminist Press, 1975.

Mattfield, Mary S. "Hawthorne's Juvenile Classics." *Discourse*, 12 (1969), 346–64.

Matthews, Harriet L. "Children's Magazines." *Bulletin of Bibliography*, 1 (April 1899), 133–36.

Maxwell, Barbara, comp. *Checklist of Children's Books, 1837–1876*. Philadelphia: Free Library of Philadelphia, 1975 (mimeo).

Meacham, Mary. *Information Sources in Children's Literature*. Westport, Conn.: Greenwood Press, 1978.

Meigs, Cornelia et al. *A Critical History of Children's Literature*. Rev. ed. New York: Macmillan, 1969.

Metzner, Seymour. *American History in Juvenile Books: A Chronological Guide*. New York: H. W. Wilson, 1966.

Miller, Bertha E. Mahoney, Louise P. Latimer, and Beulah Folmsbee. *Illustrators of Children's Books, 1744–1945*. Boston: Horn Book, 1947.

Miller, Bertha E. Mahoney, Ruth Hill Viguers, and Marcia Dalphin. *Illustrators of Children's Books, 1946–1956*. Boston: Horn Book, 1958.

Miller, Bertha E. Mahoney, and Elinor W. Field, eds. *Newbery Medal Books, 1922–1955*. Boston: Horn Book, 1955.

———. *Caldecott Medal Books, 1938–1957*. Boston: Horn Book, 1957.

Monson, Dianne L., and Bette Peltola. *Research in Children's Literature*. Newark, Del.: International Reading Association, 1976.

Mott, Frank Luther. *Golden Multitudes: The Story of Best Sellers in the United States*. New York: Macmillan, 1947.

———. *A History of American Magazines*. 6 vols. Cambridge, Mass.: Harvard University Press, 1938–68.

Newman, Joan E. *Girls Are People Too! A Bibliography of Nontraditional Female Roles in Children's Books*. Metuchen, N.J.: Scarecrow Press, 1982.

Nilsen, Alleen P. "Women in Children's Literature." *College English*, 32 (May 1971), 918–26.

Notable Children's Books, 1940–1970. Chicago: American Library Association, 1977.

Nye, Russel B. "The Juvenile Approach to American Culture, 1870–1930." In *New Voices in American Studies*. Edited by Ray B. Browne. West Lafayette, Ind.: Purdue University Press, 1966.

Osterweil, Wendy, ed. *Alternative Press Publishers of Children's Books: A Directory*. 2d ed. Madison, Wis.: Friends of Cooperative Children's Book Center, 1985.

Payne, Alma. "Louisa May Alcott (1832–1888)." *American Literary Realism*, 6 (Winter 1973), 27–43.

Pellowski, Anne. *The World of Children's Literature*. New York: R. R. Bowker, 1968.

Peterson, Linda Kauffman, and Marilyn Leathers Solt. *Newbery and Caldecott Medal and Honors Books: An Annotated Bibliography.* Boston: G. K. Hall, 1982.

Pflieger, Pat. *A Reference Guide to Modern Fantasy for Children.* Westport, Conn.: Greenwood Press, 1984.

Prager, Arthur. *Rascals at Large; or, the Clue in the Old Nostalgia.* Garden City, N.Y.: Doubleday, 1971.

Rachlin, Susan K., and Glenda L. Vogt. "Sex Roles as Presented to Children by Coloring Books." *Journal of Popular Culture,* 8 (1974), 549–56.

Rahn, Suzanne. *Children's Literature: An Annotated Bibliography of the History and Criticism.* New York: Garland, 1981.

Robinson, Evelyn R. *Readings About Children's Literature.* New York: David McKay, 1966.

Roginski, Jim, comp. *Newbery and Caldecott Medalists and Honor Book Winners: Bibliographies and Resource Material Through 1977.* Littleton, Colo.: Libraries Unlimited, 1982.

Roselle, Daniel. *Samuel Griswold Goodrich, Creator of Peter Parley: A Study of His Life and Work.* Albany: State University of New York Press, 1968.

Rosenbach, A.S.W. *Early American Children's Books.* Portland, Maine: Southworth, 1933.

Rosenberg, Judith K., and Kenyon C. Rosenberg. *Young People's Literature in Series.* 2 vols. Littleton, Colo.: Libraries Unlimited, 1972–73.

Rudman, Masha Kabakow. *Children's Literature: An Issues Approach.* Lexington, Mass.: D. C. Heath, 1976.

Sackett, S. J. "The Utopia of Oz." *Georgia Review,* 14 (Fall 1960), 275–91.

Sadker, Myra P., and David M. Sadker. *Now Upon a Time: A Contemporary View of Children's Literature.* New York: Harper and Row, 1977.

Sale, Roger. *Fairy Tales and After: From Snow White to E. B. White.* Cambridge, Mass.: Harvard University Press, 1978.

Sarkissian, Adele, ed. *Children's Authors and Illustrators: An Index to Biographical Dictionaries.* 3d ed. Detroit: Gale Research, 1981.

Sayers, Frances Clarke. *Summoned by Books.* New York: Viking, 1965.

Scharnhorst, Gary, and Jack Bales. *The Lost Life of Horatio Alger, Jr.* Bloomington: Indiana University Press, 1985.

Seelye, John. "Who Was Horatio?" *American Quarterly,* 17 (Winter 1965), 749–56.

Selecting Materials for Children and Young Adults: A Bibliography of Bibliographies and Review Sources. Chicago: American Library Association, 1980.

Shaw, John McKay, comp. *The Poems, Poets and Illustrators of St. Nicholas Magazine, 1873–1943: An Index.* Tallahassee: Florida State University Pess, 1965.

Shepard, J. P. "The Treatment of Characters in Popular Children's Fiction." *Elementary English,* 39 (November 1962), 672–76.

Simms, Rudine. *Shadow and Substance: Afro-American Experience in Contemporary Children's Fiction.* Urbana, Ill.: National Council of Teachers of English, 1982.

Sloane, William. *Children's Books in England and America in the Seventeenth Century.* New York: King's Crown Press, 1955.

Smith, Elva S. *A History of Children's Literature: A Syllabus with Selected Bibliographies.* Chicago: American Library Association, 1937. Revised and enlarged by Margaret Hodges and Susan Steinfirst. Chicago: American Library Association, 1980.

Smith, Irene. *A History of the Newbery and Caldecott Medals*. New York: Viking, 1957.

Smith, James Steel. *A Critical Approach to Children's Literature*. New York: McGraw-Hill, 1967.

Smith, Lillian H. *The Unreluctant Years: A Critical Approach to Children's Literature*. Chicago: American Library Association, 1953.

Stern, Madeleine B. *Louisa's Wonder Book: An Unknown Alcott Juvenile*. Mt. Pleasant, Mich.: Clarke Historical Library, Central Michigan University, 1975.

Subject and Title Index to Short Stories for Children. Chicago: American Library Association, 1955-.

Subject Guide to Children's Books in Print. New York: R. R. Bowker, 1970-.

Subject Index to Poetry for Children and Young People. Chicago: American Library Association, 1957-.

Sutherland, Zena, ed. *The Best in Children's Books: The University of Chicago Guide to Children's Literature, 1966–1972*. Chicago: University of Chicago Press, 1973.

Sutherland, Zena, and May Hill Arbuthnot. *Children's Books*. 7th ed. Glenview, Ill.: Scott, Foresman, 1986.

Tassin, Algernon. "Books for Children." *Cambridge History of American Literature*. 3 vols. Cambridge: Cambridge University Press, 1917–21.

Thompson, Lovell, ed. *Youth's Companion*. Boston: Houghton Mifflin, 1954.

Townsend, John Rowe. *A Sense of Story*. Philadelphia: J. B. Lippincott, 1971.

Tucker, Nicholas. *Suitable for Children? Controversies in Children's Literature*. Berkeley: University of California Press, 1976.

Turow, Joseph. *Getting Books to Children: An Exploration of Publisher-Market Relations*. Chicago: American Library Association, 1978.

Viguers, Ruth Hill. *Margin for Surprise: About Books, Children and Librarians*. Boston: Little, Brown, 1964.

Ward, Martha E., and Dorothy A. Marquardt. *Illustrators of Books for Young People*. 2d ed. Metuchen, N.J.: Scarecrow Press, 1975.

Weber, Carl J. *A Bibliography of the Published Work of Jacob Abbott*. Waterville, Maine: Colby College, 1948.

Wehmeyer, Lillian Biermann. *Images in a Crystal Ball: World Futures in Novels for Young People*. Littleton, Colo.: Libraries Unlimited, 1981.

Weitzman, Lenore J. et al. "Sex Role Socialization in Children's Picture Books." *American Journal of Sociology*, 77 (May 1972), 1125–50.

Welch, D'Alte A. "A Bibliography of American Children's Books Printed Prior to 1821." *Proceedings of the American Antiquarian Society*, 73 (1963), pt. 1:121–324, pt. 2:465–596; 74 (1964), pt. 2:260–382; 75 (1965), pt. 2:271–476; 77 (1967), pt. 1:44–120, pt. 2:281–535.

Welsh, Charles. "The Early History of Children's Books in New England." *New England Magazine*, n.s. 20 (April 1899), 147–60.

Whalley, Joyce Irene. *Cobwebs to Catch Flies: Illustrated Books for the Nursery and Schoolroom, 1700–1900*. Berkeley: University of California Press, 1975.

White, Virginia L., and Emerita S. Schulter, comps. *Books About Children's Books: An Annotated Bibliography*. Newark, Del.: International Reading Association, 1979.

Widdoes, Eleanor B., comp. *Best Books for Children: A Catalogue of 4000 Titles*. 13th ed. New York: R. R. Bowker, 1971.

Wohl, R. Richard. "The Rags to Riches Story: An Episode in Secular Idealism." In *Class, Status and Power*. Edited by Reinhard Bendix and Seymour M. Lipset. Glencoe, Ill.: Free Press, 1953.

Zuckerman, Michael. "The Nursery Tales of Horatio Alger, Jr." *American Quarterly*, 24 (May 1972), 191–209.

Periodicals

Advocate. Athens, Ga., 1982-1986.

Bibliographic Index. New York, 1938-.

Booklist and Subscription Books Bulletin. Chicago, 1905-.

Bulletin of the Center for Children's Books. Chicago, 1948-.

Children's Literature. New Haven, 1972-.

Children's Literature in Education. London, England, 1970-.

English Journal. Urbana, Ill., 1912-.

Horn Book Magazine. Boston, 1924-.

Language Arts (formerly *Elementary English*). Urbana, Ill., 1924-.

Lion and the Unicorn. Brooklyn, 1977-.

The New Advocate. Boston, 1988-.

New York Times Book Review. New York, 1896-.

Phaedrus: An International Annual of Children's Literature Research. New York, 1973-.

Publishers Weekly. New York, 1872-.

School Library Journal. New York, 1954-.

Top of the News. Chicago, 1946-.

4

Comic Books

M. THOMAS INGE

The comic book has been one of the most popular and widely read of the mass literary media in this century by both children and adults, with as many as 200 million copies a year published in the United States alone. Originated in 1933 as a vehicle for reprinting newspaper strips, the comic book soon went its separate way as a distinctive narrative art form which related the adventures of characters and super-heroes whose roots and inspiration are found in popular detective and science fiction, American folklore, and European mythology. Although the super-hero dominated the form at the start, titles were also devoted to adventure, romance, war, crime, horror, Western stories, fantasy, fairy tales, and funny animal stories (the last a direct descendant of the ancient form of the animal fable).

The peak year of 1941 saw over 160 titles in print, and while economic problems plague current publishers, the comic book has remained a significant part of America's reading matter. The characters have such a hold on the American imagination that the movie industry has turned out a seemingly endless series of motion pictures about them, such as the Superman films, Flash Gordon, Buck Rogers, the Swamp Thing, and Conan the Barbarian, or for the television screen Wonder Woman, the Hulk, Spider-Man, and Captain Marvel. In one recent film, *Breathless*, a comic book character called the Silver Surfer (along with Faulker and Jerry Lee Lewis, incidentally) holds the philosophic key to the existential meaning of the story.

What is to account for the popularity and staying power of comic book art? In the first place, it appeals to the senses: the brightly colored pages and heavily outlined figures grip the attention of the reader and like all art satisfy the urge of the eye to place the riotous colors of life into a balanced perspective. Second, it appeals to the imagination in its role as narration, and like all literature, it satisfies the thirst for vicarious adventure into worlds and experiences outside daily reality. Finally, it appeals to the mind in its effort to create rational order out of the chaos of existence by reducing conflict and complexity into a simplified and therefore less threatening moral battle between the forces of evil and good. Not all comic book art successfully achieves these three aesthetic appeals, but at its best, the comic book can simultaneously satisfy the visual, imaginative, and moral sensibilities.

HISTORIC OUTLINE

Depending upon where one begins historically, the comic book is only a little over fifty years old. While the first comic books arguably may have been the hardcover reprint collections of popular newspaper comic strips, such as *The Yellow Kid, Mutt and Jeff, Buster Brown*, and *Bringing Up Father*, published between 1897 and the late 1920s, the first comic magazine in the familiar 7 1/2″ × 10″ size printed in full color with a glossy paper cover was *Funnies on Parade* issued in 1933.

Funnies on Parade also contained Sunday newspaper reprints, but it was designed to be given away as a premium with Procter and Gamble products. The 10,000 copies went so rapidly that after several more similar premium products, the publisher issued the first number of *Famous Funnies* in 1934. Designed to be sold in chain stores for ten cents, the 35,000 copies printed were promptly sold and *Famous Funnies* became the first monthly comic magazine and continued publication for more than twenty years reaching a maximum circulation of nearly one million copies. Imitations of this successful format followed, but the comic magazine did not achieve distinction until the publishers began to commission original material for its pages, as happened with *More Fun, Detective Comics*, and *Action Comics* from National Periodical Publications.

It was the first issue of Action Comics in 1938 that guaranteed the success of the comic book and contributed to American mythology its first original super-hero since the days of Davy Crockett and Paul Bunyan—Superman. The creation of two childhood friends from Cleveland, Ohio, Jerry Siegel and Joe Shuster, and partly inspired by the protagonist of Philip Wylie's novel *Gladiator* (1930), Superman leapt into the American imagination faster than a speeding bullet. His presence as an alien from another planet, sent here by his parents from the doomed Krypton; his unlimited strength, ability to fly, and x-ray vision; and his dual identity which called for his assumption of the appearance of a mild-mannered newspaper reporter—these qualities intrigued readers like those of few other figures in American literature. Many a mild-mannered reader enjoyed imaginatively setting aside his glasses to leap into the sky with Superman as he fought for Truth, Justice, and the American way (never mind the incongruity of an interplanetary alien, without citizenship papers, fighting for our nation's principles). In *American Folklore*, Richard Dorson cites Superman as an example of how "American life glorifies brawn and muscle in contrast to mind and intellect." However, when under disguise as Clark Kent, Superman does assume the role of an intellectual, with even the stereotyped attributes of clumsiness, ineptitude, and meekness. Perhaps it is this combination of qualities, the brawn with the brain, the perfect balance of a sound body with a sound mind that was the Greek ideal, that constitutes his special appeal.

The enormous success of Superman soon spawned a multitude of imitators, literally hundreds of super-heroes who populated the pages of competing comic books, the more popular and originally conceived being Batman and Robin the Boy Wonder, the Human Torch, Sub-Mariner, Wonder Woman, Captain America, Plastic Man, Blackhawk, Daredevil, the Flash, Green Lantern, Hawkman, Green Arrow, Sandman, the Atom, Doll Man, and Blue Beetle, each characterized by a particular strength or ability, some odd physical characteristic, or a mystical secret origin.

Only one truly rivaled Superman—C. C. Beck's Captain Marvel, a satirically drawn spoof of super-heroes modeled after film actor Fred MacMurray and lovingly called by his admirers "the Big Cheese." When Captain Marvel from Fawcett Publications began to outsell Superman, National Periodical Publications began a lawsuit to claim copyright infringement, an odd allegation since among the multitude of super-heroes, Captain Marvel was the least like Superman. The case was pursued so relentlessly, however, that in 1953 Fawcett Publications cancelled their entire comic book line and relinquished the rights to the character rather than fight further in court. Ironically, twenty years later National Periodical Publications itself revived the character under the name Shazam in an effort to capitalize on the fond memories held by many older readers.

All comic books during these formative years were not devoted to flying, leaping, and fighting super-heroes. There were adventure stories about Sheena, Queen of the Jungle; the Shadow; Doc Savage; and the Spirit as beautifully rendered and carefully plotted by master artist/writer Will Eisner. There were romance and teenage comic books, best exemplified by Archie, who has remained a student at Riverdale High for over forty-five years now, surely the longest retention on record. And there were funny animal and kiddy comic books, such as *Looney Tunes and Merrie Melodies* featuring Porky Pig, Bugs Bunny, and Elmer Fudd; *Walt Disney's Comics*

and Stories featuring Mickey Mouse and the whole Disney gang, especially Donald Duck and Scrooge McDuck as strikingly developed by author/artist Carl
Barks; *Animal Comics* featuring Walt Kelly's original version of Albert Alligator
and Pogo Possum; and *Little Lulu* as charmingly recreated by John Stanley after
Marjorie Henderson Buell's *Saturday Evening Post* feature.

Most significantly there were the crime comic books, largely modeled after
the remarkable series of gangster films produced during the 1930s and prominently represented in 1942 by Charles Biro and Lev Gleason's *Crime Does Not
Pay*. In spite of explicit morals best summarized in the title, alarmed parents
were disturbed by its realistic depiction of murder and mayhem and factual accounts of how crimes were committed. This tradition was continued eight years
later by William M. Gaines under the EC (Entertaining Comics) imprint and
expanded to include horror, science fiction, and war in a series of the best written
and most imaginatively drawn comic books in the history of the medium—
*Tales from the Crypt, The Vault of Horror, The Haunt of Fear, Weird Science, Weird
Fantasy, Crime SuspenStories, Two-Fisted Tales,* and *Frontline Combat* among
them. While young readers were stirred by the stunning artwork and the carefully crafted stories with their philosophic, social, and moral messages, adults
could only see the violence, the gothic plots, and the sensually drawn women.
Thus these splendid products of the imagination were soon under the scrutiny
of a U.S. Senate Subcommittee on Juvenile Delinquency.

Before the Senate got to them, however, a psychiatrist named Dr. Fredric
Wertham was already condemning comic books. As senior psychiatrist for the
Department of Hospitals in New York City from 1932 to 1952, Dr. Wertham
had interviewed hundreds of juvenile delinquents and inevitably found that they
were eager readers of comic books. Even though he admitted that not a single
child ever told him "as an excuse for a delinquency or for misbehavior that
comic books were to blame," Wertham spun out an elaborate argument that
they were a prime stimulus for destructive and criminal behavior in his 1954
book *Seduction of the Innocent*. While his intentions were good, his proofs were
ill-conceived and simplistic. One example will suffice, an argument offered by
Dr. Wertham to a young girl for not reading Wonder Woman, an argument
which is not only illogical but at the same time contains an unconscious ethnic
slur against Latins and their eating habits and discredits the ability of a child to
distinguish between fantasy and reality:

"Supposing," I told her, "you get used to eating sandwiches made with very strong
seasonings, with onions and peppers and highly spiced mustard. You will lose your
taste for simple bread and butter and for finer food. The same is true of reading
comic books. If later on you want to read a good novel it may describe how a
young boy and girl sit together and watch the rain falling. They talk about themselves
and the pages of the book describe what their innermost little thoughts are. This is
what is called literature. But you will never be able to appreciate that if in comic-

book fashion you expect that at any minute someone will appear and pitch both of them out of the window." (Pp.64–65)

However unsound his theories, the public response to his book and the attention of the Senate Subcommittee generated so much political and economic pressure that the comic book publishers joined forces to organize a self-policing system known as the Comics Code Authority to which all material was to be submitted prior to publication. Guidelines of the authority prohibit displays of corrupt authority, successful crimes, happy criminals, the triumph of evil over good, violence, concealed weapons, the death of a policeman, sensual females, divorce, illicit sexual relations, narcotics or drug addiction, physical afflictions, poor grammar, and the use of the words "crime," "horror," and "terror" in the title of a magazine or a story. In the strangest passage of all, it appears that something called "the classic tradition" will permit the portrayal of certains kinds of evil:

Vampires, ghouls and werewolves shall be permitted to be used when handled in the classic tradition such as Frankenstein, Dracula and other high callibre literary works written by Edgar Allen [sic] Poe, Saki, Conan Doyle and other respected authors whose works are read in schools throughout the world.

Since neither Poe, Saki [H. H. Munro], nor Doyle wrote about vampires and werewolves, one wonders how their works can be used as a source of the "classic tradition."

Needless to say, these guidelines, the most severe form of censorship applied to any mass medium, prevented comic book artists and writers after 1954 from dealing with the real world in any kind of truthful fashion and from addressing themselves to any of the significant social and political problems of the modern world. The result of the code was effectively to stifle the art of the comic book from reaching the aesthetic standards towards which the EC publishing firm was moving. William Gaines quietly closed down the EC operation, took the idea behind one of his comic book titles called *Mad*, and developed it into this country's most popular satiric magazine.

The establishment of the code marked the conclusion of what historians call the Golden Age in comic book history. The only type that could thrive were the super-hero books, which depicted a world where good and evil were clearly distinguishable and justice always prevailed. In the late 1950s, under the editorship of Julius Schwartz, new artists and writers at National Periodical Publications gradually revived their stable of characters—Superman, Batman, Wonder Woman, and others—and moved from a dozen surviving titles to become once again the major comic book publisher, that is until Stan Lee came on the scene.

Beginning as an editorial assistant and copywriter at age seventeen with the Timely Comics Group, Lee worked with the firm through the 1940s as it changed names to Atlas and finally to Marvel, serving as chief editor from 1942 to 1972, when he became publisher. It was in 1961 that Lee teamed up with comic book veteran Jack Kirby to produce the first of a new breed of super-heroes more attuned to the 1960s and 1970s in *Fantastic Four* featuring a team of characters invested with human failings. The concept of the "superhero with problems" was given its most successful formulation in 1962 when Lee teamed up with artist Steve Ditko to create Spider-Man, a figure who ultimately would rival Superman's popularity and become a symbol for the youthful insecurities of the 1960s. Beset with personality problems, rejection, allergy attacks, failures, an overprotective aunt, and an unsuccessful love life, Peter Parker is accidentally bitten by a radioactive spider to become Spider-Man, an antihero among the super-powered whose successes are undermined by a series of antagonists who rob him of the respect he deserves. Their new series of titles would eventually lead Marvel into the sales arena as the only contender to National Periodical Publications in volume and readership.

While both Marvel and National Periodical Publications, now simply known as DC (after the initials of one of their most successful titles, *Detective Comics*), continued to work with the guidelines of the Comics Code Authority, some adjustments to changes in the social and political climate have been possible. In 1971, for example, the guidelines were changed to allow for stories about drug addiction, as long as it was presented as a "vicious habit" in no way pleasurable, justifiable, or easily cured. At the request of the Office of Health, Education, and Welfare in Washington, Stan Lee published a three-part story called "And Now the Goblin" beginning in the May 1971 *Amazing Spider-Man*, and the subject was handled with great tact and no misunderstanding about the harmful effects of drugs. More recently DC, in cooperation with President Reagan's drug awareness campaign, published two special issues of the currently popular title *The New Teen Titans* on the drug problem in public schools for distribution to elementary school children throughout the nation.

The newly expanded and changed marketplace for comic books has influenced the effectiveness of the Comics Code Authority. The original purpose of the code's seal of approval was to alert the newsdealer to the suitability of what was being sold to children, and the parental pressure in the dealer's own neighborhood guaranteed that no book without the seal would go on sale at the newsstand. Now many dealers do not want to sell comic books at all because of the small profit margin, and a great many comic books are sold at comic specialty shops with a large adult and teenage clientele. Stories rejected by the authority office have been known to appear in special editions without the seal at such comic shops, and numerous independent publishers have appeared who submit none of their material for approval and sell only to the shops.

In 1986 public criticism of adult-oriented material in comic books reached a new pitch on television shows, in newspaper editorials, and from fundamentalist religious groups. In response, DC Comics decided in December to inaugurate its own rating system for comic books so as to alert parents and purchasers to those titles meant for mature readers and those meant for all age groups. Many of the artists and writers for DC resigned because they had not been consulted or objected to what they saw as "in-house censorship." Whether the rating system will last or be adopted by other publishers remains to be seen. What few commentators have noted, however, is that the entire controversy is simply a sign of growth and maturation, that the artists and writers are finally addressing some of those controversial issues with which the comic book must deal if it is to realize its full potential as an art form for the remainder of the twentieth century.

A major problem in the comic book industry has always been the fact that sales figures rather than quality all too often determine whether a title will be kept in print, which is of course only a sound business practice. Another problem has been the fact that until recently most comic book work was hired out on a free-lance basis and the artists and writers maintained no reprint rights or future control of the material. The creators of Superman sold their rights to the character for $130 and after leaving the publisher received no royalties or income until recent years when public pressure led to the awarding of a retirement pension and credit for the creation. Also the pay is not high and most artists and writers stay with comic book work only until more lucrative employment develops, but it serves as an excellent showcase for their talent—the popular fantasy artist Frank Frazetta worked in comics before he became the rage of paperback and poster art. Rates of pay are now higher than they have ever been, and the publishers offer contracts which determine ownership of the original art and provide royalties on future reprint rights.

One promising development for the future of the comic book is the efforts to produce more adult-oriented and lengthier works in that format. James Warren began the trend in 1965 when he published a series of magazine-sized black-and-white comic books called *Creepy* and *Eerie*, to be joined in 1969 by *Vampirella*. Sold as adult magazines and thus outside the control of the Comics Code Authority, Warren returned to gothic and horror themes of the 1950s and produced a volume of stories which at their best rival the work in the EC line (sometimes utilizing the same artists from that firm). Paralleling this development was the publication of limited circulation underground comic books, which intentionally set out to violate every guideline of the code and many of the mores of the larger society. Although much self-indulgence and bad art ensued, the undergrounds served as a proving ground and nurtured the talents of some of the most promising and original artists of the 1970s such as Robert Crumb, Gilbert Shelton, S. Clay Wilson, Richard Corben, Art Spiegelman, Trina Robbins, Ted Richards, Victor Moscoso, Dennis Kitchen, Justin Green, and Rand Holmes among others, all brilliant in their individual ways and holding promise of finer work to come.

Although the adaptation of the comic book form to the novel and lengthy works of fiction has been underway for many years, we have witnessed recently the publication of several notable examples in this line, such as Richard Corben's *Bloodstar* (1976), Jack Katz's *The First Kingdom* (1978), *The Silver Surfer* by Stan Lee and Jack Kirby (1978), and Will Eisner's *A Contract with God and Other Tenement Stories* (1978), the last an especially impressive application of comic art to urban ethnic experiences of the 1940s. Both DC and Marvel Comics regularly publish "graphic novels" featuring their main characters, the most notable and controversial example being a futuristic version of Batman in the lengthy *The Dark Knight Returns* (1986) by Frank Miller. In another interesting development, Dutch detective novelist Janwillem van de Wetering decided to publish one of his novels in comic book form as *Murder by Remote Control* (1986), with art by American Paul Kirchner. The most serious experiment in this area, certainly in terms of subject matter, is Art Spiegelman's projected book-length treatment of the Holocaust in animal fable form, based on his brief but startling story "Maus." Chapters of the book have been appearing regularly in Spiegelman's experimental magazine *Raw*, and the first half of *Maus* appeared in 1986 as a best-selling, widely reviewed and praised paperback edition.

Perhaps the most challenging but promising development ahead lies in the direction of educational uses of the comic book. Teachers no longer fear that comic books will take students away from literature—rather we know now many children first learn to read them and then go on to more sophisticated levels of reading. Recent experiments with the use of comics in the classroom demonstrate that slow readers and children with learning disabilities can be helped through their use. Although both National Periodical Publications, especially under the leadership of publisher Jenette Kahn, and Marvel Comics have experimented with educational materials based on their properties, no one has turned out a package that successfully combines the automatic appeal of comic art with clearly articulated educational goals. Either the lesson gets lost in the art or the message subdues the entertainment value, perhaps because these materials are usually produced by teams of artists, writers, and educational consultants rather than by a single creative mind who can combine educational theory with a full grasp of the aesthetics of comic art.

Publishers have also realized the value of comic art in creating appealing textbooks. Every sort of text from freshman English rhetorics and readers to mathematics, political science, and history books, all incorporate cartoons and comic characters in order to elucidate major points and teach through humor. The most interesting example of this trend is a series of political "Documentary Comic Books" published by Pantheon Books of New York: *Marx for Beginners* by Mexican editorial cartoonist Ruis (Eduardo del Rio), *Lenin for Beginners* by Canadian novelist Richard Appignanesi and Argentine illustrator Oscar Zarate, and *The Anti-Nuclear Handbook* by British journalist Stephen Croall and American cartoonist Kaianders. Also *Einstein for Beginners* and *Freud for Beginners* have been published. Packed with information in a lively illustrated text, albeit strongly slanted in a liberal direction, the popular appeal of the books incurred the wrath of the conservative press. In an editorial on April 7, 1979, the Richmond (Va.) *News Leader* branded them "predictable Socialistic Tripe."

It may be true that the comic book has not fully reached its aesthetic potential as narrative and visual art, but the numerous bright spots and accomplishments are sufficient to suggest its genuine potential as an art form of the future. Given the fact that we are approaching a society in which the majority of information is conveyed by visual means, and if the Gutenberg revolution is indeed over as some would have us believe, the comic book of the future may remain one of our last links with the printed word.

REFERENCE WORKS

While *The Comic Book Price Guide* by Robert M. Overstreet began in 1970 as a selling price reference for dealers and collectors, it has grown through annual revisions and expansions into the single most important source of information about the history of the comic book. A comprehensive listing of comic book titles from 1933 to the present, dates of first and last issues, publishing companies, and important artists has been supplemented with updated information on comic book collecting, fan publications, comic book conventions, a history of the development of comic books, and other special features. The text is copiously illustrated with comic book covers. Overstreet's *Guide* has also served to stabilize the vigorous market that has grown up around collectors and fandom. Although neither will serve as a substitute for Overstreet's *Guide*, collectors may use with profit Marcia Leiter's *Collecting Comic Books* or Mike Benton's *Comic Book Collecting for Fun and Profit*. The pamphlet *A Guide to Collecting and Selling Comic Books*, by Raymond Carlson, is of little consequence. There are several Overstreet imitations available, but they offer no competition. The underground comic book publishing phenomenon is thoroughly documented by Jay Kennedy in *The Official Underground and Newave Comix Price Guide*.

The main body of *The World Encyclopedia of Comics*, edited by Maurice Horn, consists of more than 1,200 cross-referenced entries arranged alphabetically and devoted either to an artist, a writer, a comic strip title, or a comic book character, prepared by an international group of contributors. Additional materials include a short history of the development of comics, a chronology from the eighteenth century to 1975, an original analytic inquiry into the aesthetics of comics by Horn, a history of newspaper syndication, a glossary, a selected bibliography, and several appendixes and indexes. Unfortunately, there are many typographical errors in the text and the critical commets are often idiosyncratic or biased. A promised revised and corrected edition has never appeared. *The World Encyclopedia of Cartoons*, also edited by Maurice Horn, contains another 1,200 entires by twenty-two contributors on cartoonists, animators, editors, producers, and the works they have created in the fields of animation, gag cartoons, syndicated comic panels, editorial cartoons, caricature, and sports cartoons. Since many animated film characters are drawn from comic books, some of the material here is relevant. The entries are supplemented by an overview of caricature and cartoons, a brief history of humor magazines, a world summary of animated films, a chronology of important events in the history of cartooning, and a glossary of terms. Both of the encyclopedias are thoroughly illustrated in black and white and in color.

A standard source of biographical data on comic book artists and writers is *The Who's Who of American Comic Books* in four volumes, edited by Jerry Bails and Hames Ware. Conscientiously compiled and edited, each entry provides birth and death dates, pen names, art schools attended, major influences, and career data, including major publishers and comic book credits. Most of the information was obtained directly from the artists and writers themselves. At least two comic artists have been given comprehensive bibliographic treatment. Glenn Bray's *The Illustrated Harvey Kurtzman Index: 1939–1975* catalogs Kurtzman's innovative work for comic books (he created *Mad*), magazines, newspapers, and films, with some 200 examples of his art reprinted in an attractive, usefully arranged format. Donald M. Fiene's *R. Crumb Checklist of Work and Criticism* is a comprehensive and detailed annotated listing of practically everything underground cartoonist Robert Crumb has drawn (comic books, book illustrations, greeting cards, record covers, etc.) and everything written or drawn about him. There are a variety of indexes (titles, characters, autobiographical pieces, collaborations, etc.), a chronology of Crumb's life and career from 1943 to 1980, and numerous illustrations. Fiene's book is a model bibliographic effort for a diverse, productive, and elusive artist, probably one of the most influential of the last two decades.

The first volume of *The Encyclopedia of Comic Book Heroes* by Michael L. Fleisher contains over 1,000 entries on every major and minor character to appear in the Batman stories, with one hundred pages alone devoted to the life and adventures of Batman himself. The second and third volumes provide similar coverage for Wonder Woman and Superman respectively. Although eight volumes were announced, only three were published. *The*

Encyclopedia of Superheroes by Jeff Rovin is an alphabetically arranged catalog of information on more than 1,300 heroic figures and crime fighters from the comics, film, folklore, television, popular literature, radio, and computer games, with the great majority drawn from comic books. Each entry includes the hero's alter ego, first appearance, occupation when not fighting opponents, costume, weapons, biography, a characteristic quotation, and a commentary by Rovin, descriptive but often critical as well. While Rovin notes that superbeings and gods are as old as known history and found in all cultures, only those heroes are included in the encyclopedia who possess an extraordinary power, work for the common good rather than selfish reasons, are never vindictive, operate on Earth, and assume an alter ego and a distinctive costume. Appendixes provide data on super-hero teams, obscure and minor figures, and foreign super-heroes. There are illustrations and an index.

Also useful is Jerry Bails's *The Collector's Guide: The First Heroic Age*, an extensive effort "to list all costumed and super-heroes strips appearing from 1934 through 1947 in comic books, including reprints of newspaper strips and adaptations of heroes from pulps to radio." Publishers and artists are also listed. Complementing this volume is Howard Keltner's *Index to Golden Age Comic Books*, an alphabetically arranged index to approximately 98 percent of the Golden Age comic books of the 1940s and 1950s, with notes on publication dates, front cover and interior features, and other useful bibliographic data on over 8,000 issues of 300 titles in the super-hero line.

The Full Edition of the Complete E.C. Checklist (Revised), by Fred von Bernewitz and Joe Vucenic, focuses on the life of one publisher, Entertaining Comics, generally regarded as the producers of the best-drawn and most well-written comic books published in America during the early 1950s. The contents of all issues are listed with biographical sketches of the main artists and writers who collaborated on the series. An index would have been useful. George Olshevsky's *Marvel Comics Index* is an extensive computerized project which in fourteen projected volumes will catalog all of the super-hero stories published in Marvel comic books since November 1961 (when the first issue of the *Fantastic Four* appeared). The first ten of the volumes are devoted to the Amazing Spider-Man, Conan and the Barbarians, the Avengers and Captain Marvel, the Fantastic Four (including the Silver Surfer and the Human Torch), Doctor Strange, Thor, the Incredible Hulk, Sub-Mariner, Captain America, and Iron Man. A synopsis of each character's history, information on artists and writers, and several cross-indexes are included. A number of artist, title, and publisher checklists have been published in full and fragmentary form in scattered fan magazines and separate pamphlets, but no one has undertaken to assemble a guide to this material.

Both Marvel and DC have published valuable illustrated guides to all the characters that populate their comic book stories: *The Official Handbook of the Marvel Universe* in eight squarebound paperback volumes, and *Who's Who: The Definitive Directory of the DC Universe* as a twenty-six issue comic book series. In an effort to place their characters in a larger chronological perspective, DC has also published a two-volume *History of the DC Universe* by Marv Wolfman and George Pérez. Useful character and plot summaries, articles, and artist interviews are published in the issues of *Comics File Magazine*, each focused on specific figures, such as the X-Men, the Fantastic Four, Superman, and Spider-Man.

Although it is designed as a game book, there is a lot of information buried in *The Pow! Zap! Wham! Comic Book Trivia Quiz* by Michael Uslan and Bruce Solomon, with almost one hundred comic book covers reproduced. Other specialized reference items are *The Comic Book Custer* by Brian W. Dippie and Paul A. Hutton, an annotated checklist of the appearances of General George A. Custer in comic books and strips; and George Thomas Fisher's *The Classic Comics Index*, which indexes all authors, subjects, and topics covered in the 169-issue run of *Classics Illustrated* and related Gilberton publications. A thoroughly researched and invaluable guide to all the Classics series is *The Classics Handbook* by Charles Heffelfinger, now in its third edition. While there is much misinformation in *Cartoons and Comics in the Classroom*, edited by James L. Thomas, the book does reprint a few useful suggestions for using comic books in the teaching of reading, English, history, and languages.

The publication of fan magazines and amateur press publications about comic art began in the 1950s and reemerged in the 1960s as a significant development in the history of American magazines. Much of the pioneer scholarship about the comics first appeared in these pages, and extremely useful biographical and bibliographical information can be found there. A history of their development and a listing of titles would require more space than is available for this entire essay, and it would be almost impossible to assemble a file for back issues on most of them. The comments here will be restricted to a very few of the most professional, informative, and regularly published periodicals to which subscriptions are available.

The most widely circulated and read publication for collectors who wish to buy and sell comic books and related material is a tabloid, the *Comics Buyer's Guide*, originated in 1971 by Alan L. Light (under the title the *Buyer's Guide for Comic Fandom*). Krause Publications assumed ownership in 1983 and appointed Don and Maggie Thompson as editors. In addition to advertisements, the weekly includes feature articles, news stories, columns, reviews, cartoons, and a letter column in which readers vigorously debate issues and controversies with the editors and each other. The second most popular publication is the *Comics Journal*, a monthly magazine with lengthy essays, in-depth interviews, review columns by leading commentators on the comics, and an aggressive editorial policy that often places the magazine in the center of controversy. Both the *Guide* and the *Journal* make for lively reading.

Other publications with valuable professional and historic data include *Comics Feature*, a general interest magazine; *Amazing Heroes*, devoted to the super-hero titles; and *Comics Interview*, which offers lengthy conversations with artists, writers, publishers, and creative people. Clay Geerdes, who formerly published *Comix World*, ceased that publication to issue *Comix Wave*, a similar one-page newsletter devoted to the self-published new wave comic books and his own comments on popular culture in general. John Benson's *Squa Tront* contains thoroughy researched and critically stimulating essays about the EC comic book titles. It appears on no regular schedule but is always more than worth the wait. A good research collection should have complete runs of all these publications at a minimum.

RESEARCH COLLECTIONS

Most American libraries—public, private, and academic—never subscribed to or made any efforts to preserve comic books. They were viewed as ephemeral publications which catered to illiteracy and had little cultural or historic value. Only recently has this opinion changed; thus there are relatively few substantial collections to consult for research, and these have been built through the efforts of individuals who had the foresight to recognize their worth—not simply as investment items but as documents which relate to the cultural and social patterns of the twentieth century.

A leader in this development has been Randall W. Scott who singlehandedly has built the invaluable Russel B. Nye Popular Culture Collection at Michigan State University and assembled over 40,000 comic books with another 2,000 on microfilm. Scott has also acquired a collection of reference books and extensive files of fan publications, journals, and materials related to the history and development of the comic book. Through his efforts, the Michigan State University Library has become the major research center for the comic book anywhere in the world, and since the publishers now automatically deposit their publications there, it is likely to remain so.

What should be a major resource—the Library of Congress—has lost a large part of its copyright deposit collection over the years either through neglect or lax security. Nevertheless, it claims to own 45,000 titles and now has a program for their preservation. Other extensive files include the Bowling Green State University Library, with more than 20,000 comic books; the San Francisco Academy of Comic Art (established by Bill Blackbeard as the major research center for the comic strip) with 10,000 issues; and the libraries at Northwestern University and the University of Pittsburgh with over 8,500 issues each. Collections of between 1,000 and 2,000 comic books are found in the libraries of California State University at Fullerton, the

Comics Magazine Association of America, Southern Illinois University at Edwardsville, University of Maryland in Baltimore County, and University of Minnesota. Collections of underground comic books in excess of 2,000 issues are located at Iowa State University and Washington State University. The Library of Communication and Graphic Arts at Ohio State University, under the expert guidance of Lucy Caswell, has extensive holdings on the comic book work of Will Eisner, Milton Caniff, and others.

A useful guide to these and other collections is found in Randall W. Scott's survey "Comic Research Libraries," which includes the names of contacts, addresses, and phone numbers. This information is updated in the quarterly newsletter edited by Scott at Michigan State University, *Comic Art Collection*.

HISTORY AND CRITICISM

The earliest history and analytic study of American comic art was *The Comics* by Coulton Waugh, a practicing comic artist and devoted scholar of the subject. While many of his facts are faulty, Waugh attempted a comprehensive survey of the important movements and types of comic strips from *The Yellow Kid* through the first decade of the comic book. His insights into the reasons for the popularity of certain strips, his comments on the aesthetic principles behind them, and his early effort to define the medium make Waugh's pioneering effort a work of lasting interest, although he had little appreciation for the comic book and he appeared to accept without question some of the highbrow standards often applied to popular art by the self-appointed guardians of high culture.

The next effort on the part of a single author to chart the history of the medium was Stephen Becker's *Comic Art in America*. Becker's interests were broader than Waugh's in that he ambitiously envisioned his book, according to its subtitle, as "A social history of the funnies, the political cartoons, magazine humor, sporting cartoons, and animated cartoons." Casting his net so broadly led to much superficiality, and his commentary is often derivative, but the volume is a useful storehouse of over 390 illustrations and sample drawings. The text is kept to a minimum and the illustrations are at a maximum in *The Penguin Book of Comics* by George Perry and Alan Aldridge, aptly described in its subtitle as "a slight history." Originally published in French in conjunction with an exhibition of comic art at the Louvre, and the joint product of six contributors headed by Pierre Couperie, *A History of the Comic Strip* contains some of the best discussion and provocative comments yet ventured on the aesthetics, structure, symbolism, and themes in comic art. Another general survey undertaken by one author, comic artist Jerry Robinson, is *The Comics: An Illustrated History of Comic Strip Art*. Robinson provides a readable and interesting text complemented by thirteen original essays by eminent artists about the theories behind their work. All of these general histories contain commentary on the comic book.

Several thematic studies have been published, mostly by Maurice Horn. His *Comics of the American West* is a heavily illustrated historic survey of the major Western comic strips and books and their basic symbolic themes, and his *Women in the Comics* surveys in a similar fashion the images and roles of women as reflected in the comics. Horn's third book in this series is *Sex in the Comics*, an informal discussion of the presence of sexual behavior in comic strips and comic books of the mainstream and underground varieties primarily in the United States but in select foreign countries as well. Horn finds that despite associations of nostalgia and innocence, from the start comics have flirted with or strongly suggested sexuality and eroticism, and in the last decade through adult fantasy and science fiction comic books, writers and artists have been explicitly concerned with normal and abnormal sexual activity. Horn seldom documents his sources or mentions dates of publication, so his work is not as useful as it might be to the scholar, but his frequent use of illustrations is a major strength. *Women and the Comics* by Trina Robbins and Catherine Yronwode is a thoroughly researched first effort to chart the careers of hundreds of generally unknown women who have worked in the comic art field. The result of four years of research, this study documents the contributions of over 500 women writers and cartoonists and admirably elucidates a largely ignored area of comics history. A chapter is also devoted to female cartoonists in Europe, Japan, and Australia.

Comics: Anatomy of a Mass Medium is a broad effort by two German scholars, Reinhold Reitberger and Wolfgang Fuchs, to relate the comics to their social context and developments in other mass media. It is an admirable example of foreign scholarship, but faulty secondary sources and inaccessible primary material led to a number of factual and other errors which no one corrected in the process of translation. A British perspective is found in Denis Gifford's *The International Book of Comics*, a fully illustrated, broad survey of the cultural and historic development of comic strips and comic books in America and Great Britain, from nineteenth-century caricature and humorous periodicals through the underground comix movement. This comparative approach demonstrates the degree to which influences have worked internationally in the shaping of comic art.

The first full-length volume on the comic book was neither a history nor an appreciation. The purpose of *Seduction of the Innocent* by psychologist Fredric Wertham, published in 1954, was to prove that comic books, especially of the crime and horror variety, were a major contributor to juvenile delinquency. Although his data was scientifically invalid, Wertham's book upset many parent and teacher groups and added to the general hysteria of the McCarthy era, resulting in a congressional investigation chaired by Estes Kefauver. Anticipating the investigation, in October 1954, the Comics Magazine Association of America moved to adopt a self-regulating Comics Code Authority with the most stringent code ever applied to any of the mass media. Wertham's book, therefore, remains of significant cultural and historic interest.

A summary and chronology of the institutional attacks on juvenile delinquency and its reputed causes in American popular culture on the part of governmental agencies, political groups, sociologists, intellectuals, and parents during the 1950s is found in James Gilbert's *A Cycle of Outrage*. Gilbert focuses in particular on the crusades against films and comic books, and he analyzes the arguments of Wertham and the Kefauver Senate Subcommittee. Gilbert finds their evidence inconclusive and contradictory. The report *Juvenile Deliquency*, issued by the U.S. Congress, Senate Committee on the Judiciary, has been made available in a reprint from Greenwood Press. Martin Barker's *A Haunt of Fears* is a study of the British campaign against comic books in the 1950s. Barker discovers that the campaign was originated and covertly sponsored by the Communist party, that the comic books under question were primarily American imports, and that a large part of the campaign was inspired by nationalistic and anti-American sentiments. Comic books, along with American film and mass media, were viewed as seductive, corrupting influences on British culture during World War II. Barker provides thorough analyses of selected stories to demonstrate that the meanings were exactly opposite to the claims of the detractors but that they did seriously question the assumptions of American and British society about the nature of life, the reality of childhood, and the roots of human behavior.

Before Wertham, Gershon Legman had issued early warnings about the baneful effect of violence in the comics in *Love & Death: A Study in Censorship* in 1949. Also in tune with Wertham are the comments of Gillian Freeman in *The Undergrowth of Literature*. Freeman fears that costumed super-heroes will inspire fantasies of fetishism and sadomasochism. A chapter of Ron Goulart's *The Assault on Childhood* traces how he feels that the comic book industry "ignored its potential and became preoccupied with murder, torture, sadism and storm-tooper violence." Wertham and all his alarmist colleagues are given a gentle and good humored debunking from the Canadian perspective of novelist Mordecai Richler in a short essay that gives its title to the book *The Great Comic Book Heroes and Other Essays*.

The first writer to inaugurate what he claimed would be a full-scale history of the comic book was James Steranko, himself a talented comic book artist. Volume 1 of *The Steranko History of Comics* finds that pulp fiction of the 1930s was the single most important source of inspiration to the development of the comic book and then traces the histories of Superman, Batman, Captain America, Captain Marvel, and the DC comic books. Volume 2 continues the coverage of Captain Marvel and related Fawcett super-heroes, the Blackhawks and other airborne characters, Plastic Man and the Quality titles, and Will Eisner's Spirit. Encyclopedic in detail, there is more information in these two volumes than most readers can easily assimilate, but Steranko's contributors have a high regard for the distinctive qualities of comic book art and view it as a part and reflection of the total context of popular culture. Unfortunately, none of the promised following four volumes has appeared. Though primarily an anthology of selected stories, Jules Feiffer's *The Great Comic Book Heroes* has a lengthy introduction in which artist/author Feiffer reminisces about his days in the comic book industry and provides his personal commentary on the meaning of the super-hero. Published as a catalog for an exhibition held at Ohio State University, M. Thomas Inge's *The American Comic Book* contains a brief history of the subject, an analysis of selected stories from the EC science fiction comic books, interviews with publishers Stan Lee and Jenette Kahn, and additional essays by Stan Lee, Will Eisner, and Ray Bradbury.

A single-volume history is *Comix: A History of Comic Books in America* by Les Daniels. Daniels provides a sensible outline of the major developments and reprints over twenty stories, four of them in color. His final chapter deals with the development of underground comic books, generally called "comix" to distinguish them from the traditional publications. Partly a radical rejection of the Comics Code Authority and partly a natural development of the counterculture underground press, comix provided artists with unrestricted freedom to write and draw to the limits of their imagination, something which has seldom been possible in comic art. While shameless obscenity and bad taste abound, several striking talents emerged from the movement—Robert Crumb remains the best known—and much highly original work was accomplished. Mark James Estren attempted to produce *A History of the Underground Comics*, which is difficult to accomplish because the publishing centers have ranged from California to the Midwest to New York, and the artists have never been eager to cooperate with researchers and critics. While much of his commentary is debatable, Estren has assembled an excellent cross-section of representative art by the major figures, many of whom are allowed to speak for themselves through interviews and letters, and a useful checklist of underground titles by comix scholar Clay Geerdes concludes the volume. It is an engaging grab bag of reading matter about an important cultural development.

Ron Goulart's *Great History of Comic Books* is a richly detailed overview of the main trends and developments with attention to many often overlooked titles, characters, and artists. His breezy and personalized style belies the extensive research that goes into his writing about the comics. Focusing on the early pre-Superman years of the comic book, Charles Wooley's *History of the Comic Book 1899–1936* traces with meticulousness and careful research the development of the precursors to the modern comic book, its earliest form as a reprint publication for comic strips, and the beginning efforts to produce original material for comic book publication. In *The*

Comic Book Heroes, Will Jacobs and Gerard Jones undertake an analysis of the contents and style of the comic book from 1956, the Silver Age, to the present, with a major focus on the dominant publishers DC and Marvel. In chronologically arranged chapters, they examine the trends in super-heroes and the artists and writers who have made the comic book into a creative medium of increasing breadth and sophistication. Although marketing problems and conservative editorial practices are causes for concern, they feel that comic books remain a significant force in mainstream entertainment.

Most serious study of comic art seems to have focused on how it reflects or relates to society and the culture out of which it has grown. Only now are we witnessing the development of a body of writing that attempts to assess the comics on their own terms, by measuring their worth against their own developed standards and aesthetic principles rather than by the irrelevant yardsticks of other related arts. A collection of essays mainly on comic book super-heroes helped initiate this development, *All in Color for a Dime*, edited by Dick Lupoff and Don Thompson. Many of the essays originated in a series of fan magazine articles and still bear the stylistic and judgmental marks of their origin. A second volume, also edited by Thompson and Lupoff, *The Comic-Book Book*, is a marked improvement in this regard. In style and judgment, many of these essays are distinguished. The purpose of *Moviemaking Illustrated: The Comicbook Filmbook*, by James Morrow and Murray Suid, is to teach the technical principles of filmmaking, but the textbook utilizes nothing but frames from Marvel comic books and thereby makes many valuable points about the complex sound and visual techniques of comic art.

Will Eisner, a creator of the comic book and one of the most influential masters of comic art, discusses his ideas and theories on the practice of telling stories in graphic form in *Comics & Sequential Art*. Separate chapters, thoroughly illustrated by examples of his own work, treat imagery, timing, framing, and anatomy, and he discusses comics as a form of reading, learning, and teaching. Eisner views comics as a distinct artistic discipline and a literary/visual form, the development of which has been accelerated by advances in graphic technology and visual communication in the twentieth century. This is the best book ever written on the aesthetics of comic art, and it will remain an essential work in the field for artists and readers alike. *The Comic-Stripped American* by Arthur Asa Berger is a collection of his pieces (including discussions of Superman, Batman, and Marvel comics) on the ways comics reflect our culture, many of them stimulating and provocative but also debatable.

Ron Goulart's *The Great Comic Book Artists* showcases the work of sixty accomplished artists with a single-page biographical and appreciative essay devoted to each. Fewer artists are treated but with fuller commentary and more extensive illustration in *Masters of Comic Book Art* by P. R. Garrick.

A great deal of information about numerous comic book artists, along with full-color reproductions of forty classic covers, has been gathered in Richard O'Brien's *The Golden Age of Comic Books: 1937–1945.*

There are only two full-length books devoted to major figures in the comic book world. Frank Jacobs's *The Mad World of William M. Gaines* is partly a biography and partly a personal memoir about the publisher responsible for the distinguished EC line of comic books and later *Mad* magazine (which he began as a comic book). One half of Michael Barrier's *Carl Barks and the Art of the Comic Book* is biography and the remainder is an annotated bibliography of Barks's fine work, especially on the Donald Duck and Scrooge McDuck stories in the Disney comic books. Barks has emerged as a true master of visual narrative and satire. One of Barks's more notable creations was given his own biographical treatment in *An Informal Biography of Scrooge McDuck* by Jack Chalker. A related item is *How to Read Donald Duck: Imperialist Ideology in the Disney Comic* by Ariel Dorfman and Armand Matterlart. Originally published in South America and translated into English in 1975, this tract attempts to demonstrate how Disney comic books were used in Chile before Allende to promote capitalistic ideology. Actually, the culprits were the translators who put words into the mouths of characters not contained in the originals from Disney studios.

In *Mythmakers of the American Dream*, Wiley Lee Umphlett takes a studied look at the way fiction, the comics, movies, and television have conditioned people of his generation to view the world in new and different ways. In a lengthy and thoroughly illustrated essay, Umphlett explores his thesis that "In a way that no other popular medium could, the comic book played on the conflict between our present condition and our longing for a more idealized existence even while offering fantasies that embodied our fear of the unknown." A little explored area is the direct influence of reading comic books on popular culture figures, although a few such influences have been noted. In *Danse Macabre*, Stephen King pays tribute to the EC comic books and the way they inspired his own fiction in the horror line. In their study of Mickey Spillane, *One Lonely Knight*, Max Allan Collins and James L. Traylor discuss Spillane's early work for the comic books, and Elaine Dundy, in *Elvis and Gladys*, identifies Captain Marvel, Jr., as a source of inspiration to Elvis Presley in his dress and appearance.

ANTHOLOGIES AND REPRINTS

The reprinting of comic book material has occurred with much less frequency than of comic strips, possible because of the expense of color reproduction, which is necessary to do it properly. The first hardcover anthology of selected comic book stories was Jules Feiffer's *The Great Comic Book Heroes* in 1965, a best-selling volume which partly spurred the commercial nostalgia market development. One of the major comic book publishers, National Periodical Publications, devoted a special publication, *Famous First Edition*, to oversized, full-color, facsimile reproductions of valuable first issues: *Action* No. 1, *Detective* No. 27, *Sensation* No. 1, and *Whiz Comics* No. 2, which introduced Superman, Batman, Wonder Woman, and Captain Marvel respectively, as well as *Batman* No. 1, *Superman* No. 1, *Wonder Woman* No. 1, *Flash Comics* No. 1, and *All Star Comics* No. 3. The first five of these were issued in hardcover editions by Lyle Stuart.

Michael Barrier and Martin Williams surveyed thousands of comic book stories to make their selection for *A Smithsonian Book of Comic-Book Comics* and the result is an excellent sampler of thirty-two stories that they feel show the comic book at its very best. Brief introductions helpfully place the stories in their historic and cultural perspectives.

Under the editorship of Stan Lee, Marvel Comics has released a series of popular squarebound paperback anthologies drawing together some of the best stories about selected super-hero figures in full color. Among these are *Origins of Marvel Comics, Son of Origins of Marvel Comics, Bring on the Bad Guys, The Superhero Women, The Incredible Hulk, Marvel's Greatest Superhero Battles, The Amazing Spider-Man, Dr. Strange, The Fantastic Four, Captain America, The Invincible Iron Man, The Uncanny X-Men,* and *Mighty Marvel Team-Up Thrillers.* DC has released a similar series focusing on genres, such as *Heart Throbs* edited by Naomi Scott, *America at War* and *Mysteries in Space,* both edited by Michael Uslan, as well as several hardcover volumes devoted to major figurs, such as *Secret Origins of the DC Super Heroes,* edited by Dennis O'Neil; *Batman from the 30s to the 70s; Wonder Woman; Shazam! from the Forties to the Seventies;* and *Superman from the Thirties to the Seventies,* updated subsequently through the 1980s. In 1971 a selection from the EC titles was published in an oversized volume as *Horror Comics of the 1950s,* edited by Ron Barlow and Bob Stewart. A selection of *The Best of Archie* by John Goldwater is also available. A substantial number of collections from the underground comic books have been issued, and they will be found listed in the checklist at the end of this essay under anthologies.

Three major publication projects are underway to bring into print in oversized, hardcover volumes some of the classic works of comic book art. A complete set of all published titles in the EC comic book series is being issued by Russ Cochran Publisher, P.O. Box 469, West Plains, MO 65775, and the complete works by Carl Barks for the Walt Disney comic book titles and John Stanley for the *Little Lulu* series are coming from Another Rainbow Publishing, P.O. Box 2206, Scottsdale, AZ 85252. These are deluxe, slipcased volumes, printed on high-quality paper, and shot in black and white from the original art. They also contain excellent historical and critical introductions and essays. All the sets are indispensable for research libraries.

Many of the major paperback publishers issue from time to time collections of comic book stories, as do the smaller alternative presses supplying collectors and comic book shops. The easiest way to find out about these is to obtain the catalogs of a major distributor, such as Bud Plant, P.O. Box 1886, Grass Valley, CA 95945.

BIBLIOGRAPHY

Books and Articles

Bails, Jerry. *The Collector's Guide: The First Heroic Age*. Detroit: Jerry Bails, 1969.
Bails, Jerry, and Hames Ware, eds. *The Who's Who of American Comic Books*. 4 vols. Detroit: Jerry Bails, 1973–76.
Barker, Martin. *A Haunt of Fears: The Strange History of the British Horror Comics Campaign*. London: Pluto Press, 1984.
Barrier, Michael. *Carl Barks and the Art of the Comic Book*. New York: M. Lilien, 1981.
Becker, Stephen. *Comic Art in America*. New York: Simon and Schuster, 1959.
Benton, Mike. *Comic Book Collecting for Fun and Profit*. New York: Crown, 1985.
Berger, Arthur Asa. *The Comic-Stripped American*. New York: Walker, 1973.
Bernewitz, Fred von, and Joe Vucenic. *The Full Edition of the Complete E. C. Checklist (Revised)*. Los Alamos, N.M.: Wade M. Brothers, 1974.
Bray, Glenn. *The Illustrated Harvey Kurtzman Index: 1939–1975*. Sylmar, Calif.: Glenn Bray, 1976.
Carlson, Raymond. *A Guide to Collecting and Selling Comic Books*. New York: Pilot Books, 1976.
Chalker, Jack. *An Informal Biography of Scrooge McDuck*. Baltimore: Mirage Press, 1974.
Collins, Max Allan, and James L. Traylor. *One Lonely Knight: Mickey Spillane's Mike Hammer*. Bowling Green, Ohio: Bowling Green State University Popular Press, 1984.
Couperie, Pierre, et al. *A History of the Comic Strip*. Translated by Eileen B. Hennessy. New York: Crown, 1968.
Daniels, Les. *Comix: A History of Comic Books in America*. New York: Outerbridge & Dienstfrey, 1971.
"DC Comics Releases Comic-Book Editorial Standards." *The Comics Buyer's Guide*, no. 684 (December 26, 1986), 16–17.
Dippie, Brian W., and Paul A. Hutton. *The Comic Book Custer: A Bibliography of Custeriana in Comic Books and Comic Strips*, Bryan, Tex.: Publication No. 4 Brazos Corral of the Westerners, 1983.
Dorfman, Ariel, and Armand Mattelart. *How to Read Donald Duck: Imperialist Ideology in the Disney Comic*. Translated by David Kunzle. New York: International General, 1975.
Dorson, Richard. *American Folklore*. Chicago: University of Chicago Press, 1959.
Dundy, Elaine. *Elvis and Gladys*. New York: Macmillan, 1985.
Eisner, Will. *Comics & Sequential Art*. Tamorac, Fla.: Poorhouse Press, 1985.
Estren, Mark James. *A History of Underground Comics*. San Francisco: Straight Arrow Books, 1974.

Feiffer, Jules. *The Great Comic Book Heroes.* New York: Dial Press, 1965.

Fiene, Donald M. *R. Crumb Checklist of Work and Criticism.* Cambridge, Mass.: Boatner Norton Press, 1981.

Fisher, George Thomas. *The Classic Comics Index.* Nottingham, N.H.: Thomas Fisher, 1986.

Fleisher, Michael L. *The Encyclopedia of Comic Book Heroes.* vol. 1, *Batman.* vol. 2, *Wonder Woman.* vol. 3, *Superman.* New York: Macmillan, 1976-.

Freeman, Gillian. *The Undergrowth of Literature.* London: Thomas Nelson, 1967.

Garrick, P.R. *Masters of Comic Book Art.* New York: Images Graphiques, 1978.

Gifford, Denis. *The International Book of Comics.* New York: Crescent Books, 1984.

Gilbert, James. *A Cycle of Outrage: America's Reaction to the Juvenile Delinquent in the 1950s.* New York: Oxford University Press, 1986.

Goulart, Ron. *The Assault on Childhood.* Los Angeles: Sherbourne Press, 1969.

———. *The Great Comic Book Artists.* New York: St. Martin's Press, 1986.

———. *Great History of Comic Books.* Chicago: Contemporary Books, 1986.

Heffelfinger, Charles. *The Classics Handbook.* 3d ed. Tampa, Fla.: Charles Heffelfinger, 1986.

Horn, Maurice. *Comics of the American West.* New York: Winchester Press, 1977.

———. *Sex in the Comics.* New York: Chelsea House, 1985.

———. *Women in the Comics.* New York: Chelsea House, 1977.

———, ed. *The World Encyclopedia of Cartoons.* New York: Chelsea House, 1981.

———. *The World of Encyclopedia of Comics.* New York: Chelsea House, 1976.

Inge, M. Thomas. *The American Comic Book.* Columbus: Ohio State University Libraries, 1985.

Jacobs, Frank. *The Mad World of William M. Gaines.* New York: Lyle Stuart, 1972.

Jacobs, Will, and Gerard Jones. *The Comic Book Heroes: From the Silver Age to the Present.* New York: Crown, 1985.

Keltner, Howard. *Index to Golden Age Comic Books.* Detroit: Jerry Bails, 1976.

Kennedy, Jay. *The Official Underground and Newave Comix Price Guide.* Cambridge, Mass.: Boatner Norton Press, 1982.

King, Stephen. *Danse Macabre.* New York: Everest House, 1981.

Legman, Gershon. *Love & Death: A Study in Censorship.* New York: Breaking Point, 1949. Reprint. New York: Hacker Art Books, 1963.

Leiter, Marcia. *Collecting Comic Books.* Boston: Little, Brown, 1983.

Lupoff, Dick, and Don Thompson, eds. *All in Color for a Dime.* New Rochelle, N.Y.: Arlington House, 1970.

Morrow, James, and Murray Suid. *Moviemaking Illustrated: The Comicbook Filmbook.* New York: Hayden, 1973.

O'Brien, Richard. *The Golden Age of Comic Books: 1937–1945.* New York: Ballantine Books, 1977.

The Official Handbook of the Marvel Universe. 8 vols. New York: Marvel Comics Group, 1986–87.

Olshevsky, George. *Marvel Comics Index.* Vol. 1, *The Amazing Spider-Man.* Vol. 2, *Conan and the Barbarians.* Vol. 3, *Avengers and Captain Marvel.* Vol. 4, *Fantastic Four.* Vol. 5, *The Mighty Thor.* Vol. 6, *Heroes from Strange Tales.* Vol. 7A, *Heroes from Tales to Astonish, The Incredible Hulk.* Vol. 7B, *Heroes from Tales to Astonish, The Sub-Mariner.* Vol. 8A, *Heroes from Tales of Suspense, Captain*

America. Vol. 8B, *Heroes from Tales of Suspense, Iron Man and Others*. Toronto, Canada: G & T Enterprises, 1975-.

Overstreet, Robert M. *The Comic Book Price Guide*. Cleveland, Tenn.: Overstreet Publications, 1970 (and subsequent annual editions).

Perry, George, and Alan Aldridge. *The Penguin Book of Comics*. New York: Penguin, 1969. Rev. ed., 1971.

Reitberger, Reinhold, and Wolfgang Fuchs. *Comics: Anatomy of a Mass Medium*. Translated by Nadia Fowler. Boston: Little, Brown, 1972.

Richler, Mordecai. *The Great Comic Book Heroes and Other Essays*. Toronto, Canada: McClelland and Stewart, 1978.

Robbins, Trina, and Catherine Yronwode. *Women and the Comics*. Guerneville, Calif.: Eclipse Books, 1985.

Robinson, Jerry. *The Comics: An Illustrated History of Comic Strip Art*. New York: G. P. Putnam, 1974.

Rovin, Jeff. *The Encyclopedia of Superheroes*. New York: Facts on File Publications, 1985.

Scott, Randall W. "Comic Research Libraries." *Comic Art Collection*, no. 33 (February 2, 1987), 5–7. Reprinted in *Comics Buyer's Guide*, no. 694 (March 6, 1987), 51–52.

Steranko, James. *The Steranko History of Comics*. 2 vols. Wyomissing, Pa.: Supergraphics, 1970–72.

Thomas, James L., ed. *Cartoons and Comics in the Classroom: A Reference for Teachers and Librarians*. Littleton, Colo.: Libraries Unlimited, 1983.

Thompson, Don, and Dick Lupoff, eds. *The Comic-Book Book*. New Rochelle, N.Y.: Arlington House, 1973.

Umphlett, Wiley Lee. *Mythmakers of the American Dream: The Nostalgic Vision in Popular Culture*. Lewisburg, Pa.: Bucknell University Press, 1983.

U.S. Congress. Senate Committee on the Judiciary. *Juvenile Delinquency: Comic Books, Motion Pictures, Obscene and Pornographic Materials, Television Programs*. Westport, Conn.: Greenwood Press, 1969.

Uslan, Michael, and Bruce Solomon. *The Pow! Zap! Wham! Comic Book Trivia Quiz*. New York: William Morrow, 1977.

Waugh, Coulton. *The Comics*. New York: Macmillan, 1947. Reprinted. Brooklyn, N.Y.: Luna Press, 1974.

Wertham, Fredric. *Seduction of the Innocent*. New York: Holt, Rinehart and Winston, 1954. Reprinted. Port Washington, N.Y.: Kennikat Press, 1972.

Who's Who: The Definitive Directory of the DC Universe. 26 issues. New York: DC Comics, March 1985–April 1987.

Wolfman, Marv, and George Pérez. *History of the DC Universe*. 2 vols. New York: DC Comics, 1986.

Wooley, Charles. *History of the Comic Book 1899–1936*. Lake Buena Vista, Fla.: Charles Wooley, 1986.

Anthologies and Reprints

Barlow, Ron, and Bob Stewart, eds. *Horror Comics of the 1950s*. Franklin Square, N.Y.: Nostalgia Press, 1971.

Barrier, Michael, and Martin Williams, eds. *A Smithsonian Book of Comic-Book Comics.* Washington, D.C.: Smithsonian Institution Press, 1981.

Batman from the 30s to the 70s. New York: Crown, 1971.

The Best of the Rip Off Press. 2 vols. San Francisco: Rip Off Press, 1973–74.

Boxell, Tim. *Commies from Mars—The Red Planet, The Collected Works.* San Francisco: Last Gasp, 1985.

The Carl Barks Library. 30 vols. Scottsdale, Ariz.: Another Rainbow Publishing, 1983-.

The Complete EC Library. 53 vols. West Plains, Mo.: Russ Cochran, 1979-.

Crumb, Robert. *Fritz the Cat.* New York: Ballantine Books, 1969.

————. *Head Comix.* New York: Ballantine Books, 1970.

————. *Robert Crumb's Carload o' Comics: An Anthology of Choice Strips and Stories— 1968 to 1976.* New York: Bélier Press, 1976.

Donahue, Don, and Susan Goodrick, eds. *The Apex Treasury of Underground Comics.* New York: Quick Fox, 1974.

Feiffer, Jules, ed. *The Great Comic Book Heroes.* New York: Dial Press, 1965.

Goldwater, John. *The Best of Archie.* New York: G.P. Putnam, 1980.

Griffith, Bill, and Jay Kinney. *The Young Lust Reader.* Berkeley, Calif.: And/Or Press, 1974.

Kurtzman, Harvey, and Will Elder. *Playboy's Little Annie Fanny.* 2 vols. Chicago: Playboy Press, 1966, 1972.

Lee, Stan. *The Amazing Spider-Man.* New York: Simon and Schuster, 1979.

————. *Bring on the Bad Guys.* New York: Simon and Schuster, 1976.

————. *Captain America.* New York: Simon and Schuster, 1979.

————. *Dr. Strange.* New York: Simon and Schuster, 1979.

————. *The Fantastic Four.* New York: Simon and Schuster, 1979.

————. *The Incredible Hulk.* New York: Simon and Schuster, 1978.

————. *The Invincible Iron Man.* New York: Marvel Comics, 1984.

————. *Marvel's Greatest Superhero Battles.* New York: Simon and Schuster, 1978.

————. *Mighty Marvel Team-Up Thrillers.* New York: Marvel Comics, 1985.

————. *Origins of Marvel Comics.* New York: Simon and Schuster, 1974.

————. *Son of Origins of Marvel Comics.* New York: Simon and Schuster, 1975.

————. *The Superhero Women.* New York: Simon and Schuster, 1977.

————. *The Uncanny X-Men.* New York: Marvel Comics, 1984.

The Little Lulu Library. 1st series, 18 vols. Scottsdale, Ariz.: Another Rainbow Publishing, 1985-.

Lynch, Jay, ed. *The Best of Bijou Funnies.* New York: Links Books, 1975.

O'Neil, Dennis, ed. *Secret Origins of the DC Super Heroes.* New York: Crown-Harmony Books, 1976.

Pekar, Harvey. *American Splendor.* Garden City, N.Y.: Doubleday, 1986.

————. *More American Splendor.* Garden City, N.Y.: Doubleday, 1987.

Scott, Naomi, ed. *Heart Throbs: The Best of DC Romance Comics.* New York: Simon and Schuster, 1979.

Shazam! from the Forties to the Seventies. New York: Harmony Books, 1977.

Superman from the Thirties to the Eighties. New York: Crown, 1983.

Superman from the Thirties to the Seventies. New York: Crown, 1971.

Sutton, Laurie S., ed. *The Great Superman Comic Book Collection.* New York: DC Comics, 1981.

Uslan, Michael, ed. *America at War: the Best of DC War Comics*. New York: Simon and Schuster, 1979.
————, ed. *Mysteries in Space: The Best of DC Science Fiction Comics*. New York: Simon and Schuster, 1980.
Wonder Woman. New York: Holt, Rinehart and Winston, 1972.

Periodicals

Amazing Heroes. Agoura, Calif., 1983-.
Comic Art Collection. East Lansing, Mich., 1979-.
Comics Buyer's Guide. Iola, Wis., 1970-.
Comics Feature. Canoga Park, Calif., 1980-.
Comics File Magazine. Canoga Park, Calif., 1986-.
Comics Interview. New York, 1983-.
Comics Journal. Agoura, Calif., 1977-.
Comix Wave. Berkeley, Calif., 1984-.
Squa Tront. New York, 1986-.

5.

Detective and Mystery Novels

LARRY N. LANDRUM

Mystery and detective fiction have been among the most popular genres to emerge in Western literature. The roots of mystery fiction have been traced into antiquity, and arguments have been made for the universality of many of its characteristics. Puzzles and narrative riddles are found in the folklore of all cultures, and the investigation of wrongdoing and the search for solutions to problems found in detective fiction reaches beyond recorded history. The particular forms that such interests take are not universal; they emerge in particular cultures at particular times, pass into and come to dominate appropriate modes of expression, and reveal tendencies found in their parent cultures. Though often used interchangeably, mystery and detective fiction may be used to distinguish between two closely related forms. Detective stories demand of their protagonists keen observation, superior reasoning, and a disciplined imagination, while the immediacy of physical danger may require a strong arm, fighting skills, or a weapon. In any case the narrative must provide suitable challenge with high enough stakes so that the measures taken by the detective seem appropriate.

Mysteries are less specialized than detective stories and often verge on the gothic. While many structural similarities suggest a common origin for gothic and mystery fiction, mysteries clearly reflect the growing belief in rational explanations of mysterious causes that marked early nineteenth-century popular literature. Yet there is often some sense in which the mystery threatens to escape rational explanation and occasionally does. Such uncertainty is expressed in other ways: the narrator is vulnerable in a predatory milieu, caught in a web of intrigue, threatened by unforeseen events, or grows aware that something is terribly wrong. The central figure of a mystery is usually the narrator, and the weight of suspense allows little distance between the narrator and the reader. The suspense novel and thriller are further variations, with the former an intensified mystery and the latter exploiting possibilities for action. When the mortal stakes are raised and the mystery threatens to implode, mystery is forced into the background, resulting in what has been aptly called the suspense novel or story. Hard-boiled suspense is usually highly naturalistic in that violence becomes the inescapable consequence of the conditions of socioeconomic or psychological pressures. Suspense novels tend toward inward psychological shock, while thrillers exploit stalking action and the chase. In the detective story, distance is established by focusing the reader's attention on detection and often by placing the recorder of the experience, a Doctor Watson figure, between the reader and the detective. While these observations may be rough descriptions of types, few novels are so neatly pigeonholed and categories are often blurred.

HISTORIC OUTLINE

The origins of the detective story, it is generally agreed, are found in the work of Edgar Allan Poe. Mystery and detection figure in many of Poe's stories, but those that most influenced the detective tradition are "The Murders in the Rue Morgue" (1841), "The Mystery of Marie Rôget" (1842–43), and "The Purloined Letter" (1844). Most historians of the genre agree that nearly all the conventions of the amateur detective story achieve their earliest coherent form in this tales, though earlier tales of mystery and detection can be found throughout history. In addition to his reformulation of the logical structure of the detective story, Poe's contribution was the celebration of independent observation, of reason and imagination in the investigation of the murkier levels of human affairs. In "The Murders in the Rue Morgue," C. Auguste Dupin concludes a friend's train of thought for him by reconstructing the external clues to his thoughts. In "The Mystery of Marie Rôget" the author attempts to solve a real crime by using only the evidence available to him in the newspapers; and in "The Purloined Letter," Dupin illustrates that imagination is crucial to the solution of problems conceived by intelligent criminals. Poe himself drew on the fanciful reminiscences of François-Eugène Vidocq, a thief who became chief of the Paris police and who published his memoirs in 1828–29. Poe considered Vidocq only "a good guesser and a persevering man" who often erred because he failed to imagine the whole as well as see the parts.

Numerous writers who followed Poe failed to mark his caution and created a legion of detectives whose solutions relied heavily on luck. Others created what they felt were more realistic police detectives rather than the inspired amateur or, later, the private investigator who is available for hire. As a disinterested amateur Poe's detective avoided the exchange of money, the potential for corruption, and the rules associated with policemen. So the serious intellectual and imaginative work of fictional crime detection was given to an individual having the freedom and indepedence to see the whole picture and the leisure to pursue the unusual or bizarre. Throughout much of the rest of the nineteenth century, the narrative form in which the detective appeared remained relatively open, as if writers were willing to concede the field of the closed form to Poe. The detective's investigation tended to merge in most novels with themes from gothic fiction, domestic romance, courtroom exposition, social exposés, and picaresque adventure stories. Developments in England often appeared in America almost simultaneously through pirated editions and magazine serialization. Charles Dickens's works were eagerly awaited and often pirated within a few days of publication. Not only are his Inspector Bucket in *Bleak House* (1852–53) and the unfinished novel, *The Mystery of Edwin Drood* (published 1870 and after in a number of editions) suggestive for later writers, but his many mysterious subplots, descriptions of low life, thief-catchers, criminals, and other sharply etched characters influenced popular writers on both sides of the Atlantic. Dickens's friend Wilkie Collins seemed especially taken with the mystery; detective figures were integral to *A Woman in White* (1860), and especially *The Moonstone* (serialized in America in *Harper's Weekly* in 1868), which many feel is the first, if not the best, full-length detective novel. What Poe's stories lacked that Dickens and Collins added was a community in which the action would take place and ultimately be resolved. Poe's work undoubtedly influenced French writers, but European writers were also translated into English for American readers. These novels included the strain of social criticism introduced in France by Eugène Sue's *Les Mystères de Paris* (1842–43), characterized by gothic overtones, which influence George Lippard's *Monks of Monk Hall* (1844); and Émile Gaboriau's *L'Affaire Lerouge* (first serialized in 1863), *Le Crime d'Orcival* (1867), *Monsieur Lecoq* (1869), and others. Émile Gaboriau, especially, enjoyed a popular audience in English translation; his Inspector Lecoq (perhaps again drawing on Vidocq) used careful investigation and deduction to solve crimes.

However, like the penny dreadful in England and the *feuilleton* in France, the story papers and dime novels in the United States made early claim to adventurous detectives. The form that evolved out of the dime-novel tradition and was transformed in the pulps is the hard-boiled detective story. The figure of the detective emerged slowly and tentatively in the story papers and dime novels until the Old Sleuth first appeared as a serial titled, "Old Sleuth, the Detective; or, The Bay Ridge Mystery" in the *New York Fireside Com-*

panion in 1872. At least eighteen of Gaboriau's translated novels appeared in Munro's *Seaside Library* after 1878. Numerous American and English stories were printed in the story papers and dime novels until by 1883 the *New York Detective Library* and the *Old Cap Collier Library* were both entirely made up of detective stories. In 1885 *Old Sleuth Library* began by reprinting the 1872 "Bay Ridge Mystery." Early paper libraries featured a variety of detectives of various ages, ethnic origins, occupations, and both sexes. Of these, Old King Brady and Nick Carter became enormously popular. Though Old King Brady is now remembered mainly by collectors, over one hundred Nick Carter novels have appeared in modern paperbacks. The *Nick Carter Weekly* began in 1891 and as late as 1933 there were still 400 paper volumes in print. J. Randolph Cox counted 78 serials and 115 short stories in *Street & Smith's New York Weekly*, 282 issues of the *Nick Carter Detective Library*, 819 issues of the *Nick Carter Weekly*, 160 issues of *Nick Carter Stories*, 127 issues of *Detective Story Magazine*, and 40 issues of *Nick Carter Magazine*, as well as scattered stories elsewhere. The detective's exploits were a publisher's project written by various hands and have emerged in radio, film, and television. Nick Carter was a man of breeding, education, and polish who liked an after-dinner cigar and a glass of port, but he was also a cool man of action known for his great strength and courage. In short, he combined the attributes of the urban gentleman detective with the adventure hero.

In 1878 Anna Katharine Green's *The Leavenworth Case* appeared, combining straightforward plot and economic use of character to formulate a tightly constructed novel with three detective figures on the trails of clues. Green eliminates many of the extraneous threads of other formulas, subdues the adventure with mystery, and focuses on several strands of investigation. Her portly police investigator, Ebenezer Gryce, soon became well-known on both sides of the Atlantic. Green's long career would lead to the introduction of amateur detectives Mrs. Butterworth in *That Affair Next Door* (1897) and Violet Strange in *The Golden Slipper* (1915). Melville Davisson Post provided a scheming lawyer who separated justice from the law in *The Strange Schemes of Randolph Mason* (1896), but his Uncle Abner stories softened the skepticism. Other writers experimented with the form, but by 1890 Arthur Conan Doyle's *A Study in Scarlet* (1886), *The Hound of the Baskervilles* (1887), and others led growing numbers of British detective novels to the United States. Tightly constructed parlor mysteries, usually involving the upper class, an amateur or properly civilized policeman, an isolated setting, and an ingenious method of murder, became chiefly an import. By the turn of the century the novel of pure detection and the mystery novel whose central figure was forced into uncertain detection were distinct genres and both were popular. Sherlock Holmes in turn inspired the creation of such American detective figures as Jacques Futrelle's Professor Augustus S.F.X. Van Dusen, *The Thinking Machine* (1907). Futrelle's short story "The Problem of Cell 13" is one of the best of the locked room puzzles. The radical Bohemian subjectivism of the Dupin tradition gradually gave way to merely unusual traits in detectives, as the settings, characters, and action reflected the closure of the form. Appearing successfully in slick magazines and hardcover novels, it made its strongest appeal to the upwardly mobile middle class.

The detective novel is given a twist by Mary Roberts Rinehart, who focused on the victim or murderer, thus turning the story from the investigator back toward mystery and suspense. One of her devices was the "had I but known" formula, in which the story is told in retrospect by a narrator who has survived an ordeal. *The Circular Staircase* (1908) established Rinehart's reputation as a mystery writer, and subsequent novels made her one of America's highest paid authors. Other writers who adopted Rinehart's approach included Mabel Seeley, in such novels as *The Listening House* (1938), and Lenore Glen Offord in her frst novel, *Murder on Russian Hill* (1938). Other novelists after the turn of the century contributed to the genre's growth and enrichment. Carolyn Wells's *The Clue* (1909), the first of her Fleming Stone mysteries, led to a formulaic approach that she outlined in *The Technique of the Mystery Story* (1913). Earl Derr Biggers, best known for his Charlie Chan novels, began his mystery novels with *Seven Keys to Baldpate* (1913); Arthur Reeve created his Craig Kennedy series in both print and motion picture serials; and Jack Boyle wrote only one *Boston Blackie* (1919) novel, but it became the basis of the famous film series.

For several decades after World War I detective fiction flowered as a genre and gained millions of readers. This Golden Age of detective fiction saw considerable experimentation and innovation with characters, situations, plots, and styles. Harry Stephen Keeler's intricate mysteries began to appear with *The Voice of the Seven Sparrows* (1924). The middle-class dream of productive leisure found in many classic detective stories is apparent in the novels of Willard Huntington Wright, who wrote under the pen name of S. S. Van Dine. His detective, Philo Vance, first appeared in *The Benson Murder Case* in 1926, with the detective as a snobbish, scholarly eccentric who carried out investigations informed by psychological interpretations of personality, drawing perhaps on Poe, but also on the popularization of Watson and Freud. The investigations took place in the midst of conspicuous consumption. But if the tale of pure detection is expressed most concisely in the seemingly impossible logical problem, then its most economical form is the locked room mystery. In addition to Futrelle, other American writers explored this most closed form. Beginning with *It Walks by Night* (1930), John Dickson Carr developed a series of fascinating and often bizarre puzzles for readers. In *The Three Coffins* (1935), detective Dr. Gideon Fell presents a thesis on types of locked room situations. As Carter Dickson he is known as the author of *The Department of Queer Complaints* (1940), *The Curse of the Bronze Lamp* (1945), and others.

Fu Manchu, by English writer Sax Rohmer (Arthur Henry Sarsfield

Ward), had been serialized in slick mgazines in the United States since around 1913 and was still popular. Earl Derr Biggers's *The House Without a Key* (1925) began a series of novels that immortalized Charlie Chan, the Honolulu detective who inverted the image of an Oriental criminal mastermind. But while another influential English writer, Agatha Christie, came to dominate British and often American detective fiction in the thirties and forties, the American writers who entertained the largest number of readers for classic detective novels during this period wrote as a single detective-author—Ellery Queen. Created by Frederick Dannay and Manfred B. Lee in *The Roman Hat Mystery* (1929) and appearing in some forty novels, Ellery Queen wrote about his own cases. Dannay and Lee adopted the "fair play" rule for writers, where readers have all the necessary information available to them, and nurtured this tradition. Dannay and Lee consistently topped the best-seller lists in the thirties with such titles as *The Dutch Shoe Mystery* (1931), *The Egyptian Cross Mystery* (1932), *The Adventures of Ellery Queen* (stories, 1934), and *The Spanish Cape Mystery* (1935). Queen has appeared in numerous versions in film, radio, and television, and survives on the title of one of the most successful mystery magazines, *Ellery Queen's Mystery Magazine* (1941-). In 1929 Vincent Starrett's novels made their first appearance with *Murder on "B" Deck*, as did Elisabeth Holding's mystery, *Miasma*; Zenieth Brown's numerous classic novels appeared initially in England. Helen Reilly published her first mystery, *The Thirty-First Bullfinch*, the following year. Phoebe Atwood Taylor wrote *The Cape Cod Mystery* (1931) and others. Stuart Palmer began his Hildlegarde Withers series with *The Penguin Pool Murders* in 1931. Under the byline of George Bagby, Aaron Marc Stein published his first Inspector Schmidt novel, *Murder at the Piano* (1935), to begin a large number of crime novels. After over a dozen novels in England, Leslie Charteris found himself and *The Saint in New York* (1935). In 1938 Dolores Hitchens began, as D. B. Olsen, with *The Clue in the Clay*, Zelda Popkin published *Death Wears a White Gardenia*, Clayton Rawson published his *Death from a Top Hat*, and Anthony Boucher published his first mystery to be followed the next year with his first Fergus O'Breen novel, *The Case of the Crumpled Knave*. Margaret Scherf began her classic detective novels with *The Corpse Grows a Beard* (1940). Ruth Fenisong began a long mystery-writing career with *Murder Needs a Face* (1942). Joel Townsley Rogers supplemented his pulp stories with *Once in a Red Moon* (1923), writing for over twenty years before producing his *The Red Right Hand* (1945), which is considered a minor masterpiece. Harold Masur began his lawyer/detective series with *Bury Me Deep* (1947), and Herbert Brean published *Wilders Walks Away* (1948). Helen Nielsen's first novel was *The Kind Man* (1951), and Jean Potts wrote several novels beginning with *Go, Lovely Rose* (1954).

Many American writers turned to mysteries and suspene novels, varying their approaches from that of Rinehart to novels of quiet terror, to grim hard-boiled naturalism. Mignon Eberhart created a series of characters to center her mysteries and suspense novels around, beginning with *The Patient in Room 18* (1929). Others contributing to the form as it developed include Frances Hart with *Hide in the Dark* (1929) and others; the versatile Craig Rice (Georgiana Ann Randolph) with *Eight Faces at Three* (1930); Helen McCloy with *Dance of Death* (1938) and others has moved, in her words, "further and further away from the classic detective story pattern" in later novels. Cornell Woolrich's exceptional *Black* series of suspense stories began with *The Bride Wore Black* (1940), and as William Irish he wrote *Phantom Lady* (1942) and others. Dorothy Hughes emerged with *So Blue the Marble* (1940), and Marion Randolph (Marie Rodell) began her novels with *Breathe No More* (1940). In 1941 Kenneth Fearing published *Dagger of the Mind*. The following year Vera Caspary published *Laura* (1942), and Martha Albrand began with *No Surrender* (1942). Hilda Lawrence added the dark mystery, *Blood Upon the Snow* in 1944 and several others until her *Death of a Doll* (1947). The superb Margaret Millar began with *The Iron Gates* (1945); Charlotte Armstrong began with *The Unsuspected* (1946); and Patricia McGerr emphasized strong women in *Pick Your Victim* (1946) and *Catch Me If You Can* (1948). Shirley Jackson's *The Road Through the Wall* and Ursula Davis's *Out of the Darkness* appeared in 1948. Evelyn Piper's *The Innocent*, Dorothy Salisbury Davis's *The Judas Cat*, and Lucille Fletcher's *Sorry, Wrong Number* all appeared in 1949. Patricia Highsmith, who Julian Symons calls "the most important crime novelist at present in practice," published her first suspense novel, *Strangers on a Train*, in 1950. Nedra Tyre published *Mouse in Eternity* (1952); Joseph Hayes contributed *The Desperate Hours* (1954); Richard Stern published *The Bright Road to Fear* in 1958. Carolyn Weston wrote *Tormented* (1956); Henry Slesar published *The Gray Flannel Shroud* (1959); Robert Bloch wrote *Psycho* (1959). Gothic and/or occult elements are almost always present at least as part of the background in these novels, but with such writers as John Dickson Carr they often verge on the macabre, which is also true of the work of Stanley Ellin in such stories as "The Specialty of the House" (1954; collected 1965) and several novels.

Near the turn of the century the invention of cheaper wood pulp paper and high-speed presses, changes in the copyright law, the rise of yellow journalism, and more widespread adult literacy had created the technology and audience for pulp magazines. Bound in lurid paper jackets with fast-paced fiction printed on pulp paper, the magazines evolved into the modern digest-sized magazine and paperback book. With titles like *Argosy* (1888), *Popular Magazine* (1903), *All-Story* (1905), the magazines were inexpensive and contained a progressively urbanized, competitive perspective in moving away from the simpler adventures found in the story papers and dime novels. By the late 1910s the pulps had begun to proliferate and specialize in various genres. In 1917 there were some 30 pulps, by 1924 there were about 50, by 1929 over 120 with about 25 detective and mystery pulps. At their peak in the 1930s there may have been some 200 at one time, though life spans were often short. Detectives appearing in pulp magazines were at first extensions of those in dime novels, but soon evolved into fully urbanized figures. Flip dialogue and gritty backgrounds began to appear more authentic as Prohibition made the underworld chic and the Depression forced large numbers of people to experience failed capitalism. For many readers, exposés of city politics and gangster activities, postwar disillusionment, and literary naturalism made straight adventure seem less believable and English country house murders seem more transparently escapist. Pulp detective stories circumvented the social perspective of the classic story to deal with the rawness of American materialism from the perspective of the economic fringes. Authenticity for the detectives seemed to demand a rejection of the social complacency found in the formal story, to require a commitment that went beyond the specific investigation of a case. It is not surprising that writers should grope for a style to express feelings about the predatory quality of society nor that they should be drawn to follow the lead of writers who successfully captured them. The pattern can be seen in the detective fiction of *Black Mask* (1920–51), a magazine initially financed by George Jean Nathan and H. L. Mencken, and then quickly sold for profit. Within a few years the magazine, especially under the editorship of Joseph T. Shaw, had attracted a number of writers who refined and fashioned the violence into a style for the 1920s and 1930s. The stories of Carroll John Daly, who created the detective Race Williams, found in *The Snarl of the Beast* (1927), owed much to the dime novels, but his fiction had a grit that was rare in earlier stories; he is often considered to have written the first hard-boiled detective story. Pulps such as *Dime Detective, Detective Story, Detective Fiction Weekly*, and others picked up stories in the hard-boiled style. During the 1930s and 1940s the tough-guy style was developed in the mainstream by Hemingway, Faulkner, and others. W. R. Burnett began his gangster and hard-boiled suspense novels with *Little Caesar* (1930). Horace McCoy wrote *They Shoot Horses, Don't They?* (1935), *Kiss Tomorrow Goodbye* (1948), and others from the 1930s through the 1950s. James M. Cain's novels—*The Postman Always Rings Twice* (1934), *Serenade* (1937), *Double Indemnity* (1945), and so on—have become touchstones for hard-boiled fiction and film.

Of the 200 or so writers who made their living by selling short stories and novels to the pulps, relatively few saw their work in hardcover editions. But some could sell anything they wrote, and a few reached fame as novelists as well as pulp writers. From 1939, many writers in the pulp tradition would contribute original paperbacks. Of the detective novelists who emerged in the pulps, Dashiell Hammett is probably the most significant. His first story appeared in 1923, with *Red Harvest* (1929) introducing the Continental Op (based on his experiences with the Pinkerton Detective

Agency) to the novel. In *The Maltese Falcon* (1930) the Op becomes the private detective Sam Spade, and in the mystery *The Glass Key* (1931), Hammett explored the larger implications of the hard-boiled crime novel. His *The Thin Man* (1934) led to a number of witty husband and wife detective teams such as Richard and Frances Lockridge's *The Norths Meet Murder* (1940) and Lenore Glen Offord's *Murder on Russian Hill* (1938).

Raymond Chandler also wrote stories for *Black Mask* and other pulps and became the spokesman for the hard-boiled school with "The Simple Art of Murder." Beginning with *The Big Sleep* (1939), perhaps his masterpiece, Chandler's novels capture almost perfectly the balance between the vulnerable suspense narrator in a predatory milieu and the detective who must assert a solution to the crime. Chandler can be seen at his best in *Farewell, My Lovely* (1940), *The Lady in the Lake* (1943), and *The Long Goodbye* (1954). Rex Stout balances features of the classic story with elements of the hard-boiled story by creating a working-class Archie Goodwin to assist his opulent Nero Wolfe. Goodwin is a streetwise, updated, and sophisticated Watson figure with investigative skills of his own. Stout's fiction, beginning with *Fer-de-lance* (1934), represents a masterful balance of entertaining tales and detection. The success of Frances Noyes Hart's *The Bellamy Trial* (1927) had shown how suspense could be drawn out of a trial. Erle Stanley Gardner demonstrated with his first Perry Mason novel, *The Case of the Velvet Claws* (1933), that the hard-boiled world could be softened by moving his lawyer in front of his private detective, Paul Drake, and dramatizing Randolph Mason–type uses of the law. So successful was this approach that together with his other detective fiction Gardner sold more than a hundred million copies.

The pulps nurtured other immensely productive and versatile writers such as Willis Todhunter Ballard, who created Bill Lennox, a troubleshooter for a Hollywood studio in *Say Yes to Murder* (1942) and many other novels under a variety of bylines. Frank Gruber wrote several series of detective novels featuring colorful operators beginning with *The French Key* (1940). Jonathan Latimer's Bill Crane novels begin with *Murder in the Madhouse* (1935); George Harmon Coxe's several detectives and newsmen begin in novel form with *Murder with Pictures* (1935); Geoffrey Homes (Daniel Mainwaring) began his mystery novels with *The Doctor Died at Dusk* (1936), but is probably best known for *Build My Gallows High* (1946); Norbert Davis's enormous output of novels began with *Coffins for Three* (1938), and Hugh Pentecost's (Judson Philips) often reprinted novels began with *Cancelled in Red* (1939). Davis Dresser published in a variety of genres beginning in the early thirties, but is best known as Brett Halliday, author of Mike Shayne's adventures beginning with *Divided on Death* (1939). Starting in 1950 Richard S. Prather wrote over forty original paperbacks usually located in Los Angeles and often featuring Shell Scott; Steve Fisher wrote a variety of hard-boiled fiction such as *I Wake Up Screaming* (1941); Thomas B. Dewey created

Draw the Curtain Close (1947) and others; Frank Kane wrote the Johnny Liddell novels beginning with *About Face* (1947); Fredric Brown, also notable in science fiction, published the Ed and Am Hunter series beginning with *The Fabulous Clipjoint* (1947). John Godey (Martin Freedgood) published *The Blue Hour* (1949); Bart Spicer set his Carney Wilde novels *The Dark Light* (1949) in Pennsylvania. The crime adventure novels of Jim Thompson, dating from the late 1940s—*Nothing More Than Murder* (1949), *The Killer Inside Me* (1952), *The Getaway* (1959)—to the 1960s *Texas By the Tail*, 1965, are currently enjoying a revival. Harry Whittington included detective fiction among his numerous novels, beginning with *Slay Ride for a Lady* (1950); Kendell Foster Crossen writing as M. E. Chaber created the Milo March series beginning with *Hangman's Harvest* (1952). William Campbell Gault published his first thriller with *Don't Cry for Me* (1952) and his Brock Callahan series with *Ring Around Rosa* (1955). Ira Levin published *A Kiss Before Dying* (1953); Michael Avallone, Jr., published *The Tall Dolores* (1953); Robert Lee Martin's Ed Noone began working the Cleveland area in *Sleep My Love* (1953). William March's suspense novel, *The Bad Seed*, appeared in 1954. Stephen Marlowe (Milton Lesser) created Washington, D.C.'s Chester Drum for his paperback, *The Second Longest Night* (1955); Leonard S. Zinberg, writing as Ed Lacy, created several detectives including Toussaint Moore in *Room to Swing* (1957); Howard Browne's *The Taste of Ashes* also appeared in 1957. Dan Marlowe worked New York City in two paperback series beginning with *Doorway to Death* (1959); Talmage Powell created Tampa detective Ed Rivers in *The Killer Is Mine* (1959); and there were many more.

If one of the risks of the classic story is that it becomes too mechanistically concerned with plot, a risk of the hard-boiled story is that the detective becomes an extension of the atmosphere rather than its mediator. Dashiell Hammett's Continental Op in *Red Harvest* feels himself afflicted with the epidemic killing in "Poisonville," and Mickey Spillane's Mike Hammer, in *I, The Jury* (1947) and others, is stricken with the disease. Spillane became identified with the excesses and distortions of McCarthyism, but from 1947 to 1951 his first seven novels were best sellers and have now sold about forty million copies; he has continued to write and perform, and is best known today as a television personality found among professional athletes in beer ads. Many critics saw the formulaic expression of the hard-boiled world as a dead end, much as earlier critics had seen the puzzle story as the end of the classic detective story. Yet writers continue to produce variations on the forms of mystery, suspense, and detective fiction. The influential Ross Macdonald (Kenneth Millar) developed another variation of the detective. His early *Blue City* (1947) is close to the Hammett tradition, but his later novels show a turn to greater subtlety in which his detective, Lew Archer, is conscientiously developed as an extension of the author's moral sensibilities. In *On Crime Writing* (1973) Macdonald includes an essay on the writing of *The Galton Case* (1959), which he saw as a pivotal turn in his work. Chester Himes's detective fiction is again complex and hard-boiled, but while Spillane projects violence as a political image of the other and Macdonald compresses much of his violence into metaphor, beginning with *For Love of Imabelle* (1957) Himes infuses his Harlem police detectives Coffin Ed Johnson and Grave Digger Jones with a picaresque spirit, drawing rough humor out of trying circumstances.

Another form of the crime novel emerged immediately after World War II that would successfully compete with the classic and hard-boiled novels. The police procedural eliminated the amateur detective's independence and the private detective's ambiguous status by focusing on police work. Unlike the traditional gentleman investigator often found in the classic story or the police renegade or information source in the hard-boiled story, the lawmen in the procedural are collectively immersed in everyday police work. Violence in the procedural is externalized and response to it is placed inside the institution, thus retaining the hard-boiled atmosphere while reducing detection to procedure, highlighting the pressure and social interaction among those charged with law enforcement and lending authority to measures taken to contend with the myriad of activities to which police respond. It is a form that excludes both the amateur and private detective, with the details of police interaction serving to heighten the appearance of realism. In *V as In Victim* (1945) Lawrence Treat set a pattern that has been generally followed by subsequent authors, though *Dragnet*, when it appeared first on radio in 1948 and television in 1952, helped create an audience for the procedural (see Dove). Evan Hunter, better known as Ed McBain, author of the 87th Precinct series, exemplifies the big-city procedural, beginning with *Cop Hater, The Mugger,* and *The Pusher* in 1956. Hillary Waugh's *Last Seen Wearing* (1952) may be the best procedural yet written. Other procedural writers include Elizabeth Linington, *Case Pending* (1960, as Dell Shannon); Rex Burns, *The Alvarez Journal* (1975); Thomas Chastain, *High Voltage* (1979); Lillian O'Donnell, *The Phone Calls* (1972); Joseph Wambaugh, *The New Centurions* (1970); Collin Wilcox, *The Lonely Hunter* (1969); and Dorothy Uhnak, *The Bait* (1968).

Each of the variations on mystery fiction appeals to readers in different ways, though they may often share some of the same readers. By the sixties these fairly distinct and established subgenres were expanding further into new territories and blending in new ways. Fresh writers emerged who broadened the genre further, both spatially and through the portrayal of character and situation, and the "antidetective" novel emerged (see Tani). The amateur detective has remained healthy in the hands of Amanda Cross (Carolyn Heilbrun), *In the Last Analysis* (1964), Jane Langton, *The Transcendental Murder* (1964) and subsequent novels, Harry Kemelman beginning with *Friday the Rabbi Slept Late* (1964), and Emma Lathen (Mary Jane Latsis and Martha Henissart) beginning with *Banking on Death* (1961). Charlotte

McLeod published *Mystery of the White Knight* (1964), Phyllis Whitney began her juvenile mysteries with *The Mystery of the Haunted Pool* (1960), and Dorothy Gilman published her first Pollifax with *The Unexpected Mrs. Pollifax* (1966). As Edgar Box, Gore Vidal created several comic mysteries in the 1950s, collected in *Three By Box* (1978). The variations appear endless. Suspense also continued to thrive with Elizabeth Fenwick publishing *The Make-Believe Man* (1962) and Evelyn Berckman's *The Heir of Starvelings* appearing in 1967. Ray Russell's suspense novels, such as *The Case Against Satan* (1962), are more occult than mystery but deserve mention here. Hard-boiled and adventure detectives continued to capture large audiences in both paperback and hardcover formats. Donald Hamilton published several mysteries before launching his highly successful Matt Helm series with *Death of a Citizen* in 1960. Donald E. Westlake published *The Mercenaries* (1960) to begin a rich vein of espionage, suspense, and detective novels including the Parker series as Richard Stark, beginning with *The Hunter* (1962). Marvin Albert set his Tony Rome stories in Miami, with *Miami Mayhem* (1960); Lawrence Block published several novels in 1961, including *Death Pulls a Doublecross*. Robert L. Fish wrote *The Fugitive* (1962). Philip Atlee opened with *The Green Wound* (1963). The late John D. MacDonald wrote two fine science fiction novels in *Wine of the Dreamers* (1951) and *Ballroom of the Skies* (1952) and a host of paperback crime fiction before his Travis McGee series began with *The Deep Blue Goodbye* (1964). John Ball published his first Virgil Tibbs novel with *In the Heat of the Night* (1965). Michael Brett began his Pete McGrath series with *Kill Him Quickly, It's Raining* (1966); George Baxt began a series with *A Queer Kind of Death* (1966); Ross Thomas published *The Cold War Swap* (1966); Michael Collins (Dennis Lynds) published *Act of Fear* (1967) and others; and Floyd Salas published his prison novel, *Tattoo the Wicked Cross* (1967). Thomas Berger plays on the detective genre in *Killing Time* (1967) and *Who Is Teddy Villanova?* (1977). Leo Rosten published *A Most Private Intrigue* (1967). William F. Nolan began his Bart Challis novels with *Death is for Losers* (1968); E. Richard Johnson published his *Silver Street* (1968); Joe Gores began his detective novels with *A Time for Predators* (1968); Edward D. Hoch published *The Shattered Raven* (1969) after creating a host of distinguished short stories. Elmore Leonard, who has been touted as the best hard-boiled crime writer publishing today, began with *The Big Bounce* (1969).

The remarkably fertile 1970s began with the emergence of Ernest Tidyman's *Shaft* series set in Harlem, Lawrence Sanders's *The Anderson Tapes*, and Walter Wager's *Sledgehammer*, all in 1970. The following year Joseph Hansen's Dave Branstetter series began with *Fadeout*, Tony Hillerman introduced his Navajo policeman in *The Blessing Way* on his way to winning the Mystery Writers of America (MWA) Best Novel award for *Dance Hall of the Dead* in 1973, Francis Wynne published *The Hit*, and Ron Goulart took time from speculative fiction to begin his Johnny Easy series with *If*

Dying Was All. Since *Ask the Right Question* (1971), Michael Z. Lewin has produced a number of novels regarding the exploits of his Indianapolis detective, Albert Samson. In addition to his short stories, John Lutz produced *The Truth of the Matter* (1971); Bill Pronzini published *The Stalker* and *The Snatch* (1971); Walter Wager published *Viper Three* (1971); and A.H.V. Carr published his award-winning *Finding Maubee* the same year. Warren Kiefer won the MWA Best Novel award with *The Lingala Code* (1972), Arthur Goldstein began his Max Guttman novels with *A Person Shouldn't Die Like That* (1972), and R. H. Shimer won Best First Novel with *Squaw Point* (1972). Paul Erdman won an MWA Best First Novel for his *The Billion Dollar Sure Thing* (1973); Robert Littell won a Gold Dagger for *The Defection of A. J. Lewinter* (1973); George V. Higgins began his criminal and police novels with *The Friends of Eddie Coyle* (1972); John Ianuzzi published *Sicilian Defense* (1972); William Hallahan published *The Dead of Winter* (1972), then won Best Novel for *Catch Me, Kill Me* in 1977; and Ishmael Reed published *Mumbo Jumbo* (1972) and *The Last Days of Louisiana Red* (1974). Charles Alverson published *Fighting Back* (1973); Max Collins began his Nolan series with *Bait Money* (1973); Robert B. Parker began his Spenser private detective series with *The Godwulf Manuscript* and *God Save the Child* (1973); Roger L. Simon won the John Creasey Memorial Award for his first Moses Wine novel, *The Big Fix* (1973); K. C. Constantine published *The Man Who Liked to Look at Himself* (1973); James Jones created a very heavy detective in *A Touch of Danger* (1973); and Warren Murphy published *Subways are for Killing* (1973). Gregory McDonald won the MWA award for Best First Novel with *Fletch* (1974); Nicholas Meyer published *The Seven-Per-Cent Solution* and *Target Practice* (1974); Arthur Lyons began his Jacob Asch series with *The Dead Are Discreet* (1974); Warwick Downing began his Joe Reddman series with *The Player* (1974); Peter Israel (J. Leon Israel) began his B. F. Cage series with *Hush Money* (1974); Jackson Burke began his Sam Kelly series with *Location Shots* (1974); and Andrew Bergman published *The Big Kiss-Off of 1944* (1974). A. J. Russell published four *Caper* novels in 1975; Katherine MacLean published *Missing Man* (1975), a speculative novel; James D. Lawrence published *The Dream Girl Caper* (1975); Francis Nevins began his Loren Mensing series with *Publish and Perish* (1975); Thomas Gifford published *The Wind Chill Factor* (1975); Gardner Dozois and George Effinger published *Nightmare Blue* (1975), about the last private detective on Earth; James Crumley published *The Wrong Case* (1975); Mary Higgins Clark published *Where Are the Children?* (1975); Rex Burns (Raoul Stephen Sehler) published *The Alvarez Journal* (1975) and carried away the MWA award for the Best First Novel; Richard Brautigan published *Willard and His Bowling Trophies: A Perverse Mystery* (1975); Brian Garfield won the MWA Best Novel award for *Hopscotch* (1975); and Brad Lang published *Crockett On the Loose* (1975). Lee McGraw published *Hatchett* (1976), about ex-cop Madge Hatchett; Arthur Kaplan published *A Killing for Charity*

(1976); James Gunn published *The Magicians* (1976); Kenn Davis published *The Dark Side* (1976) with John Stanley; George Chesbro published *King's Gambit* (1976); Robert B. Parker won the MWA Best Novel award for *Promised Land*; and James Patterson's *The Thomas Berryman Number* was judged Best First Novel (1976). John Gregory Dunn published *True Confessions* (1977); Jules Feiffer published his novel *Ackroyd* (1977); Stuart M. Kaminsky published *Bullet for a Star* (1977); Marcia Muller published her novel *Edwin of the Iron Shoes* (1977); James MacDougall published *Weasel Hunt* (1977); Robert Ross won Best Novel for *A French Finish* (1977); and Mike Jahn won MWA Best Paperback for *The Quark Maneuver* (1977). Ross Spencer published *The Dada Caper* (1978); Timothy Harris worked up *Kyd for Hire* (1978); Fred Zackel published *Cocaine and Blue Eyes* (1978); and William L. De Andrea won Best First Novel for *Killed in the Ratings* (1978). William Hjortsberg published *Falling Angel* (1978) which, like Ishmael Reed's *Mumbo Jumbo*, remixes reason and the occult. David Bear published the speculative novel, *Keeping Time* (1979); Stephen Greenleaf published *Grave Error* (1979); William X. Kienzle published the first of his Father Koesler novels, *The Rosary Murders* (1979); Larry Morse published *The Flesh Eaters* (1979); Arthur Maling won the MWA Best Novel award for *The Rheingold Route* (1979); and Richard North Patterson won Best First Novel for *The Lasko Tangent* (1979).

No single writer or school of writers presently dominates detective fiction, possibly because no investigative style can very accurately reflect the generic innovation and attitudes of the times. Fictional sleuths do not, as even nineteenth-century detractors were fond of pointing out, correspond very closely to their real-life counterparts. Instead they seem to represent a way of reflecting upon the darker metaphors of life and problems in the way to their understanding. That this understanding has become more complex is reflected in the growing number of novels treating crime and criminal conspiracy as part of everyday life, and the blending of crime elements with those of international intrigue. The 1980s continue to be rich in imaginative perspectives on modern society and its forms of strain. Loren D. Estleman, whose best work is *Sugartown* (1984), began his hard-boiled Amos Walker novels with *Motor City Blue* (1980). Richard Hoyt published *Decoys* (1980); Elliott Lewis published *Two Heads Are Better* and *Dirty Linen* (1980); John Weisman published *Evidence* (1980); Kay Nolte Smith won Best First Novel with *The Watcher* (1980); and Bill Granger won Best Paperback with *Public Murders* (1980).

A. J. Quinnell published *Man on Fire* (1980); Adam Kennedy published *Debt of Honor* (1981); Charlaine Harris published *Sweet and Deadly* (1981); Barry Fantoni published *Mike Dime* (1981); Jonathan Valin published *Final Notice* and *The Lime Pit* (1981); Sara Paretsky published her first V. I. Warshawski novel, *Indemnity Only* (1982); Barney Cohen published the speculative novel *The Taking of Satcon Station* (1983); Margaret

Tracy won the MWA Best Paperback award with *Mrs. White* (1983); Orania Papazoglou published *Sweet, Savage Death* (1984), about romance publishing; Robert Reeves published *Doubting Thomas* (1985); and Tom Clancy published *Red Storm Rising* (1986).

REFERENCE WORKS

As in many other areas of popular culture, much of the available reference work has been done by fans, collectors, bibliophiles, and the writers themselves. Much work has recently gone into establishing accurate reference works, and much remains to be done. A very useful brief reference source is Chris Steinbrunner and Otto Penzler's *Encyclopedia of Mystery and Detection*, an illustrated volume important for its concise entries on authors, major works, central characters, and a wealth of other information on media treatments of the genre. *Twentieth-Century Crime and Mystery Writers*, edited by John M. Reilly, covers American and British authors, together with essays on nineteenth-century backgrounds and foreign influences. The revised edition is the single most useful reference work available for the detective and mystery authors covered in the volume. The reference book contains extensive coverage of authors to about 1980, giving several kinds of information about authors and their work. There are brief factual biographies, checklists of books, short stories, articles, and scripts, locations of papers and manuscripts, as well as critical essays of up to 1,000 words on the work of individual authors. *Detectionary: A Biographical Dictionary of Leading Characters in Detective and Mystery Fiction, Including Famous and Little-known Sleuths, Their Helpers, Rogues both Heroic and Sinister, and Some of Their Most Memorable Adventures, as Recounted in Novels, Short Stories, and Films*, edited by Otto Penzler, Chris Steinbrunner, and Marvin Lachman is described by the title. Dilys Winn's two volumes, *Murder Ink: The Mystery Reader's Companion* (and its revision) and *Murderess Ink: The Better Half of the Mystery*, provide a rich miscellany of information about authors, books, and curiosities of mystery fiction. Ordean Hagen's *Who Done It?* includes a subject guide, sections on film adaptations, plays, lists of anthologies and collections, checklists of settings and awards, a character list of some one hundred pages, and a title index. For these inclusions it is still useful, and was formerly the most comprehensive checklist, but was superseded in 1979 by Allen J. Hubin's *The Bibliography of Crime Fiction, 1749–1975: Listing All Mystery, Detective, Suspense, Police, and Gothic Fiction in Book Form Published in the English Language*, which has now been corrected, expanded to 1980 and revised for the 1984 edition, as *Crime Fiction, 1749–1980*, to include some 60,000 titles. Titles are listed under each "author's" title page name, with information given on pseudonyms; indexes are provided for titles, settings, and series, the latter two being especially useful.

H.R.F. Keating's *Murder Must Appetize* provides an author and reviewer's assessment of a wide range of mystery novels, though details are not always dependable. Robert Baker and Michael Nietzel's *Private Eyes* is an excellent source of information on private detective fiction, particularly that found in contemporary paperbacks beyond 1980. I have included the volume in reference for this reason, though the commentary is informed and thoughtful. The selection is based in part on a survey of members of the Private Eyes of America. Albert J. Menedez's *The Subject Is Murder: A Selective Subject Guide to Mystery Fiction* was not available at this writing. Betty Rosenberg's *Genreflecting* contains a chapter on the "thriller," under which she lists mystery, procedural, detective, and suspense subgenres, authors and books. Bill Pronzini and Marcia Muller's *1001 Midnights* contains generous plot synopses by twenty-six contributors for 1,001 novels and collections of suspense, detective, and espionage fiction, with occasional biographical notes on the authors. The volume is arranged alphabetically by author and covers major English, American, and some foreign writers from Poe through 1985, though coverage is strongest for contemporary and recent American authors. A coding system identifies types and gives an indication of the authors' judgments of major works.

Jacques Barzun and Wendell Hertig Taylor's *A Catalogue of Crime* is an annotated bibliography of novels and collections arranged by author, together with an annotated critical bibliography and varied miscellaneous information, primarily on classic fiction. Each author entry is accompanied by a two- or three-line impression of the work, while the bibliography is useful for unusual items. Melvyn P. Barnes's *Best Detective Fiction* is a lively annotated bibliography of some 250 authors who have written in "the classic puzzle form" and whose work centers around the "how" or "why" of murder. It is more a series of reader's impressions and plot summaries than a formally annotated bibliography. Another work for the casual reader is Eric Quayle's *The Collector's Book of Detective Fiction*, a beautifully illustrated discussion of first editions of authors and series, including some dime novels. Quayle's notes on American detective fiction are light and sometimes unreliable. Francis Lacassin's *Mythologie du roman policier* is useful for brief backgrounds on Poe, Biggers, Hammett, Chandler, Fredric Brown, Fearing, and Himes, and for the appearances of these authors' works in several media. Betty Rosenberg's *The Letter Killeth: Three Bibliographical Essays for Bibliomaniacs* is admittedly selective, tentative, and incomplete—intended as one side of a conversation, it is about crime novels involving librarians, book collectors, and authors or publishers. Jon L. Breen's *Novel Verdicts: A Guide to Courtroom Fiction* includes plot summaries and bibliographical data for novels focusing on trials. Robert Adey's *Locked Room Murders* is an anthology and annotated guide to novels and stories in this specialized form, and John E. Kramer, Jr., and John E. Kramer III's *College Mystery Novels* provides an annotated bibliography of academic mysteries, with a guide to professorial detectives in series. Related reference volumes include Donald McCormick's *Who's Who in Spy Fiction*, which covers ninety writers of spy fiction, while Myron Smith's *Cloak and Dagger Fiction: An Annotated Guide to Spy Thrillers* provides brief information on a large number of spy and espionage novels in English.

Pioneering work on pseudonyms was done by Lenore S. Gribbin in her *Who's Whodunit*, but the work contains a number of errors. Much more complete is Linda Herman and Beth Stiel's *Corpus Delecti of Mystery Fiction*, which was updated in 1977 to include new information. A more general and less complete work on pseudonyms is Frank Atkinson's *Dictionary of Literary Pseudonyms: A Selection of Popular Modern Writers in English*. Both of these works should be consulted, together with Hubin, Reilly, the Library of Congress *Catalogue*, and other standard sources. Criticism of mystery and detective fiction has grown enormously in the last two decades, and several guides have been published to identify and locate it. In addition to the above, Walter Albert has compiled and annotated *Detective and Mystery Fiction: An International Bibliography of Secondary Sources*, a useful volume based on his work published in the *Armchair Detective*. The volume is distinguished by Albert's attempt to provide international coverage of criticism, and includes a bibliography of bibliographies, a section on historical and critical works, and one on criticism related to individual authors, together with a title and name index. The title is somewhat misleading, since foreign publications, reference works, and authors are sparse, and users of the volume will be inconvenienced by the lack of a subject index to access, say, the 113 pages of articles in the section on history and criticism. There are also a number of misspellings and typos, but this is the best single-volume source available. David Skene-Melvin and Ann Skene-Melvin's *Crime, Detective, Espionage, Mystery, and Thriller Fiction and Film* is a checklist of 1,628 items, with a subject and title index, but it is by no means comprehensive. Jon L. Breen's *What About Murder?: A Guide to Books about Mystery and Detective Fiction* contains commentary on 239 critical items. Current critical bibliography can also be found in the *MLA International Bibliography* (annual), *American Literary Scholarship* (annual), and other standard literary sources.

Short stories in collections are indexed in E. H. Mundell and G. Ray Rausch's *The Detective Short Story*. This volume contains references to 7,500 short stories in 1,400 collections and is divided into sections listing espionage stories, problem and puzzle stories, and detective experiences, and includes detective lists and an author index. Michael L. Cook's *Mystery, Detective, and Espionage Magazines* provides a comprehensive listing of magazines and copyright issues, while his *Monthly Murders: A Checklist and Chronological Listing of Fiction in the Digest-Size Mystery Magazines in the United States and England* provides the most complete listing of fiction in magazines. *Dime Novel Roundup*, begun in 1931, has been the source of much useful information on dime novels, story papers, pulps, and other topics over the years, with specialized supplements on various topics. Michael L. Cook's *"Dime Novel Roundup": Annotated Index 1931–1981* is indispensable for identifying particular articles. Albert Johannsen's *The House of Beadle and Adams and Its Dime and Nickel Novels* remains the model for studies of popular periodical publishing houses, since it provides a comprehensive annotated bibliography and author biographies of contributors. Fiction published by other dime novel houses is less well-documented, but the *Dime Novel Roundup* has provided much information. For Nick Carter checklists, see J. Randolph Cox's essay and his *Roundup* supplements, *New Nick Carter Weekly* and *Nick Carter Library*. Charles Bragin's brief *Bibliography of Dime Novels, 1860–1964* is only suggestive.

Memoirs of actual detectives are often noted in the preceding sources, as are descriptions of real crimes that have provided inspiration for fiction. Thomas M. McDade's *The Annals of Murder* lists books and pamphlets on murders through about 1900. James Sandoe's anthology, *Murder: Plain and Fanciful*, contains a list of some 200 short stories and novels based on actual crimes or criminals.

HISTORY AND CRITICISM

Reviews of detective fiction are widely available in major newspapers, such as the *New York Times*, as well as such journals as the *Wilson Library Bulletin* and *Library Journal*. Retrospective as well as current reviews can be found in the *Armchair Detective* and standard periodical indexes. Steven A. Stilwell's *The "Armchair Detective" Index: Volumes 1–10, 1967–1977* provides comprehensive coverage of the varied contents of the journal. Josephine Bell and others' *Crime In Good Company* contains writers' views of current crime writing in the 1950s, mostly with regard to English fiction. Jacques Barzun's *A Book of Prefaces* contains prefaces to fifty works considered crime classics by the authors. Some of Anthony Boucher's reviews and criticism are collected in *Multiplying Villainies* and his column in the *New York Times* is indexed by Jon L. Breen in *The Girl in the Pictorial Wrapper*. Geoffrey O'Brien's *Hardboiled America* is a lively, informed discussion of the rise of paperback crime fiction, together with appropriate illustrations. Kevin B. Hancer compiled *The Paperback Price Guide*, a useful source of information about mass market paperback lines from 1939 through the 1950s. Further information on paperbacks is available in the *Paperback Quarterly*, and on detective fiction, Billy C. Lee and R. Reginald's *Murder Was Bad*. More general information on paperbacks is available in Ray Walters's column in the *New York Times Book Review*, collected in *Paperback Talk*, Piet Schreuders's *The Book of Paperbacks*, and elsewhere.

The criticism of detective and mystery novels is well represented in several useful collections. In *The Art of the Mystery Story* Howard Haycraft collected some of the best early impressions and critiques of detective fiction. The book's contents are largely oriented to the classic form with one section devoted to rules for writers, including "The Detective Club Oath," and such gems as E. M. Wrong's and Dorothy Sayers's introductions to their collections of stories. David Madden's *Tough Guy Writers of the Thirties* lent academic respectability to writers whose work was associated with the pulps as well as mainstream writers. Madden's introduction places the hard-boiled writer directly in the modern sensibility and examines the genre from a number of perspectives. Essays by Philip Durham, Robert Edenbaum, Irving Malin, Herbert Ruhm, and George Grella are especially useful. Francis N. Nevins's collection of essays, *The Mystery Writer's Art*, is much more in the Haycraft tradition of an eclectic group of contributors with a common interest in detective fiction. The twenty-one essays in the volume are organized into "Appreciations," "Taxonomy," and "Speculation and Critique," and are concerned with both classic and hard-boiled fiction, with emphasis on appreciation and description. The essays contain much useful information on individual writers. John Ball's *The Mystery Story* contains original essays on detective fiction and culture, the mystery as a form of the novel, amateur detectives, the private eye, women and ethnic representation, the police procedural, locked room stories, spy fiction, gothics, detectives in speculative fiction, series characters, criminals, and pseudonyms. *Dimensions of Detective Fiction*, edited by Larry N. Landrum, Pat Browne, and Ray B. Browne, contains twenty-three essays on various aspects of detective fiction. The volume is divided into explorations of the genre, considerations of style, and studies of detective fiction in a larger literary context. Included in the first section are essays associating the genre with myth, history, psychology, society, and literary form; the second section focuses on particular writers; the third part ties the genre to political influence and the detective figure in William Faulkner and Ishmael Reed. Robin W. Winks's *Detective Fiction* contains both often-reprinted and recent essays by W. H. Auden, Sayers, Edmund Wilson, Joseph Wood Krutch, an excerpt from Gavin Lambert (see below), George Grella, John Cawelti, Jacques Barzun, Julian Symons, Erik Routley, Ross Macdonald, Ronald Knox, and George Dove, with the editor's commentary. Glenn W. Most and William W. Stowe's *The Poetics of Murder* is a thoroughly academic collection featuring theoretical applications by Fredric Jameson, Michael Holquist, Frank Kermode, Steven Marcus, Geoffrey H. Hartman, Albert Hutter, David A. Grossvogel (see below), Stephen Knight (see below), D. A. Miller, Dennis Porter (see below), and the editors.

Collections of author criticism include Earl F. Bargainnier's *Ten Women of Mystery*, containing essays on Anna Katharine Green, Mary Roberts Rinehart, Margaret Millar, Emma Lathen, and Amanda Cross; Jane S. Bakerman's *And Then There Were Nine . . . More Women of Mystery* with essays on Dorothy Uhnak, Lillian O'Donnell, Craig Rice, Patricia Highsmith, and

Shirley Jackson; and Bernard Benstock's *Essays on Detective Fiction* with essays on Dashiell Hammett, Raymond Chandler, and Ross Macdonald. Collections of interviews with detective fiction writers are beginning to emerge. John C. Carr's *The Craft of Crime: Conversations with Crime Writers* contains interviews with Ed McBain, Jane Langton, Gregory McDonald, Robert B. Parker, Emma Lathen, and Mark Smith. Diana Cooper-Clarke's *Designs of Darkness* includes interviews with Jean Stubbs, Margaret Millar, Ross Macdonald, Patricia Highsmith, and Amanda Cross. Robin W. Winks's *Colloquium on Crime* includes comments by Rex Burns, K. C. Constantine, Dorothy Salisbury Davis, Donald Hamilton, Joseph Hansen, Tony Hillerman, Robert B. Parker, and Anne Ponder. An unusual but very useful collection of essays is Otto Penzler's *The Great Detectives*, which has authors writing about their creations. Ross Macdonald writes on Lew Archer, George Harmon Coxe on Flash Casey, Robert L. Fish on Captain José Da Silva, Carolyn Keene on Nancy Drew, Ed McBain on the 87th Precinct, Hillary Waugh on Fred Fellows, Donald Hamilton on Matt Helm, Vera Caspary on Mark McPherson, Dell Shannon on Lieutenant Luis Mendoza, Richard Lockridge on Mr. and Mrs. North, Adam Hall on Quiller, George Bagby on Inspector Schmidt, Maxwell Grant on The Shadow, Brett Halliday on Michael Shayne, John Ball on Virgil Tibbs, and Chester Gould on Dick Tracy.

Book-length criticism has become more plentiful and is perhaps best treated more or less chronologically by subject. Little scholarly attention was paid to the mystery and detective novel prior to the turn of the century. Such stories were considered a form of sensational fiction of little consequence and most of the writing done about them was in the form of brief reviews in popular periodicals. Carolyn Wells's study guide, *The Technique of the Mystery Story*, for the Home Correspondence School, translated the general features of the British style into American terms, and thus was one of the first attempts to relate formally the conventions of the mystery to aspiring writers. In 1921 E. M. Wrong collected British detective stories under the title *Crime and Detection*, and in 1926 the volume was published in the United States. In his introduction Wrong traces the roots of the detective story to ancient texts and identifies some of the salient themes of the classic detective story. He admires the action potential of what he calls "the Moriarty theme," the villain who fights back, and he is put off by the avoidance of social retribution; too many stories have the criminal punished by self-imposed or accidental means. Wrong suggests that the rise of an organized police and an attention to external detail were necessary to the emergence of the detective story, an argument that Dorothy Sayers accepts in her introduction to *The Omnibus of Crime*. Sayers also shrewdly notes that the detective story is a substitute for the romance and the adventure story in a shrinking world, and lists numerous subterfuges used by writers to make the relatively closed form work. H. Douglas Thomson's *Masters of Mystery* contains a chapter on American detective fiction featuring Anna Katharine Green, Arthur B. Reeve, Isabel Ostrander, S. S. Van Dine, and Frances Noyes Hart; Thomson finds Hammett "100% American, but little more." In 1936 the Wight House Press published *Murder Manual: A Handbook for Mystery Story Writers*, edited by Harley Franklin Wight.

Writing about the mystery story proliferated during the 1930s and early 1940s during the heyday of the genre, and as Haycraft's remarks on Dashiell Hammett suggest, by 1930 the hard-boiled genre was understood to have staked out new territory. When Raymond Chandler's famous essay, "The Simple Art of Murder," appeared in the *Atlantic Monthly* in 1944, he was not defining a new departure, but simply summarizing the development of the form over the last twenty years. Nevertheless, the time was still the heyday of the classic British detective novel. Haycraft's *Murder for Pleasure*, the first book-length history of the detective story, was published the year *Ellery Queen's Mystery Magazine* appeared. This volume is both an appreciation and a history that traces the development of the form from Poe through the late 1930s, though it is partial to the Golden Age from 1918 to 1930. *Murder for Pleasure* contains a readers' list of best fiction which later writers are fond of revising, a trivia quiz for careful readers, and a list of principal characters. The checklist of criticism is entitled "Friends and Foes." Haycraft's observations on American writers are generally sound and can be profitably read today. Abraham Soloman Burack's collection of essays by authors on writing detective fiction appeared in 1945. Sutherland Scott's *Blood In Their Ink* appeared in the United States in 1953. Scott's view on detective fiction is thoughtful, and though his focus is not on American fiction, his familiarity with it appears to be informed by eclectic reading. Fritz Wöelcken's *Der Literaiesche Mord*, an assessment of English and American crime fiction, also first appeared in 1953. David Brian Davis's *Homicide in American Fiction, 1798–1860* is concerned with the literary canon and ignores detective fiction, but it is useful background reading. Alma Elizabeth Murch's *The Development of the Detective Novel* includes one of the most thorough studies of the literary antecedents of many of the conventions of detective fiction, but it gives little indication of the direction of the fiction after the 1930s, though the Golden Age extends to the 1950s. Three-fourths of this history is devoted to a pre–Conan Doyle study of backgrounds. The author is anxious to maintain an aesthetic distance from her subject and in so doing tends to attribute too much importance to major writers and hardly anything to the great popular traditions flourishing in France, England, and the United States.

A similar problem of taste confuses Mary Noel's *Villains Galore*, which does deal directly with American story papers and dime novels. Though coverage of detective fiction and mysteries is limited, and the work lacks documentation, this is one of the few available studies of American nineteenth-century story-paper literature. Quentin Reynolds's *The Fiction Fac-*

tory fills in some of the background, but remains too general to more than hint at the needs of most investigators. The pulps are somewhat better covered, primarily through the efforts of publishers and writers themselves. Harold Hersey's *Pulpwood Editor*, an early reminiscence of the pulps by an editor and writer, is representative of the style used by most participants to disclaim any deep commitment to the pulps. Hersey thought his audience unimaginative. Frank Gruber's *The Pulp Jungle* is much more valuable for its insights into the economies of writing for the pulps and for Gruber's thoughts on structuring mysteries. Robert Turner's *Some of My Best Friends Are Writers* is another author's view on the pulps, but one that emphasizes the human problems of writing in a disposable medium. It is much easier to see from Turner's observations on writers' agencies that the differences in quality between slick and pulp fiction were not clear and in fact were often whimsical.

In 1966 Julian Symons published the first illustrated history of crime and detective fiction, as well as *Critical Occasions*, essays on fiction, both in England. *The Armchair Detective*, the most robust of the serious fan journals, began, and later grew into a scholarly journal on crime fiction and related subjects. The publication of David Madden's collection of essays, *Tough Guy Writers of the Thirties* (see above) marked a higher level of seriousness toward the pulps than any available earlier. Russel B. Nye's *The Unembarrassed Muse*, published in 1970, provided the first thorough history of the popular arts, and included a chapter on the growth of detective fiction. Tage LaCour and Harald Mogensen's *The Murder Book* is a handsomely illustrated and useful introduction to international crime fiction. Francis Nevins published his critical anthology (see above) in 1971. Erik Routley, in 1972, published *The Puritan Pleasures of the Detective Story* in England, with a highly critical chapter on American detective fiction. Ron Goulart's *Cheap Thrills* provided an informal introduction to the trends and writers in pulp magazines.

A watershed year for detective and mystery criticism was 1973. The Bouchercon published Robert E. Briney and Francis M. Nevins, Jr.'s collection of critical essays, *Multiplying Villainies*; William Vivian Butler published *The Durable Desperadoes*, a history of the gentleman outlaw in popular fiction, primarily in England from the mid–1920s through the 1930s; Ross Macdonald's influential essay, *On Crime Writing*, appeared; and the first American edition of Julian Symons's *Moral Consequences*, a modern discussion, part history and part analysis, appeared as a major attempt to bring the history of detective fiction into the 1970s. As both novelist and reviewer of detective fiction, Symons has a critical appreciation of and broad familiarity with the genre. His observations are usually fresh and perceptive, even of his own fiction. William Ruehlmann's *Saint with a Gun* is an attempt to link the private detective tradition to a broad American longing for vigilante justice. This is a one-dimensional work, but also a provocative investigation of the relationship between fiction and the varied kinds of violence that have marked recent American history. Bobbie Ann Mason's *The Girl Sleuth* is an early feminist critique of Nancy Drew and other mysteries. Margery Fisher's *The Bright Face of Danger* is primarily concerned with adventure novels for children, and contains a chapter on juvenile series detectives. In 1976 John G. Cawelti's *Adventure, Mystery, and Romance* became the most important contribution to understanding the phenomenon of popular American genres to date. Cawelti examines the structure of both classic and hard-boiled fiction and the relationships between the creator and the reader, and relates these to other genres and to the social milieu. Gavin Lambert's *The Dangerous Edge* is interesting for its background information on British fiction and its chapter on Raymond Chandler. Robert Champigny's *What Will Have Happened* considers the detective story formula as a narrative mechanism. Since he deals almost exclusively with classic puzzle writers, he does not see interrelated narrative conventions as significant; compare Champigny's approach with those of Nadya Aisenberg and Stefano Tani. Bruce Merry's *Anatomy of the Spy Thriller* applies a formalist analysis to modern spy fiction and applies several theoretical perspectives to its understanding. Nadya Aisenberg ties the motifs of detective fiction to those found in the literary tradition in *A Common Spring* and argues that this form of story reflects the fears of its audience. In *Mystery and Its Fictions* David A. Grossvogel argues that the popular detective story is only a closed play form of what might be called the premodern metaphysical mystery and postmodern forms, which resulted from writers such as Alain Robbe-Grillet having broken "the seal closing the traditional detective story" and thus opening it and bending it back toward mystery.

Jerry Palmer's *Thrillers* marks a wholly different emphasis, in that he is concerned with the contemporary ideological implications of the texts of thriller (largely spy) fiction. Palmer argues that ideology in the form of the thriller is a "combination of mystery, in the form of criminal conspiracy, and competitive individualism" as these were reflected in British society in the nineteenth century. Stefano Benvenuti and Gianni Rizzoni's *The Whodunit* is a useful introductory history with illustrations; like Tage and LaTour, the authors cover crime fiction on an international scale, and Edward Hoch's concluding essay helps bring the discussion from the 1950s to the 1970s. *Clues* began publication in 1980, and Hugh Eames's *Sleuths, Inc.* appeared with chapters on Hammett and Chandler. David Geherin's *Sons of Sam Spade* discusses Robert B. Parker, Roger L. Simon, and Andrew Bergman; R. F. Stewart's *And Always a Detective* provides useful information on nineteenth-century detective fiction and has occasional remarks on twentieth-century American detective novels. Hanna Charney's *The Detective Novel of Manners* is concerned with that quality of (particularly classic) detective fiction pointed out by George Grella in his ground-breaking essay (see Winks, 1980, or Landrum et al.)—the comedy of manners.

Charney carries the idea into the surface realism of narratives, detective figures, and other areas. Patricia Craig and Mary Cadogan's *The Lady Investigates* discusses English and American sleuths from about 1861 to the present, with chapters on early women sleuths in the United States, women spies in World War I, women sidekicks, girls' series detective novels, career women detectives, detectives' wives, and other topics. This is an area that is given suggestive and highly readable treatment here. Stephen Knight's *Form and Ideology in Crime Fiction* provides chapters on major writers of detective fiction, including Poe, Chandler, and McBain (procedurals) in order to discover fissures revealing the ideological content of detective fiction. Dennis Porter's *The Pursuit of Crime* would agree with Palmer that popular narratives reflect the anxieties of the time, but finds in detective fiction a somewhat more complex matrix of ideological play among various schools and writers. George N. Dove's *The Police Procedural* provides a history and studied discussion of the procedural. Edward Margolies's *Which Way Did He Go?* discusses the detective in the work of Dashiell Hammett, Raymond Chandler, Chester Himes, and Ross Macdonald and finds the future of the detective open-ended. A specific study of the dime novel detective is Gary Hoppenstand's *The Dime Novel Detective*. Bill Pronzini's *Gun in Cheek* is a lively discussion of, in effect, why some call detective fiction a form of subliterature. Bernard Sharratt's *Reading Relations* contains a perceptive chapter on Chandler. Robin W. Winks's *Modus Operandi* covers a broad spectrum of crime and espionage fiction with some shrewd insights, but no particular overview. Stefano Tani's *The Doomed Detective* is an interesting and provocative analysis that emphasizes hard-boiled fiction's break with the classic story. Tani sees this break as leading to postmodern writers' use of detective story conventions for literary purposes. Robert Sampson's two volumes on series characters in the early pulps, *Yesterday's Faces*, discuss Nick Carter, the devices used to create villains and numerous detective adventure heroes, and provide a good account of the emergence of detectives in the early pulps. This is an important contribution to the history of pulp magazine story conventions. David Geherin's *The American Private Eye* traces the career of the private eye through representative writers, including Carroll John Daly, Dashiell Hammett, Raoul Whitfield, Frederick Nebel, George Harman Coxe, John K. Butler, Norbert Davis, Robert Leslie Bellem, Jonathan Latimer, Raymond Chandler, Cleve Adams, Brett Halliday, Howard Browne, Wade Miller, Bart Spicer, Richard S. Prather, Mickey Spillane, Ross Macdonald, Thomas B. Dewey, William Campbell Gault, Michael Collins, Robert B. Parker, Bill Pronzini, Michael Z. Lewin, Joseph Hansen, Arthur Lyons, and Lawrence Block, and he offers reasons for the survival of the genre. Robert E. Skinner's *The Hard-Boiled Explicator* provides reference and other information for study of Dashiell Hammett, Raymond Chandler, and Ross Macdonald. John J. Winkler's *Auctor and Actor* treats Apuleius's *The Golden Ass* as a text that can be accessed as a detective story, "as an unsolved crime that may be unraveled by a somewhat unorthodox procedure in order to learn *quis ille?* ('Whodunit?')." Winkler draws on American and British detective novels for his analogies.

ANTHOLOGIES

Collected editions of detective and mystery fiction are far too numerous to list here. One of the best annual publications is *Best Detective Stories of the Year*. This series has been graced with several excellent editors including the late Anthony Boucher (William Anthony Parker White) and Allen J. Hubin. Since Hubin's editorship the annual has contained a brief bibliographical list of collections, anthologies, criticism, and "best" stories of the year. The volumes also contain a necrology and note awards given by the Mystery Writers of America. Anthologies for the classroom include Nancy Ellen Talburt and Lyna Lee Montgomery's *A Mystery Reader* and Saul Schwartz's *The Detective Story*, for high schools; Dick Allen and David Chacko's *Detective Fiction* is more clearly a college text. C.E.J. Smith's *Down a Dark Street* hard-boiled anthology of American stories for English secondary schools should be compared to those available here.

The nostalgia for the pulps that reached its peak in the early 1970s inspired several collections of pulp fiction. Tony Goodstone compiled *The Pulps*, an illustrated collection of stories, including examples of detective fiction with a very brief introduction. Ron Goulart's *The Hard-Boiled Dicks* and Herbert Ruhm's *The Hard-Boiled Detective* are more in the tradition of Joseph T. Shaw's *The Hardboiled Omnibus* and are more clearly oriented to detective fiction readers. William F. Nolan's *The "Black Mask" Boys: Masters in the Hard-Boiled School of Detective Fiction* includes commentary and stories by Dashiell Hammett, Raymond Chandler, Erle Stanley Gardner, Horace McCoy, Carroll John Daly, Frederick Nebel, Raoul Whitfield, and Paul Cain. The Ellery Queen volumes, such as *Ellery Queen's Crimes and Punishments* and the Alfred Hitchcock series, including *Alfred Hitchcock's Mortal Errors*, are perennials. Also see *Edgar Winners: 33rd Annual Anthology of the Mystery Writers of America* and *Mystery Hall of Fame: An Anthology of Classic Mystery and Suspense Stories*, edited by Bill Pronzini, and *Year's Best Mystery and Suspense Stories, 1985*. Recent thematic anthologies include *All But Impossible!: An Anthology of Locked Room and Impossible Crime Stories by Members of the Mystery Writers of America*, Ray B. Browne and Gary Hoppenstand's *The Defective Detective*, consisting of seven stories from the pulps, and Hoppenstand's *More Tales of the Defective Detective in the Pulps*. Others include J. D. Carr's *Classic Short Stories of Crime and Detection*, which contains stories from 1950 to 1973; *Midnight Specials: An Anthology for Train Buffs and Suspense Aficionados*; *Miniature Mysteries: 100 Malicious Little Mystery Stories*; *The Penguin Classic Crime Omnibus*; *A Special Kind of Crime*; *The 13 Crimes of Science Fiction*; *Women's Wiles: An Anthology of Mystery Stories by* the *Mystery Writers of America*; and Michele Slung's *Crime On Her Mind: Fifteen Stories of Female Sleuths from the Victorian Era to the Forties*. Paul E. Dow's *Criminology in Literature* is an anthology of stories grouped to illustrate accepted kinds of explanations of crime. Interest in early forms of the mystery and detective story have sparked a number of volumes that include American authors, such as Hugh Greene's series, with such volumes as *The American Rivals of Sherlock Holmes*.

RESEARCH COLLECTIONS

Manuscripts and papers of many mystery and detective novelists are available for research, and a number of libraries are building collections for the study of the genre. Listings in Lee Ash's *Subject Collections* (6th ed., 1985) and the *National Union Catalog of Manuscript Collections* suggest that several libraries have strong holdings in the manuscripts of detective writers, but these are often not cataloged or the catalogs are not easily available. The Special Collections Department of the University of Pittsburgh libraries list 400 cataloged manuscripts, Boston University's Division of Special Collections in the Mugar Memorial Library holds some 15,000 uncataloged manuscripts (for which a list is available) representing over one hundred authors, and the University of Oregon lists the manuscripts of a number of writers. Among those represented in the Boston University collection are Martha Albrand, Charlotte Armstrong, Michael Avallone, Jr., John Ball, William Ballinger, George Baxt, Evelyn Berckman, Leslie Charteris, Richard Condon, Kendell Foster Crossen, Ursula Curtiss, Jay Williams, Thomas B. Dewey, Doris Miles Disney, Mignon Eberhart, Stanley Ellin, Elizabeth Fenwick, Robert L. Fish, Deloris Stanton Forbes, Dorothy Gilman, Gordon and Mildred Gordon, Joseph Harrington, Evan Hunter, E. Richard Johnson, Frank Kane, Leonard S. Zinberg, Elizabeth Linington, Helen McCloy, Gregory McDonald, William P. McGivern, Arthur Maling, Helen Nielsen, Lillian O'Donnell, Dolores Hitchens, Barbara Mertz, Merrian Modell, Bill Pronzini, Kelley Roos, Richard Martin Stern, Phoebe Atwood Taylor, Dorothy Uhnak, Jack Vance, Donald E. Westlake, Phyllis Whitney, Collin Wilcox, and others.

The University of Oregon Library holds manuscripts and/or papers for Willis Todhunter Ballard, Francis Wynne, Frederick Nebel, Lenore Glen Offord, Margaret Scherf, Frank Ramsay Adams, Charles Alexander, Robert Wallace Grange, Mary Garden Collins, Thomas Albert Curry, John Hawkins, Jay Kalez, Jazquin L. Lait, and Louis Preston Trimble. The University of Oregon Library also holds the records of Renown Publications for 1955–72, which published the *Girl from U.N.C.L.E. Magazine* and the *Mike Shayne Mystery Magazine*. The University of California at Los Angeles holds manuscripts of Robert Leslie Bellem, Raymond Chandler, and others. Robert Bloch's manuscripts are at the University of Wyoming, as are those of

Lawrence G. Blochman, Ray Russell, and others. George Harmon Coxe's manuscripts are held by the Beinecke Rare Book and Manuscript Library, Yale University. Dorothy Salisbury Davis's manuscripts are at Brooklyn College Library, Amber Dean's manuscripts are at the University of Rochester Library, while those of August Derleth are at the State Historical Society of Wisconsin Library. The University of Pennsylvania Library holds Howard Fast's manuscripts; St. John's College, Annapolis, holds Leslie Ford's; Indiana University holds the manuscripts of Joseph Hayes and Don Pendleton. The Humanities Research Center, University of Texas, holds the vast Ellery Queen collection, and the University of Pittsburgh owns the Mary Roberts Rinehart materials. Aaron Marc Stein's manuscripts are at the Firestone Library, Princeton University, as are Willard Huntington Wright's. Richard O'Connor's papers are at the University of Maine. Most of John D. MacDonald's papers are located at the University of Florida, although the University of Colorado boasts over a thousand volumes, including audio cassettes of his work. Rex Stout's library and personal papers are at Boston College; those of Mary Roberts Rinehart are located at the University of Pittsburgh. Erle Stanley Gardner's, Dashiell Hammett's, and Ellery Queen's are at the University of Texas.

Listings for other writers can be found in John M. Reilly's edition of *Twentieth-Century Crime and Mystery Writers* and in standard reference works. Individual libraries also contain variant editions of authors' works and many contain specialized collections of popular writers. The Ira Wolff Collection at the University of California, San Diego, contains some 2,500 Erle Stanley Gardner novels in many languages, as well as a large collection of Chandler and Hammett. A collection of some 1,000 volumes of Chandler's works can be found at the Kent State University libraries at Kent, Ohio. Los Angeles's Occidental College contains the Guyman Collection of first editions of mystery and detective fiction. The Queen Collection at the University of Texas, the Sandoe Collection at Brigham Young University, the Jacques Barzun and Wendell Hertig Taylor Collection of first editions at the University of North Carolina at Chapel Hill, the Popular Culture Collection at Bowling Green State University, and others are notable. Most libraries will hold many more volumes than is at first apparent, because the volumes may not be adequately identified in subject catalogs or separated into defined collections. The Russel B. Nye Collection at Michigan State University holds some 3,500 detective and mystery novels and runs of some 28 pulp titles, and the University of Wisconsin reports some 4,000 titles, mostly of British Golden Age novels. Collections of detective fiction can be found in all public libraries, and more specialized collections can often be found in university libraries, especially those that have received gifts of large private collections.

The media for the development of much popular mystery and detective fiction—the dime novels and story papers of the nineteenth century and the pulps and paperbacks of the twentieth century—have not until recently been sought by research libraries. Now numerous libraries have attempted to collect such materials and excellent collections are available in several locations in the United States. Ash remarks that the Johannsen Collection of 1,100 volumes at Northern Illinois University's Swen Franklin Parson Library is "probably the most extensive collection [of dime novels] there is." The Library of Congress's 20,000 issues of uncataloged dime novels in the 270 series must rank as one of the most comprehensive collections, though it remains nearly unusable. Other major repositories of dime novels can be found in the Popular Library Department of the Cleveland Public Library (1,300 issues), the Huntington Library (over 2,000), Yale University Libraries, the George H. Hess Collection of 4,000 dimes novels and other books at the University of Minnesota libraries, the New York Public Libraries' collection, and Oberlin College Library's 2,200 issues of eighty-nine series.

Because pulp magazines date only from about 1895 and were printed on high acid-content paper and because they were considered subliterature, collections of them are less accessible than dime-novel collections. Many pulps are in such delicate condition that libraries should refuse to copy them with any process that generates heat; certainly care should be taken in handling the now brittle and yellowed paper where access is permitted. The University of California at Los Angeles reports 12,500 issues in 400 titles, Harvard University libraries house an extensive collection, and numerous other libraries have samples or partial collections. The Swen Franklin Parson Library at Northern Illinois University, for example, houses the Western Pulp Magazine Collection of 600 magazine titles, and the David Mullins Library at the University of Arkansas contains the Gerald J. McIntosh Dime Novel Collection. The San Francisco Academy of Comic Art claims the largest collection of pulp magazines available, together with some 12,500 hardcover detective and mystery novels.

BIBLIOGRAPHY

Books

Adams, Donald K., ed. *The Mystery and Detection Annual.* Beverly Hills: Donald Adams, 1972, 1973.

Aisenberg, Nadya. *A Common Spring: Crime Novel and Classic.* Bowling Green, Ohio: Bowling Green State University Popular Press, 1979.

Albert, Walter, ed. *Detective and Mystery Fiction: An International Bibliography of Secondary Sources.* Madison, Ind.: Brownstone Books, 1985.

Atkinson, Frank. *Dictionary of Literary Pseudonyms: A Selection of Popular Modern Writers in English.* Hamden, Conn.: Shoe String Press, 1986.

Baker, Robert, and Michael Nietzel. *Private Eyes: One Hundred and One Knights.* Bowling Green, Ohio: Bowling Green State University Popular Press, 1985.

Bakerman, Jane S., ed. *And Then There Were Nine More . . . Women of Mystery*. Bowling Green, Ohio: Bowling Green State University Popular Press, 1985.

Ball, John, ed. *The Mystery Story*. San Diego: University of California/Publisher's Inc., 1976.

Bargainnier, Earl F. *Ten Women of Mystery*. Bowling Green, Ohio: Bowling Green State University Popular Press, 1981.

Barnes, Melvyn P. *Best Detective Fiction: A Guide from Godwin to the Present*. London: C. Bingley; Hamden, Conn.: Linnet Books, 1975.

Barzun, Jacques. *A Book of Prefaces to Fifty Classics of Crime Fiction, 1900–1950*. New York: Garland, 1976.

Barzun, Jacques, and Wendell Hertig Taylor. *A Catalogue of Crime*. New York: Harper and Row, 1971.

Bell, Josephine, et al. *Crime in Good Company: Essays on Criminals and Crime-Writing*. London: Constable, 1959.

Bendel, Stephanie Kay. *Making Crime Pay: a Practical Guide to Mystery Writing*. Englewood Cliffs, N.J.: Prentice-Hall, 1983.

Benstock, Bernard, ed. *Essays on Detective Fiction*. New York: St. Martin's Press, 1984.

Benvenuti, Stefano, and Gianni Rizzoni. *The Whodunit: An Informal History of Detective Fiction*. Translated by Anthony Eyre. New York: Macmillan, 1980.

Bilker, Harvey L. *Writing Mysteries That Sell*. Chicago: Contemporary Books, 1982.

Boucher, Anthony. *Multiplying Villainies: Selected Mystery Criticism 1942–1968*. Edited by Robert E. Briney and Francis E. Nevins, Jr. Boston: Bouchercon, 1973.

Bourgeau, Art. *The Mystery Lover's Companion*. New York: Crown, 1986.

Bragin, Charles. *Bibliography of Dime Novels, 1860–1964*. Rev. ed. Brooklyn: Dime Novel Club, 1964.

Breen, Jon L. *The Girl in the Pictorial Wrapper: An Index to Reviews of Paperback Original Novels in the "New York Times" "Criminals at Large" Column, 1953–1970*. Carson, Calif.: 1972. 46 leaves.

———. *Novel Verdicts: A Guide to Courtroom Fiction*. Metuchen, N.J.: Scarecrow Press, 1984.

———. *What about Murder?: A Guide to Books about Mystery and Detective Fiction*. Metuchen, N.J.: Scarecrow Press, 1981.

Briney, Robert E., and Francis M. Nevins, Jr., eds. *Multiplying Villainies: Selected Mystery Criticism 1942–1968, by Anthony Boucher*. Boston: Bouchercon, 1973.

Browne, Ray B., and Marshall B. Fishwick. *The Hero in Transition*. Bowling Green, Ohio: Bowling Green State University Press, 1983.

Burack, Abraham Soloman, ed. *Writing Detective and Mystery Fiction*. Boston: The Writer, 1945.

Butler, William Vivian. *The Durable Desperadoes*. London: Macmillan, 1973.

Caillois, Roger. *The Mystery Novel*. Translated by Roberto Yahni and A. W. Sadler. Bronxville, N.Y.: Laughing Buddha Press, 1984.

Carr, John C. *The Craft of Crime: Conversations with Crime Writers*. Boston: Houghton Mifflin, 1983.

Cawelti, John G. *Adventure, Mystery, and Romance*. Chicago: University of Chicago Press, 1976.

Champigny, Robert. *What Will Have Happened: A Philosophical and Technical Essay on Mystery Stories*. Bloomington: Indiana University Press, 1977.

Chandler, F. W. "The Literature of Crime Detection." In *The Literature of Roguery*. Boston: Houghton Mifflin, 1907.

Chandler, Raymond. *The Simple Art of Murder*. Boston: Houghton Mifflin, 1950.

Charney, Hanna. *The Detective Novel of Manners: Hedonism, Morality and the Life of Reason*. Rutherford, N.J.: Fairleigh Dickinson University Press, 1981.

Chemistry and Crime: From Sherlock Holmes to Today's Courtroom. Washington, D.C.: American Chemical Society, 1983.

Cook, Michael L. *"Dime Novel Roundup": Annotated Index 1931–1981*. Bowling Green, Ohio: Bowling Green State University Press, 1983.

———. *Monthly Murders: A Checklist and Chronological Listing of Fiction in the Digest-Size Mystery Magazines in the United States and England*. Westport, Conn.: Greenwood Press, 1982.

———. *Murder by Mail: Inside the Mystery Book Clubs*. Bowling Green, Ohio: Bowling Green State University Popular Press, 1979; update, 1983.

———. *Mystery, Detective, and Espionage Magazines*. Westport, Conn.: Greenwood Press, 1983.

———. *Mystery Fanfare: A Composite Annotated Index to Mystery and Related Fanzines, 1963–1981*. Bowling Green, Ohio: Bowling Green State University Popular Press, 1983.

Cooper-Clark, Diana. *Designs of Darkness: Interviews with Detective Novelists*. Bowling Green, Ohio: Bowling Green State University Popular Press, 1983.

Cox, J. Randolph. "Chapters from the Chronicles of Nick Carter." *Dime Novel Roundup, May 1974, 50–55; June 1974, 62–67.*

———. *New Nick Carter Weekly, Bibliographic Listing. Dime Novel Roundup Supplement*, December 1975.

———. *Nick Carter Library, Bibliographic Listing. Dime Novel Roundup Supplement*, December 1975.

Craig, Patricia, and Mary Cadogan. *The Lady Investigates: Women Detectives and Spies in Fiction*. New York: St. Martin's Press, 1981.

Davis, David Brian. *Homicide in American Fiction, 1798–1860*. Ithaca, N.Y.: Cornell University Press, 1957.

de Vries, Peter H. *Poe and After: The Detective Story Investigated*. Amsterdam: Bakker, 1956.

Donaldson, Betty, and Norman Donaldson. *How Did They Die?* New York: St. Martin's Press, 1979.

Dove, George N. *The Police Procedural*. Bowling Green, Ohio: Bowling Green State University Popular Press, 1982.

Dow, Paul E. *Criminology in Literature*. New York. Longman, 1980.

Eames, Hugh. *Sleuths, Inc.: Studies of Problem Solvers: Doyle, Simenon, Hammett, Ambler, Chandler*. Philadelphia: J. B. Lippincott, 1980.

East, Andy. *The Cold War File*. Metuchen, N.J.: Scarecrow Press, 1983.

Fisher, Margery, *The Bright Face of Danger*. Boston: Horn Book, 1986.

Freeman, Lucy. *The Murder Mystique: Crime Writers on Their Art*. New York: Ungar, 1982.

Geherin, David. *The American Private Eye: The Image in Fiction*. New York: Ungar, 1985.

————. *Sons of Sam Spade: The Private-Eye Novel in the 70s: Robert B. Parker, Roger L. Simon, Andrew Bergman*. New York: Ungar, 1980.

Goulart, Ron. *Cheap Thrills: An Informal History of the Pulp Magazines*. New Rochelle, N.Y.: Arlington House, 1972.

Gribbin, Lenore S. *Who's Whodunit: A List of 3,218 Detective Story Writers and their 1,100 Pseudonyms*. Chapel Hill: University of North Carolina Library, 1968.

Grossvogel, David A. *Mystery and Its Fictions: From Oedipus to Agatha Christie*. Baltimore: Johns Hopkins University Press, 1979.

Gruber, Frank. *The Pulp Jungle*. Los Angeles: Sherbourne Press, 1967.

Hagen, Ordean. *Who Done It?: A Guide to Detective, Mystery and Suspense Fiction*. New York: R. R. Bowker, 1969.

Hancer, Kevin B. *The Paperback Price Guide*. New York: Harmony Books/Crown, 1980.

Haycraft, Howard. *Murder for Pleasure: The Life and Times of the Detective Story*. New York: Appleton-Century, 1941.

————, ed. *The Art of the Mystery Story: A Collection of Critical Essays*. New York: Simon and Schuster, 1946.

Herman, Linda, and Beth Stiel. *Corpus Delecti of Mystery Fiction: A Guide to the Body of the Case*. Metuchen, N.J.: Scarecrow Press, 1974; New York: R. R. Bowker, 1977.

Hersey, Harold. *Pulpwood Editor*. New York: Frederick A. Stokes, 1937.

Hoppenstand, Gary, ed. *The Dime Novel Detective*. Bowling Green, Ohio: Bowling Green State University Popular Press, 1982.

Hubin, Allen J. *Crime Fiction, 1749–1980: A Comprehensive Bibliography*. New York: Garland, 1984.

Johannsen, Albert. *The House of Beadle and Adams and Its Dime and Nickel Novels*. 3 vols. Norman: University of Oklahoma Press, 1950, 1962.

Johnson, Timothy W., and Julila Johnson. *Crime Fiction Criticism: An Annotated Bibliography*. New York: Garland, 1981.

Kalikoff, Beth. *Murder and Moral Decay in Victorian Popular Literature*. Ann Arbor, Mich.: UMI Research Press, 1986.

Keating, H.R.F. *Murder Must Appetize*. New York: Mysterious Press; London: Lemon Tree Press, 1981.

Knight, Stephen. *Form and Ideology in Crime Fiction*. Bloomington: Indiana University Press, 1981.

Kramer, John E., Jr., with John E. Kramer III. *College Mystery Novels: An Annotated Bibliography Including a Guide to Professorial Series-Character Sleuths*. New York: Garland, 1985.

Lacassin, Francis. *Mythologie du roman policier*. Paris: Union générale d'éditions, 1974.

LaCour, Tage, and Harald Mogensen. *The Murder Book: An Illustrated History of the Detective Story*. London: Allen and Unwin, 1971.

Lambert, Gavin. *The Dangerous Edge: An Inquiry into the Lives of Nine Masters of Suspense*. New York: Grossman/Viking, 1976.

Landrum, Larry N., Pat Browne, and Ray B. Browne, eds. *Dimensions of Detective Fiction*. Bowling Green, Ohio: Bowling Green State University Popular Press, 1976.

Lee, Billy C., and R. Reginald. *Murder Was Bad: Essays on Mystery and Detective Publishing from Paperback Quarterly*. San Bernardino, Calif.: Borgo Press, 1986.

Lovisi, Gary. *Science Fiction Detective Tales: A Brief Overview of Futuristic Detective Fiction In Paperback*. Brooklyn, N.Y.: Gryphon Books, 1986.

McCormick, Donald. *Who's Who in Spy Fiction*. London: Elm Tree/Hamish Hamilton, 1977.

McDade, Thomas M. *The Annals of Murder: A Bibliography of Books and Pamphlets on American Murders from Colonial Times to 1900*. Norman: University of Oklahoma Press, 1961.

Macdonald, Ross. *On Crime Writing*. Santa Barbara, Calif.: Capra Press, 1973.

Madden, David, ed. *Tough Guy Writers of the Thirties*. Carbondale: Southern Illinois University Press, 1968.

Margolies, Edward. *Which Way Did He Go? The Private Eye In Dashiell Hammett, Raymond Chandler, Chester Himes, and Ross Macdonald*. New York: Holmes and Meier, 1982.

Mason, Bobbie Ann. *The Girl Sleuth: A Feminist Guide*. Old Westbury, N.Y.: Feminist Press, 1975.

Matthews, Catlin, and John Matthews. *The Western Way: A Practical Guide to the Western Mystery Tradition*. London: Methuen, 1985.

Menedez, Albert J. *The Subject Is Murder: A Selective Subject Guide to Mystery Fiction*. New York: Garland, 1986.

Merry, Bruce. *Anatomy of the Spy Thriller*. Montreal: McGill-Queen's University Press, 1977.

Most, Glenn W., and William W. Stowe, eds. *The Poetics of Murder: Detective Fiction and Literary Theory*. New York: Harcourt Brace Jovanovich, 1983.

Mundell, E. H., and G. Ray Rausch, comps. *The Detective Short Story: A Bibliography and Index*. Manhattan: Kansas State University Library, 1974.

Murch, Alma Elizabeth. *The Development of the Detective Novel*. Port Washington, N.Y.: Kennikat Press, 1968.

Mystery Writers of America. *Mystery Writer's Handbook*. Cincinnati, Ohio: Writer's Digest Books, 1982.

Nevins, Francis N., Jr., ed. *The Mystery Writer's Art*. Bowling Green, Ohio: Bowling Green State University Popular Press, 1971.

Noel, Mary. *Villains Galore: The Heyday of the Popular Story Weekly*. New York: Macmillan, 1954.

Norville, B. *Writing the Modern Mystery*. Cincinnati, Ohio: Writer's Digest Books, 1986.

Nye, Russel B. *The Unembarrassed Muse: The Popular Arts in America*. New York: Dial Press, 1970.

O'Brien, Geoffrey. *Hardboiled America: The Lurid Years of Paperbacks*. New York: Van Nostrand Reinhold, 1981.

Palmer, Jerry. *Thrillers*. New York: St. Martin's Press, 1979.

Penzler, Otto, ed. *The Great Detectives*. Boston: Little, Brown, 1978.

Penzler, Otto, Chris Steinbrunner, and Marvin Lachman, eds. *Detectionary: A Biographical Dictionary of Leading Characters in Detective and Mystery Fiction, Including Famous and Little-known Sleuths, Their Helpers, Rogues Both Heroic and Sinister, and Some of their Most Memorable Adventures, as Recounted in Novels, Short Stories, and Films*. Woodstock, N.Y.: Overlook Press, 1977.

Pierce, Hazel Beasley. *A Literary Symbiosis: Science Fiction/Fantasy Mystery*. Westport, Conn.: Greenwood Press, 1983.

Porter, Dennis. *The Pursuit of Crime: Art and Ideology in Detective Fiction*. New Haven, Conn.: Yale University Press, 1981.

Powers, Richard Gid. *G-Men: Hoover's FBI in American Popular Culture*. Carbondale: Southern Illinois University Press, 1983.

Pronzini, Bill. *Gun in Cheek: A Study of "Alternative" Crime Fiction*. New York: Coward, McCann & Geoghegan, 1982.

Pronzini, Bill, and Marcia Muller. *1001 Midnights: The Aficionado's Guide to Mystery and Detective Fiction*. New York: Arbor House, 1986.

Quayle, Eric. *The Collector's Book of Detective Fiction*. London: Studio Vista, 1972.

Reilly, John M., ed. *Twentieth-Century Crime and Mystery Writers*. New York: St. Martin's Press, 1980; rev. ed., 1985.

Reynolds, Quentin. *The Fiction Factory: From Pulp Row to Quality Street*. New York: Random House, 1955.

Rosenberg, Betty. *Genreflecting: A Guide to Reading Interests in Genre Fiction*. Littleton, Colo.: Libraries Unlimited, 1982.

————. *The Letter Killeth: Three Bibliographical Essays For Bibliomaniacs*. Los Angeles: Kenneth Karmiole, 1982.

Routley, Erik. *The Puritan Pleasures of the Detective Story: A Personal Monograph*. London: Gollancz, 1972.

Ruehlmann, William. *Saint with a Gun: The Unlawful American Private Eye*. Washington, D.C.: American University Press, 1974.

Sampson, Robert. *Yesterday's Faces: A Study of Series Characters in the Early Pulp Magazines*. 2 vols. Bowling Green, Ohio: Bowling Green State University Popular Press, 1983–84.

Schreuders, Piet. *The Book of Paperbacks: A Visual History of the Paperback*. Translated by Josh Pachter. London: Virgin, 1981.

Scott, Sutherland. *Blood In Their Ink: The March of the Modern Mystery Novel*. New York: R. West, 1980 [1953].

Sharratt, Bernard. *Reading Relations: Structures of Literary Production: A Dialectical Text/Book*. Atlantic Highlands, N.J.: Humanities Press, 1982.

Skene-Melvin, David, and Ann Skene-Melvin. *Crime, Detective, Espionage, Mystery, and Thriller Fiction and Film: A Comprehensive Bibliography of Critical Writing Through 1979*. Westport, Conn.: Greenwood Press, 1980.

Skinner, Robert E. *The Hard-Boiled Explicator: A Guide to the Study of Dashiell Hammett, Raymond Chandler and Ross Macdonald*. Hamden, Conn.: Scarecrow Press, 1985.

Smith, Myron. *Cloak and Dagger Fiction: An Annotated Guide to Spy Thrillers*. Santa Barbara, Calif.: ABC-Clio, 1982.

Steinbrunner, Chris, and Otto Penzler. *Encyclopedia of Mystery and Detection*. New York: McGraw-Hill, 1976.

Stevenson, W. B. *Detective Fiction*. Cambridge: National Book League, 1958.

Stewart, R. F. *And Always a Detective: Chapters on the History of Detective Fiction*. North Pomfret, Vt.: David & Charles, 1980.

Stilwell, Steven A. *The "Armchair Detective" Index: Volumes 1–10, 1967–1977*. New York: Armchair Detective, 1979.

Symons, Julian. *Bloody Murder: From the Detective Story to the Crime Novel, A History*. New York: Harper and Row, 1985.

——. *Crime and Detection: An Illustrated History from 1840.* London: Studio Vista, 1966.

——. *Critical Occasions.* London: Hamish Hamilton, 1966.

——. *The Great Detectives: Seven Original Investigations.* London: Orbis, 1981.

——. *The Modern Crime Story.* Edinburgh: Tragara Press, 1980.

——. *Mortal Consequences: A History from the Detective Story to the Crime Novel.* New York: Schocken Books, 1973.

Tani, Stefano. *The Doomed Detective: The Contribution of the Detective Novel to Postmodern American and Italian Fiction.* Carbondale: Southern Illinois University Press, 1984.

Thomson, H. Douglas. *Masters of Mystery: A Study of the Detective Story.* London: Collins, 1931.

Turner, Robert. *Some of My Best Friends Are Writers, But I Wouldn't Want My Daughter to Marry One.* Los Angeles: Sherbourne Press, 1970.

Walters, Ray. *Paperback Talk.* Chicago: Academy Chicago Publishers, 1985.

Wells, Carolyn. *The Technique of the Mystery Story.* Springfield, Mass.: Home Correspondence School, 1913; rev. ed., 1929.

Wight, Harley Franklin, ed. *Murder Manual: A Handbook for Mystery Story Writers,* pt. I and Appendix by Irene E. Young. San Diego: Wight House Press, 1936.

Winkler, John J. *Auctor and Actor: A Narratological Reading of Apuleius's "Golden Ass."* Berkeley: University of California Press, 1985.

Winks, Robin W. *Modus Operandi: An Excursion into Detective Fiction.* Boston: D. R. Godine, 1982.

——, ed. *Colloquium on Crime: Eleven Renowned Mystery Writers Discuss Their Work.* New York: Scribner's, 1986.

——. *Detective Fiction: A Collection of Critical Essays.* Englewood Cliffs, N.J.: Prentice-Hall, 1980.

Winn, Dilys. *Murderess Ink: The Better Half of the Mystery.* New York: Workman, 1979.

——. *Murder Ink: Revived, Revised, Still Unrepentant.* New York: Workman, 1977; rev. ed., 1984.

Wöelcken, Fritz. *Der Literarische Mord.* Edited by E. F. Bleiler. New York: Garland, 1979.

Writing Suspense and Mystery Fiction. Boston: The Writer, 1977.

Anthologies

Adey, Robert. *Locked Room Murders.* London: Ferrett Fantasy, 1979.

Alfred Hitchcock's Borrowers of the Night. New York: Dial Press, 1983.

Alfred Hitchcock's Grave Suspicions. New York: Dial Press, 1984.

Alfred Hitchcock's Mortal Errors. New York: Dial Press, Davis Publications, 1983.

All But Impossible!: An Anthology of Locked Room and Impossible Crime Stories by Members of the Mystery Writers of America. London: R. Hale, 1981, 1983.

Allen, Dick, and David Chacko, eds. *Detective Fiction: Crime and Compromise.* New York: Harcourt Brace Jovanovich, 1974.

Asimov, Isaac. *Banquets of the Black Widowers.* Garden City, N.Y.: Doubleday, 1984.

——. *Casebook of the Black Widowers.* Garden City, N.Y.: Published for the Crime Club by Doubleday, 1980.

Asimov, Isaac, and Martin H. Greenberg, eds. *Miniature Mysteries: One Hundred Malicious Little Mystery Stories*. New York: Taplinger, 1981.

Best Detective Stories of the Year. New York: E.P. Dutton, 1945-. Annual.

Bleiler, Everett F., ed. *A Treasury of Victorian Detective Stories*. New York: Scribner's, 1979, 1982.

Breen, Jon L. *Hair of the Sleuthhound: Parodies of Mystery Fiction*. Metuchen, N.J.: Scarecrow Press, 1982.

Browne, Ray B., and Gary Hoppenstand, eds. *The Defective Detective in the Pulps*. Bowling Green, Ohio: Bowling Green State University Popular Press, 1983.

Carr, J. D., et al. *Classic Short Stories of Crime and Detection*. New York: Garland, 1983.

Cassiday, Bruce, ed. *Roots of Detection: The Art of Deduction Before Sherlock Holmes*. New York: Ungar, 1983.

Crime Wave: World's Winning Crime Stories 1981. London: Collins, 1981.

Crime Writers Association of Great Britain. *Four and Twenty Bloodhounds*. New York: Carroll and Graf, Crime Writers Association of Great Britain, anthologies edited by members, 1953-.

Dow, Paul E. *Criminology in Literature*. New York: Longman, 1980.

Gilbert, Elliot L., ed. *The World of Mystery Fiction*. San Diego: University of California Extension, University of California, San Diego; Del Mar, Calif.: Publisher's Inc., 1978.

Gilbert, Michael, ed. *Crime in Good Company: Essays on Criminals and Crime-Writing*. London: Constable, 1959.

Goodstone, Tony, ed. *The Pulps: Fifty Years of American Pop Culture*. New York: Bonanza Books, 1971.

Goulart, Ron, ed. *The Hard-Boiled Dicks: An Anthology and Study of Pulp Detective Fiction*. Los Angeles: Sherbourne Press, 1965, 1967.

Greene, Graham, and Hugh Greene, eds. *The Spy's Bedside Book*. London: Hart Davis, 1957.

Greene, Hugh, ed. *The American Rivals of Sherlock Holmes*. New York: Penguin, 1978.

———. *Cosmopolitan Crimes: Foreign Rivals of Sherlock Holmes*. New York: Pantheon, 1972.

———. *The Further Rivals of Sherlock Holmes*. New York: Pantheon, 1973.

———. *The Rivals of Sherlock Holmes: Early Detective Stories*. New York: Pantheon, 1970.

Haining, Peter, ed. *The Fantastic Pulps*. London: Gollancz; New York: St. Martin's Press, 1975.

Hoch, Edward D. *Leopold's Way: Detective Stories by Edward D. Hoch*. Edited by Francis M. Nevins, Jr., and Martin H. Greenberg. Carbondale: Southern Illinois University Press, 1985.

Hoppenstand, Gary, Garyn G. Roberts, and Ray B. Browne, intros. *More Tales of the Defective Detective in the Pulps*. Bowling Green, Ohio: Bowling Green State University Popular Press, 1985.

John Creasey's Crime Collection. 9th ed. New York: St. Martin's Press, 1985.

Larmoth, Jeanine. *Murder on the Menu*. New York: Scribner's, 1972.

McCullough, David W., ed. *Great Detectives: A Century of the Best Mysteries from England and America*. New York: Pantheon, 1984.

Meadley, Robert, ed. *Classics of Murder*. New York: Ungar, 1986.

Midnight Specials: An Anthology for Train Buffs and Suspense Aficionados. Indianapolis: Bobbs-Merrill, 1977.

Montgomery, Lyna Lee, and Nancy Ellen Talburt. *A Mystery Reader*. New York: Scribner's, 1975.

Muller, Marcia, and Bill Pronzini. *Chapter and Hearse: Suspense Stories about the World of Books*. New York: Morrow, 1985.

———. *The Web She Weaves: An Anthology of Mystery and Suspense Stories by Women*. New York: Morrow, 1983.

The Murder Mystique: Crime Writers On Their Art. New York: Ungar, 1982.

Nieminski, John. *EQMM 350: An Author/Title Index to "Ellery Queen's Mystery Magazine," Fall 1941 through January 1973*. White Bear Lake, Minn.: Armchair Detective Press, 1974.

Nolan, William F. *The "Black Mask" Boys: Masters in the Hard-Boiled School of Detective Fiction*. New York: Morrow, 1985.

The Penguin Classic Crime Omnibus. New York: Penguin, 1984.

Private Eye Writers of America. *The Eyes Have It*. Edited by Robert J. Randisi. New York: Mysterious Press, 1984.

Pronzini, Bill, ed. *The Arbor House Treasury of Detective and Mystery Stories from the Great Pulps*. New York: Arbor House, 1983.

———. *The Edgar Winners: 33rd Annual Anthology of the Mystery Writers of America*. New York: Random House, 1980.

———. *Great Modern Police Stories*. New York: Walker, 1986.

Pronzini, Bill, and Martin H. Greenberg, eds. *The Ethnic Detectives*. New York: Dodd, 1985.

Pronzini, Bill, and Barry N. Malzberg, eds. *The Arbor House Treasury of Mystery and Suspense*. New York: Arbor House, 1982.

Pronzini, Bill, et al., eds. *The Mystery Hall of Fame: An Anthology of Classic Mystery and Suspense Stories, Selected By the Mystery Writers of America*. New York: Morrow, 1984.

———. *Mystery In the Mainstream: An Anthology of Literary Crimes*. New York: Morrow, 1986.

Queen, Ellery. *Queen's Quorum: A History of the Detective-Crime Short Story as Revealed by the 106 Most Important Books Published in the Field since 1845*. Boston: Little, Brown, 1951; rev. ed., New York: Biblo and Tannen, 1969.

———, ed. *Challenge to the Reader: An Anthology*. New York: Frederick A. Stokes, 1936.

———. *Ellery Queen's Book of First Appearances*. New York: Dial Press, Davis Publications, 1982.

———. *Ellery Queen's Crimes and Punishments*. New York: Dial Press, 1984.

———. *Ellery Queen's Maze of Mysteries*. New York: Dial Press, 1982.

———. *Ellery Queen's Prime Crimes*. New York: Dial Press, Davis Publications, 1983.

———. *The Female of the Species: The Great Women Detectives and Criminals*. Boston: Little, Brown, 1943.

———. *The Great Sports Detective Stories: Sporting Blood*. Garden City, N.Y.: Blue Ribbon Books, 1946.

Reader's Digest Editors. *Great Short Tales of Mystery and Terror.* Pleasantville, N.Y.: Reader's Digest Association, 1982.

——. *Great Stories of Mystery and Suspense.* 2 vols. New York: Reader's Digest Association, 1981, 1986.

Richardson, Maurice, ed. *Novels of Mystery from the Victorian Age.* London: Pilot Press, 1945.

Rosenberg, Betty. *The Letter Killeth: Three Bibliographical Essays for Bibliomaniacs.* Los Angeles: Kenneth Karmiole, 1982.

Ruhm, Herbert, ed. *The Hard-Boiled Detective: Stories from "Black Mask" Magazine, 1920–1951.* New York: Random House, 1977.

Russell, Alan K., ed. *Rivals of Sherlock Holmes: Forty Stories of Crime and Detection from Original Illustrated Magazines.* Secaucus, N.J.: Castle Books, 1978.

——. *Rivals of Sherlock Holmes, Two: Forty-Six Stories of Crime and Detection from Original Illustrated Magazines.* Secaucus, N.J.: Castle Books, 1979.

Sandoe, James, ed. *Murder: Plain and Fanciful, with Some Milder Malefactions.* New York: Sheridan House, 1948.

Sayers, Dorothy, ed. *The Omnibus of Crime.* New York: Payson and Clarke, 1929.

Schwartz, Saul, ed. *The Detective Story: An Introduction to the Whodunit.* Skokie, Ill.: National Textbook Company, 1975.

Shaw, Joseph T., ed. *The Hardboiled Omnibus: Early Stories from "Black Mask."* New York: Simon and Schuster, 1946.

Slung, Michele, ed. *Crime on Her Mind: Fifteen Stories of Female Sleuths from the Victorian Era to the Forties.* New York: Pantheon, 1975.

Smith, C.E.J., ed. *Down a Dark Street.* London: Edward Arnold, 1973.

A Special Kind of Crime. Garden City, N.Y.: Published for the Crime Club by Doubleday, 1982.

Symons, Julian, ed. *Classic Crimes Omnibus.* New York: Penguin, 1986.

Talburt, Nancy Ellen, and Lyna Lee Motgomery. *A Mystery Reader: Stories of Detection, Adventure and Horror.* New York: Scribner's, 1975.

The 13 Crimes of Science Fiction. Garden City, N.Y.: Doubleday, 1979.

Top Crime: The Author's Choice. London: J. M. Dent, 1983.

Traylor, James T., ed. *Hollywood Troubleshooter: W. T. Ballard's Bill Lennox Stories.* Bowling Green, Ohio: Bowling Green State University Popular Press, 1984.

A Treasury of Victorian Detective Stories. New York: Scribner's, 1979.

Van Thal, Herbert, ed. *The Mamouth Book of Great Detective Stories.* Topsfield, Mass.: Salem House/Merrimack Publishers Circle, 1985.

Verdict of Thirteen: A Detection Club Anthology. New York: Harper and Row, 1978.

Vickers, Roy. *The Department of Dead Ends: 14 Detective Stories.* New York: Dover, 1978.

Wagenknecht, Edward, ed. *Murder by Gaslight: Victorian Tales.* Englewood Cliffs, N.J.: Prentice-Hall, 1949.

Women's Wiles: An Anthology of Mystery Stories by the Mystery Writers of America. New York: Harcourt Brace Jovanovich, 1979.

Wooley, John, ed. *Robert Leslie Bellem's Dan Turner Hollywood Detective.* Bowling Green, Ohio: Bowling Green State University Popular Press, 1983.

Wright, Willard Huntington, ed. *The Great Detective Stories: A Chronological Anthology.* New York: Scribner's, 1927.

Wrong, E. M., ed. *Crime and Detection*. New York: Oxford University Press, 1926.
The Year's Best Mystery and Suspense Stories, 1985. New York: Walker, annual.

Periodicals

Armchair Detective. New York, 1967-. The journal is being reprinted: Madison, Ind.: Brownstone Books, 1981-.
Clues: A Journal of Detection. Bowling Green, Ohio, 1980-.
Dime Novel Round-up. Fall River, Mass., 1931–32, 1933-.
Ellery Queen's Mystery Magazine. New York, 1941-.
New Black Mask. New York, 1985-.
Paperback Quarterly. Brownsville, Tex., 1978-.

6.

Fantasy

ROGER C. SCHLOBIN

Beginning in the late 1970s, fantasy literature has finally come to be recognized for the seminal place it has in literature and the arts, the imagination, and the creative process. In one of the few early comments about fantasy in literary scholarship, E. M. Forster identified it as "something that cuts across them [aspects of the novel] like a bar of light, that is intimately connected with them at one place and patiently illumines all the problems, and at another place shoots over or through them as if they did not exist."

Forster might have just as easily agreed with George MacDonald, who identified fantasy as the "richest source of human creativity," for it dwells at the heart of all human endeavor, be it highly creative or lowly everyday. It may not be real in any measurable sense, but it is among the most potent of thought processes.

In a few ways, it is clear why fantasy has always been powerful and popular but has not drawn its share of intellectual and scholarly attention. Simply, it is so basic that it is taken for granted. Also, the development of West European culture has frequently been inhospitable to the make-believe that so often is associated with fantasy. Certainly, religion, one of the richest indications of the human faculty to create what is not empirically real, has long been antithetical to any other fanciful constructs. Moreover, in the modern period, the pursuit of the pragmatic and the scientific has not encouraged "escapist excursions" into worlds that cannot be.

For a time, fantasy had some small, token attention. Occasionally, the Science Fiction Research Association (established in 1970) would allow the parent fantasy to visit with its younger child. The Modern Language Association and its regional associations, the Popular Culture Association, the American Studies Association, and the National Council of Teachers of English do regularly have a few panels. However, it was not until 1980 that fantasy had its own conference: the International Conference for the Fantastic in the Arts. This conference was further enhanced in 1983 and 1984 with the formation of the International Association for the Fantastic in the Arts, which assumed control over the conference. Finally, fantasy had its own home, and its varied forms and approaches have dramatically flourished in this interdisciplinary and intercultural environment (see the four volumes of *Proceedings* below, edited by Robert A. Collins and Howard D. Pearce, William Coyle, and Jan Hokenson and Howard D. Pearce). Each year the conference is bigger and its presentations more wide ranging and imposing.

In addition, a number of nonacademic groups and conferences focus on fantasy. The World Fantasy Conference has gathered together fantasy fans from throughout the world and, despite its continued inability to distinguish between fantasy and horror, has been honoring writers and holding meetings since 1975. The British Fantasy Society has been doing much the same thing on a smaller scale since 1972, and *Locus*, the "newspaper of science fiction," began polling the year's best fantasy novel in 1977. Even the World Science Fiction Conference began recognizing "Grand Masters of Fantasy" with the Gandalf Award in 1974 and added a second Gandalf for best fantasy novel in 1978 (Franson and deVore; and R. Reginald, *Science Fiction & Fantasy Awards*).

The future of fantasy's popular tradition and the International Association for the Fantastic in the Arts holds great promise. The fantasy field now has its own scholarly journal, the *Journal of the Fantastic in the Arts*. The *Fantasy Review* surveys much of the activity in the field, and there have been two special fantasy issues of more generally oriented scholarly journals (see Bibliography: Special Magazine Issues below) with a third from *Extrapolation* in spring of 1987. At this juncture, all looks generative, and no one can guess just how extensive it all may become.

HISTORIC OUTLINE

Fantasy does not yield to historical perspective. It is so elemental, so timeless, and so pervasive that its enormity overpowers thought. Even the smaller realm of American fantasy is a difficult task. Brian Attebery examines the years from Washington Irving (1819) to Ursula K. Le Guin

(1972) in his insightful survey *The Fantasy Tradition in American Literature*, but even his efforts hardly make a dent. In fact, to date there are only two book-length studies of the British tradition: Stephen Prickett's *Victorian Fantasy* and Tobin Siebers's *The Romantic Fantastic*. Most scholars avoid the historical approach and opt for the theoretical, aesthetic, or thematic. This is because fantasy is international. It pays no attention to boundaries, nationalities, or genres. It is simply everywhere. In just the American tradition alone, for example, William Burroughs's *Naked Lunch* (1959) has been considered "pornographic" and banned. Fantasy made its contribution to World War II in Theodore Pratt's *Mr. Limpet* (1942) and came back from war in Gore Vidal's *Kalki* (1978). Don Marquis's *Archy and Mehitabel* (1927) delightfully wandered into the American office and the animal kingdom, and the Second Coming arrived on a construction site in Charles Sailor's *The Second Son* (1979). Fantasy combined with utopia in Austin Tappan Wright's *Islandia* (1942) and presented confounding mysteries in John Dickson Carr's *The Burning Court* (1937), Fritz Leiber's collegiate *Conjure Wife* (1952), and Dean R. Koontz's spoof *The Haunted Earth* (1973). Gordon R. Dickson combined the epic and romance traditions (sword and sorcery) with the burlesque in *The Dragon and the George* (1976). Many fantasies draw upon folktales and mythologies from all nationalities; for example, Patricia Wrightson travels as far as Australia for the Aborigine mythology of *The Ice Is Coming* (1977), *The Dark Bright Water* (1978), and *Journey Behind the Wind* (1981), and Charles G. Finney combined numerous traditions in *The Circus of Dr. Lao* (1935). Lest anyone think fantasy untopical, the 1960s free life-styles found expression in Peter S. Beagle's urban "Lila the Werewolf" (1971) and Richard Brautigan's *Trout Fishing in America* (1967), and the absurd was greeted in Philip Roth's *The Breast* (1972; with due respect to Kafka and Woody Allen). In short, American writers have had home and the world upon which to draw, and they have.

The early stirrings of American fantasy literature have yet to be explored at length. Thomas Hooker's *The Soul's Preparation* (1632), Anne Bradstreet's *The Tenth Muse* (1650), Increase Mather's *Remarkable Providences* (1684), Cotton Mather's *Wonders of the Invisible World* (1693), Benjamin Franklin's *Poor Richard's Almanac* (1732), and Thomas Paine's *Common Sense* (1776) have remained safe from the "fantastic perspective" for the time being. However, scrutiny will one day reveal both the bright and dark fantasies of the Puritans, the Revolutionaries, and the Founding Fathers. They are there! Certainly, the early settlers brought their own folk traditions, fairy tales, literary traditions, and magics with them from the Old World. Yet as much as Thanksgiving, Manifest Destiny and the American West, and baseball distinguish the American character, its fantasy is largely indistinguishable from the rest of the world's in most senses, except for locale and age. This is undoubtedly due to America's polyglot nature and the fact that even its repressed minorities maintained the fantasy privilege. One example of this is the essentially similar treatment of the "most beautiful girl in the world" theme that is common to the widely separated (in time and place) excursions of America's *The Princess Bride* (1973), by William Goldman, and Britain's *Zuleika Dobson* (1911), by Max Beerbohm.

However, there is much agreement that modern fantasy arises in America much as it did in England. It comes primarily from the Romantic tradition (just as horror arises from the gothic and science fiction from the empirical). However, while the first "modern" fantasy in Britain, Sara Coleridge's *Phastasmion* (which was billed as fairy tale), did not appear until 1837, the roots of the American tradition began earlier with the American Romanticists: Washington Irving's *The Sketch Book of Geoffrey Crayon, Gent.* (1819–20) and *Tales of a Traveller* (1824; the latter with its obvious debt to the Brothers Grimm), Nathaniel Hawthorne's *Twice-Told Tales* (1837), and Edgar Allan Poe's *The Narrative of Arthur Gordon Pym* (1838) and *Tales of the Grotesque and Arabesque* (1840). They were quickly followed by such noteworthy works as Herman Melville's *The Confidence-Man* (1857) and Oliver Wendell Holmes's *Elsie Venner* (1861). As these varied works illustrate, American fantasy had already begun to manifest itself in a multiplicity of ways, and its continuing history includes both well-known authors and lesser-known cult authors.

Yet to say that fantasy was widespread and enormously popular in the American literary tradition prior to the late nineteenth and early twentieth centuries would be a mistake. However, as the century turned, both recognized literature and its disreputable pulp relations forever branded the American character. While Brian Attebery sees Mark Twain's *A Connecticut Yankee in King Arthur's Court* (1889) as a demonstration of "the strong hostility between [pragmatic] American thought and pure fantasy," it and the posthumously published *The Mysterious Stranger* (1916) actually demonstrate the strong antagonism between authority and virtue that is typical of much fantasy. More importantly, they mark the opening of floodgates. L. Frank Baum's Oz books (1900–1920) and their many imitators, Edgar Rice Burroughs's Mars/Barsoom series (1917–64), and James Branch Cabell's twenty-volume *Biography of Manuel* (1919–23) demonstrate an ongoing American fascination that continues to this day.

Curiously, the twentieth century continues a sharp division within fantasy. At one time, fantasy was considered fairy tales and children's fare and was set against "real, adult" literature (and still is in some circles). Beginning in the early 1920s, another chasm appears between "serious" and "pulp" literatures. On one hand are respectable, accepted works: Ben Hecht's *Fantazius Mallare* (1922) and *The Kingdom of Evil* (1924); Thorne Smith's humorous and satiric Topper books (1926, 1932); John Erskine's *Adam and Eve* (1927); Thornton Wilder's *The Skin of Our Teeth* (1942); James Thurber's *The White Deer* (1945), *The 13 Clocks* (1950), and *The Wonderful O* (1957); John Collier's *Fancies and Goodnights* (1951); John Updike's *The Centaur*

(1963); Thomas Tryon's *The Other* (1971); John Barth's *Giles Goat-Boy* (1966) and *Chimera* (1972); Robert Coover's *The Universal Baseball Association, Inc.* (1968); Donald Barthelme's *The Dead Father* (1975); and John Crowley's *Little, Big* (1981), among those mentioned earlier.

On the other hand, buried in those yellowed magazines and paperbacks were works that were making sword-and-sorcery and fantasy household words in places far away from the intellectuals and college faculties. These included Abraham Merritt's *The Ship of Ishtar* (1927), L. Sprague de Camp and Fletcher Pratt's Incomplete Enchanter series (1941–60), Robert E. Howard's *Conan the Conqueror* (1950), Poul Anderson's *The Broken Sword* (1954), H. P. Lovecraft's *The Dream-Quest of Unknown Kadath* (1955), Fritz Leiber's *Two Sought Adventure* (1957), Andre Norton's Witch World series (1963-), and Ray Bradbury's *Something Wicked This Way Comes* (1962). In addition, DAW Books has, since 1975, enjoyed success with an annual series called *The Year's Best Fantasy Stories*. However, it's clear that even this "subliterary" tradition is finding respectability. These works and many like them have found their ways into college classrooms, and Stephen R. Donaldson's Chronicles of Thomas Covenant the Unbeliever (1977–83), Terry Brooks's *The Sword of Shannara* (1977), and Piers Anthony's pun-ridden Xanith books (1977-) have appeared with prominence in the *New York Times* best-seller list (without even mentioning the successes of Stephen King's horror fiction).

Much seems to be coming together for fantasy as it lives in the American consciousness. Its long and varied tradition is finding a far greater home than many may have imagined, but which others have foreseen.

REFERENCE WORKS

The "beginning place" for any serious exploration of any subject is where the basic tools can be found. Up until 1972, fantasy scholars had to be content with the scattered and unsystematic listing in the Prose Fiction sections of the annual bibliographies of *Publications of the Modern Language Association*. However, in 1972, when Thomas D. Clareson (the longtime editor of the journal *Extrapolation*) published *Science Fiction Criticism: An Annotated Checklist*, he inspired the beginning of science fiction's and fantasy's ongoing secondary bibliography, "The Year's Scholarship in Science Fiction, Fantasy, and Horror Literature." Conceived in 1975 by Roger C. Schlobin and Marshall B. Tymn and continued by Tymn and a team of scholars since Schlobin's retirement from the project with the 1980 annual (published in 1983), this seminal tool has appeared in a variety of forms: within the pages of *Extrapolation*, as separate monographs from Kent State University Press, and in two book-length cumulations from Kent State University Press. Originally just devoted to fantasy and science fiction scholarship and with an emphasis on literature, it has expanded over the years to include the horror genre and media (i.e., film). It is well divided into categories and is indexed and annotated. Since 1984, however, the annotations have become occasional (due to its increasing size), making it somewhat less valuable.

The highly energetic researcher will supplement "The Year's Scholarship" with Hal W. Hall's *Science Fiction Index: Criticism: An Index to English Language Books* and *Articles about Science Fiction and Fantasy* and *Science Fiction and Fantasy Research Index*. Both list various publications (i.e., amateur magazines, book reviews, etc.) that are not included in "The Year's Scholarship."

The early years of primary book lists, checklists, and bibliographies were distinguished by the highly enthusiastic efforts of selfless and frequently ignored pioneers. Bradford Day's *The Checklist of Fantastic Literature in Paperback Books* and *The Supplemental Checklist of Fantastic Literature*, E. F. Bleiler's *The Checklist of Fantastic Literature: a Bibliography of Fantasy, Weird and Science Fiction Books Published in the English Language* (revised by Bleiler as *The Checklist of Science-Fiction & Supernatural Fiction*), R. Reginald's *Stella Nova: The Contemporary Science Fiction Authors*, and Donald H. Tuck's *The Encyclopedia of Science Fiction and Fantasy through 1968* gave valuable direction and resources to fields that were frequently ignored by traditional scholars. Their contributions insured that fantasy research survived its early dark ages.

However, early primary bibliography suffered from an indiscriminate approach that often tossed fantasy literature into too large a pile, and these early efforts mirror the early difficulty with definition. Much of this was cleared up with the publication of Roger C. Schlobin's *The Literature of Fantasy: A Comprehensive, Annotated Bibliography of Modern Fantasy Fiction*. To date, it is the recognized, seminal listing of fantasy fiction from 1837 to 1979. Its 1,249 annotated and indexed entries reflect the efforts of 800 authors and 100 editors and include 721 novels, 244 collections, 100 anthologies, and 3,610 short stories. It also includes what one review called "the best short introduction to the nature of fantasy in the field."

However, Schlobin's *The Literature of Fantasy* should be supplemented by less comprehensive, if sometimes more fully annotated or more author-exhaustive works. The best of these are Marshall B. Tymn, Kenneth J. Zahorski, and Robert H. Boyer's *Fantasy Literature: A Core Collection and Reference Guide*, which has longer annotations but significantly less coverages, anad two unannotated bibliographies that include more titles: L. W. Currey's *Science Fiction and Fantasy Authors: A Bibliography of First Printings of Their Fiction and Selected Nonfiction* and R. Reginald's *Science Fiction and Fantasy Literature: A Checklist, 1700–1974 with Contemporary Science Fiction Authors II*. Also, while its nonselectivity harks back to the pioneering days of bibliographies of fantastic fiction, E. F. Bleiler's *The Guide to Supernatural Fiction: A Full Description of 1,775 Books from 1750 to 1960, Including Ghost*

Stories, Weird Fiction, Stories of Supernatural Horror, Fantasy, Gothic Novels, Occult Fiction, and Similar Literature with Author, Title, and Motif Indexes is a treasure trove of titles, not mentioned elsewhere, with valuable annotations. Another similarly unusual bibliography, without which any discussion of fantasy bibliograhy would be incomplete (and significantly less entertaining), is George Locke's *A Spectrum of Fantasy: The Bibliography and Biography of a Collection of Fantastic Literature.* This eccentric and enjoyable compilation will be a pleasure for any avid pursuer of the unusual and the arcane. One further primary bibliography that deserves mention is Stuart W. Wells III's *The Science Fiction and Heroic Fantasy Author Index.* Unannotated and outdated, it nonetheless is a handy pocket guide to the very popular sword-and-sorcery fantasy.

Those primarily interested in children's and young adults' fantasy should consult Ruth Nadelman Lynn's *Fantasy for Children: An Annotated Checklist and Reference Guide.* Some may find its categories questionable and its annotations too brief, but its coverage of this important part of fantasy's literary tradition is extensive (expecially in the much improved second edition).

Researchers will find any of the bibliographies listed above valuable. However, Diana Waggoner's *The Hills of Faraway: A Guide to Fantasy* and Betty Rosenberg's *Genreflecting: A Guide to Reading Interests in Genre Fiction* (which includes a section on fantasy) should be ignored for the flawed and inaccurate compilations they are.

For a variety of reasons, many types of literature that have caught the popular taste, like fantasy, are filled with authors who use pseudonyms. While many of the bibliographies listed here do include these, there are so many that specialized studies are often very helpful. The best and most current of these is Susannah Bates's *The Pendex: An Index to Pen Names and House Names in Fantastic, Thriller, and Series Literature.* Also valuable is Barry McGhan's shorter and less current *Sciencefiction [sic] and Fantasy Pseudonyms.*

Finally, for those very serious fantasy mavens and scholars who would like to do their own, original research, Michael Burgess's *A Guide to Science Fiction and Fantasy in the Library of Congress Classification Scheme* is an invaluable aid.

Among the more valuable tools available are those that seek to survey large blocks of authors or works. These frequently provide extraordinarily helpful introductions (when they are done well). They offer biographical information, critical commentary of varying length and depth, and bibliographic detail. The current leader in this area is E. F. Bleiler's two-volume *Supernatural Fiction Writers: Fantasy and Horror.* Arranged by a combination of nationality and chronology, its essays survey a significant number of authors (from Apuleius to Roger Zelazny with stress on British and American) and are written by scholars of varying distinction. While some have found it interesting for the authors omitted as much as for those included, the essays do provide valuable insights and information.

Of a considerably briefer nature (although with more author coverage) than Bleiler's *Supernatural Fiction Writers*, Mike Ashley's alphabetical *Who's Who in Horror and Fantasy Fiction* contains 400 short bio-bibliographic entries with very brief critical commentary. It is a far more satisfactory attempt than Baird Searles, Beth Meacham, and Michael Franklin's *A Reader's Guide to Fantasy*, which is too inaccurate to be trusted.

RESEARCH COLLECTIONS

Because of fantasy's unrecognized nature among traditional library categories, numerous significant collections remain unknown. For example, I found many titles in Indiana University's Lilly Library when working on *The Literature of Fantasy*, titles unknown to the library staff. Hal W. Hall's *Science/Fiction Collections: Fantasy, Supernatural & Weird Tales* has done much to give details of the recognized collections, such as those in the Spaced Out Library in Montreal and the J. Lloyd Eaton Collection at the University of California at Riverside, among others. Significant collections are also in private hands. The good researcher will check libraries even when nothing is supposed to be there.

HISTORY AND CRITICISM

Fantasy history and criticism have been growing rapidly in the past decade and receiving far more attention than ever before. However, while fantasy theory, in general, and the British branch, in particular, have prospered, American treatments have not. This is not so surprising. Fantasy fiction, because of its international nature, does not lend itself to boundaries, and within a context that stretches from *Gilgamesh* to yesterday, the American portion is small. Also, much of American literature is already placed in traditional categories; for example, it is not unusual to read or hear discussions of Nathaniel Hawthorne and Edgar Allan Poe that do not even allude to the concept of fantasy. The only major book-length study that does focus specifically on American fantasy is Brian Attebery's *The Fantasy Tradition in American Literature from Irving to Le Guin*. Drawing heavily on fantasy's popular folk origin, fairy tales, and legends and on the American development of its own fairyland, Attebery ranges intelligently among such seemingly dissimilar authors as Edgar Allan Poe, Nathaniel Hawthorne, Herman Melville, L. Frank Baum, Ray Bradbury, James Thurber, and H. P. Lovecraft. His landmark study has offered challenges to American literature scholars that are still largely unmet. For example, the aforementioned early American literature is untouched. Of related interest for the contemporary era is Ann Swinfen's *In Defence of Fantasy: A Study of the Genre in English and American Literature since 1945.*

In general, the nature of fantasy still has not surrendered to a definitive study by a single author. It is unlikely that it ever will; it is too expansive and seminal to yield to a single point of view. However, two collaborate efforts have made valiant and significant tries at the entire genre. The well-received *The Aesthetics of Fantasy Literature and Art,* edited by Roger C. Schlobin, attempts to survey fantasy in both literature and art with a series of essays by the major scholars in the field. Its discussions of such varied aspects as the fantasy reader response, lost-race fantasy, fantasy book illustration, high fantasy, children's fantasy, utopian fantasy, and fantasy's relationships with earlier traditions attempt to provide a primer to the genre.

The five-volume *Survey of Modern Fantasy Literature,* edited by Frank N. Magill, takes a different approach, and its strong critical essays are arranged by titles (with author and title indexes). While it suffers from an annoying inability to distinguish between fantasy and horror (see Roger C. Schlobin's "Fantasy Versus Horror," Magill, V, 2259–66), its 500 entries, especially the general ones in volume 5, are a vast compendium of useful and easy to use information that covers authors from a variety of nationalities as well as extensively treating American and British ones.

However, the potentially most valuable source is the continuing proceedings of the International Conference for the Fantastic in the Arts (see Collins and Pearce; Coyle; and Hokenson and Pearce). Published under varying titles and with varying editors by Greenwood Press, these volumes reflect the vast scope and vitality of the International Association for the Fantastic in the Arts, the sponsoring organization. In fact, the interdisciplinary and cross-cultural contents of these volumes, both present and forthcoming, defy any attempt at classification and will long be rich sources for understanding fantasy and the fantastic in all media. A similar effort, although reflecting only a single event, is the far less expansive *Bridges to Fantasy,* edited by George E. Slusser, Eric S. Rabkin, and Robert Scholes, which is the proceedings of the one J. Lloyd Eaton Conference that focused, in part, on fantasy.

Among those scholars who have not been daunted by the challenges fantasy presents to the single mind, four are most respected (for a valuable overview of fantasy theory, see Gary K. Wolfe's "Contemporary Theories of Fantasy," Magill, V, 2220–34). W. R. Irwin's *The Game of the Impossible: A Rhetoric of Fantasy* is formidable in its literary and philosophical approach. It draws heavily on Victorian and modern literary thought to comment significantly on the intellectual nature of fantasy, especially as it relates to the conspiratorial bond that fantasy demands during the reader's engagement with the authors and their fictions. Colin N. Manlove's *The Impulse of Fantasy Literature* and *Modern Fantasy: Five Studies* contain some of the most clearly conceived and sensitive reactions to modern fantasy. Many of the guidelines he establishes have become almost givens among fantasy scholars and are especially valuable for the insight they provide into the Romantic and gothic modes of thought and the nineteenth- and twentieth-century British fantasists (Charles Kingsley, George MacDonald, C. S. Lewis, J.R.R. Tolkien, and Mervyn Peake). Eric S. Rabkin's *The Fantastic in Literature* has been among the most popular of the major examinations of modern fantasy, perhaps because it is among the most readable. His approach is sociological and ranges widely among such topics as fairy tales, optical illusions, mysteries, Henry James, and wish fulfillment. While the nature of the reversal of reality that Rabkin discusses has come under attack in recent years, *The Fantastic in Literature* is still considered by some to be one of the touchstones. Tzvetan Todorov's *The Fantastic: A Structural Approach to a Literary Genre* is among those works that serious students of fantasy return to again and again to discuss. Its often complicated approach to the rhetorical tactics of fantasy and the response to it (which Todorov calls "hesitation") appear to many to identify too general a technique, one which does not identify fantasy specifically enough. Still, it would be hard to measure the pervasive influence Todorov's work has had on modern critical thought.

In *Fantasists on Fantasy: A Collection of Critical Reflections by Eighteen Masters of the Art*, editors Robert H. Boyer and Kenneth J. Zahorski (both important scholars in their own right) take a different approach than any of the aforementioned works. Theye have selected important discussions of the art by the artists themselves. While each of these authors frequently demonstrates that there is a marked difference between doing something and understanding what's being done, it is nonetheless enlightening and revealing to discover what George MacDonald, G. K. Chesterton, H. P. Lovecraft, Sir Herbert Read, James Thurber, J.R.R. Tolkien, August Derleth, C. S. Lewis, Félix Martí-Ibáñez, Peter S. Beagle, Lloyd Alexander, Andre Norton, Jane Langton, Ursula K. Le Guin, Mollie Hunter, Katherine Kurtz, Michael Moorcock, and Susan Cooper think of fantasy literature and what they were trying to do in their own creative moments. It is, for example, intriguing to contrast the authors' views with those of a more intellectual (and perhaps more objective) approach, such as Colin Wilson's *The Strength to Dream: Literature and the Imagination*.

One additional work, which is too often neglected, is Harvey Cox's *The Feast of Fools: A Theological Essay on Festivity and Fantasy*. It very clearly demonstrates the bond between fantasy and the two vital human elements of worship and play and is one of those works that goes directly to the heart of the intricate nature of creativity in its most elemental and primordial forms.

Among the more recent theoretical studies that have not yet reached the recognized status of those above, Kathryn Hume's *Fantasy and Mimesis: Responses to Reality in Western Literature* is the most helpful and insightful.

Deftly building on earlier research and paying valuable attention to the reader-text relationship, Hume places fantasy within its long literary tradition and shows extensive parallels with representations of reality and nonreality within many historical contexts. Christine Brook-Rose's *A Rhetoric of the Unreal: Studies in Narrative and Structure, Especially the Fantastic* works from Todorov's earlier study and extends it further into the areas of structuralism, poststructuralism, formalism, and the nature of literary reality. Rosemary Jackson, another follower of Todorov, seeks in her Freudian and psychoanalytic *Fantasy: The Literature of Subversion* to specifically define fantasy as a distinct historical and didactic form of narrative with strong thematic identifications. T. E. Apter's *Fantasy Literature: An Approach to Reality* also takes a psychoanalytic approach and contends that fantasy, rather than distorting or hiding reality, actually exposes it. It is particularly valuable for its discussions of Joseph Conrad and Nathaniel Hawthorne. All of these studies, like most that seriously explore fantasy, impress one with their range and their disregard for traditional literary classifications.

Among the studies of fantasy, there are those that focus on special topics. For example, Raymond H. Thompson extensively illustrates the ample use of one of the Western world's major legends in combination with fantasy in *The Return from Avalon: A Study of the Arthurian Legend in Modern Fiction*, and Don D. Elgin brings a modern concern to the forefront in *The Comedy of the Fantastic: Ecological Perspectives on the Fantasy Novel*. Hazel Beasley Pierce demonstrates the aforementioned ability of fantasy to shine across the entire spectrum of literary genres in *A Literary Symbiosis: Science Fiction/Fantasy Mystery*.

One specialized area in which fantasy has received extensive attention is children's literature. This is expected; fantasy has always been associated with the reading affections of the young (it's one of the major misapprehensions and prejudices). For example, even though Bruno Bettelheim's *The Uses of Enchantment: The Meaning and Importance of Fairy Tales* was probably intended for a different audience, its Freudian excursions into the internal psychology of children and their most-loved stories are popular among students of fantasy. More specifically related to children's fantasy literature (as is Ruth Nadelman Lynn's bibliography, which was discussed earlier), one of the more intriguing critical discussions is Jane Yolen's *Touch Magic: Fantasy, Faerie and Folklore in the Literature of Childhood*. This series of light essays is, like Bettelheim's study, more directed toward understanding children's reactions. Yet it too addresses issues of fantasy and its literature that are at the bedrock of the development of human culture. This trend of examining the childhood mind and discovering things about fantasy is continued in the conversational *Pipers at the Gates of Dawn: The Wisdom of Children's Literature*, by Jonathan Cott, in its explorations of the creative processes of Dr. Seuss, Maurice Sendak, William Steig, Astrid Lindgren, Chinua Achebe, and P. L. Travers. Considering that fantasy is one of the most elemental of human characteristics, none of the discoveries about fantasy through children's fantasy fiction should amaze. This point is further amplified and stressed by Marion Lochhead's *The Renaissance of Wonder in Children's Literature*, which is a unified discussion of children's literature, George MacDonald and other nineteenth-century writers, C. S. Lewis, J.R.R. Tolkien, and, most significantly, Celtic mythology. However, it would be interesting to know what the reactions of such traditional scholars of children's literature, fantasy, and psychology would be to Jack Zipes's *Breaking the Magic Spell: Radical Theories of Folk & Fairy Tales*. This valuable historical study, after carefully exploring the generative nature of folk and fairy tales, moves into the current day and discusses their modern subversion to materialism and marketing.

One of the more striking contrasts in the consideration of the scholarly efforts to explore fantasy is how much the older, amateur efforts pale in comparison. Once thought to be important critical contributions, little is heard anymore of Lin Carter's *Imaginary Worlds: The Art of Fantasy* (whose Ballantine Adult Fantasy series gave the genre a strong popular boost during the 1970s) or L. Sprague de Camp's *Literary Swordsmen and Sorcerers: The Makers of Heroic Fantasy*. There might be some error in neglecting such works, however, because they frequently do provide historical insights that are unavailable elsewhere.

Individual author studies present a quandary. In many ways, they reflect the popular taste: there are more studies of J.R. R. Tolkien and the Inklings (Charles Williams and C. S. Lewis, especially) than almost the entire remaining corpus of fantasy scholarship. The lengths of Richard C. West's major Tolkien bibliography, *Tolkien Criticism: An Annotated Checklist*, and Joe R. Christopher's annual Inklings bibliographies in the journal *Mythlore* attest to this. Add the numerous articles written on Ursula K. Le Guin, which in given years was the longest author entry in "The Year's Scholarship in Science Fiction, Fantasy and Horror Literature," and the preponderance is overwhelming. Thus, this discussion is limited to those series within which valuable author studies regularly appear.

The Starmont House Reader's Guides to Contemporary Science-Fiction, Fantasy, and Horror Authors (series editor, Roger C. Schlobin) is the largest of the continuing examinations of these three genres. It follows a uniform format that provides strong introductions for those who are looking for author surveys. Each volume includes a chronological chart, a biography and career overview, discussions of major works, group discussions of minor works, and annotated primary and secondary bibliographies. With almost forty volumes in print and some sixty more under contract, it should continue to supply readers for some time. Among those currently in print, the following will be of interest to the student of fantasy: Gary K. Wolfe's *David Lindsay*, Brian Murphy's *C. S. Lewis*, Lahna Diskin's *Theodore Sturgeon*, Robert A. Collings's *Piers Anthony*, Mary T. Brizzi's *Philip José Farmer*,

Rosemary Arbur's *Marian Zimmer Bradley*, and Carl B. Yoke's *Roger Zelazny*.

Greenwood Press's Contributions to the Study of Science Fiction and Fantasy (series editor, Marshall B. Tymn) is almost as large as the Starmont series, but its volumes are more thematic in nature. This is the series that contains the proceedings of the International Conference for the Fantastic in the Arts as well as the aforementioned *A Literary Symbiosis*, by Hazel Beasley Pierce; *The Return from Avalon*, by Raymond H. Thompson; and *The Comedy of the Fantastic*, by Don D. Elgin. Another volume of interest is Don Herron's critical anthology, *The Dark Barbarian: The Writings of Robert E. Howard*.

Another series in which fantasy titles occasionally appear is Writers of the 21st Century (Taplinger; Joseph D. Olander and Martin Harry Greenberg, general editors). Olander and Greenberg have edited *Ursula K. Le Guin*, and Tim Underwood and Chuck Miller have guest edited *Jack Vance*. Sadly, the G. K. Hall series of author bibliographies, once edited by L. W. Currey and Marshall B. Tymn, seems to be fallow or defunct. However, there have been a number of valuable titles released: Kenneth J. Zahorski and Robert H. Boyer's *Lloyd Alexander, Evangeline Walton Ensley, Kenneth Morris*; Lahna F. Diskin's *Theodore Sturgeon*; Roger C. Schlobin's *Andre Norton*; and Joseph L. Sanders's *Roger Zelazny*.

PERIODICIALS

Prior to the publication of Marshall B. Tymn and Mike Ashley's *Science Fiction, Fantasy, and Weird Fiction Magazines*, trying to discover the contents of the numerous magazines that have existed since the pulp explosions of the 1920s and 1930s involved searching out a large stack of separate volumes (many of them quite rare). Tymn and Ashley's 970-page monster gathers together the efforts of a number of scholars to describe and highlight the contents of 660 international magazines by category. Researchers will still have to go to other research tools for actual indexes to the magazines (which are indicated in the Tymn-Ashley volume), but this volume has made entry into the realm of periodic fiction so much easier that there is just no comparison with past agonies. Five important current periodicals are listed in the bibliography that follows.

BIBLIOGRAPHY

Books

Apter, T. E. *Fantasy Literature: An Approach to Reality*. Bloomington: Indiana University Press, 1982.

Arbur, Rosemary. *Marian Zimmer Bradley: A Reader's Guide*. Mercer Island, Wash.: Starmont House, 1985.

Ashley, Michael. *Who's Who in Horror and Fantasy Literature*. London: Elm Tree, 1977; New York: Taplinger, 1978.

Attebery, Brian. *The Fantasy Tradition in American Literature from Irving to Le Guin*. Bloomington: Indiana University Press, 1980.

Bates, Susannah. *The Pendex: An Index to Pen Names and House Names in Fantastic, Thriller, and Series Literature*. New York: Garland, 1981.

Bettelheim, Bruno. *The Uses of Enchantment: The Meaning and Importance of Fairy Tales*. New York: Knopf, 1976.

Bleiler, Everett F. *The Checklist of Science-Fiction & Supernatural Fiction*. Glen Rock, N.J.: Firebell, 1978. Supersedes *The Checklist of Fantastic Literature: A Bibliography of Fantasy, Weird and Science Fiction Books Published in the English Language*. 1948, 1972.

————. *The Guide to Supernatural Fiction: A Full Description of 1,775 Books from 1750 to 1960, Including Ghost Stories, Weird Fiction, Stories of Supernatural Horror, Fantasy, Gothic Novels, Occult Fiction, and Similar Literature with Author, Title, and Motif Indexes*. Kent, Ohio: Kent State University Press, 1983.

————, ed. *Supernatural Fiction Writers: Fantasy and Horror*. 2 vols. New York: Scribner's, 1985.

Boyer, Robert H., and Kenneth J. Zahorski, eds. *Fantasists on Fantasy: A Collection of Critical Reflections by Eighteen Masters of the Art*. New York: Avon, 1984.

Brizzi, Mary T. *Philip José Farmer: A Reader's Guide*. Mercer Island, Wash.: Starmont House, 1980.

Brook-Rose, Christine. *A Rhetoric of the Unreal: Studies in Narrative and Structure, Especially the Fantastic*. Cambridge: Cambridge University Press, 1981.

Burgess, Michael (also see R. Reginald below). *A Guide to Science Fiction and Fantasy in the Library of Congress Classification Scheme*. San Bernardino, Calif.: Borgo Press, 1984.

Carter, Lin. *Imaginary Worlds: The Art of Fantasy*. New York: Ballantine, 1973.

Clareson, Thomas D. *Science Fiction Criticism: An Annotated Checklist*. Kent, Ohio: Kent State University Press, 1972.

Collings, Robert A. *Piers Anthony: A Reader's Guide*. Mercer Island, Wash.: Starmont House, 1984.

Collins, Robert A., and Howard D. Pearce, eds. *The Scope of the Fantastic—Theory, Technique, Major Authors: Selected Essays from the First International Conference on the Fantastic in Literature and Film*. Westport, Conn.: Greenwood Press, 1985.

————. *The Scope of the Fantastic—Culture, Biography, Themes, Children's Literature: Selected Essays from the First International Conference on the Fantastic in Literature and Film*. Westport, Conn.: Greenwood Press, 1985.

Cott, Jonathan. *Pipers at the Gates of Dawn: The Wisdom of Children's Literature*. New York: Random House, 1981.

Cox, Harvey. *The Feast of Fools: A Theological Essay on Festivity and Fantasy*. Cambridge, Mass.: Harvard University Press, 1969.

Coyle, William, ed. *Aspects of Fantasy: Selected Essays from the Second International Conference on the Fantastic in Literature and Film*. Westport, Conn.: Greenwood Press, 1986.

Currey, L. W. *Science Fiction and Fantasy Authors: A Bibliography of First Printings of Their Fiction and Selected Nonfiction.* Boston: G. K. Hall, 1979.

Day, Bradford. *The Checklist of Fantastic Literature in Paperback Books.* Denver, N.Y.: Science Fiction & Fantasy, 1965; New York: Arno, 1975.

————. *The Supplemental Checklist of Fantastic Literature.* Denver, N.Y.: Science Fiction & Fantasy, 1963; New York: Arno, 1975.

De Camp, L. Sprague. *Literary Swordsmen and Sorcerers: The Makers of Heroic Fantasy.* Sauk City, Wis.: Arkham, 1976.

Diskin, Lahna F. *Theodore Sturgeon: A Primary and Secondary Bibliography.* Boston: G. K. Hall, 1980.

————. *Theodore Sturgeon: A Reader's Guide.* Mercer Island, Wash.: Starmont House, 1981.

Elgin, Don D. *The Comedy of the Fantastic: Ecological Perspectives on the Fantasy Novel.* Westport, Conn.: Greenwood Press, 1985.

Forster, E. M. *Aspects of the Novel and Related Writings.* 1927; repr. London: Edward Arnold, 1974.

Frane, Jeff. *Fritz Leiber: A Reader's Guide.* Mercer Island, Wash.: Starmont House, 1980.

Franson, Donald, and Howard DeVore. *A History of the Hugo, Nebula, and International Fantasy Awards.* rev. ed. Dearborn, Mich.: Misfit Press, 1985.

Hall, Hal W., ed. *Science Fiction and Fantasy Research Index.* Vol. 2. Bryan, Tex.: SFBRI, 1982.

————. *Science/Fiction Collections: Fantasy, Supernatural & Weird Tales.* New York: Haworth, 1983.

————. *Science Fiction Index: Criticism: An Index to English Language Books and Articles about Science Fiction and Fantasy.* Bryan, Tex.: Privately Printed, 1980.

Herron, Don, ed. *The Dark Barbarian: The Writings of Robert E. Howard.* Westport, Conn.: Greenwood Press, 1985.

Hokenson, Jan, and Howard D. Pearce, eds. *Forms of the Fantastic: Selected Essays from the Third International Conference on the Fantastic in Literature and Film.* New York: Greenwood Press, 1986.

Hume, Kathryn. *Fantasy and Mimesis: Responses to Reality in Western Literature.* New York: Methuen, 1984.

Irwin, W. R. *The Game of the Impossible: A Rhetoric of Fantasy.* Urbana: University of Illinois Press, 1976.

Jackson, Rosemary. *Fantasy: The Literature of Subversion.* New York: Methuen, 1981.

Kennard, Jean E. *Number and Nightmare: Forms of Fantasy in Contemporary Fiction.* Hamden, Conn.: Archon/Shoe String, 1975.

Lochhead, Marion. *The Renaissance of Wonder in Children's Literature.* Edinburgh: Canongate, 1977.

Locke, George. *A Spectrum of Fantasy: The Bibliography and Biography of a Collection of Fantastic Literature.* Upper Tooting, London: Ferret Fantasy, 1980.

Lynn, Ruth Nadelman. *Fantasy for Children: An Annotated Checklist and Reference Guide.* 2d ed. New York: R. R. Bowker, 1983.

MacDonald, George. "The Imagination, Its Functions and Its Culture." In *The Imagination and Other Essays.* Boston: Lothrop, 1883.

McGhan, Barry. *Sciencefiction [sic] and Fantasy Pseudonyms.* Dearborn, Mich.: Misfit Press, 1976.

Magill, Frank N., ed. *Survey of Modern Fantasy Literature*. 5 vols. Englewood Cliffs, N.J.: Salem, 1983.

Manlove, Colin N. *The Impulse of Fantasy Literature*. Kent, Ohio: Kent State University Press, 1983.

———. *Modern Fantasy: Five Studies*. Cambridge: Cambridge University Press, 1975.

Murphy, Brian. *C. S. Lewis: A Reader's Guide*. Mercer Island, Wash.: Starmont House, 1983.

Olander, Joseph D., and Martin Harry Greenberg, eds. *Ursula K. Le Guin*. New York: Taplinger, 1979.

Pierce, Hazel Beasley. *A Literary Symbiosis: Science Fiction/Fantasy Mystery*. Westport, Conn.: Greenwood Press, 1983.

Prickett, Stephen. *Victorian Fantasy*. Bloomington: Indiana University Press, 1979.

Rabkin, Eric S. *The Fantastic in Literature*. Princeton: Princeton University Press, 1976.

Reginald, R[obert], pseud. [Michael Burgess]. *Science Fiction & Fantasy Awards*. San Bernardino, Calif.: Borgo Press, 1981.

———. *Science Fiction and Fantasy Literature: A Checklist, 1700–1974 with Contemporary Science Fiction Authors II*. 2 vols. Detroit: Gale Research, 1979.

———. *Stella Nova: The Contemporary Science Fiction Authors*. Los Angeles: Unicorn & Son, 1970. Rpt. as *Contemporary Science Fiction Authors: First Edition*. New York: Arno, 1975.

Rosenberg, Betty. *Genreflecting: A Guide to Reading Interests in Genre Fiction*. Littleton, Colo.: Libraries Unlimited, 1982.

Sanders, Joseph L. *Roger Zelazny: A Primary and Secondary Bibliography*. Boston: G. K. Hall, 1980.

Schlobin, Roger C., ed. *The Aesthetics of Fantasy Literature and Art*. Notre Dame, Ind.: Notre Dame University Press, 1982.

———. *Andre Norton: A Primary and Secondary Bibliography*. Boston: G. K. Hall, 1980.

———. *The Literature of Fantasy: A Comprehensive, Annotated Bibliography of Modern Fantasy Fiction*. New York: Garland, 1981.

Searles, Baird, Beth Meacham, and Michael Franklin. *A Reader's Guide to Fantasy*. New York: Avon, 1982.

Siebers, Tobin. *The Romantic Fantastic*. Ithaca, N.Y.: Cornell University Press, 1984.

Slusser, George E., Eric S. Rabkin, and Robert Scholes, eds. *Bridges to Fantasy*. Carbondale: Southern Illinois University Press, 1982.

Swinfen, Ann. *In Defence of Fantasy: A Study of the Genre in English and American Literature since 1945*. Boston: Routledge and Kegan Paul, 1984.

Thompson, Raymond H. *The Return from Avalon: A Study of the Arthurian Legend in Modern Fiction*. Westport, Conn.: Greenwood Press, 1985.

Todorov, Tzvetan. *The Fantastic: A Structural Approach to a Literary Genre*. Translated by Richard Howard. Ithaca, N.Y.: Cornell University Press, 1973.

Tuck, Donald H. *The Encyclopedia of Science Fiction and Fantasy Through 1968*. 2 vols. Chicago: Advent, 1974, 1978.

Tymn, Marshall B., Kenneth J. Zahorski, and Robert H. Boyer. *Fantasy Literature: A Core Collection and Reference Guide*. New York: R. R. Bowker, 1979.

Tymn, Marshall B., et al. *The Year's Scholarship in Science Fiction, Fantasy and Horror*

Literature 1974-. In various forms: separate cumulations (1972–1975 and 1976–1979) and individual books from Kent State University Press and annuals in *Extrapolation*, 1976-. Earlier title: "The Year's Scholarship in Science Fiction and Fantasy."

Tymn, Marshall B., and Mike Ashley, eds. *Science Fiction, Fantasy, and Weird Fiction Magazines*. Westport, Conn.: Greenwood Press, 1985.

Underwood, Tim, and Chuck Miller, eds. *Jack Vance*. New York: Taplinger, 1980.

Waggoner, Diana. *The Hills of Faraway: A Guide to Fantasy*. New York: Atheneum, 1978.

Wells, Stuart W. III, comp. *The Science Fiction and Heroic Fantasy Author Index*. Duluth, Minn.: Purple Unicorn, 1978.

West, Richard C. *Tolkien Criticism: An Annotated Checklist*. Rev. ed. Kent, Ohio: Kent State University Press, 1981.

Wilson, Colin. *The Strength to Dream: Literature and the Imagination*. Boston: Houghton Mifflin, 1962; repr. Westport, Conn.: Greenwood Press, 1973.

Wolfe, Gary K. *David Lindsay: A Reader's Guide*. Mercer Island, Wash.: Starmont House, 1982.

Yoke, Carl B. *Roger Zelazny: A Reader's Guide*. Mercer Island, Wash.: Starmont House, 1979.

Yolen, Jane. *Touch Magic: Fantasy, Faerie and Folklore in the Literature of Childhood*. New York: Philomel, 1981.

Zahorski, Kenneth J., and Robert H. Boyer. *Lloyd Alexander, Evangeline Walton Ensley, Kenneth Morris: A Primary and Secondary Bibliography*. Boston: G. K. Hall, 1981.

Ziolkowski, Theodore. *Disenchanted Images: A Literary Iconology*. Princeton, N.J.: Princeton University Press, 1977.

Zipes, Jack. *Breaking the Magic Spell: Radical Theories of Folk & Fairy Tales*. Austin: University of Texas Press, 1979.

Special Magazine Issues

Extrapolation. Spring 1987. Special fantasy issue.
Kansas Quarterly. 16, no. 3 (1984). Special fantasy issue.
Mosiac. Winter 1977. Special fantasy issue.

Periodicals

Extrapolation. Wooster, Ohio, 1959-.
Fantasy Review. Boca Raton, Fla., 1978-.
Journal of the Fantastic in the Arts. Armonk, N.Y., 1988-.
Locus: The Newspaper of the Science Fiction Field. San Francisco, 1968-.
Mythlore. Los Angeles, 1969-.

7

Gothic Novels

KAY MUSSELL

The gothic novel had its greatest popularity in a relatively brief period of literary history, the end of the eighteenth and the beginning of the nineteenth centuries. It was originally a British literary form, although authors and readers in other countries quickly adopted gothic fiction and its conventions for their own. The influence of the gothic in fiction, however, has been much more significant than its relatively short period of great popularity would indicate. Gothic conventions influenced the detective novel, science fiction, horror stories, the popular melodrama, and the works of such writers as Edgar Allan Poe, Nathaniel Hawthorne, Washington Irving, Henry James, and William Faulkner. The gothic also continued as a form in itself, although much less well defined and pervasive than it had been in its heyday. The audience for the gothic novel, from the work of Ann Radcliffe in eighteenth-century England to that of Phyllis Whitney in twentieth-century America, has been largely female. Women are attracted to gothic novels by the combination of romance and terror, a blend that has remained relatively constant over the past 200 years.

Although the gothic as a form is capable of containing and exploring sensitive and sophisticated questions, as in the works of Poe and Hawthorne, in its popular version it has been a formulaic and predictable kind of fiction. It posits a fictional world in which life itself is precarious, but especially for young women. The worldview of the gothic novel offers vicarious danger and romantic fantasy of a type that is particularly appealing to female readers. Heroines are cast as victims in a man's world; but through the demonstration of feminine virtues, the victim proves herself worthy of the love of the hero, who becomes her deliverer from the terrors to which she is vulnerable. The gothic villain, who manipulates terrifying props and produces fear and danger, is defeated by the power of true love. The gothic novel over two centuries reaffirms the romantic belief in love as cure for and defense against evil.

HISTORIC OUTLINE

Scholarly consideration of the gothic novel in America is long overdue, but the study has been hampered by a variety of legitimate difficulties beyond the traditional resistance to the study of popular art forms. The term *gothic* does not lend itself to easy definition and has not been consistently applied. In the eighteenth century, the gothic novel (of Horace Walpole, for example) was synonymous with supernatural horror; but within a few years, the gothic took on more sentimental and romantic characteristics, almost as if a novel by Samuel Richardson had been overlaid with gothic props. In Ann Radcliffe's works, the "supernatural" was explained as the manipulations of a gothic villain who threatened the lovers. Clara M. Reeve's gothic novels were historical romances that used the exotic trappings of medieval chivalry to provide excitement. It was these two latter types of the gothic that were most influential in America.

After the early nineteenth century, the word *gothic* was not consistently applied to formula novels until the early 1960s, when Gerald Gross, an editor at Ace Books, used the term as the title for a paperback series of romantic mysteries designed for women readers. From 1960 to the mid–1970s, the modern gothic novel was one of the most active and lucrative areas of publishing. The gothic boom, however, was not wholly dependent on new material; many popular titles had been published long ago and either were never out of print or were returned to print to satisfy a new readership. The gothic novel may have been submerged or out of vogue before 1960, but it was never entirely absent from the literary scene.

Beyond the problem of definition, another impediment to serious study of gothic fiction is that its audience has been primarily female, relatively inarticulate, and lacking in access to outlets for critical expression. The forms influenced by the gothic, on the other hand, have been more thoroughly studied. When the original gothic novels lost their vitality for readers, the tradition splintered. Poe was influenced by the gothic in both his stories of detection and his stories of horror. Science fiction was indebted to gothic fiction for its premise of the seemingly supernatural rationally explained. The stage melodrama often resembled gothic novels in worldview as well as conventions. Some critics have even suggested that the Western was influenced by the gothic, especially in its use of Indians and the dangers of the wilderness as a form of American gothic terror. In Europe, although more rarely in America, gothics influenced the development of horror stories, such as *Frankenstein* and *Dracula*. However, all of these uses of the gothic go beyond the imaginative world posited by the original gothic novelists.

Literary formulas might be defined as fiction with a characteristic worldview supported by a particular set of conventions. A gothic novel consists of a story set in a remote place or a remote time in which a usually improbable and terrifying mystery is completely intertwined with a successful love story. Unlike detective stories, gothic novels do not offer a logical solution to the mystery; to the contrary, the mystery and the love story are so coincidentally interconnected that it is virtually impossible to separate them. The solution of the mystery removes the impediments to the successful conclusion of the romance. Heroines in gothics are doubly victimized: they are vulnerable to the plots of gothic villains and they are subordinate in the love story (that is, they cannot take the lead in resolving the romance). The novels depend on a setting in which the social structure is hierarchical; the conventions of gothic fiction, such as mysterious inheritances, hidden identities, lost wills, family secrets, inherited curses, incest and illegitimacy, require a world in which social mobility takes place through family identity and marriage rather than individual worth. Conclusions explicitly resolve the conflict in both strands of the plot, by linking triumph over evil with marriage.

For the late eighteenth and early nineteenth centuries, as well as for the mid-twentieth century, scholars are in relatively firm agreement on how to define a gothic novel. The definitions from the two periods are not entirely congruent, however, and for the century and a half between them there is no such agreement. The first gothic novels, those of Horace Walpole, Ann Radcliffe, Clara M. Reeve, Monk Lewis, and others, were read in America and influenced American fiction. The rise of the novel in America coincided with the peak popularity of gothic fiction in Britain; and since early American fiction was often derivative of British models, American novels were variously influenced by the gothic. Most influential in America were the works of writers like Ann Radcliffe, whose books had strong love interests and used supernatural terrors with rational explanations. Another influential gothic strain, exemplified by Clara M. Reeve, romanticized the past, usually with anachronistic elements, using the exoticism of a remote time to heighten the atmosphere of terror. More supernatural gothics, like those of Walpole and Lewis, influenced serious writers in America; but the horror novel never developed fully in this country for the audience apparently preferred terrors with rational explanations to explorations of the irrational or the psychological.

Although the gothic was influential in America, its creative energy was European. The American society and landscape did not provide the necessary settings of sinister castles and corrupt monasteries or the hierarchical social structure so necessary to the novels. American antipathy to novels as "not true" and "not instructive" impeded serious consideration of fiction into the nineteenth century. Additionally, in the absence of international copyright laws, it was simpler and cheaper for American printers to pirate the works of British popular authors than to pay American writers for original material. For more than a century, American fiction writers were hampered by the competition of British authors, who, in turn, complained loudly about the lack of payment for their work. Even today, the most popular gothic writers are usually British, and American gothic authors frequently use British settings.

Charles Brockden Brown was the first major American writer to employ the gothic in his fiction. He was particularly influenced by the horror mode, although he often supplied rationalistic or quasi-scientific explanations for apparently supernatural effects, drawing on terrorizing material to explore psychological states. His novels, including *Wieland* (1798), *Ormond* (1799), and *Edgar Huntly* (1799), have American settings. A lesser contemporary of Brown was Isaac Mitchell, who wrote one of the most popular novels of his day, *The Asylum, or Alonzo and Melissa* (1804), a romance about the opposition of a father to his daughter's proposed marriage. To heighten the gothic atmosphere in an American setting, Mitchell located his book in a medieval castle on the shore of Long Island Sound. Another book that derives from British models, *Julia, or the Illuminated Baron* (1800) by Sally Wood, is set in eighteenth-century France. The plot depends on the hidden identities of Julia and her suitor, who are revealed to be aristocrats; but in deference to American democratic sentiment they renounce their titles. Other similar novels by Wood are *Dorval, or the Speculator* (1801), *Amelia; or the Influence of Virtue: an Old Man's Story* (1802?), and *Ferdinand and Elmira: A Russian Story* (1804). Other gothic novelists of the early period, some anonymous, include Ann Eliza Bleecker and the women who used the pseudonyms "A Lady of Massachusetts" and "A Lady of Philadelphia." Chapbooks and magazines also published gothic fiction. George Lippard's *The Quaker City, or The Monks of Monk's Hall* (1844) used many gothic conventions.

Because the American democratic and practical mind was never quite comfortable with the gothic novel of terror, the true heirs of the original gothics can be found in the women's novels of the nineteenth and twentieth centuries. In the first half of the nineteenth century, some American women authors wrote novels of the Puritan period with heroines who were threatened both by the dangerous frontier environment and by an oppressive patriarchal society. Many writers of sentimental romances wrote novels that today would be called *gothics*, novels that are dependent on the models of

Radcliffe or the Brontës for their plot and their worldview. Probably the most important of these writers was Mrs. E.D.E.N. Southworth, author of *The Hidden Hand* (1859) and *The Curse of Clifton* (1852). Another was Bertha M. Clay, the pseudonym for a group of writers, beginning with Charlotte M. Breame, who wrote women's gothics for Street and Smith's dime-novel series. So popular was the gothic in this period that a major dime-novel publisher, Norman Munro, once printed Walpole's *Castle of Otranto* in a story paper without acknowledging either author or title. Nine-teenth-century gothics were usually very long, written in a highly romantic style, and full of coincidences in plot and anachronisms in setting.

The turn of the century saw a great increase in interest in historical romances, many of which drew on gothic models. Some followed the tradition of Clara M. Reeve and others in Britain, mining the past ages of Europe for romantic and exotic material. But by the end of the nineteenth century, many historical gothics were no longer set in the Middle Ages. Colonial America and the Revolutionary War, as well as the Civil War, were also remote enough in time to provide appropriate settings. Mary Johnston, the Virginia author, wrote several novels of this type. Her *To Have and To Hold* (1900), one of the most popular historical romances in American publishing, is set in Jamestown. Authors of the early twentieth century who used gothic material included Mary Roberts Rinehart, Mignon Eberhart (both better known as mystery writers), Kathleen Norris, Emilie Loring, and Kathleen Winsor. These authors and others have never been studied with consistency, although some of their books are still in print.

In the early 1960s, publishers began actively to seek new gothic novels, but the roots of the recent gothic revival were evident at least as early as the 1930s with the immense popularity of Daphne du Maurier's *Rebecca* (1938). Recent gothic writers include two Americans, Phyllis Whitney and Anya Seton, who published their first books in the 1940s; but once again British writers were most significant. In 1960, the first novel by Victoria Holt (a pseudonym of Eleanor Burford Hibbert) was published in America. *Mistress of Mellyn*, which resembled *Jane Eyre*, sparked interest in gothic fiction, creating a renewed market for British writers (Mary Stewart, Barbara Cartland, Dorothy Eden, and Hibbert herself) and for the romantic mysteries of Americans like Whitney, Seton, and Daoma Winston.

In the mid–1970s, a new version of the gothic gained popularity. Novels by such authors as Rosemary Rogers, Kathleen Woodiwiss, Claire Lorimer, and Lolah Burford were original paperbacks, usually very long, with historical settings, and including far more sexual and violent material than gothics since Walpole or Lewis. In Rogers's *Wicked, Loving Lies* (1976), the heroine is raped innumerable times, almost always by the same man (who is, of course, the hero). She is, for a time, Napoleon's mistress, a prisoner in a harem, a British noblewoman, a quadroon slave, and an heiress. These books are more sexually explicit than other gothics, but their worldview remains similar, indicating that the twentieth-century audience is more tolerant of sexual deviation in heroines but still wishes some of its vicarious romance in gothic form.

Although there has been some change, the value system of gothic novels has remained relatively stable over the years. The stories still occur in a world in which marriage appears to be the best of all possible states for women, although difficult to achieve, and in a world which, because women have very little control over their lives, is especially precarious for them. In their domestic context, gothics have always offered to women readers a particularly female form of adventure with the anachronisms of sinister mansions, corrupt aristocrats, disguised identities, lost heirs, rationalized supernatural effects, and melodramatic reconciliations.

REFERENCE WORKS

Most reference works on fiction do not include a category for gothic authors and titles, and researchers must often read between the lines in searching out materials. A useful source book, although almost entirely devoted to eighteenth-century British gothic fiction, is Dan J. McNutt's *The Eighteenth-Century Gothic Novel: An Annotated Bibliography of Criticism and Selected Texts*. The book provides brief annotations of bibliographies and secondary sources, including background materials, specialized studies, and other items of interest. It is current through 1971. Although the focus in this volume, as in so many others, is on British versions of the gothic and serious literary consideration rather than popular culture, it is still indispensable. The only other specialized bibliography of the early gothic is less useful. Montague Summer's *A Gothic Bibliography* lists primary works to 1916. McNutt says: "An essential book, yet one to be used with caution." Frederick S. Frank's *Guide to the Gothic: An Annotated Bibliography of Criticism* is an exhaustive and excellent guide to writings on the gothic. Organized topically (by national literature and special issues), the book includes succinct annotations to more than 2,000 books and articles, some of which are directly relevant to popular gothic works.

Many general books on early American fiction provide titles, authors, and publishing information about gothic novels written in America. Among the best of these are Lyle H. Wright's *American Fiction 1774–1850* and *American Fiction 1774–1900*. The volumes are listings of American fiction included in major collections in the United States. Entries include place, date of publication or the printer, if known, along with location of copies. Some books have descriptive annotations, and there is an index of unexamined titles, as well as a title index. Although much of the listed material is not gothic, the volumes are well worth consulting. Arthur Hobson Quinn's *American Fiction: An Historical and Critical Survey* includes a great number of plot summaries and can be used to find forgotten novels with gothic elements. Less useful but worth consulting is John Williams Tebbel's *A History of Book Publishing in the United States* for information on publishers, best sellers, and copyright laws.

Much of the gothic fiction of the mid to late nineteenth century was published in dime novels, story papers, and women's sentimental novels. There is no comprehensive guide to such material and some of the best collections are uncataloged. However, there are a few good places to start. Quentin Reynolds's *The Fiction Factory* is a history of the publications of Street and Smith and provides much solid information on authors, titles, and bibliographic data. The book is marred by the lack of a good annotated bibliography and information on the location of primary source material. A better bibliographical guide is Albert Johannsen's *The House of Beadle and Adams*. Although neither of these books is devoted exclusively, or even primarily, to gothic material, both contain information about particular authors and series. For example, Bertha M. Clay was a pseudonym used by Street and Smith authors of a particular kind of women's novel with strong gothic characteristics. Unfortunately, given the current state of dime-novel and story-paper bibliography, the only effective way to discover what gothic material was published by a given source is to go to the collections and search. In an uncataloged collection, the task can be immense.

Several specialized volumes are also of use in searching for gothic fiction in America. Because most gothic novels are set in the past, reference works on historical fiction may include relevant titles and authors. Especially useful is A. T. Dickinson, Jr.'s *American Historical Fiction*, a briefly annotated checklist by period of history. The book includes author-title and subject indexes, and the annotations are extensive enough to suggest whether the book is a gothic novel. Ernest E. Leisy's study, *The American Historical Novel*, is an excellent guide to titles and authors. Ordean A. Hagen's *Who Done It? A Guide to Detective, Mystery, and Suspense Fiction* includes many modern gothic authors and titles, usually categorized under suspense. A final useful volume is Alice Payne Hackett and James Henry Burke's *80 Years of Best Sellers*. Again, it is most helpful when a particular author is known in advance, but its lists of mystery and detective fiction include some gothic fiction as well.

In the past decade, two newer fields of research—popular culture and women's studies—have produced specialized bibliographical tools relevant to gothic fiction. *Twentieth-Century Crime and Mystery Writers*, edited by John M. Reilly, includes modern gothic writers like Joan Aiken, Dorothy Eden, Elizabeth Peters, Phyllis Whitney, and Mary Stewart. Each entry has a critical essay and a full bibliography of the author's works, with variant titles and pseudonyms. Similarly organized, *Twentieth-Century Romance and Gothic Writers*, edited by James Vinson, is the single best bibliographic source on modern gothic authors. The forthcoming *International Encyclopedia of Communications*, published through the Annenberg School of Communication at the University of Pennsylvania, will include relevant entries. The demand for better research sources on women produced the four-volume *American Women Writers*, edited by Lina Mainiero. Each entry includes biographical and bibliographical information as well as a critical essay. Another important source is Narda Lacey Schwartz's *Articles on Women Writers, 1960–1975: A Bibliography*, which cites work on some gothic writers in popular and scholarly sources. Kay Mussell's *Women's Gothic and Romantic Fiction: A Reference Guide* covers material on gothic and romance fiction through 1979.

RESEARCH COLLECTIONS

American popular gothic fiction is found in great profusion in research collections in the United States, although it is rarely identified as such nor is it systematically cataloged under "Gothic." Because the rise of fiction in America coincided with the peak influence of the gothic, collections of early American fiction are fruitful sources. The Lee Ash guide, *Subject Collections*, lists major collections of early American fiction at the American Antiquarian Society, New York University, the Athenaeum of Philadelphia, and the University of Pittsburgh, which has the Hervey Allen Collection of 2,000 volumes and related manuscripts in American historical fiction. The most extensive collection of books and manuscripts is at the New York Public Library, which contains over two million volumes as well as catalogs of lending libraries and booksellers in the eighteenth and nineteenth centuries. Many libraries, including the Library of Congress, own volumes listed in the Wright bibliographies of early American fiction.

Dime-novel and paperback fiction collections offer another useful source of popular gothic fiction. The Library of Congress's uncataloged collection of dime novels includes 20,000 titles. Some of the series contained there consist of gothic romances, including books by Mrs. E.D.E.N. Southworth. Street and Smith's Bertha Clay Library is also available there. Ash lists other collections of dime novels at the University of California at Los Angeles, Yale University, the New York Public Library, and New York University. Northern Illinois University, DeKalb, has the Albert Johannsen Collection of 1,100 cataloged volumes and some related material; the University of Alberta, Canada, collection is especially strong in penny dreadfuls and gothics. Both Oberlin College and the Cleveland Public Library have collections; Cleveland is especially good in nineteenth-century romances. The Hess Collection at the University of Minnesota holds 70,000 dime novels.

Major collections of gothic novels, although not mainly American, include the Sadleir-Black Gothic Collection at the University of Virginia (2,000 volumes—see Robert Kerr Black, "The Sadleir-Black Gothic Collection"), the Yale University Library, and the University of California at

Los Angeles (300 volumes). Two brief published anthologies that contain American material and are worth noting are *Gothic Tales of Terror*, edited by Peter Haining, and *Seven Masterpieces of Gothic Horror*, edited by Robert Donald Spector. Another collection, G. Richard Thompson's *Romantic Gothic Tales 1790–1840*, contains an excellent introduction with a summary of scholarship and an extensive definition of distinct types of gothic fiction. A series of facsimile reprints, *Gothic Novels*, edited by Devendra P. Varma, is in progress by Arno Press.

Major authors of gothic popular fiction in America are rarely taken seriously enough to have their papers and manuscripts collected by a library. However, the papers of Mrs. E.D.E.N. Southworth are in the Duke University Library, those of Mary Johnston can be seen at the University of Virginia Library, and those of Mary Roberts Rinehart (who wrote a few gothics as well as mysteries) are at the University of Pittsburgh. The Barnard College Library includes manuscripts and volumes by American women authors (Bertha Van Riper Overbury Gift). The Library of Congress Manuscript Division contains the Ernest E. Leisy Collection of the American historical novel. The collection is composed of manuscripts and related material c. 1923–50 from work on Leisy's published study, *The American Historical Novel*. Because so much fiction of the nineteenth century was serialized, another valuable, although uncataloged, source is nineteenth-century newspapers and story papers. Southworth, for example, wrote for the *New York Ledger*, the *National Era*, the *Saturday Evening Post*, the *New York Weekly* (Street and Smith), and the *Baltimore Saturday Visiter*.

Twentieth-century gothic fiction is less systematically available. The Popular Culture Library at Bowling Green State University has a large cataloged collection of popular fiction, including gothics. At Michigan State University, the Russel B. Nye Popular Culture Collection includes romances and mysteries, although acquisition in these areas is not active. Robert G. Sewell, in "Trash or Treasure? Pop Fiction in Academic and Research Libraries," suggests that many libraries disdain women's popular fiction (gothics and romances) even when they collect other popular novels. For modern gothic novels, the best source for current titles (besides *Publishers Weekly*) is a mass market bookstore; novels since the recent publishing boom began in 1960 may be found in used bookstores or paperback sections of public libraries.

HISTORY AND CRITICISM

Until recently, most critical consideration of gothic novels in America occurred in articles and books on more general or related topics. Only a few authors directly confront the subject, although there is much valuable critical material in both standard and specialized volumes. *Cheap Book Production in the United States, 1870–1891* by Raymond H. Shove provides important information about the publishing of popular novels in America. Shove's book is especially valuable for its discussion of the economics of pirating and the impact of the International Copyright Law of 1891 on American book publishing. General studies on popular literature with criticism of the gothic and related literature include James D. Hart's *The Popular Book: A History of America's Literary Taste*, a chronological study of popular publishing, and Russel Nye's excellent critical survey *The Unembarrassed Muse*. The methodology suggested by John G. Cawelti in *Adventure, Mystery, and Romance* is particularly fruitful for the study of formulaic literature, the gothic novel included.

For the early gothic novel, there is much critical work available; unfortunately, most of it relates to the study of American popular gothic material only as background. If American authors are considered at all, they are invariably Poe and Hawthorne, not the popular authors of whom Hawthorne complained so eloquently that if that "d——d mob of scribbling women" did not lose its hold on the public, his work would never be appreciated. Three specialized studies of the gothic novel in England are Eino Railo's *The Haunted Castle*, Montague Summers's *The Gothic Quest*, and Devendra P. Varma's *The Gothic Flame*. Railo is especially thorough in his description of the various strains of the gothic in England. Summers is far too much the ideologue and bibliophile for the book to be of critical use; he is interested in "spreading the faith" rather than analysis. Varma offers a lucid discussion of the gothic novel in England and discusses the various ways that the gothic was diffused in other forms of literature after its heyday. An appendix analyzes the influence of the gothic on the detective novel, and Varma's bibliography is extensive. Elizabeth MacAndrew's *The Gothic Tradition in Fiction* traces British gothic conventions from Walpole through the nineteenth century, with some analysis of popular fiction and gothic examples in other national literatures. Edith Birkhead's *The Tale of Terror* is excellent on the supernatural in English gothic fiction, but traces the gothic in America only through Charles Brockden Brown, Poe, Hawthorne, and Irving; she is more interested in the influence of the gothic on serious literature than on popular culture. Michael Sadleir's " 'All Horrid?': Jane Austen and the Gothic Romance" describes the novels Austen satirized in *Northanger Abbey*.

Some studies discuss gothic fiction in a broader cultural context. The chapter "Literary Influences" in Kenneth Clark's *The Gothic Revival: An Essay in the History of Taste* links the Graveyard Poets and gothic novelists with the gothic revival in architecture in England. A more recent work that links fiction and art is Linda Bayer-Berenbaum's *The Gothic Imagination: Expansion in Gothic Literature and Art*. Although the book centers on early gothicism, one chapter deals with Mary Shelley's *Frankenstein* and Victoria Holt's *On the Night of the Seventh Moon* as complementary gothic tales.

Dorothy Blakey's *The Minerva Press 1790–1820* is a basic study of a British publishing house that issued gothic material. Worthy of note is Lowry Nelson, Jr.'s "Night Thoughts on the Gothic Novel," especially for its suggestive discussion of the gothic hero/villain. Margot Northey's *The Haunted Wilderness: The Gothic and the Grotesque in Canadian Fiction* suggests that both American and Canadian gothic fiction developed outside the European tradition.

General studies of American literature that are especially good on the gothic include Alexander Cowie's *The Rise of the American Novel*. Cowie says that the American novel never really developed a gothic tradition (a debatable assumption), but his analysis of Charles Brockden Brown, Lippard's *The Quaker City*, and Mitchell's *Alonzo and Melissa* is particularly fine. Edward Wagenknecht in *Cavalcade of the American Novel* has an excellent chapter on women novelists, emphasizing their use of sensational material, although he does not call it specifically *gothic*. His expanded comments on the novels of Mary Johnston appear in an essay entitled "The World and Mary Johnston." Two studies of the early American novel are also interesting. Lily D. Loshe's 1907 book, *The Early American Novel*, covers the period from 1789 to 1830. In 1971, it was superseded by Henri Petter's *The Early American Novel*, which analyzes American uses of gothic conventions in the chapter "Mystery and Terror." Petter also covers the attack on novel reading in the period, which often was aimed at women's novels in general and the gothic in particular. Most critics complained that novels were a "waste of time" and "not true," although the supposedly pernicious influence of such fiction on suggestive young female minds also came in for its share of opprobrium. Leslie A. Fiedler's *Love and Death in the American Novel* suggests a link between death and the orgasm in gothics, with the approach of danger representing a strong sexual urge toward death. Since in most gothic fiction the culmination of the love story and the salvation from danger are simultaneous, his argument seems relevant.

Some recent feminist criticism has focused on specifically female manifestations of gothic fiction. Ellen Moers, in her influential book *Literary Women*, argues that women authors employ the gothic to portray a particularly female version of vulnerability. She discusses the gothic tradition throughout the book, especially in the chapters "Female Gothic" and "Traveling Heroinism: Gothic for Heroines." Juliann E. Fleenor's anthology, *The Female Gothic*, was designed to elaborate Moers's ground-breaking study. It argues that the gothic is appropriate to female literary purposes in both serious and popular works. Among the authors covered in the volume are Victoria Holt, Margaret Atwood, Emily Brontë, Mary Shelley, and Isak Dinesen. Fleenor's introduction provides an excellent analytical survey of scholarly theories about women and the gothic tradition. Sandra M. Gilbert and Susan Gubar's important study, *The Madwoman in the Attic: The Woman*

Writer and the Nineteenth-Century Literary Imagination, examines the gothic in the work of the Brontës and also suggests that Emily Dickinson's poetry contains gothic elements.

Other studies are variously useful. Oral Sumner Coad's "The Gothic Element in American Literature Before 1835" is an influential survey. Jane Lundblad's *Nathaniel Hawthorne and the Tradition of the Gothic Romance* shows how Hawthorne adapted gothic elements in his own work. G. H. Orians's "Censure of Fiction in American Magazines and Romances 1789–1810" provides useful background on American attitudes toward the novel. Of specific value in the study of early American gothic fiction is Sister Mary Mauritia Redden's *The Gothic Fiction in the American Magazines (1765–1800)*. She includes definitions of the characteristics of British and American gothic fiction and plot summaries of gothic fiction in American magazines. She says that the gothic first appeared in American magazines in 1785; almost all of the stories in the period were anonymous imitations of Ann Radcliffe. The appendixes include magazine lists, bibliography, and a chronological listing of stories.

On the dime novels and the "scribbling women," there are several good critical studies, including Herbert Ross Brown's classic *The Sentimental Novel in America, 1789–1860*. Brown's study deals with gothic novelists and conventions in a general survey of sentimental fiction. Helen Waite Papashvily's *All the Happy Endings* covers the same ground, although she is probably too breezy and her strong proto-feminist slant sometimes gets in the way of objective analysis. Her argument that women's escape fiction in the period was a way of getting back at a male society seems too facile. The bibliography of secondary sources is good up to 1954 but is not annotated. The book also lacks a good list of primary material. An essay-length study of similar usefulness is Alexander Cowie's "The Vogue of the Domestic Novel." On periodical literature, the most comprehensive work is Mary Noel's *Villains Galore: The Heyday of the Popular Story Weekly*. The book is useful on publishers and publications, but it lacks a bibliography.

Other studies in related areas offer useful perspectives. Katharine West's *Chapter of Governesses: A Study of the Governess in English Fiction 1800–1949* is especially relevant since so many gothic novels have governesses as protagonists. She suggests that a governess is an appropriate heroine for novels about women as victims because of her anomalous place in the household and her task of finding a domestic circle of her own through vicarious involvement in her employer's family. M. Jeanne Peterson's "The Victorian Governess: Status Incongruence in Family and Society" also addresses the social status of governesses. Barbara Welter's "The Cult of True Womanhood" delineates the feminine ideal for the nineteenth century and indicates how certain types of escape fiction might have filled female psychological needs. Chapter eight of David Grimsted's *Melodrama Unveiled*

includes pertinent discussion of the worldview of nineteenth-century thea-
ter, which closely resembles that of the gothic.

For individual authors, very few specialized studies exist. An exception
is Regis Louise Boyle's *Mrs. E.D.E.N. Southworth, Novelist*. The only full-
length study of this author or of any of her contemporaries, it is especially
rich in bibliographic material. Boyle notes that contemporary reviewers of
Southworth compared her work to that of Currer Bell (Charlotte Brontë).
Jan Cohn's *Improbable Fiction: The Life of Mary Roberts Rinehart* is a fine
critical biography of Rinehart's life and work.

Until recently, analyses of modern gothic novels appeared most often in
journalistic sources. Phyllis Whitney, Susan Howatch, and Mary Stewart
all wrote how-to articles for the *Writer* magazine. *Time* and *Newsweek* covered the gothic revival and some of its authors in "Extricating Emily" and
Martha Duffy's "On the Road to Manderley" in *Time* and "Heathcliff:
Cliff-Hangers" in *Newsweek*. A satirical piece in the *New York Times Book
Review* by Gary Jennings, "Heathcliff Doesn't Smoke L and M's," offers a
male view of the excesses of women's gothic fiction. A sidebar by Lewis
Nichols, "The Gothic Story," cites figures and facts about gothic publication in 1969. *Publishers Weekly* since the early 1960s has included both
advertisements and reviews of gothic novels; because *Publishers Weekly*
serves the book trade, it offers the best source of information on the economics of publishing.

Recently, some scholars and critics have published analyses of gothic
fiction for women. Among articles in the *Journal of Popular Culture* are Joanna
Russ's "Somebody's Trying to Kill Me and I Think It's My Husband: The
Modern Gothic," Kay Mussell's "Beautiful and Damned: The Sexual
Woman in Modern Gothic Fiction," and Caesarea Abartis's "The Ugly-
Pretty, Dull-Bright, Weak Strong Girl in the Gothic Mansion." Janice A.
Radway's "The Utopian Impulse in Popular Fiction: Gothic Romances and
'Feminist' Protest" links modern gothic conventions with the quest for
female identity. Carol Thurston and Barbara Doscher's "Supermarket Er-
otica: 'Bodice-Busters' Put Romantic Myths to Bed" argues that the new
erotic gothic romances of Woodiwiss and Rogers express covert female
protest against patriarchy in a form acceptable to readers who might be
uncomfortable with overt feminism.

Several recent feminist studies of contemporary romances include con-
sideration of the gothic. Tania Modleski's *Loving With a Vengeance: Mass-
Produced Fantasies for Women* considers the gothic a powerful mode for ex-
ploration of and vicarious amelioration of female victimization in patriarchy.
Kay Mussell's *Fantasy and Reconciliation: Contemporary Formulas of Women's
Romance Fiction* places gothics in the context of other popular women's
formulas as an expression of popular entertainment for women. Janice A.
Radway's *Reading the Romance: Women, Patriarchy, and Popular Literature*

studies gothics in a wide-ranging book that includes ethnographic research on women readers. Helen Hazen's *Endless Rapture: Rape, Romance, and the Female Imagination* includes a chapter on gothics in a book that defends apparent sexual violence in romances against the feminist critique of popular fiction for women. It is evident that serious critical consideration of gothic fiction in America has begun in recent years, although much remains to be done, both in comprehensive critical analysis of the formula and in the basic bibliographic work that would serve to define and locate additional research material.

BIBLIOGRAPHY

Abartis, Caesarea. "The Ugly-Pretty, Dull-Bright, Weak Strong Girl in the Gothic Mansion." *Journal of Popular Culture*, 13 (Fall 1979), 257–63.

Ash, Lee. *Subject Collections: A Guide to Special Book Collections and Subject Emphases as Reported by University, College, Public, and Special Libraries and Museums in the United States and Canada.* 4th ed. New York: R. R. Bowker, 1974.

Bayer-Berenbaum, Linda. *The Gothic Imagination: Expansion in Gothic Literature and Art.* Rutherford, N.J.: Fairleigh Dickinson University Press, 1982.

Birkhead, Edith. *The Tale of Terror.* New York: E. P. Dutton, 1921; Russell and Russell, 1963.

Black, Robert Kerr. "The Sadleir-Black Gothic Collection." An Address Before the Bibliographic Society of the University of Virginia, University of Virginia Library. Charlottesville: University Press of Virginia, 1949.

Blakey, Dorothy. *The Minerva Press 1790–1820.* London: Oxford University Press, 1939.

Boyle, Regis Louise. *Mrs. E.D.E.N. Southworth, Novelist.* Washington, D.C.: Catholic University Press, 1939.

Brown, Herbert Ross. *The Sentimental Novel in America, 1789–1860.* Durham, N.C.: Duke University Press, 1940; New York: Octagon, 1975.

√ Cawelti, John G. *Adventure, Mystery, and Romance: Formula Stories as Art and Popular Culture.* Chicago: University of Chicago Press, 1976.

Clark, Kenneth. *The Gothic Revival: An Essay in the History of Taste.* London: Constable, 1928, 1950; Murray, 1962; New York: Holt, Rinehart and Winston, 1962; Humanities Press, 1970.

Coad, Oral Sumner. "The Gothic Element in American Literature Before 1835." *Journal of English and Germanic Philology*, 24 (January 1925), 72–93.

Cohn, Jan. *Improbable Fiction: The Life of Mary Roberts Rinehart.* Pittsburgh: University of Pittsburgh Press, 1980.

Cowie, Alexander. *The Rise of the American Novel.* New York: American Book, 1948, 1951.

———. "The Vogue of the Domestic Novel." *South Atlantic Quarterly*, 41 (October 1942), 416–25.

Dickinson, A. T., Jr. *American Historical Fiction.* 3d ed. Metuchen, N.J.: Scarecrow Press, 1971.

Duffy, Martha. "On the Road to Manderley." *Time*, 97 (April 12, 1971), 95–96.

"Extricating Emily." *Time*, 87 (April 22, 1966), 88.

Fiedler, Leslie A. *Love and Death in the American Novel*. New York: Criterion, 1960; Dell, 1966.

Fleenor, Juliann E., ed. *The Female Gothic*. Montreal: Eden Press, 1983.

Frank, Frederick S. *Guide to the Gothic: An Annotated Bibliography of Criticism*. Metuchen, N.J.: Scarecrow Press, 1984.

Gilbert, Sandra M., and Susan Gubar. *The Madwoman in the Attic: The Woman Writer and the Nineteenth-Century Literary Imagination*. New Haven, Conn.: Yale University Press, 1979.

Grimsted, David. *Melodrama Unveiled*. Chicago: University of Chicago Press, 1968.

Hackett, Alice Payne, and James Henry Burke. *80 Years of Best Sellers*. New York: R. R. Bowker, 1977.

Hagen, Ordean A. *Who Done It? A Guide to Detective, Mystery, and Suspense Fiction*. New York: R. R. Bowker, 1969.

Haining, Peter, comp. *Gothic Tales of Terror*. 2 vols. Baltimore: Penguin, 1972.

Hart, James D. *The Popular Book: A History of America's Literary Taste*. New York: Oxford University Press, 1950; Westport, Conn.: Greenwood Press, 1976.

Hazen, Helen. *Endless Rapture: Rape, Romance, and the Female Imagination*. New York: Scribner's, 1983.

"Heathcliff: Cliff-Hangers." *Newsweek* (April 24, 1966), 101–2.

Howatch, Susan. "Realism in Modern Gothics." *Writer*, 87 (May 1974), 11–13.

Jennings, Gary. "Heathcliff Doesn't Smoke L and M's." *New York Times Book Review* (July 27, 1969), 4–5, 24–25.

Johannsen, Albert. *The House of Beadle and Adams and Its Dime and Nickel Novels*. Norman: University of Oklahoma Press, 1950, 1962.

Leisy, Ernest E. *The American Historical Novel*. Norman: University of Oklahoma Press, 1950.

Loshe, Lily D. *The Early American Novel, 1789–1830*. New York: Columbia University Press, 1907; Ungar, 1966.

Lundblad, Jane. *Nathaniel Hawthorne and the Tradition of the Gothic Romance*. Cambridge, Mass.: Harvard University Press, 1946; New York: Haskell House, 1964.

MacAndrew, Elizabeth. *The Gothic Tradition in Fiction*. New York: Columbia University Press, 1979.

McNutt, Dan J. *The Eighteenth-Century Gothic Novel: An Annotated Bibliography of Criticism and Selected Texts*. New York: Garland, 1975.

Mainiero, Lina, ed. *American Women Writers: A Critical Reference Guide from Colonial Times to the Present*. 4 vols. New York: Ungar, 1979.

Modleski, Tania. *Loving with a Vengeance: Mass-Produced Fantasies for Women*. Hamden, Conn.: Archon, 1982.

Moers, Ellen. *Literary Women*. Garden City, N.Y.: Doubleday, 1977.

Mussell, Kay. "Beautiful and Damned: The Sexual Woman in Modern Gothic Fiction." *Journal of Popular Culture*, 9 (Summer 1975), 84–89.

———. *Fantasy and Reconciliation: Contemporary Formulas of Women's Romance Fiction*. Westport, Conn.: Greenwood Press, 1984.

———. *Women's Gothic and Romantic Fiction: A Reference Guide*. Westport, Conn.: Greenwood Press, 1981.

Nelson, Lowry, Jr. "Night Thoughts on the Gothic Novel." *Yale Review*, 52 (December 1962), 236–57.

Nichols, Lewis. "The Gothic Story." *New York Times Book Review* (July 27, 1969), 25.

Noel, Mary. *Villains Galore: The Heyday of the Popular Story Weekly.* New York: Macmillan, 1954.

Northey, Margot. *The Haunted Wilderness: The Gothic and the Grotesque in Canadian Fiction.* Toronto: University of Toronto Press, 1976.

Nye, Russel B. *The Unembarrassed Muse.* New York: Dial Press, 1970.

Orians, G. H. "Censure of Fiction in American Magazines and Romances 1789–1810." *PMLA*, 52 (March 1937), 195–214.

Papashvily, Helen Waite. *All the Happy Endings.* New York: Harper, 1956; Port Washington, N.Y.: Kennikat Press, 1972.

Peterson, M. Jeanne. "The Victorian Governess: Status Incongruence in Family and Society." In *Suffer and Be Still: Women in the Victorian Age.* Edited by Martha Vicinus. Bloomington: Indiana University Press, 1972.

Petter, Henri. *The Early American Novel.* Columbus: Ohio State University Press, 1971.

Quinn, Arthur Hobson. *American Fiction: An Historical and Critical Survey.* New York: Appleton-Century-Crofts, 1936, 1964.

Radway, Janice A. *Reading the Romance: Women, Patriarchy, and Popular Literature.* Chapel Hill: University of North Carolina Press, 1984.

———. "The Utopian Impulse in Popular Literature: Gothic Romances and 'Feminist' Protest." *American Quarterly*, 33 (Summer 1981), 140–62.

Railo, Eino. *The Haunted Castle.* London: George Routledge, 1927; New York: Gordon Press, 1974.

Redden, Sister Mary Mauritia. *The Gothic Fiction in the American Magazines (1765–1800).* Washington, D.C.: Catholic University Press, 1939.

Reilly, John M., ed. *Twentieth-Century Crime and Mystery Writers.* New York: St. Martin's Press, 1980.

Reynolds, Quentin. *The Fiction Factory.* New York: Random House, 1955.

Russ, Joanna. "Somebody's Trying to Kill Me and I Think It's My Husband: The Modern Gothic." *Journal of Popular Culture*, 6 (Spring 1973), 666–91.

Sadleir, Michael. " 'All Horrid?': Jane Austen and the Gothic Romance." In *Things Past.* London: Constable, 1944.

Schwartz, Narda Lacey. *Articles on Women Writers, 1960–1975: A Bibliography.* Santa Barbara, Calif.: ABC-Clio, 1977.

Sewell, Robert G. "Trash or Treasure? Pop Fiction in Academic and Research Libraries." *College and Research Libraries*, 46 (November 1984), 450–61.

Shove, Raymond H. *Cheap Book Production in the United States, 1870–1891.* Urbana: University of Illinois Press, 1937.

Spector, Robert Donald, ed. *Seven Masterpieces of Gothic Horror.* New York: Bantam, 1963.

Stewart, Mary. "Setting and Background in the Novel." *The Writer*, 77 (December 1964), 7–9.

———. "Teller of Tales." *The Writer*, 83 (May 1970), 9–12.

Summers, Montague. *A Gothic Bibliography.* London: Fortune, 1941, 1969; New York: Russell and Russell, 1964.

———. *The Gothic Quest.* London: Fortune, 1938; New York: Russell and Russell, 1964.

Tebbel, John William. *A History of Book Publishing in the United States*. 3 vols. New York: R. R. Bowker, 1972.

Thompson, G. Richard. "Introduction: Gothic Fiction in the Romantic Age: Context and Mode." In *Romantic Gothic Tales 1790–1840*. New York: Harper and Row, 1979.

Thurston, Carol, and Barbara Doscher. "Supermarket Erotica: 'Bodice-Busters' Put Romantic Myths to Bed." *Progressive* (April 1982), 49–51.

Varma, Devendra P. *The Gothic Flame*. New York: Russell and Russell, 1957, 1966.

———, ed. *Gothic Novels*. 40 vols. New York: New York Times/Arno, 1971-.

Vinson, James, ed. *Twentieth-Century Romance and Gothic Writers*. London: Macmillan, 1982.

Wagenknecht, Edward. *Cavalcade of the American Novel*. New York: Holt, Rinehart and Winston, 1952.

———. "The World and Mary Johnston." *Sewanee Review*, 44 (April–June 1936), 188–206.

Welter, Barbara. "The Cult of True Womanhood." *American Quarterly*, 18 (Summer 1966), 151–74.

West, Katharine. *Chapter of Governesses: A Study of the Governess in English Fiction 1800–1949*. London: Cohen and West, 1949.

Whitney, Phyllis A. "Writing the Gothic Novel." *Writer*, 80 (February 1967), 9–13, 42–43.

Wright, Lyle H. *American Fiction 1774–1850*. San Marino, Calif.: Huntington Library, 1939.

———. *American Fiction 1774–1900*. Louisville, Ky.: Lost Cause Press, 1970.

8.

Historical Fiction

R. GORDON KELLY

Any consideration of historical fiction begins with the troublesome matter of definition. What is a historical novel? Sir Walter Scott, whose Waverly novels effectively established a model adhered to by writers for nearly a century afterward, was less dogmatic on the subject than some of his successors. In giving to *Waverly* the subtitle "It Is Sixty Years Past," Scott implied a setting at least two generations in the past. In his preface to *Ivanhoe*, he offered few prescriptions for the historical novel, concentrating rather on defending his practice against anticipated charges of "polluting the well of history with modern inventions." Ernest E. Leisy, author of the principal study of American historical fiction, adopted the broadest of definitions— "A historical novel is a novel the action of which is laid in an earlier time"— and reduced Scott's half century in the past to a generation, "so rapid are changes [in the United States]." And Avrom Fleishman, with Georg Lukács, one of the most theoretically oriented commentators on the historical novel, accepts essentially the same definition, adding only the specification that "real" historical persons be present in the story: "When life is seen in the context of history, we have a novel; when the novel's characters live in the same world with historical persons, we have a historical novel."[1] For the purposes of this essay, however, the broader definition is preferable in order to avoid excluding those costume historical romances that might not qualify under Fleishman's slightly more restrictive definition. Because it is with the *popular* historical novel that we shall be concerned in this essay, little attention is given to those classic works of American fiction—*The Scarlet Letter* or *The Red Badge of Courage*, for example—which a broad definition of historical fiction would otherwise warrant incuding.

HISTORIC OUTLINE

The historical novel has been a staple of American publishing since the first quarter of the nineteenth century, when the call for a national literature and an American Scott was explicit in Rufus Choate's oration "The Importance of Illustrating New England History by a Series of Romances like the Waverly Novels" (1810). The form was especially popular with readers in the 1820s and 1830s, again at the turn of the century, and in the 1930s and 1940s. With *The Spy* (1821), James Fenimore Cooper successfully demonstrated that Scott's methods could be applied to American materials. Dramatizing the fratricidal nature of the Revolution in his depiction of the Warren family's divided loyalties, Cooper laid the foundations for an international reputation and encouraged a host of imitators. So well-received were *The Spy* and *The Pilot* (1823) that Cooper projected a series of thirteen historical novels, one for each of the Revolutionary colonies, although he completed only one, *Lionel Lincoln* (1825). His subsequent historical fiction included *The Wept of Wishton-Wish* (1829), set during King Philip's War; *Wyandotte* (1843), set in western New York State during the Revolution; and *The Oak Openings* (1848), set in frontier Michigan during the War of 1812. He also wrote three novels with European settings in which he deliberately set out to show the differences between his and Scott's perceptions of the same things: eighteenth-century Venice (*The Bravo*, 1831); Germany on the eve of the Reformation (*The Heidenmauer*, 1832); and Switzerland in the early eighteenth century (*The Headsman*, 1883). Cooper's Leatherstocking novels are too well known to require description.

By the mid–1820s, "with Waverly galloping over hill and dale; the 'Spy' lurking in every closet; the mind everywhere supplied with 'Pioneers' on the land and soon to be with 'Pilots' on the deep," American writers were rushing to imitate Cooper.[2] Faced with the number of historical novels coming to market as early as 1824, a critic for the *North American Review* began a review of *The Wilderness, or Braddock's Time* on a note of asperity:

It has been a question seriously agitated among our cisatlantic literati, even at so late a period as since the publication of this journal [begun in 1815] whether America did or did not afford sufficient materials for a new and peculiar historical romance; yet now, so prolific are we in this species of production that the reader who keeps pace with the outpourings of the press . . . must have some industry and a great deal of patriotism.[3]

Among the most successful with the reading public were Southern romancers like William A. Caruthers in *The Cavaliers of Virginia* (1834) and John Pendleton Kennedy, who found in the Virginia planter an American analogue to Scott's English noble or Scottish laird in *Swallow Barn* (1832) and *Horse Shoe Robinson* (1835). The most prolific of Southern historical novelists was William Gilmore Simms, who drew judiciously on Scott and Cooper for structural elements and on his own early experience, as well as on research, for convincing detail in describing early colonial South Carolina in *The Yemassee* (1835), for example, a novel of Indian warfare that still repays reading for its treatment of the Yemassee Indians and their allies. In Simms's wake, John Esten Cooke continued to romanticize Southern life until well past mid-century, by which time the historical romance, increasingly out of fashion because of the rise of literary realism, became ever more hackneyed and conventionalized.

The three most popular historical novels published before the Civil War are instructive of the principal ways in which American writers made use of the past. Two of the novels exploited the nation's constitutive conflicts—warfare with the Indian and separation from the British. Robert Montgomery Bird dramatized the former in his bloody, widely read account of frontier revenge, *Nick of the Woods* (1837), while Judge Daniel P. Thompson's *The Green Mountain Boys* (1839) celebrated his forebears' struggle to defend their homes, first against land speculators and then against Burgoyne and his soldiers. The third best-selling historical romance of the antebellum period, Joseph Holt Ingraham's *The Prince of the House of David* (1855), depicted the chief episodes in the life of Jesus as seen by a young Jewish girl and demonstrated the profits to be made from tapping the populace's religious idealism, as romances of the Revolution had already amply demonstrated with regard to nationalism and patriotism.

The mid–1850s to the mid–1880s was a period of lessened popularity for historical fiction as a genre. The historical romance continued to attract readers, but the decades were without conspicuous best-selling historical novels. A number of works from the 1870s and 1880s were informed by realism and the increasing preoccupation with local color: for example, Edward Eggleston's *The Circuit Rider* (1874); Mary Hartwell Catherwood's novels of France's New World colonies such as *The Romance of Dollard* (1888); George Washington Cable's *Old Creole Days* (1879) and *The Grandissimes* (1880); and Harold Frederic's *In the Valley* (1890), a tale of the Mohawk Valley in the French and Indian War. By the mid–1890s, however, the historical romance was once more the reigning form of popular fiction. Frank Luther Mott, the principal historian of best sellers, claims that fully half of the best-selling fiction of the period 1894–1902 consisted of historical romances. The revival of the genre's popularity began quietly enough in 1880 with the publication of a religious novel set in Rome at the time of Christ, which was dismissed initially by reviewers as anachronistic. By

1896, however, a nationwide survey revealed that *Ben-Hur: A Tale of the Christ*, by the Civil War general Lew Wallace, was circulated more than any other book in eight out of ten libraries. Widely imitated (for example, Marie Corelli's *Barrabbas*, 1894; and Florence Kingsley's *Titus, A Comrade of the Cross*, 1894), *Ben-Hur* eventually appeared in editions that were authorized by the Holy See as well as retailed by Sears, Roebuck—an achievement probably without precedent in American publishing. Combining the historical values of Scott and the moral values of the genteel tradition, it has been credited with battering down the last vestiges of prejudice against fiction.[4] With this last resistance overcome, with Robert Louis Stevenson and Rudyard Kipling reviving the romance in England, and with patriotism in this country aroused by our adventuring in Cuba and the Philippines, the historical romance flourished and dominated popular fiction until the 1920s.

The stream of historical fiction flowed in several channels at the turn of the century. The commercial success of Anthony Hope's *The Prisoner of Zenda* (1894), set in the mythical Balkan kingdom of Ruritania, established a vogue for costume romance that lasted a decade and encouraged a number of American imitators, among the more successful of whom are Richard Harding Davis in *The Princess Aline* (1889) and Harold McGrath in *Arms and the Woman* (1899) and *The Puppet Crown* (1901). However, the Ruritanian formula was most successfully exploited by George Barr McCutcheon, an obscure Indiana journalist, in *Graustark* (1901), a tale that combined love and adventure with the unabashed celebration of the American virtues of its clean-cut hero. The inordinate popularity of the pseudohistorical romance waned as sales of *Graustark* tailed off—McCutcheon's sequel *Beverly of Graustark* (1904) failed to surpass *Graustark*'s sales. The publication in 1907 of George Ade's parody of the Ruritanian romance, *The Slim Princess*, put an end to the popularity of that formula. In the same year, however, the publication of Elinor Glyn's *Three Weeks* presaged the form's survival in the "bosom and bravado" historical novels of the 1930s, by adding sex—three weeks of lovemaking in a Graustarkian setting—to the Hope-Mc-Cutcheon formula.

Romances with historical European settings, as opposed to the misty midregions of Ruritania, were also popular with American readers at the turn of the century. F. Marion Crawford wrote more than forty novels with European settings, for example, *Via Crucis* (1898) and *In the Palace of the King* (1900); S. Weir Mitchell's *The Adventures of François* (1898) was set during the French Revolution; Robert Chambers's *Ashes of Empire* (1898) was based on the Franco-Prussian War; and Charles Major's *When Knighthood Was in Flower* (1898) told in archaic language of Mary Tudor's love for a man who was her social inferior. All were best sellers and were more credible historical fiction than the Ruritanian romances.

American settings predominated, however, and among the writers who both rode the crest of the historical romance's popularity and distinguished themselves somewhat from the mass of journeymen writers on the basis of their narrative skill and historical knowledge were S. Weir Mitchell, Paul Leicester Ford, Winston Churchill, Mary Johnston, and Maurice Thompson, author of the very popular tale of the Revolution in the Old Northwest, *Alice of Old Vincennes* (1900). Mitchell's revolutionary war tale of a free or fighting Quaker, *Hugh Wynne* (1898), was not only a commercial success but also an influential model for writers seeking psychological realism. Paul Leicester Ford brought the knowledge and research skills of a trained historian to his writings of *Janice Meredith* (1899), a tale of the Revolution set in New Jersey.

Winston Churchill won acclaim for three novels especially: *Richard Carvel* (1899), a story of the Revolution, in which the Annapolis-trained Churchill presented a virtuoso description of the battle between John Paul Jones's *Bonhomme Richard* and the British man-of-war *Serapis; The Crisis* (1901), in which Churchill portrayed the bitter division of feeling in Missouri, particularly in St. Louis, before and during the Civil War; and *The Crossing* (1904), a story of George Rogers Clark's campaign in the Northwest Territory during the Revolution.

Mary Johnston, the daughter of a Confederate officer, wrote more than twenty historical novels mostly set in the South during the Revolution or the Civil War. Beginning her career with *The Prisoners of Hope* (1898), she hit her stride in *To Have and To Hold*, a best seller in 1900. In *The Long Roll* (1911) and in *Cease Firing* (1912), she traced the course of the Civil War with meticulous research and evident Southern sympathies.

So great was the popularity of historical fiction that a number of writers whose earlier works were in a different vein temporarily joined the ranks of historical novelists. Mary E. Wilkins Freeman's *The Heart's Highway* appeared in 1900, the year that saw the publication, too, of Edward Bellamy's *The Duke of Stockbridge*, a story of Shays's Rebellion that had appeared as a magazine serial in 1879. The following year saw the publication of Sarah Orne Jewett's *The Tory Lover*. Frank Stockton's *Kate Bonnet* was published in 1902.

By 1905, the extraordinary popular appeal of the historical novel was waning and did not really revive until the 1930s, when enthusiasm for Hervey Allen's sprawling tale of the Napoleonic era, *Anthony Adverse* (1933), proved to be a prelude to the unprecedented popularity of Margaret Mitchell's *Gone with the Wind* (1936). Nevertheless, interest in the historical novel had increased in the wake of World War I, and the 1920s saw the publication of a number of notable historical novels: James Boyd's *Drums* (1925) and *Marching On* (1928), which dealt with the Revolution and Civil War respectively and were informed by a soldier's knowledge of military tactics; Walter D. Edmonds's *Rome Haul* (1929), a painstakingly accurate portrayal of life along the Erie Canal in its heyday; and Edna Ferber's *Cimarron* (1930).

The Revolution and the Civil War, pioneer life, and the opening of the West would continue to furnish historical novelists with their staple subjects.

A new note in the historical fiction of the 1930s was the blend of scrupulous historical research and unconventional interpretation of men and events, exemplified in the work of Kenneth Roberts, who produced a half-dozen well-crafted, exciting novels during the decade. In *Arundel* (1930), Roberts's hero is none other than tradition's archtraitor Benedict Arnold; and in *Oliver Wiswell* (1940), Roberts presented the Revolution from the loyalist point of view. Even more revisionist in orientation was the work of Howard Fast, whose *The Last Frontier* (1941) was an indictment of the Indian Wars of the 1870s, and whose *The American* presented a defense of John Peter Altgeld, the Illinois governor maligned for his pardon of the convicted Haymarket anarchists. Fast's special interest, however, was the Revolution, which he explored in five novels: *Two Valleys* (1933), *Conceived in Liberty* (1939), *The Unvanquished* (1942), *Citizen Tom Paine* (1943), and *The Proud and the Free* (1950).

Fiction of the flashing rapier and heaving bosom school also enjoyed a considerable measure of popularity during the 1940s, paced by such commercial successes as Kathleen Winsor's *Forever Amber* (1944), a lineal descendant of Elinor Glyn's pioneering *Three Weeks*; by Thomas Costain's costume pieces such as *The Black Rose* (1945) and *The Silver Chalice* (1952); and by the indefatigable Frank Yerby, whose *The Foxes of Harrow* (1946) was followed by twenty-two more novels, which have sold some twenty million copies to date.

Although the popularity of *Gone with the Wind* has not been matched by any other subsequent historical novel, that fact should not obscure the considerable popularity of the form down to the present day. According to Russel B. Nye, at least one historical novel has reached the best-seller lists every year since 1931, and he estimates that 10 percent of all books published in paperback today may be considered historical fiction.[5] The extraordinary popularity of John Jakes's multivolume saga of an American family, beginning with *The Bastard* (1976), offers convincing proof that *mutatis mutandis* the spirit of nationalism that Cooper and his contemporaries so successfully exploited is alive and well.

By 1986, *The Kent Family Chronicles*, in eight volumes, had sold more than thirty-six million copies, and television adaptations of such works as *The Seekers* (1983) and *North and South* (1982) had extended Jakes's audience and popularity. Testifying to the undiminished popularity of the historical romance, new practitioners of the form have recently appeared: Laurie McBain, whose paperback originals for Avon have sold in the millions; Parris Afton Bonds, whose contributions to the Silhouette Intimate Moments series are set in the American Southwest; and Anne Carsley.

With the publication of *Lincoln* in 1984 and *Empire* in 1987, Gore Vidal has established himself as the foremost historical novelist of American politics currently writing, but other prominent literary figures have recently produced notable historical novels: e.g., William Styron, *Sophie's Choice* (1979), and Norman Mailer, *Ancient Evenings* (1983). James Michener chronicled 500 years of South African history in *The Covenant* (1981), and Mary Lee Settle received a National Book Award in 1978 for *Blood Tie*. And throughout the last ten years, there has been a steady stream of well-crafted historical novels by such writers as George Garrett, *The Succession* (1983); Jane Gilmore Rushing, *Covenant of Grace* (1982), based on the life of Anne Hutchinson; Thomas Fleming, *Spoils of War* (1985), which deals with the aftermath of the 1876 presidential election; and Nora Lofts, *Anne Boleyn* (1979), an alternate Literary Guild selection. From all appearances, the historical novel continues to hold its own in the 1980s.

REFERENCE WORKS

There is no general agreement over where the boundaries of historical fiction should be drawn. An indispensable guide to the problems of definition and categorization is Joseph W. Turner, "The Kinds of Historical Fiction: An Essay in Definition and Methodology." Turner's proposal for a taxonomy of historical novels is informed by a thorough knowledge of the controversy. Harry E. Shaw's "An Approach to the Historical Novel," the introduction to his study of Scott, *The Forms of Historical Fiction*, complements Turner. Also valuable is Cushing Strout's *The Veracious Imagination*, especially the chapter "Hazards of the Border Country," which explores the relationship between history and historical fiction. Despite the lack of agreement over the nature of historical fiction, a number of bibliographies, based on varying definitions, offer guidance to the researcher, although there exists no truly comprehensive bibliography of historical fiction by American authors.

Dickinson's American Historical Fiction by Virginia Brokaw Gerhardstein (formerly *American Historical Fiction* by A. T. Dickinson, Jr.), now in its fifth edition, lists and briefly annotates over 3,000 titles but includes only novels set in the United States and published since 1917. An extensive subject index as well as an author-title index makes *American Historical Fiction* an indispensable guide within the limitations noted earlier. *Dickinson's* is best supplemented by reference to Leisy's standard study discussed below, *The American Historical Novel*, to which is appended a selective list of historical novels not treated in his text, and by reference to Otis W. Coan and Richard G. Lillard's *America in Fiction*, now in its fifth edition, an annotated list, primarily of novels, organized under regional and topical headings: the frontier, farm and village, politics, and so on. Like many other compilers, Coan and Lillard invoke minimum standards of literary excellence and so exclude popular but "unenduring" writers (F. Marion Crawford, Frank

Yerby, and others) who are of particular interest to cultural historians and students of popular culture.

A Guide to Historical Fiction, in its tenth edition, compiled now by Leonard B. Irwin following the death of its originator, Hannah Logasa, includes historical novels set abroad, but the list is designed primarily to identify relatively "good" books, published primarily since 1940, "for the use of schools, libraries, and the general reader." *World Historical Fiction Guide* by Daniel D. McGarry and Sarah Harriman White is a selective guide to historical novels by American and European authors published before 1900 and organized broadly by period and geographical area, with alphabetical listing by author within each subdivision. Inclusion in the *Guide* is based on literary criteria that discriminate against popular historical fiction.

Brief but helpful checklists of historical fiction can be found in Howard Mumford Jones and Richard M. Ludwig's well-known *Guide to American Literature and Its Backgrounds Since 1890* and in the original edition of the *Harvard Guide to American History* by Oscar Handlin and others, which also includes a compressed but thoughtful discussion on the scholarly uses of historical fiction. Older bibliographies that may still be profitably consulted on occasion include Jonathan Nield's *A Guide to the Best Historical Novels and Tales*, fifth edition, which is heavily weighted toward British historical fiction but which includes the most extensive bibliography in print of commentary on historical fiction for the period 1890–1929; Reverend James R. Kaye's *Historical Fiction Chronologically and Historically Related*; Ernest A. Baker's *A Guide to Historical Fiction*, which like Nield's is heavily British but which lists some juvenile historical fiction that more recent compilers ignore; and William M. Griswold's *A Descriptive List of Novels and Tales Dealing with the History of North America*.

Specialized bibliographies of historical fiction include the list of over 500 Civil War novels published before 1950 appended to Robert A. Lively's excellent study, *Fiction Fights the Civil War*; Rebecca W. Smith's "Catalogue of the Chief Novels and Short Stories . . . Dealing with the Civil War and Its Effects, 1861–1899"; Harold U. Ribalow's selective bibliography "Historical Fiction on Jewish Themes"; and checklists of writings by and about Kenneth Roberts by George Albert and Ruth Stemple.

RESEARCH COLLECTIONS

Despite the popularity of historical fiction and its long history as a staple of the American publishing industry, libraries appear to have made little effort to establish extensive, broadly based research collections of historical novels. In addition, few private collectors appear to have interested themselves in the form, in contrast to the intense interest shown in, and the significance of private collections of, such other popular forms as the detective novel, the comic book, and literature for children. The Wilmer

Collection of Civil War novels at the University of North Carolina, Chapel Hill, the basis for Lively's *Fiction Fights the Civil War*, testifies to the idiosyncratic enthusiasm of one collector, Richard H. Wilmer, Jr. Consisting of over one hundred titles when it was given to the library in 1946, the Wilmer Collection has been systematically augmented over the years. A more broadly based collection, emphasizing American historical fiction, is the University of Pittsburgh's Hervey Allen Collection, numbering some 2,000 volumes. A number of more specialized collections devoted to particular authors are relevant to the study of popular historical fiction. Among these are collections of materials relating to James Lane Allen in the Margaret I. King Library, University of Kentucky; Winston Churchill in the Dartmouth College Library; Mary Johnston in the University of Virginia Library; John Pendleton Kennedy at the Peabody Institute of the City of Baltimore, a collection described by Lloyd Griffin in "The John Pendleton Kennedy Manuscripts"; George Barr McCutcheon and Charles Major, both of whose literary manuscripts are in the Purdue University Library, the latter collection described by W. M. Hepburn in "The Charles Major Manuscripts in the Purdue University Libraries"; F. Van Wyck Mason in the Houghton Library, Harvard University; S. Weir Mitchell in the University of Pennsylvania Library; Kenneth Roberts in the Library of Congress as well as in the library of Phillips Exeter Academy; and William Gilmore Simms at the University of South Carolina, a collection described by John R. Welsh in "The Charles Carroll Simms Collection."

HISTORY AND CRITICISM

There are few major studies of the historical novel as a form, and the best of these—combining theoretical sophistication, substantial scholarship, and critical acumen—have tended, until recently, to be European or British. Still a readable essay, and a good place to begin thinking about the issues raised by historical fiction, is Herbert Butterfield's *The Historical Novel* (1924). Although Butterfield treats the British historical novel, and primarily the great Victorian romancers, his discussion of the relationship between history as a scholarly endeavor and history in and through fiction, as well as his efforts to formulate an appropriate critical approach to the historical novel, deserve attention. The most formidable history and criticism of the genre remains Georg Lukács's *The Historical Novel*. Written in 1936, it was translated into Russian and published in Moscow the following year, but was not available in an English translation in the United States until 1963. Lukács has had little discernible influence on American students of the historical novel. Cooper, the only American novelist that he considers, receives only two pages of discussion; but Lukács's erudition and theoretical framework make *The Historical Novel* an indispensable work. A more recent study, one designed in part to correct Lukács's picture of English historical fiction, is Avrom Fleishman's *The English Historical Novel: Walter Scott to Virginia Woolf.* Fleishman prefaces the substantive chapters of his study with a controversial discussion of the problems inherent in formulating a critical theory of historical fiction. In *The Forms of Historical Fiction: Sir Walter Scott and His Successors*, Harry E. Shaw proposes an alternative approach to those of Butterfield, Fleishman, and Lukács, insisting that the nature of historical fiction is inherently problematic and distinct from "standard" fiction. Shaw does not analyze any American historical novel, but his detailed examination of Scott merits attention.

The principal study of American historical fiction, Ernest E. Leisy's *The American Historical Novel*, was preceded by several highly selective discussions. Arthur Hobson Quinn, in *American Fiction*, devotes the better part of a chapter to the "romance of history" in the last two decades of the nineteenth century and examines the historical novels of F. Marion Crawford and S. Weir Mitchell in his chapters on those popular authors. In *Cavalcade of the American Novel*, Edward Wagenknecht describes the revival of historical fiction in the 1930s; Alexander Cowie devotes a chapter in *The Rise of the American Novel* to a discussion of Cooper and the historical romance; and Carl Van Doren discusses the development of the historical romance in two chapters of *The American Novel*. Nevertheless, Leisy was substantially correct when he claimed in 1950 that *The American Historical Novel* was the first comprehensive treatment of the popular, but greatly neglected, form of American fiction. Leisy organized his work by historical period—colonial America, the Revolution, the westward movement—arguing that this arrangement would best serve his readership, "the intelligent lay reader who is interested in the nation's past and who wants a rather full account of the materials and methods of American historical fiction." Brief chapter introductions are followed by descriptions and evaluations of historical novels, grouped under topical headings and usually taken up in the order of publication. Leisy typically provides 300 to 500 words of plot summary and commentary on any given novel, a practice that leads inevitably to superficial description and dogmatic-seeming judgments: for example, John Esten Cooke's *Henry St. John* "blends history and romance better than its predecessor, but is too attenuated for the modern reader." A short introductory chapter, "History Vivified," and a cursory conclusion offer Leisy's generalizations about the development and cultural function of the form. As an extensively annotated catalog, *The American Historical Novel* retains its significance. No one in the thirty-five years since its publication has sought to bring it up to date or to build upon it. Harry B. Henderson's *Versions of the Past: The Historical Imagination in American Fiction* provides a corrective to Leisy's view that historical novels present merely "fictionalized" history and so are best categorized in terms of the events they portray. Henderson concentrates his attention on a select group of classic American novels, proposing "to treat *Satanstoe, The Scarlet Letter,*

Billy Budd, A Connecticut Yankee in King Arthur's Court, The Red Badge of Courage and *Absalom! Absalom!* as though they belonged in significant respects to the same literary category," namely historical fiction, in order "to create an appreciation of the self-awareness and complexity of the historical imagination of American writers."

Adopting a strategy reminiscent of such critics as Vernon L. Parrington, Philip Rahv, and others, Henderson posits two structures of the historical imagination in the nineteenth century—two "theories of social representation" implicit in the work—on the one hand, of the "progressive" historians George Bancroft and John L. Motley and, on the other, the "holistic" historians William H. Prescott and Francis Parkman. By "progressive" Henderson means to designate "the historian's ruling belief that the historical treatment of a subject should be constantly informed by the notion of historical progress and improvement in human affairs." "Holistic" historians, by contrast, "were less interested in selecting those social institutions which might most clearly illustrate the theme of Progress than they were in creating an illusion of a whole civilization or culture, in which each institution or characteristic of a society might be seen as integral to the total culture." Henderson's close reading of classic American texts is richer and more exciting than these two ideal types might suggest, however; and his views on the relationships between fiction and history can be usefully contrasted to those of David Levin's *In Defense of Historical Literature*.

The history of the popular historical novel remains to be written, but Frank Luther Mott, in *Golden Multitudes*, identifies and describes best-selling historical novels in the chapters "History for the Millions, 1830–1870" and "The Romantic Parade." Scattered references to popular historical fiction can be found in James D. Hart's engaging work *The Popular Book*, and Russel Nye touches briefly on the genre in *The Unembarrassed Muse*.

The Civil War has been the inspiration for more historical novelists than any other event in the nation's history, with the possible exception of the Revolution; and the Civil War novel and the effect of the war on American letters have been the subject of excellent studies. A good place to begin considering the subgenre of Civil War fiction is Bernard DeVoto's compressed but intelligent essay "Fiction Fights the Civil War," the title, too, of Robert A. Lively's superb examination of 512 Civil War novels. Lively, a historian who taught at Vanderbilt and Wisconsin before moving to Princeton, writes incisively and provocatively on the social function of Civil War fiction and attempts to answer what he calls "the simplest questions": who wrote Civil War fiction and from what perspectives; what shifts of interest and interpretation have occurred; and what historical methods were employed by the novelists. A brief final chapter, "The Uses of Fictional History," is a concise, informed discussion of the value of historical novels. Three subsequent articles offer useful footnotes to Lively's study: Sam Pickering's "A Boy's Own War," which considers the juvenile fiction of Horatio

Alger, Harry Castelmon (Charles A. Fosdick), and Oliver Optic (William Taylor Adams); Robert L. Bloom's "The Battle of Gettysburg in Fiction," which assesses the historical accuracy of novelists' accounts of that battle; and Richard B. Harwell's "Gone with Miss Ravanel's Courage; or Bugles Blow So Red: A Note on the Civil War Novel."

Daniel Aaron's *The Unwritten War: American Writers and the Civil War* contains only limited reference to the Civil War novels analyzed by Lively. Aaron seeks to reveal how the war "more than casually touched and engaged a number of writers" although, paradoxically, with a few notable exceptions, writers have said little that was very revealing about the meaning of the conflict, in Aaron's view.

Although the American Revolution has long been the subject of historical novels, no study analogous to Lively's has been written until recently. Michael Kammen's *A Season of Youth: The American Revolution and the Historical Imagination* explores the ways in which historical novelists since Cooper have conceptualized the nation's rite of passage and the degree to which historical novelists anticipated professional historians in their emphasis on various aspects and interpretations of the war. An acute, but sharply limited, discussion of fiction on the Revolution is Donald A. Ringe's "The American Revolution in American Romance," which compares the work of Cooper, Kennedy, and Simms with that of their now less well-known contemporary John Neal. Complementing and extending Kammen's work is Joel Taxel's probing essay "The American Revolution in Children's Fiction," which analyzes thirty-two novels recommended for children, published between 1899 and 1976. By looking closely at both form and content, Taxel sought to isolate implicit as well as explicit interpretations of the Revolution as presented in juvenile trade books. A number of other articles that analyze the Revolution as depicted in the writings of individual authors are cited below, in the section that discusses scholarship on selected popular historical novelists.

Surprisingly little attention has been given to historical novels set in Puritan New England. Adelheid Staehelin-Wackernagel's *The Puritan Settler in the American Novel Before the Civil War* traces changing attitudes toward the Puritans; describes the treatment of various character types such as the magistrate, the minister, the merchant, and women; and concludes with a discussion of Puritan "features"—piety and resignation, fanaticism and bigotry, intolerance and persecution. The persisting figure of the Virginia cavalier is traced by Ritchie Devon Watson, *The Cavalier in Virginia Fiction*, through the historical novels of George Tucker, John Pendleton Kennedy, William Alexander Caruthers, John Esten Cooke, Thomas Nelson Page, Mary Johnston, James Branch Cabell, Ellen Glasgow, William Styron, and Garrett Epps. The dilemma faced by the Virginia writer, Watson argues, has always been how to translate the aristocratic ideal of the Virginia gentleman "into a character capable of living in harmony with the nation's fundamental political and social ideals."

STUDIES OF POPULAR HISTORICAL NOVELISTS

Given the lack of both scholarly and critical interest in popular historical fiction, it is not surprising that relatively little substantial work has been done on individual practitioners of the form, particularly those noted primarily for the popularity of their work with the reading public rather than for their literary skill: a devalued product does not inspire interest in the producer. With a few notable exceptions, commentary on authors of historical novels runs in well-worn, conventional channels: assessments of the historical accuracy of a work, analyses of an author's use of sources, or his interpretations of the events or era that forms the setting for a work. Following is a representative cross-section of commentary on authors of popular historical fiction, most of it in the form of essays in professional literary and historical periodicals. Hervey Allen's *Anthony Adverse* provoked charges of plagiarism in 1933 from some critics, charges that Allen himself answered in an article cited elsewhere in this essay. Allen's research methods are analyzed by H. K. Siebeneck in "Hervey Allen and Arthur St. Clair." In "George Washington Cable and the Historical Romance," R. B. Eaton argues that the difficulties many critics have had in coming to terms with Cable's *The Grandissimes* stem from his efforts to assimilate two distinct genres in the work. Cable's work as an "historical romancer" is surveyed in a chapter of Louis D. Rubin's authoritative study, *George Washington Cable: The Life and Times of a Southern Heretic.*

Winston Churchill, the most popular American novelist in the first fifteen years of this century, is treated by Robert W. Schneider in *Novelist to a Generation: The Life and Thought of Winston Churchill.* "Winston Churchill: A Study in the Popular Novel" is an incisive essay by Richard Hofstadter and Beatrice Hofstadter, who see Churchill absorbed with the split between business values and human values at the turn of the century although the full weight of this concern is felt more in his political novels, for example, *Coniston* (1906), than in the historical fiction for which he is better known.

Commentary on James Fenimore Cooper, who was acclaimed the American Scott by his admiring contemporaries, is very extensive; and there is no need here to reproduce citations that are readily accessible elsewhere—for example, in James F. Beard's comprehensive and judicious bibliographical essay on Cooper in *Fifteen American Authors Before 1900.* Two articles of particular relevance, owing to the renewed interest in the depiction of the Revolution by historical novelists, are James F. Beard's "Cooper and the Revolutionary Mythos" and H. D. Peck's "Repossession of America: The Revolution in Cooper's Trilogy of Nautical Romances" (*The Pilot,*

The Red Rover, and *The Water Witch*). Peck argues that the novels reveal not only the pscyhological basis out of which Cooper's later conservatism grew; they also show his successful solution to the problem that history posed for his art. William P. Kelly's study of Cooper's Leatherstocking novels, *Plotting America's Past*, is an effort to rescue their "historiographic dimension," which Kelly argues has been obscured by a series of influential mythic readings.

The work of Walter D. Edmonds, best known for *Rome Haul* and *Drums Along the Mohawk*, both carefully researched romances set in his native New York State, is briefly and approvingly surveyed by Dayton Kohler in "Walter D. Edmonds: Regional Historian." Edmonds's description of his own working habits and preparation for writing historical fiction is cited below. The historical fiction of Mary Johnston is sensitively discussed by Edward Wagenknecht in "The World and Mary Johnston" as well as in *Cavalcade of the American Novel*. In " 'As Much History as . . . Invention' " Charles H. Bohner assesses John Pendleton Kennedy's use of surviving historical documents in writing *Rob of the Bowl*. William S. Osborne takes up the same issue in another Kennedy novel, "John Pendleton Kennedy's *Horse Shoe Robinson*: A Novel with 'the Utmost Historical Accuracy.' "

As might be expected, Margaret Mitchell's *Gone with the Wind* has received a great deal of attention. In "Tara Twenty Years After," Robert Y. Drake, Jr., tries valiantly to encourage critics to take a second, more careful, look at the novel as "an epic treatment of the fall of a traditional society." The general critical estimate of the novel, however, is more nearly exemplified in Floyd C. Watkins's "*Gone with the Wind* as Vulgar Literature," which condemns Mitchell's novel for, among other things, its oversimplified regionalism, its prudery, and its false picture of the South and of human nature. J. W. Mathews's "The Civil War of 1936: *Gone with the Wind* and *Absalom! Absalom!*" contrasts sales figures and reviews without coming to any very interesting conclusions. Dawson Gaillard's "*Gone with the Wind* as Bildungsroman, or Why Did Rhett Butler Really Leave Scarlett O'Hara?" discusses the heroine as a "new woman" at odds with the older social type of the Southern lady. Finis Farr's *Margaret Mitchell of Atlanta* does not probe sufficiently into the novel's popularity or into Mitchell's relationship with her publisher, among other aspects. Mitchell's correspondence concerning the novel, from its publication in 1936 to her death in 1949, was published in 1976 as *Margaret Mitchell's "Gone with the Wind" Letters*, edited by Richard Harwell.

Commentary on Philadelphia's physician–novelist S. Weir Mitchell has generally ignored his historic fiction to concentrate on his use of psychological themes, but in "Weir Mitchell and the Genteel Romance," Kelly Griffith, Jr., provides a useful account of the tradition of historical romance at the turn of the century and assesses Mitchell's contribution to it.

Conrad Richter has received disproportionately more attention than other popular twentieth-century historical novelists. In addition to the Twayne series study, *Conrad Richter* by Edwin W. Gaston, Jr., there is *Conrad Richter's America* by Marvin J. LaHood, which groups Richter's novels in terms of their geographical setting, and *Conrad Richter's Ohio Trilogy: Its Ideas, Themes, and Relationships to Literary Tradition* by Clifford D. Edwards.

A useful introduction to the work of Kenneth Roberts is the collection of essays "For the Quinquennial of Kenneth Roberts," by A. H. Gibbs and others. A brief, but judicious, assessment of Roberts's efforts to blend historical "fact" and entertaining "fiction" is Grace Lee Nute's review of *Northwest Passage*.

One of the more impressive essays on historical fiction is M. D. Bell's "History and Romance Convention in Catharine Sedgwick's *Hope Leslie*." Bell moves away from a simplistic concern with Sedgwick's fidelity to historical "fact" to considerations of how she shaped her material to the existing conventions of romance and what she sought to communicate in and through those conventions.

A good deal of attention has been focused on William Gilmore Simms in the last twenty years, as scholars have sought to legitimate his canonical status. C. Hugh Holman, whose unpublished dissertation deals with Simms's theory and practice of historical fiction, provides a starting point for a consideration of Simms's revolutionary war fiction in "William Gilmore Simms' Picture of the Revolution as a Civil Conflict." Holman's essay can be supplemented by R. J. Bresnahan's "William Gilmore Simms' Revolutionary War: A Romantic View of Southern History," which contains some interesting material on the author's changing ideas about his region's past, to the interpretation of which Simms contributed extensively both in fiction and in historical writing. Simms scholarship up to 1973 is comprehensively described and evaluated by Charles S. Watson in "William Gilmore Simms: An Essay in Bibliography."

Despite the influence of *Ben-Hur* in the late nineteenth century, interest in that novel and in Wallace has been minimal. Brief references in Mott aside, the best source of information is Irving McKee's biography *"Ben-Hur" Wallace: The Life of General Lew Wallace*.

The work of William Ware, a Unitarian minister and the author of three widely read antebellum historical novels, is analyzed by Curtis Dahl in "New England Unitarianism in Fictional Antiquity: The Romances of William Ware." Like M. D. Bell's essay on *Hope Leslie* cited above, Dahl's is a stimulating exploration of the ideological uses to which historical fiction has been put, in this case in the service of liberal religious opinion.

The novels of Frank Yerby, one of the most consistently successful of contemporary popular historical romancers since the publication of *The Foxes of Harrow*, were long ignored. Recently, however, critics became interested in how Yerby, an expatriate black American, was depicting race relations in his fiction, the audience for which was largely white. Jack B.

Moore's "The Guilt of the Victim: Racial Themes in Some Frank Yerby Novels" challenges earlier critics, contending that Yerby "in no way turned his back upon his race" after his first popular success. Another view of Yerby's work is provided by Darwin Turner in "Frank Yerby as De-bunker," which discusses Yerby's efforts to undermine historical myths, the persistence of which, Turner argues, can be traced to historical novelists less critical than Yerby.

Authors of historical fiction have often felt obliged to explain or defend the significance and value of their works, especially during the last seventy-five years, a period generally of unremitting critical contempt for the genre. Scott's preface to *Ivanhoe*, which sets out a view of historical fiction that was influential for over a century, is still a valuable place to begin and invites comparison with Simms's preface in his revised version of *The Yemassee*. F. Marion Crawford's lengthier discussion of historical fiction in *The Novel—What It Is* also deserves mention. In *A Certain Measure: An Interpretation of Prose Fiction*, Ellen Glasgow describes her intentions and methods in writing *The Battleground* (1902), the first in a series of novels designed to compose a social history of Virginia from 1850. A particularly thoughtful and reflective piece on the writing of historical fiction is G. P. Garrett's "Dreaming with Adam: Notes on Imaginary History," in which he discusses the develop-ment of his ideas for *Death of the Fox: An Imaginary Version of the Last Days of Sir Walter Raleigh* (1971). Garrett concludes: "I came to cling to the notion that the proper subject and theme of historical fiction is what it is—the human imagination in action, itself dramatized as it struggles with surfaces, builds structures with facts, deals out and plays a hand of ideas, and most of all, by conceiving of the imagination of others, wrestles with the angel . . . of the imagination."

A more conventional point of view, emphasizing the historical novelist's dependence on extensive research, is expressed by Hervey Allen in "The Sources of *Anthony Adverse*," a spirited reply to the critics who accused him of plagiarism; by Walter D. Edmonds in "How You Begin a Novel," a concise account of his research for *Drums Along the Mohawk*, his widely read tale of the Mohawk Valley of New York during the Revolution; in MacKinlay Kantor's dogmatic and defensive lecture "The Historical Novel," delivered at the Library of Congress; and by one of the masters of the swashbuckling romance, Rafael Sabatini, in "Historical Fiction," in which he discusses his writing as embodying three distinct approaches to the historical novel. Esther Forbes, who wrote widely acclaimed historical fiction for both adults and children, discusses her decision to write historical fiction in "Why Not the Past?" A. B. Guthrie addresses the same question in his essay "The Historical Novel." In "The Novel of Contemporary History," John R. Hersey discusses the clarifying function of fiction in modern life, listing and briefly describing the "valid motives" that presum-ably inform his own work.

Much of the discussion of historical fiction implies, when it does not overtly turn on, familiar oppositions that are rooted in common usage: fact and fiction, observation and imagination, real and unreal, truth and—what? Falsehood is perhaps too strong, but it comes near enough the mark, even today, reminding us of a residual common-sense skepticism concerning the truth claims of "fiction." Historical fiction invites the historian's scorn for playing fast and loose with the facts, even while literary critics denigrate it for its slavish subservience to the documentary record—"mere" fact. And both historian and critic have nothing but contempt for the costume romances—*Forever Amber* in a thousand guises—devoid of both historical accuracy and literary value that bulk so large in the history of the genre. In "The Views of the Great Critics on the Historical Novel," Ernest Bernbaum traces the Victorian critics' scorn for historical fiction to a naive empiricism, but his judicious essay and implicit warning failed to have any appreciable impact on the terms in which the genre tended to be discussed during the 1930s and 1940s, as the following citations make clear. Bernard DeVoto, for example, emphasized the novelist's obligation to historical fact in offering qualified approval to the changes that he perceived taking place in the best historical novels of the 1930s in "Fiction and the Everlasting *If.*" Edmund Fuller, himself a historical novelist, made much the same point in distinguishing "interpretive" novels (good) from "romantic" novels (bad) in "History and the Novelists." Orville Prescott, in the essays "Popularity" and "The Art of Historical Fiction" included in *In My Opinion*, is only slightly more complex, developing a fivefold categorization, the largest— and worst—group made up of novels based on superficial research and cheaply sensational plots, the smallest group composed of works that combine exhaustive research and a high order of literary skill. In essentially the same terms, Jay Williams claims in "History and Historical Novels" that the good historical novelist deserves to be recognized and valued as a synthesizer and illuminator of the past.

The publication in 1968 of William Styron's *The Confessions of Nat Turner* evoked a firestorm of criticism. All of the knotty problems associated with the interpretation and evaluation of historical fiction are on display in the controversy that ensued. Black writers were outraged by Styron's portrayal of Turner: "the Nat Turner created by William Styron has little resemblance to the Virginia slave insurrectionist who is a hero to his people," wrote John H. Clarke, in his introduction to *William Styron's Nat Turner: Ten Black Writers Respond*. The dimensions of the controversy can be explored in three essays conveniently collected in *The Achievement of William Styron*, edited by Robert K. Morris with Irving Malin: George Core, "*The Confessions of Nat Turner* and the Burden of the Past"; Ardner R. Cheshire, Jr., "The Recollective Structure of *The Confessions of Nat Turner*"; and Mary S. Strine, "*The Confessions of Nat Turner*: Styron's 'Meditation on History' as Rhetorical Act." J. R. Huffman defends Styron's portrait from charges that it reproduces the discredited thesis of Stanley Elkines or that Styron yields to Freudian reductionism: "Psychological Redefinition of William Styron's *The Confessions of Nat Turner.*" Noting that Styron's use of particular sources was ignored in the controversy, A. D. Casiato and J.L.W. West III analyze Styron's annotated copy of *The Southhampton Insurrection*, one of the novelist's principal historical sources. In "This Unquiet Dust: The Problem of History in Styron's *The Confessions of Nat Turner,*" J. M. Mellard examines *The Confessions* as a novel which both represents the consciousness of its subject and addresses the problem of historical knowledge. The value of the novel lies less in its (disputed) historical veracity than in its potential for creating awareness of a traumatic episode in the nation's past.

NOTES

1. Avrom Fleishman, *The English Historical Novel* (Baltimore: Johns Hopkins University Press, 1971), p. 4.

2. Lydia M. Child, *Hobomok, a Tale of Early Times,* quoted in Ernest E. Leisy, *The American Historical Novel* (Norman: University of Oklahoma Press, 1950).

3. *North American Review,* 19 (July 1824), 209.

4. James D. Hart, *The Popular Book* (New York: Oxford University Press, 1950), p. 184.

5. Russel B. Nye, *The Unembarrassed Muse* (New York: Dial Press, 1970), p. 46.

BIBLIOGRAPHY

Aaron, Daniel. *The Unwritten War: American Writers and the Civil War.* New York: Alfred A. Knopf, 1973.

Albert, George. "Bibliography of Kenneth Lewis Roberts." *Bulletin of Bibliography,* 17 (September and October 1942), 191–92, 218–19; 18 (January and February 1943), 13–15, 34–36.

Allen, Harvey. "The Sources of Anthony Adverse." *Saturday Review of Literature,* 10 (January 13, 1934), 401, 408–10.

Baker, Ernest A. *A Guide to Historical Fiction.* London: George Routledge, 1914.

Beard, James F. "Cooper and the Revolutionary Mythos." *Early American Literature,* 11 (Spring 1976), 84–104.

———. "James Fenimore Cooper." In *Fifteen American Authors Before 1900.* Edited by Robert A. Rees and Earl N. Herbert. Madison: University of Wisconsin Press, 1971.

Bell, M. D. "History and Romance Convention in Catharine Sedgwick's *Hope Leslie.*" *American Quarterly,* 22 (Summer 1970), 213–21.

Bernbaum, Ernest. "The Views of the Great Critics on the Historical Novel." *PMLA,* 41 (June 1926), 424–41.

Bloom, Robert L. "The Battle of Gettysburg in Fiction." *Pennsylvania History,* 43 (October 1976), 309–27.

Bohner, Charles H. " 'As Much History as . . . Invention': John P. Kennedy's *Rob of the Bowl.*" *William and Mary Quarterly,* 17 (July 1960), 329–40.

Bresnahan, R. J. "William Gilmore Simms' Revolutionary War: A Romantic View of Southern History." *Studies in Romanticism*, 15 (Fall 1976), 573–87.

Butterfield, Herbert. *The Historical Novel: An Essay*. Cambridge: Cambridge University Press, 1924.

Casiato, A. D., and J.L.W. West III. "William Styron and *The Southhampton Insurrection*." *American Literature*, 52 (January 1981), 564–77.

Clarke, John H., ed. *William Styron's Nat Turner: Ten Black Writers Respond*. Boston: Beacon Press, 1968.

Coan, Otis W., and Richard G. Lillard. *America in Fiction*. 5th ed. Palo Alto, Calif.: Pacific Books, 1967.

Cowie, Alexander. *The Rise of the American Novel*. New York: American Book, 1951.

Crawford, F. Marion. *The Novel—What It Is*. New York: Macmillan, 1893.

Dahl, Curtis. "New England Unitarianism in Fictional Antiquity: The Romances of William Ware." *New England Quarterly*, 48 (March 1975), 104–15.

DeVoto, Bernard. "Fiction and the Everlasting *If*: Notes on the Contemporary Historical Novel." *Harper's*, 177 (June 1938), 42–49.

———. "Fiction Fights the Civil War." *Saturday Review of Literature*, 17 (December 18, 1937), 3–4.

Drake, Robert Y., Jr. "Tara Twenty Years After." *Georgia Review*, 12 (Summer 1958), 142–50.

Eaton, R. B. "George Washington Cable and the Historical Romance." *Southern Literary Journal*, 8 (Fall 1975), 84–94.

Edmonds, Walter D. "How You Begin a Novel." *Atlantic Monthly*, 158 (August 1936), 189–92.

Edwards, Clifford D. *Conrad Richter's Ohio Trilogy: Its Ideas, Themes, and Relationship to Literary Tradition*. The Hague: Mouton, 1970.

Farr, Finis. *Margaret Mitchell of Atlanta: The Author of "Gone with the Wind."* New York: William Morrow, 1965.

Fleishman, Avrom. *The English Historical Novel: Walter Scott to Virginia Woolf*. Baltimore: Johns Hopkins University Press, 1971.

Forbes, Esther. "Why the Past?" In *What is a Book?* Edited by Dale Warren. Boston: Houghton Mifflin, 1935.

Fuller, Edmund. "History and the Novelists." *American Scholar*, 16 (Winter 1946–47), 113–24.

Gaillard, Dawson. "*Gone with the Wind* as Bildungsroman, or Why Did Rhett Butler Really Leave Scarlett O'Hara?" *Georgia Review*, 28 (Spring 1974), 9–18.

Garrett, G. P. "Dreaming with Adam: Notes on Imaginary History." In *New Directions in Literary History*. Edited by Ralph Cohen. Baltimore: Johns Hopkins University Press, 1974.

Gaston, Edwin W., Jr. *Conrad Richter*. New York: Twayne, 1965.

Gerhardstein, Virginia Brokaw. *Dickinson's American Historical Fiction*. Metuchen, N.J.: Scarecrow Press, 1986.

Gibbs, A. H. et al. "For the Quinquennial of Kenneth Roberts." *Colby Library Quarterly*, 6 (Summer 1962), 83–132.

Glasgow, Ellen. *A Certain Measure: An Interpretation of Prose Fiction*. New York: Harcourt Brace, 1943.

Griffin, Lloyd W. "The John Pendleton Kennedy Manuscripts." *Maryland Historical Magazine*, 48 (December 1953), 327–36.

Griffith, Kelly, Jr. "Weir Mitchell and the Genteel Romance." *American Literature*, 44 (May 1972), 247–61.

Griswold, William M. *A Descriptive List of Novels and Tales Dealing with the History of North America*. Cambridge, Mass.: Griswold, 1895.

Guthrie, A. B. "The Historical Novel." In *Western Writing*. Edited by G. W. Haslam. Albuquerque: University of New Mexico Press, 1974.

Handlin, Oscar et al., eds. *Harvard Guide to American History*. Cambridge, Mass.: Harvard University Press, 1954.

Hart, James D. *The Popular Book: A History of America's Literary Taste*. New York: Oxford University Press, 1950.

Harwell, Richard B. "Gone with Miss Ravenel's Courage; or Bugles Blow So Red: A Note on the Civil War Novel." *New England Quarterly*, 35 (June 1962), 253–61.

———, ed. *Margaret Mitchell's "Gone with the Wind" Letters, 1936–1949*. New York: Macmillan, 1976.

Henderson, Harry B. *Versions of the Past: The Historical Imagination in American Fiction*. New York: Oxford University Press, 1974.

Hepburn, W. M. "The Charles Major Manuscripts in the Purdue University Libraries." *Indiana Quarterly for Bookmen*, 2 (July 1946), 71–81.

Hersey, John R. "The Novel of Contemporary History." In *The Writer's Book*. Edited by H. R. Hull. New York: Harper, 1950.

Hofstadter, Richard, and Beatrice Hofstadter. "Winston Churchill: A Study in the Popular Novel." *American Quarterly*, 2 (Spring 1950), 12–28.

Holman, C. Hugh. "William Gilmore Simms' Picture of the Revolution as a Civil Conflict." *Journal of Southern History*, 15 (November 1949), 441–62.

———. "William Gilmore Simms' Theory and Practice of Historical Fiction." Ph.D. dissertation, University of North Carolina, 1950.

Huffman, J. R. "Psychological Redefinition of William Styron's *The Confessions of Nat Turner*." *Literary Review*, 24 (Winter 1981), 279–307.

Irwin, Leonard B., comp. *A Guide to Historical Fiction*. 10th ed. Brooklawn, N.J.: McKinley Publishing, 1971.

Jones, Howard Mumford, and Richard M. Ludwig. *Guide to American Literature and Its Backgrounds Since 1890*. 4th ed. Cambridge, Mass.: Harvard University Press, 1972.

Kammen, Michael. *A Season of Youth: The American Revolution and the Historical Imagination*. New York: Alfred A. Knopf, 1978.

Kantor, MacKinlay. *The Historical Novelist's Obligation to History*. Macon, Ga.: Wesley College, 1967.

———. "The Historical Novel." In *Literary Lectures Presented at the Library of Congress*. Washington, D.C.: Library of Congress, 1973.

Kaye, James R. *Historical Fiction Chronologically and Historically Related*. Chicago: Snowdon Publishing, 1920.

Kelly, William P. *Plotting America's Past: Fenimore Cooper and the Leatherstocking Tales*. Carbondale: Southern Illinois University Press, 1983.

Kohler, Dayton. "Walter D. Edmonds: Regional Historian." *English Journal*, 27 (January 1938), 1–11.

LaHood, Marvin J. *Conrad Richter's America*. The Hague: Mouton, 1975.

Leisy, Ernest E. *The American Historical Novel*. Norman: University of Oklahoma Press, 1950, 1962.

Levin, David. *In Defense of Historical Literature*. New York: Hill and Wang, 1957.

Lively, Robert A. *Fiction Fights the Civil War*. Chapel Hill: University of North Carolina Press, 1957.

Lukács, Georg. *The Historical Novel*. Translated by Hannah and Stanley Mitchell. Boston: Beacon, 1963.

McGarry, Daniel D., and Sarah Harriman White. *World Historical Fiction Guide*, 2d ed. Metuchen, N.J.: Scarecrow Press, 1973.

McKee, Irving. *"Ben-Hur" Wallace: The Life of General Lew Wallace*. Berkeley: University of California Press, 1947.

Major, Charles. *When Knighthood Was in Flower*. Indianapolis: Bobbs-Merrill, 1898.

Mathews, J. W. "The Civil War of 1936: *Gone with the Wind* and *Absalom! Absalom!*." *Georgia Review*, 21 (Winter 1967), 462–69.

Mellard, J. M. "This Unquiet Dust: The Problem of History in Styron's *The Confessions of Nat Turner*." *Mississippi Quarterly*, 36 (Fall 1983), 525–43.

Moore, Jack B. "The Guilt of the Victim: Racial Themes in Some Frank Yerby Novels." *Journal of Popular Culture*, 8 (Spring 1975), 746–56.

Morris, Robert K., with Irving Malin, eds. *The Achievement of William Styron*. Rev. ed. Athens: University of Georgia Press, 1981.

Mott, Frank Luther. *Golden Multitudes: The Story of Best Sellers in the United States*. New York: Macmillan, 1947.

Nield, Jonathan. *A Guide to the Best Historical Novels and Tales*. 5th ed. New York: Macmillan, 1929.

Nute, Grace Lee. "Northwest Passage." *Minnesota History*, 19 (March 1938), 76–78.

Nye, Russel B. *The Unembarrassed Muse: The Popular Arts in America*. New York: Dial Press, 1970.

Osborne, William S. "John Pendleton Kennedy's *Horse Shoe Robinson*: A Novel with 'the Utmost Historical Accuracy.' " *Maryland Historical Magazine*, 59 (September 1964), 286–96.

Peck, H. D. "A Repossession of America: The Revolution in Cooper's Trilogy of Nautical Romances." *Studies in Romanticism*, 15 (Fall 1976), 589–605.

Pickering, Sam. "A Boy's Own War." *New England Quarterly*, 48 (September 1975), 362–77.

Prescott, Orville. *In My Opinion*. Indianapolis: Bobbs-Merrill, 1952.

Quinn, Arthur Hobson. *American Fiction*. New York: Appleton-Century, 1936.

Ribalow, Harold U. "Historical Fiction on Jewish Themes: A Selected Bibliography." In *Jewish Book Annual*, 23 (1965–66), 63–39.

Ringe, Donald A. "The American Revolution in American Romance." *American Literature*, 49 (November 1977), 352–65.

Rubin, Louis D. *George Washington Cable: The Life and Times of a Southern Heretic*. New York: Pegasus, 1969.

Sabatini, Rafael. "Historical Fiction." In *What Is A Book?* Edited by Dale Warren. Boston: Houghton Mifflin, 1935.

Schneider, Robert W. *Novelist to a Generation: The Life and Thought of Winston Churchill*. Bowling Green, Ohio: Bowling Green State University Popular Press, 1976.

Scott, Walter. Preface to *Ivanhoe*. Philadelphia: M. Carey, 1820.

Shaw, Harry E. *The Forms of Historical Fiction: Sir Walter Scott and His Successors.* Ithaca, N.Y.: Cornell University Press, 1983.

Siebeneck, H. K. "Hervey Allen and Arthur St. Clair." *Western Pennsylvania History Magazine*, 30 (September 1947), 73–94.

Simms, William Gilmore. Preface to *The Yemassee*. Rev. ed. New York: Redfield, 1853.

Smith, Rebecca W. "Catalogue of the Chief Novels and Short Stories by American Authors Dealing with the Civil War and its Effects, 1861–1899." *Bulletin of Bibliography*, 16 (October 1939), 193–94; 17 (January-April 1940), 10–12, 33–35, 53–55, 73–75.

Staehelin-Wackernagel, Adelheid. *The Puritan Settler in the American Novel Before the Civil War.* Bern, Switzerland: Francke, 1961.

Stemple, Ruth. "Kenneth Roberts: A Supplementary Check-List." *Bulletin of Bibliography*, 22 (October 1959), 228–30.

Strout, Cushing. *The Veracious Imagination: Essays on American History, Literature and Biography.* Middletown, Conn.: Wesleyan University Press, 1981.

Taxel, Joel. "The American Revolution in Children's Fiction: An Analysis of Historical Meaning and Narrative Structure." *Curriculum Inquiry*, 14 (Spring 1984), 7–55.

Turner, Darwin. "Frank Yerby as Debunker." *Massachusetts Review*, 9 (Summer 1968), 569–77.

Turner, Joseph W. "The Kinds of Historical Fiction: An Essay in Definition and Methodology." *Genre*, 12 (Fall 1979), 333–55.

Van Doren, Carl. *The American Novel, 1789–1959.* Rev. ed. New York: Macmillan, 1940.

Wagenknecht, Edward. *Cavalcade of the American Novel.* New York: Holt, Rinehart and Winston, 1952.

———. "The World and Mary Johnston." *Sewanee Review*, 44 (April-June 1936), 188–206.

Watkins, Floyd C. "*Gone with the Wind* as Vulgar Literature." *Southern Literary Journal*, 2 (Spring 1970), 86–103.

Watson, Charles S. "William Gilmore Simms: An Essay in Bibliography." *Resources for American Literary Study*, 3 (Spring 1973), 3–26.

Watson, Ritchie Devon. *The Cavalier in Virginia Fiction.* Baton Rouge: Louisiana State University Press, 1985.

Welsh, John R. "The Charles Carroll Simms Collection." *South Atlantic Bulletin*, 31 (November 1966), 1–3.

Williams, Jay. "History and Historical Novels." *American Scholar*, 26 (Winter 1956–57), 67–74.

9

Popular History and Biography

JOHN SCOTT WILSON

School windows in February decorated with hatchets and cherry trees cut from paper, the still expanding numbers of people in cemeteries and archives looking for their "roots"—these are indications of the impact of popular history and biography in American culture. The story of George Washington and the cherry tree is a part of our folklore, invented for the first biography of the Father of Our Country. Alex Haley's *Roots*, both in its printed form and in the overwhelmingly successful television presentation in 1978, demonstrates the appeal of history written for and to the general public rather than professional historians.

Popular history and biography are those works written for a general audience, either by an amateur, a professional writer, or even a professional historian. These works tend to focus on traditional subjects, attempt a dramatic style of writing, are presented as a narrative, and usually have little scholarly apparatus, such as footnotes. Such works have circulated from the beginning of our history, yet few scholars have examined them and their impact on our culture.

Professional historians are familiar with and study the development of historical writings, but that study tends to focus on scholarly work, books designed for the profession. Books written for the mass audience are usually ignored, even when written by members of the profession. Popular history is dismissed as not being serious. That Parson Weems invented the story of the cherry tree and that Haley's book is filled with invented material, what he calls "factions," history as it should have been even if it did not happen, help explain this attitude. Yet as a few analysts have noted, popular history and biography can give important clues, not to the development of historiography, but to the development of the culture itself. This is an open area for study.

HISTORIC OUTLINE

While a sense of history, the study of change over time, developed slowly in this country, Americans from the beginning were interested in the past.[1] The culture was dominated by Protestant Christianity, which placed primary emphasis on the Bible as the source of Christian belief. Those who would understand their faith must study the Old and New Testaments. Trained ministers used their sermons to trace their audiences' faith from Abraham through Jesus. And in the surge of evangelicalism of the Second Great Awakening at the beginning of the nineteenth century, individuals pored over their Bibles to learn for themselves what events 2,000 and 3,000 years ago meant in their lives in modern times. The climax of this, perhaps, was Alexander Campbell's adage of his new denomination, the Christian Church, "where the Bible speaks we speak. Where the Bible is silent, we are silent."[2] This pattern of finding religious revelation in a historical text was so engrained that Joseph Smith's assertion of God's continuing revelation to His Latter Day Saints was proved in the *Book of Mormon*, a history of the Lost Tribes of Israel in North America.[3]

In addition to this religious culture, historians have begun to call attention to the political culture in the early years of the republic, a culture called Republicanism. The foundation of this political current was the radical Whig criticism of the outcome of the Glorious Revolution of 1688. This criticism of Britain's dominant Whig establishment used historical incidents in politics to conclude that usurpation of power and corruption were undermining British liberties in the colonies, as well as the mother country. History was used to advance and buttress the political ideology of the Revolution.[4]

These historical tendencies in both the religious and political cultures were intensified, of course, by the uniqueness of the United States. The struggle to maintain their liberties led the American people to the creation of a new nation in 1776. The nation came into existence as an act of will, at a particular time, and independence was secured by a bitter, costly war. The United States did not evolve out of history, it appeared in history. Just as Protestants felt compelled to return to the Bible to understand and renew their faith, so Americans returned to the revolutionary era to understand and sustain their nation.

A need to hold on to the Revolution as a means of defining the new nation was widespread at the end of the nineteenth century. Its heroes were immortalized in the cities and counties across the country which incorporated the names of Knox and Greene and Sumter and Hamilton in their own, and reached an apogee in the naming of the new capital, Washington, the District of Columbia. Noah Webster's speller devised an American orthography and Jededia Morse an American geography. It was natural that attempts be made to capture the history of that event and the lives of its creators.

These first-generation historians were primarily patriots and their work established a pattern which dominated the writing of American history for a century. The Revolution, whether in David Ramsey's *History of the Revolution in South Carolina* (1785) or the second volume of Jeremy Belknap's *History of New Hampshire*, was a struggle for liberty on both the local and national scene. A Whig interpretation of history was established from the beginning. The event, its supporters, and the culture demanded that.

They also seemed to demand the moral lessons of the first of the great popularizers of our past. In 1800 Mason Locke Weems expanded his sermon on the death of George Washington into a brief biography. As edition followed edition, Weems expanded his work, not by research into the first president's life but by embellishing that life with anecdotes and moral lessons which, whether true or not, would inculcate virtue in American youth. In 1806 the fifth edition of *A History of the Life and Death, Virtues and Exploits of General George Washington* had expanded from the original 80 pages to 250. It included for the first time the story of the cherry tree. Weems's *Life of Washington* went through twenty editions during his lifetime and over seventy by the beginning of the twentieth century. While originally designed for the young, the book was read by millions and fixed the image of Washington in the American mind.[5]

Weems proved that popular history pays off. Although an Episcopal clergyman, he supported himself as a bookseller, making extensive tours from Savannah to New York. He was a success as a drummer, including his own work, earning enough money to maintain a comfortable plantation in Virginia. The story of the cherry tree might not be true, but it should be, and it sold.

Weems also learned from his contact with the public some of the characteristics that history needed in order to be popular. He became an agent for John Marshall's *Life of Washington* (1804–1807), the first attempt to write such a biography from Washington's own papers. The first volume was long, dull, and political. Subscriptions dropped sharply. Weems was dismayed to learn that the publishers intended to cut costs and the resulting appearance of later volumes. He wrote them that he could sell the books if he had "regiments upon regiments in red and gold to flash around me.

The *name*—the *noise*—the Eclate is EVERYTHING." The parson was right. Instead of the anticipated sale of 30,000 sets, only 8,000 were sold.[6] Appearance would always be a potent way to increase sales.

The American interest in the past, caused by religious and historical forces, was strengthened in the early nineteenth century by that cultural movement called Romanticism. This phenomenon, which dominated Western culture for decades, used history as a way of displaying the Romantic concern with the unique, the exotic, and the distant. Distance in time was useful for poets like Walter Scott as distance in space was for a Coleridge or Byron.

Scott's shift in 1814 from poetry to historical fiction increased his influence on American writers. The better writers like Washington Irving and James Fenimore Cooper turned to their own nation's experience for material and settings for their fiction. And Irving combined his interest in Spain and his homeland in biographies of Washington and Columbus.

While historical fiction, whether overt or disguised as history, acquired a wide audience in the United States, the Romantic interest in the past and increasing standards of scholarship led to the appearance of the first great American historian of this country. George Bancroft acquired a great audience yet held to the highest standards of his time. His career proved that at least one man with a brilliant imagination and ability to write could maintain two vocations. Bancroft was deeply involved with the affairs of the Democratic party while he wrote a lengthy study of the origins of the United States. His work, *A History of the United States* (10 vols., 1834–74; last revised by the author into 6 vols., 1883–85), was a great success. By 1874, when the last volume was published, Bancroft was recognized as America's greatest historian, and he had become wealthy.

Even though Bancroft is no longer read, he is still acknowledged as the first of our great historians because of his use of primary material. But his popularity in his lifetime rested upon his ideas and his writing style. The professional rejection of both is an indication of the cleavage between professional historians and those who appeal to the mass audience; Bancroft's work recounted the long history of the American people from the founding of the English colonies to the Revolution in a romantically written narrative. Even though his final revision in the 1800s toned down the florid prose, it remains too rich for our eyes.

But current historians reject Bancroft for another quality which made him attractive in his day. Although a historian, he was frankly a presentist. While he attempted to base his understanding of the seventeenth and eighteenth centuries on documents from the era, he wrote of their histories as leading to the American Revolution and the birth of the new nation. This patriotic interpretation, of course, is as acceptable to current readers as it was in his day. Less acceptable today, perhaps, was his insistence that this progressive development toward liberty and freedom was the unfolding of a divine will. Providence had set aside this continent as a reserve for the creation of a nation that would kindle the flame of liberty in the world. Romanticism was fused with patriotism and religion in a brilliant narrative. Clearly Bancroft's narrative skills, his ability to set a scene and use events to move his action, are as important as his subject and the assumptions that underlay his study. It was this ability to tell a tale and bring the dramatic past into life in the present that accounts for the wide acclaim given to the other great nineteenth-century historians such as Francis Parkman, historian of the struggle between France and Britain for North America, or William Hicklin Prescott, who enchanted readers with his studies of Spain in the Americas.[7]

These brilliant historians were men of leisure who wrote history as an avocation. They attracted a wide audience among the educated and those with money to buy their multivolume series. While there were not many Americans in this group, they were sufficiently numerous to provide income for these historians who could already afford a life of culture. Bancroft, Parkman, and Prescott reflected the cultural currents of their time, and the massive acceptance of their work suggests that their views on the racial superiority of the Anglo-Saxon were widely shared by hundreds. No questions were asked about their values.[8]

Even before Bancroft finished his monumental study of the origins of the American nation, his type of history was becoming outmoded among other historians. A new approach, calling itself scientific history because it relied on careful analysis of documents, replaced the sweeping, romantic narratives of the great mid-nineteenth-century historians. This scientific history was based on the methods taught in German universities. Shortly after the Civil War, seminars at the graduate level were established at the University of Michigan, Johns Hopkins, and Harvard. Here bright young men were introduced to this new close study of primary material which culminated in the Ph.D. dissertation. Instead of rich New Englanders who studied history with a romantic emphasis and concentrated on narratives covering sweeping topics, the young graduates of these seminars came from all parts of the country, from various classes, and supported themselves in their new professions as teachers of history at the college level. They tended to write for each other and not the general public.[9]

This new scientific history tended to focus on political issues and institutional development. The seminar room at Johns Hopkins was decorated with E. A. Freeman's aphorism, "History is past politics. Present politics is future history." And monographs came out of these new universities exploring, in elaborate detail with elaborate footnotes, the political issues of American institutions. These monographs found their readers, and their market, among other professional historians. The subjects, the methods, the manner of presentation made demands that even the best educated of the general public could not or would not meet, and professional history became separate from popular history.

The separation was not absolute, of course. There were those scholars with academic credentials whose writings attracted general audiences. John Fiske, lecturer and historian, demonstrated this. Fiske's original interest was in the ideas of Herbert Spencer and he made himself a spokesman and popularizer of the British philosopher, trying to reconcile his evolutionary ideas with religion. At the end of the 1870s Fiske became a professional lecturer and gradually expanded his subjects to include American history. In the middle of the next decade he began to revise his lectures and published several popular studies such as *Washington and His Country* (1889), *The Critical Period of American History* (1888), and *The American Revolution* (1891). The lectures and the books reinforced each other. By the turn of the century Fiske was America's most famous and popular historian.

Fiske considered himself a scientific historian, but this view was based on his attempt to apply the new theories of evolution to history. Professional historians based their claims to science on their methods of analyzing documents and reaching convincing interpretations. Fiske primarily relied on secondary works, such as scientific monographs, although he did utilize documents to some extent. The split between the academic and the popular historians was not absolute, however. Fiske was invited to join the new American Historical Association and was considered for its important offices. He chose to ignore the academic side of history. Later academic historians would ignore popularizers.

Fiske's role and reputation are useful in giving a sense of the appeal of popular history at the turn of the last century. One of his biographers concludes that there was an overlap between people who attended his lectures and those who purchased his books. The lecture was most popular in the northeastern part of the country and in those areas and cities where there were large numbers of people from New England. They were from upper-income levels and either were responding to the ancestral appeal of that region or were attracted to its cultural reputation. Fiske did lecture in the South, but he was not comfortable there, nor were his audiences taken with his New England slant. The market for popular history, at least that by Fiske, was an elite group.[10]

Fiske was not simply fileopietistic, however. His histories incorporated his evolutionary thought with regional and national patriotism. New England was the foundation of liberty in America and was consequently responsible for the desire of self-government in the New World. The growth of liberty in the United States, now in the nineteenth century, was leading the world to a better life. Fiske used New England's past to congratulate his audience on the present and dazzle them with their future. The response was sufficient to earn him a long-term publishing contract, access to the largest circulating quality magazines, an enthusiastic lecture audience, and a celebrity status. By 1891 his income reached $12,000 a year.[11]

While history did not attract the great masses of Americans at the turn of the century, it did draw large numbers of readers. The circulation of the *Century Magazine* nearly doubled to 225,000 by 1885 in the first year of the famous "Battles and Leaders" series. This four-year run of articles on Civil War battles by the opposing generals and their memoirs of the war culminated in a four-volume work that sold 75,000 copies and earned the Century Publishing Company a million dollars.[12]

Illustrations were part of the attraction of the *Century* series, and publishers at the end of the century recognized that illustrations could sell magazines. Ida Tarbell's "Napoleon" in *McClure's Magazine* in 1894 had twenty-two etchings, and Woodrow Wilson's two-volume *History of the American People* (1902) was packed with pictures.

The magazine industry's success in picture reproduction coincided with other technical innovations that made it possible to produce thousands of copies quickly and cheaply. These could be distributed to a national audience through the U.S. mail and the new magazine syndicates which exploited the nationwide railway system. With large profits from advertisers, editors were able to pay high prices for publication. *Harper's Magazine* agreed to pay Woodrow Wilson, then president of Princeton, $1,000 per chapter for his *History of the American People* before it reached book form.[13] Ida Tarbell, an editor for *McClure's*, contributed sensationalism, soberly guised as history, in her *History of the Standard Oil Company* (2 vols., 1904), which ran in her magazine before being published in book form. The title, insisting this was a history, intensified the impact of her exposé of the rise of the great monopoly.

General circulation magazines were the primary mass outlet for popular history in the period between 1890 and 1920. Such histories, historical sketches, and biographies were cobbled up by journalists as historians abandoned the market. Certain themes and subjects such as the Revolution or Civil War maintained a level of popularity, and certain figures drew attention with periodic outbreaks of intense interest. Between 1900 and 1904 the *Readers' Guide to Periodical Literature* lists thirty-eight citations of all sorts on Lincoln. During the period surrounding the centennial of his birth, 1905–1909, 169 items were published. In the period 1910–14 those items listed declined to fifty-eight with an additional nine poems. George Washington attracted steady attention during this time. Between 1900 and 1904 there were thirty-six items; between 1905 and 1909, thirty-five; and between 1910 and 1914, twenty-seven items. (Napoleon was also a steady topic: 1900–1904, fifty-one items; 1905–1909, thirty-one items; 1910–1914, thirty-nine items.)

Popular history continued to focus on patriotic themes at the turn of the century, but professional historians debated important alternatives proposed to their focus on political history. Frederick Jackson Turner encouraged looking at social history, and his provocative and influential Frontier Thesis asserted that the key to the American democratic experience was the continuing involvement with the ongoing frontier. The general public paid little attention to the debate that developed among academic historians and encountered Turner's thesis in diluted forms, such as Owen Wister's famous western, *The Virginian* (1906). Even more controversial was Charles A. Beard's assertion in 1913 that the Founding Fathers at the Constitutional Convention were motivated by economic interests rather than detached patriotism. There was uproar in the academy, but the flashes of the lightning of that distant thunder reached the general audience only as it was reflected in the textbooks of the following decades.

Beard's thesis, presented in his *An Economic Interpretation of the Constitution* (1913), can be seen as a part of the early twentieth-century reform movement called Progressivism. His interpretation suggested that the Constitution did not encode laissez-faire economics. But his book can also be seen as one of the opening guns by young intellectuals against the stuffy, conservative establishment's worship of the past. Here was one of the first revelations of the clay feet of the Founding Fathers. In the 1920s there was a rejection of the excessive jingoism of World War I that manifested itself in a movement to "debunk" American institutions and heroes.

In her autobiography, *The Promised Land* (1912), Mary Antin recounts how, as a young immigrant to the United States, she felt when she encountered the school presentation of George Washington and the cherry tree. How could she, an immigrant child, live up to his moral standards? Yet new American as she was, she and Washington were fellow citizens.[14] While Antin as a child knew she could never live up to Washington, as an adult she might have learned from W. E. Woodward's *George Washington; The Image and the Man* that she could live down to him, if she worked at it. Woodward's Washington was an ambitious land speculator, who carefully married a rich widow, and lusted after his best friend's wife.

In contrast to Albert Bigelow Paine's gentle study of America's favorite humorist, *Mark Twain* (1912), the first biography to reach the new bestseller list,[15] in *The Ordeal of Mark Twain* (1920) Van Wyck Brooks used Twain's life to attack the puritanical restrictions that America's materialistic culture placed on artistic genius. Henry Ford might say "History is bunk," but bright young men were using history as a way to correct the mistakes of their elders. And to a certain extent, the public responded eagerly. Claude G. Bowers's best-selling *Jefferson and Hamilton* (1925) and *The Tragic Era* (1929) presented our past with Southern and Democratic assaults on the standard New England and Republican versions of our past.

While debunking was a temporary fad, it usefully corrected a tendency toward hero worship and strengthened an interest in social history among the general audience. Bowers's Reconstruction was melodrama as he used details of life in post–Civil War America to move his argument. Other writers with journalistic backgrounds used their writing skills to attract audiences that academic historians seemed to scorn. One volume of Carl

Sandburg's six-volume *Abraham Lincoln* (1926–39) won a Pulitzer Prize and public acceptance as did Bernard DeVoto for his study of the westward movement, *Across the Wide Missouri* (1947). These writers of popular history had limited acceptance in the academic world, among historians who could not or would not write dramatic narrative studies. While Bruce Catton's military studies of the Civil War were generally accepted by academic historians, only Allen Nevins achieved full acceptance, and he did this partly by joining the profession.

The debunking fad of the 1920s coincided with another development in popular history, an interest in recent history and in the social and popular aspects of that history. Change was so rapid that events a quarter of a century ago seemed distant. In 1926 the first volume of Mark Sullivan's *Our Times* (6 vols., 1926–35) made the best-seller list. Sullivan wrote not only of the foreign and domestic events of the first decades of the century but also of the music, the dances, and the books and newspapers that people read. The development of a consumer culture was a theme, if not clearly articulated.

In 1931 Frederick Lewis Allen published his best-selling *Only Yesterday: A History of Our Time*. The paperback version continues to attract readers by its breezy account of the roaring twenties. Allen's book not only confirms the popular myths of the Jazz Age, but it is largely responsible for those myths. Allen used the newspaper interest in the popular and faddish and contrasted the gaiety of the 1920s with the soberness of the 1930s, the irresponsible politics of the Harding gang with the moral idealism of the Wilson administration. Even professional historians have difficulty giving up the view of the 1920s of Allen and F. Scott Fitzgerald.[16]

But Allen's focus ignores the questions raised by the great popularity of H. G. Wells's *Outline of History* (2 vols., 1922). Or were the hundreds of thousands of people who bought the two volumes at first $10.50 and then $5.00 or the one-volume edition for $1.00 laying up knowledge to be tapped in emergency just as the Yale Club laid up a fifteen-year supply of liquor for Prohibition? By 1976 the *Outline* would be the fourth best-selling history book in our nation's history, selling 2,020,170 copies in various versions.[17] Or what about the even larger popularity at that time of Henrick Willen van Loon's *Story of Mankind* (1922)? Though the book seemed designed for children, their parents read it in quantities. It went through thirty-two printings in five years and earned van Loon an estimated half million dollars.[18]

And Allen's book paid scant attention to the appearance in 1926 of the Book-of-the-Month Club (BOMC), which chose his history as a selection in 1931. While the BOMC and its competitors would be subjected to withering scorn from time to time as middle-brow pandering to the taste of a poorly educated middle class, the book clubs made books available in areas without bookstores in that long period before the national bookstore chains.[19] The book clubs, the paperback book industry, and the chain bookstores all helped to make the book a mass commodity on a national level, just as television blanketed the country.

Mass distribution of books, talking movies, and television all developed in a world of increasingly frequent crises. Wars and depressions, the threat of nuclear destruction, famine, and political and religious savagery were inescapable, either as they directly affected people or as they were brought into the home by magazines and television. In the period after World War II nonfiction began to sell larger numbers of books than the old fiction staple. And much of that nonfiction was history as people attempted to understand the past to understand the present.

Pictures added an immediacy to events, current and past, that was exploited in popular histories. As the process of photoduplication improved along with color reproduction techniques, new means of attracting audiences were devised. In 1950 *Life* successfully published *Life's Picture History of World War II* and sold 450,000 copies with a direct mail campaign to the magazine's readers.[20] At the end of the decade Time set up a book division which would directly solicit buyers and use the vast photographic resources of the originators of photojournalism. Volume after volume of series such as *The Old West* (26 vols., 1978–79) and *World War II* (16 vols., 1979–83) were churned out. The *Old West* series went back into circulation in 1986. Time-Life sent out seven million mailings advertising its *Epic of Man* series and received 300,000 initial orders.[21]

Time-Life used many of the same techniques as one of the nation's most successful history magazines, *American Heritage* (1954–). While not the first history magazine, *American Heritage* proved there was a market for studies of our past when written clearly and profusely illustrated. Since its beginning it has sold about 33,000 copies per issue. In its first twelve years the separate book division issued 200 titles with sales of fifty-seven million.[22] *American Heritage* gave its readers what was promised in 1954; entertainment, stories to "bring to life again the vivid exciting story of our country's past." At its peak of circulation it had nearly 320,000 subscribers willing to pay the high subscription rates. The success of *American Heritage* has led to similar publications such as *American History Illustrated* (1966–) and *Civil War Times Illustrated* (1961–). In 1980 a history magazine for children, *Cobblestone* (1980–), began circulation.

Popular history can serve a variety of functions, information, entertainment, even memorial. In 1970, John F. Kennedy's *Profiles in Courage* had become the best-selling popular history of all time with 5,490,000 copies in print. While the book had been a best seller and a Pulitzer Prize winner when it was first published, most of these sales came after the president's assassination.[23] One suspects the readers were less concerned about the problems John Quincy Adams faced in voting for the embargo in 1807 than about commemorating the death of a hero president. They probably did not care that Kennedy did not write the book himself.[24]

And popular history served the same role at the time of our bicentennial as it did when Parson Weems was writing. It could still be used to instill pride by celebrating the characters of our ancestors. The civil rights movement stimulated deep interest among academic historians in black American history as popular black historians insisted that Afro-Americans should be proud, not ashamed, of their past. While popular books by historians like Lerone Bennett and John Hope Franklin sold well, primarily in the black community, the great sensation, of course, was *Roots*. The book achieved best-seller status even before the sensational response to the television mini-series taken from its characters. Within a two-year period 4,850,000 copies had been printed and thousands of people, white and black, were inspired to search out their own family histories.[25] They ignored the fact that Alex Haley's book had only a tenuous claim to history. He himself called his data "factions." Professional genealogists and historians called his work historical fiction.[26] But it taught lessons that should have been true, even if they were not. And it was popular. Parson Weems would have been proud.

REFERENCE WORKS

Popular history and biography have rarely been considered subjects in themselves. As weak, if not disreputable, examples of the discipline, they have received little historiographical attention. There are no specific guides to the field at this time, although examples can be sifted out of standard reference works by looking at specific topics such as military history, the Revolution, the Civil War, the 1920s, or Afro-American history.

With this in mind, the researcher will start with the standard bibliographical and historical guides. A logical starting point is Eugene Sheehy, *Guide to Reference Books*, which, with its supplements, lists various reference books, including bibliographies, guides, and handbooks. There is an author, title, and subject index. A second standard source is Frank Friedel, ed., *The Harvard Guide to American History*, which lists materials by types such as "Biographies and Personal Records" and "Histories of Special Subjects." Works are also organized by time periods.

A new work that may be of use, since major historians did write popular history from time to time, is the series edited by Clyde N. Wilson: *American Historians, 1607–1865*, *American Historians, 1866–1912*, and *Twentieth-Century American Historians*, volumes 30, 47, and 17 respectively of the *Dictionary of Literary Biography*.

Of particular use for locating secondary material is *Recently Published Articles*, published annually by the American Historical Association since

1976, and *Social Science Index* and *Humanities Index* 1974– (formerly *International Index*, 1907–64, and *Social Science and Humanities Index*, 1964–74), which lists scholarly articles.

The twenty-volume *Dictionary of American Biography* edited by Allen Johnson and Dumas Malone, gives scholarly biographies of deceased Americans. The bibliographical references may be of use.

There are several surveys of best-selling books which include material on popular histories and biographies. Frank Luther Mott's *Golden Multitudes: The Story of Best Sellers in the United States* covers the period to 1945, and Alice Payne Hackett and James Henry Burke's *80 Years of Best Sellers, 1895–1975* brings together the figures Hackett compiled for *Publishers Weekly* for many years. *Publishers Weekly* presents a list of hardbound and paperback best sellers each spring which includes nonfiction as well as fiction titles. Those interested in books for young people should see Seymour Metzner's *American History in Juvenile Books: A Chronological Guide*. Charles Lee, *The Hidden Public: The Story of the Book-of-the-Month Club*, gives the titles of the primary selections of this crucial book distribution system.

RESEARCH COLLECTIONS

There are no specific collections of popular history and biography in libraries since these are usually considered by both librarians and historians as books on particular topics and are cataloged and shelved with similar works. George H. Callcott remarks that when he was doing research for his *History in the United States, 1800–1860*, he found it useful to supplement his bibliography by walking through a section of the library stacks picking out books with bindings that looked as if they might fit. The way materials in popular history are organized may make that system somewhat useful to the researcher.

While the great standard research libraries are obvious locations of popular histories and biographies, one may find them concentrating on scholarly works rather than those directed at the general or marginal reader. Public libraries, which focus attention on readers of this type, may be more useful than research libraries. Those which began to buy with the rapid expansion of book publishing in the last half of the nineteenth century are most likely to have popular histories and biographies. The popular histories will be indexed and shelved with more scholarly books on the topic.

Specialized, specific collections may well include books which could be characterized as popular history and biography. The American Antiquarian Society has been adding to its research collection since its founding in 1812 and has approximately 30,000 printed volumes of biography, many of which are of the popular sort. Equally interesting is the printed material in the society's local history collection. While the primary strength of the collection is in New England material, every state is represented in the collection of 55,000 items. As Keith Arbour, the head of reader's services, notes, "Local histories are almost by definition 'popular' works, or at least were until recent decades."[27]

Arbour's remark suggests a way to investigate topics in popular history, by looking at local and regional history collections. While these research collections tend to concentrate on manuscripts and official documents, they usually attempt to include as much secondary, printed material as possible. These are often popular histories and biographies. Some collections in various regions that might be of use include the Maryland Department of the Enoch Pratt Free Library in Baltimore. Included in this division are about 40,000 volumes concerning the history of Maryland and its subdivisions, particularly Baltimore. The Afro-American collection consists of about 6,000 volumes including biographies in addition to manuscripts and periodicals.

The Tutwiler Collection of Southern History and Literature at the Birmingham Public Library, Alabama, has 37,000 printed volumes with strong materials in state and local histories, Civil War and Reconstruction studies, and black histories. Other Southern collections with strong printed materials in regional history and biography include the Filson Club in Louisville, Kentucky; the McClung Library in Knoxville, Tennessee; and the Louisiana State University Library in Baton Rouge.

The history departments at public libraries such as Cleveland, Ohio, and Minneapolis, Minnesota, contain extensive materials on city and regional histories of the old Northwest and the trans-Mississippi West.

For the West itself, the Kansas State Historical Society prides itself on its collection of histories of that state and region, while the Kansas Collection at the University of Kansas Library covers Kansas, Nebraska, Colorado, Oklahoma, and Missouri. The Baker Texas History Center at the University of Texas at Austin collects not only manuscript material but also printed works on Texas and the Southwest.

For the Pacific Slope the University of Washington and the Oregon Historical Society are essential for the Northwest, and the public libraries in San Francisco and Los Angeles supplement the materials in the research collections of the University of California at Berkeley and Los Angeles.

In addition to these regional collections, the scholar looking at popular histories and biographies should consult the great research collections which include published materials among their holdings. The Library of Congress is comprehensive, as is the New York Public Library. One must have some knowledge of what one wants before ordering titles from the stacks. Special collections in such libraries may cover specific topics. The Schomburg Center for Research in Black Culture, a part of the New York Public Library, includes the sweep of published histories of black Americans in its 58,000 volumes. The local and family history section of the Newberry Library in Chicago has one of the most extensive manuscript collections in this country on those topics, and has printed materials also.

CRITICISM AND HISTORY

The study of popular history as a subject in intellectual and cultural history is a recent development. One recent book that indicates the usefulness of such study is Michael Kammen, *A Season of Youth: The American Revolution and the Historical Imagination*. Kammen looks at the changing views of the Revolution as they were reflected in 200 years of popular culture. To establish a base for his study Kammen begins with that founding event as seen in popular history and then looks at how those views were reflected in poetry, art, and historical fiction. The changes in the treatment of the Revolution, he believes, reflect the growing conservatism of the nation. That conservatism is seen most clearly in historical fiction where it becomes a rite of passage for the protagonist. He reads this as an attempt to make the Revolution unique, distinctively different from the other revolutions that have swept the world. Our Revolution was not a revolution but a coming of age and maturity for a nation.

A widely read study using popular history as a means of examining a social issue is Frances Fitzgerald, *America Revised: History Schoolbooks in the Twentieth Century*. She concludes that the history textbook remains bland and uninteresting because it has been, in our century, "a kind of lowest common denominator of American tastes . . . that reflects . . . a compromise, an America sculpted and sanded by the pressures of diverse constituents and interest groups." Her study attempts to explain why and how the publishing industry and teachers deal with the forces that operate in our society. A complementary dissertation on the themes in American popular histories is Jack C. Thompson's "Images for Americans in Popular Survey Histories, 1829–1912."

In biography Merrill D. Peterson looked at popular as well as scholarly biographies to track the shifting estimations of Thomas Jefferson in his *The Jefferson Image in the American Mind*. He concludes that Jefferson's reputation rose and ebbed as political currents shifted in the nineteenth century, and only in the recent half-century did Jefferson move above the political scene into general acceptance.

Thomas L. Connelly relied on popular histories and estimations to follow the rise of Robert E. Lee from rebel or Southern patriot to his present position as American hero in his biography-social history *Marble Man: Robert E. Lee and His Image in American Society*. Studies such as this and Peterson's tell us about the shifts in our culture as biographies change their emphases and stress different issues in their characters' lives.

In 1985 Roy Rosenweiz published "Marketing the Past: *American Heritage* and Popular History in the United States, 1954–1984" in *Radical History*. The article is preliminary to a book-length study of this amazingly successful history magazine. At the height of its popularity *American Heritage* focused on the characters of our history, ordinary people with some sort of interesting quirk. It ignored the great events, looking at them only from the sideline. It presented human interest material, lavishly illustrated, reflecting the influence of *Life*. What few major stories were presented by historians came from conservatives. There was little notice of women, blacks, and workers. The form rather than the content attracted the readers, according to Rosenweiz. He concludes that the audience was made up of people from the upper middle class who had moved away from their home areas and were deracinated. The general, unchallenging material in *American Heritage* gave them a sense of place and time.

In a recent paper James B. Jones has looked at the most simple of popular histories, the state-owned, roadside historical markers. By categorizing the markers in Tennessee, he confirms the assertion that this sort of history is "constituent" history, that the white male elites of that state have focused on public's attention on white male Southerners and the events they controlled from the Revolution into the middle of this century. He notices, with some dismay, that 5 percent of the Tennessee markers are concerned with Nathan Bedford Forrest—slave trader, Confederate general, and head of the first Ku Klux Klan.

Popular history as a subject matter is a new concept, and collections and anthologies of paperback examples are rare. Reprints of popular histories are common, for extremely popular works such as Frederick Lewis Allen's *Only Yesterday*. Other books such as Mark Sullivan's *Our Times*, are reissued in paperback from time to time. The best examples are found on the shelves of libraries and in used bookstores and sales.

NOTES

1. Dorothy Ross, "Historical Consciousness in Nineteenth Century America," *American Historical Review*, 89 (October 1984), 909–28.

2. David Edwin Harrell, Jr., *The Quest for Christian America: The Disciples of Christ and American Society to 1866*, vol. 1 (Nashville, Tenn.: Disciples of Christ Historical Society, 1966), p. 6 and passim for the importance of the biblical foundation of the movement.

3. Leonard J. Arrington and Davis Bitton, *The Mormon Experience* (New York: Alfred A. Knopf, 1979), p. 14.

4. Gordon S. Wood, "Republicanism as a Revolutionary Ideology," in John R. Howe, Jr., ed., *The Role of the Ideology in the American Revolution* (New York: Holt, Rinehart and Winston, 1970), pp. 83–91.

5. Harold Kellock, *Parson Weems and the Cherry Tree* (facsimile reprint of the 1928 edition; Ann Arbor, Mich.: Gryphon Books, 1971), p. 97.

6. Ibid., p. 134.

7. Russel Nye, *Geoorge Bancroft* (New York: Twayne, 1964), pp. 156–74; David Levin, *History as Romantic Art: Bancroft, Prescott, Motley, and Parkman* (New York: Harcourt, Brace and World, 1959).

8. Nye, *George Bancroft*, pp. 126–59.

9. Michael Kraus and David D. Joyce, *The Writing of American History* (Norman: University of Oklahoma Press, 1985), pp. 136–51.

10. Milton Berman, *John Fiske: The Evolution of a Popularizer* (Cambridge, Mass.: Harvard University Press, 1961), pp. 221–22, 240–42.

11. Ibid., p. 223.

12. Stephen Davis, "A Matter of Sensational Interest: The *Century* 'Battles and Leaders' Series," *Civil War History*, 27 (December 1981), 338–49.

13. Arthur Link, ed., *The Papers of Woodrow Wilson*, vol. 2, *1890–1900* (Princeton, N.J.: Princeton University Press, 1971), pp. 360–65.

14. Mary Antin, *The Promised Land*, 2d ed. (Princeton, N.J.: Princeton University Press, 1969), p. 224.

15. Alice Payne Hackett and James Henry Burke, *80 Years of Best Sellers* (New York: R. R. Bowker, 1977), p. 76.

16. Kenneth S. Lynn, "Only Yesterday," *American Scholar*, 49 (Autumn 1980), 513–18.

17. Hackett and Burke, *80 Years of Best Sellers*, p. 19.

18. Gerard Willen van Loon, *The Story of Henrick Willen van Loon* (Philadelphia: J. B. Lippincott, 1972), pp. 128–29.

19. Charles Lee, *The Hidden Public: The Story of the Book-of-the-Month Club* (Garden City, N.Y.: Doubleday, 1958).

20. "Around the World with Time-Life Books," *Publishers Weekly*, 208 (December 8, 1975), 22–25.

21. "Time, Inc. Books; Marketing, Editing, Designing for a Mass Market," *Publishers Weekly*, 182 (August 6, 1962), 88–89.

22. "American Heritage Starts Trade Book Division," *Publishers Weekly*, 194 (July 15, 1968), 33.

23. Hackett and Burke, *80 Years of Best Sellers*, p. 12.

24. Herbert Parmet, *Jack: The Struggles of John F. Kennedy* (New York: Dial Press, 1980), p. 333.

25. "The Best Sellers," *Publishers Weekly*, 215 (February 20, 1978), 54–58.

26. Richard N. Current, "Fiction as History: A Review Essay" *Journal of Southern History*, 52 (February 1986), 77–90.

27. Letter from Keith Arbour, Head of Reader's Services, American Antiquarian Society, to John Scott Wilson, July 10, 1986.

BIBLIOGRAPHY

Allen, Frederick Lewis. *Only Yesterday: An Informal History of the Nineteen-twenties.* New York: Harper and Row, 1964.

"American Heritage Starts Trade Book Division." *Publishers Weekly*, 194 (July 15, 1968), 33.

Antin, Mary. *The Promised Land.* 2d ed. Princeton, N.J.: Princeton University Press, 1969.

"Around the World with Time-Life Books." *Publishers Weekly*, 208 (December 8, 1975), 22–25.

Arrington, Leonard J., and Davis Bitton. *The Mormon Experience*. New York: Alfred A. Knopf, 1979.

Bancroft, George. *A History of the United States*. 6 vols. Port Washington, N.Y.: Kennikat Press, 1967.

Banson, Susan Ponter, Stephen Brier, and Roy Rosenweiz, eds. *Presenting the Past: Essays on History and the Public*. Philadelphia: Temple University Press, 1986.

Beard, Charles A. *An Economic Interpretation of the Constitution*. New York: Macmillan, 1960.

Berman, Milton. *John Fiske: The Evolution of a Popularizer*. Cambridge, Mass.: Harvard University Press, 1961.

"The Best Sellers." *Publishers Weekly*, 215 (February 20, 1978), 54–58.

Bowers, Claude G. *Jefferson and Hamilton*. Boston: Houghton Mifflin, 1925.

———. *The Tragic Era*. Boston: Houghton Mifflin, 1962.

Brooks, Van Wyck. *The Ordeal of Mark Twain*. New York: E. P. Dutton, 1970.

Callcott, George H. *History in the United States, 1800–1860: Its Practice and Purpose*. Baltimore: Johns Hopkins University Press, 1970.

Connelly, Thomas L. *Marble Man: Robert E. Lee and His Image in American Society*. New York: Alfred A. Knopf, 1977.

Current, Richard N. "Fiction as History: A Review Essay." *Journal of Southern History*, 52 (February 1986), 77–90.

Davis, Stephen. " 'A Matter of Sensational Interest'; The *Century* 'Battles and Leaders' Series." *Civil War History*, 27 (December 1981), 338–49.

DeVoto, Bernard. *Across the Wide Missouri*. Boston: Houghton Mifflin, 1947.

Fiske, John. *The American Revolution*. Boston: Houghton Mifflin, 1891.

———. *The Critical Period of American History, 1783–1789*. Boston: Houghton Mifflin, 1888.

———. *New France and New England*. Boston: Houghton Mifflin, 1902.

———. *Washington and His Country*. Boston: Ginn, 1889.

Fitzgerald, Frances. *America Revised: History Schoolbooks in the Twentieth Century*. Boston: Little, Brown, 1979.

Friedel, Frank, ed. *The Harvard Guide to American History*. Cambridge, Mass.: Harvard University Press, 1976.

Hackett, Alice Payne, and James Henry Burke. *80 Years of Best Sellers*. New York: R. R. Bowker, 1977.

Haley, Alex. *Roots*. New York: Doubleday, 1976.

Harrell, David Edwin, Jr. *The Quest for Christian America: The Disciples of Christ and American Society to 1866*. vol. 1. Nashville, Tenn.: Disciples of Christ Historical Society, 1966.

Howe, John R., Jr., ed. *The Role of Ideology in the American Revolution*. New York: Holt, Rinehart and Winston, 1970.

Irving, Washington. *Columbus, His Life and Voyages*, condensed by the author. New York: G. P. Putnam's Sons, 1897.

———. *Life of Washington*. 5 vols. in 3. Boston: Twayne, 1980–81.

Johnson, Allen, and Dumas Malone, eds. *Dictionary of American Biography*. 20 vols. and Index. New York: Scribner's, 1928–37.

Jones, James B. "An Analysis and Interpretation of Historical Markers and National

Register Listings in Tennessee." Paper presented at the Popular Culture Association in the South annual meeting. Chattanooga, Tennessee, 1986.

Kammen, Michael. *A Season of Youth: The American Revolution and the Historical Imagination.* New York: Alfred A. Knopf, 1978.

Kellock, Harold. *Parson Weems and the Cherry Tree.* Ann Arbor, Mich.: Gryphon Books, 1971.

Kennedy, John F. *Profiles in Courage.* New York: Harper and Row, 1964.

Kraus, Michael, and David D. Joyce. *The Writing of American History.* Norman: University of Oklahoma Press, 1985.

Lee, Charles. *The Hidden Public: The Story of the Book-of-the-Month Club.* Garden City, N.Y.: Doubleday, 1958.

Levin, David. *History as Romantic Art: Bancroft, Prescott, Motley, and Parkman.* New York: Harcourt, Brace and World, 1959.

Life editors. *Life's Picture History of World War II.* New York: Time-Life Books, 1950.

Link, Arthur, ed. *The Papers of Woodrow Wilson.* vol. 2. *1890–1900.* Princeton, N.J.: Princeton University Press, 1971.

Lynn, Kenneth S. "Only Yesterday." *American Scholar,* 49 (Autumn 1980), 513–18.

Metzner, Seymour. *American History in Juvenile Books: A Chronological Guide.* New York: H. W. Wilson, 1966.

Mott, Frank Luther. *Golden Multitudes: The Story of Best Sellers in the United States.* New York: Macmillan, 1947.

Nye, Russel. *George Bancroft.* New York: Twayne, 1964.

Paine, Albert Bigelow. *Mark Twain: A Biography.* 3 vols. New York: Harper, 1912.

Parmet, Herbert. *Jack: The Struggles of John F. Kennedy.* New York: Dial Press, 1980.

Peterson, Merrill D. *The Jefferson Image in the American Mind.* New York: Oxford University Press, 1960.

Ramsey, David. *History of the Revolution in South Carolina.* Trenton, N.J.: Issac Collins, 1785.

Rosenweiz, Roy. "Marketing the Past: *American Heritage* and Popular History in the United States, 1954–1984." *Radical History,* 32 (March 1985), 7–29.

Ross, Dorothy. "Historical Consciousness in Nineteenth Century America." *American Historical Review,* 89 (October 1984), 909–28.

Sandburg, Carl. *Abraham Lincoln,* 6 vols. New York: Scribner's, 1926–39.

Sheehy, Eugene. *Guide to Reference Books.* 9th ed. Chicago: American Library Association, 1982.

Sullivan, Mark. *Our Times, 1900–1925,* 6 vols. New York: Scribner's, 1926–35.

Tarbell, Ida. *History of the Standard Oil Company.* 2 vols. New York: Peter Smith, 1950.

Thompson, Jack C. "Images for Americans in Popular Survey Histories, 1829–1912." Ph.D. dissertation, University of Michigan, 1976.

"Time, Inc. Books: Marketing, Editing, Designing for a Mass Market." *Publishers Weekly,* 182 (August 6, 1962), 88–89.

van Loon, Gerard Willen. *The Story of Henrick Willen van Loon.* Philadelphia: J. B. Lippincott, 1972.

van Loon, Henrick Willen. *The Story of Mankind.* New York: Liveright, 1951.

Weems, Mason Locke. *A History of the Life and Death, Virtues and Exploits of Gen. George Washington*. Georgetown: Greene & English, 1800.

Wells, H. G. *An Outline of History*, 2 vols. New York: Garden City Books, 1961.

Wilson, Clyde N., ed. *American Historians, 1607–1865*. vol. 30 of *Dictionary of Literary Biography*. Bruccoli-Clark Books. Detroit: Gale Research, 1984.

———. *American Historians, 1866–1912*. vol. 47 of *Dictionary of Literary Biography*. Bruccoli-Clark Books. Detroit: Gale Research, 1983.

———. *Twentieth-Century American Historians*. vol. 17 of *Dictionary of Literary Biography*. Bruccoli-Clark Books. Detroit: Gale Research, 1983.

Wister, Owen. *The Virginian: A Horseman of the Plains*. New York: Macmillan, 1902.

Woodward, W. E. *George Washington: The Image and the Man*. New York: Liveright, 1946.

10

Pulps and Dime Novels

BILL BLACKBEARD

HISTORIC OUTLINE

Until about twenty years ago, the terms *pulp, pulp magazine*, and *pulp fiction* were writers' and publishers' trade terms, little known to or used by the general public. Readers who bought such magazines as *Dime Detective, Argosy, Blue Book*, and *Weird Tales* in the 1930s and 1940s did not think of these popular titles as pulps, but just as fiction magazines, or more generically, according to subject matter, as detective story magazines, adventure story magazines, fantasy magazines, etc. Infrequent and casual articles in such magazines as *Esquire* and *Vanity Fair* dealing with the phenomenon of the popular fiction magazines did, of course, use the term *pulp*, but it did not gain broad usage. From the point of view of the general reader, who once absorbed reams of pulp fiction as he does hours of television today, the paper on which his reading matter was printed was simply irrelevant. A Western novel serialized in the slick paper magazine *Saturday Evening Post* could, in his eyes, be quite as entertaining as another printed on pulp paper in *Wild West Weekly*. He read the latter magazine largely because the more eclectic *Post* did not publish enough Western fiction to satisfy his specialized cravings over a given period of time.

To the magazine publisher and his potential advertisers, however, the quality of paper used was a vital concern. So-called slick paper, made of rag content stock, afforded a highly desirable surface for the reproduction of advertisements, particularly those involving a lavish use of color. Unfortunately, slick paper was a costly item and was economically feasible only for very large circulation magazines, such as the *Saturday Evening Post, Collier's,* or *Life,* of low newsstand cost supported in large part by their advertising revenue or for more highly priced "quality" magazines, such as *Esquire,* the *New Yorker,* or *Vanity Fair,* with an "elite" appeal, again substantially supported by their advertisements. Pulp paper, on the other hand, prepared from a wood-fiber base and also called *newsprint,* largely in newspaper publishing circles, was much cheaper than *slick* or coated paper, and its use made it possible for publishers so inclined to reach a mass reading market at low prices without any substantial financial aid from advertisers. (For this reason, "radical" political journals, that tended to alienate advertisers per se, almost always appeared on the cheapest kind of pulp paper stock, generally called *butcher paper* by its left-wing users of the time.)

Many different kinds of magazines with low advertising content utilized pulp paper: the early color comic strip magazines (or comic books); political and cultural journals of all sorts (some of which, like *Harper's* and the *Atlantic,* used a high grade of wood-based paper, called *book paper* in the publishing field); newspaper book review and entertainment supplements; scholastic, library, and book trade publications, etc. However, only the popular fiction or all-fiction magazine acquired the name *pulp* from its writers and editors in the decades following the turn of the present century, and it is, of course, with this widely circulated, enormously varied body of publications that we are concerned here.

In referring to the pulp fiction magazine in these pages, we are speaking of a specific, readily defined kind of periodical, found only in six sizes and forms, all of which share in common wood-pulp paper and a two-column text. The most frequently encountered form of pulp magazine is a sheaf of several octavo signatures, stapled together at two equidistant points near the spine, enclosed with a slick paper cover attached with glue over the flat area of the spine, and usually featuring interior illustrations, as well as color printing on the outside of the cover. This basic form of pulp magazine is found in three sizes: the large "flat" of about 8½" × 11", usually about ¼ to 1 inch thick with trimmed page edges, and composed of three to four signatures (or, very occasionally, perfect bound, with or without staples); the median, standard size (representing the vast majority of all pulps) of 10" × 7" untrimmed, or about 9" × 6½" trimmed, averaging ⅓ to ½ inch in thickness (some exceptional pulps of this size can go to 2 inches or more of thickness), made up of six to twelve signatures (or again, in rare instances, dozens of signatures); and the "digest" size, of about 7½" × 5", ¼ to ½ inch thick (with some rare titles reaching an inch or more), almost always trimmed, and involving six to eight signatures (or perfect bound, with or without staples).

A much less frequent form of pulp magazine is the saddle-stitched, single signature variety. The standard binding (at 9" × 6½") for most of the nickel thrillers of the 1880s and later, as well as for virtually all comic books, saddle-stitching (two staples inserted at the signature fold) is most often encountered in pulps in the form of the under-the-counter sex story magazines of the 1920s and 1930s (with marked variations in the 9" × 6½" measurements cited for nonpulp formats). Saddle-stitching is also to be seen, although very uncommonly, in some digest science fiction and detective pulps, mostly in the 1950s.

The all-fiction magazine, by its nature, emphasized a basic broad appeal in its writing and narrative content. Here and there, especially in its later, closing years, the pulp magazine might chance a "difficult," experimental piece of fiction, because of real editorial enthusiasm and a feeling that one such item in a given issue would not alienate finicky readers provided with a half dozen other standard pieces of fiction. Even in such work some kind of straightforward narrative progress had to be in evidence, so that while as bizarre a writer as H. P. Lovecraft or Joel Townsley Rogers could (and did) appear regularly in pulps, a post-*Dubliners* James Joyce or a contemporary equivalent of John Barth probably would not. Basically, the all-fiction magazines provided a market for genre fiction that, often because of peculiar editorial biases as much as any real lack of intrinsic merit, failed to sell to the very limited but higher-paying slick paper magazine markets. While much of the pulp magazine content was, understandably, a mass-produced, stereotyped product seized upon by editors desperate to fill the endless pages of twenty or more titles a month in publishing house after publishing house, virtually all of the fine fiction written in America between the turn of the century and the close of the 1940s found print in these magazines if it could not find it in the slicks or literary journals. Much worthwhile material is still being uncovered today and reprinted to critical applause; indeed, in the case of some long-neglected writers, separate publishing houses with a largely academic clientele have been founded essentially to republish the works of such authors complete in successive, highly priced volumes.

It should be kept in mind, however, that the widespread belief that pulp paper magazines printed popular fiction for vast masses of readers, while slick paper magazines published quality material for more tasteful, elite readers, is simply wrong. The reverse, in fact, was true. While such magazines as the *Saturday Evening Post, Collier's, Ladies' Home Journal, Cosmopolitan,* and the *American Magazine* sold in the many millions of issues monthly at generally very low prices, the pulps in general retailed at their higher prices only in the low tens of thousands at best, with such primary titles as *Argosy* or *Blue Book* barely 80,000 or 90,000 copies per issue at peak circulation in the prosperous 1920s. While the nickel slicks were bought by literally everybody—the millions who stare at television today bought the slicks then to marvel at the full-color story illustrations and the endless pages of color ads, without really reading much of the text—the pulps were bought by a small elite of fiction devotees who *really* read what they bought, and wanted *much* more of the detective stories, air war stories, Westerns, or fantasies that the general fiction slicks brought them only in small quantities in any given issue. These people, many of them well educated, often academics, often writers themselves, often simply the brightest kids in a given school, numbered at best only a few hundred thousand out of a populace of a hundred million or more. Many saved and shelved their pulps over the years, while the multitudinous readers of the slicks tossed their magazines out every week or so. Thus pulp fiction was in fact the choice of the bulk of the real reading public of its time, just as today the best genre fiction in paperback is loyally supported by the tiny minority of people who still love to read in a nation inundated by cable television, VCRs, and such mindless mass circulation magazines as *People Today* and the contemporary *Esquire*. Today, old pulps sell to highly literate collectors at fancy prices—some select and rare titles can fetch upwards of $200 to $300 apiece in fine condition—while the million-issue slicks of the 1950s and earlier can generally be sold for the appeal of their cover art (Norman Rockwell, etc.) or their bountiful color ads for Coca-Cola and the like. The pulps were truly elite fiction, seen as trash only by the "proper" citizenry who read little of anything. (Unfortunately, the great majority of the people who determined public library subscription policy at the time were made up of precisely these "proper" types, which is why every library from here to Hoboken still has shelf after shelf laden with unread, dusty volumes of the *Saturday Evening Post* and similar genteel, "decent" large-circulation magazines, while possessing not a single copy of the really exciting and pioneering pulp fiction magazines of the same period.)

Although the pulp magazine, as we have been discussing it, was essentially a product of the first half of the present century, the popular, all-fiction magazine as a viable commodity appeared early in the nineteenth century in both England and America, and was largely printed on rag content paper (then much cheaper than it was to become by the 1880s). The American rag paper "story papers" of the 1850s and later, weekly publications the size of today's newspapers, running eight to twelve pages apiece of text and illustration, and bearing such excitingly etched logos as *Boys of New York, Banner Weekly, Young Men of America*, and *New York Weekly*, were crammed cheek to inky jowl with endless columns of sensational fiction by such worthies as Nick Carter, Horatio Alger, and Ned Buntline, and sold into the many thousands of copies at five or six cents each (although these papers were primarily designed for home subscription, being too large for full-cover display at most newsstands). Their enormous black-and-white cover illustrations, replete with blood and thunder of a Western, detective, or science fiction orientation, were matched by those of the considerably smaller English penny dreadfuls of the same period. These were illustrated penny serial parts, published weekly and sold singly or in groups in book stalls, usually eight pages long, 7″ × 10″, and kept in print so long as the continuing story in each title, often spun out to inordinate length in 200–300 parts, continued to sell profitably. When sales slumped, the stories were brought to a hurried halt, and the authors turned to new titles and characters. Popular titles in these series included *Boy Detective, Varney the Vampire, Wild Boys of London,* and *Blue Dwarf,* their notorious authors including Thomas Pecket Prest, Augustus Sala, and Pierce Egan, Jr., son of the man whose 1821 adult work, *Life in London,* was the first best-selling English novel-in-parts. A bit later, and overlapping the vogue for penny-dreadful part fiction, the English equivalents of the American story papers appeared. Weekly compilations of serials and short stories adorned with sensational cover illustrations like their Yankee kin, the English papers were much smaller in format, generally consisting of sixteen to twenty pages and measuring about 8½″ × 11″. Typical early titles in this immediately popular field were *Lads of the Village, Gentleman's Journal,* and *Boy's Herald.* Noticeably more restrained at the outset than their American cousins, the British all-fiction journals speedily plunged into horrific sensationalism as it became evident that what sold the penny-dreadful parts would also sell the boys' journals, and the deuce with what might upset the odd parent here or there. By the 1880s there were two dozen or more such magazines, such as *Boys of the Empire, Comrades, Champion,* and *Ching-Ching's Own,* some of them reprinting the texts and illustrations of the new popular boys' periodical form which had largely supplanted the story papers in the States, the so-called dime novel.

The term dime novel was coined to describe the pocket-sized original novels (measuring 6¼″ × 4″) of one hundred pages or so published by the New York firm of Beadle and Adams for the reading convenience of Civil War soldiers. Published monthly from the 1860s on, and originally intended for adult and young adult readers, with such titles as *The Rival Scouts, The Outlaw Brothers, The Deer-Hunters,* and *The Dacotah Queen,* the Beadle's Dime Novels line was chiefly concerned with Western and frontier adventure until well into the 1870s, when such titles as *The Phantom Hand, or, The Heiress of Fifth Avenue* of 1877 anticipated the urban detective thrillers that would rival the Western stories in popularity in the 1880s and after. The ten-cent pocket-novel format continued through the 1870s, with some minor size variations and rival publishers (such as George Munro), but was eventually eclipsed when Beadle and Adams introduced a larger format dime novel weekly series in 1878, with a gripping cover picture similar to those on the story papers. Measuring 12″ × 8½″, and running to between twenty and forty pages of triple-columned, closely printed text, the new series, called Beadle's New York Dime Library, opened with a detective story, titled *The Spotter Detective, or, The Girls of New York,* switched to a

Western yarn in the next number, and featured both narrative forms for the remainder of its weekly (and occasionally biweekly) 1,009 novels.

Although the Beadle and Adams dime pocket-sized books and weekly dime magazines were aimed at the adults, millions of boys had devoured them from the 1860s on. Realizing this, and knowing that many boys found a dime very hard to come by, the publishers decided to introduce a nickel publication, to be named Beadle's Half Dime Library, in 1877. Although the stories were about half of the length of those in the dime magazine, running to between sixteen and twenty-four pages, and were intended to attract nickel-bearing boys, there was no perceptible difference in the quality of the stories or their sensational cover art: certainly there were no great number of boy heroes in the Half Dime Library, and most of the Dime Library authors wrote for the new magazine as well. Opening with a *Deadwood Dick* yarn, the Half Dime Library ran for 1,168 issues, closing down operations (like its companion Dime Library) only with the end of the nineteenth century.

The five-cent price was a sensational success, and other publishers entered the popular fiction field with a flood of new titles of all sorts, all selling for a nickel and all with garish, shocking covers of action and brutality (augmented by full color in the late 1890s). Publishers later to be famed in the pulp fiction era to follow, such as Street and Smith (who owned story papers in the 1870s), were active in printing what the juvenile readers called nickel (or "nickul") thrillers (although their censorious parents, unconcerned about precise niceties of price, kept on calling them, as they had their predecessors, "dime novels," forcing the term on the entire nickel fiction field to follow). Among the plethora of new titles which flooded the newsstands from the 1880s through the 1910s were such generalized fiction rivals of the Half Dime Library as Wide Awake Library, Morrison's Sensational Series, and The Boys' Star Library; and such specialized fiction series (anticipating the variety of narrative emphasis in the pulps to come) as The Red Raven Library (pirate stories), The War Library, Diamond Dick Library (Westerns), The New York Detective Library, Old Sleuth Library, Nick Carter Library, and a host of others. By the 1890s, the feature hero series of nickel thrillers was in great vogue (again anticipating a major pulp category), with such detectives and Western heroes and outlaws as Nick Carter, Buffalo Bill, Young Wild West, Old Sleuth, Young and Old King Brady, Dick Dobbs (the millionaire detective), Jesse and Frank James, the Youngers, Wild Bill Hickok, etc., as well as a sports hero, Frank Merriwell, and a pair of science fiction forerunners of Tom Swift: Tom Wright and Frank Reade, Jr. (At least two of these characters were later to be featured in their own pulp magazines: Frank Merriwell and Nick Carter, the latter in *two* different pulps.)

Kids adored these magazines, read them to pieces, collected them, traded them, and generally behaved like the comic book juveniles (adolescent and adult) of today. They were almost universally read by boys in their time, and when their readers in many instances grew up to become men of substance, the old nickel thrillers were ferreted out of attics and basements and the back rooms of second-hand magazine stores and traded and sold again, often for quite high prices, in the 1920s and later. Many of these men ignored the contents of the much better written pulps of their adult years and gave their spare reading time over to "catching up" on the "dimes" they'd missed as kids. Most of these early readers are dead now, and the old nickel thrillers languish long in dealers' hands (when they do still turn up) until an institutional collector picks them up for fifty cents or a dollar apiece. Too antiquated and alien to appeal to even the phony nostalgia-gripped yuppies of today (who buy up the more garishly covered pulps avidly), the sensational weeklies of the gaudy era before 1910 are chiefly of interest to popular fiction researchers. Oddly, although virtually all of these magazines were printed on pulp paper stock (the rag content story papers also turned to pulp paper to save printing costs in the late 1870s), the term *pulps* is held to apply only to the specific group of magazines we will examine at considerable length shortly, while the *dime novel* misnomer continues to identify the dreadful popular American shockers of the Gilded Age.

In moving from the nickel thrillers of the nineteenth century to the pulps of the twentieth, we are, of course, passing from fiction of minimal literacy aimed almost entirely at juvenile readers, or the most naive of uneducated adults, to a narrative prose intended for a mature mass readership not satisfied by the relatively small amount of genre fiction available in quality or general content magazines, or in inexpensive paperback book reprints. Interestingly, the first periodical to establish the profitable existence of such a mature mass readership (initially in England rather than America) was not printed on pulp paper at all, nor was it an all-fiction publication. This was the widely famed, slick paper magazine of George Newnes, the *Strand*, in which such fictional figures as Sherlock Holmes and Bulldog Drummond appeared in series after series of novelettes and novels, together with sensational adventure and mystery fiction of all kinds, all profusely illustrated, often with color plates in holiday issues. Sandwiched in was a respectable (though peripheral) stock of nonfiction pieces on prominent personalities, exotic places, pets, and patriotism, so that despite its bounty of popular fiction, parlors that had previously accepted only such dull slick paper periodicals as *Blackwood's, Good Words,* and the *Leisure Hour* now received the *Strand*.

Ambitious imitators of the *Strand* appeared almost at once in England, all bounteously illustrated (at the rate of about one cut for every two pages) and replete with thrilling action or detective fiction written by such masters as H. Rider Haggard, R. Austin Freeman, Guy Boothby, E. Phillips Oppenheim, and many others; among these new and sensationally popular magazines were the *Windsor Magazine, Pearson's, Cassell's, Harmworth's* (later the *London Magazine*), and the *Idler*. Many of these published American editions to protect their copyrights in the United States, and their popular impact was much the same here as in England, although direct American imitations were not at all immediately evident (the earliest, possibly, being *Cosmopolitan* after 1905, when it was purchased by William Randolph Hearst and immediately took an engaging turn toward broadly popular fiction in great and well-illustrated quantity). American publishers of general magazines, dominated by the images of the more serious *Harper's* and *Scribner's* magazines at the close of the century, seemed to eschew the kind of fun-and-games fiction featured in the new group of British publications, and certainly they avoided any broad body of it in their pages at all times. Even the popularly oriented weekly slick paper magazines of wide dimensions, such as *Collier's* and *Saturday Evening Post* of the 1890s and 1900s, in which the Sherlock Holmes and Raffles stories were reprinted for American consumption, ran only one or two pieces of fiction per issue, with but one or two illustraions apiece, and placed their heavier editorial emphasis on journalistic nonfiction and illustrations of various kinds.

The would-be American consumer of quantitatively published popular action fiction was thus frustrated on two fronts: the imported British magazines, such as the *Strand* and *Pearson's*, were too highly priced for the mass reading public's budget even in American reprint form, while the cheaper popular American magazines, such as *Collier's* and *Saturday Evening Post*, ran about a single evening's worth of engaging fiction per week between them. The stage was thus set in the United States for the emergence of what was to be the single most successful medium for the merchandising of cheap fiction to a mass audience in the history of publishing: the pulps. It was an idea whose time had come, and if one publisher had not developed the concept, another would have in short order. As it happened, however, the man who published the first definitive pulp fiction magazine in 1896, the *Argosy*, did so only as one more step to save a foundering magazine, not as a calculated move in opening a new publishing frontier. Frank Andrew Munsey, who first converted his feebly conceived children's weekly of 1882, the *Golden Argosy*, into a boy's adventure story paper called simply the *Argosy* in 1888, then into a general illustrated monthly magazine of the same name in 1894, finally tried making it a monthly all-fiction adult adventure story magazine companion to his previously successful, general, illustrated *Munsey's Magazine* of 1891. By printing his new 1896 version of *Argosy* on pulp paper and omitting all illustrative art, Munsey found he could provide a fat bundle of reading matter for a dime, well below the quarter charged at the time by slick paper magazines of similar bulk, such as *Harper's* or *Century*. Moreover, a great deal of the normal editorial content of such general magazines was pictorial, while in their fastidious prose, nonfiction usually had a marked edge in pages over fiction. On the average, it would be safe to say that a single monthly issue of *Argosy* of 1896 held more fiction than any six of the leading general monthlies of the time—and it was virtually *all* sensational adventure and mystery fiction of reasonably mature quality.

That this kind of magazine was exactly what the mass adult reading public of the 1890s wanted was at once evidenced by the steep increase in *Argosy*'s circulation. From a rock-bottom low of 9,000 in 1894, the new *Argosy*'s sales figures quickly soared to 80,000, gradually ascending to a peak of half a million by 1907, a mere decade from its start. The *Argosy* was not long alone in its pulp paper splendor, but it was some time before its burgeoning imitators equalled or surpassed it in overall story quality. The inspired early editorial work in the post–1895 *Argosy* was not that of Munsey, who was much more involved in *Munsey's Magazine* and other projects by that time, but that of Matthew White, Jr., who had joined the Munsey staff in 1886 (and who was later closely aided by Robert "Bob" Davis, a Munsey editor hired in 1904). That White's judgment was sound is indicated by the impressive roster of writers whose early work was printed in *Argosy* between 1896 and 1910: James Branch Cabell, Upton Sinclair, Mary Roberts Rinehart, William Sydney Porter (later O. Henry), Susan Glaspell, George Allen England, Albert Payson Terhune, Joseph Louis Vance, Frank L. Packard, William MacLeod Raine, and Ellis Parker Butler, many of whom became regular contributors to the prestigious *Saturday Evening Post* of the upcoming century.

Among the earliest of *Argosy*'s technical rivals were two other Munsey adventure fiction pulps, *All-Story* of 1905 (later *All-Story Weekly*) and *Cavalier* of 1908. Both monthlies and both essentially duplicates of the *Argosy* with interchangeable authors and cover artists, these two new publications in effect put an over 220-page, all-fiction Munsey magazine on the newsstands three times a month; and when *All-Story* combined with *Cavalier* and went weekly in 1913, there were *five* Munsey adventure pulps for sale every month—and they all sold, voluminously. There seemed to be plenty of people able to devour 1,200 closely printed pages of Munsey fiction per month—and more, if the sales of other publishers' action fiction pulps are added to those of the Munsey magazines. It must be kept in mind that ten cents in the 1900s would buy about what a dollar will buy today, at a time when most actual incomes were smaller in real purchasing power. It can accordingly be assumed that most buyers of the early pulps rarely bought on impulse or just to read one or two stories by favorite authors; they read their money's worth out of every magazine purchased. A persistent point made in letters to the editors at this time and later is that the readers read every story in every issue; many even rated them in terms of enjoyment derived. Contemporary authors can only weep for that once vast reading public, a public that sustained the pulps for fifty years.

Among the early and most substantial imitators of *Argosy* were such other 7″ × 10″ quarto pulp magazines containing roughly 150 to 200 pages of adventure and action fiction as Street and Smith's *Popular Magazine* of 1904, which reached a quarter million in circulation by 1905; *Gunter's Magazine*, also of 1904, another Street and Smith response to *Argosy* (with a leavening of romantic fiction in an attempt to appeal to some female readers), which became *New Magazine* under another publisher in 1910, then returned to Street and Smith as *New Story Magazine* in 1912; *People's Magazine*, a third Street and Smith undertaking of 1906 with an early emphasis on detective fiction rather than straight adventure; *Top-Notch* of 1910, a final Street and Smith effort in the general action story field issued in an initial dime-novel format, with a bias toward the sports fiction story; *Blue Book* of 1907 (originally titled *Monthly Story Magazine* in its 1905 inauguration), a companion magazine to the women-oriented *Red Book* and the later, theater-slanted *Green Book* of the same period; *Short Stories* of 1910, previously an all-fiction reprint magazine of high price and slick paper; and *Adventure* of 1910, the first issue of which actually appeared on slick paper, apparently for promotional reasons. Some of these newcomers carried a fifteen-cent price, justifying it by a modicum of interior illustrations, while the early *Top-Notch*, the smallest in length of the lot, tried for a nickel, but none ever surpassed the enormous circulation lead attained by *Argosy* or attempted to emulate the weekly publication of *All-Story* (later merged with *Argosy* into a single Munsey pulp adventure fiction weekly in 1920, after *Argosy* itself had been a weekly since 1917), although *Popular, Short Stories, Adventure*, and *Top-Notch* eventually went to twice a month publication for varying periods of time.

It soon became evident to some of these pulp fiction entrepreneurs that the needs of their newly tapped reading pubic might not be wholly met by action fiction in bulk, and that many readers, as indicated by a growing demand in libraries and bookstores, wanted to read rather narrowly along one line of popular fiction, most notably in the 1910s that of detective and mystery narrative, although a spreading interest in Western fiction was not far behind. Street and Smith, of course, had earlier noted this phenomenon in their nineteenth-century nickel library series, where tens of thousands of copies of the weekly *Nick Carter* detective and *Buffalo Bill* Western thrillers vanished off the newsstands every seven days. Munsey, however, was the first to investigate specialized fiction interests when he launched the *Railroad Man's Magazine* in 1906. A monthly pulp, this publication featured much more nonfiction than the other men's adventure magazines and was actually more of a fraternal journal for railroad employees and locomotive buffs than anything else; it lasted until 1919 and was revived by Munsey in 1929. More typical of the specialized fiction pulp was a second Munsey effort in this direction, the *Ocean* of 1907. Here, although there was considerable nonfiction, sea stories predominated, with as many as four serials running every month. Munsey's estimate of the public's interest in salt water narratives was misguided, however (in fact, there was never to be a really successful sea story pulp at any time), and he was forced to fold the venture after only a year.

Street and Smith, experimenting a little later in the game, had much better luck. In 1915, they decided to convert the old *Nick Carter* nickel thriller into a new ten-cent semimonthly pulp magazine of detective fiction, called *Detective Story Magazine*. Nick Carter stories, often serialized, were still featured, but the bulk of the new magazine's contents were purchased from the same free-lance authors then supplying the other pulps. Initially only a slim 128 pages, *Detective Story Magazine* quickly fattened to 160 pages, then switched to a weekly schedule at 144 pages with a steadily mounting circulation through the 1920s. Encouraged by their initial success, Street and Smith proceeded in 1919 to alter their successful *Buffalo Bill* weekly nickel thriller into another specialized pulp, this one called *Western Story Magazine*. Like *Detective Story Magazine*, *Western Story Magazine* was launched as a semimonthly ten-cent publication of 128 pages. By 1920, however, circulation had swelled to such an extent that *Western Story Magazine*, like its predecessor, became a 144-page dime weekly. Then at 300,000 circulation, it later reached a half million in sales in the mid–1920s when the extraordinarily popular fiction of the hyper-prolific Max Brand (Frederick Faust) began to run in its pages at the rate of two or three serials at a time. A third Street and Smith attempt at a specialized fiction magazine, the fabled *Thrill Book* of 1919, failed because of a lack of courageous editorial direction. Clearly meant to be a magazine emphasizing the weird, bizarre, and fantastic in popular fiction (material which had already proven its wide popularity through its repeated appearance in *Argosy*, where writers famed for fantastic narratives, such as Edgar Rice Burroughs, Abraham Merritt, George Allen England, J. U. Geisy, Francis Stevens, and many others, were acclaimed headliners), *Thrill Book* lacked the nerve to limit its contents to science fiction and fantasy and, by actually taking on the amorphous shape of just another general action pulp, failed to attract the steadfast band of followers who were later to adhere faithfully to such undiluted exponents of fantastic fiction as the *Weird Tales* of 1923 and *Amazing Stories* of 1926. The *Thrill Book* did run some unusual and memorable fantasy—notably Francis Stevens's "The Heads of Cerebus"—but not enough to catch the notice of the multitude of readers who were regularly buying *Argosy* and *All-Story* for the same thing.

Street and Smith continued with their pioneering creation of specialized genre fiction pulps in the 1920s and introduced the long-lived and vastly popular *Love Story Magazine* in 1921 as a 144-page, fifteen-cent weekly— and as a cheaper companion to two older Street and Smith romantic fiction monthlies, *Smith's Magazine* and *Ainslee's Magazine*, once aspiring slicks, but now down-at-the-heel twenty-cent pulps. The following year Street and Smith made their own attempt at a salt spray magazine with *Sea Stories* (which had to be abandoned by 1930 and converted to a mystery-adventure pulp called *Excitement*); they also introduced the nation's first magazine of collegiate fiction in *College Stories*, anticipating the later peak success in that field of *College Humor*. *Sport Story* was first published in 1923, as a companion to the sports-oriented *Top-Notch*, while by 1927 another long-established nickel-thriller weekly (actually then selling at seven cents), Harry E. Wolff's *Wild West Weekly*, with its feature novels about Young Wild West, was taken over by Street and Smith as a straight Western fiction weekly with the same name.

In the meantime, other publishers had been busy, particularly in the detective and Western fiction fields. H. L. Mencken and George Jean Nathan, engaged in developing their famed *Smart Set Magazine*, merrily launched three deliberate potboiler magazines in the 1910s to bring in supportive funds for *Smart Set*. The first two of these "louse" magazines, as Mencken and Nathan called them, were routine spicy story pulps of the innocent sort prefigured by Street and Smith's *Live Stories* of 1913 or their earlier *Yellow Book* of 1897, the kind of magazine which sold well in wartime; and Mencken and Nathan's *Parisienne* of 1915 and *Saucy Stories* of 1916 were specifically created with the young, war-excited American in mind. Both were immediate hits, with the second giving the leading naughty story magazine of the time, *Snappy Stories*, strong competition for its position. (It might be mentioned at this point that some variety of risqué pulp fiction was always on sale under dozens of different titles from the turn of the century through the 1950s, many published and distributed in legally sub rosa operations. Notable titles in the 1920s and 1930s were *La Paree Stories, Bedtime Stories, 10-Story Book, Saucy Movie Stories, Vice Squad Detective, Spicy Mystery Stories*, and *Hollywood Detective*. There were dozens of other titles, and none ever failed financially; every last one was, in fact, ultimately suppressed only by the authorities.) Mencken and Nathan's third "louse" magazine, however, proved to be quite a different matter from the first two; in fact, its reputation eventually overshadowed that of *Smart Set* itself.

Created several years later in 1920, this new monthly action pulp was titled *Black Mask*, and its initial orientation was toward stories of crime, horror, and the quasi-supernatural. Deliberately sensational in title and content, the feisty magazine was intended to attract readers who wanted more fearsome fare than they could find in the relatively sedate *Detective Story Magazine* and *Mystery Magazine* (the latter being a Frank Tousey venture of 1919, a thirty-two-page, 8" × 11" dime publication featuring cheaply acquired fiction by minor writers). A pitch was made for women readers by the early subtitle wording, "A Magazine of Mystery, Romance, and Adventure," but there was little of the boy-girl romancing that packed the pages of *Ainslee's* or *Love Story Magazine* of the following year; indeed, the cover of the October 1920 issue depicted a young woman cowering from a hot branding iron that has *already* branded her cheek with a livid, smoking image. Although there were a number of generally straightforward detective problem stories in the early issues, these probably reflected the kind of rejects from *Detective Story Magazine* the editors were initially forced to buy, and the obviously desired theme was powerfully rendered in blood and thunder. There was, needless to say, little hint of the restrained, coldly realistic, well-paced fiction that *Black Mask* was later to personify in the writing of Dashiell Hammett, Raymond Chandler, Paul Cain, Raoul Whitfield, and others. Indeed, *Black Mask*, for all of its fame as a pioneering hard-boiled detective story magazine in the 1920s, was in fact a long time in finding its real focus. For most of the 1920s, *Black Mask* was described in its cover subtitle variously as a magazine of air, Western, adventure, and he-man fiction, as well as of detective fiction, and its contents reflected that description. Such later noted writers of tough crime fiction as Whitfield and Horace McCoy initially wrote little but air and Western stories for *Black Mask*. It was not, in fact, until the public impact and circulation rise of the very late 1920s that accompanied the major Hammett serials, such as *Red Harvest* and *The Maltese Falcon*, that *Black Mask* became wholly a magazine of tough detective fiction. In the meantime, there was little influence exerted on other pulp magazines, and the first out-and-out *Black Mask* imitator, *Black Aces*, did not appear until 1931, while such strong and lasting parallel crime fiction magazines as *Dime Detective* and *Detective Tales* did not reach their peaks of quality until the middle 1930s.

In the 1920s, following the advent of *Black Mask* and the minor curiosity called *Mystery Magazine*, the only notable introductions in detective story magazines were Munsey's first move into the field in 1924 with the weekly *Flynn's* (later *Flynn's Weekly Detective Fiction* and finally *Flynn's Detective Fiction Weekly*), starting out with 200 pages for a dime; Edwin Baird's somewhat earlier *Detective Tales* of 1923, an oddly old-fashioned magazine which quickly jumped to an 8½" × 11¼" format (the size of the "true" detective and "confession" slicks of the period), but retained its pulp paper as its title changed to a twenty-five-cent *Real Detective Tales & Mystery Stories* in 1924; the Priscilla Company's *Mystery Stories* of 1925, a quality twenty-five-cent magazine of 160 pages, emphasizing true crime accounts and crime action fiction; W. M. Clayton's *Clues: A Magazine of Detective Stories* of 1926, which directly paralleled *Detective Story Magazine* and ran twice a month for a while in the late 1920s at fifteen cents; Dell's short-lived *Crime Mysteries* of 1927, a fifteen-cent 120-page monthly which featured much of the interest in the horrific and grisly which characterized the early *Black Mask*; and Harold Hersey's *Dragnet Magazine* of 1928, a twenty-cent, 128-page monthly which was later (in 1931) to become the famed *Ten Detective Aces*, in which such top pulp writers as Lester Dent and Norvell Page wrote monthly novelettes about continuing feature characters in deliberately fantastic and gruesome adventures. The great bulk of the pulps jamming the newsstands of the 1920s were adventures and Westerns, with detectives a slim third, and a random spotting of other early genre pulps, such as *Ghost Stories, Weird Tales, Amazing Stories, Secret Service Stories, Sky Birds*, and the like. The earlier adventure pulps had been augmented by such 1920s titles as *Danger Trail, Complete Stories, Five-Novels Monthly, Tropical Adventures, Thrills, Romance, Ace-High Magazine*, etc., while the Western fiction deluge inaugurated by *Western Story Magazine* counted among its 1920s arrivals the *Frontier, Lariat, Cowboy Stories, West, Rangeland Stories, Western Trails*, and many others.

It was at the close of the 1920s, however, that the real torrent of new pulps (and fresh varieties of pulps) took place. Suddenly, by 1929, all sorts of new kinds of pulp magazines were appearing—World War I action fiction, in such titles as *War Stories* (actually dating from 1926), *Submarine Stories, Navy Stories, Triple-X Magazine, War Novels, Over the Top*, and a subgenre which quickly outgrew its parent: air war fiction featuring *Airplane Stories, Wings, Sky Birds, Aces, Air Stories, Eagles of the Air, Sky Riders, Zeppelin Stories*; gangster fiction, typified by such new titles as *Racketeer Stories, Gun Molls, Speakeasy Stories, Gang World, Gangster Stories, Gangland Stories, Underworld*; and science fiction, reflected by *Amazing Stories, Science Wonder Stories, Air Wonder Stories, Scientific Detective Monthly*, and (just around the corner in 1930) *Astounding Stories of Super-Science*. The quality of pulp fiction had become speedier and breezier, too, with a general dumping of the kind of prolix description and circumlocution which had filled many of those earlier, endless pages in *Argosy* and *Detective Story Magazine*, and reflected the general tenor of turn-of-the-century fiction. Those writers who had anticipated the looser, swifter style, such as Edgar Rice Burroughs, Max Brand, Dashiell Hammett, Robert E. Howard, and Erle Stanley Gardner, continued to flourish in the decade ahead, while many others stodgily prominent in the 1910s and 1920s vanished completely from the fast-action pulps of the 1930s, much as certain silent film idols, such as John Gilbert and Ramon Navarro, had essentially slipped from view with their own passing medium.

The rising tide of new pulp variations surged into the 1930s, seeing the birth of such minor one-pulp genres as *Prison Stories, New York Stories, Courtroom Stories, Fire Fighters, Jungle Stories, Northwest Stories, Front Page Stories*, and similar titles as well as the introduction of many FBI pulps, such as *Federal Agent, Public Enemy, G-Men, G-Men Detective, Ace G-Man Stories, Feds*; the formal mixing of genre themes and risqué fiction in such mid–1930s magazines as *Spicy Mystery Stories, Spicy Detective Stories, Spicy Adventure Stories, Spicy Western Stories, Saucy Detective, Saucy Movie Tales, Scarlet Adventures, Hollywood Detective*; the unleashing of a number of sadistic horror fiction magazines, such as *Dime Mystery Magazine, Horror Stories, Terror Tales, Uncanny Tales, Eerie Stories, Thrilling Mystery, Ace Mystery Magazine*; plus even more new detective pulp titles—*Popular Detective, Thrilling Detective, Dime Detective, Detective Tales, New Detective, Crime*

Busters, Private Detective Stories, Black Book Detective, Double Detective, Strange Detective Mysteries; Westerns—*Western Aces, Mavericks, 10-Story Western, Popular Western, Dime Western Magazine, All Western Magazine, Nickel Western, Thrilling Western, Thrilling Ranch Stories*; adventures—*Action Stories, Thrilling Adventures, All-American Fiction, Dynamic Adventures, Excitement, Northwest Stories, Golden Fleece, Oriental Stories, Magic Carpet*; air war—*Air War, Dare-Devil Aces, Sky Aces, Battle Birds, War Birds, Sky Fighters, Sky Devils, George Bruce's Contact, George Bruce's Squadron*; and science fiction—*Miracle Science and Fantasy Stories, Thrilling Wonder Stories, Startling Stories, Marvel Science Stories, Dynamic Stories, Planet Stories*.

Many of the multitude of new magazines were the product of freshly formed pulp chain publishers who carried as many as thirty or more pulp titles apiece; others were the releases of older publishers attracted to the market by the sizable and rising profits in an economic recession (for a nation out of work had little choice but to drink or read, and with bootleg whisky at a quarter a shot, many chose to read cheap fiction much of the time). Among the major publishers who flooded the newsstands with pulps in the wake of Munsey and Street and Smith were Dell Publishing, Fiction House, the Hersey Magazines, Clayton Magazines, Popular Publications, Thrilling Publications, Culture Publications, Standard Publications (later Better Publications), and A. A. Wynn magazines, and others, including spinoffs or front publishers set up by established houses to bring out yet more strings of pulps, such as Fictioneers, backed by Popular Publications, or Trojan Publishing, established by Culture Publications. At the helms of many of the pulps fielded by these publishers, sometimes editing as many as a dozen or more at once, were a number of talented and canny men, such as the much acclaimed Joseph T. "Cap" Shaw of the later *Black Mask*; Harold Brainerd Hersey of *Thrill Book, Ace-High Magazine, Danger Trail, Clues-Detective*, and *Dragnet*; John W. Campbell, Jr., of *Astounding Science Fiction* and *Unknown Worlds*; John L. Nanovic of numerous Street and Smith titles; Ken White of *Dime Detective*; Farnsworth Wright of *Weird Tales* and *Oriental Stories*; Leo Margulies of the Thrilling chain, who shone in his handling of *Thrilling Wonder Stories* and *Startling Stories*; Henry Steeger of Popular, who supervised almost three dozen titles from *Horror Stories* to *Glamorous Love Stories*; Rogers Terrill, direct editor of all Popular titles under Steeger; Hugo Gernsback of *Amazing Stories* and *Wonder Stories*; Daisy Bacon of *Love Story Magazine*; F. Orlin Tremaine of *Top-Notch* and *Astounding Stories*; A. A. Wynn of *Ten Detective Aces*; Donald Kennicott of *Blue Book*; and others of equal capacity and accomplishment.

Probably the most notable and memorable achievement of the large pulp chain publishers and their editors in the 1930s was the fostering of the rebirth of the hero novel, once so central to the prosperity of the nickel thriller magazines of the 1890s. The first of these new monthly pulps was Gilbert Patten's little known *Swift Story Magazine* of November 1930, which, aside from its twenty-cent price and digest pulp size, itself unusual and innovative for the time, anticipated the content and format of the other hero pulps that followed in every detail: 128-page length, a recurrent hero in a monthly feature novel dominating the magazine—Derek Dane, Sky Sleuth in this case—several illustrations in the lead novel, a group of short stories in the closing pages, a department for the readers, and a lurid cover featuring the hero. Next, five months later, was Street and Smith's *Shadow Magazine* of April 1931, which introduced the dual-identity outlaw crime fighter to the hero pulps; then came Standard Publications' *Phantom Detective* of February 1933, a *Shadow* imitation; Street and Smith's *Doc Savage* and *Nick Carter* of March 1933, covering the themes of exotic, fantastic adventure and the private detective respectively; Standard's *Lone Eagle* of September 1933, featuring a World War I air ace; Popular's *Spider* and *G–8 and His Battle Aces* of October 1933, presenting yet another masked crime fighter (the best of the lot) and a second World War I air ace cum spy respectively; Street and Smith's *Pete Rice* of November 1933, showcasing the first cowpoke sheriff in the hero pulps; Rose Wyn's *Secret Agent "X"* of February 1934, carrying the fourth hidden-identity avenger of crime; Street and Smith's *Bill Barnes*, also of February 1934, a pulp with a contemporary aviation hero like Derek Dane; Popular's *Operator #5* of April 1934, introducing an American master spy facing contemporary enemy operations and foreign invasions; Popular's *Dusty Ayres and His Battle Birds* of July 1934, the first science fiction hero pulp, featuring a future interplanetary war; Popular's *Secret Six* of October 1934, multiplying the dual–identity crime fighter by six; Ranger Publications' *Masked Rider* Western of December 1934, starring an imitation of the Lone Ranger of radio; Dell's *Doctor Death* of February 1935, introducing the first criminal lead character, à la Fu Manchu, in a hero pulp; and Fawcett Publications' *Terence X, O'Leary's War Birds* of March 1935, a second science fiction air war hero pulp.

The astonishing average was one new hero pulp every two months between January 1933 and April 1935, most of which kept going for the remainder of the decade. Nor did the pace slacken; these seventeen stalwart openers of the heroic way were followed by as many more over the next few years: *Wu Fang, Dr. Yen Sin, G-Men, Public Enemy* (later *Federal Agent*), *Whisperer, Skipper, Captain Satan, Captain Hazzard, Captain Combat, Captain Danger, Mavericks, Jungle Stories, Ka-Zar, Lone Ranger, Masked Detective, Ghost* (later *Green Ghost Detective*), *Octopus, Scorpion, Wizard,* and others, including three short-lived newspaper comic strip adaptations: *Flash Gordon, Dan Dunn,* and *Tailspin Tommy.* Only the paper shortages of World War II reduced the tide, but even after the war, in the increasing ebb that ultimately foundered almost all the pulps, a few more hero pulps were expectantly launched, such as *Hopalong Cassidy, Captain Zero,* and *Sheena, Queen of the Jungle,* a comic book adaptation. The last hero pulp to succumb was the third to be created, *Phantom Detective* of 1933, which expired with its 170th quarterly issue in the summer of 1953. In number of issues, however, it was sur-passed by *Doc Savage*, with 181 numbers to the summer of 1949, and the twice-a-month *Shadow*, with 325 issues to the same date. The magazine that pioneered the pulp hero concept and format, *Swift Story Magazine* of 1930, curiously, lasted just one issue.

Illustrating the hero pulps, as well as the pulp chain titles in general, was nearly as important for sales by the 1930s as the lurid covers of nickel thrillers had been for their prosperity at the turn of the century. While the earliest pulps (the Munsey titles, *Popular*, *Short Stories*, etc.) were chary of interior illustrations when they carried them at all and generally garbed themselves in thematic covers featuring adventurous or sporting males in static poses with little or no relation to specific stories within, the number and quality of interior drawings increased sharply through competition in the 1920s, while direct story delineation on covers—initiated by the Munsey magazines in the 1910s—gradually became the norm. While a very few well-budgeted pulps ran virtually an illustration to a page by the mid-1920s and 1930s (notably the stunning *Blue Book Magazine*, which also ran many illustrations in colored ink, *Real Detective Tales*, and the Spicy chain) and a number of others tried to continue with a minimal number of illustrations or none at all (*Best Detective, Great Detective Stories, Scotland Yard, Dragnet,* and *War Stories* were typical), the vast majority carried at least one lead illustration for every story (very short stories were usually excepted) and between two to four for novelettes and novels, plus continuing department heads. Supplying this considerable quantity of artwork was the task of a few dozen well-worked professional ink, watercolor, and oil artists, who varied in quality and reputation from the dreariest kind of scrawlers and daubers who worked for Desperation Row (as the skin-of-their-teeth pulp houses were called) to a number of fine artists of international fame who did occasional or regular pulp magazine illustration for bread-and-butter money. Most, of course, were journeymen artists of reasonable competence and occasional flairs of real genius. Among the renowned artists who did a notable amount of pulp cover or interior work were N. C. Wyeth, Rock-well Kent, John Newton Howitt, J. Allen St. John, Gordon Grant, John R. Neill, Jonn Clymer, Austin Briggs, Nick Eggenhoffer, J. C. Leyden-decker, and Herbert Morton Stoops; while the most outstanding and pop-ular of the journeymen numbered such memorable talents as Hubert Rogers, Walter M. Baumhofer, Jerome Rozen, Virgil Finlay, Paul Orban, John Fleming Gould, Frederick Blakeslee, Hannes Bok, Elliot Dold, Edd Cartier, Joseph Doolin, Frank R. Paul, H. W. Wesso, R. G. Harris, Norman Saun-ders, H. W. Scott, Rudolph Belarski, William Parkhurst, Frank Tinsley, Harold S. DeLay, and Margaret Brundage. Some indifferent comic strip art was introduced experimentally into a few pulps in the 1930s and later, but never with a notable effect on sales or lingering impact, with the possible exception of the classically silly *Sally the Sleuth* in *Spicy Detective Stories*.

The writers, of course—the kids just in from the prairies with their heavy office typewriters in cardboard boxes unloaded on wooden tables in shabby Manhattan furnished rooms, the wealthy top-wordage pulp kings writing from their estates around the world, the 5,000-words-a-day steady producers in their suburban homes on Long Island or in southern California—these were the mainstay of the whole pulp operation. Following on the early group of pioneer pulp writers in the old Munsey magazines already mentioned, and writing in the 1940s or before, were such gifted and entertaining fictioneers as Edgar Rice Burroughs, whose highly contagious visions of Tarzan and Mars first overwhelmed the mass reading public in Munsey's *All-Story* between January and November 1912; Zane Grey, many of whose best-known novels ran in *Popular, Argosy*, and *All-Story*; Max Brand, who galloped to fame in virtually every early pulp, from *Argosy* and *Blue Book* through *Black Mask* and *Ace High* to *Western Story* and the *Railroad Man's Magazine*; Frank L. Packard, who introduced the dual-identity outlaw crime fighter to detective fiction in his Jimmie Dale series for *People's Magazine* and later *Detective Fiction Weekly*; Abraham Merritt, who gripped two generations of readers with his splendid fantasy adventures, such as *The Moon Pool* and *The Ship of Ishtar*, in the Munsey titles; Joel Townsley Rogers, one of the most bizarre writers of suspense prose in American fiction, who wrote both aviation and crime fiction for such disparate magazines as *Wings, Adventure*, and *New Detective*; George Bruce, the finest author of air war fiction in the pulps, who was the first writer to have a pulp named for his work—and not just one pulp, but three (*George Bruce's Aces*, 1930; *George Bruce's Squadron*, 1933; and *George Bruce's Contact*, 1933); H. P. Lovecraft, the finest American writer of macabre fiction since Poe, whose stories had enormous reader impact in *Weird Tales* and *Astounding Stories* and now constitute the base of a small publishing industry; Lester Dent, who wrote most of the *Doc Savage* hero pulps, of which over one hundred have been reprinted in top-selling paperback editions in the 1970s; Dashiell Hammett, who introduced his Continental Op, Sam Spade, and other characters in fresh, hard-bitten prose through the pages of *Black Mask, Brief Stories*, and *Argosy-All-Story*; Carroll John Daly, who created the lone private eye concept in *Black Mask* and augmented it through *Dime Detective, Detective Story, Detective Fiction Weekly*, and a dozen other pulps; Robert E. Howard, the freshest writer of adventure prose since Jack London, who wrote for an endless number of pulps from *Weird Tales* to *Argosy*, and whose work is being avidly reprinted here and abroad in over a hundred hardcover and paperback books; Norvell Page, creator of the *Spider* hero pulp, most powerful and memorable of the hero pulp writers and a regular contributor to many other pulps from *Unknown* to *Dime Mystery Magazine*; Raymond Chandler, who added his own bittersweet cachet to crime fiction in *Black Mask* and *Dime Detective* and even experimented with fantasy in *Unknown*; Ray Bradbury, one of the most noted contemporary American authors, who wrote much of his best fiction for

Weird Tales, Startling Stories, Detective Tales, and other pulps; Walter B. Gibson, creator of the *Shadow* hero pulp and the indefatigable author of over 300 novels about his cloaked hero, now in active reprint, as well as of other pulp hero series for such magazines as *Crime Busters* and *Mystery Magazine*; and a host of others of almost equal worth and importance: Robert A. Heinlein, Clark Ashton Smith, Steve Fisher, Frank Gruber, John D. MacDonald, Frederick C. Davis, Raoul Whitfield, Paul Cain, Henry S. Whitehead, Clifford D. Simak, Fritz Leiber, Robert Bloch, Luke Short, H. Bedford Jones, Victor Rousseau, Malcolm Jameson, C. L. Moore, Henry Kuttner, Ted Copp, Vincent Starrett, Erle Stanley Gardner, Frederick Nebel, William J. Makin, Cornell Woolrich, Norbert Davis, Donald Wandrei, Howard Wandrei, Harry Sinclair Drago, Fred MacIsaac, Theodore Tinsley, Theodore Sturgeon, John W. Campbell, Jr., Emile C. Tepperman, Cyril Kornbluth, Eric Temple Bell, David H. Keller, Robert J. Hogan, Paul Ernst, J. J. des Ormeaux, Clarence E. Mulford, Walt Coburn, Paul Chadwick, Huge B. Cave, Jack Kofoed, E. E. Smith, Rex Stout, A. E. Van Vogt, Isaac Asimov—a heady roster of famous names (and some no longer so famous), but one that literally cuts away only some of the cream of the pulps' exciting literary fraternity. There are at least fifty more names as well-known or representing as competent a body of work as any on the preceding list. Some—particularly the writers in the science fiction field and the *Black Mask* school—will be mentioned in other essays in this volume; others will have to wait for a longer study to be properly cited.

As can be seen from the authors noted, almost every area of popular American literature was blanketed by the pulps, and nearly always the involvement was both intimate and massive, leaving a major and permanent impression behind. There never was a time before or since that more good, engaging prose fiction (with, admittedly, a sizable, perhaps essential admixture of rubbish) has been available as cheaply to so many people. It lasted more than half a century, but when it entered its decline, the end came quickly. Many pulp readers of the time could see it coming, although the bulk of the editors and publishers in those later years did not seem so prescient. Since it was, by and large, their new policies and approaches to the fiction they were packaging that hastened the ruin of the pulps, this is perhaps not too surprising.

What happened is that the war years of the 1940s not only led to a reduction in the size of the pulps, their frequency of publication, their abundance of titles, and their very sturdiness (many issues had to be published with only one staple to conserve metal), but to the dismemberment of much of the established editorial staffs as well, with many going into the armed forces or war work. In most cases, these veterans of the great pulp boom of the 1930s, often with little formal schooling and sharing many of the tastes and needs of their readers, were replaced by young, draft-exempt people direct from college with liberal arts degrees in hand, who had rarely had the time or inclination to open a pulp for four or more years previously. Instead of feeling that they were the new, fortunate custodians of a marvelously varied treasure house of ongoing accomplishments and exciting possibilities, most seemed to believe that they had been put in charge of horrendously lowbrow products in antiquated packaging, badly in need of immediate improvement. The improvement they felt necessary, unfortunately, was the discarding of the lurid, raffish veneer, which attracted the bulk of their readership, and supplanting it with a neat, trimmed, proper, respectable, "distinguished" look which would permit the pulp editors to hold their heads up along Publishers Row in the future. The most extreme steps along this line were taken at what had become the economic mainstay of the shortage-racked pulp chains, Street and Smith, and when the prosperous flagship threw the Jolly Roger and the cutlasses overboard and broke out the doilies and teacups, it was really all over for the pulps. Through the 1940s, they were improved to death; in the 1950s, the corpses were interred.

The tragedy was compounded by the fact that, while the Street and Smith pulp packages were being upgraded to invisibility so far as the public was concerned, and their contents made increasingly unpalatable (the editorship of the classic *Detective Story Magazine* was taken over in the 1940s by Daisy Bacon, whose whole previous experience and orientation had been derived from her decades with *Love Story Magazine*), the general level of pulp writing elsewhere was improving enormously. A fresh generation of fine young pulp writers, who had cut their creative eye-teeth on the pulps as kids, was entering the field: Frederic Brown, John D. MacDonald, David Goodis, John McPartland, David Karp, Jack Vance, Philip K. Dick, Harlan Ellison, Evan Hunter, James Causey, Robert Turner, Day Keene, Richard S. Prather, Louis L'Amour, and a great many others. Their beautifully written, highly imaginative, and innovative stories filled many of the surviving pulps, notably those of the hardily conservative Popular chain, as well as most of the burgeoning science fiction pulps. It was to no avail; as the sales of the top-selling Street and Smith chain tumbled in the wake of the deadly new garb of neat propriety imposed on its pulps, national magazine distributors grew more nervous and reluctant about carrying any pulps at all. Individual dealers gave over more newsstand space to the proliferating comic books and cut back on that afforded the slower-selling pulps, often stacking them in odd corners rather than giving them cover display. What people did not see, or did not see well, they were less inclined to look for and buy. (It must be kept in mind, too, that the hard-core, devoted purchasers of particular pulp titles were always in a minority among the largely impulsive pulp public. If *Argosy*, say, was prominently displayed, it sold to some extent through familiarity with the title and the look of the cover; hidden from immediate sight, it was not sought out enough to sustain anything like the previous level of sales.) Basically, the public simply wanted light entertainment. If comic books and the exploding new field of paperback fiction (which demanded less space from dealers than pulps) were more visible than the pulps, the public's money was largely spent in these areas. When one of the two major national distributors of magazines refused to carry pulps any more in the early 1950s, it was all over for the chain publishers. A colorful handful of pulps survived, largely because of strong specialized markets (such as *Ranch Romances'* healthy newsstand pull in the Midwest and Northwest, and the tendency of devoted science fiction fans to buy all of the titles in their field as if they were one publication), but almost all had to adopt the digest pulp size to get even a hope of display at the newsstands. One or two, such as *Argosy* and *Blue Book*, gave up their pulp format and contents altogether and began fresh careers as general slick magazines with male appeal.

Although the bulk of their outlets were gone by the mid–1950s, the new writers remained. Those turning out science fiction had no real problem, for most of their old markets kept publishing, often as the only pulp titles left in the reorganized chains, but other writers had to find fresh sources of income. One or two new digest-size pulps were created with some success to carry some of this material in the crime, detective, and Western fiction fields, notably in Flying Eagle's *Manhunt, Murder!, Alfred Hitchcock's Mystery Magazine*, and *Gunsmoke*, but by and large the more adaptable writers turned to the brand-new markets for original paperback book fiction, such as Fawcett's Gold Medal Books, Atlas News's Lion Books, and similar title lines at Signet and Dell. These markets were almost exclusively for book-length novels, but paid very well in contrast to the penny-a-word rate still prevailing with most pulps at their demise. A few old-line pulp writers tried these new outlets, as well as the field of hardcover publishing to which most went. Lester Dent of *Doc Savage* tried both, for example, but generally speaking, it was the postwar group of newcomers, such as Day Keene, John D. MacDonald, and David Goodis, who flourished handsomely in the original paperback field.

Still, the pulps as they had been known in their heyday had irrevocably passed from the land. The sight, feel, and smell of them is no more, apart from the shelves of collectors, rare book dealers, and institutions. Only the living heart of their contents beats healthily in the myriad of briskly selling reprints that continue to be unearthed in great quantity from their yellowing pages both here and abroad where—notably in France and Japan—a youthful cabal of interest has sprung up in recent years. The pulps are dead, but at no time has literary and critical awareness of them been livelier than today.

RESEARCH COLLECTIONS

Larry Landrum's listing of major library research collections of pulps and dime novels in his essay on detective and mystery novels in this volume has well anticipated any similar listing that I might make, and although I will augment his listing here, there is no point in my repeating it. Primarily, I will use this space to discuss briefly certain problems likely to be encountered in making use of institutional pulp collections.

The State Historical Society of Wisconsin at Madison holds the August Derleth pulp collection, largely comprising fantasy and science fiction pulps, some in incomplete runs, together with many detective and other genre pulps to which the prolific Derleth contributed material; some of these latter items are relatively rare.

The San Francisco Academy of Comic Art contains what has been described as the finest cross-genre collection of pulps and dime novels in any public institution, holding key or first issue examples of virtually every pulp, as well as many complete runs of titles in all pulp areas. The academy also provides the researcher with the unique opportunity to study pulps in close conjunction with large special collections in *all* other areas of the popular narrative arts, from comic strips through hardcover and paperback detective, Western, adventure, and science fiction, children's books, comic books, films, drama, general fiction, story papers, general periodicals in all areas, extensive bound newspaper runs, Sherlockiana, Dickensiana, etc., all housed and indexed for efficient cross-reference. The academy can provide a perfect, bound facsimile of any pulp on high quality paper, including reproductions of the original color covers, for any fellow institution or serious researcher, at about $20 an issue.

The researcher interested in examining detective, Western, science fiction, or other genre pulps in the institutional collections listed here and elsewhere in this volume should bear the following information in mind.

1. No comprehensive pulp collection exists (although that at the San Francisco Academy of Comic Art comes closest in breadth of material represented); all suffer frequent and wide gaps in various areas. The researcher may well have to go to a number of widely separated institutions in order to locate a given group of titles and dates, and even then there may be some he will not be able to find. Science fiction pulp collections tend to be the most complete, however, due to the assiduity of the private collectors whose files have now entered public institutions.

2. Pulp collections are in varying degrees of accessibility. The Library of Congress pulps, once they are ferreted out, can be one or two days in reaching the Main Library from the warehouse where they are stored, and they are also in dangerously bad condition. The pulps in Special Collections at the University of California at Los Angeles are usually brought promptly, but they are kept in a large number of boxes and often filed out of logical genre or title sequence in these boxes, so that the researcher, usually limited to one box at a time, can spend much time going through successive boxes if he wishes to examine any considerable number of pulps. It would be wise, accordingly, to discuss accessibility factors with the institutions prior to visiting them, in order to have a reasonable idea of how much time will

have to be expended. It is quite likely to be more than one would spend in looking at an equivalent number of hardcover books from the stacks of most institutions.

3. The readability condition of pulps will usually vary greatly within the confines of each collection. Few institutions, unfortunately, have the budgets or the inclination to replace poor copies of pulps received as parts of donated collections with better ones, so that these poor copies steadily deteriorate to the degree that they are used and according to the condition under which they are stored. The researcher and librarian may well find that a pulp vital to the former's concerns is so browned and brittle with age that it literally cannot be further used without falling to pieces, so that the researcher will have to find another copy at some other institution—if he can. The librarian, meanwhile, will remove the pulp from the stacks and put it away to await restoration or duplication, but will rarely check the collection further to locate similarly aged pulps, which will accordingly continue to stay on the institution's actively accessible list until they also are discovered at the worst possible time. One rarely will be able to learn about the condition of pulps in advance of a visit (many of these collections are not used by anyone for years at a time), so that this is a hazard to be met at any institution.

4. Since study time is understandably limited at most institutions, one will frequently want to leave pulps with stories marked for reproduction by the library. Since reproductive equipment can vary greatly in quality from place to place, it will be wise to sample this by making some few copies of pulp material on the premises, although more and more institutions are acquiring fine reproductive equipment which will provide stunning copies.

5. If one hopes to conduct pulp research with the concurrent aid of critical and historical texts, it would be advisable either to bring along copies of these works or check the institution's general reference stacks prior to arrival. The fact that a library holds a large, donated pulp collection (almost no institution has actually built its own collection from scratch) is no guarantee it will own many specialized reference books in the field—or, indeed, that any of the institution staff will themselves have much knowledge of, or interest in, their pulp holdings.

HISTORY AND CRITICISM

This essay is concerned with the pulps as a publishing phenomenon, rather than with specific works or even bodies of work which appeared in the pulps. Accordingly, these notes reflect that concern and deal only with those texts that relate in some substantial way to the history of pulps or of some variety of pulps. Texts largely concentrating on single writers who happened to appear in the pulps, or on extant popular literary forms which of necessity were represented by pulp genre titles, are not discussed, although a number of such works are covered by other chapters in this volume.

Very little of consequence has been written about the pulps as a publishing form in books from the major trade or academic publishers, either in the past or present. A good deal more has been done in limited edition texts, often in paper wrappers, from small publishers, while a small number of relevant and informative pieces do appear from time to time in a few academic and amateur press periodicals devoted to various aspects of the popular arts.

As a display case of pulp covers, Chelsea House's large volume simply titled *The Pulps*, edited by Tony Goodstone, has considerable merit. Limited in its referential scope and in the representative value of the individual covers reproduced (all in full color) to the resources of the editor's small collection, the book nevertheless provides a reasonably good visual introduction to the newsstand impact and appeal of the pulps over much of their existence. The book's greatest flaw lies in its concentration on the pulp covers of the 1930s (the area of the editor's personal interest), its slighting of the pulps of the 1920s and earlier, and its all but total ignoring of the pulps of the 1940s and later. In its accompanying textual pages, a very abbreviated and inept "history" of the pulps is set forth, together with a largely unimaginative selection of pulp fiction and interior art over the decades. The emphasis in the latter often seems to be on "name" authors regardless of the worth of the material selected (where shortness seems to be a primary factor); for example, a dreadfully bad early piece by Tennessee Williams from *Weird Tales* is included, apparently just because it is by Williams. Similarly, bad to poor pieces by such fine writers as H. P. Lovecraft, Robert E. Howard, Dashiell Hammett, Ray Bradbury, Max Brand, and others are included; on the other hand, relatively good stories by Edgar Rice Burroughs, Clark Ashton Smith, Malcom Jameson, and others are to be found. The interior art selected runs the gamut from fine to dreadful, with much more of the latter than the former, while the reproduction is uniformly poor.

Another pulp text from a major trade publisher is Quentin Reynolds's history of Street and Smith, *The Fiction Factory: From Pulp Row to Quality Street*. Chiefly of use for its interesting, though not very thoughtful or selective, series of pulp cover reproductions in color and black and white, this volume is primarily a puff job, bought and paid for by Street and Smith. The general thrust of the Reynolds text, as implied in the subtitle, is that Street and Smith has "made it" into big-time publishing by shucking its dismal old line of pulps and developing such paragons of periodical excellence as *Mademoiselle, Charm,* and *Living for Young Homemakers.* (Nevertheless, Random House was astute enough, in trying to find *some* sales for the prefinanced vanity job, to splash plenty of pulp covers on the glossy wraparound jacket.) Reynolds's history is dull, circumspect, often misinformed, and obviously the result of a few weeks' cramming before the writing. It does, however, represent the only extant history of any real length covering a major pulp publisher as such, aside from the three generally unsatisfactory texts dealing with the Munsey Company.

The first of these is an autobiographical work by Frank Munsey himself, *The Founding of the Munsey Publishing House*, which is colorful and lively with regard to Munsey's vicissitudes and triumphs in the publishing business through 1906, but of little use with regard to the texts and art of the Munsey magazines themselves. The same is largely true of George Britt's posthumous study of Munsey, *Forty Years, Forty Millions*, where references to the Munsey pulps—the book is basically concerned with Munsey's newspaper activity—are primarily for background color and anecdote, rather than celebration or critical concern. Neither book has much to offer in the way of illustrative data on the Munsey pulps. The same is unfortunately true of Frank Luther Mott's account of the Munsey Company in his generally exhaustive, five-volume *History of American Magazines*. Mott, as in most of his lengthy pieces on major American magazines, is much more concerned with the relatively trivial data of financing and the musical chair ins and outs of editors and publishers than with the physical contents from year to year of the magazines he is discussing. In personal taste, he is not overly interested in fiction and not at all in pulp fiction; accordingly, he slights even those occasional pulp titles published by the slick paper magazine companies with which his work is primarily concerned. His piece on Munsey in volume 4 of his set represents his work's only coverage of a pulp publisher, and even here his emphasis is on Munsey's one major slick, the relatively feeble *Munsey's Magazine*. The bulk of the data in the piece is derived from the Munsey and Britt works cited, and it too is largely valid for reference to the limited extent it deals with the Munsey pulps at all.

Excellent as anecdotal color relevant to the creative lives and commerce of the pulp writers in the 1930s and 1940s are two fine works: Frank Gruber, *The Pulp Jungle*, and Robert Turner, *Some of My Best Friends Are Writers, But I Wouldn't Want My Daughter to Marry One*. Turner, however, is much more reliable in areas of strict fact than Gruber, wherein anecdotes are often attributed to the wrong writers or editors or to the wrong time and place. There is a good deal of interesting critical commentary on many of the pulps in both books, although Turner is, again, more astute here than Gruber. Neither book, unfortunately, carries an index or illustrations, although Gruber has a nice display of pulp covers on its wraparound jacket. Harold Hersey's *Pulpwood Editor* is rather superficial and a bit confused in its relatively brief attempt to blanket what was obviously a very complex and exciting career in pulp editing that involved over fifty pulps, but nevertheless of great value in illustrating the capacity and intelligence necessarily involved in mass pulp editing. (Hersey's later, long article in *Golden Atom* for 1953, "Looking Backward into the Future," which emphasizes his science fiction and fantasy pulp work, is much more precise and interesting than his formal hardcover book.) The book is well indexed, although un-illustrated, and has a partial listing of Hersey's pulps. An interesting but unfortunately latter-day look at the work of pulp agents (the focus is almost wholly on sales to Gold Medal Books and other paperback replacements of the pulps) is to be found in Donald McCampbell's *Don't Step on It—It Might Be a Writer*. Again, there are no illustrations, but there is a useful index. In a class by itself is the only serious study of a single pulp magazine issued by a major publisher, Philip José Farmer's *Doc Savage: His Apocalyptic Life*. It has no index or illustrations, but contains a series of highly inform-ative appendixes.

Among formal instructional texts on pulp and general fiction writing between 1900 and 1930, few provide much worthwhile data on pulps per se, aside from the transient editorial requirements prevailing at the time of the book's publication. (While a study of such requirements can obviously be very informative, they are much better researched in the numerous writers' magazines of the period on a month-to-month basis than by leap-frogging among the various how-to-write texts.) The handful of writing manuals that do contain a good bit of information about the pulp magazines and pulp writers as such are *This Fiction Business*, by H. Bedford Jones; *The Fiction Factory*, by John Milton Edwards (pseudonym for William Wallace Cook); *Love Story Writer*, by Daisy Bacon; and *Science Fiction Handbook*, by L. Sprague deCamp.

Book-length studies of detective fiction or collections of shorter studies rarely mention any pulps other than *Black Mask*, and they are usually mis-informed about even that title, thinking it was wholly a detective fiction magazine from the start. A partial exception is David Madden's anthology of articles by various writers, *Tough Guy Writers of the Thirties*, in which *Black Mask* nominally receives a long and separate discussion by Philip Durham. Durham is aware of *Black Mask*'s early multigenre aspect and mentions it, but too quickly becomes involved in an exegesis on his King Charles' Heads, Dashiell Hammett and Raymond Chandler (despite the assignment of special articles—all the studies in the book were written to order—on Hammett and Chandler to other hands), to say much of interest about the magazine itself. (Even in discussing Chandler, Durham seems unaware that the best of Chandler's pulp detective fiction appeared in *Dime Detective*—which he does not mention—rather than in *Black Mask*.) Oth-erwise, despite the book's assumed focus on the style of writing that pre-vailed in the detective pulps from 1930 on, there is no other discussion of pulps in any of the articles in the volume; there is not even an entry for "pulps" or "pulp magazines" in the index.

The few books to deal seriously with Western fiction neglect the pulps similarly, excepting only John G. Cawelti's *The Six-Gun Mystique*, in which the importance of Western pulps is at least acknowledged, and a number of major pulp titles are listed (oddly including *Doc Savage*), but little informative comment about the pulps themselves is made in the text. Similarly, Max Brand's and Zane Grey's pulp sales are duly noted in books on the authors (the two best are *Max Brand: The Big "Westerner,"* by Robert Easton, and *Zane Grey*, by Frank Gruber), but little or nothing is said about the pulps involved, not even such relevant matters as the kind and amount of illustrative art given to major pulp works by the writers discussed. In the area of science fiction, on the other hand, an abundance of talented and scholarly minded "fans," who literally grew up with the pulps of that genre, have seen to it that the central relevance of the pulps to the development of science fiction in the twentieth century has received its just dues in a vast number of amateur, small press, and generally published titles. In fact, there is virtually no text on science fiction as a genre in which the pulps are not discussed in often intimate and highly informative length. (Since a great number of these will doubtless be analyzed and listed in the essay on science fiction in this volume, I will avoid extensive repetition here, mentioning only a few titles in the following passages dealing with small press publications on the pulps.) Aside from texts on detective fiction, Western fiction, science fiction, and fantasy, little has appeared from general or academic publishers in book form covering fictional genres prominent in the pulps (there has been no study, for example, of adventure fiction as such, or of popular war fiction, etc.), so that the relevant pulp facets here remain as unexamined on this level as in detective and Western fiction.

Some of the very few texts which touch knowledgeably on the fields of periodical popular fiction which preceded the pulps might advantageously be mentioned here. These would include, certainly, the monumental study of the first dime-novel publishing house, *The House of Beadle and Adams and Its Dime and Nickel Novels*, by Albert Johanssen; *Dime Novels*, by Edmund Pearson; *Books in Black and Red*, by Edmund Pearson; *Villains Galore*, by Mary Noel; *Virgin Land*, by Henry Nash Smith; *Bang! Bang!*, by George Ade; *Penrod Jashber*, by Booth Tarkington; and (largely for impressionistic humor) *A Plea for Old Cap Collier*, by Irvin S. Cobb.

In the small press area, several works of direct and important relevance to the pulp fiction magazine field have appeared in recent years, while more will apparently continue to appear, thanks to the development over the past decade of a new, concentrated body of interest among bibliophiles in the contents, sequences, and fine points of differentiation to be found in the pulps. This growth of interest has been augmented by the appearance in recent years of several small journals devoted wholly to the pulps, their contents, and collection. Prominent among the small press works which serve this interest is a fine impressionistic study of several pulp genres, with no pretense to formal history, popular fiction writer Ron Goulart's engaging *Cheap Thrills*. Goulart quickly covers most of the major pulp genres with an engaging gloss and includes a number of black-and-white pages of pulp cover and interior art. Some very pertinent information about pulp writing and editing can be found in the several pages of direct quotes obtained by Goulart from surviving pulp writers which close this book. More informative in the sense of its organized emphasis on a single pulp subject is Robert Kenneth Jones's *The Shudder Pulps* from a mail-order book business, Fax Collector's Editions. This data- and quotation-packed text deals wholly with the sex-and-sadism pulps of the 1930s, includes a great many reduced black-and-white pulp cover and interior art cuts, and is meticulously indexed (although, curiously, no checklist of the pulps covered is included). In *The "Weird Tales" Story*, also from Fax, Robert Weinberg similarly focuses on a single pulp subject, the development of the famed fantasy magazine between 1923 and 1973. Although this work lacks the fine index of the Jones title, it includes a large number of black-and-white photos and reproductions of covers and interior art from *Weird Tales*. As with the Goulart book, a number of short but worthwhile quotations from writers and artists associated with the magazine are included. Alva Rogers's *A Requiem for "Astounding,"* from Advent Publishers, a mail-order house developed within science fiction fandom in the 1950s, deals engagingly with the history of the central science fiction pulp, *Astounding Stories*, through all of its literary and titular permutations, and includes both a detailed index and an excellent selection of cover and interior art in black-and-white reproduction.

The foregoing small press titles are hardcover in the original editions. Among paperback (and generally smaller) texts from this source, one of the most notable works is Lohr McKinstrey and Robert Weinberg's *The Hero Pulp Index*. This painstaking and nearly inclusive compilation by story title and date of all the issues of all the hero pulps in the 1930s and later has been a vital reference guide to research in this important area of pulp publishing. Included are a number of black-and-white pulp cover reproductions, and summaries of the themes of each pulp covered. Some separate (and generally well done) studies of individual hero pulps are *The Man Behind Doc Savage*, by Robert Weinberg; *America's Secret Service Ace*, by Nick Carr, which deals with *Operator #5*; *Gangland's Doom*, by Frank Eisgruber, Jr., covering *The Shadow*; and *The Many Faces of the Whisperer*, by Will Murray. None of these texts, published by Weinberg with no separate press name, has indexes, but all are well and appropriately illustrated with black-and-white cuts from the pulps covered and contain full lists of the issues discussed.

Among the small reprint publishers almost wholly devoted to hardcover republication of important works from the pulps (many of which are often reprinted profitably by major paperback houses in several editions) are Arkham House of Wisconsin, founded in 1939 and the forerunner of all such publishers, with nearly one hundred titles to its credit, and largely concerned with pulp material from *Weird Tales* and the science fiction and fantasy pulps (particularly the work of H. P. Lovecraft, Clark Ashton

Smith, and August Derleth); Donald M. Grant of Rhode Island, who has published over twenty-six titles to date that are largely involved with the pulp works of Robert E. Howard and Talbot Mundy; Fax Collector's Editions, which reprints memorable fiction from the broad range of pulps in a myriad of hardcover and paperback volumes; and Carcosa of North Carolina, which specializes in large, definitive anthologies of the pulp work of major writers in all genres. The science fiction field fostered a number of such pulp reprint publishers in the postwar decades, notably Gnome Press, Fantasy Press, Shasta Publishers, and Hadley Publishing (later Grant-Hadley, now Donald M. Grant); all but the last are now moribund, the large paperback houses having taken over science fiction and fantasy pulp reprinting directly. Popular Press, of Bowling Green State University in Ohio, has emerged in recent years as an important publisher of general pulp studies, bibliographies, and scholarly anthologies in the field, with several new titles appearing annually.

Of important contemporary periodicals concerned in whole or in part with the study of pulps (excluding science fiction fan publications, which are a highly specialized field of their own), it is necessary to mention Nils Hardin's *Xenophile*, Will Murray's *Duende*, Ray B. Browne's *Journal of Popular Culture*, Robert Weinberg's *Weird Tales Collector* and *Pulp*, Allen J. Hubin's *Armchair Detective*, J. Randolph Cox's *Dime Novel Round-up*, and Donald Halpern's *Antaeus*. Of these, in 1987 only the *Journal of Popular Culture*, the *Armchair Detective*, and the *Dime Novel Round-up* are being regularly published. The two Weinberg titles and *Duende* are now only irregularly issued, with long (years-long) gaps between issues, while *Xenophile*, perhaps the best of the lot, has been discontinued for many years now. *Antaeus*'s pulp interest appears to have been short-lived; its present focus is little-magazine "fine writing."

In addition to the works discussed above, all of which appeared prior to 1978, the subsequent decade has seen the publication of a number of excellent volumes by the publishers cited, as well as by some houses new to the field. Remarkable in its ambition and accomplishment is Robert Sampson's six-volume *Yesterday's Faces*, subtitled *A Study of Series Characters in the Early Pulp Magazines*. For Sampson, "early" means largely the pulps printed in the 1920s and before; consequently, he is concerned primarily with the general-content pulps such as *Argosy, Blue Book*, and *Adventure*, although some early genre titles such as *Detective Story Magazine* and *Weird Tales* are well covered. The great bulk of Sampson's fascinating subject matter has never been discussed in print before, and his pioneering examination in depth of the exotic creatures he parades before us in volume after volume is—thanks to the author's lively, humorous style—endlessly absorbing. From Nick Carter to Wu Fang, by way of Semi Dual, Fantomas, and John Carter, Sampson paints a series of garishly arresting portraits; his brisk, witty summation of the kill-and-rescue plots of the Tarzan novels (in volume 2) is the best such recounting I have ever read. Another fact-packed study by Sampson, colorfully surveying the 326-novel career of the Shadow and called *The Night Master*, is the leading work among recent books dealing with hero pulp figures, such as Tom Johnson and Will Murray's incisive *Secret Agent "X": A History* and Nick Carr's absorbing study of *G–8 and His Battle Aces*, titled *The Flying Spy*.

Excellent biographies of major pulp writers have appeared, notably Peter Berresford Ellis's account of Talbot Mundy's life, *The Last Adventurer*, and two penned by L. Sprague de Camp: *Lovecraft: A Biography*, and (with Catherine Crook de Camp and Jane Whittington Griffin) *Dark Valley Destiny: The Life of Robert E. Howard*. Glenn Lord's *The Last Celt: A Bio-Bibliography of Robert Ervin Howard* deals with both the life and works of Howard in loving detail, much as an earlier work by Darrell C. Richardson, titled *Max Brand: The Man and His Work*, covers the life and work of its subject in roughly equal parts. Notable volumes in still another novel form, which might be termed the bio-bibliography-anthology, are Douglas G. Greene's engaging *The Door to Doom and Other Detections* by John Dickson Carr (although Carr was only infrequently a writer for the pulps, the emphasis in this text is on this peripheral, periodical work), and Donald M. Grant's *Talbot Mundy: Messenger of Destiny*, which combines articles about Mundy's life and work with an excellent bibliography.

A pair of superficial works derived from (rather than seriously studying) the English parallels of the American dime novel and nickel thriller (called variously penny dreadfuls, penny bloods, and shilling shockers), and chiefly made up of numerous reproductions of the illustrations and color covers of these periodicals, have appeared during the past decade. These are Michael Anglo's *Penny Dreadfuls and Other Victorian Horrors*, and Peter Haining's *The Art of Horror Stories* (which includes a good deal of American pulp horror fiction art in its later pages). Two other titles in this arcane area by Haining are extremely useful anthologies with all too brief prefactory matter called *The Penny Dreadful* and *The Shilling Shockers*. A light but informed study in some depth of this material is to be found in E. S. Turner's *Boys Will Be Boys*, where the reader will want to consult both the first (1948) and the current (1975) editions, since the two versions contain much dissimilar but equally informative matter. Two worthwhile anthologies of dime novel texts are E. F. Bleiler's *Eight Dime Novels* and Gary Hoppenstand's *The Dime Novel Detective*. The Hoppenstand volume includes bibliographies of such long-running dime novel characters as Nick Carter, Old Sleuth, and Secret Service, while the Bleiler is marvelously informed with the editor's characteristic knowledge of all aspects of nineteenth-century esoterica. Daryl Jones's fine study, *The Dime Novel Western*, is a genuinely gripping and entertaining account in detail of a previously underdiscussed body of bizarre writing.

By far the most outstanding work of scholarship in the pulp and dime novel field to date is Michael L. Cook's superbly edited and comprehensively encyclopedic *Mystery, Detective, and Espionage Magazines*, in which numerous experts (including Robert Sampson, Nick Carr, and others discussed above) have written succinctly definitive entries about virtually every crime-suspense dime novel or pulp title published over the past century, making it the one absolutely indispensable reference work for any student of the pulp and dime novel. Since it was published in 1983, many of its entries for more obscure titles have already become obsolete due to continued discoveries about these titles, and the doubtless forthcoming revised edition should prove even more invaluable a reference work than the present volume. Another work edited by Cook, of literally endless use to the critical researcher in popular fiction history, is *Mystery Fanfare: A Composite Annotated Index to Mystery and Related Fanzines 1963 to 1981*, in which some seventeen old, current, major, and obscure publications devoted to pulps (as well as another twenty-eight titles about mystery fiction in general, but often touching on pulps) are indexed through some 441 pages and several thousand articles. A vitally related and more extensive work is Walter Albert's *Detective and Mystery Fiction: An International Bibliography of Secondary Sources*, which lists and discusses (often in considerable detail) all books and many articles in selected general and fan magazines which deal with mystery fiction in hardcover, paperback, pulps, and dime novels in any way at all (although, for space considerations, most Sherlockiana has been excluded). Many long-promised pulp indexes continue in preparation in various places, but two crucial works indexing *Black Mask* and *Dime Detective* have at last been printed. E. R. Hagemann's *A Comprehensive Index to "Black Mask," 1920–1951* is an excellent formal indexing by author of every story and many articles published in that doyen of detective pulps (although an earlier and more obscure work compiled by E. H. Mundell—*"Black Mask": an Index*—is of much greater use to the collector and institution that has to decide which issues to purchase from dealers who list by date only, since it prints the contents page of every issue from volume 1, number 1, through volume 36, number 2, in simple sequence, exactly as each one appeared in each issue with all titles and authors included, an indexing concept particularly vital at this time in a field with so few complete reference runs of non–science fiction pulps accessible to researchers with the Hagemann type of index in hand). James L. Traylor's *Dime Detective Index* wisely combines both forms of indexing in his masterfully accomplished volume, a model for future pulp indexes (including, one hopes, those long needed for the *Argosy-All-Story-Cavalier* composite Munsey run; *Adventure; Blue Book; Detective Tales*—and I do mean *both* versions of this popular title; the *Spicy-Speed-Private* and *Super Detective* group of titles, so tightly interrelated; the *Popular;* and a considerable number of other long-lived and vital titles in the field).

BIBLIOGRAPHY

Books and Articles

Ade, George. *Bang! Bang!* New York: J. H. Sears, 1928.

Albert, Walter. *Detective and Mystery Fiction: An International Bibliography of Secondary Sources.* Madison, Ind.: Brownstone Books, 1985.

Anglo, Michael. *Penny Dreadfuls and Other Victorian Horrors.* London: Jupiter Books, 1977.

Bacon, Daisy. *Love Story Writer.* New York: Hermitage House, 1954.

Bedford-Jones, Henry. *This Fiction Business.* New York: Covici-Freide, 1929.

Bleiler, E. F., ed. *Eight Dime Novels.* New York: Dover, 1974.

Britt, George. *Forty Years, Forty Millions: The Career of Frank A. Munsey.* New York: n.p., 1935.

Browne, Ray B., and Gary Hoppenstand, eds. *The Defective Detective in the Pulps.* Bowling Green, Ohio: Bowling Green State University Popular Press, 1983.

Carr, Nick. *America's Secret Service Ace (Operator #5).* Oak Lawn, Ill.: Robert Weinberg, 1974.

————. *The Flying Spy (G–8).* Chicago: Robert Weinberg, 1978.

Cawelti, John G. *The Six-Gun Mystique.* Bowling Green, Ohio: Bowling Green State University Popular Press, 1970.

Cobb, Irvin S. *A Plea For Old Cap Collier.* New York: George H. Doran, 1921.

Cook, Michael L., ed. *Mystery, Detective, and Espionage Magazines.* Westport, Conn.: Greenwood Press, 1983.

————. *Mystery Fanfare: A Composite Annotated Index to Mystery and Related Fanzines, 1963–1981.* Bowling Green, Ohio: Bowling Green State University Popular Press, 1983.

Cook, William Wallace [John Milton Edwards]. *The Fiction Factory.* Ridgewood, N.J.: The Editor Co., 1912.

Day, Donald B. *Index to the Science-Fiction Magazines: 1926–1950.* Portland, Oreg.: Perri Press, 1952.

De Camp, L. Sprague. *Science Fiction Handbook.* New York: Hermitage House, 1953. rev. ed. Philadelphia: Owlswick Press, 1975.

————. *Lovecraft: A Biography.* New York: Doubleday, 1975.

De Camp, L. Sprague, Catherine Crook de Camp, and Jane Whittington Griffin. *Dark Valley Destiny: The Life of Robert E. Howard.* New York: Bluejay Books, 1983.

Easton, Robert. *Max Brand: The Big "Westerner."* Norman: University of Oklahoma Press, 1970.

Eisgruber, Frank, Jr. *Gangland's Doom: The Shadow of the Pulps.* Oak Lawn, Ill.: Robert Weinberg, 1974.

Ellis, Peter Berresford. *The Last Adventurer: The Life of Talbot Mundy 1879–1940.* West Kingston, R.I.: Donald M. Grant, 1984.

Etulain, Richard W., and Michael T. Marsden, eds. *The Popular Western: Essays Toward a Definition.* Bowling Green, Ohio: Bowling Green State University Popular Press, 1974.

Farmer, Philip José. *Doc Savage: His Apocalyptic Life.* Garden City, N.Y.: Doubleday, 1973.

Farsace, Larry. *Golden Atom*. New York: Golden Atom Publications, 1955.

Goodstone, Tony, ed. *The Pulps*. New York: Chelsea House, 1970.

Goulart, Ron. *Cheap Thrills: An Informal History of the Pulp Magazines*. New Rochelle, N.Y.: Arlington House, 1972.

Grant, Donald M., ed. *Talbot Mundy: Messenger of Destiny*. West Kingston, R.I.: Donald M. Grant, 1983.

Greene, Douglas G., ed. *The Door to Doom and Other Detections*, by John Dickson Carr. New York: Harper and Row, 1980.

Gruber, Frank. *The Pulp Jungle*. Los Angeles: Sherbourne Press, 1967.

———. *Zane Grey*. Cleveland, Ohio: World, 1970.

Hagemann, E. R. *A Comprehensive Index to "Black Mask," 1920–1951*. Bowling Green, Ohio: Bowling Green State University Popular Press, 1982.

Haining, Peter, ed. *The Art of Horror Stories*. Secaucus, N.J.: Chartwell Books, 1986.

———. *The Art of Mystery and Detective Stories*. Secaucus, N.J.: Chartwell Books, 1986.

———. *The Penny Dreadful*. London: Victor Gollancz, 1975.

———. *The Shilling Shockers*. New York: St. Martin's Press, 1978.

Heins, Henry Hardy. *A Golden Anniversary Bibliography of Edgar Rice Burroughs*. West Kingston, R.I.: Donald M. Grant, 1964.

Herron, Don, ed. *The Dark Barbarian: The Writings of Robert E. Howard*. A Critical Anthology. Westport, Conn.: Greenwood Press, 1984.

Hersey, Harold. "Looking Backward into the Future." *Golden Atom* (1953), 45–68.

———. *Pulpwood Editor*. New York: Frederick A. Stokes, 1937.

Hoppenstand, Gary, ed. *The Dime Novel Detective*. Bowling Green, Ohio: Bowling Green State University Popular Press, 1982.

Johanssen, Albert. *The House of Beadle and Adams and Its Dime and Nickel Novels*. Norman: University of Oklahoma Press, 1950. Supplement, 1962.

Johnson, Tom, and Will Murray. *Secret Agent "X": A History*. Oak Lawn, Ill.: Robert Weinberg, 1980.

Jones, Daryl. *The Dime Novel Western*. Bowling Green, Ohio: Bowling Green State University Popular Press, 1978.

Jones, H. Bedford. *This Fiction Business*. New York: Covici-Fried, 1929.

Jones, Robert Kenneth. *The Shudder Pulps: A History of the Weird Menace Magazines of the 1930s*. West Linn, Oreg.: Fax Collector's Editions, 1975.

Lord, Glenn. *The Last Celt: A Bio-Bibliography of Robert Ervin Howard*. West Kingston, R.I.: Donald M. Grant, 1976.

McCampbell, Donald. *Don't Step On It—It Might Be a Writer: Reminiscences of a Literary Agent*. Los Angeles: Sherbourne Press, 1972.

McKinstrey, Lohr, and Robert Weinberg. *The Hero Pulp Index*. Evergreen, Colo.: Opar Press, 1971.

Madden, David, ed. *Tough Guy Writers of the Thirties*. Carbondale: Southern Illinois University Press, 1968.

Mott, Frank Luther. *A History of American Magazines*, volume 4. Cambridge, Mass.: Harvard University Press, 1957.

Mundell, E. H. *"Black Mask": An Index*. Portage, Ind.: Mundell, 1969.

Munsey, Frank. *The Founding of the Munsey Publishing House*. New York: Munsey, 1907.

Murray, Will. *The Many Faces of the Whisperer*. Pulp 7. Oak Lawn, Ill.: Robert Weinberg, 1975.

———. *Secrets of Doc Savage*. Greenwood, Mass.: Odyssey Publications, 1981.

Noel, Mary. *Villains Galore: The Heyday of the Popular Story Weekly*. New York: Macmillan, 1954.

Pearson, Edmund. *Books in Black and Red*. New York: Macmillan, 1923.

———. *Dime Novels*. Boston: Little, Brown, 1929.

Porges, Irwin. *Edgar Rice Burroughs: The Man Who Created Tarzan*. Provo, Utah: Brigham Young University Press, 1975.

Reynolds, Quentin. *The Fiction Factory: From Pulp Row to Quality Street*. New York: Random House, 1955.

Richardson, Darrell C. *Max Brand: The Man and His Work*. Los Angeles: Fantasy Publishing, 1952.

Roberts, Garyn G. *A Cent a Story! The Best from Ten Detective Aces*. Bowling Green, Ohio: Bowling Green State University Popular Press, 1986.

Rogers, Alva. *A Requiem for "Astounding."* Chicago: Advent, 1964.

Sampson, Robert. *The Night Master*. Chicago: Pulp Press, 1982.

———. *Yesterday's Faces: A Study of Series Characters in the Early Pulp Magazines*. Vols. 1, 2 & 3 of a projected six. Bowling Green, Ohio: Bowling Green State University Popular Press, 1983, 1985, and 1986.

Shine, Walter, and Jean Shine. *A Bibliography of the Published Works of John D. MacDonald*. Gainesville: University of Florida, 1980.

Smith, Henry Nash. *Virgin Land: The American West as Symbol and Myth*. Cambridge, Mass.: Harvard University Press, 1950, 1970.

Tarkington, Booth. *Penrod Jashber*. Garden City, N.Y.: Doubleday, 1929.

Traylor, James L. *Dime Detective Index*. New Carrolton, Md.: Pulp Collector Press, 1986.

Turner, E. S. *Boys Will Be Boys: The Story of Sweeney Todd, Deadwood Dick, Sexton Blake, Billy Bunter, Dick Barton, et al.* London: Michael Joseph, 1975.

Turner, Robert L. *Some of My Best Friends Are Writers, But I Wouldn't Want My Daughter to Marry One!* Los Angeles: Sherbourne Press, 1970.

Weinberg, Robert. *The Man Behind Doc Savage: A Tribute to Lester Dent*. Oak Lawn, Ill.: Robert Weinberg, 1974.

———. *The "Weird Tales" Story*. West Linn, Oreg.: Fax Collector's Editions, 1977.

Periodicals

Antaeus. New York. Issues undated.

Armchair Detective. New York, 1967–.

Dime Novel Round-up. Fall River, Mass., 1931–.

Duende. North Quincy, Mass., 1977–.

Journal of Popular Culture. Bowling Green, Ohio, 1977–.

Weird Tales Collector. Chicago, 1977–.

Xenophile. St. Louis, Mo., 1974–.

11

Romantic Fiction

KAY MUSSELL

As defined by publishers and readers, the popular romantic novel is a tale about the courtship and marriage of two main characters. It may take the form that Robert Palfrey Utter and Gwendolyn Bridges Needham described as "the typical plot of the English novel," which "has love for the starting-post and marriage for the finish line." Or, the plot can concern the problems of an already-achieved marriage, with difficulties between husband and wife resolved when the wife is rewarded with a better marriage to her current husband or a new marriage with a new lover. In addition, some romantic novels, more accurately called "anti-romances," invert the love plot while reinforcing the assumptions of the form. In "anti-romances" the value structure is unchanged, but the heroine behaves in such a way that she cannot be rewarded with marriage in the end. These, too, are romances, although they serve as cautionary tales rather than as models to be emulated. Because the tensions and issues inherent in love stories are traditionally women's concerns, romantic fiction is almost entirely a female form of escape.

Many novels in literary history revolve around these questions of love, courtship, and marriage imagined from a woman's perspective. The tension for a woman in the process of achieving identity through a lasting marriage has been dramatized in fiction extensively from Samuel Richardson's *Pamela* (1741) to the most recent issue of *Redbook* or *Good Housekeeping*, or to this month's selection of Harlequin Romances. Significantly, however, the shape and conventions of the popular romantic novel have remained similar over time.

The plot of a romantic novel begins with an assumption—unquestioned and unexamined except in a few books—that the necessary, preordained, and basic goal of any woman is to achieve a satisfying, mature, and all-fulfilling marriage. The primacy of romantic love, in defining a woman's place and value in the world, is rarely in doubt in these books. The plot may appear diffuse, but it never loses sight of that goal. Although other kinds of events and actions by the protagonist may take up much of the novel, those events are always related eventually to the woman's marital status and condition of happiness at the end of the book. Thus, although much of the action of *Gone with the Wind* (1936) concerns Scarlett O'Hara's experiences during the Civil War and Reconstruction, the underlying value structure of the novel is prescribed by Scarlett's relationships with men. Similarly, Maria Susanna Cummins's *The Lamplighter* (1854) traces the childhood and young adulthood of its main character, Gertie, showing how she learned to be a worthy and moral young woman through the influence of various other characters on her life. In the end, however, the novel confirms her struggle for identity when she marries the hero, who has figured only infrequently through much of the plot.

Romantic fiction actually represents a group of literary formulas, not just one. Romances intersect with several other kinds of popular fiction: the gothic, the historical, the juvenile, the sentimental, the domestic, and the seduction. But romances cannot be entirely identified with any of these other formulas. Recently, critical work on romantic fiction has begun to emerge in scholarship, and scholars disagree on both definitions and interpretations. A major difficulty in dealing with the romance is that it is such an ephemeral form. Some examples are so widely popular and so often reprinted that they come to mind immediately: Susanna Rowson's *Charlotte Temple* (1791) or Margaret Mitchell's *Gone with the Wind* (1936). Others have certainly been lost forever as the last cracked and crumbling copy, published by a local printer as a favor to a neighboring author, has disappeared in the trash after an attic was cleaned. Romantic novels are almost never reviewed, unless they are highly publicized blockbusters. Authors who write them tend to be relatively private persons who, until recently, were rarely interviewed or written about. Many authors of romantic novels are very prolific, publishing several books a year, making large amounts of money from their work, but reaping little acclaim except from readers.

Romantic novels are the fare of public libraries, which have large circulations for these books but which do not rebind or reorder most of them when they wear out. Such books are also commonplace in drugstores and grocery stores. Romantic fiction is a staple in women's magazines today, as it has been for almost two centuries. It has been common in subscription series of novels sold by dime novel publishers in the nineteenth century and as named series (Harlequin Romances, Silhouette Special Editions, Barbara Cartland's Library of Love) in the twentieth century. It is easy to find current examples of the form; it was probably as easy to find them in 1880 as it is today. But it is difficult today to find 1880 examples or even 1920 or 1930 versions because many of these novels leave very little trace, and many are impossible to identify as romances from a mere title or author's name.

HISTORIC OUTLINE

The first example of a popular romantic novel in America was probably Susanna Rowson's *Charlotte Temple*, one of the great best sellers of literary history. First published in Britain by a woman who moved to America to set up a school for young ladies, *Charlotte Temple* went through more than 200 editions, 40 before the author's death in the 1820s. The first American edition was published in Philadelphia in 1794. As recently as the early twentieth century, it was still in print; one 1905 edition was illustrated by photographs, including one of Charlotte's reputed grave in New York City. *Charlotte Temple* was a classic seduction novel about a young girl who allowed herself to be carried off to America by an officer; when she became pregnant, he abandoned her, and she died after giving birth to a daughter, whose life was later chronicled by Rowson in *Lucy Temple*, also known as *Charlotte's Daughter* (1828).

Many other seduction novels were written in the early nineteenth century. Hannah W. Foster's *The Coquette* (1797), Eliza Vicery's *Emily Hamilton* (1803), and several anonymous novels, such as *Fidelity Rewarded* (1796) and *Amelia, or the Faithless Briton* (1798), told the familiar story. Most of these, incidentally, were presented to the public as true stories, thinly disguised by changing names and places. Since seduction stories served so consciously as cautionary tales, the claim for their truth is logical, although it might be just as reasonable to conclude that the novels claimed a factual basis to combat the contemporary prejudice against fiction as harmful because it was made up of lies. After the early nineteenth century, a full-blown seduction story was hard to find. The tensions of the precarious position of "loose women" were still important in later romantic novels; but the explicit warning about men, the specific if somewhat euphemistic story about sexuality, was less significant in romantic fiction.

From the 1820s until after the Civil War, romantic fiction was dominated by a group of women novelists usually referred to as the "domestic sentimentalists." They included writers such as Catharine Maria Sedgwick, Lydia Maria Child, Fanny Fern (Ruth Payton Willis), Mary Jane Holmes, Ann Sophia Stephens, Maria Susanna Cummins, and others. The work of these women has been more thoroughly documented than that of any other romantic novelists, and new critical studies of their work emerge every year with the impetus of the women's studies movement in scholarship. Although critics disagree about the meaning of "domestic sentimentalism," the novels are structured as love stories and almost all the heroines are married, happily, at the end of the books. Between the beginning and the end, males may be less in evidence than females, as the heroines spend their time solving domestic difficulties and improving their characters, saving souls, and learning to be "true women." But despite the trials of domestic life, the reconciliation with woman's place in a good marriage is where the plots end.

These were the novels that prompted Nathaniel Hawthorne's heartfelt cry in a letter to his publisher in 1855, a few years after *The Scarlet Letter* (1850) had been virtually ignored by the mass reading audience:

American is now wholly given over to a d----d mob of scribbling women, and I should have no chance of success while the public taste is occupied with their trash— and should be ashamed of myself if I did succeed. What is the mystery of these innumerable editions of the "Lamplighter," and other books neither better nor worse?—worse they could not be, and better they need not be, when they sell by the 100,000. . . .

After the Civil War, romantic fiction was found in dime-novel series and story papers, as well as in full-length novels, which were often serialized in newspapers and magazines before book publication. Augusta Jane Evans Wilson's *St. Elmo* (1867) and novels by Mrs. E.D.E.N. Southworth were especially popular, although the work of the domestic sentimentalists was still in print and widely read. Since there are few studies of romantic fiction in this period, it is more difficult to identify titles and authors. Laura Jean Libbey's novels about working girls and the historical novels of Mary Johnston used romance elements. A particularly interesting writer of romantic fiction, who also wrote numerous advice books, popular history and Bible studies, and edited a magazine, was Isabella Alden (known as "Pansy"). Her niece, Grace Livingston Hill, was to become one of the best-selling romance writers of the twentieth century.

Lists of best sellers are available from 1895 onward, so it becomes an easier task to identify romantic novels that did well in the marketplace. Those books that did not sell widely enough to appear in these compilations are still hard to retrieve, but enough information is available to indicate that the love story was in style. Kathleen Norris's novels of family and domestic drama were especially popular during the first thirty years of the twentieth century. Grace Livingston Hill's novels of romance and traditional religion were popular alongside the racier books of Fannie Hurst and Faith Baldwin. Emilie Loring also sold widely. Only a very few romantic novels, however, were great best sellers until the 1930s. *Gone with the Wind* appealed to a much wider audience than most—to men as well as to women. The 1977 edition of the best-seller lists, Alice Payne Hackett and James Henry Burke's *80 Years of Best-Sellers*, lists it as the number 11 book on the all-time hardbound best-seller list; it is the top fiction book on the list after several cookbooks, Kahlil Gibran's *The Prophet*, and five Dr. Seuss books. Incidentally, the number 12 book on the all-time list is also a romance—Anya Seton's *The Winthrop Woman* (1958), a book about the Massachusetts Bay Colony, which seems to be an enduring setting in popular romantic fiction.

Following *Gone with the Wind*, the next romance best-seller was Daphne du Maurier's *Rebecca* (1938), the work of a British author who has always been very popular in this country. Kathleen Winsor's *Forever Amber* (1944) was also important. Most recently, Rosemary Rogers's *Dark Fires* (1975) has reached the all-time list of books that have sold more than two million copies. It is significant to note that two of these books, *Gone with the Wind* and *Forever Amber*, are inversions of the classic romantic story with heroines who do not deserve a happy marriage and who are left alone by the men they love. It appears probable that this inversion holds more appeal for male readers than does a more straightforward love story.

The post–World War II period has been very fruitful for the popular romantic novel in America. Novels by British writers have been readily available in paperback and have been widely read. There is little sense in trying to separate the works of British and American authors during this period, except for the record, since both sell widely in both countries and are almost routinely published on both sides of the Atlantic. Particularly popular in the last three decades have been British authors Georgette Heyer, Barbara Cartland, and Dorothy Eden, as well as the Americans Anya Seton, Rosemary Rogers, and Janet Dailey. The Harlequin romances, inexpensive paperback originals published in Canada by arrangement with the British firm of Mills and Boon, have also been widely read and imitated. These books, like the dime novels of the nineteenth century, are sold on book racks as well as by subscription. Most are straightforward romances—love stories set in interesting or exotic places or about people with interesting or exotic lives.

In 1980, after Harlequin's American distribution agreement with Simon and Schuster broke down, the American firm created a new series of paperback romances entitled Silhouette. Based on extensive reader research, Silhouette Romances employed an agressive advertising campaign on television, reader panels to approve manuscripts, and blatant imitation of Harlequin design and plot types. So closely was the series modeled on Harlequin Presents that Silhouette was forced by a court decision to redesign its cover. Some of the most successful Mills and Boon/Harlequin authors—most notably Anne Hampson and Janet Dailey—were lured from Harlequin to Silhouette. Other publishing firms also began new series of paperback romances or repackaged older ones to compete more effectively with Harlequin and Silhouette. For a few years in the early 1980s, the market became glutted with series romances, including those in the Dell Candlelight Ecstasy series, the Jove Second Chance at Love series, and the Bantam Loveswept series. Competition led to a rapid change in the level of sophistication for series books, especially in a widening of the range of character types and a loosening of the traditional restraints on premarital sex. After a serious loss of market share, Harlequin ended the most intense competition by buying Silhouette and continuing to publish all the competing series from both companies.

Magazines have also flourished on love stories in their fiction pages, from the most serious and uplifting of the women's magazines such as *Godey's Lady's Book* in the nineteenth century to *Good Housekeeping* in the twentieth. Confession magazines, love comics, and pulps are twentieth-century versions of the nineteenth-century story papers.

The drama of courtship and marriage has had a strong hold on the imaginations of American women readers for two centuries. The specifics of the plot have changed over the years, but the value structure and shape of the narrative have changed relatively little. Amber does not die for her adultery as does Charlotte Temple, but the lesson of the two novels is clearly related. Melanie is alowed a happy and fulfilling marriage that is denied to Scarlett, even though Scarlett may have had the greater love, since Rhett is so much more passionate than Ashley. In domestic sentimental novels, women spend their time in domestic trivia rather than in the social whirl of more recent romantic novels by Georgette Heyer and others, but their behavior and their reward for virtue remain similar. Although heroines of contemporary series romances may now be allowed premarital sexual experience and professional ambition, at heart they remain as committed to marriage and family as were their predecessors.

REFERENCE WORKS

Until recently, there were few reference guides or bibliographical works that could be used to identify romantic novels or to survey criticism about them. Even now, much useful information is still most easily found in standard references and bibliographies that include such fiction. One excellent reference guide to contemporary romance authors and titles, James Vinson's *Twentieth-Century Romance and Gothic Writers*, was published in 1982. An important tool for finding romantic novels is a massive twenty-five-volume guide entitled *Bibliography of English Language Fiction in the Library of Congress Through 1950*, subdivided into three separate and complete bibliographies compiled by R. Glenn Wright. These volumes are composed of reproduced cards from the Library of Congress shelf list. The sets are organized, respectively, by author, title, and chronology; and because the cards themselves are reproduced, they contain much information that might not be available in a standard bibliographical format. The guides are organized within each of the three sets by nationality and include indexes to translators and translations. For the early period, when few novels were being published in America, the chronological bibliography is most useful. Later, once a researcher has identified an author as having written romantic fiction, the author bibliography is most helpful because it lists an entire survey of the author's work in the Library of Congress. Although not all books written in English are represented (since the Library of Congress does not catalog all copyrighted works it receives), the bibliography cannot be used for constructing definitive lists of works, but the collection is comprehensive enough to make it a good place to start.

Several general studies of American fiction provide information about popular novels that include romantic works. Henri Petter's *The Early American Novel* is an excellent monograph with valuable bibliographical sections for works before 1820. He includes synopses of novels, a useful tool for identifying types of fiction; there are also bibliographies of novels of the period, sources from the period, and modern criticism.

Surveys of popular culture in America also provide good sources for titles and authors of romantic fiction. The definitive work is Russel B. Nye's *The Unembarrassed Muse*. Other sources include James D. Hart's *The Popular Book* and Frank Luther Mott's *Golden Multitudes*, both studies of the best seller in America. For materials since 1895, R. R. Bowker's periodic updates of best-seller lists by Alice Payne Hackett are the best sources available. These, however, list only books that achieved best-seller status, so many popular formula novels do not appear on the lists. In 1979, Harlequin Books issued a paperback history which lists all its titles and authors for the first thirty years.

Since there has been so little critical work on the novels, there is very little of bibliographical interest in critical essays and books. One specialized bibliography, *They Wrote for a Living: A Bibliography of the Works of Susan Bogert Warner and Anna Bartlett Warner*, by Dorothy Hurlbut Sanderson, was recently published. A 1978 monograph by Nina Baym, *Woman's Fiction: A Guide to Novels by and about Women in America 1820–1870*, also contains some useful bibliographical materials. For Susanna Rowson, R.W.G. Vail's *Susanna Haswell Rowson, the Author of "Charlotte Temple": A Bibliographical Study* is comprehensive and standard. Kay Mussell's *Women's Gothic and Romantic Fiction: A Reference Guide* covers criticism through 1979.

RESEARCH COLLECTIONS

There are no research collections devoted strictly to romantic fiction, which makes the researcher's job difficult. However, there are collections of popular American novels, as well as some paper and manuscript collections, that should be consulted. As the U.S. copyright depository, the Library of Congress collection is excellent, particularly in the Rare Book

Room, where there is an (unfortunately) uncataloged collection of more than 20,000 paperback dime novels. Finding romantic novels in this collection is a hit-or-miss process since the finders' guide lists the collection by series title; but some lists are descriptive and will aid in locating book titles and authors' names. The Rare Book Room also has more than a dozen separate editions of Rowson's *Charlotte Temple*, including a dime-novel reprint with an "authentic" portrait of Charlotte in high Victorian dress. The general fiction collection at the library also contains a wealth of materials. In many cases, fairly complete hardbound collections of particular authors' works exist virtually untouched on the shelves of the PZ3 category. If an author who wrote romantic fiction can be identified, the chances are that works published in the twentieth century will be available.

Several special collections in the New York Public Library include popular fiction. The Berg Collection of English and American literature is excellent; the Rare Book Division offers both the Frank P. O'Brien Collection of Beadle Dime Novels (1,400 volumes) and a chapbook file. The Arents Collection of books in parts (including serials, shilling shockers, and penny dreadfuls) also includes romantic fiction.

Elmira College in Elmira, New York, has a one hundred–volume cataloged collection entitled "Genteel Women's Reading, 1855–1955." The Bertha Van Riper Overbury Gift at Barnard College consists of nearly 2,000 books, mostly rare, written by American women, as well as almost 1,000 manuscripts. The Cleveland Public Library collection has dime novels and other nineteenth-century romances. In Portland, Maine, the Westbrook College Library has a collection of 1,200 volumes written by Maine women writers. The collection is especially noteworthy for some rare editions of novels by Mme. Wood, one of the earliest American writers of romantic and gothic fiction. The Bowling Green State University Library also has some romances in its collection of paperback fiction.

Manuscripts and personal papers for writers of romantic fiction are even more difficult to find, although library collections are beginning to reflect the scholarly interest in popular culture materials. Boston University's Mugar Memorial Library, for example, is collecting literary and personal papers, correspondence, and published articles by and about more than 1,000 modern published authors, including materials on several romance writers such as Anya Seton, Dorothy Eden, Phyllis Whitney, and Faith Baldwin. A complete list of authors included is available from the curator of the Division of Special Collections.

Some individual authors are represented by their papers and manuscripts in major research collections. Ellen B. Brandt, author of a recent biography of Susanna Rowson, notes that the best collection of Rowson material is at the American Antiquarian Society, although she also found items at the University of Pennsylvania Rare Book Room, the Pennsylvania Historical Society, the Philadelphia Free Library, and the New York Historical Society, among other standard research libraries. Catharine Maria Sedgwick, who wrote *Hope Leslie* (1827) and *A New England Tale* (1822) among others, lived in Stockbridge, Massachusetts, where her papers, manuscripts, and other memorabilia are to be found in the Stockbridge Library Association's Sedgwick Family Collection. Caroline Lee Hentz has diaries and letters in the Southern Historical Collection at the University of North Carolina at Chapel Hill, as well as letters in the Chamberlain Collection of the Boston Public Library.

Lydia Maria Child wrote prolifically in many forms other than romance; her romantic fiction includes *Hobomok* (1824) and *A Romance of the Republic* (1867). Her papers are in the Hofstra University Library, which includes some manuscripts; letters are in the Ellis Gray Loring Collection of the New York Public Library, the F. G. and S. B. Shaw Papers of the Houghton Library at Harvard University, and the Schlesinger Library at Radcliffe College. Mrs. E.D.E.N. Southworth, one of the most prolific of the romantic writers, can be studied at the Duke University Library or the Library of Congress Manuscript Division. Susan Warner and her sister Anna, authors of a number of books separately and together, lived on Constitution Island in the Hudson River, near West Point. The Constitution Island Association maintains their home and some memorabilia and papers. Susan (under the name Elizabeth Wetherell) wrote one of the period's most popular novels, *The Wide Wide World* (1850). The memorabilia of Mary Jane Holmes, author of more than forty books between 1854 and 1905, is in the Seymour Library in Brockport, New York.

Helen Hunt Jackson, who wrote *Ramona* (1884), is represented in the collections of the Huntington Library and the Jones Library in Amherst, Massachusetts; the latter collection does not circulate. Amelia E. Barr emigrated to the United States from England and wrote more than sixty novels, some romantic and some historical. Her papers are in the Archives Division of the Texas State Library; the collection is restricted. Papers of Harriet Prescott Spofford are in the Historical Society of Pennsylvania and the Essex Institute in Salem, Massachusetts. The New York Public Library has the letters of Laura Jean Libbey.

Mary Johnston, the Virginia author of historical and romantic fiction, donated her papers to the University of Virginia; the collection contains more than 4,000 items. Kathleen Norris's papers are at Stanford University. Frances Parkinson Keyes had a long career as a writer; her papers from 1952 to 1963 are in the University of Virginia Library. Materials on Fannie Hurst can be found at the Olin Library, Washington University, St. Louis, at the Special Collections of the Goldfarb Library at Brandeis University, and at the University of Texas Library.

Materials relating to Margaret Mitchell can be found in the Atlanta Public Library (access is restricted), at Agnes Scott College in Georgia, and at Boston University and Harvard University. The manuscripts of Marcia

Davenport are in the Manuscript Division of the Library of Congress. There are approximately 3,500 items, including literary manuscripts, galley proofs, press clippings, working drafts, notes, and one hundred items of correspondence with Maxwell Perkins, her editor on her major work of romantic fiction, *The Valley of Decision* (1942). Legal briefs and records of the attempt by the Commonwealth of Massachusetts to ban Kathleen Winsor's *Forever Amber* on grounds of obscenity can be found in the Library of Congress Law Library. Additional materials on Margaret Mitchell and Kathleen Winsor are in the Macmillan Collection at the New York Public Library.

HISTORY AND CRITICISM

In recent years, the impetus of women's studies in scholarship has spurred the study of romantic fiction, both as part of larger studies of women and as a subject in itself. Until the experience of women in America was subject to this reinterpretation, critical work on romantic fiction, although often excellent, was random. An occasional dissertation or antiquarian work appeared, and many general works on American fiction included at least brief sections on romantic fiction. Scholars, however, reached little firm agreement about what the novels should be called or on how they should be evaluated.

Background material for understanding popular romantic fiction comprises an enormous number of works, but only a few need citation. Most studies of the medieval romance are far too specialized to be applicable to popular romantic fiction in America; the worlds of the two types of literature are far apart. A notable exception, however, is the small volume by Gillian Beer, *The Romance*, a formalistic approach to the genre. It deals almost entirely with European and pre–1800 romances, but its brief analysis of the relation between the romance and its readers is suggestive for further study of all types of romantic fiction. Two monographs on English fiction are more directly applicable to American popular romantic fiction. J.M.S. Tompkins's *The Popular Novel in England (1770–1800)* has a chapter on romantic and historical fiction in the period that is exceptionally good for understanding the English backgrounds of the emerging American novel. Robert Kiely's *The Romantic Novel in England* deals with aesthetic definitions of romantic fiction but does not make invidious comparisons between serious and popular fiction. Although none of these three books refers to American fiction at all, each is important.

Much more directly relevant is a reprinted 1935 monograph by Mary Sumner Benson, *Women in Eighteenth-Century America*. Benson's chapter "Women in Early American Literature" is a good survey of novels, plays, and magazines as they related to American women, although she consciously ignores "numerous second-rate novels of romantic adventure."

Lily D. Loshe's *The Early American Novel, 1789–1830* was first published in 1907. The author attempts definition of the forms of the first fiction in America. More thorough and analytical is Henri Petter's *The Early American Novel*. Petter has a long section on "the love story," in which he discriminates among types and conventions. Also helpful is Alexander Cowie's *The Rise of the American Novel*, which includes good individual sections on a number of relevant novels and authors. Michael Davitt Bell's *Hawthorne and the Historical Romance of New England* traces the connections between Hawthorne and contemporary women writers in their use of the Puritan past.

A few general studies of popular fiction are also good sources. Carl Bode's *Anatomy of American Popular Culture* analyzes romantic fiction, among other phenomena, during the 1840s. The most recent comprehensive work is also the best: Russel B. Nye's *The Unembarrassed Muse*. His discussion of romantic fiction suggests formulaic definitions and mentions numerous titles and authors as examples. The major theoretical work is John G. Cawelti's *Adventure, Mystery, and Romance*. Cawelti is exceptionally insightful on the definition of the popular romance and particularly suggestive on the relationship between the romance and what he calls the "social melodrama."

A different kind of data can be obtained from studies of book publishing, library policies, and censorship in America. John W. Tebbel's *A History of Book Publishing in the United States* offers valuable material on publishers and copyright laws, vital for understanding the close parallels and overlaps between British and American popular romantic fiction. Kenneth C. Davis's *Two-Bit Culture: The Paperbacking of America* offers a fine history of the mass-market paperback book in America, including some discussion of romance novels. G. H. Orians's "Censure of Fiction in American Magazines and Romances 1789–1810" delineates the reasons for the outcry against the novel in America, presenting the arguments of those who believed that it was subversive of public values because it was untrue and immoral. Dee Garrison's essay "Immoral Fiction in the Late Victorian Library" is a study of an 1881 questionnaire by the American Library Association (ALA) to seventy major public libraries about the fiction they censored. Of the list of "questionable" authors cited by the ALA, ten were writers of women's romances. Garrison tries to show why some librarians considered these women subversive of the public morality. *Fiction in Public Libraries 1876–1900* by Esther J. Carrier provides some insight into the popularity of Mrs. E.D.E.N. Southworth and Mary Jane Holmes, among others, as well as more discussion of the censorship controversy discussed by Garrison.

A recent book that provides basic information about women's magazine fiction—a relatively neglected area—is Mirabel Cecil's *Heroines in Love 1750–1974*. Cecil surveys magazine romance fiction over more than two centuries, providing in each chapter a breezy overview of a particular era as well as an excerpt or a representative story. She covers both British and American fiction. The work is comprehensive, but it contains no bibliography or analysis. It is more suggestive than useful, but it is essential nonetheless since these stories are not surveyed elsewhere.

Before recent feminist approaches to nineteenth-century popular romantic fiction, there were a few excellent critical sources that still cannot be overlooked. The best is Herbert Ross Brown's *The Sentimental Novel in America, 1789–1860*, published in 1940 and only partially superseded in 1987 by Nina Baym's study to be discussed below. Helen Waite Papashvily's *All the Happy Endings* is a more popularized book; it is a prefeminist approach to the domestic romance, arguing that the books are actually submerged revolts against the male-dominated culture. Her book has a good unannotated bibliography of secondary material prior to 1954, but no list of primary sources. Alexander Cowie's "The Vogue of the Domestic Novel" is an excerpt from his larger study published several years later, F. L. Pattee's *The Feminine Fifties* has a survey chapter on the "scribbling women." Beatrice Hofstadter's "Popular Culture and the Romantic Heroine" is an analysis of the heroines of six popular novels from the mid-nineteenth century to the mid-twentieth century.

Three works on women in fiction before the women's studies movement also have valuable information. *Pamela's Daughters* by Robert Palfrey Utter and Gwendolyn Bridges Needham discusses images of women in British fiction, with some minimal attention given to American books. It focuses on types of women in novels and is particularly worthy of attention in its excellent analysis of women's economic and domestic roles portrayed in fiction, as well as its argument that the precariousness of those roles made the love plot particularly attractive and significant for women readers. Dorothy Yost Deegan's *The Stereotype of the Single Woman in American Novels* uses lists of significant American books and analyzes them for stereotypes. William Wasserstrom's *Heiress of All the Ages: Sex and Sentiment in the Genteel Tradition* argues that in genteel fiction from the 1830s to World War I, the function of sex is domesticated in marriage. He refers almost entirely to serious literature, but his analysis is also relevant to popular fiction.

Fairly recent work in the emerging field of popular culture has also dealt with romantic fiction. In a collection of essays written by members of a graduate seminar in popular culture at Michigan State University, *New Dimensions in Popular Culture*, edited by Russel B. Nye, two of the papers relate directly to the subject. Ellen Hoekstra's "The Pedestal Myth Reinforced: Women's Magazine Fiction 1900–1920" surveys major magazines and reports that most of the stories were of the "boy-meets-girl" type. Leslie Smith's essay, "Through Rose-Colored Glasses: Some American Victorian Sentimental Novels," is about Mary Jane Holmes, Mrs. E.D.E.N. Southworth, and Sylvanus Cobb, Jr. Another former graduate student at Michigan State, Kathryn Weibel, published her dissertation as *Mirror, Mirror: Images of Women Reflected in Popular Culture*. The first chapter of this excellent study is an analytical history of women in popular fiction and is particularly perceptive on romantic fiction. Henry Nash Smith in "The Scribbling Women and the Cosmic Success Story" and Ann D. Wood in "The 'Scribbling Women' and Fanny Fern: Why Women Wrote" place the domestic sentimentalists in the context of their wider culture.

Until Janice A. Radway's recent work, a major omission in the study of romantic fiction was direct analysis of the readers themselves. Impressionistic evidence strongly indicates that the audience for love stories is almost entirely female; but the expertise to study that audience is more the province of sociologists than of literary or historical critics. It is noteworthy, then, that sociologist Peter H. Mann in Great Britain has been working on popular romantic fiction and its readers for some time. Mann used the mailing list of subscribers to the Mills and Boon romance series in England, sending two long questionnaires—one in 1968 and the other four or five years later. Mann received a good rate of return for a mail questionnaire, indicating a high level of interest on the part of the respondents. The reports show that the readership is overwhelmingly female, represents a wide range of age levels and occupations as well as housewives, and has a much higher level of education than the surveyors had expected. This material is particularly interesting since the Mills and Boon novels are marketed in the United States and Canada as Harlequin Romances. The evidence gathered in Great Britain is, of course, not directly valid in the United States, but it is at least suggestive. Mann's reports are offered and evaluated in *The Romantic Novel: A Survey of Reading Habits* and *A New Survey: The Facts about Romantic Fiction*. An American study, Jan Hajda's "A Time for Reading," confirms many of Mann's conclusions in its survey of women readers in Baltimore. Further information about reading in America, which includes romance reading as a category, can be found in the Yankelovich, Skelly, and White survey, *Consumer Research Study on Reading and Book Purchasing*, conducted for the Library of Congress Center for the Book. In 1984, Janice Radway's *Reading the Romance* offered an important ethnographic study of a group of avid romance readers in the United States.

In the past fifteen years, the influence of women's studies in scholarship has become apparent in approaches to romantic fiction. The studies range from the blindly political to the brilliantly innovative, and the number of new essays and monographs seems to increase geometrically. An early anthology of material on women in popular culture contains some good, although uneven, work. *Images of Women in Fiction: Feminist Perspectives*, edited by Susan Koppelman Cornillon, appeared in 1972. Although many of the articles are relevant and worth consulting, the most interesting is a suggestive essay by Joanna Russ, "What Can a Heroine Do? or Why Women Can't Write." Russ argues that the useful myths that inform literary works are male myths and that women exist in them only as reflected entities; thus, the central experience for women in fiction is courtship and marriage.

The rest of women's lives cannot be conventionally portrayed in fiction. Ellen Moers's *Literary Women* defined the conventions, concerns, and experiences of women that take shape in literature by women. Many of these are issues that relate to romantic fiction. The book is especially suggestive in its discussion of what Moers refers to as "female heroinism," her term for the heroic possibilities and limits for female protagonists of novels written by women. In describing "heroinism," Moers goes a long way toward evaluating the reasons why romance in the popular sense is primarily a women's genre.

A growing list of works by women scholars, primarily nineteenth-century historians interested in New England, has added greatly to our knowledge of romantic fiction between 1820 and 1870. Some of these studies are not directly about popular fiction, but they all approach women in American culture in ways that illuminate the fiction; many of them discuss the fiction as an integral part of the work. Barbara Welter's article, "The Cult of True Womanhood," has been very influential on later scholars. In her introduction to a collection of writings by American women, *The Oven Birds: American Women on Womanhood, 1820–1920*, Gail Thain Parker discusses the problems of women who lacked heroinic models and how this affected their writing. Kathryn Kish Sklar's excellent biography *Catharine Beecher: A Study in American Domesticity* adds much to an understanding of the woman as writer in the period. A more general study is Susan P. Conrad's *Perish the Thought: Intellectual Women in Romantic America 1830–1860*. Conrad argues that the work of the popular novelists, with its emphasis on home and love and marriage, reinforced the problems of female intellectuals in America.

Ann Douglas's *The Feminization of American Culture* suggests that both nineteenth-century clergymen and women experienced a progressive loss of power leading to a debased religious sensibility. Women turned to fiction to work out the implications of daily problems, resulting in a pervasive and evasive sentimentality and convention. There is a great deal of excellent background material on women's romantic fiction, especially in its more sentimental forms. Nina Baym's *Women's Fiction: A Guide to Novels by and about Women in America 1820–1870* provides long plot descriptions and analyses for a number of important forgotten romantic novels. She uses all the available biographical sources and feminist scholarship, although she is most interested in close readings of the works themselves. Although the book is very important in the field and is exceptionally thorough and useful, Baym sometimes strains her analysis by trying to make too strong a case for "her" authors as opposed to writers of seduction or gothic fiction; thus, she minimizes many of the essential similarities between them. More recently, Mary Kelley's studies of nineteenth-century writers have added to our understanding of female authorship. Kelley argues in "The Sentimentalists: Promise and Betrayal in the Home" that women authors felt serious conflict between their intentions and the form of their fiction. Her book, *Private*

Women, Public Stage: Literary Domesticity in Nineteenth-Century America, is a study of twelve major writers: Maria Susanna Cummins, Charlotte Perkins Gilman, Caroline Lee Hentz, Mary Jane Holmes, Maria McIntosh, Sara Parton, Catharine Maria Sedgwick, Mrs. E.D.E.N. Southworth, Harriet Beecher Stowe, Mary Virginia Terhune, Susan Warner, and Augusta Evans Wilson.

Other studies of groups of individual romantic writers are unscholarly and superficial, but even they provide useful data about the writers and their works, and the occasional biography or dissertation is sometimes remarkably useful. A New York editor, Grant Overton, published two volumes entitled *The Women Who Make Our Novels*, composed of journalistic ballyhoo for the writers, but there is also some solid information about such women as Mary Roberts Rinehart, Kathleen Norris, Mary Johnston, Amelia E. Barr, Temple Bailey, Faith Baldwin, Margaret Culkin Banning, Fannie Hurst, Margaret Widdemer, and other writers who are mostly ignored by scholars.

On individual novels, the available information is variable and sketchy. There has been much interest in Susanna Rowson in recent years because her *Charlotte Temple* inspired so many imitators, even though it was derivative in its turn of Samuel Richardson's *Clarissa*. The introduction by William S. Kable in *Three Early American Novels* is a basic introduction to Rowson; the volume also anthologizes two works by Charles Brockden Brown. A recent book by Ellen B. Brandt, *Susanna Haswell Rowson: America's First Best-Selling Novelist*, is a serious, heavily researched biography with a critical analysis of Rowson's books and a good bibliography. Three previous studies of Rowson are also significant. Elias Nason's *A Memoir of Mrs. Susan Rowson* is Victorian hagiography. But *The Romance of the Association; or, One Last Glimpse of Charlotte Temple and Eliza Wharton* by Caroline Wells Dall is a fascinating example of Charlotte-mania in that the author in 1875 was trying to provide historical background to the actual events of both *Charlotte Temple* and Foster's *The Coquette*, two popular seduction novels reputedly based on fact. R.W.G. Vail's *Susanna Haswell Rowson, the Author of "Charlotte Temple": A Bibliographical Study* is a guide to the various editions of the book and has been the definitive source since its publication in 1933 by the American Antiquarian Society.

Interest in Catharine Maria Sedgwick has been somewhat higher, although her major works are not in print. In 1871, Mary E. Dewey's *Life and Letters of Catharine M. Sedgwick* was issued. This remained the standard source, supplemented by a dissertation in 1937, Sister Mary Michael Welsh's *Catharine Maria Sedgwick: Her Position in the Literature and Thought of Her Time up to 1860*, until Edward Halsey Foster's volume for the Twayne series, *Catharine Maria Sedgwick*. An interesting article is Michael Davitt Bell's "History and Romance Convention in Catharine Sedgwick's *Hope Leslie*." One major writer of the period about whom a major biographical, critical, and bibliographical study is long overdue is Mrs. E.D.E.N. South-worth; the only full-length study is still Regis Louise Boyle's 1939 dissertation, *Mrs. E.D.E.N. Southworth, Novelist.*

Occasional materials relating to romantic novelists come from local history organizations or institutions. The Constitution Island Association, which preserves the home of the Warner sisters, compiled a book about the island for a meeting of the Garden Club of America in 1936. A brief essay, "Susan and Anna Warner: 'The Brontë Sisters of America,' " is included. More general, but more revealing of contemporary attitudes, is Nathaniel Hall's laudatory *A Sermon. Preached in the First Church, Dorchester, on the Sunday (October 8, 1866) Following upon the Decease of Maria S. Cummins.* He portrays the author of *The Lamplighter* (the book that prompted Hawthorne's imprecations about "d——d scribbling women") as a female paragon. Two published dissertations are the only full-length treatment of two other authors: Elizabeth K. Halbeisen's *Harriet Prescott Spofford: A Romantic Survival* and William Perry Fidler's *Augusta Evans Wilson 1835–1909.* Both are basic, if uninspired. Grace Livingston Hill was the subject of a highly flattering memoir by Jean Karr, *Grace Livingston Hill: Her Story and Her Writings.* Margaret Widdemer was discussed in Dorothy Scarborough's *Margaret Widdemer, a Biography* in 1925.

Although no major critical work has yet been done on Margaret Mitchell and *Gone with the Wind*, there are some useful works. A 1954 thesis by William Carter Pollard, available on microcard, "*Gone with the Wind*: Story of a Best Seller," is a substantial study of the popularity of the book. The Macmillan Company issued a self-congratulatory volume on the twenty-fifth anniversary of the book's publication, "*Gone with the Wind*" *and Its Author Margaret Mitchell*, containing some surprisingly interesting information. Finis Farr's chatty biography, *Margaret Mitchell of Atlanta*, is particularly good on the subject of how the book was published. William Pratt's *Scarlett Fever* is a large-sized picture book about the book as phenomenon, including much valuable material on the making of the film. Richard Harwell edited *Margaret Mitchell's "Gone with the Wind" Letters 1936–1949*, a collection of letters written to her about the book, which gives valuable insight into the book's audience.

Autobiographical materials by romantic writers are probably even less reliable than the journalistic approaches available, but they are at least sources for basic materials that can be further investigated. Isabella M. Alden's *Memories of Yesterdays* is an autobiography edited by her niece Grace Livingston Hill. Other memoirs include Amelia E. Barr's *All the Days of My Life* and Fannie Hurst's long and fascinating *Anatomy of Me.* More useful than most is the autobiographical writing by Frances Parkinson Keyes. *The Cost of a Best Seller* is her description of the emotional and physical toll on the writer. The best two volumes on the backgrounds of her writing are *Roses in December* and *All Flags Flying: Reminiscences of Frances Parkinson*

Keyes; together they constitute a long autobiography, the latter incomplete on her death. Kathleen Norris, who married a brother of Frank Norris and whose sister married William Rose Benét, wrote two very interesting autobiographical volumes that incidentally give insight into American letters in the period as well as into her own life. *Noon: An Autobiographical Sketch* describes her life through middle age; *Family Gathering* is a lengthy and comprehensive work. Mary Virginia H. Terhune called her reminiscences *Marion Harland's Autobiography*, after her pen name. Margaret Widdemer's *Golden Friends I Had* is not only an autobiography but also a fairly thorough set of sketches of most major literary figures of the twentieth century, including a few romantic writers. One more biography, *Susan Warner*, by Anna B. Warner, is actually more like a joint autobiography since the Warner sisters collaborated on many writings.

Beginning in the late 1970s, when competition among paperback romance publishers increased, romance authors began to seek professional affiliations and publicity for themselves. After establishment of the Romance Writers of America, authors had an organization with a newsletter, *Romance Writers Report*, to keep in touch with the field; and the association's annual convention brought together both published and unpublished writers with editors, publishers, and agents. "How-to-write-a-romance" books proliferated. Much valuable information on changing contemporary romance formulas can be found in books like Marilyn M. Lowery's *How to Write Romance Novels That Sell*, Yvonne McManus's *You Can Write a Romance! And Get It Published!*, Kathryn Falk's *How to Write a Romance and Get It Published*, and Helene Schellenberg Barnhart's *Writing Romance Fiction for Love and Money*. *Romantic Times* is a popular newsletter for romance readers, including information on favorite authors and upcoming titles. Additional journalistic information on romances can be found regularly in the pages of *Publishers Weekly*.

Scholars, too, have shown more interest in contemporary romances and romance writers, although their approaches vary widely. Ann Douglas attacked romances as "soft porn" in "Soft-Porn Culture," an article in the *New Republic*. Tania Modleski's *Loving with a Vengeance: Mass-Produced Fantasies for Women* argues that such female entertainment forms as romances, gothic novels, and soap operas are fantasies that contain strategies for release of covert anger against men and a patriarchal culture. Helen Hazen, in *Endless Rapture: Rape, Romance, and the Female Imagination*, defends romances on similar grounds to the critiques of Douglas and Modleski. Hazen suggests that the aspects of romances that most offend feminists—the implied violence against women, rape fantasies—are precisely the needs and desires of women that feminists conventionally ignore. Margaret Ann Jensen's *Love's $weet Return: The Harlequin Story* is a study of the Canadian firm of Harlequin Books, the current leader among romance publishers. Lillian S. Robinson's essay, "On Reading Trash," describes the work of Georgette Heyer as a modern fantasy that appeals to some readers who also enjoy Jane Austen. Janice A. Radway's *Reading the Romance: Women, Patriarchy, and Popular Literature* studies romances as a phenomenon of reading, using information on publishing, distribution, and reader response to assess the role of romances in the life of readers. Kay Mussell's *Fantasy and Reconciliation: Contemporary Formulas of Women's Romance Fiction* argues that romances respond to female interests and concerns that are only rarely met in the society at large.

Criticism of romantic fiction stands today at a particularly interesting moment. The autobiographical and journalistic sources provide some detail about the writers; the basic literary and historical works to give background are emerging; and women's studies provide the interest and the climate for further scholarly work in the field.

BIBLIOGRAPHY

Books and Articles

Alden, Isabella M. [Pansy]. *Memories of Yesterdays*. Edited by Grace Livingston Hill. Philadelphia: J. B. Lippincott, 1931.

Barnhart, Helene Schellenberg. *Writing Romance Fiction for Love and Money*. Cincinnati, Ohio: Writer's Digest Books, 1983.

Barr, Amelia E. *All the Days of My Life: An Autobiography*. New York: D. Appleton, 1913.

Baym, Nina. *Woman's Fiction: A Guide to Novels by and about Women in America 1820–1870*. Ithaca, N.Y.: Cornell University Press, 1978.

Beer, Gillian. *The Romance*. London: Methuen, 1970.

Bell, Michael Davitt. *Hawthorne and the Historical Romance of New England*. Princeton, N.J.: Princeton University Press, 1971.

———. "History and Romance Convention in Catharine Sedgwick's *Hope Leslie*." *American Quarterly*, 22 (Summer 1970), 213–21.

Benson, Mary Sumner. *Women in Eighteenth-Century America*. New York: Columbia University Press, 1935; AMS Press, 1976.

Bode, Carl. *Anatomy of American Popular Culture, 1840–1861*. Berkeley: University of California Press, 1959.

Boyle, Regis Louise. *Mrs. E.D.E.N. Southworth, Novelist*. Washington, D.C.: Catholic University Press, 1939.

Brandt, Ellen B. *Susanna Haswell Rowson: America's First Best-Selling Novelist*. Chicago: Serbra Press, 1975.

Brown, Herbert Ross. *The Sentimental Novel in America, 1789–1860*. Durham, N.C.: Duke University Press, 1940; New York: Octagon Books, 1975.

Carrier, Esther J. *Fiction in Public Libraries 1876–1900*. New York: Scarecrow Press, 1965.

Cawelti, John G. *Adventure, Mystery, and Romance: Formula Stories as Art and Popular Culture*. Chicago: University of Chicago Press, 1976.

Cecil, Mirabel. *Heroines in Love 1750–1974*. London: Michael Joseph, 1974.

Chase, Richard. *The American Novel and Its Tradition.* Garden City, N.Y.: Doubleday, 1957.

Conrad, Susan P. *Perish the Thought: Intellectual Women in Romantic America 1830–1860.* New York: Oxford University Press, 1976.

Constitution Island Association. "Susan and Anna Warner: 'The Brontë Sisters of America." In *Constitution Island.* New York: Compiled for the meeting of the Garden Club of America, 1936.

Cornillon, Susan Koppelman, ed. *Images of Women in Fiction: Feminist Perspectives.* Bowling Green, Ohio: Bowling Green State University Popular Press, 1972.

Cowie, Alexander. *The Rise of the American Novel.* New York: American Book, 1948.

———. "The Vogue of the Domestic Novel." *South Atlantic Quarterly,* 41 (October 1942), 416–25.

Dall, Caroline Wells. *The Romance of the Association; or, One Last Glimpse of Charlotte Temple and Eliza Wharton: A Curiosity of Literature and Life.* Cambridge, Mass.: Press of John Wilson and Son, 1875.

Davis, Kenneth C. *Two-Bit Culture: The Paperbacking of America.* Boston: Houghton Mifflin, 1984.

Deegan, Dorothy Yost. *The Stereotype of the Single Woman in American Novels: A Social Study with Implications for the Education of Women.* New York: King's Crown Press, 1951; Octagon, 1969.

Dewey, Mary E., ed. *Life and Letters of Catharine M. Sedgwick.* New York: Harper, 1871.

Douglas, Ann. *The Feminization of American Culture.* New York: Alfred A. Knopf, 1978.

———. "Soft-Porn Culture." *New Republic,* 183 (August 30, 1980), 25–29.

Falk, Kathryn. *How to Write a Romance and Get It Published.* New York: Crown, 1983.

Farr, Finis. *Margaret Mitchell of Atlanta.* New York: Morrow, 1965.

Fidler, William Perry. *Augusta Evans Wilson 1835–1909.* University: University of Alabama Press, 1951.

Foster, Edward Halsey. *Catharine Maria Sedgwick.* New York: Twayne, 1974.

Garrison, Dee. "Immoral Fiction in the Late Victorian Library," *American Quarterly,* 28 (Spring 1976), 71–89.

Hackett, Alice Payne, and James Henry Burke. *80 Years of Best Sellers.* New York: R. R. Bowker, 1977.

Hajda, Jan. "A Time for Reading." *Trans-Action,* 4 (June 1967), 45–50.

Halbeisen, Elizabeth K. *Harriet Prescott Spofford: A Romantic Survival.* Philadelphia: University of Pennsylvania Press, 1935.

Hall, Nathaniel. *A Sermon. Preached in the First Church, Dorchester, on the Sunday (October 8, 1866) Following upon the Decease of Maria S. Cummins.* Cambridge, Mass.: Riverside Press (private distribution), 1866.

Harlequin Books. *Harlequin 30th Anniversary: 1949–1979.* Toronto: Harlequin Books, 1979.

Hart, James D. *The Popular Book: A History of America's Literary Taste.* New York: Oxford University Press, 1950; Westport, Conn.: Greenwood Press, 1976.

Harwell, Richard, ed. *Margaret Mitchell's "Gone with the Wind" Letters 1936–1949.* New York: Macmillan, 1976.

Hazen, Helen. *Endless Rapture: Rape, Romance, and the Female Imagination.* New York: Scribner's, 1983.

Hofstadter, Beatrice. "Popular Culture and the Romantic Heroine." *American Scholar* 30 (Winter 1960–61), 98–116.

Hurst, Fannie. *Anatomy of Me.* Garden City, N.Y.: Doubleday, 1958.

Jensen, Margaret Ann. *Love's $weet Return: The Harlequin Story.* Toronto: Women's Educational Press, 1984.

Kable, William S., ed. *Three Early American Novels.* Columbus, Ohio: Charles E. Merrill, 1970.

Karr, Jean. *Grace Livingston Hill: Her Story and Her Writings.* New York: Greenberg, 1948.

Kelley, Mary. *Private Women, Public Stage: Literary Domesticity in Nineteenth-Century America.* New York: Oxford University Press, 1984.

———. "The Sentimentalists: Promise and Betrayal in the Home." *Signs,* 4 (Spring 1979), 434–46.

Keyes, Frances Parkinson. *All Flags Flying: Reminiscences of Frances Parkinson Keyes.* New York: McGraw-Hill, 1972.

———. *The Cost of a Best Seller.* New York: Julian Messner, 1950.

———. *Roses in December.* Garden City, N.Y.: Doubleday, 1960.

Kiely, Robert. *The Romantic Novel in England.* Cambridge, Mass.: Harvard University Press, 1972.

Koch, Donald A. Introduction. In *Tempest and Sunshine* by Mary Jane Holmes and *The Lamplighter* by Maria Susanna Cummins. New York: Odyssey, 1968.

Loshe, Lily D. *The Early American Novel, 1789–1830.* New York: Columbia University Press, 1907; Ungar, 1966.

Lowery, Marilyn M. *How to Write Romance Novels That Sell.* New York: Rawson Associates, 1983.

McManus, Yvonne. *You Can Write a Romance! and Get It Published!* New York: Pocket Books, 1983.

Macmillan Co. *"Gone with the Wind" and Its Author Margaret Mitchell.* New York: Macmillan, 1961.

Mann, Peter H. *A New Survey: The Facts about Romantic Fiction.* London: Mills and Boon, 1974.

———. *The Romantic Novel: A Survey of Reading Habits.* London: Mills and Boon, 1969.

Modleski, Tania. *Loving with a Vengeance: Mass-Produced Fantasies for Women.* Hamden, Conn.: Archon, 1982.

Moers, Ellen. *Literary Women.* Garden City, N.Y.: Doubleday, 1977.

Mott, Frank Luther. *Golden Multitudes.* New York: Macmillan, 1947.

Mussell, Kay. *Fantasy and Reconciliation: Contemporary Formulas of Women's Romance Fiction.* Westport, Conn.: Greenwood Press, 1984.

———. *Women's Gothic and Romantic Fiction: A Reference Guide.* Westport, Conn.: Greenwood Press, 1984.

Nason, Elias. *A Memoir of Mrs. Susanna Rowson.* Albany, N.Y.: Joel Munsell, 1870.

Norris, Kathleen. *Family Gathering.* Garden City, N.Y.: Doubleday, 1959.

———. *Noon: An Autobiographical Sketch.* Garden City, N.Y.: Doubleday, Page, 1925.

Nye, Russel B. *The Unembarrassed Muse.* New York: Dial Press, 1970.

———, ed. *New Dimensions in Popular Culture*. Bowling Green, Ohio: Bowling Green State University Popular Press, 1972.

Orians, G. H. "Censure of Fiction in American Magazines and Romances 1789–1810." *PMLA*, 52 (March 1937), 195–214.

Overton, Grant. *The Women Who Make Our Novels*. New York: Moffet, Yard, 1918; rev. and enl. ed., New York: Dodd, Mead, 1928.

Papashvily, Helen Waite. *All the Happy Endings*. New York: Harper, 1956; Port Washington, N.Y.: Kennikat Press, 1972.

Parker, Gail Thain, ed. *The Oven Birds: American Women and Womanhood, 1820–1920*. Garden City, N.Y.: Doubleday, 1972.

Pattee, Fred Lewis. *The Feminine Fifties*. New York: D. Appleton, 1940.

Petter, Henri. *The Early American Novel*. Columbus: Ohio State University Press, 1971.

Pollard, William Carter. "*Gone with the Wind*: Story of a Best Seller." Microcard thesis, Florida State University, 1954.

Pratt, William. *Scarlett Fever*. New York: Macmillan, 1977.

Radway, Janice A. *Reading the Romance: Women, Patriarchy, and Popular Literature*. Chapel Hill: University of North Carolina Press, 1984.

Robinson, Lillian S. "On Reading Trash." In *Sex, Class, and Culture*. Bloomington: Indiana University Press, 1978.

Sanderson, Dorothy Hurlbut. *They Wrote for a Living: A Bibliography of the Works of Susan Bogert Warner and Ann Bartlett Warner*. West Point, N.Y.: Constitution Island Association, 1976.

Scarborough, Dorothy. *Margaret Widdemer, a Biography*. New York: Harcourt, Brace, 1925.

Sklar, Kathryn Kish. *Catharine Beecher: A Study in American Domesticity*. New Haven: Yale University Press, 1973.

Smith, Henry Nash. "The Scribbling Women and the Cosmic Success Story." *Critical Inquiry*, 1 (September 1974), 47–70.

Tebbel, John W. *A History of Book Publishing in the United States*. New York: R. R. Bowker, 1972.

Terhune, Mary Virginia H. *Marion Harland's Autobiography*. New York: Harper, 1910.

Tompkins, J.M.S. *The Popular Novel in England (1770–1800)*. London: Methuen, 1932, 1969.

Utter, Robert Palfrey, and Gwendolyn Bridges Needham. *Pamela's Daughters*. New York: Macmillan, 1936; Russell and Russell, 1972.

Vail, R.W.G. *Susanna Haswell Rowson, the Author of "Charlotte Temple": A Bibliographical Study*. Worcester, Mass.: American Antiquarian Society, 1933.

Vinson, James, ed. *Twentieth-Century Romance and Gothic Writers*. London: Macmillan, 1982.

Warner, Anna B. *Susan Warner*. New York: G. P. Putnam's Sons, 1909.

Wasserstrom, William. *Heiress of All the Ages: Sex and Sentiment in the Genteel Tradition*. Minneapolis: University of Minnesota Press, 1959.

Weibel, Kathryn. *Mirror, Mirror: Images of Women Reflected in Popular Culture*. Garden City, N.Y.: Doubleday, 1977.

Welsh, Sister Mary Michael. *Catharine Maria Sedgwick: Her Position in the Literature and Thought of Her Time up to 1860*. Washington, D.C.: Catholic University Press, 1937.

Welter, Barbara. "The Cult of True Womanhood." *American Quarterly*, 18 (Summer 1966), 151–74.

Widdemer, Margaret. *Golden Friends I Had*. Garden City, N.Y.: Doubleday, 1964.

Wood, Ann D. "The "Scribbling Women' and Fanny Fern: Why Women Wrote." *American Quarterly*, 23 (Spring 1971), 3–24.

Wright, R. Glenn, comp. *Author Bibliography of English Language Fiction in the Library of Congress Through 1950*. Boston: G. K. Hall, 1973.

———. *Chronological Bibliography of English Language Fiction in the Library of Congress Through 1950*. Boston: G. K. Hall, 1974.

———. *Title Bibliography of English Language Fiction in the Library of Congress Through 1950*. Boston: G. K. Hall, 1976.

Yankelovich, Skelly, and White, Inc. *Consumer Research Study on Reading and Book Purchasing*. Darien, Conn.: The Group, 1978.

Periodicals

Publishers Weekly. New York, 1872-.

Romance Writers Report. Houston, Tex., 1981-.

Romantic Times. Brooklyn Heights, N.Y., 1982-.

12

Science Fiction

MARSHALL B. TYMN

Once exiled to comic strips, pulp magazines, and late-night movies, science fiction is now the most popular of the specialized literary genres in the United States today.[1] Its enthusiasts range from onmivorous devourers of paperbacks to serious scholars who probe, analyze, and discuss the characteristics and significance of works old and new.

The reason for this explosion of interest is not just fascination with exotic settings and futuristic worlds. Science fiction is a literature which prepares us to accept change, to view change as both natural and inevitable, and since change is fast becoming one of the few constants in our society, the attractiveness of this genre is both understandable and encouraging. Add the popular appeal that science fiction has as pure entertainment, and it becomes clear why this literature is attracting vast numbers of readers of all ages and from all stations of life.

HISTORIC OUTLINE

Science fiction is a literature with a heritage reaching back into ancient times, to a prescientific world inhabited by peoples whose myths, legends, and superstitions became a way of thinking about and explaining the wonders of the universe. The seeds of science fiction were planted thousands of years ago, as the human species dreamed of the great unknown.

Science fiction had its beginnings at least as early as the second century with a Greek named Lucian who satirized his own society through the device of an imaginary moon voyage. Although fantastic voyages and other writings containing elements of science fiction appear in Western literature over the centuries, it was not until the beginning of the Industrial Revolution in the eighteenth century, with its vision of a future altered by technology, that science fiction could exist as a viable literary form. Suddenly there seemed to be a very real possibility that tomorrow might bring a better world, and the new science fiction fostered the idea that mankind might learn to control his own destiny.

As the Industrial Revolution burst upon the Victorian world, people began to write fantastic tales based upon the possibilities of scientific discovery and the now-evident fact that the world was changing. By the nineteenth century the world had come to believe in the limitless miracles of science, and the seeds were sown for the development of science fiction.

Brian W. Aldiss, the noted British writer and critic, contends in *Trillion Year Spree* that science fiction had its beginnings in the English Romantic movement with the publication of Mary Shelley's *Frankenstein: or, The Modern Prometheus* in 1818. When Shelley wrote her novel, she started a trend that left behind the supernatural elements of the gothic horror tale and introduced "science" as an ingredient of fiction. Many historians consider *Frankenstein* the first science fiction novel. It was certainly the first truly outstanding science fiction success, not only as a novel but also on the London stage. *Frankenstein* demonstrated the theme of man creating life and the inevitable retribution which follows. The novel warned that the scientist is responsible for anticipating the future effects his inventions may have on the world. This theme was echoed in the pulp magazines of the 1920s and 1930s and is still with us today.

The nineteenth century was fascinated with ideas of science and progress, and its mood was generally one of optimism. The machine age had been inaugurated, and its impact on fiction was tremendous. Popular magazines, such as *Century, Cosmopolitan, Harper's, Atlantic Monthly*, and *Saturday Evening Post*, kept the public interest keen with stories featuring new mechanical devices and scientific marvels. The groundwork was laid by such writers as Nathaniel Hawthorne, Edgar Allan Poe, Fritz-James O'Brien, Edward Bellamy, Ambrose Bierce, and Mark Twain, who produced a group of tales that constitute the first important American contributions to the growth of science fiction. Nearly every major writer in America and many in Europe experimented with writing stories about the new science and the possibilities of the future, but Jules Verne was the first to devote more than part-time effort to the task.

Jules Verne (1828–1905) was the almost archetypal expression of the nineteenth-century's romantic interest in science and technology. His life spanned the great age of invention, and his work represents the high tide of European delight in the marvels and possibilities of science. Verne championed the revolution in transportation with such works as *Five Weeks in a Balloon* (1863), *From the Earth to the Moon* (1865), *Twenty Thousand Leagues Under the Sea* (1870), and *Around the World in Eighty Days* (1873).

Verne's success as a writer of fantastic adventure helped pioneer a genre. His blend of science and invention in his "voyages extraordinaires" insured the survival of science fiction, and his fertile imagination made it exciting. Verne was not a great innovator of science fiction ideas, but he captured the optimistic spirit of the century when he made technological achievements a subject for fiction. Thus science fiction, though not yet named, gained its own identity and a measure of respectability as defined by Verne's prolific and highly profitable output. His worlds seem limited, though, when compared with the work of another nineteenth-century writer, H. G. Wells.

With his background as scientist, teacher, and journalist, Herbert George Wells (1866–1946) published his first "scientific romance," *The Time Machine*, in 1895. Not only was this novel a vehicle for an extraordinary journey through time, but more important, the work contained social commentary. Wells criticized the exploitation of the working classes by attacking the English class system which divided workers from the leisured rich. He challenged nineteenth-century notions of progress and asked far-reaching questions about the directions in which progress would take us.

A one-time student of Thomas Huxley, Wells was deeply affected by Charles Darwin's theory of evolution, which triggered Wells's own ideas of evolution and progress, later to be expressed in his greatest and most famous works. *The Time Machine* (1895), *The War of the Worlds* (1898), *The Island of Dr. Moreau* (1896), *The Invisible Man* (1897), *When the Sleeper Awakes* (1899), and *First Men in the Moon* (1901) all warn that there are limits to progress which man should not surpass because of the detrimental changes which might result.

Through a variety of motifs and new perspectives H. G. Wells made startling insinuations about the significance of man in the universe. With Wells, science fiction began to take form and direction, becoming more a medium of ideas than a variety of adventure. He became one of the most respected writers of the early twentieth century. He not only showed that fiction can anticipate the power of science to change the world; he also predicted that scientific discoveries would change people's view of their place in the universe. Wells tempered his vision of the future, as seen in his science fiction stories and novels, by pessimism, unlike Jules Verne, who was invariably optimistic in his tales of the wonders of a new scientific age.

Although stories heralding the new technology popularized by Verne and others constitute the early core of science fiction, other motifs had emerged by the turn of the century.[2] As a response to a movement in England calling for the reorganization of the armed forces to meet the threat of global war, the future war motif, characterized by George Chesney's "Battle of Dorking" (1871), established imaginary warfare as a viable theme for science fiction writers, with the warring nations depicted in Chesney's tale eventually replaced by alien invaders.

The interplanetary voyage motif, which had existed in various guises since David Russen's *Iter Lunare: Or, A Voyage to the Moon* (1703), has adopted the more technological orientation that remains a staple of modern science fiction. Stories of catastrophes evolved from works such as Mary Shelley's *The Last Man* (1826), in which plague destroys the human race, and from threats of world destruction as portrayed in Wells's *The War of the Worlds* (1898), to an Earth devastated by atomic war, overpopulation, or pollution, as depicted in post–World War II works. Contemporary science fiction has focused not so much on the catastrophe itself, but on the kinds of society developed after the catastrophe (or holocaust). Mature versions of this motif are George R. Stewart's *Earth Abides* (1949), Walter M. Miller's *A Canticle for Leibowitz* (1960), Brian W. Aldiss's *Greybeard* (1964), and Vonda N. McIntyre's *Dreamsnake* (1978).

By far the most popular of the early motifs on both sides of the Atlantic was the lost race, which developed out of the interest in geology, archeology, paleontology, and exploration. Escape was the keynote of science fiction in the early years of the twentieth century, and tales of exotic lands and lost races provided readers with a temporary release from the cares of the mundane world. H. Rider Haggard was the pioneer, but Edgar Rice Burroughs (1875–1950) was the most popular writer in this motif. Burroughs was a master storyteller whose works were packed with solid entertainment and whose Tarzan series made him the most widely read author in the English language.[3] Many of the Tarzan novels centered on lost cities and lost races. Burroughs also wrote a series of novels set on Mars, where the remnants of a once mighty civilization were depicted with great color, vigor, and exotic splendor. Other series took the reader to Venus, the Moon, and to the center of the Earth. His adventures were light, his characterizations superficial, and his science almost nonexistent; but his striking settings and spellbinding adventures offered readers an escape from the gloom of industrialized cities and the realities of World War I. A greedy audience, and the inclination of pulp magazine editors to publish escape fiction, not only enhanced Burroughs's reputation but also gave science fiction another popular outlet.

It was not until Hugo Gernsback (1884–1967), a Luxembourg immigrant, began publishing a series of electrical magazines[4] which regularly featured science fiction that the contemporary label *science fiction* evolved.[5] Science fiction entered a new phase when, in 1926, Gernsback placed the first issue of *Amazing Stories* on the newsstands. It was the first magazine devoted exclusively to science fiction ("scientifiction," as Gernsback first termed it), and it was an instant success. With *Amazing Stories* the pulp era of science fiction began. This form of literature separated itself from the mainstream by isolating itself within a long line of specialist pulp titles, and remained virtually the only outlet for science fiction writers until after World War II. By the 1930s, other science fiction magazines were appearing regularly, competing with *Amazing* and other Gernsback titles for the growing number of science fiction readers.[6]

Gernsback steadfastly promoted science fiction, as he filled his issues with reprints of classic tales by Verne, Wells, and Poe. Later, he featured the stories of Edward E. Smith, Ray Cummings, Jack Williamson, Edmond Hamilton, and Murray Leinster, among others. Most of the science fiction appearing in *Amazing Stories* emphasized the wonders of science and were filled with futuristic hardware and fantastic adventure—another brand of escape fiction. One of the most famous writers of the Gernsback era was Edward E. "Doc" Smith, whose Skylark series, with its indestructible heroes and super villains, interacting on a galactic scale, popularized the term *space opera*. Other pulp adventure magazines of the 1930s and 1940s entered the field with stories of space exploration, robots, catastrophes, and alien encounters. Like Verne and Burroughs before them, these writers leaned heavily on romance and adventure.

In 1952 Hugo Gernsback was the guest of honor at the World Science Fiction Convention in Chicago. The following year, at the Philadelphia convention, popular works of science fiction were awarded silver rockets named "Hugos," in honor of the man who invented the term *science fiction* and encouraged the development of new writers in the field.

Science fiction began to change shape and direction when, late in 1937, John W. Campbell, Jr., assumed the editorship of *Astounding Stories*.[7] Campbell, a regular contributor to that magazine, recruited writers who could write more realistically about science and scientists and demanded from them greater sophistication of style and technique, and greater rigor of ideas. Writers refined their plots and characters, while emphasizing human relationships, and were encouraged by Campbell to tap psychology, philosophy, politics, and other soft sciences and areas of specialization. *Astounding* gradually became the foremost science fiction magazine and one of the few to survive the economic hardships and wartime shortages of the 1930s and 1940s.

Campbell's position in the field, at the head of the best-paying and highest-circulation magazine, gave him the advantage of pre-eminence: writers looked to him as their primary market, wrote their ideas to him and accepted his suggestions, sent him their stories first, and often rewrote them to his order. Campbell also had the good fortune to become an editor when science fiction was responding to a new wave of popularity, through the publication of a growing number of new science fiction magazines. Among the new writers to appear in the pages of *Astounding* during the early years of Campbell's editorship were Isaac Asimov, Robert A. Heinlein, A. E. van Vogt, Theodore Sturgeon, Lester del Rey, and Clifford D. Simak, most of whom are still active in the field. Guided by Campbell's demands for quality and serious scientific conjecture, science fiction matured, and entered what fans refer to as its Golden Age, roughly the period from 1938 to 1950. *Astounding* changed its name to *Analog* in 1960 as part of an alteration of its overall format, and is today still one of the world's leading science fiction magazines. The Golden Age endured until 1950, when the field broadened and improved as influential magazines such as the *Magazine of Fantasy and Science Fiction* (1949), under the editorship of Anthony Boucher and J. Francis McComas, and *Galaxy* (1950), edited by Horace L. Gold, appeared, and as science fiction spilled over into the paperbacks.

While prewar science fiction had concentrated on the technical wonders suggested by scientific advances, writers in the post–World War II period began to examine the human consequences of these advances and the fear that we might become the victims of our own creations. Science fiction experienced a new direction of growth as the social sciences became important subjects for writers in the 1950s and 1960s. The dystopian future became a staple plot of 1950s pulp science fiction. Frederik Pohl and Cyril Kornbluth satirized a society dominated by advertising corporations in *The Space Merchants* (1953), which is perhaps the most famous work of this generation of science fiction writers. So prominent was the dystopian image in magazine science fiction of this period that an entire body of works dealing with this theme was produced over a twenty-year period, not only in the pulps but in a remarkable number of varied dystopian novels, such as Ray Bradbury's *Fahrenheit 451* (1953), Cyril M. Kornbluth's *Not This August* (1955), Anthony Burgess's *A Clockwork Orange* (1962), Harry Harrison's *Make Room! Make Room!* (1966), and John Brunner's *Stand on Zanzibar* (1968).

The response to social issues was intensified in the 1960s by British and American writers such as Michael Moorcock, J. G. Ballard, Brian W. Aldiss, Norman Spinrad, Harlan Ellison, Samuel R. Delany, Joanna Russ, and Thomas M. Disch. The New Wave, as this group came to be called, warned of the chaos and despair threatened by the potential for war and internal corruption in a technological society. New Wave writers also lent a fresh approach to the writing of science fiction, which, by the end of the 1950s, had become set in its ways. Eventually the New Wave was absorbed into the system, but before the movement faded, it was responsible for several important and permanent changes in the quality of science fiction writing, and helped to establish science fiction as a literature of serious social comment.

Science fiction continued to grow and develop in the 1970s. Robert Silverberg hit his stride with *Time of Changes* (1971) and *Dying Inside* (1972) and six other major novels published during the period 1970–72.[8] Ursula K. Le Guin's *The Left Hand of Darkness* (1969) and *The Dispossessed* (1974) became symbols of the high standards of quality of which writers in the field were capable. Philip K. Dick, who died in 1982, left behind a great legacy of works, including *Flow My Tears, the Policeman Said* (1973) and *A Scanner Darkly* (1977). One of the least predictable of science fiction writers, Brian W. Aldiss, continued to explore new territory with works like *Frankenstein Unbound* (1974) and *The Malacia Tapestry* (1977). A British writer, his influence in the United States has been pervasive. It was Frederik Pohl, however, who had the greatest impact in the 1970s. Following a period of low productivity and indifferent success, Pohl powerfully reestablished his reputation with his novels *Man Plus* (1976), *Gateway* (1977), and *JEM* (1979), each of which has won major awards in the field. He has continued this prolific production of enduring works into the present day.

Among the writers whose careers began (or who first achieved recognition) in the 1970s are George R. R. Martin, *Dying of the Light* (1977); James Tiptree, Jr., *Up the Walls of the World* (1978); Vonda N. McIntyre, *Dreamsnake* (1978); Joe Haldeman, *The Forever War* (1975); John Varley, *The Persistence of Vision* (1978); Gregory Benford, *In the Ocean of the Night* (1977); C. J. Cherryh, *Brothers of Earth* (1976); Gene Wolfe, *The Fifth Head of Cerberus* (1972); Joan D. Vinge, *The Outcasts of Heaven Belt* (1978); Michael Bishop, *The Catacomb Years* (1979); and British authors Christopher Priest, *Inverted World* (1974); Ian Watson, *The Jonah Kit* (1975); and Brian Stableford, *The Halcyon Drift* (1976). Many other writers entered the field during the 1970s; it was a fruitful decade for science fiction.

The decade of the 1980s holds high promise, with more writers entering the field than ever before in its history, and pioneers such as Isaac Asimov, Arthur C. Clarke, and Robert A. Heinlein reaffirming their popularity with new works. To list all of the bright new stars of the current decade would be impossible here; but among those who have carved enduring reputations among the readers are David Brin, Greg Bear, Connie Willis, Kim Stanley Robinson, Bruce Sterling, William Gibson, Lucius Shepard, and Orson Scott Card. Science fiction has come a long way since the 1930s and 1940s when the pulp magazines provided the sole training ground for new talent. In many ways the literature is still growing, altering its forms, modifying its techniques and subject matter. This willingness to adapt to changes in style and direction is typical of a literature that, above all else, is concerned with evaluating the forces affecting the shape the future may take and providing a vision of possibilities open to society and the human race.

REFERENCE WORKS

Alongside the growth of science fiction as a popular literature has been its gradual emergence and acceptance as an academic discipline. Science fiction's gradual climb to academic respectability began in the late 1950s with three significant events: in 1958, Scott Osborne of Mississippi State University organized the first Conference on Science Fiction at the Modern Language Association meeting in New York; a year later the first academic journal, *Extrapolation*, was founded by Thomas D. Clareson at the College of Wooster; and at Princeton University in 1959, Kingsley Amis, a recognized English poet and author, presented a series of lectures in which he proclaimed his longtime admiration for science fiction. A year later the lectures appeared as *New Maps of Hell*, and various surprised popular media, reviewing the book, began to reconsider their own policy of consistently ignoring or denigrating the science fiction which had somehow reached their desks.[9]

The genre was given further impetus when the Science Fiction Research Association was established in 1970 to serve as a gathering point for those concerned with some phase of the study of science fiction. At about the same time, courses in science fiction began to proliferate, with a noticeable increase in the publication of works of criticism and reference to meet the demands of the scholar and teacher. Special sections on science fiction are now regular features on the programs of academic organizations such as the Modern Language Association, the National Council of Teachers of English, the Popular Culture Association, and their regional and state affiliates. Scholarly journals such as *Extrapolation, Science-Fiction Studies*, and *Foundation* serve the needs of a worldwide science fiction community.

In 1980 the International Conference for the Fantastic in the Arts was established by Robert A. Collins and a staff at Florida Atlantic University. Now the largest conference of its kind in the world, its annual meetings (which, in 1985, began to rotate among various geographical locations under the direction of the International Association for the Fantastic in the Arts) are now the major focal points for the dissemination of scholarship in fantasy, science fiction, and horror literature among a wide range of specialized and traditional disciplines.

The acceptance of science fiction as a proper subject for scholarly investigation was preceded by several decades of research activity by dedicated amateurs. Many of these early attempts at indexing and classifying materials appeared in fan magazines with small distributions or were published as pamphlets in severely limited editions now difficult to locate. Few of these amateur researchers were trained in bibliographic methodology; compiling indexes, checklists, and bibliographies was largely a labor of love, an activity which reflected the particular enthusiasms of the compilers rather than any systematic exploration of the genre. These fan projects nonetheless helped to establish the bibliography as a mainstay in science fiction research, and commercial publishers are now receptive to this kind of scholarly endeavor. These pioneer efforts constitute an important body of core documents, many of which have been indispensable to contemporary researchers in their efforts to establish bibliographic control for the science fiction field.

Robert E. Briney and Edward Wood's *SF Bibliographies* in 1972 was the first attempt to publish information on early bibliographic work in the field. This forty-nine-page booklet supplied exhaustive coverage of bibliographic reference tools, listing and annotating approximately one hundred books and pamphlets published during the period 1923–71. A later work, *A Research Guide to Science Fiction Studies*, compiled by Marshall B. Tymn, Roger C. Schlobin, and L. W. Currey, summarized science fiction scholarship in book and pamphlet form. This work supplements and in some cases supersedes citations in *SF Bibliographies*, and provides the researcher with a comprehensive, annotated listing of the important scholarly tools published in the United States and England through 1976.

The pioneer bibliography of primary works in science fiction and fantasy is Everett F. Bleiler's *The Checklist of Fantastic Literature*, first published in 1948. The result of seven years of research, the volume contains approximately 5,300 prose titles published from 1764 through 1947. This seminal work has remained an indispensable reference tool for this period, when the publication of fantastic fiction was scattered and erratic. In 1978 Bleiler issued a revised version of this earlier work under the title *The Checklist of Science-Fiction and Supernatural Fiction*.

Of the dozen or so checklists and bibliographies of science fiction and fantasy that have appeared since 1948, only two works can be compared to the Bleiler volume in terms of their scope of coverage. The first major title to appear was Donald H. Tuck's three-volume *The Encyclopedia of Science Fiction and Fantasy Through 1968* (1974, 1978, 1982), which was the accumulation of over twenty years of research. Tuck stresses that both his 1974 and 1978 volumes complement the 1948 Bleiler checklist and "can be considered as a sort of continuation of that book." The Tuck bibliography consists of alphabetical listings of authors, anthologists, editors, artists, and others, with biographical sketches when available, and compilations of their works, in most cases all known editions and forms, including foreign translations. Full listings of the contents of story collections and anthologies, as well as series descriptions, are an important feature of this work. Although the author checklists are now several years out of date, the scope of this compilation is immense and it is likely to remain an important reference tool for many years.

Thus far, the most important comprehensive general bibliography is R. Reginald's two-volume *Science Fiction and Fantasy Literature*. Although no science fiction researcher should rely on a single source of information, this work comes close to being the "essential" checklist for science fiction. Volume 1 lists 15,884 English-language first editions of books published between 1700 and 1974; volume 2 presents 1,443 biographical sketches of both living and deceased authors of the modern period. Reginald's work is a remarkable achievement and a major contribution to scholarship in the field. An update is badly needed, however. Until the first supplement is issued, the field lacks a checklist of science fiction and fantasy works for the decade beginning 1975.

Science fiction magazines have been well indexed since the publication of Donald B. Day's pioneering work, *Index to the Science-Fiction Magazines 1926–1950*. This volume indexes the contents of fifty-eight science fiction magazines from their first issues through December 1950. Day's work remains the standard index for science fiction magazines of this period. The 1951–65 period is covered by Erwin S. Strauss's *The MIT Science Fiction Society's Index to the S-F Magazines, 1951–1965*, which indexes the contents of one hundred English-language magazines. The New England Science Fiction Association (NESFA) subsequently issued a five-year index compiled by Anthony Lewis, *Index to the Science Fiction Magazines 1966–1970*, which includes all of the American and British magazines published during the period. Commencing with the 1971–72 supplement, coverage was extended to include original anthologies. The NESFA has issued annual volumes at irregular intervals since 1972 (although none have been issued since 1984); they have become the standard magazine indexes for science fiction and fantasy.

The most comprehensive reference work yet published for magazines in the field is *Science Fiction, Fantasy, and Weird Fiction Magazines*, edited by Marshall B. Tymn and Mike Ashley. This massive work collects the publishing histories of 279 English-language magazines that publish science fiction, fantasy, and weird fiction in the twentieth century. The volume gives full coverage of the pulp age of science fiction and fantasy, beginning with the general pulp magazines such as *Argosy*, which was first published in 1882, through the decades of specialist pulp titles that began with the publication of *Weird Tales* in 1923, up to the contemporary pulps of the early 1980s. It provides sustained commentary, not only for titles for which information is partially available but for those titles which have never before been researched, along with details of each magazine's publishing history, location, and reprint sources, and relevant critical studies. Sections on anthology series, academic periodicals, fanzines, and non–English-language magazines round out the volume.

Complementing the magazine indexes is William Contento's *Index to Science Fiction Anthologies and Collections*, which contains full contents listings of 1,900 books containing 12,000 different English-language stories by 2,500 authors. This 1978 work was followed in 1984 by an update covering the period 1977–83.

Three reference works have been published that together comprise an essential set of resources for locating biographical, critical, and bibliographical information on hundreds of science fiction writers, past and present.

Twentieth-Century American Science-Fiction Writers, compiled by David Cowart and Thomas L. Wymer, contains biographical-critical studies of ninety authors who began writing after 1900 and before 1970. Each entry provides up-to-date biographical and bibliographical material together with a synthesis of the critical response to the author's works. Curtis C. Smith's *Twentieth-Century Science-Fiction Writers* is a reference handbook which provides information on more than 600 writers (the 1986 revised edition adds 50 writers). Each entry consists of a brief biography, a bibliography, and a short critical essay. This work is valuable for the scope of its coverage. Everett F. Bleiler's *Science Fiction Writers: Critical Studies of the Major Authors from the Early Nineteenth Century to the Present Day* contains studies of the life and works of seventy-six important science fiction writers. Each essay provides basic biographical information, commentary on major works, historical background, and a selected bibliography. In many instances the critical studies comprise the first extended coverage of the subject author.

Some general reference works that are important guides to the science fiction field as a whole should be mentioned at this point. The one which appeals to the largest audience is Neil Barron's *Anatomy of Wonder: A Critical Guide to Science Fiction*. This guide critically annotates almost 1,700 English-language books, fiction and nonfiction, and contains essays which provide historical contexts for the annotations. Coverage of film and television, science fiction art, the magazines, and teaching aids, as well as foreign-language science fiction, is also included. *Anatomy of Wonder* is the major source for content descriptions of science fiction novels, story collections, and anthologies.

A one-volume work covering all aspects of the science fiction field is Peter Nicholls's *The Science Fiction Encyclopedia*. Most entries are brief, but over 2,800 items are listed, covering authors, themes, magazines, films, publishers, series, terminology, awards, conventions, and much more. This volume is unmatched in scope by any other book in the field. Marshall B. Tymn's *The Science Fiction Reference Book* is a comprehensive handbook and guide to the history, literature, scholarship, and related activities of the science fiction and fantasy fields. While it is not as broad in its coverage as the Nicholls volume, its background essays, reading lists, and discussions of current resources make this an ideal companion for the classroom teacher and student.

The most ambitious survey of the genre ever published is the five-volume *Survey of Science Fiction Literature*, edited by Frank N. Magill. The set comprises 513 essay-reviews representing 280 authors, including about 90 foreign-language titles written by 72 authors. The works have been carefully chosen, with most major works in the field represented. *Anatomy of Wonder* annotates twice as many works but with briefer commentary.

Science fiction and fantastic film has been thoroughly documented by science fiction researchers. The single most valuable index to the fantastic film is Walt Lee's *Reference Guide to Fantastic Films*. This three-volume work lists over 20,000 films produced in more than fifty countries since about 1900. Each citation includes date of release, country of production, length, cast, credits, content notes, source of film story, and references to reviews. Lee's guide is praised in *Anatomy of Wonder* as "an extraordinary achievement characteristic of the best of fan scholarship." An update is badly needed, for no other film reference work of this scope exists. The 1972–83 period is covered by another reference work, *Horror and Science Fiction Films II* and *Horror and Science Fiction Films III*, by Donald C. Willis. Sequels to an earlier volume which overlaps with Lee's *Reference Guide to Fantastic Films*, Willis's volumes list over 3,100 titles from the period, with data and commentary, and together comprise the most comprehensive index for the modern period of science fiction film.

Of all the science fiction film reference books published during the last decade, by far the best is Phil Hardy's *The Film Encyclopedia: Science Fiction*, part of a projected nine-volume series issued by Aurum Press (London) and William Morrow, which will cover the principal film categories or genres which have developed since the birth of the industry. What distinguishes the Hardy volume from others is its scope, which is truly encyclopedic, and its structure. The heart of the book is some 1,300 entries devoted to individual films. These entries range from a hundred to a thousand words in a direct reflection of the film's interest and/or historical importance in the development of the science fiction film. As far as possible, each entry comprises fully researched credits, a brief synopsis of the plot, and informed critical comment on the film. In addition to the entries, the encyclopedia also contains numerous appendixes, including a Critics' Top Ten, a ranking of science fiction films by their rental earnings, and a list of Oscars won by science fiction films. Taken together, the appendixes comprise the most comprehensive statistical overview of the genre ever published. Even more significant is the wide range of films included. In contrast to previous works which have concentrated almost exclusively on British and American films, Hardy covers in depth the science fiction cinema of such countries as Japan, Italy, Mexico, and Spain, as well as Eastern Europe. With over 450 black-and-white stills and sixteen pages of color plates, this spectacular volume now ranks as the standard reference on the science fiction film, and should remain so for many years.

The complete record of books reviewed in science fiction is H. W. Hall's *Science Fiction Book Review Index*, which has been published by Hall annually since 1970. *SFBRI* indexes book reviews in the science fiction magazines, selected fanzines, and in general reviewing media such as *Library Journal, Publishers Weekly*, and *Choice*. During the period 1974–79, *SFBRI* cited 16,700 reviews to over 5,000 books. These six issues were published as *Science Fiction Book Review Index, 1974–1979* in 1979. An earlier compilation,

Science Fiction Book Review Index, 1923–1973, appeared in 1975. A third volume covering the period 1980–84 was issued in 1985.

CRITICAL STUDIES

The volume of criticism published for the science fiction field since 1970 has been literally overwhelming and impossible for any one person to know in its entirety. Over the years scholars committed to the genre have published works of high quality which have been accepted by a wide audience.

The first comprehensive background study was J. O. Bailey's 1947 *Pilgrims Through Space and Time*, a survey of the scientific and utopian romance in English, emphasizing fiction published prior to 1914. Still a standard work, its chief value is the thematic arrangement of the material. One of the earliest symposiums on science fiction, *Modern Science Fiction*, edited by Reginald Bretnor, is an important document on the Golden Age of the literature. The first full-length commentary on the genre by a critic from outside the science fiction community, Kingsley Amis's *New Maps of Hell: A Survey of Science Fiction*, gave direction to current criticism of science fiction by emphasizing its role as an instrument of social diagnosis and warning. H. Bruce Franklin's *Future Perfect: American Science Fiction of the Nineteenth Century*, a fiction anthology with extensive critical commentary by the editor, remains the most perceptive survey of science fiction written by American literary figures of the period.

These early efforts have been continued with several works published in the 1970s and 1980s, the first of which was Robert M. Philmus's *Into the Unknown: The Evolution of Science Fiction from Francis Godwin to H. G. Wells*, a survey of English science fiction of the eighteenth and nineteenth centuries, which relates the genre to utopian satire and to a mythological view of life. Donald A. Wollheim's *The Universe Makers: Science Fiction Today* is a personal statement of the place of science fiction in literature and an excellent introduction to the genre for the beginning student. Thomas D. Clareson has been responsible for bringing together a multitude of critical viewpoints on the literature of science fiction. His pioneer anthology, *SF: The Other Side of Realism*, illustrates the diverse ways in which the study of science fiction may be approached; and his *Many Futures, Many Worlds* integrates views on the study of science fiction from starting points as diverse as philosophy, mythology, theology, and technology.

An important landmark in the treatment of science fiction history is Brian W. Aldiss's *Billion Year Spree: The True History of Science Fiction*, which surveys the development of the genre from its nineteenth-century beginnings through contemporary writings of the 1950s and 1960s. Aldiss released in 1986 his *Trillion Year Spree*, a revised and updated version of the earlier volume. Following the Aldiss study was James Gunn's *Alternate Worlds:*

The Illustrated History of Science Fiction, an informed study of the scientific, social, and philosophical climate that brought forth and shaped science fiction from its early beginnings to the present. *Science Fiction: History, Science, Vision*, by Robert Scholes and Eric S. Rabkin, is a textbook survey of science fiction that offers a synthesis of the historical, scientific, and thematic elements that constitute the genre. In his 1978 autobiography, *The Way the Future Was*, Frederik Pohl offers a delightful and absorbing account of his career as fan, writer, editor, anthologist, and literary agent, while providing an inside view of the development of the genre from the late 1920s to the present. Another important genre survey is Barry Malzberg's *The Engines of the Night: Science Fiction in the Eighties*, which looks at the state of the art in science fiction today, and in the process offers a thoughtful consideration of science fiction's classic past, the Golden Age of the pulps and the seminal editors, fandom and conventions, and the practices of the modern science fiction scene. The most recently published commentary on the contemporary science fiction scene is *Age of Wonders: Exploring the World of Science Fiction*, by David Hartwell, one of America's leading science fiction editors and an influential voice in its publishing industry. Hartwell examines a number of issues, including the experience of discovering and becoming addicted to science fiction, the phenomenon of fandom, science fiction publishing, the academic treatment of science fiction, and science fiction as a reflection of contemporary culture. Most recently, Thomas D. Clareson shows how science fiction was a popular response to world events during the period 1870–1930 in his *Some Kind of Paradise: The Emergence of American Science Fiction*, as he explores the intellectual and social milieu which produced and shaped the genre during the period under study. Brian Stableford's *Scientific Romance in Britain 1850–1950* argues that there grew up in Britain at the end of the last century an important and distinctive kind of science fiction writing, constituting a tradition quite separate from science fiction in America at the same period. This book promises to be a seminal work in science fiction history.

The growing interest in theoretical criticism is represented by several key works. David Ketterer's *New Worlds for Old: The Apocalyptic Imagination, Science Fiction, and American Literature* is an attempt to place the literature of science fiction within the broader category of the "apocalyptic"—literature that concerns itself with the "destruction of an old world and the coming of a new order." Ketterer maintains that "because of a common apocalyptic quality and a common grounding in the romance, science fiction and mainstream American literature share many significant features." This is an important scholarly study and the first book-length treatment of science fiction to give sustained explication of contemporary texts, Gary K. Wolfe's *The Known and the Unknown: The Iconography of Science Fiction* is a significant advance over the general surveys which dominated studies of science fiction until the mid–1970s. Wolfe examines the evolution and meaning of several key images—spaceships, the city, wastelands, robots, and monsters; in relating these images to the fundamental beliefs and values of the genre, Wolfe reveals a complex and sophisticated ideology concerning the meaning of technology and the role of humanity in the universe. Darko Suvin's *Metamorphoses of Science Fiction: On the Poetics of a Literary Genre* is a serious and insightful examination of what the author calls "the fiction of cognitive estrangement." The first part of this study is an elaboration of the concepts of cognition (science) and estrangement (fiction) in which Suvin sets the science fiction genre apart from either naturalistic fiction or the supernatural. The second part, on the historical tradition, deals with science fiction in Europe and America from Thomas More to H. G. Wells, with references to earlier writers as well as Slavic science fiction up to the 1950s. This work is a major contribution to the intellectual history of science fiction and to theoretical studies of the genre.

One of the most far-reaching of the recent body of theoretical criticism is Casey Fredericks's *The Future of Eternity: Mythologies of Science Fiction and Fantasy*. This study of the impact of mythology on modern science fiction and fantasy ranges broadly in interdisciplinary fashion over many of the most popular theories and concepts of modern thought: myth theory, history and philosophy of science, Freudian and Jungian psychology, narratology and fiction theory, along with current developments in science fiction criticism. Fredericks emphasizes three speculative confrontations of crucial interest to the twentieth-century imagination: man/superman, man/machine, and human/alien. This is a pioneer work which will form the basis of future studies of science fiction as an interdisciplinary genre.

The growing interest in subject studies of the science fiction genre is represented in several important works. The first systematic study of twentieth-century dystopian fiction is *The Future as Nightmare: H. G. Wells and the Anti-Utopians*, by Mark R. Hillegas. A more detailed and wide-ranging examination of the dystopian trend in contemporary science fiction is Harold L. Berger's *Science Fiction and the New Dark Age*, which includes works that have previously received little critical attention. A well-documented study concerned with the uses to which science fiction writers put linguistics is Walter E. Meyers's *Aliens and Linguistics: Language Study and Science Fiction*. Meyers's approach is speculative, but firmly grounded in current techniques of language analysis and is informed by a wide acquaintance with science fiction literature. Patricia Warrick's *The Cybernetic Imagination in Science Fiction* is the first in-depth treatment of artificial intelligence (robots and computers) in science fiction. Based on a study of 225 short stories and novels written between 1930 and 1977, the work is both a history of cybernetic science fiction and an analysis of its recurring images, patterns, and meanings. This theme is continued in two later works, edited by Richard D. Erlich and Thomas P. Dunn. *The Mechanical God: Machines in Science Fiction* treats the subject of mechanization in science fiction, while *Clockwork*

Worlds: Mechanized Environments in SF, with its focus on mechanized environments, serves as a companion volume to *The Mechanical God*.

Until recently, the full-length critical study of individual authors was a neglected area of science fiction scholarship. The earliest attempts at author coverage were two works by historian Sam Moskowitz: *Explorers of the Infinite: Shapers of Science Fiction*, with chapters on pre–World War II writers who influenced the developing genre; and *Seekers of Tomorrow: Masters of Modern Science Fiction*, with chapters on twenty-one modern writers. The tradition established by Moskowitz has been continued by Thomas D. Clareson, with his three *Voices for the Future* volumes, which are collections of critical essays by various academics on major writers of science fiction whose careers had begun by World War II or later. A second series, Writers of the 21st Century, edited by Joseph D. Olander and Martin Harry Greenberg, was an important landmark in science fiction author studies. The first two volumes in the series, collections of essays on Isaac Asimov and Arthur C. Clarke, were published in 1977; additional volumes were released in 1978 (Robert A. Heinlein), 1979 (Ursula K. Le Guin), 1980 (Ray Bradbury and Jack Vance), and 1983 (Philip K. Dick), the final volume in the series.

Studies of science fiction writers are appearing with increasing frequency, not only as isolated publications, but also as part of existing series devoted to author studies. Three ongoing series which comprise a ready market for single-authored studies of science fiction writers are *The Milford Series: Popular Writings of Today* (Borgo Press), edited by R. Reginald, which began publication in 1977; *The Starmont Reader's Guides to Contemporary Science Fiction and Fantasy Authors* (Starmont House), edited by Roger C. Schlobin, which was launched in 1979; and *Recognitions* (Frederick Ungar), edited by Sharon Jarvis, which released its first volume in 1980. The Greenwood Press *Contributions* series, discussed below, has also published a number of author studies, and will continue to make this an important emphasis in the series.

Although pulp magazines have not been completely neglected by science fiction historians, more critical studies of the pulps need to be done. Two pioneering works, both by Sam Moskowitz, are *Science Fiction by Gaslight: A History and Anthology of Science Fiction in the Popular Magazines, 1891–1911* and *Under the Moons of Mars: A History and Anthology of "The Scientific Romance" in the Munsey Magazines, 1912-1920*. The thirty-six-page introduction to *Science Fiction by Gaslight* is one of Moskowitz's most important contributions to the study of science fiction history. He charts the early development of the mass-circulation, general-interest, English-language magazine and, through his historical survey and representative fiction selections, examines the themes and extent of a popular literary form of the period. *Under the Moons of Mars* is, in part, a continuation of *Gaslight*, though here the study is restricted to American periodicals with emphasis on the

Munsey group. In a valuable 154-page historical survey, Moskowitz traces the influence of Edgar Rice Burroughs, whose scientific romances sacrificed verisimilitude for romantic adventure. The scientific romance was a dominant literary form during this transitional period, and the popular fiction magazine was the major vehicle for this type of fiction.

In 1974–75 and 1977–78, the New English Library issued four volumes of a series edited by Michael Ashley. Each volume of *The History of the Science Fiction Magazine* examines a decade of magazine publication (the series covers the period 1926–65) through historical commentary by Ashley and story selections from the magazines. The series, as far as it goes, provides the first balanced, compact overview of the development of this specialized magazine genre.

A welcome addition to pulp magazine history, Paul A. Carter's *The Creation of Tomorrow: Fifty Years of Magazine Science Fiction* is a historical survey of thematic trends apparent in pulp science fiction since magazines devoted entirely to the genre began to be published. Complementing the Carter study is a new series dealing with series characters in the pulp magazines. Two of a projected four volumes, written by Robert Sampson, have been released: *Yesterday's Faces: A Study of Series Characters in the Early Pulp Magazines*, volume 1: *Glory Figures* and volume 2: *Strange Days*. Frank Ciofi's *Formula Fiction? An Anatomy of American Science Fiction, 1930–1940* is an application of formula analysis to magazine science fiction, with an emphasis on *Astounding*, relating his findings to the social reality of the 1930s. Researchers are also reminded that *Science Fiction, Fantasy, and Weird Fiction Magazines*, discussed above under reference works, is not only a reference tool but a comprehensive history of magazine science fiction.

There are two "central clearinghouses" for those who have ideas for scholarly books on science fiction and fantasy. These clearinghouses take the form of two critical series, which, taken together, support the work of a large number of researchers and scholars in the science fiction field. The first of these series, *Alternatives*, is published by Southern Illinois University Press and is edited by Eric S. Rabkin, Martin Harry Greenberg, and Joseph D. Olander. The first volume in the series was published in 1980, and eight books of criticism have so far been released, the latest in 1986; all are essay collections.

The second series is *Contributions to the Study of Science Fiction and Fantasy*, published by Greenwood Press and edited by Marshall B. Tymn. The focus of the series is on selected historical topics, author studies, and thematic studies. Twenty-four volumes have been published since 1982, making this the largest science fiction and fantasy critical series in the English language and the major focal point for the dissemination of scholarship in these fields. This series also publishes an annual proceedings volume for the International Association for the Fantastic in the Arts, thus providing a ready and viable outlet for conference papers. Both the *Alternatives* and the *Contributions* series were established to serve the growing critical audience of science fiction and fantasy fiction.

The study of the science fiction film continues to be a viable area of interest on the part of both fans and scholars. There has been no shortage of books on this subject since the first serious study was published in 1970 by John Baxter. *Science Fiction in the Cinema* outlines the history of the science fiction film from 1895 to 1968. The coverage is broad and informed, especially for the period 1900 to 1940. William Johnson's *Focus on the Science Fiction Film* contains essays by American, British, and European critics covering three historical periods: 1895–1940, the 1950s, and the 1960s. Philip Strick's *Science Fiction Movies* is an informative text which includes an unusually wide and interesting range of films and treats all the popular themes. Equal to the Strick study, if not superior to it, is John Brosnan's *Future Tense: The Cinema of Science Fiction*. This scrupulously researched and exhaustively detailed work is a comprehensive historical survey of 400 films that includes plot summaries, developments in technical mastery and special effects, the difference between written and filmed science fiction, and a history of the genre. Vivian Carol Sobchack's *The Limits of Infinity: The American Science Fiction Film 1950–75* is an aesthetic study which focuses on the American science fiction film from its birth as a critically recognized genre in the early 1950s through 1975 and the genre's current renaissance in popularity. Sobchack investigates the relationship between the science fiction and horror film, discusses science fiction imagery, and explores a previously neglected area, the sounds of the science fiction movie (dialogue, music, sound effects). A well-reviewed and popular recent work is Bill Warren's *Keep Watching the Skies! American Science Fiction Movies of the Fifties*, a survey of every film produced in the United States between 1950 and 1957 that has some element of science fiction important to the plot. This book gives not a history but a personal reaction to each movie, articulated by a knowledgeable fan and expert in the field. Each film is discussed in essay style, with film data relegated to an appendix. An insightful book, *Shadows of the Magic Lamp*, edited by George E. Slusser and Eric S. Rabkin, is testimony to the serious interest among scholars in the science fiction and fantasy film. This volume contains essays by fourteen critics who, using very different methods, span cinematic history from its beginning to the present and offer their independent speculations as to the importance of science fiction in film. The most recent work on genre film criticism is Donald Palumbo's *Eros in the Mind's Eye: Sexuality and the Fantastic in Art and Film*. This essay collection offers a wide-ranging exploration of the erotic and the fantastic over six decades of science fiction and horror film and will be of interest to the student of both film history and popular culture.

How does one keep track of the vast amount of scholarship now being published in science fiction and fantasy? There is no standard library reference work which indexes all of the articles and books in the field, as is the case with some of the traditional disciplines. The first person to compile a guide to the literature was Thomas D. Clareson. His *Science Fiction Criticism: An Annotated Checklist* covered books and articles published in the English language prior to 1972. The chronological continuation of Clareson's bibliography is an annual listing, "The Year's Scholarship in Fantastic Literature," edited by Marshall B. Tymn, which appears in the journal *Extrapolation*, published by the Kent State University Press.[10] "The Year's Scholarship" is an ongoing secondary bibliography created to serve the needs of the scholarly community. It cites all books, pamphlets, Ph.D. dissertations, periodical articles, essays in critical anthologies, chapters in reference works, and instructional media published for a given year. Citations are grouped under the following categories: bibliography and reference, history and criticism, author studies, writing and publishing, film and television, art and artists, and teaching resources. It thus serves the scholar in many ways: as an aid to individual research, as a guide to personal or library acquisition, and as a comprehensive survey of current trends in the scholarship of science fiction and fantasy. These bibliographies were collected and published in 1979 and 1983 as *The Year's Scholarship in Science Fiction and Fantasy: 1972–1975* and *The Year's Scholarship in Science Fiction and Fantasy: 1976–1979*.

The recent proliferation of fantasy and science fiction research activity and the popular interest in the field as a whole have prompted academic libraries to develop systematic collections of primary and secondary titles. The first attempt to compile a listing of such holdings was Hal Hall's preliminary list in the April 1972 issue of the *SFRA Newsletter*, in which thirty-five American, four Canadian, and two British collections were identified. Hall updated this listing in "Library Collections of Science Fiction and Fantasy" (*Anatomy of Wonder*) and again in "Library and Private Collections of Science Fiction and Fantasy" (*Anatomy of Wonder*, 2d ed.). The reader should also consult Elizabeth Cummins Cogell's "Science Fiction and Fantasy Collections in U.S. and Canadian Libraries," in *The Science Fiction Reference Book*, edited by Marshall B. Tymn. The Cogell chapter contains a valuable user's guide to the contents of one hundred collections and is the most comprehensive listing of science fiction and fantasy library holdings ever compiled. Another valuable access tool is the *Dictionary Catalog of the J. Lloyd Eaton Collection of Science Fiction and Fantasy Literature* (G. K. Hall, 1982). This three-volume work lists more than 12,000 books and 4,100 issues of pulp magazines, encompassing all forms of science fiction and fantasy from the late seventeenth century to the present. The Eaton Collection at the University of California at Riverside has grown to become one of the world's largest and most important collections of its kind in the world, and this published catalog provides researchers, bibliographers and collectors with unprecedented access to its contents.

H. W. Hall's *Science Fiction Collections: Fantasy, Supernatural & Weird Tales* highlights a number of significant private and library science fiction collections and is the first such survey ever published.

As this survey has attempted to show, science fiction has achieved acceptance as an academic discipline during the past decade, with its reference works and critical studies acquired by private and institutional libraries, as well as a growing number of readers and scholars. The scope and quality of recent science fiction scholarship have been impressive. Seasoned scholars and qualified newcomers must continue the effort to develop and permanently establish science fiction as a legitimate genre of scholarly inquiry.

NOTES

1. Portions of this essay appeared in "Science Fiction: A Brief History and Review of Criticism," *American Studies International*, 23 (April 1985), 41–66.

2. For additional commentary on early motifs, see Thomas D. Clareson's introduction in his *A Spectrum of Worlds* (New York: Doubleday, 1972).

3. *Tarzan of the Apes*, Burroughs's second published novel, first appeared in the October 1912 issue of *All-Story*. His first novel, *Under the Moons of Mars*, appeared in the February 1912 issue of the same magazine and ran as a six-part series; for its book publication in 1917 the title was changed to *A Princess of Mars*.

4. Gernsback published science fiction as early as 1911, when his own story, "Ralph 124C41 +," appeared in *Modern Electrics*. He also published science fiction in *Electrical Experimenter* (1915–20), *Science and Invention* (1920–28), *Radio News* (1919–28), and the *Experimenter* (1924–26).

5. The term was first used in Gernsback's editorial, "Science Wonder Stories," in the premiere issue of *Science Wonder Stories*, dated June 1929.

6. Gernsback launched *Amazing Stories Annual* in 1927, *Amazing Stories Quarterly* in 1928, and *Science Wonder Stories* in 1929. These were followed by *Air Wonder Stories, Scientific Detective Monthly*, and *Science Wonder Quarterly*; in 1953 he published his last title, *Science Fiction Plus*, a large-format magazine.

7. *Astounding Stories of Super Science* began publication in January 1930 under the editorship of Harry Bates; the next editor was F. Orlin Tremaine (1933–37), who was replaced by John W. Campbell. The magazine changed its name to *Astounding Science Fiction* in 1938, and to *Analog Science-Fact Fiction* in 1960, with a minor change to *Analog Science Fiction-Science Fact* in 1965.

8. *Downward to the Earth* (1970), *Tower of Glass* (1970), *A Time of Changes* (1971), *The World Inside* (1971), *Son of Man* (1971), *The Second Trip* (1972), *Dying Inside* (1972), and *The Book of Skulls* (1972).

9. James Gunn cites this example of the Kingsley Amis lectures in "From the Pulps to the Classroom," in *The Science Fiction Reference Book*, ed. Marshall B. Tymn (Mercer Island, Wash.: Starmont House, 1981).

10. "The Year's Scholarship in Science Fiction and Fantasy" was first compiled by Marshall B. Tymn and Roger C. Schlobin as annual articles in *Extrapolation* covering the period 1974–79. They were published as separate monographs for the years 1980–82 under the title *The Year's Scholarship in Science Fiction, Fantasy, and Horror Literature*, edited by Marshall B. Tymn. The bibliography has now returned

to *Extrapolation*, and beginning with the 1986 installment, will be known as "The Year's Scholarship in Fantastic Literature."

BIBLIOGRAPHY

Books

Aldiss, Brian W. *Billion Year Spree: The True History of Science Fiction*. Garden City, N.Y.: Doubleday, 1973.

Aldiss, Brian W., with David Wingrove. *Trillion Year Spree: The History of Science Fiction*. New York: Atheneum, 1986.

Amis, Kingsley. *New Maps of Hell: A Survey of Science Fiction*. New York: Harcourt, Brace, 1960; Arno Press, 1975.

Ashley, Michael. *The History of the Science Fiction Magazine*. 4 vols. London: New English Library, 1974–75, 1977–78.

Bailey, J. O. *Pilgrims Through Space and Time: Trends and Patterns in Scientific and Utopian Fiction*. New York: Argus Books, 1947; Westport, Conn.: Greenwood Press, 1972.

Barron, Neil, ed. *Anatomy of Wonder: Science Fiction*. New York: R. R. Bowker, 1976; rev. ed., 1981, as *Anatomy of Wonder: A Critical Guide to Science Fiction*.

Baxter, John. *Science Fiction in the Cinema*. London: Zwemmer, 1970.

Berger, Harold L. *Science Fiction and the New Dark Age*. Bowling Green, Ohio: Bowling Green State University Popular Press, 1976.

Bleiler, Everett F. *The Checklist of Fantastic Literature: A Bibliography of Fantasy, Weird and Science Fiction Books Published in the English Language*. Chicago: Shasta, 1948; West Linn, Oreg.: Fax Collector's Editions, 1972.

———. *The Checklist of Science-Fiction and Supernatural Fiction*. Glen Rock, N.J.: Firebell Books, 1978.

———, ed. *Science Fiction Writers: Critical Studies of the Major Authors from the Early Nineteenth Century to the Present Day*. New York: Scribner's, 1982.

Bretnor, Reginald, ed. *Modern Science Fiction: Its Meaning and Its Future*. New York: Coward-McCann, 1953.

Briney, Robert E., and Edward Wood. *SF Bibliographies: An Annotated Bibliography of Bibliographical Works on Science Fiction and Fantasy Fiction*. Chicago: Advent, 1972.

Brosnan, John. *Future Tense: The Cinema of Science Fiction*. New York: St. Martin's Press, 1979.

Carter, Paul A. *The Creation of Tomorrow: Fifty Years of Magazine Science Fiction*. New York: Columbia University Press, 1977.

Ciofi, Frank. *Formula Fiction? An Anatomy of American Science Fiction, 1930–1940*. Contributions to the Study of Science Fiction and Fantasy, No. 3. Westport, Conn.: Greenwood Press, 1982.

Clareson, Thomas D. *Science Fiction Criticism: An Annotated Checklist*. Kent, Ohio: Kent State University Press, 1972.

———. *Some Kind of Paradise: The Emergence of American Science Fiction*. Westport, Conn.: Greenwood Press, 1985.

———. *A Spectrum of Worlds*. New York: Doubleday, 1972.

————, ed. *Many Futures, Many Worlds: Theme and Form in Science Fiction*. Kent, Ohio: Kent State University Press, 1977.

————. *SF: The Other Side of Realism: Essays on Modern Fantasy and Science Fiction*. Bowling Green, Ohio: Bowling Green State University Popular Press, 1971.

————. *Voices for the Future: Essays on Major Science Fiction Writers*. 3 vols. Bowling Green, Ohio: Bowling Green State University Popular Press, 1976, 1979, 1984 (last volume co-edited with Thomas L. Wymer).

Contento, William. *Index to Science Fiction Anthologies and Collections*. Boston: G. K. Hall, 1978.

————. *Index to Science Fiction Anthologies and Collections 1977–1983*. Boston: G. K. Hall, 1984.

Cowart, David, and Thomas L. Wymer, eds. *Twentieth-Century American Science-Fiction Writers*. 2 vols. Detroit: Gale Research, 1981.

Day, Donald B. *Index to the Science-Fiction Magazines: 1926–1950*. Portland, Oreg.: Perri Press, 1952; rev. ed., Boston: G. K. Hall, 1982.

Dictionary Catalog of the J. Lloyd Eaton Collection of Science Fiction and Fantasy Literature. 3 vols. Boston: G. K. Hall, 1982.

Dunn, Thomas P., and Richard D. Erlich, eds. *The Mechanical God: Machines in Science Fiction*. Contributions to the Study of Science Fiction and Fantasy, No. 1. Westport, Conn.: Greenwood Press, 1982.

Erlich, Richard D., and Thomas P. Dunn, eds. *Clockwork Worlds: Mechanized Environments in SF*. Contributions to the Study of Science Fiction and Fantasy, No. 7. Westport, Conn.: Greenwood Press, 1983.

Franklin, H. Bruce, ed. *Future Perfect: American Science Fiction of the Nineteenth Century*. New York: Oxford University Press, 1966; rev. ed., 1978.

Fredericks, Casey. *The Future of Eternity: Mythologies of Science Fiction and Fantasy*. Bloomington: Indiana University Press, 1982.

Gunn, James. *Alternate Worlds: The Illustrated History of Science Fiction*. Englewood Cliffs, N.J.: Prentice-Hall, 1975.

Hall, H. W. *Science Fiction Book Review Index, 1923–1973*. Detroit: Gale Research, 1975.

————. *Science Fiction Book Review Index, 1974–1979*. Detroit: Gale Research, 1979.

————. *Science Fiction Book Review Index, 1980–1984*. Detroit: Gale Research, 1985.

————, ed. *Science/Fiction Collections: Fantasy, Supernatural & Weird Tales*. New York: Haworth, 1983.

Hardy, Phil. *The Film Encyclopedia: Science Fiction*. New York: William Morrow, 1984.

Hartwell, David. *Age of Wonders: Exploring the World of Science Fiction*. New York: Walker, 1984; McGraw-Hill, 1985.

Hillegas, Mark R. *The Future as Nightmare: H. G. Wells and the Anti-Utopians*. Carbondale: Southern Illinois University Press, 1967, 1974.

Johnson, William, ed. *Focus on the Science Fiction Film*. Englewood Cliffs, N.J.: Prentice-Hall, 1972.

Ketterer, David. *New Worlds for Old: The Apocalyptic Imagination, Science Fiction, and American Literature*. Bloomington: Indiana University Press, 1974.

Lee, Walt. *Reference Guide to Fantastic Films: Science Fiction, Fantasy, & Horror*. 3 vols. Los Angeles: Chelsea-Lee Books, 1972–74.

Lewis, Anthony. *Index to the Science Fiction Magazines 1966–1970*. Cambridge, Mass.: New England Science Fiction Association, 1971.

Magill, Frank N., ed. *Survey of Science Fiction Literature: Five Hundred 2,000-Word Essay Reviews of World-Famous Science Fiction Novels with 2,500 Bibliographical References*. 5 vols. Englewood Cliffs, N.J.: Salem Press, 1979.

Malzberg, Barry. *The Engines of the Night: Science Fiction in the Eighties*. Garden City, N.Y.: Doubleday, 1982; Bluejay Books, 1984.

Meyers, Walter E. *Aliens and Linguistics: Language Study and Science Fiction*. Athens: University of Georgia Press, 1980.

Moskowitz, Sam. *Explorers of the Infinite: Shapers of Science Fiction*. Cleveland, Ohio: World, 1963; Westport, Conn.: Hyperion Press, 1974.

———. *Seekers of Tomorrow: Masters of Modern Science Fiction*. Cleveland, Ohio: World, 1966; Westport, Conn.: Hyperion Press, 1974.

———, ed. *Science Fiction by Gaslight: A History and Anthology of Science Fiction in the Popular Magazines, 1891–1911*. Cleveland, Ohio: World, 1968; Westport, Conn. Hyperion Press, 1974.

———. *Under the Moons of Mars: A History and Anthology of "The Scientific Romance" in the Munsey Magazines, 1912–1920*. New York: Holt, Rinehart and Winston, 1970.

Nicholls, Peter, ed. *The Science Fiction Encyclopedia*. Garden City, N.Y.: Doubleday, 1979.

Palumbo, Donald, ed. *Eros in the Mind's Eye: Sexuality and the Fantastic in Art and Film*. Contributions to the Study of Science Fiction and Fantasy, No. 21. New York: Greenwood Press, 1986.

Philmus, Robert M. *Into the Unknown: The Evolution of Science Fiction from Francis Godwin to H. G. Wells*. Berkeley: University of California Press, 1970, 1983.

Pohl, Frederik. *The Way the Future Was: A Memoir*. New York: Ballantine Books, 1978.

Rabkin, Eric S., Martin Harry Greenberg, and Joseph D. Olander, eds. *Alternatives* (series). Carbondale: Southern Illinois University Press, 1980–present.

Reginald, R., ed. *The Milford Series: Popular Writers of Today*. San Bernardino, Calif.: Borgo Press, 1977–present.

———. *Science Fiction and Fantasy Literature: A Checklist, 1700–1974*. 2 vols. Detroit: Gale Research, 1979.

Sampson, Robert. *Yesterday's Faces: A Study of Series Characters in the Early Pulp Magazines*, vol. 1: *Glory Figures*. Bowling Green, Ohio: Bowling Green State University Popular Press, 1983.

———. *Yesterday's Faces: A Study of Series Characters in the Early Pulp Magazines*. vol. 2: *Strange Days*. Bowling Green, Ohio: Bowling Green State University Popular Press, 1984.

Schlobin, Roger C., ed. *The Starmont Reader's Guides to Contemporary Science Fiction and Fantasy Authors*. Mercer Island, Wash.: Starmont House, 1979–present.

Scholes, Robert, and Eric S. Rabkin. *Science Fiction: History, Science, Vision*. New York: Oxford University Press, 1977.

Slusser, George E., and Eric S. Rabkin, eds. *Shadows of the Magic Lamp*. *Alternatives* Series. Carbondale: Southern Illinois University Press, 1985.

Smith, Curtis C., ed. *Twentieth-Century Science-Fiction Writers*. New York: St. Martin's Press, 1981; 2d ed., Chicago: St. James Press, 1986.

Sobchack, Vivian Carol. *The Limits of Infinity: The American Science Fiction Film 1950–75*. Cranbury, N.J.: A. S. Barnes, 1980.

Stableford, Brian. *Scientific Romance in Britain 1850–1950*. New York: St. Martin's Press, 1985.

Strauss, Erwin S. *The MIT Science Fiction Society's Index to the S-F Magazines, 1951–1965*. Cambridge, Mass.: MIT Science Fiction Society, 1965.

Strick, Philip. *Science Fiction Movies*. London: Octopus, 1976.

Suvin, Darko. *Metamorphoses of Science Fiction: On the Poetics of a Literary Genre*. New Haven, Conn.: Yale University Press, 1979.

Tuck, Donald H. *The Encyclopedia of Science Fiction and Fantasy Through 1968*. 3 vols. Chicago: Advent, 1974, 1978, 1982.

Tymn, Marshall B., ed. *Contributions to the Study of Science Fiction and Fantasy* (series). Westport, Conn.: Greenwood Press, 1982–present.

Tymn, Marshall B., and Mike Ashley, eds. *Science Fiction, Fantasy, and Weird Fiction Magazines*. Westport, Conn.: Greenwood Press, 1985.

Tymn, Marshall B., and Roger C. Schlobin. *The Year's Scholarship in Science Fiction and Fantasy: 1972–1975*. Kent, Ohio: Kent State University Press, 1979.

———. *The Year's Scholarship in Science Fiction and Fantasy: 1976–1979*. Kent, Ohio: Kent State University Press, 1983.

Tymn, Marshall B., Roger C. Schlobin, and L. W. Currey. *A Research Guide to Science Fiction Studies: An Annotated Checklist of Primary and Secondary Sources for Fantasy and Science Fiction*. New York: Garland, 1977.

Tymn, Marshall B., ed. *The Science Fiction Reference Book: A Comprehensive Handbook and Guide to the History, Literature, Scholarship, and Related Activities of the Science Fiction and Fantasy Fields*. Mercer Island, Wash.: Starmont House, 1981.

Warren, Bill. *Keep Watching the Skies! American Science Fiction Movies of the Fifties*. vol. 1: *1950–1957*. Jefferson, N.C.: McFarland, 1982.

Warrick, Patricia. *The Cybernetic Imagination in Science Fiction*. Cambridge, Mass.: MIT Press, 1980.

Willis, Donald C. *Horror and Science Fiction Films: A Checklist*. Metuchen, N.J.: Scarecrow Press, 1972.

———. *Horror and Science Fiction Films II*. Metuchen, N.J.: Scarecrow Press, 1982.

———. *Horror and Science Fiction Films III*. Metuchen, N.J.: Scarecrow Press, 1984.

Wolfe, Gary K. *The Known and the Unknown: The Iconography of Science Fiction*. Kent, Ohio: Kent State University Press, 1979.

Wollheim, Donald A. *The Universe Makers: Science Fiction Today*. New York: Harper and Row, 1971.

Periodicals

Algol: The Magazine about Science Fiction, New York, 1963–.

Amra. Philadelphia, 1956–.

Ariel. New York, 1976–.

Cinefantastique. Oak Park, Ill., 1970–.

CSL: The Bulletin of the New York C. S. Lewis Society. Ossining, N.Y., 1969–.

Delap's F&SF Review. West Hollywood, Calif. 1975–.

Extrapolation. Wooster, Ohio, 1959–.

Foundation: The Review of Science Fiction. Essex, England, 1972-.

Locus: The Newspaper of the Science Fiction Field. San Francisco, 1968-.

Luna. Oradel, N.J., 1969-.

Mythlore: A Journal of J.R.R. Tolkien, C. S. Lewis, and Charles Williams. Los Angeles, 1969-.

Orcrist: A Journal of Fantasy in the Arts. Madison, Wis., 1966/67-.

Riverside Quarterly. Gainesville, Fla., 1964-.

The Science-Fiction Collector. Calgary, Alberta, Canada, 1976-.

Science Fiction Review. Portland, Oreg., 1972-.

Science-Fiction Studies. Terre Haute, Ind., 1973-.

SF Commentary. Melbourne, Australia, 1969-.

Whispers. Chapel Hill, N.C., 1973-.

Xenophile. St. Louis, Mo., 1974-.

13

Verse and Popular Poetry

JANICE RADWAY and PERRY FRANK

While virtually every field in popular culture studies is plagued by the problems inherent in defining and identifying a proper object for analysis, these difficulties become particularly acute, in fact almost prohibitive, when the subject under scrutiny is popular poetry and verse. Several individual poets have become extraordinarily "popular" figures during the course of American cultural development, in the sense that they were, or are now, personally familiar to a large portion of the population. However, very few single volumes of actual poetry have ever achieved best-seller status at the time of their publication.

Frank Luther Mott, who conservatively defines the best seller as a work purchased in the decade of publication by 1 percent of the total population of the continental United States, lists only seven individual volumes of poetry by American poets as best sellers in the years from 1662 to 1945. Included in this list, however, is Walt Whitman's *Leaves of Grass* (1855), of which only a few hundred copies were actually sold in the year of publication itself. Mott is able to retain the work on his list only because, through cheap reprints, the requisite number of copies was eventually sold in the course of the entire decade. But there is an obvious and significant difference between Whitman's status as a popular poet and that of Henry Wadsworth

Longfellow, whose *Hiawatha* (1855) sold 2,500 copies during the week of publication alone and nearly 18,000 more during the next three months.

Although Mott's figures are therefore of little help to the researcher interested in identifying America's popular poets, assistance is not easily found elsewhere. Even if one could decide on an appropriate measure for the popularity of this genre, which has never approached the novel in sales, such publication figures for volumes of poetry are not readily available. Many literary historians of the eighteenth and nineteenth centuries do include poets now unfamiliar to us in their dictionaries and encyclopedias, but there is almost no way of determining whether such figures were truly popular or only minor poets who produced elitist verse of secondary quality.

The problem is further compounded by the fact that nearly every newspaper and popular magazine published in the United States has, at one time or another, included poetry that cannot be termed "elite" or "artistic." On the other hand, many of these same versifiers have neither produced an entire volume of poetry nor reached a national audience transcending regional, economic, and social limits. As a result, one has to question whether such poetry should be included in a study of popular forms, or whether it ought to be excluded as a variant of American folk culture.

These problems are of more than incidental significance because the way this field of study is delineated necessarily affects the character and validity of the conclusions drawn. Any thesis, therefore, about the place, development, or significance of poetry in the popular culture of the United States is, in reality, little more than a highly speculative hypothesis that can only be tested through further research.

The poets mentioned in the following survey have, accordingly, been selected on the basis of a fairly rigorous procedure. All of those occasional versifiers whose extant work is now limited to individual poems found in magazines, newspapers, or anthologies have been excluded. Of the remaining professional poets, only those for whom substantial sales figures or other indications of general popularity are available will be found in this history. In the case of the eighteenth- and nineteenth-century poets, it was necessary to rely heavily on Rufus Wilmot Griswold's *The Poets and Poetry of America,* a best-selling literary encyclopedia, which itself went through more than sixteen editions. If Griswold includes a poet, refers to his or her popularity, and that popularity could be confirmed in some other source, then that poet has been added as well. Although the resulting list is therefore quite limited, these few figures are the only American poets whose work can be readily identified as poetry read by more than a very small portion of the population.

HISTORIC OUTLINE

In the years immediately following the settlement of the American colonies, two distinct forms of verse emerged as the basis of a popular poetic tradition. While religious and practical considerations tended to diminish interest in the high art of poesy as it was then practiced in England, the early colonist found definite merit in religious poetry of a didactic nature and in informational verse designed for the circulation of news. Accordingly, it is not surprising to discover that the first truly popular American poems were those of the *Bay Psalm Book* (1640) and the numerous "broadsides" hawked by street peddlers.

While the two kinds of verse appeared vastly different on the surface, they exhibited a common interest in content as well as a very obvious disinterest in matters of aesthetic form. Indeed, the editors of the *Bay Psalm Book* apologized for the rustic quality of their verse with the observation that "if therefore the verses are not always so smooth and elegant as some may desire or expect; let them consider that God's Altar needs no polishing."

Like the broadside verse that told of specific crimes, births, deaths, and holidays, early American religious poetry was thus designed to refer explicitly to the world inhabited by its reader. Language was not something to be manipulated for its own sake, but rather a tool to be used for instruction and information. It is this exclusive emphasis on the referential aspect of language that has continued to differentiate America's popular verse from her more self-conscious, deliberately aesthetic poetry of the elite tradition.

Throughout the late seventeenth and early eighteenth centuries, most of the poetry read by the majority of the populace was amateur verse published outside the three major literary centers of Philadelphia, New York, and Boston. Such verse was highly topical and therefore largely ephemeral. It was published by a local printer in pamphlet form and financed by the author himself. Much of the verse, like the "Massachusetts Liberty Song," centered about the revolutionary war, although religious teaching continued to be the primary subject of American amateur verse for the next 150 years. A vast quantity of this sort of verse was included in the almanacs that began to appear as early as 1639 and that quickly became an indispensable guide for every colonial home.

Two professional poets, however, did reach a relatively large audience even before growing industrialization began to revolutionize the printing industry. As far as can be determined, Michael Wigglesworth's *Day of Doom* (1662) was the most popular poem in America for well over one hundred years. The first edition of 1,800 copies was exhausted in the year of publication, a remarkable achievement considering the sparse population of the colonies at the time. While Wigglesworth's verse was certainly more accomplished than that of his amateur contemporaries, the poem probably achieved popular status because its theological content was remarkably expressive of the people's beliefs.

That this was the case with John Trumbull's "McFingal" (1775) is obvious since none of the poetry he later produced ever excited the interest of readers as did this patently political, Hudribrastic attack on the manners and men

of Tory America. The poem went throught thirty editions during the next
century and, according to one literary historian, furnished many popular
proverbs that were quoted long after the war that had sparked it had ended.
"McFingal's" patriotic sentiments were quoted by innumerable political
orators, and the poem itself was a standard entry in both poetic anthologies
and school textbooks for the next hundred years.

Until Lydia Huntley Sigourney's poetry began to dominate the scene,
most eighteenth-century Americans read little more verse than that appearing in the almanacs. Occasionally, a poem by a professional poet would
strike the popular imagination and it would then be widely circulated and
much discussed. It is, however, difficult to determine exactly how well-
known such figures as William Treat Paine, John Pierpont, or James Gates
Percival ever became. Paine's publication of *Adams and Liberty* earned him
$750, a very large sum for any book in 1797. Pierpont's "The Airs of
Palestine" (1816) seems to have attracted a great deal of attention, as did
Percival's sentimental Byronic epic, "The Suicide," which occupied twelve
long magazine pages. While it is fairly certain that these men were widely
known and read outside the small literary community of the period, none
ever achieved the general popularity enjoyed by Sigourney, the "Sweet
Singer of Hartford."

Lydia Huntley Sigourney began writing poetry in 1798, published forty-
six volumes of poetry in her lifetime, and, until the appearance of Longfellow, was America's most popular poet. Her first verse collection, *Moral
Pieces in Prose and Verse* (1816), made it abundantly clear that for her, poetry
was not a mere ornament to life, but rather a direct vehicle for moral
instruction. Although her poems dealt with nearly every subject imaginable,
each was designed to instruct the reader in the inestimable value of the
chaste and moral Christian life. Her *Letters to Young Ladies* (1833) was
especially popular—it eventually went through twenty American editions—
and was followed by the equally popular *Letters to Mothers* (1838).

Sigourney was one of the first American poets to compose lines upon
request for the commemoration of special events. Her "occasional" poems
memorialized many of her dedicated readers, whose relatives sought solace
for their loss in her highly "poetical" sentiments and "uplifting language."
It is important to note that although Sigourney's poetry always referred
directly to the world, it did so in language that clearly set itself off from
the mundane discourse of everyday life. She was extraordinarily adept at
striking a balance between the events of this world and the meaning they
were thought to have in the more important ethereal realm of the spirit.
While it is not completely accurate to think of American popular poetry as
a "formula," Sigourney's combination of the sublime with the small seems
to have set a pattern followed fruitfully thereafter by nearly every popular
American bard.

Lydia Sigourney's extraordinary popularity was challenged for a time in the 1830s by that of another occasional poet, Charles Sprague. He first attracted attention in 1829 when he delivered the Phi Beta Kappa poem at Harvard University's commencement. Although the poem was a highly conventional treatment of the forms "Curiosity" could take, it seems to have struck a popular chord, for it was widely circulated during the next ten years. Sprague thereafter wrote many odes for public and private occasions, including one "written on the accidental meeting of all the surviving members of a family."

Although William Cullen Bryant never became as popular a figure as Longfellow, he was able to earn a substantial living on the basis of his poetry publication. By 1842, he could command a fifty-dollar fee for a single magazine poem, while his individual volumes sold at the respectable rate of 1,700 copies per year. His work seems not to have excited as much general interest as that of some of his contemporaries, for he is included less often in anthologies and textbooks than either Sigourney, Sprague, or the remarkable Longfellow. Still, he appears to have been generally known and popularly appreciated.

It was, however, Henry Wadsworth Longfellow who established himself most successfully in the minds of his fellow Americans as the country's unofficial poet laureate. At a time when the poetic vocation was still scorned as a generally ornamental, effeminate occupation, he was able to command respect as a spokesman for the American spirit. His first volume of poetry, *Voices of the Night* (1839), sold 900 copies in thirty days, 4,300 in a single year. This seems to have set a precedent, for Longfellow earned more than $7,000 in royalties on *Hiawatha* alone in the next ten years. In fact, every volume he produced after the first was subject to advance sale. *Evangeline* (1847) sold 6,050 copies in the first two years after publication; 20,000 copies of *Hiawatha* (1855) were purchased in the first three months alone; and in London, 10,000 copies of *The Courtship of Miles Standish* (1858) were sold in a single day.

No doubt many factors contributed to Longfellow's unprecedented popularity, not the least of which was the skill with which he played the part demanded of him by his readers. However, it is also certain that his ability to combine European erudition and a sense of the past with a characteristically American enthusiasm and optimism was also widely appreciated. This variation of Sigourney's method, characterized by the combination of the elevated with the ordinary, served Longfellow well. He produced innumerable very learned poems, complete with classical allusions, on ordinary topics familiar to his mass of readers. He was generally extolled for his high moral sentiment, for the depth of his feeling, and for the breadth of his knowledge. It did not matter to most of his readers that his versification was conservative or that his poetic treatment occasionally bordered on the sentimental or the melodramatic. What was of primary importance to them was his ability to comment on the higher meaning of their daily lives in an easily comprehensible style. As Russel B. Nye has suggested in *The Unembarrassed Muse,* it was Longfellow's clarity and ability to unravel apparent complexities that most endeared him to his huge audience.

Longfellow was aided in his task of satisfying the young country's need for poetic interpretation and edification by men such as James Russell Lowell, Oliver Wendell Holmes, Josiah Gilbert Holland, and John Greenleaf Whittier. Although none ever came close to Longfellow's popularity, each was called on again and again to comment publicly on the "meaning" of the American experience.

Holmes was a well-known occasional poet who produced lines on commencements, feasts, town meetings, births, deaths, and special holidays. Lowell also produced topical poetry, but he was best known for his satirical verse in *The Biglow Papers* as well as for his extravagant historical epic *The Vision of Sir Launfal* (1848), which sold nearly 175,000 copies during the decade after publication. Holland began his career as a poet in the magazines but graduated soon thereafter to complete volumes of verse. His 200-page epic, *Bittersweet* (1858), setting forth the thesis that evil is part of the Divine Plan, first made his reputation as a poet of the people. When he composed the *Life of Abraham Lincoln* in 1865, 80,000 readers snatched up his eulogy. Like his poetic forefathers, Holland's goal was didactic, and his message emphasized the need for religion in American life.

But even though Holmes, Lowell, and Holland were thus well-known, their poetry did not touch the hearts of their fellow Americans in the exact way that the verses of John Greenleaf Whittier did. Indeed, Whittier's preoccupation with the pastoral values of rural existence seems to have endeared him all the more to America because it appeared at that precise moment when industry and urbanization were becoming a serious threat to a disappearing way of life. Although his first volume, *Lays of My Home* (1843), was well received, it was "Snowbound" (1866) which solidified Whittier's reputation with the masses. The poem's homely but sincere language, its nostalgic sentimentality, and detailed evocation of the hardship of country life made it especially attractive to a swiftly urbanizing people who were anything but sure that they wished to put the past behind them. Twenty-eight thousand copies of "Snowbound" were sold during the first year, and Whittier eventually realized more than $100,000 in royalties from its sale alone. As Van Wyck Brooks has pointed out, "Snowbound" was the safeguard of America's memory and the touchstone of its past. Whittier, like Longfellow and Sigourney before him, was remarkably good at couching America's highest sentiments about God, country, and the family in language slightly but definitely removed from the vernacular of the people. As a result, he was quoted and deferred to unceasingly throughout the nineteenth century as one of America's most honored sages.

Although Alice and Phoebe Cary never achieved the status of American sages, they did produce more than fifteen volumes between them that reached a specific segment of the American population. Born in Cincinnati, Ohio, the sisters composed verses on motherhood, family, and farm life that were especially well known among women and in the midwestern United States. While their verse was neither so refined nor so polished as that of their better-known contemporaries, the sentiments they expressed were almost identical to those of Holmes, Holland, or Whittier. In fact, these lines from Alice's poem "Dying Hymn" (1865), while a bit more effusive, are not very different from numerous poems composed by the other three:

> That faith to me a courage gives
> Low as the grave, to go:
> I know that my Redeemer lives:
> That I shall live, I know.

> The palace walls I almost see,
> Where dwells my Lord and King:
> O grave, where is thy Victory!
> O death, where is thy sting!

Although many other poets like the Carys achieved regional popularity during the middle decades of the nineteenth century, none seems to have developed a reputation comparable to that of Bryant, Longfellow, or Whittier. John Godfrey Saxe, "the witty poet," was read for his satirical comments on the follies of social life, but he actually made his reputation by traveling throughout the country giving oral presentations. Nathaniel Parker Willis published nine volumes of verse throughout his lifetime, but he was better known as an editor, literary fop, and travel writer. In addition, many versifiers developed a following during the Civil War, when poetic sentiments were in particular demand. But as the war ended, and the broadsides in which they were published disappeared, so too did the poets.

This situation did not alter drastically in the last half of the century either. Thomas Bailey Aldrich achieved a measure of popularity with his "Ballad of Babie Bell" (1858) and thereafter published numerous poems on love, God, and the ubiquitous family. Still, he was most widely celebrated for his fiction and criticism, produced while he was editor of the *Atlantic Monthly*. Bayard Taylor, also an editor, produced a great deal of poetry that sold fairly well. However, his reputation was not strong enough to guarantee the success of any of his verse, for several of his epic poems, including "Lars, a Pastoral of Norway" (1873) and "The Prophet" (1874), were definite failures.

Perhaps the one poet of the late nineteenth century who came closest to rivaling the popular reputations of Longfellow and Whittier was James Whitcomb Riley, whose rustic Hoosier dialect and homespun philosophy struck a responsive chord in the now almost-wholly urban America. His idealizations of farm and country life were enormously popular throughout the country, despite the fact that the peculiar language he employed was nearly incomprehensible to some. Riley produced fourteen volumes of cheerful poetic sentiment, all of which were characterized by regular rhythms and easily memorized rhymes. Like nearly all of America's popular poets, he was obsessed with the family, childhood, and days gone by. His poetry, like Whittier's and Longfellow's, embodied the vision of America in which his fellow Americans most wanted to believe. The fact that the vision existed only in the poetry troubled almost no one, least of all Riley.

During the final decades of the century, three poets developed national reputations similar to Riley's in that they were identified with a unique section of the country. Will Carleton, a Michigan newspaperman, began his poetic career with "Betsy and I Are Out," a ballad about lost love, first published in the *Toledo Blade* in 1871. When newspapers across the country reprinted the poem, it was an immediate success. Three years later, Carleton published *Farm Ballads* (1873), a collection full of lavish sentiment and careful descriptions of the farming Midwest. The combination was perfectly suitable for the popular demand, and by his death in 1912, more than 600,000 copies of the book had been sold.

Madison Cawein of Louisville, Kentucky, was never as popular as either Carleton or Riley, but his thirty-six volumes of verse did make him the most prolific Southern writer of the decade. Although most of his lyrics were as sentimental, patriotic, and religious as those of nearly every other poet of the period, his realistic description of the Southern landscape tended to set his work apart as something quite unique.

Joaquin Miller was not, like Cawein, known for the precision of his imagery. Indeed, he was extravagantly praised as the one American poet capable of capturing the grandeur of the magnificent West. Something of a showman, Miller exploited his frontier roots, traveling about the country dressed in buckskins to give poetry readings. Except for his evocative portrayal of the desert and the life of the American Indian, Miller's poetry is indistinguishable from the "heartfelt lyrics" of Carleton or Cawein.

This characteristic emphasis on sentimentality continued throughout the first years of the twentieth century. Most of the American popular verse published in 1900 was as closely centered about the home and family as it had been a century earlier. Although the kind of subject matter that could be treated in a poem had been extended and realistic description tended to appear more often, rhyme was still a necessary component, as was a lightly lilting rhythm. No doubt this was, in part, due to the continuing use of poetry for recitations in the schools and for orations at official occasions.

During the latter years of the nineteenth century more and more poets found their major audience in periodicals and newspapers of the period—there was hardly a major daily that did not publish verse after 1890, and many poets of the period were known primarily through these channels. The public and rhetorical function of verse began to disappear, and the advent of modernism marked the beginning of a deepening schism between elite and popular poetry. While major poets of the nineteenth century found expression in forms that were enjoyed by elite and popular audiences alike, when elite verse struck out for the avant-garde and an allusiveness unknown to nineteenth-century bards, most of the reading public was left behind, as remains the case today. Popular verse in the first half of the twentieth century took a number of different forms. Some poets adopted the subjective tone of elite poetry while retaining referential imagery and pronounced rhyme schemes. Others specialized in witty, clever poetry that pricked the foibles of society, while still another brand of popular poet produced homilies about God, home, and nature of the type that had also been a staple of nineteenth-century verse.

The shift to new genres was noticeable at the end of the century in newspaper poets such as Eugene Field and Ella Wheeler Wilcox. Field, who was associated with the city of Chicago, was particularly good at producing poetry about the innocence and beauty of childhood and was perhaps best known for "Little Boy Blue" (1887) and "Dutch Lullaby: Wynken, Blynken, and Nod" (1895). Wilcox, like Field, was adept at describing the inner life in studied but sentimental terms and once remarked that her purpose was "to raise the unhappy and guide those who need it."

The new tone was also apparent in the response to World War I in popular verse. Poetry enjoyed something of a renaissance after 1915, when large numbers of people were willing to purchase single volumes of verse in addition to the traditional anthologies that had continued in popularity throughout the early years of the century. This increase in the "demand" for verse that spoke to the people is also evident in both the local newspapers and national magazines of the period. While many of the poems were written by the "mothers," "fathers," and "sisters" of the American soldier, by far the largest segment of verse was produced by the young infantrymen who had gone to Europe to "make the world safe for democracy." Among the most well known were John McCrae ("In Flanders Field," 1919), Alan Seeger ("I Have a Rendezvous with Death," 1917), and Joyce Kilmer ("Trees," 1913), all of whom were killed on the battlefields of France.

None of the soldier-poets, however, could match the popularity of the Michigan newspaper poet, Edgar A. Guest, who extended his early regional reputation by publishing large quantities of verse about the war. Although Guest did not participate in the conflict, it was the implicit subject behind most of his poetry. Indeed, his primary concern during the years 1914–17 was the war experience as it was lived by those on the home front. Then, throughout the 1920s, he consolidated his national reputation by continuing to write about home, work, and God. He rightly conceived of his verse as a "mirror" of the values adhered to by his audience, and that audience ratified his conception by purchasing his volumes in increasingly large numbers.

While Guest and most of the popular war poets did not aim for a sophisticated or literary audience, many of the early twentieth-century popular poets did. Ogden Nash, who epitomized the genre, was a master of light wit and was widely read in periodicals of the 1920s and 1930s. Known for his outrageous rhymes and trenchant comments on the modern world, he also published thirteen books of verse between 1931 and 1953.

Berton Braley, another light poet, was widely read in newspapers during the 1920s. Braley had a narrative gift somewhat reminiscent of Edwin Arlington Robinson and a knack for capitalizing on current issues. His collection *Suffragette,* for example, includes the first-person narrative of the debutante who joins the suffrage movement mostly out of curiosity, focuses on the impression made by her clothes, and finds a boyfriend in the cause. Although the poem would hardly find favor today, it was widely admired and is still amusing.

Morris Bishop published light verse in the *Saturday Evening Post* and the *New Yorker,* combining the avocation with a post in romance languages at Cornell. His rhymed couplets poked fun at solemn occasions and technology. A fellow New Yorker, Arthur Guiterman, produced humorous verse and ballads dealing with American history and legend. Guiterman was deeply influenced by Longfellow and spun tales about early New York; his poems were published in popular magazines such as *Woman's Home Companion.*

Samuel Hoffenstein, who wrote mock-heroic verse in rhymed couplets, was a master of parody, turning out poems on slight subjects studded with literary and historical allusions. While not all of his readers may have understood the literary apparatus embedded in his verse, they did understand that he was making fun of pedantry and of the difficult modernist poetry then in vogue among elite audiences. Hoffenstein, a native Pennsylvanian, made his living as a New York journalist and published in the leading periodicals of his day. He also brought out five volumes of verse between 1916 and 1946.

Another periodical poet who captured the public imagination, especially that of women, was Margaret Fishback. She published light verse focusing on matters of the heart and family in such magazines as *Ladies' Home Journal, Saturday Evening Post,* and *Redbook.* Three books of her verse were published during the 1930s.

A far more sophisticated woman poet who achieved wide readership in the 1930s was Dorothy Parker. Parker's gift was a humorous but morbid one, and she often wrote about death. Born in New Jersey and raised a Catholic, she shucked the social constraints of her class and period and traveled widely. While her early periodical verse drew her many fans, her first book, *Enough Rope,* was a phenomenal success when it was published in 1927.

Beginning in the early 1950s with the proliferation of television, popular culture in America underwent a marked change that affected verse and other literary forms as well. Prior to the 1950s, much fun and family entertainment derived from the serialized fiction and light verse that appeared in popular periodicals, as well as on radio and in film. Television influenced not only the radio serials that mesmerized children and adults of the 1930s and 1940s, but also the content, and ultimately the circulation, of the newspapers and magazines that had been the most important outlet for light verse for fifty years. Popular poetry rarely appeared in major dailies after 1955, and magazines that had been the staple of the genre, such as *Collier's* and the *Saturday Evening Post,* folded or sharply curtailed their offerings in the 1960s. The women's magazines that survive still include watered-down fiction and an occasional light poem, but the heyday of periodicals as a vehicle for popular verse, particularly of the witty variety, has long passed.

A few popular poets span the quite distinct periods of the first and second halves of the twentieth century. One of these is Don Blanding, who was born in Oklahoma and ran away from home at the age of fifteen. Becoming the quintessential American vagabond, he lived in Hawaii, Florida, the northwest, and California, and wrote about all his habitats. His first book, *Leaves from a Grass House,* based on his experiences in Hawaii, was self-published and sold 2,000 copies overnight. The book went through twelve printings in four years, making him a literary lion of sorts. Over the years Blanding produced fifteen volumes of thumping, vivid verse that shows the influence of Kipling, or, perhaps, Vachel Lindsay. He was able to evoke a sense of place, and no doubt owed his popularity partly to his Bohemian mystique, which he promoted in his collection *Vagabond's House.* The public bought the romantic image of a hobo who was somehow conveniently never out of money (thanks to the steady sales of his books throughout his life), and who celebrated the still-exotic parts of America while not questioning too deeply or explicitly mainstream American values or experience.

Another popular poet who spans the 1930s through the 1960s is Phyllis McGinley, one of the most prolific and gifted light versifiers of the century. Born in Ontario, Oregon, McGinley grew up in Utah and began writing verse after marrying and moving to New Rochelle, New York, in 1929. McGinley was an adept craftsman and far from naive in her use of literary and historical materials; her wit and pointed aphorisms caught the exact spirit of her corner of society, summing up for many the experience of suburbia, marriage, family, travel, and ordinary life at mid-twentieth century. Although she won a Pulitzer Prize in 1960, her poetry found a broad audience and is very different from the modernist and postmodernist verse of the same period.

A final figure who attained popularity in the 1930s and enjoys a continuing vogue among college students today is the cult figure Kahlil Gibran. Gibran first developed a large audience in the 1920s, when his Oriental mysticism satisfied the American public's interest in the exotic and the Bohemian. He wrote eleven volumes before he died in 1931, all of which included a curious mix of parables, aphorisms, verses, and short narratives. His best-known book, however, is *The Prophet* (1923), which was resurrected in the 1960s as a kind of handbook for the counterculture. To date, *The Prophet* has sold more than three million copies.

The number of popular poets who began writing after 1940 and achieved wide success is considerably smaller than in the previous century. The genre of extremely clever and sophisticated verse exemplified by Nash, Parker, and McGinley has virtually passed away, while the inward, sentimental strain of Eugene Field and Edgar Guest is sustained in popular verse and songs of varying quality.

The most prolific and widely read modern poet of this variety is Rod McKuen, who has probably sold more volumes than any other popular poet of the twentieth century. McKuen's poetry has been especially (one might say exclusively) read by the young. His first book, *Stanyan Street and Other Sorrows,* appeared in 1954 to a decidedly indifferent reception. But when *Listen to the Warm* was published in 1963, it immediately made the best-seller list, and McKuen became an instant celebrity. His verse differs somewhat from traditional popular poetry in that it is explicitly erotic, written in a free-verse style, and lacks any kind of end-rhyming. However, the language is as referential and familiar as that of Longfellow, Riley, or Guest, in that it describes the inner emotional life of the modern adolescent. Although his themes—loneliness, lost love, and the need for human communication—are slightly different from those of his poetic forebears, the generally hopeful note sounded by his sentimental conclusions is not. In that sense, it is possible to see a direct line of development in American poetry extending from Lydia Huntley Sigourney through Henry Wadsworth Longfellow, Riley, Guest, and McKuen.

In somewhat the same mode but for a slightly more mature audience, Walter Benton created a one-book sensation in the 1950s with his long narrative *This Is My Beloved,* a poem that was first published in 1943. Benton's free-verse soft-core pornographic chronicle of a love affair went through several printings and was a favored gift of would-be lovers before its appeal waned in the wake of more explicitly erotic material in the 1960s.

A final figure who should be mentioned during this period is Allen Ginsberg, who is usually classed as a minor but elite poet in the manner of Whitman. Ginsberg's first and most famous book, *Howl,* published in 1956, took stock of mid-century values in unflattering terms, ushering in the Beat generation and ultimately the counterculture of the 1960s. Like Gibran, Ginsberg might more properly be considered a cult than a popular figure, but the distinction is a thin one, especially considering his large sales and status as a self-promoting celebrity.

The widely read popular poets of the post–1950s era are dissimilar in every way except one: all appeal to youth in one way or another, capitalizing on sex, mysticism, the counterculture, or adolescent woes. As has been mentioned, the advent of television, and, more recently, other forms of home entertainment, has cut into the market for the periodicals that previously published popular verse. Thus, the adult, often well-educated audience that formerly followed the versifiers described above may have fallen out of the habit of reading light verse. Perhaps, also, the clever approach to human problems and societal foibles that sustained popular verse of the 1920s, 1930s, and 1940s, seems irrelevant in a post-Watergate world that has turned to black humor and other genres to express its dis-ease. Additionally, the extremely difficult tack that poetry has taken in the last fifty years may have discouraged readers of popular as well as elite verse— Americans are simply not in the habit of writing or reading verse today for pleasure or edification.

Although it can be argued that popular verse as practiced and read in the first half of the twentieth century has continued to decline in the 1960s, 1970s, and 1980s, another avenue of approach is to search for popular verse in a different form—specifically, in the popular and rock music of the 1960s through the present. A number of critics have noted that the lyrics of the Beatles, Simon and Garfunkel, Leonard Cohen, Bob Dylan, and Joni Mitchell have captured the imagination of Americans for over a generation. The subjective, sentimental, but often wryly humorous commentary on modern life found in many of these ballads places them in the tradition of popular poetry; it may be that many of the talents that previously would have found an outlet in popular verse are today being put to service in the music industry.

Meanwhile, popular verse in the traditional sense of limericks, solemn didactic poetry, and naive verse on topics of family, nature, and God continues to be written. A small amount appears in women's magazines, church publications, and journals of special interest groups, but the major outlet is in anthologies of one kind or another. *The Clover Collection of Verse,* for example, published in Washington, D.C., in 1969, contains 300 examples of popular verse of this type. *From Sea to Sea in Song,* a collection published in 1972 by the American Poetry League to commemorate the group's founding in 1922, contains sentimental, nature-oriented poetry. The Pennsylvania Poetry Society published *Prize Poems,* an anniversary volume containing a mix of popular and elite verse, in 1969. *The Golden Anniversary Anthology,* published by the Poetry Society of Virginia in 1974, includes both elite and better-known popular poets, such as Rod McKuen and Phyllis McGinley. *Best Loved Poems,* published in 1983, contains popular religious and spiritual verse from the nineteenth century to the present. Another spiritually oriented anthology, *Virginia Originals,* published by the United Methodist Women in 1982, contains topical verse, prayers, and occasional pieces.

One of the largest recent anthologies of popular verse is *Today's Greatest Poems,* an oversize book of 665 pages published in 1983. The volume contains thousands of popular limericks and poems, printed as many to the page as possible. The crowded format suggests what is probably true for other anthologies of the type described above as well: namely, that writers of such verse today are composing largely for themselves and each other, and that the largest bulk of sales of these volumes is probably made up of contributors.

REFERENCE WORKS

American popular poetry has, until recently, excited very little serious critical attention. As a consequence of this state of neglect, there is no full-length reference work available that is devoted solely to the "poets of the people." However, a good introduction to the field can be found in Russel B. Nye's comprehensive history of the popular arts, *The Unembarrassed Muse.* Nye's chapter on "Rhymes for Everybody" is a historical survey that is both more detailed and complete than the one provided here. While Nye does not list all the volumes published by the authors he cites, the essay is a good starting point in any attempt to identify those poets who did achieve a measure of popularity in the United States.

Frank Luther Mott's *Golden Multitudes* and Alice Payne Hackett's *Fifty Years of Best Sellers* are both useful in that they provide specific figures for some of the most popular poets. However, neither volume goes much beyond the two or three poets who could compete with American novelists in overall sales. James Hart's *The Popular Book* includes a few names and details missing from these other general studies, and as a result, it is a useful supplement. His *The Oxford Companion to American Literature* also includes short paragraphs on a small number of popular versifiers, but once again his comments are generally limited to the most obvious and best-documented among them.

Biographical sketches and bibliographical listings are scattered throughout a number of sources. Perhaps the most useful volume for the earliest poets is Rufus Wilmot Griswold's *The Poets and Poetry of America,* initially published in 1842 and revised through 1872. Although Griswold only occasionally identifies his poets as popular, he includes many minor figures whose renown can usually be verified elsewhere. This volume is particularly noteworthy because it includes selections from poets whose work might otherwise be hard to locate.

The Cyclopaedia of American Literature by Evert and George Duyckinck is another good guide to America's early popular poets. The Duyckincks include biographical and critical sketches on many minor figures although, unfortunately, they usually make no reference to the popularity of the poetry. If this volume is supplemented by Frank McAlpine's *Our Album of Authors* and Oscar F. Adam's *A Dictionary of American Authors,* a fairly good picture can be developed of the major popular poets through the early years of the twentieth century. Additional biographies can then be found in Stanley J. Kunitz and Howard Haycraft's *American Authors, 1600–1900,* which is particularly useful because it lists major works and secondary sources about the figures it includes.

Jacob Blanck's *Bibliography of American Literature* includes complete bibliographic listings for many important popular poets. In addition, full-length studies have been produced on a number of the figures discussed above. For Edgar Guest, the best source is Royce Howes's biography, *Edgar Guest,* while for Gibran, the volume to check is *Kahlil Gibran: Wings of Thought, the People's Philosopher,* by Joseph P. Ghougassin. No fewer than four books have been written about Dorothy Parker: *You Might as Well Live: The Life and Times of Dorothy Parker,* by John Keats, *Dorothy Parker,* by Arthur F. Kinney, *Dorothy Parker,* by Marian Meade, and *The Late Mrs. Dorothy Parker,* by Leslie Ronald Frewin. One book is in print dealing with the poetry and life of Ogden Nash (*Ogden Nash,* by David Stuart), and a biography has been written on Phyllis McGinley (*Phyllis McGinley,* by Linda Welshimer Wagner). For others, introductions to posthumous collections of poems provide the best information: one example would be *The Best of Bishop,* edited with an introduction by Charlotte Putnam Reppert and a foreword by David McCord.

Besides these sources, there are several volumes available devoted exclusively to poetry produced in colonial America. While much of the verse that is documented is elite, anonymous, or folk, the listings are complete and thus include those works that achieved a national reputation. The single best source here is Oscar Wegelin's *Early American Poetry,* which has been supplemented by Roger Stoddard's *A Catalogue of Books and Phamphlets Unrecorded in Oscar Wegelin's "Early American Poetry."* Leo Lemay's *A Calendar of American Poetry in the Colonial Newspapers and Magazines* extends the list supplied by Wegelin and Stoddard, while William J. Scheick and Jo Ella Doggett's *Seventeenth-Century American Poetry: A Reference Guide* provides a comprehensive survey of the criticism devoted to the period.

Until recently, there was no comparable guide to popular verse in the twentieth century; however, since 1981 three volumes have been published that contain indexes to poems that appeared in periodicals between 1915 and 1929 (*Index to Poetry in Periodicals: American Poetic Renaissance, 1915–1919*; *Index to Poetry in Periodicals, 1920–1924*; and *Index to Poetry in Periodicals, 1925–1929*). The number of periodicals covered has expanded from 122 in the first volume to over 300 in the third, and over 20,000 poems are cited in all. Since periodicals were rich in popular verse during the years covered, these volumes are undoubtedly an important bibliographic contribution to the subject.

A second recent bibliographical source is *The Newspaper Poets: An Inventory of Holdings in the John M. Shaw Collection,* by John Mackay Shaw and Frederick Korn, published in 1983 by the Robert M. Strozier Library at Florida State University. This volume describes the works of a number of newspaper and periodical poets of the 1920s and 1930s. The poets are listed alphabetically, and each citation includes a biographical sketch, an example of verse, and a critical assessment. The writers listed are Franklin Adams Pierce, Thomas Augustine Daly, Jake Falstaff (Herman Fetzler), Hans Hertzberg, Stoddard King, Richard Henry Little, Donald Robert Perry Marquis, Christopher Darlington Morley, Keith Preston, and Bert Leston Taylor.

RESEARCH COLLECTIONS

American popular verse is well represented in several major research collections devoted more generally to American poetry at large. The most comprehensive among these is the Harris Collection of American Poetry housed at Brown University. This extraordinary collection includes more than 100,000 volumes of poems and plays, many of which were written by poets forgotten long ago. A complete, twelve-volume catalog to the collection was issued in 1972 by G. K. Hall.

The New York Public Library also possesses a major collection of American poetry, although its holdings are confined largely to the years 1610 to 1820. A catalog to this grouping was compiled and published by J. G. Frank in 1917. The Van Pelt Library at the University of Pennsylvania also houses a large collection relating to American poetry, including many first editions and hard-to-locate volumes of the popular poets. There are two catalogs, neither of which, however, is completely up to date. *The Checklist of Poetry by American Authors Published in the English Colonies* lists only those works printed before 1865. *Literary Writings in America: A Bibliography* is a photo-offset of the card catalog at Van Pelt Library, prepared as a WPA project from 1938 to 1942. This bibliography, however, does not list anything the library acquired after 1942, nor does it list its extensive holdings of secondary sources relating to America's poets.

In his *Subject Collections* (fourth edition, 1974), Lee Ash lists several other concentrations of books of major interest to any researcher concerned with popular American poetry. The New York State Library in Albany holds a 10,000-volume collection of American poetry, strong in both the minor poets and early broadside ballads. The Florida State University at Tallahassee possesses a Childhood in Poetry Collection, which includes the works of "hundreds of minor poets" relating specifically to childhood. A five-volume catalog of the holdings by John Mackay Shaw was published by the Gale Research Company in 1967. In addition, the Poetry Society of America at the Van Voorhis Library in New York maintains a 4,000-volume collection of poetry, while the Beloit College Library in Wisconsin holds 3,000 volumes of contemporary American poetry published by vanity presses.

The manuscripts and papers of America's popular poets, like those of most of her authors, are scattered throughout the country. The Houghton Library at Harvard University, however, possesses at least one or two manuscripts or letters by every important popular poet. Its most significant holdings are the papers of Longfellow, Lowell, and Whittier, although it also has substantial portions of the papers of Thomas B. Aldrich, Eugene Field, Joyce Kilmer, Charles Sprague, Alan Seeger, and Bayard Taylor.

The Huntington Library in San Marino, California, also holds large numbers of manuscripts and letters by America's popular poets. Among its large collections are papers relating to Alice and Phoebe Cary, Eugene Field, Joaquin Miller, James Whitcomb Riley, Lydia Huntley Sigourney, Bayard Taylor, Nathaniel Parker Willis, and Ella Wheeler Wilcox. In addition to these collections at Harvard and the Huntington, there is another major concentration of papers at the Alderman Library at the University of Virginia. It numbers among its holdings significant portions of the papers of the Cary sisters, Joyce Kilmer, James Russell Lowell, Joaquin Miller, John Godfrey Saxe, Charles Sprague, and Nathaniel Parker Willis.

The New York Public Library holds most of the papers of William Cullen Bryant and Josiah Gilbert Holland, while those of Oliver Wendell Holmes are located at the Library of Congress. All of Will Carleton's papers are held by the Hillsdale College Library in Hillsdale, Michigan, while most of Madison Cawein's papers are split between the Bentley Historical Library at the University of Michigan and Yale University. Yale also possesses most of the papers of James Gates Percival, John Pierpont, and Lydia Huntley Sigourney, as well as some by Holland, Saxe, Miller, Taylor, and Willis. The Rutgers University Library holds four scrapbooks relating to Joyce Kilmer, while the Indiana University Library holds a 6,200-piece collection pertaining to James Whitcomb Riley. The few extant papers of Michael Wigglesworth can be found at the Massachusetts Historical Society and the Indiana University Library.

Poetry anthologies are also a good source for anyone interested in American popular verse. In addition to the recent, somewhat specialized collections mentioned above, a number of anthologies have attempted to collect the best of popular verse published during this and previous centuries. The best known of these are probably Burton Stevenson's *The Home Book of Verse* and Hazel Felleman's *The Best Loved Poems of the American People*. Both of these have gone through several printings. Others of note include Slason Thompson's *The Humbler Poets,* George Cheever's *The American Commonplace Book of Poetry,* Henry M. Coates's *The Fireside Encyclopedia of*

Poetry, Brander Matthews's *American Familiar Verse,* and Roy J. Cook's *One Hundred and One Famous Poems.* The most recent and one of the most entertaining of these is Russell Baker's collection, *Light Verse,* published in 1986. Like all of these anthologies, Baker's book is organized by subject rather than by poet; Baker has developed an innovative classification scheme that includes "Bile," and "Money, Money, Money," and the book contains many old favorites along with fresh offerings.

HISTORY AND CRITICISM

Although Russel B. Nye's chapter in *The Unembarrassed Muse* is currently the only analysis available that focuses on the entire history of American popular poetry, several more general volumes on American literature treat the poets in question in a more than cursory manner. Most notable among these is perhaps Van Wyck Brooks's four-volume study, *Makers and Finders: A History of the Writer in America, 1800–1915.* Although Brooks's subject is all of American literature, he mentions many of the country's popular writers and is generally sensitive to the qualities in their work that appealed to a large portion of the population.

Equally, if not more, valuable to the student of popular poetry is James Lawrence Onderdonk's *History of American Verse, 1610–1897.* Onderdonk also covers "all" of America's poetry, but his definition of the canon is much broader than that of modern literary historians. As a result, he includes most of the country's nationally popular poets and attempts to discern the peculiar "excellence" he believes they must have had in order to warrant such popularity. His opinions are an excellent guide to the sort of middle-of-the-road taste in the nineteenth century that understood the significance of Whitman and Dickinson but actually preferred the work of Bryant, Longfellow, and Whittier.

Alfred Kreymborg also treats several of America's popular poets in *A History of American Poetry: Our Singing Strength,* but his critical evaluations are all affected by the typical twentieth-century bias toward the avant-garde. As a result, he tends to dismiss as insignificant any poetry that was formally conservative. This sort of bias is not so evident in Fred Lewis Pattee's *A History of American Literature Since 1870,* which includes sympathetic treatments of Will Carleton, Madison Cawein, James Whitcomb Riley, and Eugene Field, among others. Pattee's long discussion of Joaquin Miller is especially interesting since he considers Miller a major figure in contemporary American letters. His opinion, indeed, often seems to accord with that of the populace at large—a fact that confers a sort of "guide" status on the volume.

Another more specific historical study of use to the student of popular verse is Carlin T. Kindilien's *American Poetry in the 1890's.* Based on the Harris Collection at Brown University, Kindilien's study covers "the general state of poetry during the decade," including, as a consequence, both anthology and newspaper verse, the work of the most familiar popular poets, and that of several "lost" elite poets as well. His initial chapter on "The Literary Scene" treats poetry publication in the decade as part of an overall state of affairs or tradition, and his analysis of the "average" poetry anthology produced from within that tradition is most interesting. Kindilien treats both Joaquin Miller and Madison Cawein at some length, as representative figures of the dominant romantic tendency in the poetry of the period. His evaluations, while not uncritical, are judicious and careful in their attempt to discover those elements that made this poetry appealing to so many. Kindilien is also quite sympathetic to the work of Carleton and Riley since he is willing to accord validity and legitimacy to the tradition of rural humor in which they worked.

Although Howard Cook covers most of America's elite poets in *Our Poets of Today* (1919), he also includes many popular figures as well, such as John McCrae, Joyce Kilmer, Alan Seeger, Edgar Guest, and Ella Wheeler Wilcox. His analysis generally involves a biographical sketch, a selection of verse, and critical assessment, which once again attempts to determine the reasons for the people's verdict.

Another historical study that covers a limited period of American poetry production is Harold S. Jantz's *The First Century of New England Verse*. This volume includes a historical and critical discussion of many unknown early poets and poems, as well as selections and an extensive bibliography. While most of the material Jantz treats was not "popular" in the sense that it was read by large numbers of people, most of the poets he treats were amateur versifiers writing for their own personal reasons and thus cannot be included in the "high-art" tradition.

Two last historical studies, while not devoted exclusively to popular poetry, can be of some use to the student of the subject. These are William Charvat's *Literary Publishing in America, 1790–1850* and *The Profession of Authorship in America, 1800–1870*. The first volume provides some interesting background material on the rise of an American publishing industry that was always concerned with the desires of its audience. Charvat extends his interest in the relationship between publisher and public in the second volume, where he specifically considers "The Popularization of Poetry" in the early nineteenth century and then attempts to measure the extent and reasons for Longfellow's popularity. Charvat here includes a discussion of Longfellow's earnings as a poet as well as sales figures for nearly all the poetry he produced in his lifetime.

A bibliographic search for more recent full-length critical studies turned up practically no works dealing with popular verse from either an aesthetic or cultural perspective. This is largely due to the fact that contemporary critical analysis of American popular poetry has reflected the pervasive influence of the New Criticism, and as a result, it has been limited to studies of individual poets and poems. One volume, *American Poetry and Culture,* by Robert von Hallberg, makes the point that the media are probably responsible for the decline of the popularity of poetry, if not of popular poetry itself. He goes on to argue that the avant-garde poets who wrote in the 1950s and were read in the 1960s—most notably Allen Ginsberg—should be accorded "popular" status, especially in view of their large sales.

A number of articles published early in the century treat popular verse seriously, and many of these can still be of use to the student interested in the American popular poetic tradition. Two of the most interesting are A. C. Henderson's "The Folk Poetry of These States" and R. Z. Deats's "Poetry for the Populace," both of which attempt some sort of definition of the aims and purposes of "poetry for the people." Henderson tends to collapse the distinctions between folk and popular poetry and thus considers James Whitcomb Riley, Bret Harte, and James Russell Lowell as indigenous American folk poets. Nevertheless, his article is of use because of its willingness to consider verse appreciated by large audiences as a literary tradition related to, but distinct from, classical "art" poetry.

Deats's essay is an examination of the poetry printed in America's popular magazines in an attempt to determine the nature of America's "thought patterns" in 1942. As a result, he focuses on the themes and moods of the poetry rather than on its verse patterns or language. His perspective on the poetry is thus much closer to that of the people who enjoy it, and he is accordingly quite sympathetic to the popular poets' attempt to keep the "spirit and flame of poetry" alive in a "prosy age."

A third, more recent essay, Alan Goldings's "History of American Poetry Anthologies," which is included in Robert Von Hallberg's *Canons,* sheds light on the formation of literary taste through the selection of poets, popular and otherwise, for inclusion in major collections. In the process Goldings comments on the confusion of popular and elite forms in anthologies of verse. and suggests reasons for the more programmatic form of verse in the nineteenth century.

Because so little bibliographic work has been done on American popular poetry, there are no comprehensive guides to reviews of individual poets, secondary sources, or essays on popular verse. Some of the relevant articles are listed, however, in Lewis Leary's *Articles on American Literature, 1900–1950* and *1950–1967.* For more recent essays, the *MLA Bibliography* is a good source. Leary is particularly useful for the early, more general articles, while the *MLA Bibliography* yields many interesting essays if one focuses on the individual author listings. For example, the 1984 *Bibliography* lists three articles on Longfellow and one on James Whitcomb Riley; however, listings for twentieth-century popular poets are sparse. Little turns up under the popular literature heading, but such titles as Louraine Buell's "Literature and Scripture in New England Between the Revolutionary and Civil Wars"

(1983), and Ronald McFarland's "Idaho's Pioneer Poetry" (1984) would be possible sources of new information.

The *Journal of Popular Culture,* which is not indexed by MLA, is notable for its lack of treatment of popular poetry—in an issue devoted to popular literature published in 1982, poetry was not even touched upon. Two issues contained articles on Bob Dylan ("Dylan as *Auteur,*" by Leland Poague, and "Bob Dylan and the Pastoral Apocalypse," by Gregg M. Campbell), and one article suggests that Chicano poetry can be seen as a popular statement ("A Popular Manifesto," by Frank Pino).

American doctoral dissertations are also a good source of historical, critical, and biographical material on popular poets and poetry. In fact, there are so many of these that it is impossible to survey them here. However, all those completed before 1965 can be found in Lawrence McNamee's *Dissertations in English and American Literature,* while more recent ones are listed in the MLA's yearly bibliographies. There are biographical and critical dissertations on many of the popular poets considered here, as well as more general historical treatments of themes, trends, and traditions.

Perhaps one of the most significant of these, because it specifically treats the subject of popular poetry as well as the problems involved in defining it, is Wilma J. Clark's "The Levels of Poetry: An Exploration of the Dichotomy between Nineteenth-Century American Popular Poetry and Elitist Poetry." Aside from the more general theoretical issues Clark treats, she also includes critical discussions of the work of Lydia Huntley Sigourney, Ella Wheeler Wilcox, Bayard Taylor, Will Carleton, and Henry Wadsworth Longfellow. Delwyn L. Sneller's "Popular and Prophetic Traditions in the Poetry of John Greenleaf Whittier" is also of note, because, like Clark, Sneller directly confronts the "problem" of a popular poetic tradition and the nature of its relationship to the more widely known and studied elite tradition.

A check of *Dissertation Abstracts International* shows works on individual poets, especially of the nineteenth century. Listings under either Popular Literature or Popular Culture categories are sparse, although a few titles, such as Mary Karen Guilar's "Allen Ginsberg and the Development of Popular Poetry," are suggestive.

All in all, it appears that modernism on the one hand and the media on the other have contributed to a decline in the production of popular verse as it has traditionally been known in America, although the continuing proliferation of popular song lyrics and their evident meaning for large segments of the population may constitute a renaissance of sorts. The exploration of the evolution of popular verse in the twentieth century and its connection with elite traditions and other elements of the culture by historians and literary critics is long overdue.

BIBLIOGRAPHY

Adams, Oscar F. *A Dictionary of American Authors*. 5th ed. Boston: Houghton Mifflin, 1905.

Ash, Lee. *Subject Collections: A Guide to Special Book Collections and Subject Emphases as Reported by University, College, Public, and Special Libraries and Museums in the United States and Canada*. 4th ed. New York: R. R. Bowker, 1974.

Axford, Lavonne B. *An Index to the Poems of Ogden Nash*. Metuchen, N.J.: Scarecrow Press, 1972.

Baker, Russell, ed. *Light Verse*. New York: W. W. Norton, 1986.

Baxt, George. *The Dorothy Parker Murder Case*. New York: St. Martin's Press, 1984.

Best Loved Poems. New Rochelle, N.Y.: Salesian Missions, 1983.

Bishop, Morris. *The Best of Bishop*. Edited by Charlotte Putnam Reppert. Ithaca, N.Y.: Cornell University Press, 1980.

Blanck, Jacob. *Bibliography of American Literature*. New Haven, Conn.: Yale University Press, 1955–.

Brooks, Van Wyck. *Makers and Finders: A History of the Writer in America, 1800–1915*. 4 vols. New York: E. P. Dutton, 1956.

Brown University Library. *Dictionary Catalogue of the Harris Collection of American Poetry and Plays*. 12 vols. Boston: G. K. Hall, 1972.

Campbell, Gregg M. "Bob Dylan and the Pastoral Apocalypse." *Journal of Popular Culture*, 8 (Spring 1975), 696–707.

Charvat, William. *Literary Publishing in America, 1790–1850*. Philadelphia: University of Pennsylvania Press, 1959.

———. *The Profession of Authorship in America, 1800–1870*. Columbus: Ohio State University Press, 1968.

Checklist of Poetry by American Authors Published in the English Colonies of North America and the United States through 1865 in the Possession of the Rare Book Collection at the University of Pennsylvania. Compiled by Albert von Chorba, Jr. Philadelphia: University of Pennsylvania Press, 1951.

Cheever, George B. *The American Commonplace Book of Poetry*. Boston: Carter, Hendee, 1831.

Clark, Wilma J. "The Levels of Poetry: An Exploration of the Dichotomy between Nineteenth-Century American Popular Poetry and Elitest Poetry." Ph.D. dissertation, Michigan State University, 1972.

Coates, Henry M. *The Fireside Encyclopedia of Poetry*. Philadelphia: Porter and Coates, 1879.

Cook, Howard. *Our Poets of Today*. New York: Moffat, 1919.

Cook, Roy J. *One Hundred and One Famous Poems*. Rev. ed. Chicago: Cable, 1929.

Deats, R. Z. "Poetry for the Populace." *Sewanee Review*, 50 (July 1942), 374–88.

Dissertation Abstracts International. Ann Arbor, Mich.: University Microfilms International, 1969–.

Duyckinck, Evert, and George Duyckinck. *The Cyclopaedia of American Literature*. New York: Scribner's, 1856.

Early American Poetry, 1610–1820, a List of Works in the New York Public Library. Compiled by J. G. Frank. New York: New York Public Library, 1917.

Felleman, Hazel. *The Best Loved Poems of the American People*. New York: Garden City Publishing, 1936.

Frewin, Leslie Ronald. *The Late Mrs. Dorothy Parker.* New York: Macmillan, 1986.

Ghougassin, Joseph P. *Kahlil Gibran: Wings of Thought, the People's Philosopher.* New York: Philosophical Library, 1973.

The Golden Anniversary Anthology of Poets by Member Poets. Williamsburg: Poetry Society of Virginia, 1974.

Goldings, Alan. "A History of American Poetry Anthologies." In *Canons.* Edited by Robert Von Hallberg. Chicago: University of Chicago Press, 1984.

Griswold, Rufus Wilmot. *The Poets and Poetry of America.* New York: James Miller, 1872.

Guilar, Mary Karen. "Allen Ginsberg and the Development of Popular Poetry." Ph.D. dissertation, Temple University, 1984.

Hackett, Alice Payne. *50 Years of Best Sellers, 1895–1945.* New York: R. R. Bowker, 1945.

Hart, James. *The Oxford Companion to American Literature.* 4th ed. New York: Oxford University Press, 1965.

————. *The Popular Book.* Berkeley: University of California Press, 1961.

Henderson, A. C. "The Folk Poetry of These States." *Poetry,* 16 (August 1920), 264–73.

Howes, Royce. *Edgar Guest: A Biography.* Chicago: Reilly and Lee, 1953.

Index to Poetry in Periodicals: American Poetic Renaissance, 1915–1919. Great Neck, N.Y.: Granger, 1981.

Index to Poetry in Periodicals, 1920–1924. Great Neck, N.Y.: The Company, 1983.

Index to Poetry in Periodicals, 1925–1929. Great Neck, N.Y.: The Company, 1984.

Jantz, Harold S. *The First Century of New England Verse.* Worcester, Mass.: American Antiquarian Society, 1962.

Journal of Popular Culture, 16 (Summer 1982).

Keats, John. *You Might as Well Live: The Life and Times of Dorothy Parker.* New York: Simon and Schuster, 1970.

Kindilien, Carlin T. *American Poetry in the 1890's.* Providence, R.I.: Brown University Press, 1956.

Kinney, Arthur F. *Dorothy Parker.* Boston: Twayne, 1978.

Kreymborg, Alfred. *A History of American Poetry: Our Singing Strength.* New York: Tudor, 1934.

Kunitz, Stanley J., and Howard Haycraft. *American Authors, 1600–1900.* New York: H. W. Wilson, 1938.

Leary, Lewis. *Articles on American Literature, 1900–1950,* and *1950–1967.* Durham, N.C.: Duke University Press, 1954, 1970.

Lemay, Leo. *A Calendar of American Poetry in the Colonial Newspaper and Magazines.* Worcester, Mass.: American Antiquarian Society, 1972.

Literary Writings in America: A Bibliography. WPA Project at the University of Pennsylvania. Millwood, N.Y.: Kto Press, 1977.

Lyon, Mabelle A. *From Sea to Sea in Song.* Orange, Calif.: American Poetry League, 1972.

McAlpine, Frank. *Our Album of Authors: A Cyclopedia of Popular Literary People.* Philadelphia: Elliot and Beezley, 1886.

McNamee, Lawrence. *Dissertations in English and American Literature, 1865–1964.* New York: R. R. Bowker, 1968.

Matthews, Brander. *American Familiar Verse.* New York: Longmans, Green, 1904.

Meade, Marian. *Dorothy Parker*. New York: Villard Books, 1988.

MLA International Bibliography of Books and Articles on the Modern Languages and Literatures. New York: Modern Language Association of America, 1922-.

Mott, Frank Luther. *Golden Multitudes*. New York: Macmillan, 1947.

Nye, Russel B. *The Unembarrassed Muse: The Popular Arts in America*. New York: Dial Press, 1970.

Onderdonk, James Lawrence. *History of American Verse, 1610–1897*. Chicago: A. C. McClurg, 1901.

Pattee, Fred Lewis. *A History of American Literature Since 1870*. New York: Century, 1921.

Pennsylvania Poetry Society. *Prize Poems*. Harrisburg, Pa.: Keystone Press, 1969.

Petry, Evelyn. *The Clover Collection of Verse*. Washington, D.C.: Clover, 1968.

Pino, Frank. "A Popular Manifesto." *Journal of Popular Culture,* 6 (Spring 1973), 718–30.

Poague, Leland. "Dylan as *Auteur*: Theoretical Notes, and an Analysis of 'Love Minus Zero/No Limit.' " *Journal of Popular Culture,* 8 (Summer 1974), 53–58.

Scheick, William J., and Jo Ella Doggett. *Seventeenth-Century American Poetry: A Reference Guide*. Boston: G. K. Hall, 1977.

Schmittroth, John. *New Poets, New Music*. Cambridge, Mass.: Winthrop, 1970.

Shaw, John Mackay. *Childhood in Poetry: A Catalogue of the Books of English and American Poets in the Library of the Florida State University*. Tallahassee: Robert M. Strozier Library, Florida State University, 1967.

Shaw, John Mackay, and Frederick Korn. *The Newspaper Poets: An Inventory of the Holdings in the John M. Shaw Collection*. Tallahassee: Robert Manning Strozier Library, Florida State University, 1983.

Sneller, Delwyn L. "Popular and Prophetic Traditions in the Poetry of John Greenleaf Whittier." Ph.D. Dissertation, Michigan State University, 1972.

Stevenson, Burton. *The Home Book of Verse, American and English, 1850–1920*. 6th ed. New York: Henry Holt, 1930.

Stoddard, Roger. *A Catalogue of Books and Pamphlets Unrecorded in Oscar Wegelin's "Early American Poetry."* Providence, R.I.: Friends of the Library of Brown University, 1969.

Stuart, David. *Ogden Nash*. New York: Stein and Day, 1987.

Thompson, Slason. *The Humbler Poets: A Collection of Newspaper Poets and Periodical Verse*. Chicago: Jansen, McClurg, 1886.

Today's Greatest Poems. Edited by John Campbell. Sacramento, Calif.: World of Poetry Press, 1983.

Von Hallberg, Robert. *American Poetry and Culture, 1945–1980*. Cambridge, Mass.: Harvard University Press, 1985.

Wagner, Linda Welshimer. *Phyllis McGinley*. New York: Twayne, 1971.

Wegelin, Oscar. *Early American Poetry: A Compilation of the Titles and Volumes of Verse and Broadsides by Writers Born or Residing in North America*. New York: P. Smith, 1930.

14

Westerns

RICHARD W. ETULAIN

HISTORIC OUTLINE

Until the 1950s little had been written about the Western, for it, like most types of American popular culture, was not considered worthy of scholarly scrutiny. The rise of the American studies movement of the 1950s and the birth of the Popular Culture Association in the late 1960s, however, have encouraged students and teachers to examine the form and content of popular literary genres, such as the Western. During the 1970s and 1980s, interest in the Western as a form of popular culture has continued to grow. It is now acceptable in many English, history, and American studies departments to undertake a study of the Western for a thesis or dissertation. Some of this new interest in the Western has found its way into a series of recently published books and essays. Still, while systematic study of this genre is growing, much remains to be done.

The following essay deals with the popular Western, the formula fiction of such authors as Owen Wister, Max Brand, Zane Grey, Ernest Haycox, Luke Short, and Louis L'Amour. These writers follow the patterns of action, romance, and the clash of heroes and villains familiar to the Western. Their plots are predictable; they confirm rather than challenge or satirize American culture. Writers of Westerns do not produce the less stylized western novels of Willa Cather, John Steinbeck, Wallace Stegner, and Larry McMurtry. To make these distinctions between the *Western* and the *western novel* is not to denigrate the former and praise the latter but to make clear the subject of the following pages.

In recent treatments of the Western, two points of view about its historical development have emerged. One group argues that the Western is strongly tied to several nineteenth-century sources: the *Leatherstocking Tales* of James Fenimore Cooper, dime novels, and western local color writing. Another group asserts that though these early roots are significant for a large understanding of popular literature about the West, the Western is primarily the product of the dynamic climate of opinion surrounding 1900. The present account leans toward the second point of view while trying not to overlook the earlier influences upon the Western.

Many Americans did not take a positive view of the frontier until the last decades of the eighteenth century. Before that time, the earliest settlers and their descendants saw the frontier as a region for expansion but also as a forbidding and evil wilderness. As Richard Slotkin has pointed out in his book *Regeneration Through Violence,* it was not until John Filson published his legend-making volume, *The Discovery, Settlement and Present State of Kentucke* (1784), that Americans were provided with a western hero in the author's account of Daniel Boone.

In the fifty years following the publication of Filson's work, other information necessary for the creation of a western literature became available. Even before Thomas Jefferson became president, he was encouraging exploration of the West, and after he was elected, he sent Lewis and Clark to traverse the West and to provide written records of what they saw and experienced. The publication of their journals and the accounts of such travelers as Josiah Gregg, Jedediah Smith, and Stephen H. Long convinced many Americans that the empty spaces beyond the frontier were indeed a "passage to India" and part of the nation's "untransacted destiny."

The stage was set for an imaginative writer who could synthesize the information available about the West and the emotions that these facts and rumors had inspired. James Fenimore Cooper was able to use these materials to create the earliest full-blown hero of western fiction in Natty Bumppo (or Leatherstocking, the Long Rifle, or the Deerslayer). Many interpreters argue that Cooper produced the first widely read novels about the West and hence deserves to be called the father of the western novel.

Cooper used many ingredients in his fiction that later became standard parts of the Western. In the first place, his hero, Leatherstocking, embodied several of the virtues of the Romantic hero. He was a man of nature who loved animals, forests, and good Indians (Cooper made sharp distinctions between what he considered good and bad Indians) and was at home in the wilderness. Although Natty was interested in the women his creator provided for him, when he had the opportunity to choose between these heroines and the forest, he selected the frontier rather than hearth, home, and domesticity. On numerous occasions Leatherstocking conflicted with white men or Indians who challenged his sense of territory or what he thought to be his rights. These conflicts foreshadowed the famous walkdowns that appeared later in such novels as *The Virginian*. And anyone acquainted with the modern Western will recognize its indebtedness to the chase-and-pursuit plot that Cooper utilized in his *Leatherstocking Tales*.

Cooper's western novels attracted thousands of readers throughout the world, and thus it is not surprising that several American authors rushed in to imitate his work. Such writers as James Hall, Charles Webber, Mayne Reid, and Emerson Bennett turned out dozens of adventure novels set in the West. By the Civil War, American readers were widely acquainted with the frontier West through the fiction of Cooper and other novelists. Then, in the next three decades, two developments changed the content and direction of western fiction and helped pave the way for the rise of the modern Western.

The first of these innovations was the appearance of the earliest dime novels shortly before the Civil War. Sales of the dime novel rose spectacularly until the late 1880s. And, as one might expect, authors of this new popular fiction, in their search for salable materials, made wide use of themes and formats contained in earlier writing about the West. Some writers sensationalized the deeds of historical persons, such at Kit Carson and Buffalo Bill; others like Edward Wheeler and Edward S. Ellis created the fictional characters Deadwood Dick and Seth Jones. As demands for the dime novel increased, writers were less inclined to stick to the Leatherstocking figure inherited from Cooper and fashioned instead heroes more adventurous and less reflective. Gradually the actions of these heroes—and heroines—were melodramatized beyond belief, and the potential power of the western setting was lost in the drive to turn out hundreds of dime novels in which action and adventure were paramount. The dime novel popularized the West, but its lurid sensationalism revealed a lack of serious intent in dealing with the western materials introduced earlier in the nineteenth century.

The other development that influenced writing about the West was the rise of the local color movement after the Civil War. In the first decades following Appomattox many American writers began to emphasize local dialect, customs, and settings in their fiction. Bret Harte was a well-known participant in this movement; indeed, his stories about Californian mining camps and prostitutes and hard-bitten miners with hearts of gold were pathbreaking developments in the local color movement. Other writers like Joaquin Miller, Mary Hallock Foote, and Alfred Henry Lewis wrote poems, stories, and novels about explorers, engineers, and cowpunchers. These authors, whose works never sold as widely as those of the dime novelists, were more serious of purpose and proved that literary treatment of the West need not fall victim to sensationalism.

In addition to the rise of the dime novel and the local color movement, several other developments in late nineteenth-century America prepared the way for Owen Wister and the Western. Not the least of these was the realization of many Americans that the frontier was gone or rapidly disappearing. As the wide-open spaces vanished, cities, industrialism, and numbers of immigrants seemed to increase; and writers, sensing the public's desire to hold onto the frontier, began to write about the cowboy and other symbols of an older West. The same nostalgic mood helped popularize Buffalo Bill's Wild West show, which played to large audiences in the United States and abroad. The show included real Indians, cowboys, and sharpshooters, and it aided in keeping alive an era that was rapidly disappearing. Probably the most important of the cultural happenings leading to the birth of the western novel was the discovery of the cowboy. A few dime novelists, journalists, and travelers mentioned the cowboy before 1890, but during the 1890s and early 1900s the fiction of Wister and the illustrations of Frederic Remington and Charles Russell helped to make the cowboy a new cultural hero worthy of a major literary treatment.

And Wister was the man worthy of the task. Philadelphia-born and Harvard-educated, Wister first saw the West in the 1880s during a series of trips designed to relieve his boredom and restore his health. At first, he was satisfied to wander throughout the West as a dilettantish sightseer, but at the suggestion of his friends he began to record in his journals what he saw and experienced. Wister was a keen observer and talented writer—he had already published on a variety of subjects—and his first Western stories published in magazines in the early 1890s attracted a good deal of attention. By the turn of the century, Wister was known as a prominent writer about western subjects.

Wister's position in 1900 was similar to Cooper's in 1820: he had at his disposal the materials necessary for significant works of fiction, and his previous writings proved he could produce work that attracted readers. His first Western books *Red Men and White* (1896) and *Lin McLean* (1897) dealt with cowboys, although these heroes were most often picaresque protagonists who were not as adventurous and winsome as many Romantic heroes. But in *The Virginian*, published in 1902, Wister put his brand on the most popular Western ever written, and after its publication Western writing was never the same.

The Virginian occupies the central position in the historical development of the Western. The novel not only contains the action, adventure, romance, and good-versus-bad characters that had become standard parts of nineteenth-century western fiction; the work also reveals how much its creator was a participant in several cultural currents at the turn of the century. Wister's novel is shot through with nostalgia. From the prefatory note to the closing pages of the book, the tone is elegiac. The Virginian and the other cowboys are dealt with as symbols of a vanishing frontier. Wister also treats the West as another (perhaps the final) arena in which Anglo-Saxons can prove their superiority through vigorous competition with other people and the environment. In *The Virginian,* the hero and setting are used to illustrate these ideas: the Virginian is the Anglo-Saxon protagonist who wins his competition with others and who proves his superiority through conflict.

And yet there is an ambivalent strain in the novel. Although Wister seems drawn to the openness, the challenge, the romance of the West, he also implies that life in Wyoming may turn men brutal and careless in their treatment of land, horses, and people. And it is necessary for Molly Wood, the eastern schoolmarm, to bring civilization (as eastern women had often done in earlier western fiction) to the West in the form of literature and culture. Finally, the marriage of the East (Molly) and West (the Virginian) is a union of the best qualities of each region and a union that bodes well for the future of America.

If Wister provided in *The Virginian* a paradigm for the modern Western, B. M. Bower (Bertha Muzzy Sinclair Cowan), Zane Grey, Max Brand (Frederick Faust), and Clarence Mulford followed his lead and produced hundreds of novels that hardened the ingredients of Wister's novel into a durable formula. Although each of these writers turned out numerous works—most of which were notable for their predictable plots, stereotyped characters, and conventional morality—they exhibited individual talents and tendencies.

B. M. Bower, the only woman to produce a string of notable Westerns, is best known for her characters in *Chip of the Flying U.* She dealt authentically with the details of cattle ranching, and reviewers noted her use of humor and her varied plots. Like Wister, she used East-versus-West conflicts and tried to capture the complexities of a closing frontier. Her heroines were more convincing than those of her contemporaries, but the organization of her novels was often chaotic, and conflicts between characters were too easily resolved. Even more damaging to her reputation was the fact that she seemed unable to deal with serious cultural or social issues and during her long career was reluctant to make changes in her plots and ideas.

Zane Grey was a much more well-known writer than Bower. In fact, between 1910 and 1930 he did more than any other writer to popularize the Western. Not only did several of his works top the best-seller lists, but he also portrayed a West of picturesque and restorative power that appealed to Americans increasingly distraught with urban, industrial, and international problems. The public seemed convinced that Grey's West, which was pictured as able to redeem effete Easterners, was a marvelous and wonderful place. His descriptive and narrative abilities were particularly alive in novels such as *Riders of the Purple Sage* (1912), *The U.P. Trail* (1918), and *The Vanishing American* (1925). Grey's popularity has endured, and many readers when asked to define the Western point to Grey's works as epitomizing the elements of the formula Western.

Max Brand (the most popular of Frederick Faust's seventeen pen names) was much less interested than Grey in specific settings, natural or historical, and Brand never placed a high value on his Westerns. While Grey was convinced that his novels should place him among the leading writers of his time, Brand referred to his novels set in the West as "Western stuff" or "cowboy junk." He was interested, however, in showing human nature in conflict, and to enlarge the significance of these battles he frequently made his heroes titan-like. Between the early twentieth century and his death in 1944, Brand turned out more than 500 books, more than 100 of which were Westerns.

Another writer, Clarence Mulford, was more serious than Brand in his approach to writing Westerns. Mulford prided himself on his careful research into the historical backgrounds of his fiction. He gathered a large library and boasted of knowing intimately the West even though most of his writing was carried out in Maine. Early in his career he introduced Hopalong Cassidy, a wise, humorous, and appealing cowboy, who appeared later in many of Mulford's Westerns and became one of the well-known series characters in Western fiction. Hopalong was a working cowboy and rancher—much different from the image of Cassidy that William Boyd depicted in Western movies.

By the early 1930s these novelists, in addition to such writers as Stewart Edward White, Emerson Hough, W. C. Tuttle, and Eugene Manlove Rhodes, had helped to identify the Western as a separate fictional type. Reviewers and readers were now aware of what the term *Western* meant when it was applied to a novel. Unfortunately, for many critics *Western* denoted a subliterary type that they considered beneath their scholarly interests.

Part of this negative reaction arose because the Western was associated with the pulp magazines of the 1920s and 1930s. Publishers found that after the demise of the dime novel and the popular story weeklies in the years surrounding the turn of the century, there was still a large audience for adventure fiction about the West. Firms such as Munsey's, Doubleday, and Street and Smith capitalized on this huge market. *Love Story, Detective Story, Western Story,* and *Adventure* were four of the most widely read pulps, but Western stories and magazines were the most popular. By 1930, more than thirty Western magazines were on the market, and writers like Frank C. Robertson, Frank Richardson Pierce, W. C. Tuttle, and Max Brand especially dominated the pulp Western scene.

From the middle 1930s until his death in 1950, Ernest Haycox was the premier figure among another group of writers of Westerns. Haycox had served his apprenticeship in the pulps during the 1920s, and by the mid–

1930s his stories and serials were appearing in *Collier's,* which, along with *Saturday Evening Post,* was considered the leading slick magazine. When Zane Grey lost his place in the major serial markets in slick magazines, Haycox quickly moved into his vacated slot and won the attention of editors and many readers. Several writers of Westerns who began their careers in the 1940s and 1950s were later to testify that they learned their craft by reading and studying the Haycox serials in *Collier's.*

Haycox was interested in producing more believable Westerns. Not only did he try to create more persuasive characters, he also tinkered with the stereotyped characterizations of the Western by using two or more heroes and heroines and thereby added a measure of complexity to an uncomplex genre. In addition, Haycox began to people his Westerns with what one interpreter calls *Hamlet heroes.* These protagonists were reflective men who often wrestled with their consciences in deciding what was the right course of action. These heroes were far more serious and contemplative than the leading men in the Westerns of Grey and Brand.

Finally, Haycox added a historical dimension to several of his Westerns. He was convinced that by resting his fiction on historical events he could increase the realism of the Western. In such novels as *The Border Trumpet* (1939), *Alder Gulch* (1942), and particularly in his novel on General Custer, *Bugles in the Afternoon* (1944), he carefully gathered data on historical occurrences and based his plots on recorded events. Because of his tinkerings with and his additions to the format of the Western, Ernest Haycox occupies a large niche in the development of the popular genre.

No single writer can be said to have inherited Haycox's mantle, but three authors of the last three decades have attracted more attention than other writers of Westerns. Henry Wilson Allen, who writes under the pen names of Will Henry and Clay Fisher, has adhered closely to the historical Western that Haycox popularized in the 1940s. Particularly in his Will Henry Westerns, Allen demonstrates an experienced hand in joining history and fiction to produce high caliber Westerns. His Clay Fisher Westerns, on the other hand, emphasize action and adventure and rarely deal with specific historical events. (Allen, by the way, argues that this division of his works into Will Henry and Clay Fisher Westerns is not tenable.) Among the best of the Will Henry novels are *From Where the Sun Now Stands* (1959), *The Gates of the Mountains* (1963), and *Chiricahua* (1972).

Frederick Glidden, better known by his *nom de plume,* Luke Short, was probably the most popular writer of Westerns during the 1950s and 1960s. Short emphasizes action, and he packs his Westerns with suspense. His novels are tightly written with carefully structured adventure. In several of his works, Short draws upon his knowledge of frontier and western occupations to make his caracters more believable. Sometimes he sets a Western in a twentieth-century mining town, but most of his settings are frontier communities of no specific location. Short frequently deals with town life, although he seems little interested in using historical characters or events in his novels. He is skillful in handling women and knows how to picture some of his heroes as good men who have made a mistake in the past and are now bent on redeeming themselves. In the 1950s Short's Westerns began to appear as original paperbacks after markets for magazine serials had disappeared. Since that time most Westerns have been printed as original paperbacks.

The third of the triumvirate of contemporary writers of Westerns is Louis L'Amour. During the early 1970s L'Amour became the most widely published writer of Westerns in the history of the genre. Readers of L'Amour's novels praise his abilities as a storyteller. His speedy narratives seem to contain fresh stories within the familiar format of the Western. One survey of nearly two dozen of L'Amour's Westerns (he has written 90 books, more than 400 stories, and about 100 television scripts) noted a pattern in L'Amour's fiction: his emphasis on families, their origins and characteristics, and their historic roles in settling the West. Another critic stressed L'Amour's use of violence; in ten randomly selected Westerns, 156 persons were killed, not counting those destroyed in massacres and other mass killings. The same commentator observed that most of the heroes of L'Amour's Westerns are self-made men who espouse traditional and popular causes. It seems clear that L'Amour has gained his audience primarily because he produces Westerns that contain predictable characters, plots, and endings. His narrative skills hold his readers while he relates stories strongly tied to the familiar structure of the Western.

If Allen, Short, and L'Amour have made, at the most, tinkering changes with the content and format of the Western, other writers and film producers have given the popular genre a total overhaul. These people appear certain that the Western—like much of popular culture of the 1960s, 1970s, and 1980s—has not been very relevant to an understanding of America. Yet they also seem convinced that because the nature of the Western is so well-known, parodies of its tone, structure, and focus could be used to reveal dangerous tendencies in the formula Western and the popular genre's inadequacies as a moral and ethical base for American ideology.

In the 1960s such books and films as *The Rounders* (Max Evans, 1960), *Little Big Man* (Thomas Berger, 1964), *Cat Ballou* (1965), *North to Yesterday* (Robert Flynn, 1967), and *Soldier Blue* (1970) satirized the Western. Some of the treatments were gentle: *The Rounders* dealt with a pair of cowpokes cavorting about as drunken and lusting failures; *Cat Ballou* pictured a renowned Western gunslinger as a drunk (Lee Marvin) and utilized a pretty and naive schoolmarm (Jane Fonda) as protagonist; *North to Yesterday* described a cattle drive which arrived two decades late in a midwestern cattle town. (The novels of Richard Brautigan also seem, in part, gentle satires of the ingredients of the popular Western.) Other accounts are more biting:

Little Big Man portrays General Custer as a vicious killer of Indians and suggests, on the other hand, that the Indians were *the* Western heroes (the film based on Berger's novel was even more harsh and pro-Indian than the book); *Soldier Blue* implied that the army on the frontier was little more than a pack of killers who slaughtered Indians.

In 1960, E. L. Doctorow prefigured this attack on the Western in his first novel *Welcome to Hard Times*. Through his narrator-historian, Blue, Doctorow hints that early western experiences were, at best, depressing and more often savage. Most of the residents of Hard Times are grotesques: ludicrous whores, grasping merchants, and violent killers—all of whom rip into one another and show little or no sense of community. Another author, John Seelye, is equally devastating in his attack on the Western in his brief novel *The Kid* (1972). Seelye, who dedicates his work to Leslie Fiedler and who is obviously indebted to the writing of Mark Twain and Herman Melville, pictures a frontier Wyoming town ripe with violence, racism, and perversion. In addition to parodying the usual makeup of the Western, Seelye hints at the detrimental impact that violence, racism, and sexual prejudices have had on America. Thus, *The Kid* undercuts the form and content of the Western while it also attacks what the author sees as the major weaknesses of American culture. Although parodies of the Western continued to be popular into the 1970s, interest in this approach to the popular genre has fallen off during the last decade. Perhaps satiric Westerns have now run their course; at least the predominant tone and plot types of fictional and cinematic Westerns produced since the late 1970s point towards this conclusion.

Finally, there are other small signs the Western is changing. Writers are dealing more explicitly with sex. For example, Playboy Press is publishing its line of Jake Logan Westerns, which emphasize the hero's abundant sexual prowess. Other recent Westerns treat homosexuality. Women are playing a more conspicuous role; the protagonists in some Westerns are women (see Jack Bickham's novels dealing with a female character named Charity Ross and a paperback series by Stephen Overholser starring a female detective and marshal). More and more writers are avoiding picturing their heroines as merely pawns of their men; even several of L'Amour's Westerns feature strong leading women. Moreover, the treatment of Indians, blacks, and Mexican Americans is more balanced than in earlier Westerns. Indians, for example, are often described in these recent novels as embodying a culture different from white society, and it is obvious that these differences will lead to conflict, but the Indians who fight their white enemies are not portrayed as inferior people or as savages.

These innovations suggest that the Western is reflecting the changing ideas and customs of the United States during the last decade or so. If this surmise is true, the Western remains a valuable source for attempting to understand the American popular mind.

REFERENCE WORKS

In the last decade or two, the growing number of general reference guides on the Western and on individual writers is another indication of the expanding interest in the study of popular culture in the United States. While no compilation of secondary sources dealing with the Western appeared until the 1960s, several works containing selective listings of Westerns and commentaries on the Western and individual authors have been published since that time. An extensive bibliography containing the titles of all works by the leading writers of the Western is still much needed.

The most extensive and best source of information on the American Western is the thick volume edited by Englishman James Vinson, *Twentieth-Century Western Writers*. This fact-filled volume contains brief bio-bibliographical essays on about 300 western authors, including such well-known authors as Jack London, Willa Cather, John Steinbeck, and Wallace Stegner, as well as sections on a host of authors writing popular Westerns. Each entry includes nearly exhaustive bibliographies of a writer's published work, evaluations of his or her career, and lists of pertinent secondary materials for major writers. The essays were prepared by nearly eighty writers, many of whom are specialists in western studies. This is now *the* reference source with which to begin serious study of the Western.

A similar volume, *Encyclopedia of Frontier and Western Fiction*, by Jon Tuska and Vicki Piekarski, while not as extensive and valuable as Vinson's book, nonetheless includes helpful entries for most major writers of Westerns. The discussions include brief commentaries on the authors, listings of their most notable works, and sometimes names of films based on these Westerns. Except for the tendency of the editors to be too dogmatic in their evaluations and assertions, this volume is a handy guide to the Western and other pertinent, closely related topics.

Tuska and Piekarski, again with the aid of a few others, have prepared another useful reference volume, *The Frontier Experience: A Reader's Guide to the Life and Literature of the American West*. The extended section on "Western Fiction" (pp. 239–334) purports to be "a brief literary history," but when it deals with twentieth-century authors of Westerns, it is more a string of plot summaries and iconoclastic assertions and asides than a well-formed, sound literary history. This section also includes annotations on the major books treating the American literary West and concludes with a nine-page bibliography of Western fiction.

A book that parallels somewhat the format of these volumes is Fred Erisman and Richard W. Etulain's *Fifty Western Writers: A Bio-Bibliographical Guide*. While most of the essays in this reference volume treat western novelists, it also includes essays on Owen Wister (by Neal Lambert), Emerson Hough (Delbert E. Wylder), Zane Grey (Gary Topping), Max Brand (William Bloodworth), Ernest Haycox (Robert L. Gale), Luke Short (Richard W. Etulain), Louis L'Amour (Michael T. Marsden), and Jack Schaefer (Michael Cleary). Each of these essays includes biographical, thematic, and critical commentaries and concludes with selective listings of primary and secondary sources on each author.

Another useful source of information on the Western is Clarence Gohdes, *Literature and Theatre of the States and Regions of the U.S.A.: An Historical Bibliography*. This state-by-state listing also includes a special section on the Western. A few entries are annotated. Some overlapping occurs among the sections on western states, regionalism, and the Western; and Gohdes's definition of the Western is fuzzy, but if one is acquainted with the names of writers of Westerns, this bibliography will be useful. For articles and books that have been published since Gohdes's volume, one should consult two listings in the winter issues of *Western American Literature,* the scholarly journal of the Western Literature Association. The "Annual Bibliography of Studies in Western American Literature" lists books and essays about specific topics and individual writers, and "Research in Western American Literature" notes theses and dissertations. These bibliographies are particularly helpful because most research and writing about the Western has been so recent.

Richard W. Etulain has provided two other bibliographies. His "Western American Literature: A Selective Annotated Bibliography" emphasizes secondary works published since 1960. Divided into four sections (Bibliographies, Anthologies, History and Criticism—Books, and History and Criticism—Articles), this list contains brief annotations on more than sixty items, about fifteen of which deal with the popular Western. Much more extensive are the listings in Etulain's *A Bibliographical Guide to the Study of Western American Literature.* This book-length compilation contains sections on bibliographies, anthologies, general books and essays, specific listings on fictional and cinematic Westerns, and lists of secondary materials on more than 350 writers. The part on fictional Westerns lists more than 130 items—books, essays, theses, dissertations, and book review essays. Notable among the bibliographies on specific writers are those on Wister, Haycox, Brand, and Grey. Etulain's bibliography includes works published through 1981. Although the bibliography is not annotated or exhaustive, it does attempt to bring "together in one volume . . . [citations to] the most important research on the literature of the American West." Two other regional bibliographies add beneficial information on the Western, numerous regional writers, and general backgrounds for two subregions of the West: John Q. Anderson et al., eds., *Southwestern American Literature: A Bibliography,* and Gerald Nemanic, ed., *A Bibliographical Guide to Midwestern Literature.*

In "The Western: A Selective Bibliography," Michael D. Gibson lists twenty-six books and dissertations and eighty-one essays. He includes general items on Western fiction and film as well as materials on specific authors.

His entries are not annotated, and he includes materials published through 1972. Some of the same items are listed in "Suggestions for Further Research" in *The Western Story: Fact, Fiction, and Myth,* edited by Philip Durham and Everett L. Jones. The most recent brief bibliography of interpretive treatments of western literature is that in Rodman W. Paul and Richard W. Etulain, *The Frontier and American West.* The section on western writing contains nearly one hundred unannotated items, a good portion of which treat the popular Western.

Except for the scattered listings on individual authors in the reference volumes noted above and below and in the National Union Catalogue (NUC), no comprehensive bibliography of Westerns is in print. The most extensive checklist—other than the brief listings in the NUC—is that of Jack VanDerhoff, *A Bibliography of Novels Related to American Frontier and Colonial History.* VanDerhoff deals with areas other than the trans-Mississippi frontier, and his definition of the Western includes such unlikely choices as Walter Van Tilburg Clark's *The City of Trembling Leaves.* Sometimes he lists but one or two novels to illustrate an author's works, but the major writers of Westerns are well represented: Zane Grey (fifty items), Ernest Haycox (twenty-seven), and Max Brand (seventy-nine). Another incomplete listing of Westerns is that by Philip Durham and Everett L. Jones. Published from 1969 to 1970 in the *Roundup,* the house organ of the Western Writers of America (WWA), their bibliography includes only the works of then-present members of WWA. Thus, Wister, Grey, Brand, and Haycox are not cited, but Nelson Nye and Luke Short are among those who are. Most of the items listed are novels, but nonfiction works are included for authors who have written little or no fiction.

Although there is no comprehensive bibliography of Westerns, checklists on individual writers are available. Dean Sherman provides the most useful published listing of Owen Wister's fiction, nonfiction, shorter pieces, and books in "Owen Wister: An Annotated Bibliography." Most of the annotations are summary in nature. Complementing Sherman's work is Sanford E. Marovitz's outstanding compilation "Owen Wister: An Annotated Bibliography of Secondary Material." Reliable and thoroughly annotated, Marovitz's listing is arranged chronologically from 1887 to 1973. This bibliography, which contains hundreds of items and a very useful author index, will remain *the* source of commentary on Wister's life and writings. Lists of Wister's writings and citations to many essays and books about him are contained in John L. Cobbs, *Owen Wister,* and Darwin Payne, *Owen Wister: Chronicler of the West, Gentleman of the East.*

On Frederick Faust (Max Brand), Darrell C. Richardson has provided an extensive bibliography in his *Max Brand: The Man and His Work.* Richardson's bibliography is an exhaustive listing of Faust's writings including work he published under several pen names. Noted are books, novelettes, short stories, other magazine and newspaper work, and several magazine articles about Faust. Meant to be complete through 1950, the checklist contains enormous amounts of information, but it is a bit disorganized and difficult to follow. Less extensive but easier to use is the bibliography contained in Robert Easton, *Max Brand: The Big "Westerner."* Organized chronologically, this list contains American original publications only and includes books and magazine and newspaper writings, as well as work published under his numerous pseudonyms. Helpful listings of essays and books about Faust and Faust's works used in film, radio, and television are included. The section on Faust in Vinson's *Twentieth-Century Western Writers* also includes a long list of Faust's novels and short stories.

The most significant works on Zane Grey also include bibliographies. In *Zane Grey,* Carlton Jackson lists novels, manuscripts, and articles in periodicals (the latter contains only six items). In addition, he produces a helpful map indicating the settings of Grey's Westerns. Jackson lists but eleven secondary items on Grey. Another writer, Frank Gruber (*Zane Grey: A Biography*), includes a listing of Grey's numerous novels with an indication of prior appearances as magazine serials, and he provides a more extensive listing of magazine pieces (largely nonfiction and juveniles) than Jackson. An annotated bibliography of Grey's works appears in Jean Karr's *Zane Grey: Man of the West*. These annotations, which deal with novels, juveniles, and outdoor books, are not analytical but provide useful information on settings and plots. Karr does not list Grey's numerous short stories. A brief bibliography is contained in Ann Ronald's pamphlet, *Zane Grey,* in the Boise State Western Writers Series. She lists the novels alphabetically and also notes juveniles, outdoor books, and general and specific studies about Grey. But now supplanting all these reference works on Grey is Kenneth W. Scott, *Zane Grey: Born to the West,* an exhaustive and very useful guide to the Zane Grey industry.

Selective bibliographies of the works of Luke Short, Henry Wilson Allen, and Louis L'Amour appear in the recent Twayne volumes on each of these writers by Robert L. Gale. Even more extensive are the listings in Vinson's volume and in some of the entries in Tuska and Piekarski's *Encyclopedia*. Bibliographies on Ernest Haycox also appear in the last sources, and his writings are conveniently listed in Jill Haycox and John Chord, "Ernest Haycox Fiction—A Checklist." This excellent compilation contains information on novels, anthologies, paperback anthologies and reprints, and short stories in periodicals, and include a helpful index. The authors provide dates for serial appearances and further information on each novel.

RESEARCH COLLECTIONS

The three largest research collections pertaining to the Western are those at the university libraries of Oregon, Wyoming, and UCLA. For at least three decades these libraries have been collecting the manuscripts and correspondence of writers of Westerns. In addition, they have useful collections of western novels.

The University of Oregon library houses several manuscript collections dealing with the Western. Not only does it have a growing assemblage of the papers of Ernest Haycox and Luke Short, it also has numerous letters concerning the origin and development of the WWA. Some of these letters are contained in the correspondence of Charles Alexander, Brian Garfield, Dwight Newton, John and Ward Hawkins, Thomas Thompson, and Robert O. Case.

An even larger number of writers are represented at the University of Wyoming library. The Western History Center in the library at Laramie contains numerous small collections of letters and manuscripts. The Jack Schaefer Collection is particularly useful, as is the correspondence dealing with the WWA. And the original western journals of Owen Wister are on deposit at Wyoming.

The UCLA library houses a large collection of Westerns, and it too contains useful information about the WWA. The collections at this library and those at Bowling Green State University in Ohio, the New York Public Library, and the Library of Congress are the most notable gatherings of Westerns. The Huntington Library in San Marino, California, has a large collection of dime novels.

The papers of other leading writers of Westerns are scattered throughout the United States. The Max Brand collection is at the Bancroft Library in Berkeley, and the largest collection of Owen Wister correspondence is on file at the Library of Congress. The Huntington Library contains the papers of Eugene Manlove Rhodes and Eugene Cunningham. Most of Emerson Hough's letters are housed in the Iowa State Department of History and Archives in Des Moines. Nearly all of Zane Grey's manuscripts and correspondence are in the private collection of Zane Grey, Inc., in Pasadena, California.

Other useful materials are still in the hands of publishers. Little, Brown and Company holds a sizable collection of Haycox's letters, and some of Grey's correspondence is on file with Harper and Row. Dodd, Mead and Condé Nast Publications (successor to Street and Smith) have Brand letters, and Houghton Mifflin has some of the correspondence of Andy Adams and Jack Schaefer. Unfortunately, many of the papers of Street and Smith, *Collier's, Saturday Evening Post,* and Doubleday and Company are not available or easily accessible. These collections will be necessary sources for a full-scale history of the Western.

HISTORY AND CRITICISM

Although a few authors dealt with facets of the Western prior to the appearance of Henry Nash Smith's *Virgin Land,* that book has stimulated more research and writing about popular western literature than any other volume. First of all, Smith was one of the first scholars willing to study, as literature, several types of writing that previous scholars had relegated to the nonliterary categories of history, propaganda, and pulp novels. Through careful analysis of a wide variety of fiction and nonfiction about the West, Smith outlined what Americans came to believe about the western frontier. Second, he described the symbols and myths about the West that fascinated Americans. He was able to show how the West as a "passage to India," as a stage for the "sons of Leatherstocking," and as a desert and a garden, was a large part of Americans' mental image of the West in the nineteenth century. Third, Smith demonstrated one way that scholars could approach popular literature in his probing discussion of dime-novel Westerns. No scholar who aims at completeness in his research on western writing can afford to overlook Smith's brilliant book.

If Smith opened the door for early studies of western writing, John G. Cawelti has recently marked out one corridor students could follow in pursuing the Western. First in *The Six-Gun Mystique* and then in *Adventure, Mystery, and Romance,* he has encouraged systematic thinking about the nature of popular fiction about the West. He urges scholars to study the Western as a species of formula literature (he defines formulas as "structures of narrative conventions which carry out a variety of cultural functions in a unified way") to see how these patterns change over time as they respond to the culture that produces them. Although Cawelti provides useful sketches of the historical development of the Western, he is more concerned with the social and cultural implications of the formulas he finds in Westerns. In Cawelti's volumes, the plots and characters of novels by Cooper, Wister, and Grey are scrutinized and used to illustrate what Cawelti believes to be the major themes of the authors' cultural environments. *Adventure, Mystery, and Romance,* which in addition to dealing with the Western treats crime novels, detective stories, and social melodramas, incorporates much information from Cawelti's earlier volume, but it also includes extensive treatments of nineteenth-century western fiction and recent Western films. In fact, Cawelti is satisfied to break off discussion of the fictional Western after his treatment of Zane Grey. One wishes he had chosen to deal with Haycox, Short, and L'Amour. Still, his books are necessary beginning points for all serious study of the Western.

The volume that comes nearest to being a brief history of the twentieth-century Western is *The Popular Western: Essays Toward a Definition,* edited by Richard W. Etulain and Michael T. Marsden. The book contains, in addition to brief introductory and concluding sections, eight essays and a selective bibliography. Some of the articles deal with individual topics and writers, such as the dime-novel Western, B. M. Bower, Zane Grey, Clay Fisher, Will Henry, Luke Short, and Jack Schaefer; another essay traces the historical development of the Western, and in a superb piece Don D. Walker argues for more rigorous application of standard methods of literary criticism to the Western. The authors of the essays approach their subjects from their training in history, literature, and American studies, but their major emphasis has been to show how their topic or author contributes to an understanding of the development of the Western. The editors are now preparing a full-scale history of the Western that will supersede this slim volume.

In additon to these books on the Western, several other volumes offer useful background information on the popular genre. Two books by Richard Slotkin—*Regeneration Through Violence* and *The Fatal Environment*—and Edwin Fussell's *Frontier: American Literature and the American West* do not focus on the Western but provide lengthy discussions of the treatment of the frontier in American imaginative literature published before 1900. Slotkin's massive volumes—nearly 700 and 650 pages—trace Americans' feelings about the frontier from the first settlers to the end of the nineteenth century. He is particularly interested in writers' attitudes toward land, Indians, and pioneers who moved west, and in the important roles of such heroes as George Armstrong Custer. Fussell centers on the major American authors of the Romantic era and shows how they wrote about their complicated responses to the frontier. His chapters on Cooper, Thoreau, and Whitman are particularly stimulating.

In his book *The Western Hero in History and Legend,* Kent Ladd Steckmesser offers another perspective for students of the Western. He outlines how four historic characters—Kit Carson, Billy the Kid, Wild Bill Hickok, and George Armstrong Custer—became legendary figures. Working his way through large amounts of history, literature, and propaganda, Steckmesser points out what writers, ideas, and events shaped the legendary lives of these four men. Along the way, he discusses the role of a few Westerns in helping to make these reputations, but more importantly, his book outlines the manner in which historical figures can and have been used in popular literature. Joseph G. Rosa does the same for one Western type in his study, *The Gunfighter: Man or Myth?* Both of these authors—in research method and findings—owe a great deal to *Virgin Land.*

Two other studies comment upon the early historical and literary treatments of the cowboy. E. Douglas Branch's *The Cowboy and His Interpreters* was a pioneer work and has been largely superseded in Joe B. Frantz and Julian E. Choate, Jr., *The American Cowboy: The Myth and the Reality.* Although these authors employ a narrow and misleading definition of myth—that is, the opposite of historical fact—they do provide useful summaries of cowboy novels published from about 1890 to 1920. Even more useful is William W. Savage, Jr.'s study of varying roles of the cowboy in American popular culture in his *The Cowboy Hero: His Image in American History and Culture,* which includes chapters on such topics as history, literature, music, athletics, and selling the cowboy. Another volume that collects eight essays about the images of cowboys in early movies, recent films, and music and their associations with Indians and dude ranching is the lively book edited by Charles W. Harris and Buck Rainey, *The Cowboy: Six-Shooters, Songs, and Sex*. Only the book by Savage, however, approaches the full-scale study we need of the cowboy in the Western and other kinds of American literature.

Russel Nye's brief history of the Western in *The Unembarrassed Muse* and that of Tuska and Piekarski in *The Frontier Experience* are the best brief accounts of the origins and flowering of the popular genre. In fact, these two sections should be the starting points for students of the Western. Cooper's role in the rise of the Western is covered in *Virgin Land*, in Cawelti's two books, in James K. Folsom's *The American Western Novel*, and in a host of other essays and books. The classic study of the dime novel is Albert Johannsen's three-volume *House of Beadle and Adams and Its Dime and Nickel Novels*, but Daryl Jones's *The Dime Novel Western* is thorough, well written, and illuminating and is now the best concise study of the dime novel. No complete study of the pulp Western has been published, but Quentin Reynolds offers a helpful volume on Street and Smith in *The Fiction Factory*. Also useful is John A. Dinan, *The Pulp Western*. Much narrower in scope and less analytical and also more personal in tone is Frank Gruber's *The Pulp Jungle*.

In the past decade or so, as much scholarship on the film Western as on the fictional Western has appeared, and several of these more recent studies are useful for scholars undertaking research on writers. The still useful standard history of the film Western is George N. Fenin and William K. Everson, *The Western: From Silents to the Seventies*, which is comprehensive, detailed, and well-illustrated. Equally helpful is Jon Tuska's encyclopedic, chatty, and lively book *The Filming of the West*. Both of these volumes are stronger on the silent, B-Western, and classic Western films than on those produced after 1960. Two other indispensable reference guides to the Western are Brian Garfield, *Western Films*, and Phil Hardy, *The Western*. Garfield's volume is organized alphabetically and is more iconoclastic in tone, while Hardy arranges his coverage by date and includes less extensive commentaries on each film discussed. One should also consult Jon Tuska, *The American West in Film*, for a series of "critical approaches" to the Western.

Jenni Calder attempts to discuss the myths and reality of Western films in her book, *There Must Be a Lone Ranger*. Along with treatments of such filmmakers as John Ford, Sam Peckinpah, and Howard Hawks, she includes analyses of the Westerns of Brand, Grey, Haycox, and Short. A sociologist who employs the structural insights of Vladimir Propp and Claude Lévi-Strauss, Will Wright deals with such well-known films as *Stagecoach, Shane, High Noon, Rio Bravo, Butch Cassidy and the Sundance Kid*, and *True Grit* in his *Sixguns and Society*. His comments about narrative formats are illuminating for those interested in the formulas endemic to many Westerns. Another fine example of the numerous recent studies of Western films is *Horizons West* by Jim Kitses, who analyzes the films of Anthony Mann, Budd Boetticher, and Sam Peckinpah. In an adjacent field, Ralph and Donna Brauer have provided the first book-length study of the television Western in their volume, *The Horse, the Gun and The Piece of Property*. But the best one-volume treatment of recent Westerns is John H. Lenihan's *Showdown: Confronting Modern America in the Western*, which persuasively views Westerns as cultural indexes of their times. Lenihan's study is particularly provocative for those dealing with racial, foreign relations, and sociocultural themes in the post–World War era. Essays treating the full historical development of the Western film are gathered in Richard W. Etulain, *Western Films: A Brief History*, which also contains a bibliographical essay by the editor on "Recent Interpretations of the Western Film." For the most extensive listings of publications about Western films, however, one must consult John G. Nachbar, *Western Films: An Annotated Critical Bibliography*, a very useful listing that is now, unfortunately, somewhat dated.

The select number of scholars who have dealt with larger topics of western American literature have not devoted much attention to the fictional Western. Among these overviews, James K. Folsom's *The American Western Novel* is a good summary. His chapters are largely topical in nature with emphases on Indians, western heroes, and agrarian novels. He treats major writers like Cooper, Garland, and Clark, and he discusses the Westerns of Wister, Grey, and Alan LeMay; but he does not reveal how the writings of the latter group differ from the works of major western novelists like Cather and Steinbeck. His handy book would have been even more stimulating had he chosen to make some of these distinctions. Another recent study, John R. Milton's *The Novel of the American West*, contains an unenthusiastic chapter on the popular Western but illuminating chapters on several major western writers. Richard W. Etulain discusses several other interpretations of western literature and the Western in his essay "The American Literary West and Its Interpreters: The Rise of a New Historiography."

Although a book-length study of the Western has not been published, several studies of individual writers have appeared. Darwin Payne has just published a smoothly written biography of Owen Wister, which treats the subject's literary career without providing a great deal of commentary on Wister's writings. Much less successful is *Owen Wister*, by John L. Cobbs, a book that makes no use of the indispensable Wister collection in the Library of Congress and that provides readings too tied to the author's predilections for it to be the much-needed literary study of Wister. Ben M. Vorpahl's *My Dear Wister* contains a lively account of Frederic Remington's friendship with and influence upon Wister. Even more useful as a model for understanding Wister as a man, a writer, and a cultural figure is G. Edward

White's penetrating book, *The Eastern Establishment and the Western Experience*. White reveals how Wister became an integral part of a cultural consensus of the East and West in the decades surrounding 1900. A short summary of Wister's life and western writings is presented in Richard W. Etulain, *Owen Wister*.

Judging solely on the numbers of studies published, Zane Grey has fared much better with scholars than Wister. Jean Karr, Frank Gruber, Carlton Jackson, Kenneth W. Scott, and Candace C. Kant have written books on Grey, but the first two are weak on interpretation and the third lacks sufficient critical insights to be labeled *the* literary study of Grey. As noted, Scott's volume is a notable reference guide to Grey and his career. Meanwhile, Kant's book, *Zane Grey's Arizona,* while narrowly focused and a bit too accepting of Grey's view of his world, is nonetheless a thorough work on the influence of Arizona settings on Grey's writings. Another writer, Gary Topping, provides a more searching analysis of Grey's Westerns in his essays and dissertation. His articles should be gathered, expanded, and published as a book. Frederick Faust's son-in-law, Robert Easton, has produced a fine biography in his *Max Brand: The Big "Westerner."* No one will need to cover that ground again, but, unfortunately, Easton does little with Faust as a writer of Westerns. He is reluctant to evaluate Faust's novels and is unaware of the scholarship available on Western writing. Eugene Manlove Rhodes is the subject of W. H. Hutchinson's lively book, *A Bar Cross Man*. Hutchinson is more interested in biography and in presenting long sections of Rhodes's valuable letters than he is in evaluating Rhodes as a writer, but the book is nonetheless rewarding reading. Useful as a brief introduction to Rhodes's life and writings is Edwin W. Gaston, Jr.'s pamphlet in the Boise State Series. Other writers, such as B. M. Bower, Clarence Mulford, and Stewart White, merit extended monographs, but no published book-length studies of their lives and works have appeared.

More than two decades ago, Richard W. Etulain prepared the first literary study of a writer of Westerns in his unpublished dissertation on Ernest Haycox. Chapters of the dissertation have been published as essays, but Haycox deserves a full-length volume that is not yet published. Meanwhile, one should utilize Robert Gale's essay on Haycox in Erisman and Etulain, *Fifty Western Writers*. At the same time, no one has yet written the needed book on Jack Schaefer's notable career. Until that volume is completed scholars should utilize Gerald Haslam's pamphlet, which reviews Schaefer's life and major works.

In the last decade, Robert L. Gale of the University of Pittsburgh has done the most to deal with the careers of recent writers of Westerns. In addition to his essay on Haycox and his helpful pamphlet on Henry Wilson Allen, he has recently completed volumes on Allen, Luke Short, and Louis L'Amour for the Twayne United States Authors Series. Each of these volumes gives evidence of Gale's thorough reading, his thoughtful consideration of these writers' talents as novelists and historians, and their varied uses of plot, setting, and characterization. If the tone of the volume on Allen is the most sympathetic and personal and that on L'Amour the least friendly, his study of Short is perhaps the most balanced of these three important studies. Altogether these books are models of clarity and reasoned readings. One hopes they may become paradigms for similar volumes on such authors as B. M. Bower, Clarence Mulford, Zane Grey, Max Brand, and Ernest Haycox.

ANTHOLOGIES AND REPRINTS

There are few collections of Western stories in print—largely because little demand exists for such books among general readers and for use in classrooms. In addition, short story collections most often lose out in the stiff competition with reprints of older novels and the new paperback originals. If one wishes to make money writing Westerns, one must turn out novels; neither the skimpy remuneration available to short story writers nor the moderate interest of general readers in short fiction is enough to encourage the publication of many collections of short stories. There are, however, a few anthologies of stories worthy of mention.

The best anthology of Western fiction—*The Western Story: Fact, Fiction, and Myth,* edited by Philip Durham and Everett L. Jones—is currently out of print. This collection was designed as a text for college courses—for freshman composition courses and for classes concentrating on the Western. The book is divided into three sections: *fact*—five primary essays dealing with cowboys, cattlemen, and the cattle country dating from the time of Theodore Roosevelt to the present; *fiction*—sixteen stories from Bret Harte's "Tennessee's Partner" to Walter Van Tilburg Clark's "The Indian Well"; and *myth*—six interpretive essays on Western fiction and films. This is a useful anthology even though the editors' reasons for selecting the stories are not clear. The editors include the works of popular Western writers, such as Mulford, Grey, Haycox, Short, and Thomas Thompson, but, strangely, they also have chosen stories by Jack London, Vardis Fisher, and Walter Van Tilburg Clark that are not good examples of the Western. A brief introduction and lists of discussion questions after each selection will help students and teachers to reflect on the nature of the Western. An insightful publisher should secure new editors, update the collection, and reprint it.

Another notable collection is J. Golden Taylor's *Great Stories of the West,* which appeared originally as a hardcover book, *Great Western Short Stories.* Taylor has organized his anthology into ten divisions that move chronologically from Indians to contemporary Westerners. Among the twenty-eight stories are works by Will Henry, Emerson Hough, Max Brand, Owen Wister, E. M. Rhodes, and Conrad Richter. Wallace Stegner's essay "History, Myth, and the Western Writer" is a first-rate introduction. Unfortunately, Taylor's book has been too often out of print.

Another fine collection currently not in print is Harry E. Maule's *Great Tales of the American West*. Maule, who edited pulp magazines in the 1920s and 1930s and later became an executive with Doubleday and Random House, appreciates the historical development of the Western (as his brief introduction demonstrates) and senses which authors have made the largest contributions to the popular genre. His book contains eighteen stories from Harte to Clark and includes works from Wister, Rhodes, Grey, Raine, Mulford, Short, Haycox, and Brand. The stories are judiciously chosen; Maule has selected the best stories from the most important writers of Westerns.

Two other anthologies reprint stories that appeared first in two periodicals. E. N. Brandt has edited *The Saturday Evening Post Reader of Western Stories,* and Ned Collier has collected short stories from the pulp magazine *West* in his book, *Great Stories of the West*. Brandt's volume, which contains eighteen stories and two novelettes from leading Western writers, demonstrates how well the *Post* did in securing the best Western fiction for its pages. Collier reprints fourteen pieces that are not as well written as those in Brandt's volume, but the *West* stories illustrate the kinds of fiction that appeared in a leading pulp periodical of the 1920s and 1930s.

Three other earlier anthologies should be mentioned because they reprint stories from the best Western writers of the first half of the twentieth century. They are William Targ's *Western Story Omnibus,* William MacLeod Raine's *Western Stories,* and Leo Margulies's *Popular Book of Western Stories*.

One should note too the anthologies of short Western fiction published by the WWA, which the WWA sponsored from the 1950s through the 1970s. The first books in the series used reprinted stories, but the more recent anthologies contain original pieces written by members of the WWA for specific collections. These volumes reflect changing trends in Western fiction of the last twenty-five years, but one cannot say the anthologies always contain the best Western writing, for the works of Luke Short and Louis L'Amour, for example, have not appeared in recent volumes. A later collection that attempts to illustrate the accomplishments of the WWA is edited by August Lenninger, *Western Writers of America: Silver Anniversary Anthology*. The editor has chosen twelve novelettes and stories and two poems. Most of his selections appeared first in the 1940s and 1950s, but two stories are original publications. Among the authors included are Luke Short, S. Omar Barker (author of the two poems), Elmer Kelton, and Nelson Nye. The introduction contains a brief account of the WWA's dealings with outlets for the publications of Western fiction in the 1940s, 1950s, and 1960s.

Among the most recent anthologies, the best is Jon Tuska's *The American West in Fiction*. Collecting twenty stories from such authors as Twain, Harte,

Cather, and Walter Van Tilburg Clark, the editor also includes works by Wister, Rhodes, Grey, Brand, Short, L'Amour, Will Henry, and Elmer Kelton. In addition to a useful but very opinionated and spread-eagle introduction, Tuska provides instructive introductions to each story and a brief appended section of "Suggested Further Reading." This is the best in-print anthology. While *The Arbor House Treasury of Great Western Stories,* edited by Bill Pronzini and Martin H. Greenberg, contains thirty-three stories, thus allowing them to illustrate more of the diversity and historical development of short Western fiction, the introductory comments by John Jakes and the comments prefacing each selection are neither insightful nor very useful. The same editors have compiled *The Western Hall of Fame: An Anthology of Classic Western Stories Selected by the Western Writers of America.* This collection contains even fewer editorial aids, but the balance of contents between the classics of Crane, Twain, Harte, and O. Henry with the works of the popular writers such as Haycox, Grey, Brand, Clay Fisher, Lewis B. Patten, and Thomas Thompson make this anthology useful for classroom use.

The recent publication of these collections, the appearance of several books and numerous essays on the Western in the last decade, and the ongoing interest in popular images of the West attest to the continuing fascination of Americans—as well as readers and audiences around the world—with things Western. While few new Western films are being produced, reruns of classic Westerns on television and their availability on videotape, the millions of readers who devour the Westerns of Louis L'Amour, and the enduring fashionableness of Western music, art, dress, and lifestyles reinforce one's conviction that the Western and popular images of the West will continue to be important icons of American popular culture in the years to come.

BIBLIOGRAPHY

Books and Articles

Anderson, John Q. et al., eds. *Southwestern American Literature: A Bibliography.* Chicago: Swallow Press, 1980.

Bloodworth, William. "Literary Extensions of the Formula Western." *Western American Literature,* 14 (Winter 1980), 287–96.

———. "Max Brand's West." *Western American Literature,* 16 (Fall 1981), 177–91.

———. "Zane Grey's Western Eroticism." *South Dakota Review,* 23 (Autumn 1985), 5–14.

Bold, Christine. *Selling the Wild West: Popular Western Fiction, 1860–1960.* Bloomington: Indiana University Press, 1987.

Branch, E. Douglas. *The Cowboy and His Interpreters.* New York: D. Appleton, 1926, 1961.

Brandt, E. N., ed. *The Saturday Evening Post Reader of Western Stories*. Garden City, N.Y.: Doubleday, 1960; New York: Popular Library, 1962.

Brauer, Ralph, with Donna Brauer. *The Horse, the Gun and the Piece of Property: Changing Images of the TV Western*. Bowling Green, Ohio: Bowling Green State University Popular Press, 1975.

Calder, Jenni. *There Must Be a Lone Ranger: The American West in Film and in Reality*. New York: Taplinger, 1975.

Cawelti, John G. *Adventure, Mystery, and Romance: Formula Stories as Art and Popular Culture*. Chicago: University of Chicago Press, 1976.

————. *The Six-Gun Mystique*. Bowling Green, Ohio: Bowling Green State University Popular Press, 1971.

Cobbs, John L. *Owen Wister*. Boston: Twayne, 1984.

Collier, Ned, ed. *Great Stories of the West*. Garden City, N.Y.: Doubleday, 1971.

Dinan, John A. *The Pulp Western*. San Bernardino, Calif.: Borgo Press, 1983.

Durham, Philip, and Everett L. Jones, eds. *The Western Story: Fact, Fiction, and Myth*. New York: Harcourt Brace Jovanovich, 1975.

Easton, Jane Faust. *Memories of the '20s and '30s*. Santa Barbara, Calif.: n.p., 1979.

Easton, Robert. *Max Brand: The Big "Westerner."* Norman: University of Oklahoma Press, 1970.

Erisman, Fred, and Richard W. Etulain, eds. *Fifty Western Writers: A Bio-Bibliographical Guide*. Westport, Conn.: Greenwood Press, 1982.

Etulain, Richard W. *The American Literary West*. Manhattan, Kans.: Sunflower University Press, 1980.

————. "The American Literary West and Its Interpreters: The Rise of a New Historiography." *Pacific Historical Review*, 45 (August 1976), 311–48.

————. *A Bibliographical Guide to the Study of Western American Literature*. Lincoln: University of Nebraska Press, 1982.

————. "Changing Images: The Cowboy in Western Films." *Colorado Heritage*, 1 (1981), 37–55.

————. "The Literary Career of a Western Writer: Ernest Haycox, 1899–1950." Ph.D. dissertation, University of Oregon, 1966.

————. *Owen Wister*. Western Writers Series, No. 7. Boise, Idaho: Boise State University, 1973.

————. "Western American Literature: A Selective Annotated Bibliography." In *Interpretive Approaches to Western American Literature*. Edited by Daniel Alkofer et al. Pocatello: Idaho State University Press, 1972.

————. *Western Films: A Brief History*. Manhattan, Kans.: Sunflower University Press, 1983.

Etulain, Richard W., and Michael T. Marsden, eds. *The Popular Western: Essays Toward a Definition*. Bowling Green, Ohio: Bowling Green State University Popular Press, 1974.

Fenin, George N., and William K. Everson. *The Western: From Silents to the Seventies*. New York: Grossman, 1973.

Folsom, James K. *The American Western Novel*. New Haven, Conn.: College and University Press, 1966.

————, ed. *The Western: A Collection of Critical Essays*. Englewood Cliffs, N.J.: Prentice-Hall, 1979.

Frantz, Joe B., and Julian E. Choate, Jr. *The American Cowboy: The Myth and the Reality*. Norman: University of Oklahoma Press, 1955.

Fussell, Edwin. *Frontier: American Literature and the American West*. Princeton, N.J.: Princeton University Press, 1965.

Gale, Robert L. *Louis L'Amour*. Boston: Twayne, 1985.

————. *Luke Short*. Boston: Twayne, 1981.

————. *Will Henry/Clay Fisher*. Western Writers Series, No. 52. Boise, Idaho: Boise State University, 1982.

————. *Will Henry/Clay Fisher (Henry W. Allen)*. Boston: Twayne, 1984.

Garfield, Brian. *Western Films: A Complete Guide*. New York: Rawson Associates, 1982.

Gaston, Edwin W., Jr. *Eugene Manlove Rhodes: Cowboy Chronicler*. Southwest Writers Series, No. 11. Austin, Tex.: Steck-Vaughn, 1967.

Gibson, Michael D. "The Western: A Selective Bibliography." In *The Popular Western*. Edited by Richard W. Etulain and Michael T. Marsden. Bowling Green, Ohio: Bowling Green State University Popular Press, 1974.

Gohdes, Clarence. *Literature and Theatre of the States and Regions of the U.S.A.: An Historical Bibliography*. Durham, N.C.: Duke University Press, 1967.

Gruber, Frank. *The Pulp Jungle*. Los Angeles: Sherbourne Press, 1967.

————. *Zane Grey: A Biography*. Cleveland, Ohio: World, 1970.

Hardy, Phil. *The Western: The Complete Film Sourcebook*. New York: William Morrow, 1983.

Harris, Charles W., and Buck Rainey, eds. *The Cowboy: Six-Shooters, Songs, and Sex*. Norman: University of Oklahoma Press, 1976.

Haslam, Gerald. *Jack Schaefer*. Western Writers Series, No. 20, Boise, Idaho: Boise State University, 1975.

Haycox, Jill, and John Chord. "Ernest Haycox Fiction—A Checklist." *Call Number* (University of Oregon), 25 (Fall 1963/1964), 5–27.

Hutchinson, W. H. *A Bar Cross Man: The Life and Personal Writings of Eugene Manlove Rhodes*. Norman: University of Oklahoma Press, 1956.

Jackson, Carlton. *Zane Grey*. New York: Twayne, 1973.

Johannsen, Albert. *The House of Beadle and Adams and Its Dime and Nickel Novels*. 3 vols. Norman: University of Oklahoma Press, 1950, 1962.

Jones, Daryl. *The Dime Novel Western*. Bowling Green, Ohio: Bowling Green State University Popular Press, 1978.

Kant, Candace C. *Zane Grey's Arizona*. Flagstaff, Ariz.: Northland Press, 1984.

Karr, Jean. *Zane Grey: Man of the West*. New York: Greenberg, 1949.

Kitses, Jim. *Horizons West: Anthony Mann, Budd Boetticher, Sam Peckinpah: Studies of Authorship Within the Western*. Bloomington: Indiana University Press, 1969.

Klaschus, Candace. "Louis L'Amour: The Writer as Teacher." Ph.D. dissertation, University of New Mexico, 1983.

Lenihan, John H. *Showdown: Confronting Modern America in the Western Film*. Urbana: University of Illinois Press, 1980.

Lenninger, August, ed. *Western Writers of America: Silver Anniversary Anthology*. New York: Ace Books, 1977.

McDonald, Archie P., ed. *Shooting Stars: Heroes and Heroines of Western Film*. Bloomington: Indiana University Press, 1987.

Margulies, Leo, ed. *Popular Book of Western Stories*. New York: Popular Library, 1948.

Marovitz, Sanford E. "Owen Wister: An Annotated Bibliography of Secondary Material." *American Literary Realism 1870–1910*, 7 (Winter 1974), 1–110.

Marsden, Michael T. "The Concept of Family in the Fiction of Louis L'Amour." *North Dakota Quarterly*, 46 (Summer 1978), 12–21.

———. "The Modern Western." *Journal of the West*, 19 (January 1980), 54–61.

Maule, Harry E., ed. *Great Tales of the American West*. New York: Random House, 1945.

Milton, John R. *The Novel of the American West*. Lincoln: University of Nebraska Press, 1980.

Nachbar, John G., ed. *Western Films: An Annotated Critical Bibliography*. New York: Garland, 1975.

Nemanic, Gerald, ed. *A Bibliographical Guide to Midwestern Literature*. Iowa City: University of Iowa Press, 1981.

Nesbitt, John D. "Change of Purpose in the Novels of Louis L'Amour." *Western American Literature*, 13 (Spring 1978), 65–81.

———. "A New Look at Two Popular Western Classics." *South Dakota Review*, 18 (Spring 1980), 30–42. (Haycox and L'Amour.)

Nolan, William F., ed. *Max Brand's Best Western Stories*. New York: Dodd, Mead, 1981.

Nye, Russel. "Sixshooter Country." In *The Unembarrassed Muse: The Popular Arts in America*. New York: Dial Press, 1970.

Paul, Rodman W., and Richard W. Etulain. *The Frontier and American West*. Goldentree Bibliographies in American History. Arlington Heights, Ill.: AHM Publishing, 1977.

Payne, Darwin. *Owen Wister: Chronicler of the West, Gentlemen of the East*. Dallas, Tex.: Southern Methodist University Press, 1985.

Pronzini, Bill, and Martin H. Greenberg, eds. *The Arbor House Treasury of Great Western Stories*. New York: Arbor House, 1982.

———. *The Best Western Stories of Steve Frazee*. Carbondale: Southern Illinois University Press, 1984.

———. *The Best Western Stories of Wayne D. Overholser*. Carbondale: Southern Illinois University Press, 1984.

———. *The Western Hall of Fame: An Anthology of Classic Western Stories Selected by the Western Writers of America*. New York: William Morrow, 1984.

Raine, William MacLeod, ed. *Western Stories*. New York: Dell, 1949.

Reynolds, Quentin. *The Fiction Factory*. New York: Random House, 1955.

Richardson, Darrell C., ed. *Max Brand: The Man and His Work*. Los Angeles: Fantasy Publishing, 1952.

Ronald, Ann. *Zane Grey*. Western Writers Series, No. 17. Boise, Idaho: Boise State University, 1975.

Rosa, Joseph G. *The Gunfighter: Man or Myth?* Norman: University of Oklahoma Press, 1969.

Savage, William W., Jr. *The Cowboy Hero: His Image in American History and Culture*. Norman: University of Oklahoma Press, 1979.

Scott, Kenneth W. *Zane Grey: Born to the West*. Boston: G. K. Hall, 1979.

Sherman, Dean. "Owen Wister: An Annotated Bibliography." *Bulletin of Bibliography*, 28 (January-March 1971), 7–16.

Slotkin, Richard. *The Fatal Environment; The Myth of the Frontier in the Age of Industrialization, 1800–1890.* New York: Atheneum, 1985.

———. *Regeneration Through Violence: The Mythology of the American Frontier, 1600–1860.* Middletown, Conn.: Wesleyan University Press, 1973.

Smith, Henry Nash. *Virgin Land: The American West as Symbol and Myth.* Cambridge, Mass.: Harvard University Press, 1950, 1970.

Sonnichsen, C. L. *From Hopalong to Hud: Thoughts on Western Fiction.* College Station: Texas A & M University Press, 1978.

Speck, Ernest B. *Benjamin Capps.* Western Writers Series, No. 49. Boise, Idaho: Boise State University, 1981.

Steckmesser, Kent Ladd. *The Western Hero in History and Legend.* Norman: University of Oklahoma Press, 1965.

Targ, William, ed. *Western Story Omnibus.* Cleveland, Ohio: World, 1945. (An abridged edition appeared as *Great Western Stories.* New York: Penguin, 1947.)

Taylor, J. Golden, ed. *Great Stories of the West.* 2 vols. New York: Ballantine Books, 1971. (The American West Publishing Company printed the hardcover version as *Great Western Short Stories,* Palo Alto, Calif., 1967).

Taylor, J. Golden, Thomas J. Lyon, et al. *A Literary History of the American West.* Fort Worth: Texas Christian University Press, 1987.

Topping, Gary. "The Rise of the Western." *Journal of the West,* 19 (January 1980), 29–35.

———. "Zane Grey: A Literary Reassessment." *Western American Literature,* 13 (Spring 1978), 51–64.

———. "Zane Grey's West." In *The Popular Western.* Edited by Richard W. Etulain and Michael T. Marsden. Bowling Green, Ohio: Bowling Green State University Popular Press, 1974.

———. "Zane Grey's West: Essays in Intellectual History and Criticism." Ph.D. dissertation, University of Utah, 1977.

Tuska, Jon, ed. *The American West in Fiction.* New York: New American Library, 1982.

———. *The American West in Film: Critical Approaches to the Western.* Westport, Conn.: Greenwood Press, 1985.

———. *The Filming of the West.* Garden City, N.Y.: Doubleday, 1976.

Tuska, Ron, and Vicki Piekarski, eds. *Encyclopedia of Frontier and Western Fiction.* New York: McGraw-Hill, 1983.

———. *The Frontier Experience: A Reader's Guide to the Life and Literature of the American West.* Jefferson, N.C.: McFarland, 1984.

VanDerhoff, Jack. *A Bibliography of Novels Related to American Frontier and Colonial History.* Troy, N.Y.: Whitston, 1971.

Vinson, James, with D. L. Kirkpatrick, eds. *Twentieth-Century Western Writers.* London: Macmillan, 1982.

Vorpahl, Ben M. *My Dear Wister.* Palo Alto, Calif.: American West Publishing Co., 1972.

Walker, Dale, ed. *Will Henry's West.* El Paso: Texas Western Press, 1984.

White, G. Edward. *The Eastern Establishment and the Western Experience: The West of Frederic Remington, Theodore Roosevelt, and Owen Wister.* New Haven, Conn.: Yale University Press, 1968.

"The Works of Elmer Kelton." *Southwestern American Literature,* 9 (Spring 1984), 5–52.

Wright, Will. *Sixguns and Society: A Structural Study of the Western.* Berkeley: University of California Press, 1975.

Periodicals

Roundup. Sheridan, Wyo., 1953.

Western American Literature. Logan, Utah, 1966–.

Zane Grey Collector. Williamsport, Md., 1968–.

15

Young Adult Fiction

ALLEEN PACE NILSEN
and KEN DONELSON

There is no hard and fast definition for *adolescent literature*. In fact, there is little agreement on which of several terms, e.g., *teenage books, adolescent literature, juvenile fiction,* or *young adult literature,* should be used. In 1980, we polled one hundred people nationally recognized for their work with books and young people to see which term they preferred. We assumed that the different terms, all of which appear in the literature, were based on the age of the reader. *Juvenile fiction* would refer to books for preteens, *junior* or *teen novels* would be for slightly older readers, *adolescent literature* would refer to books with more substance for older high school students, and *young adult literature* would be books published as adult books but often read by advanced high school and beginning college students.

Not one respondent agreed completely with our definitions nor categorized the twenty sample books we had listed in the same way we did. Nor did respondents agree on the ages of readers belonging to this group. They mentioned "fourteen and up," "eleven or twelve and up," "thirteen to eighteen group," "twelve to nineteen," "teenagers over sixteen," and "tenth to twelfth graders." Much of the disagreement about the terms related to background training and current occupation. English teachers used the term *adolescent literature,* which editors and authors identified as having "academic overtones"; people in publishing were more likely to use the term *juvenile fiction*; and librarians overwhelmingly preferred the term *young adult literature*. Of the seventy-six people who responded and cataloged the twenty titles, *young adult literature* was listed as a preferred term 496 times; *adolescent literature*, 248 times; *junior (or teen) novel*, 211 times; and *juvenile fiction*, 189 times.

Junior and *juvenile* were identified as old-fashioned terms with slightly negative connotations. *Adolescent* was said to have "the ugly ring of pimples and puberty" and "to suggest immature in a derogatory sense." Reasons given for preferring *young adult literature* included such statements as "It lends a sense of dignity to the book," "It makes young readers feel respected," and "It is becoming an umbrella term for anything teens read including nonfiction and books published for adults."

This latter definition is the one we prefer and use in our own work with books and teenagers, but readers should be aware that many people in the field restrict themselves to books published by the juvenile division of a publishing house. Part of this is undoubtedly a matter of territorial boundaries; for example, it is a convenience to publications such as the *New York Times Book Review* to avoid duplication by limiting the reviewers in the "Children's Books" section to books released by a juvenile division. However, this limitation causes publications to miss out on many of the new books most popular with teenage readers because television and other mass media have eroded the boundaries between what young people and their parents read and view. In some ways we are returning to an earlier period when there were only books for children and books for adults. People in between made their own choices of which side of the fence to stand on.

School Library Journal handles the problem of today's teenagers reading books produced especially for them alongside books produced for a general adult audience by publishing an annual list of the year's best juvenile books, noting those recommended for grade six and above, with another list of best books published by adult divisions of publishing houses but recommended by the journal editors for teenagers. On its annual list, the Young Adult Services Division of the American Library Association makes no overt distinction between adult and juvenile titles, and frequently includes more "adult" than "juvenile" releases. Additional complicating factors in deciding what is young adult literature are the many best sellers from previous decades, e.g., *A Tree Grows in Brooklyn*, *The Catcher in the Rye*, and *Gone with the Wind*, which are kept alive because there is always a new crop of teenagers to read them.

An alternate way of defining young adult literature is to look at its structure. In an October 1983 article in *School Library Journal*, English teachers Maia Pank Mertz and David K. England identified the following as characterizing modern adolescent literature:

1. Adolescent fiction will involve a youthful protagonist.
2. It often employs a point of view which presents the adolescent's interpretation of the events of the story.

3. It is characterized by directness of exposition, dialogue, and direct confrontation between principal characters.

4. It is characterized by such structural conventions as being generally brief, taking place over a limited period of time and in a limited number of locales, having few major characters, and resulting in a change or growth step for the young protagonist.

5. The main characters are highly independent in thought, action, and conflict resolution.

6. The protagonists reap the consequences of their actions and decisions.

7. The authors draw upon their sense of adolescent development and the concomitant attentions to the legitimate concerns of adolescents.

8. Adolescent fiction strives for relevance by attempting to mirror current societal attitudes and issues.

9. The stories most often include gradual, incremental, and ultimately incomplete "growth to awareness" on the part of the central character.

10. The books are hopeful.

If stories are judged according to these criteria rather than by whether or not a specific label has been attached by a publisher, young adult literature is nothing new. It has been around as long as people have been telling stories.

For several reasons, teenagers make good protagonists in popular literature. They are physically attractive, and readers or listeners enjoy identifying with them. They are at a psychological stage in their lives when their emotions are especially intense. And because they are faced with making major decisions about how they will live their lives apart from their parents, there is ample material for developing interesting plots. The result is a myriad of folk and fairy tales, legends, and myths telling about young people setting out on adventures which lead to personal growth, e.g., Dorothy in *The Wizard of Oz,* Joseph in the Old Testament, and Snow White in the folktale.

This common story pattern resembles the formal initiation that some cultures have for making a young person's passage from childhood to adulthood. The young and innocent person is separated from the nurturing love of family and friends. During the separation he or she undergoes a test of courage and stamina that may be either physical, mental, or emotional. After passing the test, the person is reunited with family and friends but in a new role with increased respect.

In spite of the long-standing existence of stories fitting into the literary mold of adolescent or young adult literature, formal recognition of such stories as being particularly appropriate or being specifically prepared for teenage readers is relatively recent. It coincides with the development of adolescence itself as a unique period of one's life. Puberty is universal but adolescence is not. This period between childhood and adulthood has been created by industrialization and the complexities of modern life. Before the Civil War in the United States and even today in some nontechnological societies, the change from childhood to adulthood occurred fairly rapidly. Children were considered adults as soon as they could begin contributing to the economic well-being of the family. But today the careers that many young people aspire to require such high-level skills that they are likely to be in training long past their teenage years. This lengthening of time before one is considered a full-fledged adult has brought many changes to society, but this discussion focuses on only one such change—the creation and marketing of books specifically for readers caught between being children and adults.

HISTORIC OUTLINE

In the 1986 May Hill Arbuthnot lecture, English critic and novelist Aidan Chambers said,

The family of literature for young readers has its own parentage to live out. It was born of a humble, well-intentioned mother named Simple Didactics, and sired by a cunning but aggressive father called Cheap Commerce. Many children of the family inherited the worst of the genes from both sides. Even now, they stick close to home and carry on the business of telling readers what to think in off-the-shelf stories more notable for the craft of their marketing than the skill of their crafting.[1]

Chambers's comment, unhappily but not surprisingly, applies to most adolescent literature, past and present, just as it applies to most popular literature.

Prior to 1800, literature read by adolescents consisted largely of religious novels like John Bunyan's *Pilgrim's Progress* and pietistic tracts like Hannah More's *Repository Tracts*, which warned of the brevity of life and the wrath of God to come. After 1800, adolescent reading remained somber and didactic, but more often it hinted at the possibility of a longer and more satisfying life here on earth. In part, the change came from the decreasing infant mortality. In part, it came from our national expansion and a society which was increasingly urban and less agrarian. Sermons on becoming a better person mixed with heavy doses of the Protestant ethic and lessons on patriotism were common, particularly in the works of the prolific and didactic Samuel Goodrich—who wrote 170 books under the pen name of Peter Parley—and the even more prolific and equally sermonistic Jacob Abbott—who wrote more than 200 books, 28 of them about noble but tiresome Rollo. The title of the 1838 Rollo book, *Rollo at Work, or The Way for a Boy to Learn to Be Industrious,* sounds the tenor of the book, the series, and the time.

The favorite reading of young women in the 1850s through the 1880s was domestic novels. Born out of the belief that humanity was redeemable, the domestic novel preached the glories of suffering, women's submission to men, and a religion of the heart and the Bible, and made several women writers rich. Susan Warner's *The Wide, Wide World* (1850) was both the first domestic novel and the form's prototype. Ellen Montgomery's mother is dead and her father improvident so off she goes to her aunt's home. There she finds a faithful friend, the daughter of the minister, who showers Ellen with pity, piety, and platitudes. Tears flow constantly as Ellen surmounts insurmountable problems, and during those rare moments when Ellen is not weeping, someone is cooking or talking about food. Later domestic novels, particularly the best-selling of them all, Augusta Jane Evans Wilson's *St. Elmo* (1867), added more melodramatic gothic devices like mysterious deaths, disappearing wills, evil men, frightened virgins, and trances, but they maintained the domestic novel's belief in morality, religion, suffering, and the possibility of redemption here on earth.

As girls avidly read domestic novels, boys were equally fascinated by dime novels. When Beadle and Adams published the first dime novel, Ann S. Stephen's *Malaeska: The Indian Wife of the White Hunter* (1860), and the even more successful eighth dime novel later that year, Edward S. Ellis's *Seth Jones,* it assumed the likely audience was men. Some time later, Beadle and Adams recognized the obvious, that the primary audience was boys, and the price was dropped to a nickel. Action-packed dime novels grabbed readers immediately. The lurid cover was followed by a first sentence that announced thrills and chills to come, and readers were rarely disappointed. If the plots were ridiculous and exaggerated, written by hacks who had no idea of the real West, countless boys were hooked on the adventures of Buffalo Bill, Diamond Dick, or Young Wild West. Detective dime novels were no more sensible, but readers followed the wild exploits of Young Sleuth and Nick Carter novel after novel. And boys learned what real heroism on the baseball field was like as they read amazing stories featuring Frank Merriwell and Fred Fearnot. Boys learned through dime novels what adults learned through their reading of the time, that success awaited any person who was willing to fight to get ahead. Family and social position counted for little. Ambition and hard work counted for everything.

Two writers for adolescents stand out in the last half of the nineteenth century. Louisa May Alcott and Horatio Alger both wrote about youngsters moving from childhood to early maturity, but any similarities end there. Alcott wrote about happy families while Alger wrote about broken or unhappy families. Alcott wrote honestly about the problems of growing up. Alger's books were romantic fantasies about life as he wished it might be, for himself and his heroes. Alcott's *Little Women* (1868–69) retains its vitality and joy and popularity today. Other books—*Little Men* (1871), *Eight Cousins* (1875), and *Jo's Boys* (1886)—are inferior to *Little Women,* but they remain in print and are still read. Alger's best book was also his first try at an adolescent novel, *Ragged Dick, or Street Life in New York* (1868). The plot, as in other Alger books, is a series of semiconnected episodes illustrating a boy's first step toward maturity, respectability, and affluence. Typically, Alger is not content to let Dick rise through pluck but adds a fortuitous bit of luck which allows Dick to speed along faster toward success. About 119 books followed, all much the same.

Of the many other writers for adolescents of the time, a few are still readable. Under the pen name of Susan Coolidge, Sarah Chauncey Woolsey wrote a series of books about tomboy Katy which once rivaled Alcott's books in popularity and sales—*What Katy Did* (1873), *What Katy Did at School* (1874), and *What Katy Did Next* (1886). Howard Pyle's *Otto of the Silver Hand* (1888) and *Men of Iron* (1892) are occasionally read. John Meade Falkner's *Moonfleet* (1898) once captivated readers with its tale of smuggling and a cursed diamond. And, of course, Robert Louis Stevenson's *Treasure Island* (1883) and *Kidnapped* (1886) and Mark Twain's *The Adventures of Tom Sawyer* (1876) and *Adventures of Huckleberry Finn* (1884) remain basic adventure reading for adolescents today.

Incredibly popular at the time, almost unbelievably so for most readers today, were several girls' books about terribly brave and noble young women. Martha Finley's *Elsie Dinsmore* (1867) was the first of a long series preaching love and obedience to adults, no matter how little Finley's grownups deserved either. Far worse, and an adult best seller for two consecutive years, was Eleanor Porter's *Pollyanna* (1913), a tiresome tale of a child who delights in playing the "glad game" and saving unfortunates for miles around. Fortunately, two potentially sticky but ultimately refreshing novels were available as antidotes to the sugary Elsie and Pollyanna, Kate Douglas Wiggin's *Rebecca of Sunnybrook Farm* (1903) and L. M. Montgomery's *Anne of Green Gables* (1908).

By the early 1900s, Edward Stratemeyer's Literary Syndicate was both the major producer of adolescent novels and a perpetual irritation to librarians and teachers who wanted the young to read better, more honest, and less melodramatic books. After learning the publishing business by editing a Street and Smith children's magazine and working with Alger and other writers for adolescents, Stratemeyer wrote *Under Dewey at Manila, or, The War Fortunes of a Castaway* (1898), which reached bookstores in time to capitalize on Admiral Dewey's victory. The book, like those that followed, was melodramatic morality with a young boy (or boys) proving his manhood and his equality with—or superiority to—adults. After completing several series for boys, Stratemeyer decided that he was faster at creating plots than in finishing books, so he advertised for writers to develop his plots into books. He then edited the writing to ensure that the book dovetailed with earlier books in a series. His series under many pseudonyms about the wondrous exploits of Baseball Joe, the Rover Boys, the Moving Picture Boys, the Moving Picture Girls, Bomba the Jungle Boy, and more were extremely popular, but his greatest successes came with three series—Tom Swift, the Hardy Boys, and Nancy Drew, the latter two likely to go on forever.

The school/sports novels of Ralph Henry Barbour and William Heyliger were far more honest about real boys, but the success of the form created its own formulas and stereotypes. Beginning with *The Half-Back* (1899), Barbour wrote about boys entering eastern private schools and playing various sports. The books soon became repetitious, but early books like *The Crimson Sweater* (1906) advanced the cause of adolescent literature through honest portraits of real boys with real problems. William Heyliger followed Barbour's formula in his early books, but later novels like *High Benton* (1919) and *High Benton, Worker* (1921) brought school and sports together with the world of work. Girls' school stories were rarely as successful or popular though Marjorie Hill Allee's *Jane's Island* (1931) and *The Great Tradition* (1937) intelligently mixed romance with college life. Even better was Mabel Louise Robinson's *Bright Island* (1937) for its warmth, charm, and delight in describing a loving family on a small island off the Maine coast.

The development of juvenile divisions in many publishing companies and the first use of "junior novels" came in the 1930s. Rose Wilder Lane's *Let the Hurricane Roar* (1933) had first been marketed for adults by Longmans, Green. Late that year, the publishers began to advertise the novel as the first in their series of Junior Books. Their reasoning is obvious. The novel tells of a young married couple and their hard, dangerous, but always loving life on the North Dakota plains. In only a few pages, Lane made readers—old and young—care about two likable young people. By 1937 other publishers had followed suit as John Tunis learned when he submitted a draft of *Iron Duke* (1938) to Harcourt. Tunis was invited to the publisher's office, met a somewhat evasive Mr. Harcourt, and soon was marched out and taken to the head of the juvenile division. Shortly to become *the* sports novelist for adolescents, the bewildered Tunis had no idea what a "juvenile" book was, though it was a term he hated throughout his career.

By the 1940s adolescent literature appeared in almost every major publisher's catalog. More important than mere quantity, the quality rose steadily. The popularity of series books, save the ubiquitous Nancy Drew and the Hardy Boys, fell because of the increasing education and sophistication of adolescents. Much of the material continued to celebrate the wonders and problems of high school years, but other themes appeared. Esther Forbes's *Johnny Tremain* (1943) told of a cocky young silversmith who gets his comeuppance and learns about himself. Social issues, rarely noticed in earlier adolescent literature, were the center of books by two important novelists. Florence Crannell Means's earlier books, *Tangled Waters* (1936) and *Shuttered Windows* (1938), brought minority characters into a field which had almost entirely ignored them, save as servants or menials, but *The*

Moved Outers (1945) was even more powerful. The story of a forced relocation of Japanese-American families after Pearl Harbor shocked readers then and still has bite. John Tunis deeply believed in American democracy, and his tales of corruption in sports, presumably the bastion of fairness and equality, were moral lessons and at the same time exciting accounts of games and heroes. If his inclination toward preaching sometimes made him forget his story, as in *A City for Lincoln* (1945), readers stayed with Tunis because he knew what locker rooms smelled like and he knew the game and its players. *All-American* (1942) is a remarkable football story about racial prejudice, and *Yea! Wildcats!* (1944) and *Go, Team, Go!* (1954) are perceptive novels about the evil and corruption that can arise out of small-town basketball mania.

Romance and love along with a small bit of discreet sex remained popular with girls, and few authors since have done better at portraying that first love of an innocent young girl than Maureen Daly's *Seventeenth Summer* (1942). Mary Stolz's books are still worth reading, particularly *To Tell Your Love* (1950), her first novel and an introspective story of a girl waiting vainly for *that* phone call from *that* boy; *A Love, or a Season* (1964), a story of a love that nearly gets out of hand; and *Pray Love, Remember* (1954), the story of a popular girl who does not like herself and Stolz's most distinguished novel.

Daring as these novels were by 1940s and 1950s standards, they continued the moral strain of earlier adolescent literature, though they were less obviously didactic. Their excellence is surprising given the unwritten but widely known taboos for adolescent literature of the time. Many writers fought the taboos, others (supposedly librarians) supported the taboos, and publishers, happily or not, enforced the taboos on manuscripts aimed at adolescents. These taboos were simple, direct, and negative—no smoking, no drinking, no divorce, no profanity, no suicide, no violence, no pregnancy, no protests about anything significant, no comments on social or racial unrest, no scenes showing young people disagreeing with parents or other authority figures on serious matters, and on and on. In effect, adolescent literature allowed for little reality. Means, Tunis, Daly, Stolz, and a few others may have skirted the edges of the taboos. Others either went along with the taboos or believed in them.

Movies had broken through the sterility of the Hays Office Code, so American writers were writing about serious adult themes without apology, and since paperacks of fine adult books like *The Catcher in the Rye, 1984, Brave New World, Of Mice and Men,* and *A Farewell to Arms* were easily available and much read by adolescents, it is surprising that the taboos endured into the 1960s. Then in 1967–68, several ground-breaking adolescent novels took care of most of the taboos by ignoring them. Ann Head's *Mr. and Mrs. Bo Jo Jones* (1967), in which a young couple *do it* and *have* to get married, seems innocuous now, but it shocked many adults, one of whom announced at a gathering of parents that "this is an evil book because teenagers are too young to learn about pregnancy." Ridiculous as the comment is, it reflects a mental set which held back the growth and honesty of adolescent literature.

Three other novels from 1967–68 are far better literature and still read. Robert Lipsyte's *The Contender* (1967) is a compassionate story of a black ghetto teenager who believes that boxing is his way to a better life. S. E. Hinton's *The Outsiders* (1967) tells of a sensitive young man living on the edge of gang warfare who endures while his friends do not. And Paul Zindel's *The Pigman* (1968) portrays two lonely and alienated youngsters desperately trying to find a reason to hope in a selfish world. All three novels describe a world that adolescent readers recognized as real, not a perfect world nor the world many adults had described, but a real world. Protagonists in all three books used language that shocked some adults but rarely fazed adolescents. Protagonists sought what adolescents really wanted—acceptance, love, honesty—most of all, honesty. And all three books caused problems in communities where adults fought to keep honesty out of adolescent literature.

As more freedom in themes and language was granted by publishers, often grudgingly, to writers for adolescents, the gap between the talented and the hack became wider and more apparent. Good writers produced better and more honest books while poorer writers used the freedom to write books about social problems with a few characters and a bit of plot attached.

Good adolescent literature today does not allow readers to feel comfortable or complacent. It engages readers and forces them to see themselves and other people and the state and nature of humanity a little more perceptively. Good adolescent literature respects its readers, neither condescending nor pandering to the lowest common denominator of taste or intelligence. It gives readers the ultimate satisfaction that things and people are not always right or good but that the book is about honesty and reality.

Four themes dominate adolescent literature today just as they dominate good adult literature.

First, the need of young people to find who and what they are in books as good as Alan Garner's *The Owl Service* (1968), Barbara Wersba's *Run Softly, Go Fast* (1970), Robert Newton Peck's *A Day No Pigs Would Die* (1972), Leon Garfield's *The Sound of Coaches* (1974), Katherine Paterson's *Jacob Have I Loved* (1980), and Monica Hughes's *Hunter in the Dark* (1983).

Second, the need of young people to find something or someone to love in books as good as Isabelle Holland's *The Man without a Face* (1972), Alice Childress's *A Hero Ain't Nothin but a Sandwich* (1973), Norma Foz Mazer's *A Figure of Speech* (1973), Mildred Taylor's *Roll of Thunder, Hear My Cry* (1976), Sue Ellen Bridgers's *Notes for Another Life* (1981), and Todd Strasser's *Friends Till the End* (1981).

Third, the need of young people to search for the truth and fight for what they believe in books as good as James Forman's *Ceremony of Innocence* (1970), Paula Fox's *The Slave Dancer* (1973), Robert Cormier's *The Chocolate War* (1974) and *Beyond the Chocolate War* (1985), Robert Westall's *The Machine Gunners* (1976), Walter Wangerin, Jr.'s *The Book of the Dun Cow* (1978), and Harry Mazer's *The Last Mission* (1979).

Last, the need of young people to laugh at themselves and recognize that the world is sometimes mad in books as amusing as Leon Garfield's *The Strange Affair of Adelaide Harris* (1971), Bruce Clements's *I Tell a Lie Every So Often* (1974), E. Ernesto Bethancourt's *The Dog Days of Arthur Cane* (1976), Benjamin Lee's *It Can't Be Helped* (1979), Judie Angell's *Suds* (1983), and Robert Kaplow's *Alex Icicle: A Romance in Ten Torrid Chapters* (1984).

Robert Cormier is the premier writer for adolescents in the United States, though critics disagree on whether *The Chocolate War* (1974), his first book, is better than *I Am the Cheese* (1977) or *After the First Death* (1979). Other writers highly regarded in America include Sue Ellen Bridgers, Alice Childress, Paula Fox, Robin McKinley, Katherine Paterson, and Mildred Taylor.

In England, the four major writers are Leon Garfield, Alan Garner, Rosemary Sutcliff, and Robert Westall. Other highly respected writers include Aidan Chambers, Peter Dickinson, Jane Gardam, Mollie Hunter, Jan Mark, and Jill Paton Walsh.

REFERENCE WORKS

There is no standard bibliography of adolescent literature. Virginia Haviland's *Children's Literature: A Guide to Reference Sources* is helpful as is Jane Bingham and Grayce Scholt's *Fifteen Centuries of Children's Literature: An Annotated Chronology of British and American Works in Historical Context*. Both works, however, mix children's books and adolescent literature, a problem common to most reference works in the field, and make scholarly work unnecessarily complicated and difficult. The recent and scholarly *Children's Fiction, 1876–1984* inevitably covers any one item so briefly that its usefulness is limited.

Two checklists provide excellent coverage for areas previously difficult to work with. Harry K. Hudson's *A Bibliography of Hard-Cover Boys' Books* is limited in scope, covering only boys' series largely of the first half of the present century, but it is a pioneer in the field. *Girls' Series Books: A Checklist of Hardcover Books Published 1900–1975* is more scholarly, the work of researchers and librarians at the University of Minnesota.

A recent dictionary attempts to cover the entire scope of adolescent and children's books. Alethea K. Helbig and Agnes Regan Perkins's two-volume *Dictionary of American Children's Fiction* contains entries for authors, book titles, and major characters in the most significant novels covering the period from 1859 to 1984 and provides useful details and contemporary criticism.

The major scholarly reference works in adolescent literature are historical. Two general histories of the field, again mixed with children's literature as well, are basic sources for the scholar. Cornelia Meigs, Anne Thaxter Eaton, Elizabeth Nesbit, and Ruth Hill Viguers's *A Critical History of Children's Literature* is long and occasionally ponderous. Far more readable, if sometimes slanted more toward British than American material, is John Rowe Townsend's *Written for Children: An Outline of English-Language Children's Literature*. Townsend's perceptive and succinct criticism and his ability as a novelist make his work both scholarly and entertaining. Three chapters (13–15) in Alleen Pace Nilsen and Kenneth L. Donelson's *Literature for Today's Young Adults* attempt to cover the history of adolescent literature, unmixed with children's books, from 1800 to today. Two brief booklets, neither likely to be easily found, are most satisfying British accounts of the history of adolescent/children's literature. Christine A. Kloet's *After Alice: A Hundred Years of Children's Reading in Britain* was prepared for an exhibition to celebrate the centenary of the British Library Association. Even better is John Rowe Townsend's *25 Years of British Children's Books,* a sixty-page annotated list of books, alphabetized by authors Townsend considered most important in the field.

Less significant histories are Elva S. Smith's *The History of Children's Literature,* though a ground-breaker when it appeared in 1937, and Mary F. Thwaite's *From Primer to Pleasure in Reading: An Introduction to the History of Children's Books in England from the Invention of Printing to 1914 with an Outline of Some Developments in Other Countries.*

Scholars seeking information about adolescent literature in America prior to 1900 have several fine books to consult. William Sloane's *Children's Books in England and America in the Seventeenth Century* is a standard source, always scholarly and accurate. Bernard Wishy's *The Child and the Republic: The Dawning of Modern American Child Nurture* is obviously more concerned with children than adolescents, but it is a book no scholar working in early adolescent literature can afford to ignore. A.S.W. Rosenbach's *Early American Children's Books* is precisely what the title suggests, children's books, but Rosenbach's pioneer work in a hitherto largely ignored field and his fascination with his material are contagious. Also scholarly and equally enthusiastic is Jacob Blanck's *Peter Parley to Penrod: A Bibliographical Description of the Best-Loved American Juvenile Books.*

Scholars working with nineteenth-century children's and adolescent books must consult two basic tools. Monica Kiefer's *American Children through Their Books, 1700–1835* and Anne Scott MacLeod's *A Moral Tale: Children's Fiction and American Culture, 1820–60.* Raymond L. Kilgour's *Lee and Shepard: Publishers for the People* is more limited in interest, but since this publisher mined adolescent literature, scholars should know of Kilgour's work. Richard L. Darling's *The Rise of Children's Book Reviewing in America, 1865–1881* is superb and illustrates the kind of historic research that remains to be done in the field. Esther Jane Carrier's *Fiction in Public Libraries, 1876–1900* is mainly devoted to adult literature, but the material on adolescent literature and the problems it caused is worth consulting.

Almost any history of the American novel would touch on the domestic novel, but two histories are especially good, Herbert Ross Brown's *The Sentimental Novel in America, 1789–1860* and Fred Lewis Pattee's *The Feminist Fifties*. The most enjoyable source is Helen Waite Papashvily's *All the Happy Endings: A Study of the Domestic Novel in America, the Women Who Wrote It, the Women Who Read It, in the Nineteenth Century*.

The standard source on the dime novel is Albert Johannsen's three-volume *The House of Beadle and Adams and Its Dime and Nickel Novels: The Story of a Vanished Literature*. Daryl Jones's *The Dime Novel Western* is broader in scope and better written. Henry Nash Smith's *Virgin Land: The American West as Symbol and Myth* is basic for any study of the Western novel or the dime novel. Chapter 8, "The Dime Novel Tradition," in Russel Nye's *The Unembarrassed Muse: The Popular Arts in America*, is an excellent and brief introduction to the dime novel.

Of the many biographies of Louisa May Alcott, Madeleine Stern's *Louisa May Alcott* is both sensible and well written though some critics have argued for Martha Saxton's *Louisa May: A Modern Biography of Louisa May Alcott*. While dated, Ednah D. Cheney's edition of *Louisa May Alcott: Her Life, Letters and Journals* is still helpful. Alma J. Payne's "Louisa May Alcott (1832–1888)" in *American Literary Realism, 1870–1910* is a model of bibliographical information.

Most of the material on Horatio Alger is dubious or worse. Gary Scharnhorst's *Horatio Alger, Jr.* for the Twayne United States Authors Series corrects a mass of historic misinformation. Scharnhorst and Jack Bales's *Horatio Alger, Jr.: An Annotated Bibliography of Comment and Criticism* is essential in an area that has been largely chaotic.

Of the writings on Edward Stratemeyer's Literary Syndicate, Deidre Johnson's *Stratemeyer Pseudonyms and Series Books: An Annotated Checklist of Stratemeyer and Stratemeyer Literary Syndicate Publications* serves as a sound introduction, suggesting some of the intricacies of working through problems in popular culture. Bobbie Ann Mason's *The Girl Sleuth: A Feminist Guide* is a delightful way of looking at Nancy Drew (and others) through a particular literary eyeglass. And Leslie McFarlane's *Ghost of the Hardy Boys: An Autobiography of Leslie McFarlane* is a chatty history of his relationship with the syndicate.

Although their work mixes children's and adolescent literature, English historians and critics have provided us with a number of helpful books. E.J.H. Darton's *Children's Books in England: Five Centuries of Social Life* is standard if a bit stuffy. Alec Ellis's *A History of Children's Reading and*

Literature and Roger L. Green's *Tellers of Tales: British Authors of Children's Books from 1800 to 1964* are standard if unexciting. More stimulating and psychologically perceptive about young people and their books are Frank Eyre's *British Children's Books in the Twentieth Century* and Marcus Crouch's *Treasure Seekers and Borrowers: Children's Books in Britain, 1900–1960* and *The Nesbit Tradition: The Children's Novel in England, 1945–1970*.

Two works deserve particular attention in an area that is sometimes stuffy if not downright boring. Gillian Avery's *Childhood's Pattern: A Study of the Heroes and Heroines of Children's Fiction 1700–1950* is wise and witty, and Mary Cadogan and Patricia Craig's *You're a Brick, Angela! A New Look at Girls' Fiction from 1839 to 1975* is as delightful and thoughtful as the title suggests.

Edward Salmon's *Juvenile Literature as It Is* was published in 1888, long before adolescent literature (or children's literature, for that matter) was considered a respectable or wholesome enterprise for a grown-up. Salmon's book is a delight no matter what the age of the book, and anyone curious about the field misses a necessary and fascinating book if Salmon is ignored.

Canadian adolescent literature is covered brilliantly in Sheila Egoff's *The Problem of Childhood: A Critical Guide to Canadian Children's Literature in English*. Scholars seeking the standard coverage of European adolescent literature will find much that is helpful in Bettina Hurlimann's *Three Centuries of Children's Books in Europe*.

Biographical information is readily accessible. Anne Commire's *Something about the Author*, a multivolume work, is standard and valuable, if sometimes little more than chatty. Far more detailed, although in its early multivolume stage, is Adele Sarkissian's *Something about the Author: Autobiography Series*, which devotes more pages to each author. D. L. Kirkpatrick's *Twentieth-Century Children's Writers* is a model of the one-volume biographical tool, comprehensive yet allowing authors of individual entries to condense the biographies and include some brief but often pointed criticism.

Less valuable biographical data can be found in Brian Doyle's *The Who's Who of Children's Literature*, Stanley J. Kunitz and Howard Haycraft's *The Junior Book of Authors*, Muriel Fuller's *More Junior Authors*, and Doris DeMontreville and Donna Hill's *Third Book of Junior Authors*.

Of the several collections of interviews with authors of adolescent books, the best are Justin Winkle and Emma Fisher's *The Pied Pipers: Interviews with the Influential Creators of Children's Literature* and M. Jerry Weiss's *From Writers to Students: The Pleasures and Pains of Writing*.

Biographical data along with critical assessment of nineteenth-century writers for adolescents can be found in Glenn E. Estes's *American Writers for Children before 1900*. Later writers are treated in John Cech's *American Writers for Children, 1900–1960*. The multivolume *Children's Literature Review* is the standard source for criticism of adolescent literature.

Booklists are a commonplace in various journals concerned with adolescent books. Standard book-length lists include G. Robert Carlsen's *Books and the Teenage Reader; Books for You,* published by the National Council of Teachers of English approximately every five years for high school students and teachers; and *Your Reading,* from the same source and at approximately the same interval, for junior high students and teachers. Barbara Dodds Stanford and Karima Amin's *Black Literature for High School Students* and Anna Lee Stensland's *Literature by and about the American Indian, An Annotated Bibliography* are basic specialized lists.

RESEARCH COLLECTIONS

Irvin Kerlan, a Washington, D.C., doctor who had graduated from the University of Minnesota medical school, collected rare books including Caldecott Medal winners. Eventually his interest included the process of bookmaking, and he collected editorial correspondence as well as various stages of manuscripts and illustrations. In 1949, he began donating material to the University of Minnesota library. When he died in 1963, his collection went to the library to form the base of the Kerlan Collection, *the* leading research center for children's books in the United States. A catalog of holdings printed in 1985 is available for $30 from the Children's Literature Research Collection, 109 Walter Library, University of Minnesota, Minneapolis, MN 55455.

Although Kerlan's initial interest was in children's books, the collection has since been expanded to include literature for teenagers. All material is available for use in the Kerlan Collection Reading Room. Among the manuscripts are Judy Blume's *Are You There God? It's Me Margaret* (1970), Lois Duncan's *Stranger with My Face* (1981), Bette Greene's *Summer of My German Soldier* (1973), Felice Holman's *Slake's Limbo* (1974), M. E. Kerr's *Dinky Hocker Shoots Smack* (1972), Robert Lipsyte's *The Contender* (1967), Robert C. O'Brien's *Z for Zachariah* (1975), and Katherine Paterson's *Jacob Have I Loved* (1980).

The second largest collection is the Lena Y. deGrummond Collection at the University of Southern Mississippi in Hattiesburg. Lena deGrummond was the supervisor of school libraries in Louisiana. Upon her retirement in 1965, she joined the faculty of the Library School at Hattiesburg and soon began asking authors for their manuscripts and correspondence. The response surprised even deGrummond, and, according to curator John Kelly, the collection now contains 27,000 items from over 1,000, authors, editors, and illustrators. Ninety percent of the collection is children's books, but in the other 10 percent is manuscripts from such young adult writers as Madeleine L'Engle, Isabelle Holland, Richard Peck, and Ouida Sebestyen. Researchers are welcome to work with the materials.

During the late 1960s and 1970s, the University of Oregon under the leadership of librarian Ed Kemp searched for books, manuscripts, correspondence, and illustrations. Most of the material concerns children's books, but there are six shelf-feet of papers from young adult author Hila Colman and fifteen from nonfiction writer Milton Meltzer. Maureen Daly's papers are in the collection, dating from 1938 to 1973.

A different kind of collection is one devoted to a few authors or to a single author, for example, the collection of Robert Cormier's published and unpublished manuscripts, correspondence, taped speeches, and newspaper columns at Fitchburg State College in Massachusetts. Wheaton College in Illinois has fifty-seven volumes of Madeleine L'Engle manuscripts dating from childhood through 1978. Boston University has eighty-eight manuscript boxes of material from John Tunis. The University of Louisville has over 6,000 items related to Edgar Rice Burroughs and the Tarzan series. Iowa writers Jeannette Eyerly and Henry Gregor Felsen donated their papers to the University of Iowa Library.

Authors whose work was published for a general audience but found a special place with teenage readers include Jack London, the focus of 395 volumes in the Oakland Public Library, and Harriet Beecher Stowe, whose papers are preserved at the Stowe-Day Foundation in Hartford, Connecticut. Mark Twain is featured in eleven different libraries, notably the University of California at Berkeley for general information and the Buffalo and Erie County Public Library for items on *Huckleberry Finn*. Robert Louis Stevenson is the subject of collections at the University of California in Los Angeles, Yale University, and the University of Texas at Austin. The Silverado Museum in St. Helena, California, has 7,000 items related to Stevenson.

Many libraries have extensive historical collections of materials on authors who purposely set out to win young adults as readers in the 1800s. Seven libraries have collections of Louisa May Alcott papers including Harvard University, the Library of Congress, and the Orchard House Museum in Concord, Massachusetts. Twelve libraries have Horatio Alger collections, the largest being the Library of Congress; the others include the Free Library of Philadelphia, Northern Illinois University of Dekalb, the University of Southern Mississippi in Hattiesburg, and Ohio University in Athens.

Other historical collections are organized by type of material rather than by individual authors. The largest such collections contain dime novels, and probably the largest of the dime novel collections is one named for collector George H. Hess, Jr., who in 1954 donated 75,000 items to the University of Minnesota Library. Besides dime novels, the Hess collection contains story papers, pulps, periodicals, and boys' and girls' series books. More fragile items have recently been microfilmed, but most materials are available for researchers. Other libraries with extensive collections of dime novels include the University of Arkansas in Fayetteville, San Diego Public, Northern Illinois University in DeKalb, Brandeis University, and Michigan State Library.

Libraries with collections of serialized stories for young readers include Bowdoin College in Brunswick, Maine, with the Rollo books of Jacob Abbott, the New Hampshire State Library in Concord with the Tom Swift books, Dartmouth College with books by Horatio Alger, the Donnell Center of the New York Public Library with books by Abbott and Alger, and Indiana University with Susan Coolidge's *Katy* books, and the Public Library of Cincinnati and Hamilton County with a complete 245-volume set of the Frank and Dick Merriwell sports stories. Northern Illinois University in DeKalb has complete runs of *Beadle's Monthly, Beadle's Weekly, Saturday Journal,* and the *Young New Yorker,* while the American Antiquarian Society in Worcester, Massachusetts, has an extensive collection of periodicals published between 1700 and 1876 including *Parley's Magazine* and *Youth's Companion.*

For scholars of young adult literature, working in research collections is often depressing because the books for teens are Johnny-come-latelies and sometimes treated like poor relations. As one curator reported, "Of course I keep track of [scholarship dealing with] children's literature first and foremost, but we do try to be watchful and in fact have a clipping folder of articles on YA lit."

The prime reason that young adult literature takes a backseat to children's books in most research collections is simply that it is relatively new. It does not have traditions such as the Newbery and Caldecott medals, nor are young adult books illustrated. Many research collections were originally based on someone's interest in gathering illustrations and then the accompanying manuscripts.

Ironically, just as manuscripts for young adult books are beginning to be sought by collectors, the word processor has changed the way authors write. Ann Seymour, library assistant at the Kerlan Collection, said that changes are already evident. They have received a few "perfect" manuscripts fresh off a word processor. Other authors have sent in an early and a late word-processed copy so that a careful reader can compare changes made but not nearly as easily as with the old typed copies filled with authors' penciled changes.

HISTORY AND CRITICISM

The criticism of adolescent literature falls mainly into four types: historical, pedagogical or promotional, social, and literary. The critic who writes from a historical viewpoint analyzes books of a certain period or compares books from one period with books from another or shows how the books of a particular period reflect the culture of that period. Many of the outstanding books of this type are mentioned above under Reference Works.

Pedagogical criticism is written from the viewpoint of educators, mainly librarians and teachers of reading or English who want to encourage young people to read. The Russian launching of Sputnik in 1957 jarred Americans into taking a new look at the way their children were educated. One result was the National Defense Education Act, which in the 1960s and 1970s provided financial support for school libraries. Publishers responded by printing large numbers of books designed to entice both children and teenagers into extensive leisure-time reading. The public was supportive, as shown by the popularity of two books written to help adults bring books and teenagers together. Daniel Fader's 1966 *Hooked on Books* recounted his successful experiment introducing large quantities of paperback books to boys in a training school in Michigan. G. Robert Carlsen's *Books and the Teenage Reader* went through seven Bantam printings between its publication in April 1967 and a revised edition in December 1971. Fader's and Carlsen's philosophies had a common belief, that if a knowledgeable adult will get the right book to the right student, something almost magical will happen as young people take steps toward becoming lifelong readers.

Many educators are less enthusiastic than Fader or Carlsen but nevertheless accept the idea that if students enjoy what they are reading, they will read more and consequently develop into better readers. Critics who serve as defenders of using adolescent literature in the schools say that when compared to what has been traditionally assigned for class reading, the best young adult literature is more appealing because of its contemporary settings, plots, and diction. Comfortable readers become emotionally involved with interesting characters of their own age. Of course, teachers and librarians do not intend to limit young people to adolescent novels but rather to use adolescent literature as a bridge to more complex, adult literature.

The first of several college textbooks introducing teachers to the genre was Dwight L. Burton's 1970 *Literature Study in the High Schools*. A collection of articles edited by Richard A. Meade and Robert C. Small, Jr., *Literature for Adolescents: Selection and Use,* was published in 1973. Later textbooks for college classes of potential or in-service teachers included Sheila Schwartz's *Teaching Adolescent Literature: A Humanistic Approach* published in 1979, the Nilsen and Donelson text mentioned earlier and first published in 1980, Ruth Cline and William McBride's *A Guide to Literature for Young Adults: Background, Selection, and Use* in 1983, and Arthea J. S. Reed's *Reaching Adolescents: The Young Adult Book and the School* in 1985.

The interest of English teachers, who for the most part had snubbed the "junior novel," is reflected in the founding of ALAN (Assembly on Literature for Adolescents) by a small group of teachers who in 1973 gathered as part of the National Council of Teachers of English (NCTE) annual conference. ALAN now has approximately 2,000 members, holds an annual

November two-day workshop attended by 400 people, and three times a year publishes a journal. The *ALAN Review* has articles by and about young adult authors as well as reviews of dozens of recently published books. Another indication of the interest of English teachers in young adult books is the inclusion on a regular basis of reviews as well as frequent articles on them in the *English Journal*.

Several NCTE state affiliates have published special issues of their journals devoted to adolescent literature including the *Arizona English Bulletin* in April 1972 and April 1976, the Southeastern Ohio Council's *Focus* in Winter 1977, the *Iowa English Bulletin* in Spring 1980, the *Connecticut English Journal* in Fall 1980, and *English in Texas* in Winter 1981.

Teachers of reading also began taking a more serious look at adolescent literature because with falling reading scores, many high schools created reading classes, not just for remedial students but for everyone. Elective courses such as individualized reading, science fiction, and black (or women's or Hispanic or Indian, etc.) studies forced teachers to search for new books that students would like. The International Reading Association's *Journal of Reading* began a regular review column of young adult books.

During this same period, more libraries opened young adult rooms or sections and membership climbed in the Young Adult Services Division of the American Library Association. Its annual list of Best Books increased in length, and as the quality of books coming from juvenile divisions of publishing houses increased, more titles were included on the annual list. *Booklist, Wilson Library Bulletin, Top of the News,* and *School Library Journal* gave more attention to young adult books. Margaret A. Edwards's 1969 classic, *The Fair Garden and the Swarm of Beasts,* a how-to for young adult librarians wanting to encourage reading, was reissued in an expanded 1974 version. In 1978 librarian Jana Varlejs edited *Young Adult Literature in the Seventies: A Selection of Readings,* and in 1980 the American Library Association published *Young Adult Literature: Background and Criticism,* edited by Millicent Lentz and Ramona M. Mahood. In the same year, the H. W. Wilson company published Joni Bodart's *Booktalk! Booktalking and School Visiting for Young Adult Audiences.*

The enthusiasm of librarians and teachers was shared by publishers and by producers of television and movies, who in a youth-oriented society were looking for relatively simple stories that could be dramatized within the time limitations of television. Many books written for teenagers became either films or television programs. Librarians, teachers, and publishers capitalized on the interest through media-related paperbacks, which could be used in promotional efforts.

Even though the primary goal of most of the people described above was to promote reading, evaluation was still a part of the matter as they tried to decide which books to promote. A popular form of research was to conduct reading preference surveys among young people to find which books they enjoyed the most. These could then be recommended for purchase by other schools and libraries. The best known is the University of Iowa Book Poll founded by G. Robert Carlsen in 1971. Research assistants take new books out to area high schools where students read then and have conferences about them with the researchers. Results from this poll have been published in the *English Journal* every December or January since 1973.

A goal quite different from that of matching "the right book with the right reader" to increase pleasure and promote widespread reading is that of using books to influence readers to whatever social beliefs and behaviors the critic thinks are desirable. The social consciousness that rose out of the turmoil of the 1960s found its way into the criticism of young adult literature as did the backward swing of the pendulum in the 1980s. The result has been tremendous variety both in the types of groups and individuals involved in social criticism and in the recommendations they make.

During the 1980s, scholarly, religious, civic, and political organizations have all been involved in criticizing particular young adult books. None admit to being censors, yet all have protested certain titles because of the social messages that the books carried. Critics have presented well-prepared cases against the stereotyping of parents in teenage books, the glorification of violence for young men, the demeaning portrayals of minorities, the absence of good books about handicapped people, and most recently the unrealistic expectations promoted by popular romance novels.

By far the most influential and well known of several groups criticizing from a social issues viewpoint is the Council on Interracial Books for Children (CIBC), founded in the mid–1960s. The CIBC believes that books should "become a tool for the conscious promotion of human values that lead to greater human liberation." Its checklist for evaluation includes such categories as racism, sexism, elitism, materialism, ageism, cultural authenticity, and positive vs. negative images of females and minorities. Reviews and articles in its *Interracial Books for Children Bulletin* focus on such matters. As might be expected, their reviews are often controversial, for example, this sentence in a review of Lawrence Yep's *Dragonwings* (1975): "The book, though highly recommended, does have a weakness. While oppression and racism are well described, blame is not placed squarely on the economic system which then, as now, used non-whites for maximum profit."

Books by individuals writing from a social issues viewpoint include Dorothy Broderick's 1973 *Images of the Black in Children's Fiction*, Bob Dixon's 1977 *Catching Them Young: Political Ideas in Children's Fiction* and *Catching Them Young: Sex, Race and Class in Children's Fiction*, Donnarae MacCann and Gloria Woodward's 1972 *The Black American in Books for Children: Readings on Racism*, and Masha Kabakow Rudman's 1976 *Children's Literature: An Issues Approach*. Most social issues critics take a positive approach by recommending books whose messages they like. For example, the American Council on Education and the National Council of Teachers of English have for decades jointly sponsored the publication of *Reading Ladders for Human Relations,* a 400-page book edited by Eileen Tway now in its sixth edition. Its goal is "to advance the cause of better human relations." The method it espouses is reading and discussing books—both children's and young adult—under such ladders as "Interacting in Groups," "Appreciating Different Cultures," and "Coping in a Changing World."

Voice of Youth Advocates (*VOYA*) was founded in 1978 by Dorothy M. Broderick and Mary K. Chelton to change the traditional linking of young adult services from children's to adult sections of libraries. As part of its anticensorship stand, *VOYA* reviews and promotes the use of books dealing with all kinds of previously taboo topics.

An extensive body of literature has grown up around the problem of censorship of books for young readers, for example, *Censors in the Classroom: The Mind Benders,* by Edward B. Jenkinson; *Limiting What Students Shall Read,* published jointly by the Association of American Publishers, the American Library Association, and the Association for Supervision and Curriculum Development; and the NCTE publications *The Students' Right to Read*; *The Students' Right to Know,* by Lee Burress and Edward B. Jenkinson; and *Dealing with Censorship,* edited by James E. Davis.

A quite different approach to young adult books is that of literary criticism similar to that applied to the best adult books. This criticism is about the books themselves and the relationships between the authors and what they have written, patterns that appear, techniques that authors use, and themes and underlying issues. Two pioneer dissertations exemplifying this kind of criticism were A. Stephen Dunning's "A Definition of the Role of the Junior Novel Based on Analyses of Thirty Selected Novels," completed in 1959, and Dorothy J. Petitt's "A Study of the Qualities of Literary Excellence Which Characterize Selected Fiction for Younger Adolescents," completed in 1961.

In looking for books of literary criticism one meets the same problem as in the research collections. Most critics have mixed children's and young adult books, so it takes a knowledge of the latter to pick out what is applicable. In 1975, Glenna Davis Sloan applied Northrop Frye's critical theories to children's and adolescent literature in *The Child as Critic.* A year later Rebecca Lukens wrote *A Critical Handbook of Children's Literature.* Most of her examples came from children's literature, but the literary principles she discusses are equally applicable to young adult books.

Sheila Egoff's 1981 *Thursday's Child: Trends and Patterns in Contemporary Children's Literature* proves that an intelligent critic can find plenty of intellectual meat in contemporary books for young readers. Betsy Hearne and Marilyn Kaye's 1981 *Celebrating Children's Books: Essays on Children's Literature in Honor of Zena Sutherland* does the same with papers by young adult writers Lloyd Alexander, Robert Cormier, Virginia

Hamilton, John Donovan, John Rowe Townsend, and David Macaulay. *The Arbuthnot Lectures*, edited by Zena Sutherland, is a similar collection featuring talks by John Rowe Townsend, Ivan Southall, Jean Fritz, and Sheila Egoff.

More such criticism of young adult literature is being done as the authors write books serious enough to support it. For example, the Twayne literary criticism series published by G. K. Hall recently expanded to include young adult authors. The first two volumes by Patricia J. Campbell and Alleen Pace Nilsen published in 1985 and 1986 proved that the books of Robert Cormier and M. E. Kerr are worthy of full-length analyses. Other good examples of literary criticism are David Rees's 1980 *The Marble in the Water: Essays on Contemporary Writers of Fiction for Children and Young Adults* and his 1984 *Painted Desert, Green Shade: Essays on Contemporary Writers of Fiction for Children and Young Adults,* John Rowe Townsend's 1979 *A Sounding of Storytellers: Essays on Contemporary Writers for Children,* Aidan Chambers's 1985 *Booktalk: Occasional Writing on Literature and Children,* and the 1976 collection of articles from *Children's Literature in Education* entitled *Writers, Critics, and Children,* edited by Geoff Fox et al.

One of the newest examples of literary criticism and a good one on which to end this discussion is Robert E. Probst's 1984 *Adolescent Literature: Response and Analysis*. He uses teenage books as the focus for outstanding discussions of reader response and literary analysis.

COLLECTIONS AND REPRINTS

Most major libraries have current, or near-current, adolescent books in their holdings, and many have a sprinkling of older adolescent books in their rare book or special collections.

The best early adolescent literature—Alcott's *Little Women* (1868), Twain's *The Adventures of Tom Sawyer* (1876) and *Adventures of Huckleberry Finn* (1864), and Stevenson's *Treasure Island* (1883) and *Kidnapped* (1876)—have continuously been in print since publication. Wiggin's *Rebecca of Sunnybrook Farm* (1903) and Montgomery's *Anne of Green Gables* (1908) have frequently been reprinted and are currently available in inexpensive paperback, the first from Dell and the latter from Bantam. Alger's *Ragged Dick* has been reprinted in *Struggling Upward and Other Works* (1940).

Collections of dime novels are not difficult to find. The Hess Collection is unquestionably the standard source for scholars. Austin J. McLean's "The Hess Collection of Dime Novels" in the *American Book Collector* serves as a good introduction to the holdings.

Recently, two publishers have reprinted several dime novel libraries. Garland Publishing reprinted ten volumes (the complete run) of the Frank

Reade Library. University Microfilms International has published a collection of 3,000 dime novels, mostly Westerns.

For a number of years, Charles Bragin published reprints of dime novels. Many of these can still be found. The *Dime Novel Roundup* (Edward LeBlanc, 87 School St., Fall River, MA 02720), a chatty magazine for dime novel enthusiasts that often contains invaluable information, carries advertisements for dime novels in nearly every issue.

The best of the several single-volume dime novel collections is *Eight Dime Novels*—with a Nick Carter, a Buffalo Bill, a Frank Merriwell, and an Alger—with an admirable introduction by E. F. Bleiler.

The sole attempt to reprint a large library of older books is Garland Publishing's Classics of Children's Literature, 1621–1932. Fine as the selection is by Alison Lurie and Justin G. Schiller, the 117 titles are mostly children's books. And the few adolescent titles are, with the exception of Goodrich's *Tales of Peter Parley about America* and Helen Hunt Jackson's *Nelly's Silver Mine,* relatively easy to find in second-hand bookstores.

NOTE

1. "All of a Tremble to See His Danger," *Top of the News,* 42 (Summer 1986), 415.

BIBLIOGRAPHY

Books and Articles

"Adolescent Literature." *English in Texas,* 13 (Winter 1981), Special issue.
"Adolescent Literature, Adolescent Reading and the English Class." *Arizona English Bulletin,* 14 (April 1972), Special issue.
"Adolescent Literature: Dimensions and Directions." *Iowa English Bulletin,* 29 (Spring 1980), Special issue.
"Adolescent Literature Revisited after Four years." *Arizona English Bulletin,* 18 (April 1976), Special issue.
Avery, Gillian. *Childhood's Pattern: A Study of the Heroes and Heroines of Children's Fiction 1700–1950.* London: Hodder and Stoughton, 1975.
Bingham, Jane, and Grayce Scholt. *Fifteen Centuries of Children's Literature: An Annotated Chronology of British and American Works in Historical Context.* Westport, Conn.: Greenwood Press, 1980.
Blanck, Jacob. *Peter Parley to Penrod: A Bibliographical Description of the Best-Loved American Juvenile Books.* New York: R. R. Bowker, 1956.
Bleiler, E. F., ed. *Eight Dime Novels.* New York: Dover, 1974.
Bodart, Joni. *Booktalk! Booktalking and School Visiting for Young Adult Audiences.* New York: H. W. Wilson, 1980.
Broderick, Dorothy M. *Images of the Black in Children's Fiction.* New York: R. R. Bowker, 1973.

Brown, Herbert Ross. *The Sentimental Novel in America, 1789–1860*. Durham, N.C.: Duke University Press, 1940.

Burress, Lee, and Edward B. Jenkinson. *The Students' Right to Know*. Urbana, Ill.: National Council of Teachers of English, 1982.

Burton, Dwight L. *Literature Study in the High Schools*. New York: Holt, 1970.

Cadogan, Mary, and Patricia Craig. *You're a Brick, Angela! A New Look at Girls' Fiction from 1839 to 1975*. London: Victor Gollancz, 1976.

Campbell, Patricia J. *Presenting Robert Cormier*. Boston: Twayne, 1985.

Carlsen, G. Robert. *Books and the Teenage Reader*. 2d rev. ed. New York: Harper and Row, 1980.

Carrier, Esther Jane. *Fiction in Public Libraries, 1876–1900*. Metuchen, N.J.: Scarecrow Press, 1965.

Cech, John, ed. *American Writers for Children, 1900–1960. Dictionary of Literary Biography*, vol. 22. Detroit: Gale Research, 1983.

Chambers, Aidan. *Booktalk: Occasional Writing on Literature and Children*. New York: Harper and Row, 1985.

Cheney, Ednah D., ed. *Louisa May Alcott: Her Life, Letters and Journals*. Boston: Little, Brown, 1901.

Children's Fiction, 1876–1984. 2 vols. New York: R. R. Bowker, 1984.

Children's Literature Review. Detroit: Gale Research, 1976-.

Christiansen, Jane, ed. *Your Reading: A Booklist for Junior High and Middle School Students*. Urbana, Ill.: National Council of Teachers of English, 1983.

Cline, Ruth, and William McBride. *A Guide to Literature for Young Adults: Background, Selection, and Use*. Glenview, Ill.: Scott, Foresman, 1983.

Commire, Anne, ed. *Something about the Author*. Detroit: Gale Research, 1971-.

Council on Interracial Books for Children. *Human (and Anti-Human) Values in Children's Books*. New York: CIBC, 1976.

Crouch, Marcus. *The Nesbit Tradition: The Children's Novel in England, 1945–1970*. London: Ernest Benn, 1972.

————. *Treasure Seekers and Borrowers: Children's Books in Britain, 1900–1960*. London: Library Association, 1962.

Darling, Richard L. *The Rise of Children's Book Reviewing in America, 1865–1881*. New York: R. R. Bowker, 1968.

Darton, E.J.H. *Children's Books in England: Five Centuries of Social Life*. 2d ed. Cambridge: Cambridge University Press, 1958.

Davis, James E., ed. *Dealing with Censorship*. Urbana, Ill.: National Council of Teachers of English, 1979.

DeMontreville, Doris, and Donna Hill, eds. *Third Book of Junior Authors*. New York: H. W. Wilson, 1963.

Dixon, Bob. *Catching Them Young: Political Ideas in Children's Fiction*. London: Pluto Press, 1977.

————. *Catching Them Young: Sex, Race and Class in Children's Fiction*. London: Pluto Press, 1977.

Doyle, Brian. *The Who's Who of Children's Literature*. New York: Schocken, 1968.

Dunning, A. Stephen. "A Definition of the Role of the Junior Novel Based on Analyses of Thirty Selected Novels." Ph.D. dissertation, Florida State University, 1959.

Edwards, Margaret A. *The Fair Garden and the Swarm of Beasts: The Library and the Young Adult.* Rev. ed. New York: Hawthorn, 1974.

Egoff, Sheila. *The Problem of Childhood: A Critical Guide to Canadian Children's Literature in English.* Toronto: Oxford University Press, 1967.

————. *Thursday's Child: Trends and Patterns in Contemporary Children's Literature.* Chicago: American Library Association, 1981.

Ellis, Alec. *A History of Children's Reading and Literature.* New York: Pergamon Press, 1968.

Estes, Glenn E., ed. *American Writers for Children before 1900. Dictionary of Literary Biography,* vol. 42. Detroit: Gale Research, 1985.

Eyre, Frank. *British Children's Books in the Twentieth Century.* New York: E. P. Dutton, 1971.

Fader, Daniel. *Hooked on Books.* New York: Berkley, 1966.

"Fiction for Adolescents." *Focus* (Ohio), 3 (Winter 1977), special issue.

Fox, Geoff, Graham Hammond, Terry Jones, Frederic Smith, and Kenneth Sterck, eds. *Writers, Critics, and Children.* New York: Agathon Press, 1976.

Fuller, Muriel, ed. *More Junior Authors.* New York: H. W. Wilson, 1963.

Gallo, Donald R., ed. *Books for You: A Booklist for Senior High School Students.* Urbana, Ill.: National Council of Teachers of English, 1985.

Girls' Series Books: A Checklist of Hardcover Books Published 1900–1975. Minneapolis: Children's Literature Research Collection, University of Minnesota Library, 1978.

Green, Roger L. *Tellers of Tales: British Authors of Children's Books from 1800 to 1964.* Rev. ed. New York: Franklin Watts, 1965.

Haviland, Virginia, ed. *Children's Literature: A Guide to Reference Sources.* Washington, D.C.: Library of Congress, 1966.

Hearne, Betsy, and Marilyn Kaye, eds. *Celebrating Children's Books: Essays on Children's Literature in Honor of Zena Sutherland.* New York: Lothrop, Lee and Shepard, 1981.

Helbig, Alethea K., and Agnes Regan Perkins. *Dictionary of American Children's Fiction, 1960–1984.* Westport, Conn.: Greenwood Press, 1986.

————. *Dictionary of American Children's Fiction, 1859–1959.* Westport, Conn.: Greenwood Press, 1985.

Hudson, Henry K. *A Bibliography of Hard-Cover Boys' Books.* Rev. ed. Tampa, Fla.: Data Print, 1977.

Hurlimann, Bettina. *Three Centuries of Children's Books in Europe.* Translated and edited by Brian W. Alderson. Cleveland, Ohio: World, 1968.

Jenkinson, Edward B. *Censors in the Classroom: The Mind Benders.* Carbondale: Southern Illinois University Press, 1979.

Johannsen, Albert. *The House of Beadle and Adams and Its Dime and Nickel Novels: The Story of a Vanished Literature.* 3 vols. Norman: University of Oklahoma Press, 1950–52.

Johnson, Deidre. *Stratemeyer Pseudonyms and Series Books: An Annotated Checklist of Stratemeyer and Stratemeyer Literary Syndicate Publications.* Westport, Conn.: Greenwood Press, 1981.

Jones, Daryl. *The Dime Novel Western.* Bowling Green, Ohio: Bowling Green State University Popular Press, 1978.

Kiefer, Monica. *American Children through Their Books, 1700–1835.* Philadelphia: University of Pennsylvania Press, 1948.

Kilgour, Raymond L. *Lee and Shepard: Publishers for the People.* Hamden, Conn.: Shoestring Press, 1965.

Kirkpatrick, D. L., ed. *Twentieth-Century Children's Writers.* 2d ed. New York: St. Martin's Press, 1983.

Kloet, Christine A. *After Alice: A Hundred Years of Children's Reading in Britain.* London: Library Association, 1977.

Kunitz, Stanley J., and Howard Haycraft, eds. *The Junior Book of Authors,* 2d ed. New York: H. W. Wilson, 1951.

Lentz, Millicent, and Ramona M. Mahood, eds. *Young Adult Literature: Background and Criticism.* Chicago: American Library Association, 1980.

Limiting What Students Shall Read: Books and Other Learning Materials in Our Public Schools—How They Are Selected and How They Are Removed. Washington, D.C.: Association of American Publishers, American Library Association, and Association for Supervision and Curriculum Development, 1981.

"Living with Adolescent Literature." *Connecticut English Journal,* 12 (Fall 1980), special issue.

Lukens, Rebecca J. *A Critical Handbook of Children's Literature.* Glenview, Ill.: Scott, Foresman, 1976.

McCann, Donnarae, and Gloria Woodward, eds. *The Black American in Books for Children: Readings on Racism.* Metuchen, N.J.: Scarecrow Press, 1972.

MacLeod, Anne Scott. *A Moral Tale: Children's Fiction and American Culture, 1820–1860.* Hamden, Conn.: Shoestring Press, 1975.

Mason, Bobbie Ann. *The Girl Sleuth: A Feminist Guide.* Old Westbury, N.Y.: Feminist Press, 1975.

McFarlane, Leslie. *Ghost of the Hardy Boys: An Autobiography of Leslie McFarlane.* New York: Two Continents, 1976.

McLean, Austin J. "The Hess Collection of Dime Novels." *American Book Collector,* 25 (January-February 1975), 25–29.

Meade, Richard A., and Robert C. Small, Jr., eds. *Literature for Adolescents: Selection and Use.* Columbus, Ohio: Charles E. Merrill, 1973.

Meigs, Cornelia et al. *A Critical History of Children's Literature.* Rev. ed. New York: Macmillan, 1969.

Mertz, Maia Pank, and David K. England. "The Legitimacy of American Adolescent Fiction." *School Library Journal,* 30 (October 1983), 119–23.

Nilsen, Alleen Pace. *Presenting M. E. Kerr.* Boston: Twayne, 1986.

Nilsen, Alleen Pace, and Kenneth L. Donelson. *Literature for Today's Young Adults.* 2d ed. Glenview, Ill.: Scott, Foresman, 1985.

Nye, Russel. *The Unembarrassed Muse: The Popular Arts in America.* New York: Dial Press, 1970.

Papashvily, Helen Waite. *All the Happy Endings.* New York: Harper and Brothers, 1956.

Pattee, Fred Lewis. *The Feminist Fifties.* New York: Appleton, 1940.

Payne, Alma J. "Louisa May Alcott (1832–1888)." *American Literary Realism, 1870–1910,* 6 (Winter 1973), 23–43.

Petitt, Dorothy J. "A Study of the Qualities of Literary Excellence Which Characterize Selected Fiction for Younger Adolescents." Ph.D. dissertation, University of Minnesota, 1961.

Probst, Robert E. *Adolescent Literature: Response and Analysis.* Columbus, Ohio: Charles E. Merrill, 1984.

Reed, Arthea J. S. *Reaching Adolescents: The Young Adult and the School.* New York: Holt, Rinehart and Winston, 1985.

Rees, David. *The Marble in the Water: Essays on Contemporary Writers of Fiction for Children and Young Adults.* Boston: Horn Book, 1980.

———. *Painted Desert, Green Shade: Essays on Contemporary Writers of Fiction for Children and Young Adults.* Boston: Horn Book, 1984.

Rosenbach, A.S.W. *Early American Children's Books.* 1933; New York: Kraus Reprint, 1966.

Rudman, Masha Kabakow. *Children's Literature: An Issues Approach.* Lexington, Mass.: D. C. Heath, 1976.

Salmon, Edward. *Juvenile Literature as It Is.* London: Henry J. Drane, 1888.

Sarkissian, Adele, ed. *Something about the Author: Autobiography Series.* Detroit: Gale Research, 1986-.

Saxton, Martha. *Louisa May: A Modern Biography of Louisa May Alcott.* Boston: Houghton Mifflin, 1977.

Scharnhorst, Gary. *Horatio Alger, Jr.* Boston: G. K. Hall, 1980.

Scharnhorst, Gary, and Jack Bales. *Horatio Alger, Jr.: An Annotated Bibliography of Comment and Criticism.* Metuchen, N.J.: Scarecrow Press, 1981.

Schwartz, Sheila. *Teaching Adolescent Literature: A Humanistic Approach.* Rochelle Park, N.J.: Hayden, 1972.

Sloan, Glenna Davis. *The Child as Critic.* New York: Teachers College Press, 1975.

Sloane, William. *Children's Books in England and America in the Seventeenth Century.* New York: King's Crown Press, 1955.

Smith, Elva S. *The History of Children's Literature.* Chicago: American Library Association, 1937.

Smith, Henry Nash. *Virgin Land: The American West as Symbol and Myth.* Cambridge, Mass.: Harvard University Press, 1950.

Stanford, Barbara Dodds, and Karima Amin. *Black Literature for High School Students.* Urbana, Ill.: National Council of Teachers of English, 1978.

Stensland, Anna Lee. *Literature by and about the American Indian, An Annotated Bibliography.* 2d ed. Urbana, Ill.: National Council of Teachers of English, 1979.

Stern, Madeleine. *Louisa May Alcott.* Norman: University of Oklahoma Press, 1950.

The Students' Right to Read. Urbana, Ill.: National Council of Teachers of English, 1982.

Sutherland, Zena, ed. *The Arbuthnot Lectures, 1976–1979.* Chicago: American Library Association, 1980.

Thwaite, Mary F. *From Primer to Pleasure in Reading: An Introduction to the History of Children's Books in England from the Invention of Printing to 1914 with an Outline of Some Developments in Other Countries.* Boston: Horn Book, 1972.

Townsend, John Rowe. *A Sounding of Storytellers: Essays on Contemporary Writers for Children.* New York: J. B. Lippincott, 1975.

———. *25 Years of British Children's Books.* London: National Book League, 1977.

———. *Written for Children: An Outline of English-Language Children's Literature.* 2d ed. New York: J. B. Lippincott, 1983.

Tway, Eileen, ed. *Reading Ladders for Human Relations*. Washington, D.C.: American Council on Education and National Council of Teachers of English, 1981.

Varlejs, Jana, ed. *Young Adult Literature in the Seventies: A Selection of Readings*. Metuchen, N.J.: Scarecrow Press, 1978.

Weiss, M. Jerry, ed. *From Writers to Students: The Pleasures and Pains of Writing*. Newark, Del.: International Reading Association, 1979.

Winkle, Justin, and Emma Fisher. *The Pied Pipers: Interviews with the Influential Creators of Children's Literature*. New York: Paddington Press, 1974.

Wishy, Bernard. *The Child and the Republic: The Dawning of Modern American Child Nurture*. Philadelphia: University of Pennsylvania Press, 1968.

Periodicals

ALAN Review. Urbana, Ill., 1974-.

Booklist. Chicago, 1905-.

English Journal. Urbana, Ill., 1912-.

Interracial Books for Children Bulletin. New York, 1967-.

Journal of Reading. Newark, Del., 1957-.

New York Times Book Review. New York, 1896-.

School Library Journal. New York, 1954-.

Top of the News. Chicago, 1946-.

Voice of Youth Advocates (VOYA). Virginia Beach, Va., 1978-.

Wilson Library Bulletin. Bronx, N.Y., 1914-.

Index

About the Contributors

RAY BARFIELD is a professor of English at Clemson University and author of several essays on big little books and popular culture.

BILL BLACKBEARD is director of the San Francisco Academy of Comic Art and co-editor of *The Smithsonian Collection of Newspaper Comics*.

KEN DONELSON is a professor of English at Arizona State University and co-author of *Literature for Today's Young Adults*.

RICHARD W. ETULAIN is a professor of history at the University of New Mexico and author of *Western Films: A Brief History* and numerous works on western fiction.

PERRY FRANK is a doctoral candidate in American studies at George Washington University and a free-lance writer and editor.

SUZANNE ELLERY GREENE is a professor of history at Morgan State University and author of *Books for Pleasure: Popular Fiction 1914–1945*.

M. THOMAS INGE is the Robert Emory Blackwell Professor of humanities at Randolph-Macon College and editor of the three-volume *Handbook of American Popular Culture*.

R. GORDON KELLY is director of the American studies program at the University of Maryland, author of *Mother Was a Lady: Self and Society in Selected Children's Periodicals, 1865–1890* and editor of *Children's Periodicals of the United States*.

LARRY N. LANDRUM is a professor of English at Michigan State University and author of *American Popular Culture: A Guide to Information Sources*.

KAY MUSSELL is a professor of literature and American studies at American University and author of *Women's Gothic and Romantic Fiction*.

ALLEEN PACE NILSEN is assistant dean of the graduate school at Arizona State University and co-author of *Literature for Today's Young Adults*.

JANICE RADWAY is a professor of American civilization at the University of Pennsylvania, editor of *American Quarterly*, and author of *Reading the Romance: Women, Patriarchy, and Popular Literature*.

ROGER C. SCHLOBIN is a professor of English at Purdue University and author of *The Literature of Fantasy: A Comprehensive, Annotated Bibliography of Modern Fantasy Fiction*.

ROBERT G. SEWELL is coordinator of collection management and development at the Melville Library of the State University of New York at Stony Brook.

MARSHALL B. TYMN is a professor of English at Eastern Michigan University and editor of the Contributions to the Study of Science Fiction and Fantasy series for Greenwood Press and numerous reference works on the subject.

JOHN SCOTT WILSON is a professor of history at the University of South Carolina and is working on a study of Vietnam in popular culture.